CONTEMPORARY LINGUISTICS

AN INTRODUCTION

THIRD EDITION

CONTEMPORARY LINGUISTICS

AN INTRODUCTION

THIRD EDITION

Edited by

WILLIAM O'GRADY
University of Hawaii at Manoa

and

MICHAEL DOBROVOLSKY
University of Calgary

U.S. Edition Prepared by

MARK ARONOFF
State University of New York at Stony Brook

BEDFORD/ST. MARTIN'S BOSTON ♦ NEW YORK

For Bedford/St. Martin's
Development editor: Talvi Laev
Senior editor, publishing services: Douglas Bell
Project management: Omega Publishing Services, Inc.
Production supervisor: Dennis Para
Text illustrations: Allan Moon, Valentino Sanna
Text design: Kyle Gell
Cover design: Patricia McFadden
Cover art: Susan Leopold

Library of Congress Catalog Card Number: 95-73182

Manufactured in the United States of America.

1 0
f e

For information, write:
Bedford/St. Martin's
75 Arlington Street
Boston, MA 02116
(617-399-4000)

ISBN: 0-312-13749-4

Acknowledgments

Pages 160–162: Douglas Campbell Coupland. Excerpts from *Generation X* by Douglas Campbell Coupland. Copyright © 1991 by Douglas Campbell Coupland. Reprinted by permission of St. Martin's Press Paperbacks.

Pages 225–227: Lesléa Newman. "Tiff and I." From *Sweet Dark Places* by Lesléa Newman. Copyright © 1991 Lesléa Newman. Reprinted by permission of the author.

Page 302: Table 8.23. Vowel laxing in Canadian French. Source: *The Pronunciation of Canadian French* by Douglas C. Walker. Copyright © 1984 University of Ottawa Press. Reprinted by permission of the publisher.

Page 369: Figure 9.8. Location of Indo-European Languages. Source: *Problems in the Origins and Development of the English Language,* Third Edition, edited by John Algeo (p. 84). Copyright © 1982 by Harcourt Brace & Company. Reprinted by permission.

Page 395: Figure 10.3. Bar-pressing times in sentence reading. Source: Adapted from chart by Elizabeth Stine-Morrow in "On-Line Processing of Written Text by Younger and Older Adults" in *Psychology and Aging,* 5: 68–78. Copyright © 1990 by The American Psychological Association. Adapted with permission from the author and The American Psychological Association.

Acknowledgments and copyrights are continued at the back of the book on pages 692–693, which constitute an extension of the copyright page.

Convinced at once that, in order to break loose from the beaten paths of opinions and systems, it was necessary to proceed in my study of man and society by scientific methods, and in a rigorous manner, I devoted one year to philology and grammar; linguistics, or the natural history of speech, being, of all the sciences, that which best suited the researches which I was about to commence.

–Pierre-Joseph Proudhon, *What Is Property?* (1840)

CONTENTS

five

SYNTAX: THE ANALYSIS OF SENTENCE STRUCTURE 163

ten

Psycholinguistics: The Study of Language Processing — 389

eleven

Brain and Language — 415

PREFACE

This third American edition of *Contemporary Linguistics* follows the third Canadian edition very closely. Both include a newly written chapter on second language acquisition and (for the first time) a chapter on psycholinguistics. The core chapters have been revised to reflect ongoing trends in linguistics. For example, Infl is treated as the head of S in the syntax chapter. As in previous editions, some of the specifically Canadian factual material has been deleted or replaced (though not where a Canadian example serves its pedagogical purpose as well as another might), and some specifically American material has been added, especially in the chapter on language in social contexts, where American dialects and social phenomena have been given center stage. I had hoped to be able to replace the chapter on Amerindian languages of Canada with a corresponding chapter on Amerindian languages of the United States, but time considerations prevented this and I have had to satisfy myself with an expanded section on the languages of the Americas in the chapter on language classification. The American edition continues to contain topical sections, labeled "For the Student Linguist," written from a student's perspective by Amy Schafer, a graduate student at the University of Massachusetts.

The Instructor's Manual has been updated and is available for downloading at the *Contemporary Linguistics* Web page. The page itself has links to useful resources and can be reached at <http://www.smpcollege.com/smp_english>. Printed copies of the manual can be obtained on request.

More than any other introductory linguistics textbook, *Contemporary Linguistics* is the result of a cooperative effort. It has three editors and eleven authors. There has also been some cross-fertilization between editions: in the second American edition, IPA was used as a default method of phonetic transcription. This practice was adopted in the third Canadian edition and continues in this edition. Over the years, the editors have also received helpful feedback from users of both the Canadian and American editions; we have tried to incorporate these suggestions where possible. In addition to the many individuals whose assistance is acknowledged in the first and second editions, for help specifically with the third editions I wish to express on behalf of the entire editorial team our gratitude to Francis Katamba (editor of the British edition), Norio Yamada and Shuji Chiba (editors of the Japanese edition), Byron Bender, Michael Forman, Robert Hsu, Kazue Kanno, Anatole Lyovin, Woody Mott, Joyce Hildebrand, Peter Avery, John Davison, and Patricia Shaw. Allison Teasdale revised several phonology problems and contributed additional material. Lorna Rowsell proofread several complex chapters and provided numerous corrections. Charles Ulrich offered helpful comments and suggestions. The editors also owe a debt of gratitude to the many students in introductory linguistics classes throughout the world who have continued to ask hard questions about both the textbook and the discipline. Our debt to them is greatest of all.

The following individuals contributed to the second edition of *Contemporary Linguistics,* and their assistance continues to be reflected in this edition as well: Yutaka Sato, Joyce Hildebrand, Peter Seyffert, Barbara Abbott, Howard Aronson, Byron Bender, Derek Bickerton, K. Boot, Vit Bubenik, Andrew Carnie, Vanna Condax, Eung-Do Cook, John deFrancis, Sheila Embleton, Alice Harris, Leanne

Hinton, A. Huettner, Ricky Jacobs, Kazue Kanno, Brian King, Anatole Lyovin, Barry Meislin, Yves-Charles Morin, Michael O'Grady, Terry Pratt and the students in his introductory linguistics course at the University of Prince Edward Island, Ken Rehg, Laurie Reid, Lorna Rowsell, Patricia Shaw, Albert Schuetz, Stanley Starosta, John Street, Tim Vance, Theo Vennemann, Douglas Walker, and Nava Zvaig. Several reviewers provided extensive assistance in preparing the first and second American editions: Virginia Clark, Dee Holisky, Kyle Johnson, Kostas Kazazis, Joseph Malone, Yutaka Ohno, Jennifer Peterson, and Amy Schafer.

The following reviewers provided comments and suggestions helpful in preparing the third American edition: Janet Cowal (Portland State University), Alicja Gorecka (University of Southern California), Michael Hegarty (University of Minnesota), Alan Juffs (University of Pittsburgh), Johanna Rubba (California Polytechnic State University), and Andrea Tyler (Georgetown University).

I would also like to acknowledge the assistance of a number of people here at Stony Brook in the preparation of all three American editions: Marcia Haag, Su-I Chen, Ekyoung Kim, Eriko Sato Zhu, and Yi-Lin Yin. Most of all, I owe a debt of gratitude to Janie Rees-Miller, without whose assistance with this and other editorial matters neither the third American edition nor the second might have seen the light of day.

St. Martin's Press has supported this American edition admirably since its inception. Nancy Perry and Kim Richardson held my hand during the preparation of the first edition, when I was still wet behind the ears; Joyce Hinnefeld played a similar role for the second edition. In working on this third edition, I have benefited from the assistance of Steve Debow and especially from the cheer, wit, and persistence of Talvi Laev, who has shown a dedication to this project that goes beyond professionalism.

Mark Aronoff

PREFACE TO THE FIRST EDITION

Thanks to the application of rigorous analysis to familiar subject matter, linguistics provides students with an ideal introduction to the kind of thinking we call 'scientific'. Such thinking proceeds from an appreciation of problems arising from bodies of data, to hypotheses that attempt to account for those problems, to the careful testing and extension of these hypotheses. But science is more than a formal activity. One of the great pleasures offered introductory students of linguistics is the discovery of the impressive body of subconscious knowledge that underlies language use. This book attempts to emphasize the extent of this knowledge as well as to introduce the scientific methodology used in linguistic analysis.

Although this is the first linguistics textbook designed primarily for a Canadian readership, we have tried to do much more than simply provide coverage of linguistic phenomena peculiar to Canada. As the title suggests, we have attempted an introduction to linguistic analysis as it is practised at this stage in the development of our discipline. While we do not ignore or reject other fruitful approaches to linguistics, we have taken the generative paradigm as basic for two reasons. First, generative linguistics provides a relatively coherent and integrated approach to basic linguistic phenomena. Phonetics, phonology, morphology, syntax, and semantics are viewed within this framework as perhaps in no other as fully integrated and interrelated. Secondly, the generative approach has been widely influential in its application to a broad range of other linguistic phenomena over the past twenty years.

The extent of our 'contemporariness' has been limited by the inevitable compromise between the need to present basic concepts and the demands of sophisticated and competing recent approaches. In many cases, early versions of our chapters were judged 'too contemporary' by instructors who were not specialists in the subfields in question. This led to substantial revisions and a somewhat more traditional approach to certain issues than was originally intended. Where possible, however, later sections of the chapters are used to present more contemporary material. In this way, we have attempted to provide what is promised by the title—an introductory text that provides a solid grounding in basic linguistic concepts, but one that also prepares the student to go on to current work in the discipline. For this reason, the student is introduced to multilevelled phonology (in preparation for further tiered analyses), allophonic/morphophonemic distinctions (in preparation for lexical phonology), interaction among components of the grammar (in preparation for a more extended modular approach), word formation rules in morphology, and examples of parametric variation in syntax.

To the extent possible, we have attempted to integrate the basic mechanisms outlined in the first five chapters of the book into our discussion of phenomena in later chapters. Thus, our discussion of semantics, historical linguistics, first and second language acquisition, and neurolinguistics draws to some degree on the notions presented in our introduction to generative grammar.

No textbook can be all things to all users. We hope that this book will provide students not only with a springboard to the realm of scientific linguistic analysis, but with a greater appreciation for the wonder of human language, the variety and complexity of its structure, and the subtlety of its use.

We gratefully acknowledge the assistance of Jack Chambers and Sheila Embleton, both of whom read the manuscript in its entirety and provided invaluable comments. Thanks are also due to those who have read and commented upon individual chapters and sections, including Steven Carey, Matthew Dryer, David Ingram, Gary Byma, Gary Libben, Robert Murray, R. Radhakrishnan, Ronald Southerland, Mary Pepper, Derek Bickerton, Robert Blust, Ricky Jacobs, Don Frantz, John Haiman, John Hewson, Nicole Domingue, Lydia White, George Patterson, Donna Gerdts, Elan Dresher, Keren Rice, Robert Fisher, Marilyn Philips, Lorna Rowsell, and Joyce Hildebrand. For assistance in the planning, editing, and production of the manuscript, we are grateful to Coral Sayce, Lynda Costello, Joyce Hildebrand, Brian Henderson, Patrick Burke, Les Petriw, and our project editor at Copp Clark, Margaret Larock.

LIST OF TECHNICAL ABBREVIATIONS

*	(in syntactic rules) one or more
*	(in front of words or sentences) unacceptable
#	word boundary
1	first person
1	primary stress
2	second person
2	secondary stress
3	third person
A	adjective
Abl	ablative case
Abs	absolutive case
Acc	accusative case
Adv	adverb
AdvP	adverb phrase
Af	affix
ag	agent
AP	adjective phrase
Aux	auxiliary verb
B	bound root
C	coda
C	complementizer
C	consonant
caus	cause
CG	constricted glottis
cmpl	completed action
C_o	any number of consonants
CP	complementizer phrase
CT	computerized axial tomography
CYC	Cape York Creole
DA	derivational affix
Dat	dative case
Deg	degree word
DR	delayed release
EEG	electroencephalogram
Erg	ergative case
ESL	English as a second language
FN	first name
Fut	future tense
Gen	genitive case
go	goal
H	high tone
IA	inflectional affix
indic	indicative
IPA	International Phonetic Alphabet
KT	kinterm
L	low tone
L1	first language
L2	second language
LN	last name
Loc	locative case
Loc	location
M	man
M	mid tone
N	noun
N	nucleus
Nom	nominative case
NP	noun phrase
O	(direct) object
O	onset
Obl	oblique
OE	Old English
P	preposition, postposition
Pass	passive
PC	Principal Component
PCA	Principal Components Analysis
PET	Positron Emission Tomography
PIE	Proto-Indo-European
pl	plural
PP	prepositional phrase
PR	phonetic representation
Prs	present tense
Pst	past tense
R	rhyme
R	rounded
RC	relative clause
REA	right ear advantage
recip	recipient
S	sentence
S	subject
σ	syllable
SES	socioeconomic status
SG	spread glottis
sg	singular
SLA	second language acquisition
th	theme
T	title alone
TLN	title + last name
Top	topic
UG	Universal Grammar
UR	underlying representation
UR	unrounded
V	verb
V	vowel
VP	verb phrase
W	woman
Wd	word

one

LANGUAGE: A PREVIEW

William O'Grady
Michael Dobrovolsky

The gift of language is the single human trait that marks us all genetically, setting us apart from the rest of life.

– LEWIS THOMAS, *The Lives of a Cell*

Language is many things—a system of communication, a medium for thought, a vehicle for literary expression, a social institution, a matter for political controversy, a catalyst for nation building. All human beings normally speak at least one language and it is hard to imagine much significant social, intellectual, or artistic activity taking place in its absence. Each of us has a stake in understanding something about the nature and use of language. This book provides a basic introduction to **linguistics**, the discipline that studies these matters.

1 A CREATIVE SYSTEM

What is human language? What does it mean to know a language? To answer these questions, it is first necessary to understand the resources that a language makes available to its **native speakers**, those who have acquired it as children in a natural setting.

The scope and diversity of human thought and experience place great demands on language. Because communication is not restricted to a fixed set of topics, language must do something more than provide a package of ready-made messages. It must enable us to produce and understand new words, phrases, and sentences as the need arises. In short, human language must be **creative**—allowing novelty and innovation in response to new thoughts, experiences, and situations.

Underlying the creative aspect of language is an intricate mental system that defines the boundaries within which innovation can take place. The operation of this system can be illustrated by a relatively simple phenomenon in English: the process that creates verbs (roughly, words naming actions) from nouns (roughly, words naming things).

Table 1.1 Nouns used as verbs

Noun use	*Verb use*
pull the boat onto the *beach*	*beach* the boat
keep the airplane on the *ground*	*ground* the airplane
tie a *knot* in the string	*knot* the string
put the wine in *bottles*	*bottle* the wine
catch the fish with a *spear*	*spear* the fish
clean the floor with a *mop*	*mop* the floor

As the following sentences show, there is a great deal of freedom to innovate in the formation of such verbs.

1)

a. I *wristed* the ball over the net.
b. He would try to *stiff-upper-lip* it through.
c. She *Houdini'd* her way out of the locked closet.

There are also limits on this freedom, however. For instance, a new verb is rarely coined if a word with the intended meaning already exists. Although we say *jail the robber* to mean 'put the robber in jail', we do not say *prison the robber* to mean 'put the robber in prison'. This is because the well-established verb *imprison* already has the meaning that the new form would have.

There are also special constraints on the meaning and use of particular subclasses of these verbs. One such constraint involves verbs that are created from expressions denoting a period of time such as *summer, vacation,* and so on.

2)

a. Julia *summered* in Paris.
b. Harry *wintered* in Mexico.
c. Bob *vacationed* in France.
d. Harry and Julia *honeymooned* in Hawaii.

Although the sentences in *2)* are all natural-sounding, not all time-denoting expressions can be used in this way. (Throughout this book an asterisk is used to indicate that an utterance is unacceptable.)

3)

a. *Jerome *midnighted* in the streets.
b. *Andrea *nooned* at the restaurant.
c. *Phillip *one o'clocked* at the airport.

These examples show that when a verb is created from a time expression, it must be given a very specific interpretation—roughly paraphrasable as 'to be somewhere for the period of time X'. Thus, *to summer in Paris* is 'to be in Paris for the summer', *to vacation in France* is 'to be in France for the vacation', and so on. Since *noon* and *midnight* express points in time rather than extended periods of time, they cannot be used to create new verbs of this type.

Systematic constraints are essential to the viability of the creative process. If well-established words were constantly being replaced by new creations, the vocabulary of English would be so unstable that communication could be jeopardized. A similar danger would arise if there were no constraints on the meaning of words newly derived from other words. If *They winter in Hawaii* could mean 'They make it snow in Hawaii' or 'They wish it were winter in Hawaii' or any other arbitrary thing, the production and interpretation of new forms would be chaotic and unsystematic, undermining the role of language in communication.

Some other examples

Creative systems are found in all aspects of language, including the way in which sounds are combined to form words. The forms in *4)*, for instance, are recognizable as possible names for new products or processes.

4)

a. prasp
b. flib
c. traf

Such forms contrast with the patterns in *5)*, which simply do not have the shape of English words.

5)

a. *psapr
b. *bfli
c. *ftra

The contrast between the forms in *4)* and *5)* illustrates that the set of possible sound patterns is subject to constraints that permit certain novel sound combinations, but prohibit others.

Still other constraints determine how new words can be created from already existing forms with the help of special endings. Imagine, for example, that the word *soleme* entered the English language (used perhaps for a newly discovered atomic particle). As a speaker of English, you then automatically know that something with the properties of a soleme could be called *solemic*. You also know that to make something solemic is to *solemicize* it, and you would call this process *solemicization*. Further, you know that the *c* is pronounced as *s* in *solemicize* but as *k* in *solemic*. Without hesitation, you also recognize that *solemicize* is pronounced with the stress on the second syllable. (You would say *soLEmicize*, not *SOlemicize* or *solemiCIZE*.)

Nowhere is the ability to deal with novel utterances more obvious than in the production and comprehension of sentences. Apart from a few fixed expressions and greetings, much of what you say, hear, and read in the course of a day consists of sentences that are new to you. In conversations, lectures, newscasts, and textbooks you are regularly exposed to novel combinations of words, the expression of unfamiliar ideas, and the presentation of new information. Consider, for instance, the paragraph that you are currently reading. While each of these sentences is no doubt perfectly comprehensible to you, it is extremely unlikely that you have ever seen any of them before.

The ability to produce and understand unfamiliar utterances is not without limits, however. For example, you doubtlessly find it difficult (if not impossible) to interpret the utterance in *6)*. Even though all the words used here are familiar ones, they are simply not arranged in the right way to be a sentence of English.

6)

*Frightened dog this the cat that chased mouse a.
(cf. This dog frightened the cat that chased a mouse.)

Moreover, even though you can probably understand a sentence such as *7a)*, by analogy perhaps with *7b)*, there is something about it that makes it sound less than acceptable.

7)

a. *He brought a chair in order to sit on.
b. He brought a chair to sit on.

As with other aspects of language, the ability to form and interpret sentences is subject to systematic limitations.

2 GRAMMAR AND LINGUISTIC COMPETENCE

As we have seen, speakers of a language are able to produce and understand an unlimited number of utterances, including many that are novel and unfamiliar. This ability, which is often called **linguistic competence**, constitutes the central subject matter of linguistics and of this book.

In investigating linguistic competence, linguists focus on the mental system that allows human beings to form and interpret the words and sentences of their language. This system is called a **grammar**. For the purposes of this book, we will divide the grammar into the following components.

Table 1.2 The components of a grammar

Component	*Domain*
Phonetics	the articulation and perception of speech sounds
Phonology	the patterning of speech sounds
Morphology	word formation
Syntax	sentence formation
Semantics	the interpretation of words and sentences

Linguists use the term *grammar* in a rather special and technical way. Because this usage may be unfamiliar, we will devote some time to considering several properties of the system that linguists call a grammar.

2.1 Generality: All Languages Have a Grammar

One of the most fundamental claims of modern linguistic analysis is that all languages have a grammar. This can be verified by considering a few simple facts. If a language is spoken, it must have a phonetic and phonological system; since it has words and sentences, it must also have a morphology and a syntax; and since these words and sentences have systematic meanings, there must obviously be semantic principles as well. Of course, these are the very things that make up a grammar.

It is not unusual to hear the remark that some language—Puerto Rican Spanish, Navajo, or Swahili—"has no grammar." (This is especially common in the case of languages that are not written or are not taught in universities.) Unfamiliar languages sometimes appear to an untrained observer to have no grammar simply because their grammatical systems are different from those of better-known languages. In Walbiri (an aboriginal language of Australia), for example, the relative ordering of words is so free that the English sentence *The two dogs now see several kangaroos* could be translated by the equivalent of any of the following sentences.

8)

a. Dogs two now see kangaroos several.
b. See now dogs two kangaroos several.
c. See now kangaroos several dogs two.
d. Kangaroos several now dogs two see.
e. Kangaroos several now see dogs two.

Whereas Walbiri may not restrict the order of words in the way English does, its grammar imposes other types of requirements. For example, in the sentence types we are considering, Walbiri speakers must place the ending *lu* on the word for 'dogs' to indicate that it names the animals that do the seeing rather than the animals that are seen. In English, by contrast, this information is conveyed by placing *two dogs* in front of the verb and *several kangaroos* after it.

Rather than showing that Walbiri has no grammar, such differences simply demonstrate that it has a grammar unlike that of English in certain respects. This important point is applicable to all differences among languages: although no two languages have exactly the same grammar, there are no languages without a grammar.

A similar point can be made about different varieties of the same language. As you are probably already aware, English is the language of many different communities around the world. The particular variety of English found within each of these communities has its own characteristic pronunciation, vocabulary, and sentence patterns. This is just another way of saying that each variety of English has its own grammar. Just as it is impossible to have a language without a grammar, so no variety of a language could exist if it did not have a grammar.

2.2 EQUALITY: ALL GRAMMARS ARE EQUAL

Whenever there is more than one variety of a particular language, questions arise as to whether one is somehow better or more correct than another. From the point of view of modern linguistics, it makes no more sense to say that one variety of English is better than another than it does to say that the grammar of English is better (or worse) than the grammar of Thai. All languages and all varieties of a particular language have grammars that enable their speakers to express any proposition that the human mind can produce. All varieties of language are absolutely equal as instruments of communication and thought.

Furthermore, there is no such thing as a 'primitive' or 'inferior' language. Indeed, as examples in subsequent chapters will help illustrate, some of the most complex grammatical phenomena known to linguists are found in languages spoken in societies that have neither writing nor electricity.

It is thus futile to attempt to 'rank' languages in terms of relative sophistication or superiority. A more appropriate goal for linguistic analysis is to investigate language with a view to determining what it is like and how it is used. This same point is sometimes made by noting that linguistics is **descriptive**, not **prescriptive**. This means that linguists seek to *describe* human linguistic ability and knowledge, not to *prescribe* one way of speaking in preference to another. A parallel point of view is adopted in other scientific disciplines. The first concern of all scientists is to describe and explain the facts that they observe, not to change them.

Linguists acknowledge that certain patterns (*I seen that, They was there, He didn't do nothing, He ain't here*) may be characteristic of particular socioeconomic groups within the English-speaking community. As we discuss in more detail in Chapter 14, the use of these patterns may therefore have negative social consequences: it may be harder to win a scholarship, to get a job, to be accepted in certain circles, and so forth. From a purely linguistic point of view, however, there is absolutely nothing wrong with grammars that permit such structures. Like grammars for other variants of English (and other languages), they are fully systematic, and they permit their users to express and understand the same unlimited range of thoughts.

Even though linguists reject prescriptivism, they do not deny the importance of clear expression in writing and speech. Such matters are quite rightly an object of concern among educators. However, the difficulties that arise in these areas typically result from the inconsistent or careless use of one's linguistic knowledge, not from any inherent flaw in the grammar itself. The English speakers who produced the following sentences are doubtlessly guilty of carelessness, but there is no reason to believe that they are suffering from a grammatical deficit.

9)

Don't go into darkened parking lots unless they are well lit.

You probably got a letter warning you about the dangers of lead-contaminated water in your mail.

The poet was a guest of honor at a surprise luncheon with a birthday cake thrown by several close friends in the English Department.

Molenda's last known address was not known.

In sum, linguistics does not deny either the existence or the desirability of standards. (Indeed, without standards, there might not be enough shared knowledge for language to fulfil its communicative function effectively.) Ultimately, though, any statement of the rules and conventions for speech and writing must reflect the way language is actually used, not someone's idealized vision of how it should be used. The linguist Steven Pinker offers the following metaphor to make the same point.

> Imagine that you are watching a nature documentary. The video shows the usual gorgeous footage of animals in their natural habitats. But the voiceover reports some troubling facts. Dolphins do not execute their swimming strokes properly. White-crowned sparrows carelessly debase their calls. Chickadees' nests are incorrectly constructed, pandas hold bamboo in the wrong paw, the song of the humpback whale contains several well-known errors, and the monkey's cries have been in a state of chaos and degeneration for hundreds of years. Your reaction would probably be, What on earth could it mean for the song of the humpback whale to contain an 'error'? Isn't the song of the humpback whale whatever the humpback whale decides to sing? . . . To a [linguist], of course, language is like the song of the humpback whale. The way to determine whether a construction is 'grammatical' is to find people who speak the language and ask them.

2.3 Changeability: grammars change over time

It is a well-established fact that the grammars of all languages are constantly changing. Some of these changes are relatively minor and occur very quickly (for example, the addition of new words such as *morphing, Internet, e-mail,* and *cyberspace* to the vocabulary of English). Other changes have a more dramatic effect on the overall form of the language and typically take place over a long period of time. The formation of negative structures in English has undergone this type of change. Prior to 1200, English formed negative constructions by placing *ne* before the verb and a variant of *not* after it.

10)

a. Ic ne seye not. ('I don't say.')
b. He ne speketh nawt. ('He does not speak.')

By 1400 or thereabouts, *ne* was used infrequently and *not* (or *nawt*) typically occurred by itself after the verb.

11)

a. I seye not the wordes.
b. We saw nawt the knyghtes.

It was not until several centuries later that English adopted its current practice of allowing *not* to occur after only certain types of verbs (such as *do, have, will,* and so on).

12)

a. I will not say the words. (versus *I will say not the words.)
b. He did not see the knights. (versus *He saw not the knights.)

These modifications illustrate the extent to which grammars can change over time. The structures exemplified in *11)* are archaic by today's standards and those in *10)* sound completely foreign to speakers of modern English.

Through the centuries, individuals and organizations who believe that certain varieties of language are better than others have frequently expressed concern over what they perceive to be the deterioration of English. In 1710, for example, the writer Jonathan Swift (author of *Gulliver's Travels*) lamented "the continual Corruption of our English Tongue." Among the corruptions to which Swift objected were contractions such as *he's* for *he is,* although he had no objection to *Tis* for *It is.*

In the nineteenth century, Edward S. Gould, a columnist for the New York *Evening Post,* published a book entitled *Good English; or, Popular Errors in Language,* in which he accused newspaper writers and authors of "sensation novels" of ruining the language by introducing "spurious words" like *jeopardize, leniency,* and *underhanded.* To this day, the tradition of prescriptive concern about the use of certain words continues in the work of such popular writers as Edwin Newman and John Simon, who form a kind of self-appointed language police.

Linguists reject the view that languages attain a state of perfection at some point in their history and that subsequent changes lead to deterioration and corruption. As noted above, there are simply no grounds for claiming that one way of speaking is somehow superior to another. There is therefore no reason to think that language change can or will undermine the adequacy of English (or any other language) as a medium of communication.

2.4 Universality: grammars are alike in basic ways

There are many differences among languages, as even a superficial examination of their sound patterns, vocabularies, and word order reveals. But this does not mean that there are no limits on the type of grammars that human beings can acquire and use. Quite to the contrary, current research suggests that there are important grammatical principles and tendencies shared by all human languages.

One such principle involves the manner in which sentences are negated. With unlimited variation, one would expect 'negators' (the equivalent of English *not*) to occur in different positions within the sentence in different languages. Thus, we might predict that each of the following possibilities should occur with roughly equal frequency.

13)

a. Not Pat is here.
b. Pat not is here.
c. Pat is not here.
d. Pat is here not.

As it happens, the first and fourth patterns are very rare. In virtually all languages, negative elements such as *not* either immediately precede or immediately follow the verb.

The relative ordering of other elements is also subject to constraints. To see this, we need only consider the six logically possible orders for a simple three-word statement such as *Canadians like hockey.*

14)

a. Canadians like hockey.
b. Canadians hockey like.
c. Like Canadians hockey.
d. Like hockey Canadians.
e. Hockey like Canadians.
f. Hockey Canadians like.

Interestingly, more than 95 percent of the world's languages adopt one of the first three orders for basic statements. Only a handful of languages use any of the last three orders as basic. This once again reflects the existence of constraints and preferences that limit variation among languages.

These are not isolated examples. As later chapters will show, some grammatical categories and principles are universal. And where there is variation (as in the case of word order), there is typically a very limited set of options. Contrary to first appearances, the set of grammars learned and used by human beings is limited in significant ways.

2.5 TACITNESS: GRAMMATICAL KNOWLEDGE IS SUBCONSCIOUS

Because the use of language to communicate presupposes a grammar, it follows that all speakers of a language must have knowledge of its grammar. However, this knowledge differs from knowledge of arithmetic, traffic rules, and other subjects that are taught at home or in school. Unlike these other types of knowledge, grammatical knowledge is acquired without the help of instruction when one is still a child and it remains largely subconscious throughout life. As an example of this, consider your pronunciation of the past tense ending written as *ed* in the following words.

15)

a. hunted
b. slipped
c. buzzed

Notice that whereas you say *id* in *hunted,* you say *t* in *slipped* and *d* in *buzzed.* Moreover, if you heard the new verb *flib,* you would form the past tense as *flibbed* and pronounce the ending as *d.* Although it is unlikely that you were aware of this phenomenon until now, you make these distinctions automatically if you are a native speaker of English. This is because you acquired the grammatical subsystem regulating this aspect of speech when you were a child and it now exists subconsciously in your mind.

Even more subtle phonological patterning can occur, as the following contrasts help illustrate.

16)

pint	*paynk
fiend	*fiemp
locked	*lockf
wronged	*wrongv
next	*nexk
glimpse	*glimpk

The words in the left-hand column obey an obscure constraint on the selection of consonant sequences in word-final position: when a vowel is long and followed by two consonants (*pint*) or when a vowel is short and followed by three consonant sounds (*next*, pronounced 'nekst'), the final consonant must always be one made with the tongue tip raised. (The consonants *t, d, s,* and *z* are made in this manner, but consonants such as *p, f, v,* and *k* are not.) Words that do not adhere to this phonological constraint (the right-hand column) are unacceptable to speakers of English. Linguists have to dig deeply to uncover such patterning, but in everyday language use, we routinely make decisions about the acceptability of forms based on subconscious knowledge of such constraints.

Consider one final example. Speakers of English know that there are certain structures in which the word *he* can refer to each member of a group or to a single individual outside that group.

17)

Each boy who submitted an essay thinks that he is a genius.

Sentence *17)* can mean either that each boy in the group that submitted essays thinks that he himself is a genius or that each boy thinks that a particular person not mentioned in the sentence (say, Albert Einstein) is a genius. However, only one of these interpretations is possible in the following sentence.

18)

The woman who read each boy's essay thinks that he is a genius.

In *18), he* can refer only to someone not mentioned in the sentence. In contrast with what happens in sentence *17), he* cannot refer to each individual in the group designated by the expression *each boy*. Since speakers are able to make this contrast, they must have knowledge of the relevant grammatical principle even though they are not consciously aware of it.

2.6 Grammar

In sum, linguists use the term *grammar* to refer to a subconscious linguistic system of a particular type. Consisting of several components (**phonetics**, **phonology**, **morphology**, **syntax**, and **semantics**), a grammar makes possible the production and comprehension of a potentially unlimited number of utterances. Because no language can exist without a grammar and no one can use a language without knowledge of its grammar, the study of grammatical systems has come to be the focus of contemporary linguistic analysis.

As noted above, the grammatical knowledge needed to use and understand language is acquired without the benefit of instruction and is for the most part subconscious. Since we therefore cannot investigate grammar by simply recalling prior training or by self-consultation, the study of human linguistic systems requires considerable effort and ingenuity. As is the case in all science, information about facts that can be observed (the pronunciation of words, the interpretation of sentences, and so on) must be used to draw inferences about the sometimes invisible mechanisms that are ultimately responsible for these phenomena. A good deal of this book is concerned with the findings of this research and with what they tell us about the nature and use of human language.

3 BIOLOGICAL SPECIALIZATION FOR LANGUAGE

As far as can be determined, the languages spoken in the world today cannot be traced to a common source. Rather, they seem to belong to a number of distinct families whose histories can be traced back no more than a few thousand years. Although language existed prior to that time for at least 100,000 years, virtually nothing is known about this period of linguistic prehistory or about how language originated in the first place.

Nonetheless, there is every reason to believe that humans have a special capacity for language that is not shared by other creatures. The evolutionary adaptation of certain physiological mechanisms for linguistic ends has occurred only in humans. The so-called speech organs (the lungs, larynx, tongue, teeth, lips, soft palate, and nasal passages) were—and still are—directly concerned with ensuring the survival of the organism. However, these organs have all become highly specialized for linguistic ends. The vocal folds, for example, are more muscular and less fatty in humans than in non-human primates such as chimpanzees and gorillas. Because of a very highly developed network of neural pathways, they also respond more precisely to commands from the brain. The same extensive set of neural pathways allows a high degree of control over other speech organs, such as the tongue, palate, and lips. Such control exceeds anything found in even our closest primate relatives. Table 1.3 compares the linguistic uses of the major speech organs with their primary survival functions in humans and other mammals.

There are additional indications of the evolution of linguistic vocalization. Unlike the breathing of survival respiration, speech breathing shows higher lung pressure and a longer exhalation time than respiration. Abdominal muscles that are not normally employed for respiration are brought into play in a systematic and refined manner in order to maintain the air pressure needed for speech. Again, a specialized, extensive set of neurological controls exclusive to humans makes this type of breathing possible.

There is also evidence that humans are specialized for the perception of speech. It has been suggested, for example, that we have special neural mechanisms that

Table 1.3 Dual functions of the speech organs

Organ	Survival function	Speech function
Lungs	to exchange CO_2, oxygen	to supply air for speech
Vocal folds	to create seal over passage to lungs	to produce voice for speech sounds
Tongue	to move food to teeth and back to throat	to articulate vowels and consonants
Teeth	to break up food	to provide place of articulation for consonants
Lips	to seal oral cavity	to articulate vowels and consonants
Nasal cavities	breathing	to provide nasal resonance

enable us to perceive distinctions among vowels and that these mechanisms are not found in other mammals.

We know considerably less about the evolutionary specialization for non-vocal and non-auditory aspects of language such as word formation, sentence formation, and the interpretation of meaning since the relevant grammatical mechanisms cannot be observed directly. Nonetheless, it is clear that some sort of evolutionary specialization must have occurred, since particular parts of the brain are associated with specific types of morphological, syntactic, and semantic phenomena (see Chapter 11 for discussion). This suggests that the human brain is specially structured for language, and that species with different types of brains will not be able to acquire or use the types of grammars associated with human language. We will return to this point in Chapter 16, "Animal Communication."

Summing up

Human language is characterized by **creativity**. Speakers of a language have access to a **grammar**, a mental system that allows them to form and interpret familiar and novel utterances. The grammar governs the articulation, perception, and patterning of speech sounds, the formation of words and sentences, and the interpretation of utterances. All languages have grammars that are equal in their expressive capacity, and all speakers of a language have (subconscious) knowledge of its grammar. The existence of such linguistic systems in humans is the product of unique anatomical and cognitive specialization.

Key terms

changeability
creativity
descriptive grammar
grammar
linguistic competence
morphology
native speakers
phonetics
phonology
prescriptive grammar

semantics	tacitness
syntax	universality

Sources

The discussion of word creation is based on an article by Eve Clark and Herb Clark, "When Nouns Surface As Verbs" in *Language* 55: 767–811 (1979). The Walbiri data are based on K. Hale's article "Person Marking in Walbiri" in *A Festschrift for Morris Halle*, edited by S. Anderson and P. Kiparsky (New York: Holt, Rinehart and Winston, 1973). The examples in *9)* are based on citations collected by James Kilpatrick and reported in his article "Mrs. Malaprop's Mangled Prose Set a President" in *Smithsonian* (Jan. 1995): 82–87. The quotation at the end of Section 2.2 is from the book by Steven Pinker (p. 370) cited below. The Gould book is cited in Dennis Baron's *Grammr and Good Taste* (New Haven: Yale University Press, 1982). The data on the positioning of negative elements within sentences in human language come from an article by O. Dahl, "Typology of Sentence Negation" in *Linguistics* 17: 79–106 (1979). The books by Bickerton and Pinker, cited below, provide different views of the emergence of language in the human species. The questions for this chapter were prepared by Joyce Hildebrand.

Recommended reading

Bickerton, Derek. 1990. *Language and Species*. Chicago: University of Chicago Press.

Clark, Eve, and Herb Clark. 1979. "When Nouns Surface as Verbs." *Language* 55: 767–811.

Crystal, David. 1987. *The Cambridge Encyclopedia of Language*. New York: Cambridge University Press.

Pinker, Steven. 1994. *The Language Instinct: How the Human Mind Creates Language*. New York: Morrow.

Questions

1. The following sentences contain verbs created from nouns in accordance with the process described in Section 1 of the chapter. Describe the meaning of each of these new verbs.
   a) We punk-rocked the night away.
   b) She dog-teamed her way across the Arctic.
   c) We MG'd to Oregon.
   d) They Concorded to London.
   e) He Gretzky'd his way to the net.
   f) We Greyhounded to Toronto.
   g) We'll have to Ajax the sink.
   h) He Windexed the windows.
   i) You should Clairol your hair.
   j) Let's carton the eggs.

2. Using the examples in the preceding exercise as a model, create five new verbs from nouns. Build a sentence around each new verb to show its meaning.

3. Which of the following forms are possible words of English? Solicit the help of an acquaintance and see if you agree on your judgments.
   a) mbood
   b) frall
   c) coofp
   d) ktleem
   e) sproke
   f) flube
   g) worpz
   h) bsarn

4. Imagine that you are an advertising executive and that your job involves inventing new names for products. Create four new forms that are possible words of English and four that are not.

5. Part of linguistic competence involves the ability to recognize whether novel utterances are acceptable. Consider the following sentences and determine which are possible sentences in English. For each unacceptable sentence, change the sentence to make it acceptable, and compare the two.
   a) Jason's mother left himself with nothing to eat.
   b) Miriam is eager to talk to.
   c) This is the man who I took a picture of.
   d) Colin made Jane a sandwich.
   e) Is the dog sleeping the bone again?
   f) Wayne prepared Zena a cake.
   g) Max cleaned the garden up.
   h) Max cleaned up the garden.
   i) Max cleaned up it.
   j) I desire you to leave.
   k) That you likes liver suprises me.

6. Consider the following sentences, each of which is acceptable to some speakers of English. Try to identify the prescriptive rules that are violated in each case.
   a) He don't know about the race.
   b) You was out when I called.
   c) There's twenty horses registered in the show.
   d) That window's broke, so be careful.
   e) Jim and me are gonna go campin' this weekend.
   f) Who did you come with?
   g) I seen the parade last week.
   h) He been lost in the woods for ten days.
   i) My car needs cleaned 'cause of all the rain.
   j) Julie ain't got none.
   k) Somebody left their book on the train.
   l) Murray hurt hisself in the game.

two

PHONETICS: THE SOUNDS OF LANGUAGE

Michael Dobrovolsky

Heavenly labials in a world of gutturals . . .

– WALLACE STEVENS

We do not need to speak in order to use language. Language can be written, recorded mechanically, and even produced by computers in limited ways. Nevertheless, speech remains the primary way humans encode and broadcast language. Our species spoke long before we began to write language down, and, as we saw in the first chapter of this book, this long history of spoken language is reflected in our anatomical specialization for it. Humans also appear to have specialized neural mechanisms for the perception of speech sounds. Because language and speech are so closely linked, we begin our study of language by examining the inventory and structure of the sounds of speech. This branch of linguistics is called **phonetics**.

Human languages display a wide variety of sounds, called **phones** or **speech sounds**. There are a great many speech sounds, but not an infinite number of them—the class of possible speech sounds is finite, and a portion of the total set will be found in the inventory of any human language. Certain sounds that humans are capable of producing with the vocal tract do not occur in speech, such as the sound made by inhaling through one corner of the mouth, or the 'raspberry' produced by sticking out the tongue and blowing hard across it. Nonetheless, a very wide range of sounds is found in human language, including such sounds as the click made by drawing the tongue hard away from the upper molars on one side of the mouth, or the sound made by constricting the insides of the throat as we breathe out. The class of possible speech sounds is also universal. Any human, child or adult, can learn how to pronounce these sounds.

There are two ways of approaching phonetics. One approach studies the physiological mechanisms of speech production. This is known as **articulatory phonetics**. The other, known as **acoustic phonetics**, is concerned with measuring and analyzing the physical properties of the sound waves we produce when we speak. Both approaches are indispensable to an understanding of phonetics. This chapter focuses on articulatory phonetics, but also makes some reference to the acoustic properties of sounds and to acoustic analysis.

1 PHONETIC TRANSCRIPTION

Since the sixteenth century, efforts have been made to devise a universal system for transcribing the sounds of speech. The best-known system, the **International Phonetic Alphabet (IPA)**, has been developing since 1888. This system of transcription attempts to represent each sound of human speech with a single symbol. These symbols are enclosed in brackets [ ] to indicate that the transcription is phonetic and does not represent the spelling system of a particular language. For example, the sound spelled *th* in English *this* is transcribed as [ð] (pronounced *eth*, as in *weather*). The IPA uses this symbol to represent the sound in whichever language it is heard, whether it is English, Spanish, Turkmen (a Turkic language spoken in Central Asia and written with the Cyrillic alphabet), or any other.

Table 2.1 Use of [ð] in the International Phonetic Alphabet

Language	*Spelling*	*IPA*	*Meaning*
English	this	[ðɪs]	'this'
Spanish	boda	[bɔða]	'wedding'
Turkmen	адак	[aðak]	'foot'

The use of a standardized phonetic alphabet enables linguists to transcribe languages consistently and accurately. In North American (NA) usage, though, some phonetic symbols differ from those employed by IPA transcription. For example, the sound heard at the beginning of the English word *shark* is transcribed as [ʃ] in IPA, but usually as [š] in North America. This book employs IPA transcription, but notes common North American symbols where relevant.

If you wish to start practicing the phonetic transcription of English, turn to Tables 2.16 and 2.17 for examples.

1.1 Units of representation

Anyone who hears a language spoken for the first time finds it hard to break up the flow of speech into individual units. Even when hearing our own language spoken, we do not focus attention on individual sounds as much as we do on the meanings of words, phrases, and sentences. Many alphabets, including the IPA, represent speech in the form of **segments**, or individual speech sounds like [p], [s], or [m]. Using segments, however, is only one way to represent speech. The **syllable**, presented in Chapter 3, is also represented in some writing systems (see Chapter 15, Sections 1.2, 3.2, and 4.2). In one form of Japanese writing, for example, signs such as か [ka], と [to], and み [mi] represent syllables without recourse to segmental transcription.

Segments are produced by coordinating a number of individual articulatory gestures including jaw movement, lip shape, and tongue placement. Many of these individual activities are represented as smaller subunits called **features** that segments are assumed to be made up of. Even though features are almost never represented in writing systems, they are important elements of linguistic representation. Features reflect individual aspects of articulatory control or acoustic effects produced by articulation. This chapter presents segmental transcription, since it is the most widely used way of representing speech. Features and syllables are introduced in the following chapter.

1.2 Segments

We have defined the **segment** as an individual speech sound. There are several kinds of evidence that suggest that speakers have the linguistic knowledge that makes it possible to break down a stream of speech into sound segments.

Errors in speech production provide one kind of evidence for the existence of segments. Slips of the tongue such as *Kolacodor* for *Kodacolor* and *melcome wat* for *welcome mat* show segments shifting and reversing position within and across words. This suggests that segments are individual units of linguistic structure and can be represented individually in a system of transcription.

The relative invariance of speech sounds in human language also suggests that segmental phonetic transcription is a well-motivated way of transcribing speech. It is impossible to represent all variants of human speech sounds, since no one says the same sound in exactly the same way twice. Nonetheless, the sounds of speech remain invariant enough from language to language for us to transcribe them consistently. A *p* sound is much the same in English, Russian, or Uzbek. The fact that when producing a *p* sound, English speakers press their lips together but Russian speakers draw theirs slightly inward does not make the sounds different enough to warrant separate symbols. But the sounds *p* and *t* are distinct enough from each other in languages the world over to be consistently transcribed with separate symbols.

2 THE SOUND-PRODUCING SYSTEM

Sound is produced when air is set in motion. Think of the speech production mechanism as consisting of an air supply, a sound source that sets the air in motion in ways specifically relevant to speech production, and a set of filters that modifies the sound in various ways. The air supply is provided by the lungs. The sound source is in the **larynx**, where a set of muscles called the **vocal folds** (or vocal cords) are located. The filters are the organs above the larynx: the tube of the throat between the larynx and the oral cavity, which is called the **pharynx**, the oral cavity, and the nasal cavity. These passages are collectively known as the **vocal tract**.

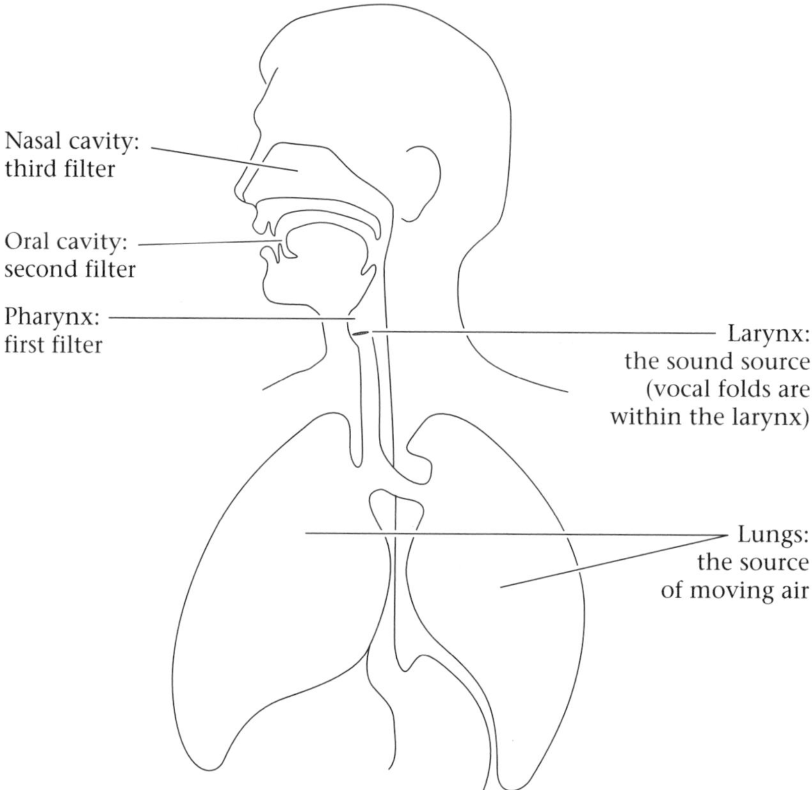

Figure 2.1 The sound producing system

2.1 THE LUNGS

In order to produce the majority of sounds in the world's languages, we take air into the lungs and then expel it during speech. (A small number of sounds are made with air as it flows into the vocal tract.) A certain level of air pressure is needed to keep the speech mechanism functioning steadily. The pressure is maintained by the action of various sets of muscles coming into play during the course of an utterance. The muscles are primarily the **intercostals** (the muscles between the ribs) and the **diaphragm** (the large sheet of muscle separating the chest cavity from the abdomen).

2.2 THE LARYNX

As air flows out of the lungs up the **trachea** (windpipe), it passes through a box-like structure made of cartilages and muscle; this is the **larynx** (commonly known as the voice box or Adam's apple). The main portion of the larynx is formed by the **thyroid cartilage**, which spreads outward like the head of a plow. The thyroid cartilage rests on the ring-shaped **cricoid cartilage**. Fine sheets of muscle flare from the inner sides of the thyroid cartilage, forming the paired vocal folds (vocal cords). The inner edges of the vocal folds are attached to the vocal ligaments. The vocal folds can be pulled apart or drawn closer together, especially at their back or posterior ends, where each is attached to one of two small cartilages, the **arytenoids**. As air passes through the space between the vocal folds, which is called the **glottis**, different glottal states are produced, depending on the positioning of the vocal folds.

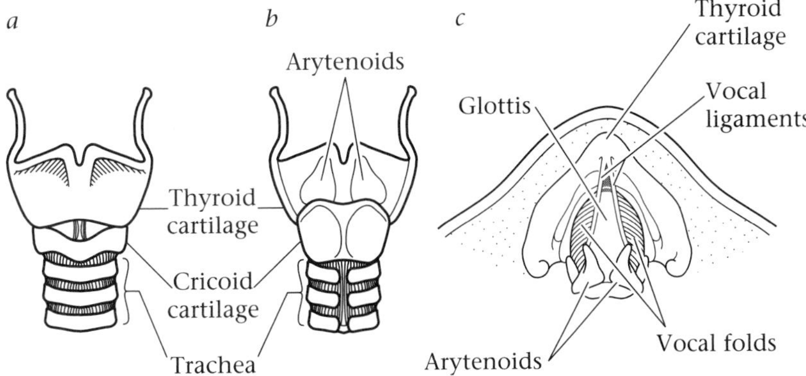

Figure 2.2 The larynx: *a* from the front; *b* from the back; *c* from above, with the vocal folds in open position. The striated lines indicate muscles, a number of which have been eliminated from the drawings in order to show the cartilages more clearly.

2.3 Glottal states

The vocal folds may be positioned in a number of ways to produce different glottal states. The first two glottal states presented in Figure 2.3 are commonly encountered in most of the world's languages. The third diagram describes the glottal state that underlies a common speech phenomenon, and the fourth illustrates one of a number of glottal states not encountered in English.

Voicelessness

When the vocal folds are pulled apart as illustrated in Figure 2.2, air passes directly through the glottis. Any sound made with the vocal folds in this position is said to be **voiceless**. You can confirm a sound's voicelessness by touching your fingers to the larynx as you produce it. You will not feel any vibration from the vocal folds being transmitted to your fingertips. The initial sounds of *fish*, *sing*, and *house* are all voiceless.

Voicing

When the vocal folds are brought close together, but not tightly closed, air passing between them causes them to vibrate, producing sounds that are said to be **voiced**. (See Figure 2.3, where the movement of the vocal folds during voicing is indicated by the wavy line.) You can determine whether a sound is voiced in the same way you determined voicelessness. By lightly touching the fingers to the larynx as you produce an extended version of the initial sounds of the words *zip* or *vow*, or any vowel, you can sense the vibration of the vocal folds within the larynx.

Whisper

Another glottal state produces a **whisper**. Whispering is voiceless, but, as shown in Figure 2.3, the vocal folds are adjusted so that the anterior (front) portions are pulled close together, while the posterior (back) portions are apart.

Murmur

Yet another glottal state produces a **murmur**, also known as **whispery voice**. Sounds produced with this glottal configuration are voiced, but the vocal folds are relaxed to allow enough air to escape to produce a simultaneous whispery effect.

These four glottal states represent only some of the possibilities of sound production at the glottis. Combined with various articulations made above the larynx, they produce a wide range of phones. Before examining these in more detail, we will first consider the three major classes of phone.

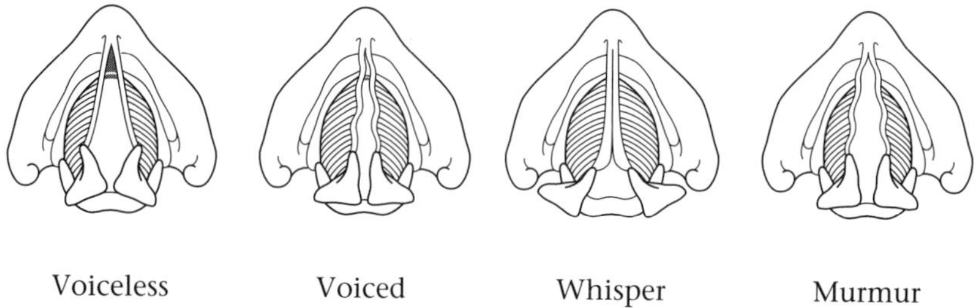

Figure 2.3 Four glottal states: the stylized drawing represents the vocal folds and glottis from above; the anterior portion at the larynx is towards the top. The small triangles represent the arytenoid cartilages, which help spread or close the vocal folds.

3 SOUND CLASSES

The sounds of language can be grouped into **sound classes** based on the phonetic properties that they share. You have already seen what some of these properties can be. All voiced sounds, for example, form a class, as do all **voiceless sounds**. The most basic division among sounds is into two major classes, **vowels** and **consonants**. Another class of sounds, the **glides**, shares properties of both vowels and consonants. Each of these classes of sounds has a number of distinguishing features.

3.1 Vowels, consonants, and glides (syllabic and nonsyllabic elements)

Vowels, consonants, and glides can be distinguished on the basis of differences in articulation, or by their acoustic properties. We can also distinguish among these elements with respect to whether they function as syllabic or nonsyllabic elements.

The articulatory difference

Consonantal sounds, which may be voiced or voiceless, are made with a narrow or complete closure in the vocal tract. The airflow is either blocked momentarily or restricted so much that noise is produced as air flows past the constriction. Vowels are produced with little obstruction in the vocal tract and are generally voiced.

The acoustic difference

As a result of the difference in articulation, consonants and vowels differ in the way they sound. Vowels are more sonorous than consonants, and so we perceive them as louder and longer lasting.

Syllabic and nonsyllabic sounds

The greater sonority of vowels allows them to form the basis of **syllables**. A syllable can be defined as a peak of sonority surrounded by less sonorous segments. For example, the words *a* and *go* each contain one syllable, the word *laughing* two syllables, and the word *telephone* three syllables. In counting the syllables in these words, we are in effect counting the vowels. A vowel is thus said to form the **nucleus** of a syllable. In Section 5.7, it will be shown that certain types of consonants can form syllabic nuclei as well. It is a good idea, therefore, to think of vowels and consonants not simply as types of articulations, but as elements that may or may not be syllabic. In *1)*, the initial sounds of the words in the left column are all consonants; those on the right are all vowels.

1)

take	above
cart	at
feel	eel
jump	it
think	ugly
bell	open

Table 2.2 sums up the differences between consonants and vowels.

Table 2.2 Major differences between syllabic and nonsyllabic elements

Vowels (and other syllabic elements)	Consonants (nonsyllabic elements)
• are produced with relatively little obstruction in the vocal tract	• are produced with a narrow or complete closure in the vocal tract
• are more sonorous	• are less sonorous

Glides

A type of sound that shows properties of both consonants and vowels is called a glide. Glides may be thought of as rapidly articulated vowels—this is the auditory impression they produce. Glides are produced with an articulation like that of a vowel. However, they move quickly to another articulation, as do the initial glides in *y̲et* or *w̲et*, or quickly terminate, as do the word-final glides in *boy̲* and *now̲*.

Even though they are vowel-like in articulation, glides pattern as consonants. For example, glides can never form the nucleus of a syllable. Since glides show properties of both consonants and vowels, the terms *semivowel* and *semiconsonant* may be used interchangeably with the term *glide*.

4 CONSONANT ARTICULATION

Airflow is modified in the oral cavity by the placement of the tongue and the positioning of the lips. These modifications occur at specific **places** or **points of articulation**. The major places of articulation used in speech production are outlined in this section. Figure 2.4 provides a midsagittal section, or cutaway view, of the vocal tract on which each place of articulation has been indicated.

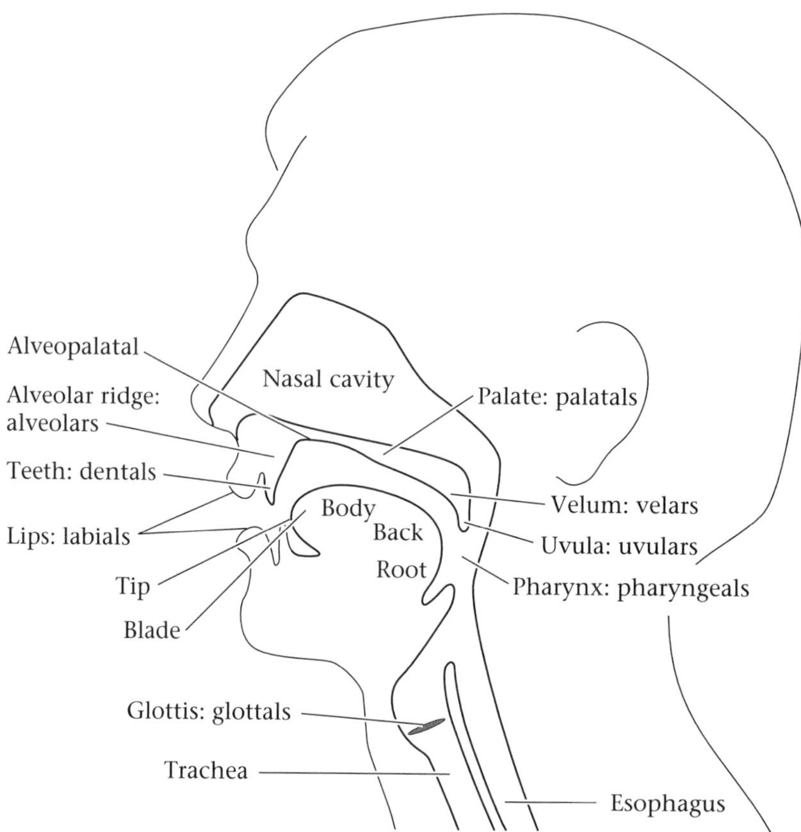

Figure 2.4 The vocal tract

4.1 THE TONGUE

The primary articulating organ is the tongue. It can be raised, lowered, thrust forward or drawn back, and even rolled back. The sides of the tongue can also be raised or lowered.

Phonetic description refers to five areas of the tongue. The **tip** is the narrow area at the front. Just behind the tip lies the **blade**. The main mass of the tongue is called the **body**, and the hindmost part of the tongue that lies in the mouth is called the **back**. The body and back of the tongue can also be referred to jointly as the **dorsum**. The **root** of the tongue is contained in the upper part of the throat (pharnyx).

4.2 PLACES OF ARTICULATION

Each point at which the airstream can be modified to produce a different sound is called a place of articulation. Places of articulation are found at the lips, within the oral cavity, in the pharynx, and at the glottis.

Labial

Any sound made with closure or near-closure of the lips is said to be **labial**. Sounds involving both lips are termed bilabial; sounds involving the lower lip and upper teeth are called **labiodentals**. English includes the bilabials heard word-initially in *peer*, *bin*, and *month*, and the labiodentals heard initially in *fire* and *vow*.

Dental

Some phones are produced with the tongue placed against or near the teeth. Sounds made in this way are called **dentals**. If the tongue is placed between the teeth, the sound is said to be **interdental**. Interdentals in English include the initial consonants of the words *this* and *thing*. (Some English speakers produce *s* and *z* as dentals; see Section 5.3 for more details.)

Alveolar

Within the oral cavity, a small ridge protrudes from just behind the upper front teeth. This is called the **alveolar ridge**. The tongue may touch or be brought near this ridge. Alveolar sounds are heard at the beginning of the following English words: *top*, *deer*, *soap*, *zip*, *lip*, and *neck*. Some languages, such as Spanish, have an *r* that is made by touching the tongue to the alveolar ridge.

Alveopalatal and palatal

Just behind the alveolar ridge, the roof of the mouth rises sharply. This area is known as the **alveopalatal** area (palatoalveolar in some books). The highest part of the roof of the mouth is called the **palate**, and sounds produced with the tongue on or near this area are called **palatals**. Alveopalatal consonants are heard in the following English words: *show*, *measure*, *chip*, and *judge*. The word-initial phone in *yes* is a palatal glide.

Velar

The soft area towards the rear of the roof of the mouth is called the **velum**. Sounds made with the tongue touching or near this position are called **velars**. Velars are heard in English at the beginning of the words *call* and *guy*, and at the end of the word *hang*. The glide heard word-initially in *wet* is called a **labiovelar**, since the tongue is raised near the velum and the lips are rounded at the same time.

Uvular

The small fleshy flap of tissue known as the **uvula** hangs down from the velum. Sounds made with the tongue near or touching this area are called **uvulars**. English has no uvulars, but the *r* sound of standard European French is uvular.

Pharyngeal

The area of the throat between the uvula and the larynx is known as the pharynx. Sounds made through the modification of airflow in this region by retracting the tongue or constricting the pharynx are called **pharyngeals**. Pharyngeals can be found in many dialects of Arabic, but not in English.

Glottal

Sounds produced using the vocal folds as primary articulators are called **glottals**. The sound at the beginning of the English words *heave* and *hog* is made at the glottis.

5 MANNERS OF ARTICULATION

The lips, tongue, velum, and glottis can be positioned in different ways to produce different sound types. These various configurations are called the **manners of articulation.**

5.1 ORAL VERSUS NASAL PHONES

A basic distinction in manner of articulation is between **oral** and **nasal** phones. When the velum is raised, cutting off the airflow through the nasal passages, oral sounds are produced. The velum, however, can be lowered to allow air to pass through the nasal passages, producing a sound that is nasal. Both consonants and vowels can be nasal, in which case they are generally voiced. (Unless otherwise noted, all nasals represented in this chapter are voiced.) The consonants at the end of the English words *sun*, *sum*, and *sung* are nasal. For many speakers of English, the vowels of words such as *bank* and *wink* are also nasal.

5.2 STOPS

Stops are made with a complete and momentary closure of airflow through the vocal tract. In the world's languages, stops are found at bilabial, dental, alveolar, palatal, velar, uvular, and glottal points of articulation.

In English, bilabial, alveolar, and velar oral and nasal stops occur in the following words. Note that [ŋ] does not occur word-initially in English.

Table 2.3 English stops and their transcription

Bilabial		*Transcription*
Voiceless	span	[p]
Voiced	ban	[b]
Nasal	man	[m]
Alveolar		
Voiceless	stun	[t]
Voiced	dot	[d]
Nasal	not	[n]
Velar		
Voiceless	scar	[k]
Voiced	gap	[g]
Nasal	wing	[ŋ]
Glottal		
Voiceless	(see below)	[ʔ]

The glottal stop is commonly heard in English in the expression *uh-uh,* meaning 'no'. The two vowels in this utterance are each preceded by a momentary closing of the airstream at the glottis. In some British dialects, the glottal stop is commonly heard in place of the [t] in a word like *bottle.* This glottal stop is often spelled with an apostrophe (*bo'l*).

A grid for stops

Table 2.4 presents a grid on which the stop consonants of English are ranged horizontally according to point of articulation. As you can see, each stop, with one exception, has voiced and voiceless counterparts. The glottal stop is always voiceless. It is produced with the vocal folds drawn firmly together, and since no air can pass through the glottis, the vocal folds cannot be set in motion.

Table 2.4 English stop consonants

	Bilabial	*Alveolar*	*Velar*	*Glottal*
Voiceless	[p]	[t]	[k]	[ʔ]
Voiced	[b]	[d]	[g]	
Nasal	[m]	[n]	[ŋ]	

5.3 Fricatives

Fricatives are consonants produced with a continuous airflow through the mouth. They belong to a large class of sounds called **continuants** (a class that also includes vowels and glides), all of which share this property. The fricatives form a special class of continuants; during their production, they are accompanied by a continuous audible noise because the air used in their production passes through a very narrow opening.

English fricatives

English has voiceless and voiced labiodental fricatives at the beginnings of the words *fat* and *vat*, voiceless and voiced interdental fricatives word-initially in the words *thin* and *those*, alveolar fricatives word-initially in *sing* and *zip*, and a voiceless alveopalatal fricative word-initially in *ship*. The voiced alveopalatal fricative is rare in English. It is the first consonant in the word *azure*, and is also heard in the words *pleasure* and *rouge*. The voiceless glottal fricative of English is heard in *hotel* and *hat*.

Special note must be taken of the alveolar fricatives [s] and [z]. There are two ways that English speakers commonly produce these sounds. Some speakers raise the tongue tip to the alveolar ridge (or to just behind the upper front teeth) and allow the air to pass through a grooved channel in the tongue. Other speakers form this same channel using the blade of the tongue; the tip is placed behind the lower front teeth.

Table 2.5 The transcription of English fricatives

Glottal state	*Point of articulation*	*Transcription*
	Labiodental	
Voiceless	fan	[f]
Voiced	van	[v]
	Interdental	
Voiceless	thin	[θ]
Voiced	then	[ð]
	Alveolar	
Voiceless	sun	[s]
Voiced	zip	[z]
	Alveopalatal	
Voiceless	ship	[ʃ]
Voiced	azure	[ʒ]
	Glottal	
Voiceless	hat	[h]

A grid for fricatives

Table 2.6 presents a grid on which the fricative consonants of English are ranged according to point of articulation. As in Table 2.5, dentals are not distinguished from alveolars, since most languages have sounds with either one or the other point of articulation, but not both. Note that IPA [ʃ] and [ʒ] correspond respectively to North American [š] and [ž].

Table 2.6 English fricatives

	Labiodental	*Interdental*	*Alveolar*	*Alveopalatal*	*Glottal*
Voiceless	[f]	[θ]	[s]	[ʃ]	[h]
Voiced	[v]	[ð]	[z]	[ʒ]	

5.4 Affricates

When a stop articulation is released, the tongue moves rapidly away from the point of articulation. Some noncontinuant consonants show a slow release of the closure; these sounds are called **affricates**. English has only two affricates, both of which are alveopalatal. They are heard word-initially in *church* and *jump*, and are transcribed as [tʃ] and [dʒ], respectively.

A grid for affricates

Table 2.7 presents a grid showing the two English affricates. Note that IPA [tʃ] and [dʒ] correspond to North American [č] and [ǰ], respectively.

Table 2.7 English affricates

	Alveopalatal
Voiceless	[tʃ]
Voiced	[dʒ]

Stridents and sibilants

At the beginning of this chapter, it was noted that acoustic as well as articulatory criteria are sometimes used in describing speech sounds. An acoustic criterion comes into play to describe fricatives and affricates. These sounds are subdivided into two types, some of which are distinctly louder than others. These noisier fricatives and affricates are called **stridents**. Their quieter counterparts, such as [θ] or [ð], which have the same or nearly same place of articulation, are considered **nonstrident**. Stridents are also known as **sibilants**.

Table 2.8 Strident fricatives and affricates in English

Place of articulation	*Strident*	
	Voiceless	*Voiced*
Alveolar	[s]	[z]
Alveopalatal	[ʃ]	[ʒ]
	[tʃ]	[dʒ]

5.5 Voice lag and aspiration

After the release of certain voiceless stops in English, you can sometimes hear a lag or brief delay before the voicing of a following vowel. Since the lag in the onset of vocalic voicing is accompanied by the release of air, the traditional term for this phenomenon is **aspiration**. It is transcribed with a small raised [ʰ] after the aspirated consonant. Table 2.9 provides some examples of aspirated and unaspirated consonants in English (some vowel symbols are introduced here as well). Notice that the sounds that have both aspirated and unaspirated varieties are all voiceless stops. In other languages, voiceless fricatives and affricates may also be aspirated or unaspirated.

Table 2.9 Aspirated and unaspirated consonants in English

Aspirated		*Unaspirated*	
[pʰæt]	pat	[spæt]	spat
[tʰʌb]	tub	[stʌb]	stub
[kʰowp]	cope	[skowp]	scope

Figure 2.5 shows how aspiration of a voiceless consonant takes place, using the aspirated consonant [pʰ] as an example. Though the sequence of articulations takes place continuously, the figure illustrates only certain moments.

a) As articulation of the voiceless consonant is begun, the glottis is open.

b) The closure for the consonant is released and the vowel articulation begins; however, the glottis is not yet closed enough to permit voicing to begin. Because of this, the vowel is briefly voiceless, giving the impression of an extra release of air that we call *aspiration*.

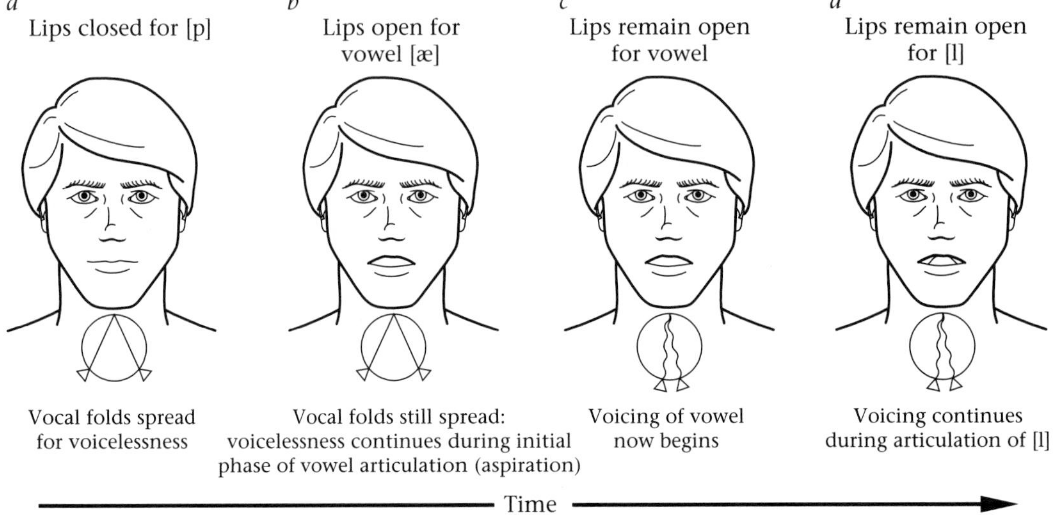

Figure 2.5 Aspirated consonant production (English *pal*)

c) After a short delay, measurable in milliseconds, voicing of the vowel begins.

d) The lips remain open and voicing continues during the articulation of the final consonant of the word.

Figures 2.6 and 2.7 show the relation between articulation and voicing for unaspirated and voiced consonants. The unaspirated consonant, such as the [p] of English

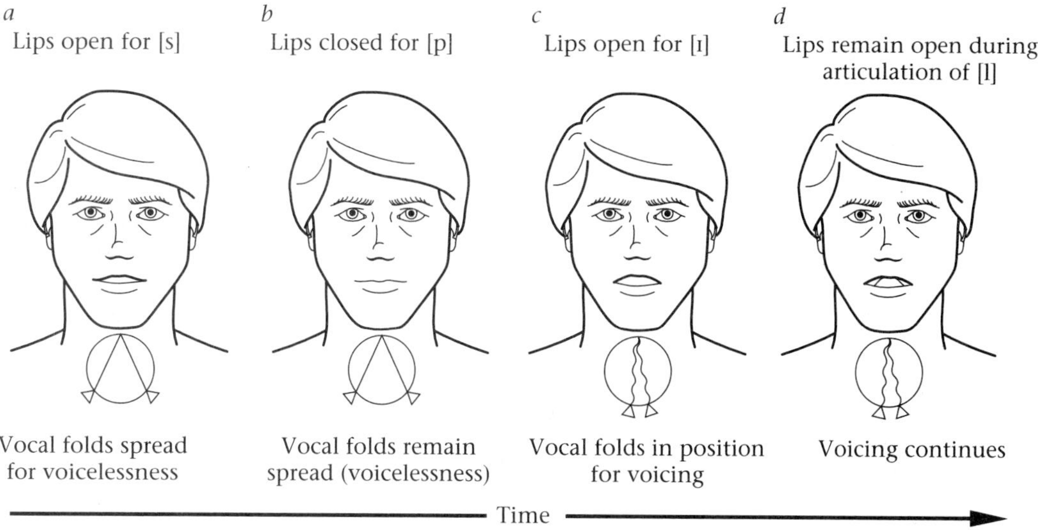

Figure 2.6 Unaspirated consonant production (English *spill*)

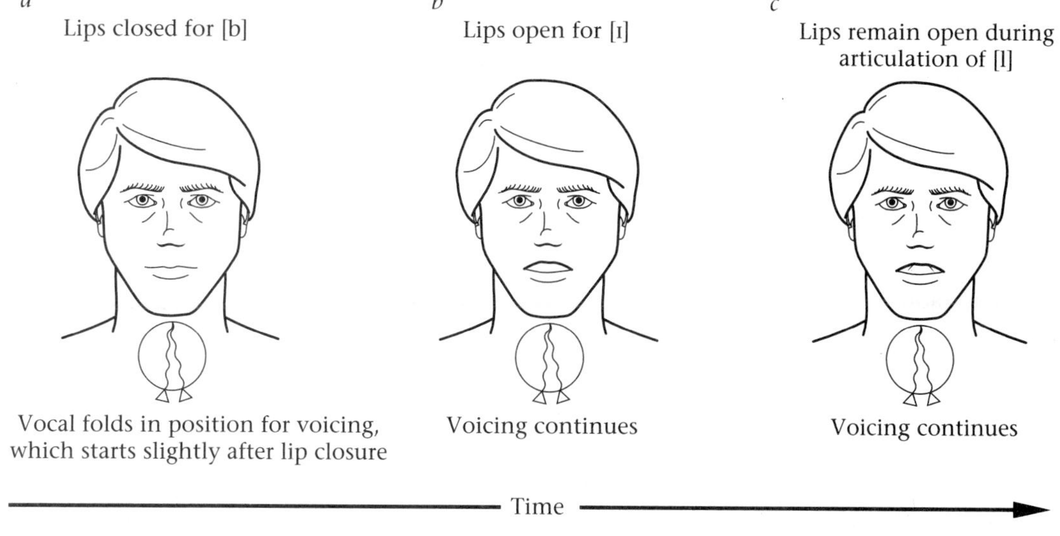

Figure 2.7 Voiced consonant release (English *bill*)

spill, shows voicing of the vowel starting very soon after release of the consonant articulation. The voiced initial [b] of English *bill* shows voicing starting just before the release of the bilabial articulation. In Figure 2.7, note how voicing precedes the release of the labial articulators.

5.6 Liquids

Among the sounds commonly found in the world's languages are *l* and *r* and their numerous variants. They form a special class of consonants known as *liquids*.

Laterals

Varieties of *l* are called **laterals**. As laterals are articulated, air escapes through the mouth along the lowered sides of the tongue. When the tongue tip is raised to the dental or alveolar position, the dental or alveolar laterals are produced. Both may be transcribed as [l].

Because laterals are generally voiced, the term *lateral* used alone usually means 'voiced lateral'. Still, there are instances of voiceless laterals in speech. The voiceless dental or alveolar lateral is written with an additional phonetic symbol, called a **diacritic**. In this case, the diacritic is a circle beneath the symbol: [l̥]. Voiceless laterals can be heard in the pronunciation of the English words *please* and *clear*.

English *r*'s

Numerous varieties of *r* are also heard in the world's languages. This section describes the types found in English.

The *r* of English as it is spoken in North America is made either by curling the tongue tip back into the mouth or by bunching the tongue upward and back in the mouth. This *r* is known as a **retroflex** *r* and is heard in *ride* and *car*. It is transcribed as [r] in this book. IPA transcription favors [ɹ] for this sound, though it also offers the symbol [r].

Another sound commonly identified with *r* is the **flap**. The flap is produced when the tongue tip strikes the alveolar ridge as it passes across it. It is heard in the North American English pronunciation of *bitter* and *butter*, and in some British pronunciations of *very*. It is commonly transcribed as [ɾ] and is generally voiced. Table 2.10 presents the laterals, *r*, *l*, and the flap of American English.

Table 2.10 English liquids

		Alveolar	
Laterals		voiced	[l]
		voiceless	[l̥]
r's	retroflex	voiced	[r]
		voiceless	[r̥]
	flap		[ɾ]

5.7 Syllabic liquids and nasals

Liquids and nasals are more sonorous than other consonants and in this respect are more like vowels than are the other consonants. In fact, they are so sonorous that they may function as syllabic nuclei. When they do so, they are called **syllabic liquids** and **syllabic nasals**. Syllabic liquids and nasals are found in many of the world's languages, including English. In transcription, they are usually marked with a short diacritic line underneath. Unfortunately for beginning linguistics students, North American transcription is not always consistent here. The syllabic *r* sound heard in words like *bird* and *her* is transcribed as a vowel-*r* sequence: [ər]. (The vowel symbol is presented in Section 6.2 of this chapter.) The IPA symbol for this sound is [ɚ].

Table 2.11 Syllabic liquids and nasals in English

	Syllabic		*Nonsyllabic*
bottle	[bɑɾl̩]	lift	[lɪft]
funnel	[fʌnl̩]	pill	[pʰɪl]
bird	[bərd], [bɚd], [br̩d]	rat	[ræt]
her	[hər], [hɚ], [hr̩]	car	[kʰar]
button	[bʌtn̩]	now	[naw]
'm-m'	[ʔm̩ʔm̩] (meaning 'no')	mat	[mæt]

5.8 Glides

Recall that a glide is a very rapidly articulated nonsyllabic segment. The two glides of American English are the jod [jɑd] (North American 'y-glide') [j] of *yes* and *boy*, and the w-glide [w] of *wet* and *now*. The [j] in IPA transcription corresponds to the [y] of North American transcription.

The [j] is a palatal glide (often cited as alveopalatal as well) whose articulation is virtually identical to that of the vowel [i] of *see*. You can verify this by pronouncing a [j] in an extended manner; it will sound very close to an [i].

The glide [w] is made with the tongue raised and pulled back near the velum and with the lips protruding, or rounded. For this reason, it is sometimes called a labio-velar. The [w] corresponds closely in articulation to the vowel [u] of *who*. This can be verified by extending the pronunciation of a [w]. We will consider [w] a rounded velar glide for purposes of description. Some speakers of English also have a voiceless (labio)velar glide, transcribed [ʍ], in the words *when*, *where*, and *which* (but not in *witch*).

English consonants

Table 2.12 provides a summary of the places and manners of articulation of English consonants.

Table 2.12 English consonants: places and manners of articulation

		Place of articulation						
Manner of articulation		*Labial*	*Labiodental*	*Interdental*	*Alveolar*	*(Alveo)palatal*	*Velar*	*Glottal*
Stop	voiceless	p			t		k	ʔ
	voiced	b			d		g	
Fricative	voiceless		f	θ	s	ʃ		h
	voiced		v	ð	z	ʒ		
Affricate	voiceless					ʧ		
	voiced					ʤ		
Nasal	voiced	m			n		ŋ	
Liquid	voiced lateral				l			
	voiced retroflex				r, ɾ			
Glide	voiced					j	w	
	(voiceless)						(ʍ)	

6 VOWELS

Vowels are sonorous, syllabic sounds made with the vocal tract more open than it is for consonant and glide articulations. Different vowel sounds (also called vowel *qualities*) are produced by varying the placement of the body of the tongue and shaping the lips. The shape of the cavity can be further altered by protruding the lips to produce rounded vowels, or by lowering the velum to produce a nasal vowel. Finally, vowels may be tense or lax, depending on the degree of vocal tract constriction during their articulation.

In the following section on vowels you are introduced to most of the basic vowels of English. Some phonetic detail is omitted that will be introduced in the following chapter.

6.1 Simple vowels and diphthongs

English vowels are divided into two major types, **simple vowels** and **diphthongs**. Simple vowels do not show a noticeable change in quality. The vowels of *pit, set, cat, bought, cut, put,* and the first vowel of *suppose* are all simple vowels.

Diphthongs are vowels that exhibit a change in quality within a single syllable. English diphthongs show changes in quality that are due to tongue movement away from the initial vowel articulation towards a glide position. This change in vowel quality is clearly perceptible in words such as *say, buy, cow, ice, lout, go,* and *boy*. The change is less easy to hear, but present nonetheless, in the vowels of words like *heed* and *lose*. Table 2.13 presents the simple vowels and diphthongs of English. The diphthongs are transcribed as vowel-glide sequences.

Table 2.13 Simple vowels and diphthongs of American English

Simple vowel		*Diphthong*		*Simple vowel*		*Diphthong*	
pit	[ɪ]	heat	[ij]	cut	[ʌ]	lose	[uw]
set	[ɛ]	say	[ej]	bought	[ɔ]	grow	[ow]
cat	[æ]	buy	[aj]	put	[ʊ]	boy	[ɔj]
pot	[ɑ]	cow	[aw]	suppose	[ə]		

In all cases, the diphthongs are somewhat longer than the simple vowels.

6.2 Basic parameters for describing vowels

Vowel articulations are not as easy to feel at first as consonant articulations, since the vocal tract is not narrowed as much. To become acquainted with vowel articulation, alternately pronounce the vowels of *he* and *paw*. You will feel the tongue move from a **high** front to a **low** back position. Once you feel this tongue movement, alternate between the vowels of *paw* and *pat*. You will feel the tongue moving from the low **back** to low **front** position. Finally, alternate between the vowels of *he* and *who*. You will notice that in addition to a tongue movement between the high front and high back position, you are also **rounding** your lips for the [uw]. Figure 2.8 shows a midsagittal view of the tongue position for the vowels [ij], [ɑ], and [uw] based on X-ray studies of speech.

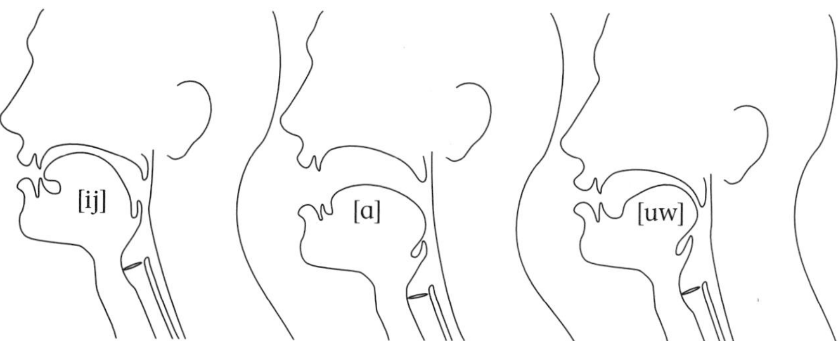

Figure 2.8 Tongue position and transcription for three English vowels

Vowels for which the tongue is neither raised nor lowered are called **mid vowels**. The front vowel of English *made* or *fame* is mid, front, and unrounded. The vowel of *code* and *soak* is mid, back, and rounded. In the case of diphthongs, the articulatory descriptions refer to the tongue position of the vowel nucleus. The vowels presented so far in this section are summed up in Table 2.14. Note that in describing the vowels, the articulatory parameters are presented in the order *height, backness, rounding*.

Table 2.14 Basic phonetic parameters for describing American English vowels

heat	[ij]	high front unrounded
fate	[ej]	mid front unrounded
mad	[æ]	low front unrounded
Sue	[uw]	high back rounded
boat	[ow]	mid back rounded
sun	[ʌ]	mid back unrounded
cot	[ɑ]	low back unrounded

Tongue positions for these vowels are illustrated in Figure 2.9. The trapezoid corresponds roughly to the space within which the tongue moves, which is wider at the top of the oral cavity and more restricted at the bottom. Nonfront vowels are traditionally divided into central and back vowels (see Figures 2.9 and 2.10); often the term *back* alone is used for all nonfront vowels.

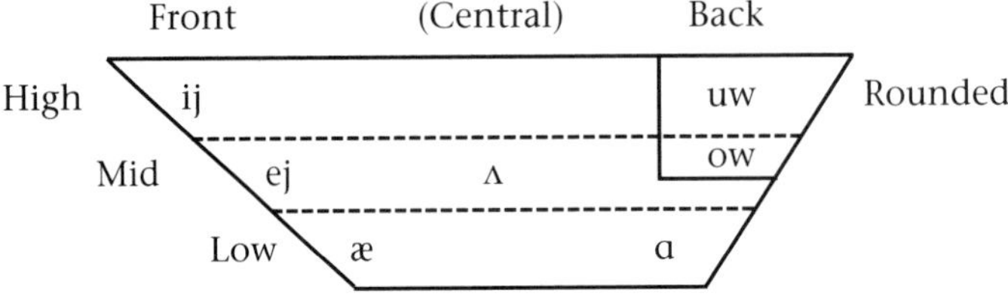

Figure 2.9 Basic tongue positions for English vowels

6.3 Tense and lax vowels

All of the vowels illustrated in Figure 2.9 except [æ] and [ʌ] are **tense vowels**; they are produced with a placement of the tongue that results in greater vocal tract constriction than that of nontense vowels; as well, tense vowels are longer than nontense vowels. Some vowels of English are made with roughly the same tongue position as the tense vowels, but with a less constricted articulation; they are called **lax vowels**.

Table 2.15 Tense and lax vowels in American English

	Tense		*Lax*
heat	[ij]	hit	[ɪ]
mate	[ej]	met	[ɛ]
—	—	mat	[æ]
shoot	[uw]	should	[ʊ]
coat	[ow]	(ought	[ɔ] in some dialects)
—	—	cut	[ʌ]
—	—	Canada	[ə]
lock	[ɑ]	—	—
lies	[aj]		
loud	[aw]		

Table 2.15 provides examples from English comparing tense and lax vowels. Note that not all the vowels come in tense/lax pairs.

The difference in two vowels illustrated in Table 2.15 is often not easy to hear at first. Both the vowel [ʌ] in *cut, dud, pluck,* and *Hun,* and the vowel [ə] of *Canada, about, tomahawk,* and *sofa* are mid, back, unrounded, and lax. The vowel of the second set of examples, called **schwa**, is referred to as a **reduced vowel**. In addition to being lax, it is characterized by very brief duration (briefer than that of any of the other vowels).

There is a simple test that helps determine whether vowels are tense or lax. In English, monosyllabic words spoken in isolation do not end in lax vowels (except for [ɔ]). We find *see* [sij], *say* [sej], *Sue* [suw], *so* [sow], and *spa* [spɑ] in English, but not *s[ɪ], *s[ɛ], *s[æ], *s[ʊ], or *s[ʌ]. Schwa, however, frequently appears in unstressed position in polysyllabic words like *sofa* [ə] and *Canada* [ə]. It should be pointed out—especially for those who think their ears are deceiving them—that many speakers produce the final vowel in the last two examples not as [ə] but as [ʌ].

The representation of vowels and their articulatory positions (Figure 2.9) is expanded in Figure 2.10 to include both tense and lax vowels.

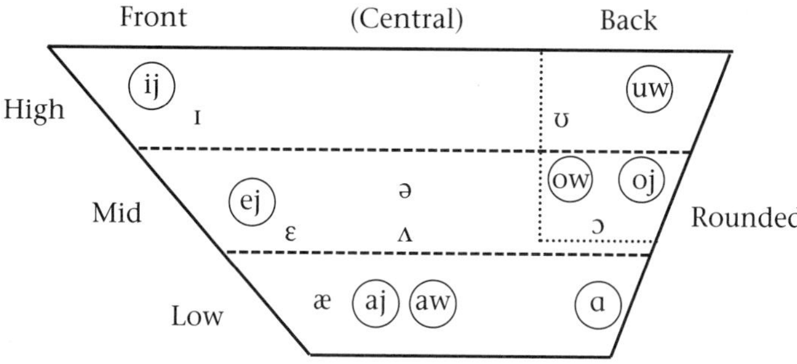

Figure 2.10 American English vowels (tense vowels are circled)

This rather formidable crowd of vowels should not intimidate you. If you are a native speaker of English, you have been using these vowels (and others, some of which you will be introduced to in the next chapter) most of your life. Learning to hear them consciously and transcribe them is not a difficult task. The next section provides more examples of the transcription of English consonants and vowels.

7 PHONETIC TRANSCRIPTION OF AMERICAN ENGLISH CONSONANTS AND VOWELS

The following tables show the phonetic symbols for consonants and vowels commonly used to transcribe American English. To show how each symbol is used, one word is transcribed completely, and then some other words in which the same sound is found are given. You will notice that in the example words, the spelling of the sound may vary. Be careful of this when you transcribe words phonetically—the sound of a word, not its spelling, is what is transcribed!

Table 2.16 Transcribing English consonants

Symbol	*Word*	*Transcription*	*More examples*
[pʰ]	pit	[pʰɪt]	pain, upon, apart
[p]	spit	[spɪt]	spar, crispy, upper, Yuppie, culprit, bumper
[tʰ]	tick	[tʰɪk]	tell, attire, terror, Tutu
[t]	stuck	[stʌk]	stem, hunter, nasty, mostly
[kʰ]	keep	[kʰijp]	cow, kernel, recur
[k]	skip	[skɪp]	scatter, uncle, blacklist, likely
[tʃ]	chip	[tʃɪp]	lunch, lecher, ditch, belch
[dʒ]	judge	[dʒʌdʒ]	germ, journal, budgie, wedge
[b]	bib	[bɪb]	boat, liberate, rob, blast
[d]	dip	[dɪp]	dust, sled, draft
[ɾ]	butter	[bʌɾər]	madder, matter, hitting, writer, rider
[g]	get	[gɛt]	gape, mugger, twig, gleam
[f]	fit	[fɪt]	flash, coughing, proof, phlegmatic, gopher
[v]	vat	[væt]	vote, oven, prove
[θ]	thick	[θɪk]	thought, ether, teeth, three, bathroom
[ð]	though	[ðow]	then, bother, teethe, bathe
[s]	sip	[sɪp]	psychology, fasten, lunacy, bass, curse, science
[z]	zap	[zæp]	Xerox, scissors, desire, zipper, fuzzy
[ʃ]	ship	[ʃɪp]	shock, nation, mission, glacier, wish
[ʒ]	azure	[æʒər]	measure, rouge, visual, garage (for some speakers), Taj Mahal
[h]	hat	[hæt]	who, ahoy, forehead, behind
[j]	yet	[jɛt]	_use, f_ew, yes
[w]	witch	[wɪtʃ]	wait, weird, queen, now
[ʍ]	which	[ʍɪtʃ]	what, where, when (only for some speakers)
[l]	leaf	[lijf]	loose, lock, alive, hail
[l̩]	huddle	[hʌɾl̩]	bottle, needle (for many speakers)
[r]	reef	[rijf]	prod, arrive, tear
[r̩]	bird	[br̩d] [bɚd], [bərd]	early, hurt, stir, purr, doctor
[m]	moat	[mowt]	mind, humor, shimmer, sum, thumb
[m̩]	'm-m'	[ʔm̩ʔm̩]	bottom, random
[n]	note	[nowt]	now, winner, angel, sign, wind
[n̩]	button	[bʌtn̩]	Jordan, batten
[ŋ]	sing	[sɪŋ]	singer, longer, bank, twinkle

Table 2.17 Transcribing English vowels

Symbol	*Word*	*Transcription*	*More examples*
[ij]	fee	[fij]	she, cream, believe, receive, serene, amoeba, highly
[ɪ]	fit	[fɪt]	hit, income, definition, been (for some speakers)
[ej]	fate	[fejt]	they, clay, grain, gauge, engage, great, sleigh
[ɛ]	let	[lɛt]	led, head, says, said, sever, guest
[æ]	bat	[bæt]	panic, racket, laugh, Vancouver
[uw]	boot	[buwt]	to, two, loose, brew, Louise, Lucy, through
[ʊ]	book	[bʊk]	should, put, hood
[ow]	note	[nowt]	no, throat, though, slow, toe, oaf, O'Conner
[oj]	boy	[boj]	voice, boil, toy
[ɔ]	fought	[fɔt]	caught, normal, all
[ɑ]	rot	[rɑt]	cot, father, rob
[ʌ]	shut	[ʃʌt]	other, udder, tough, lucky, flood
[ə]	roses	[rowzəz]	collide, hinted, telegraph, (to) suspect
[aw]	crowd	[krawd]	(to) house, plow, bough
[aj]	lies	[lajz]	my, tide, thigh, buy

8 SUPRASEGMENTALS

All phones have certain inherent **suprasegmental** or **prosodic** properties that form part of their makeup no matter what their place or manner of articulation. These properties are **pitch**, **loudness**, and **length**.

All sounds give us a subjective impression of being relatively higher or lower in pitch. Pitch is the auditory property of a sound that enables us to place it on a scale that ranges from low to high. Pitch is especially noticeable in sonorous sounds like vowels, glides, liquids, and nasals. Even stop and fricative consonants convey different pitches. This is particularly noticeable among the fricatives, as you can hear by extending the pronunciation of [s] and then of [ʃ]; the [s] is clearly higher pitched. All sounds have some degree of intrinsic loudness as well or they could not be heard. Moreover, all sounds occupy a certain stretch of time—they give the subjective impression of length.

8.1 PITCH: TONE AND INTONATION

Speakers of any language have the ability to control the level of pitch they speak on. This is accomplished by controlling the tension of the vocal folds and the amount of air that passes through the glottis. The combination of tensed vocal folds and greater air pressure results in higher voice pitch on vowels and sonorant consonants, while less tense vocal folds and lower air pressure result in lower voice pitch. Two kinds of controlled pitch movement found in human language are called **tone** and **intonation**.

Tone

A language is said to have tone or be a **tone language** when differences in word meaning are signalled by differences in pitch. Pitch on forms in tone languages functions very differently from the movement of pitch in a nontone language. When a speaker of English says *a car?* with a rising pitch, the word *car* does not mean anything different from the same form pronounced on a different pitch level or with a different pitch contour. In contrast, when a speaker of a tone language such as Mandarin pronounces the form *mà* [ma] with a falling pitch, it means 'scold', but when the same form (*ma*) is pronounced with a rising pitch, as [má], the meaning is 'hemp' (see Figure 2.13). There is no parallel to anything like this in nontone languages such as English and French.

Some tone languages show tones at only certain pitch levels. Sarcee, an Athapaskan language spoken in Canada, has tones heard at high, mid, and low pitch levels. In Figure 2.11, the uppercase letters H, M, and L stand for high, mid, and low tones, respectively. A line called an **association line** drawn from the letters to the vowel links the segments with their respective tones. (In the following example, ɬ is a voiceless lateral fricative.)

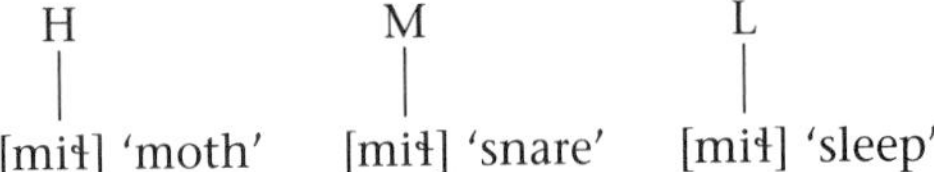

Figure 2.11 Sarcee level tones

This type of notation is known as **autosegmental** notation.

Level tones that signal meaning differences are called **register tones**: Two or three register tones are the norm in most of the world's register tone languages, though four have been reported for Mazatec, a language spoken in Mexico.

A single tone may be associated with more than one syllabic element. In Mende, a language spoken in West Africa, there are certain polysyllabic forms that show the same tone on each syllable (here, the diacritic ´ indicates a high tone and the diacritic ` indicates a low tone).

Table 2.18 High-tone and low-tone words in Mende

pɛ́lɛ́	'banana'
háwámá	'waistline'
kpàkàlì	'tripod chair'

Autosegmental notation allows us to represent the tone as characteristic of an entire form. The single underlying tone unit is associated with all vowels.

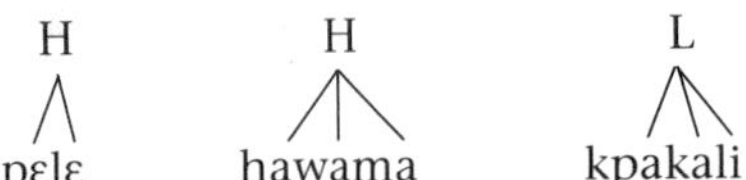

Figure 2.12 Tone as a word feature

In some languages, tones change pitch on single syllabic elements. Moving pitches that signal meaning differences are called **contour tones**. In Mandarin, both register and contour tones are heard. Contour tones are shown by pitch level notation lines that converge above the vowel, as shown in Figure 2.13.

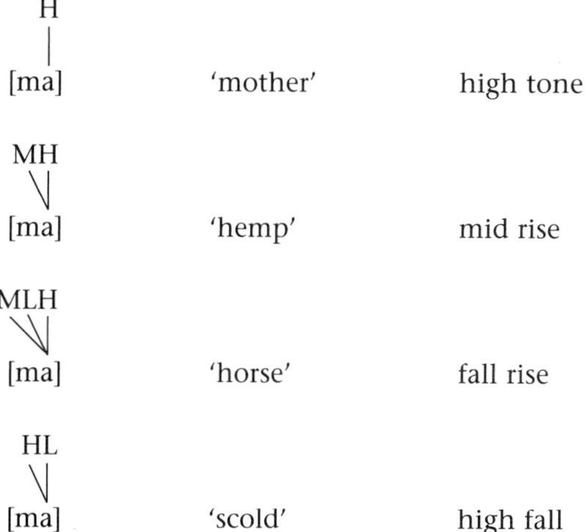

Figure 2.13 Register and contour tones in Mandarin

In Figure 2.13, there is one (high) register tone. The other tones are all contour tones.

In other languages, tone can have an even more extended function. In Bini, a language spoken in Nigeria, tone can signal differences in the tense of a verb (such as past versus present), as Figure 2.14 shows.

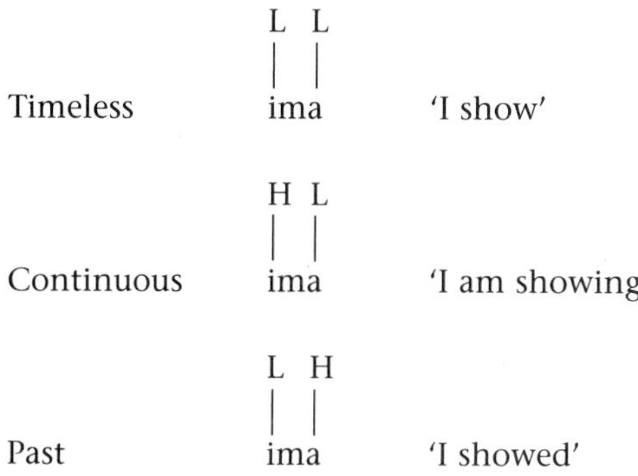

Figure 2.14 Tense and tone in Bini

Although tones may seem exotic to native speakers of Western European languages, they are very widespread. Tone languages are found throughout North and South America, Sub-Saharan Africa, and the Far East.

Intonation

Pitch movement in spoken utterances that is not related to differences in word meaning is called intonation. It makes no difference to the meaning of the word *seven*, for example, whether it is pronounced with a rising pitch or a falling pitch.

Intonation often does serve to convey information of a broadly meaningful nature, however. For example, the falling pitch we hear at the end of a statement in English such as *Fred parked the car* signals that the utterance is complete. For this reason, falling intonation at the end of an utterance is called a **terminal (intonation) contour**. Conversely, a rising or level intonation, called a **nonterminal (intonation) contour**, often signals incompleteness. Nonterminal contours are often heard in the nonfinal forms found in lists and telephone numbers.

Sally Fred Helen and Joe

two eight four two five one three

Figure 2.15 Rising nonterminal intonations in a list and a telephone number

In questions, final rising intonations also signal a kind of incompleteness in that they indicate that a conversational exchange is not finished.

Did you have a nice time

Figure 2.16 Nonterminal intonation in a question

However, English sentences that contain question words like *who, what, when,* and *how* (for example, *What did you buy?*) ordinarily do not have rising intonation. It is as if the question word itself is enough to indicate that an answer is expected.

Intonation can be represented graphically as in Figures 2.15 and 2.16. A more formal way of representing intonation is shown in Figure 2.17. Here, as in tonal representation, L and H are relative terms for differences in pitch. The letters HL are placed above the syllabic elements on which the pitch change occurs. The dotted lines indicate that the lowering pitch spreads across the remaining pitch-bearing elements.

L HL

There's an elephant in here.

Figure 2.17 A terminal contour

Rising intonation on names or requests is commonly heard in addressing people. Its use indicates that the speaker is opening a conversation or that some further action is expected from the addressee.

LH H LH

Margo? Is that you?

Figure 2.18 Two nonterminal contours

The complex uses of intonation have just been touched on here. Consider, for example, that rising intonation is often used to express politeness, as in *Please sit down*. Some linguists think that this use is an extension of the 'open-ended mode' of intonation, and that since a rising intonation indicates that further response is expected (but not demanded) of the addressee, a sentence uttered with a rising intonation sounds less like an order and so is more polite.

Intonation and tone

Tone and intonation are not mutually exclusive. Tone languages show intonation of all types. This is possible since the tones are not absolute but relative pitches. A tone is perceived as high if it is high relative to the pitches around it. As long as this relative difference is maintained, the pitch distinctions will also be maintained. Figure 2.19 shows this graphically. It represents the overall pitch of a declarative sentence in Igbo, a West African language with register tones. Note how an Igbo speaker clearly maintains the distinction among the pitch registers even as the overall pitch of the utterance falls. Each high tone is always lower than the preceding high tone, but higher than the low tone that immediately precedes it. This phenomenon is known as **downdrift**.

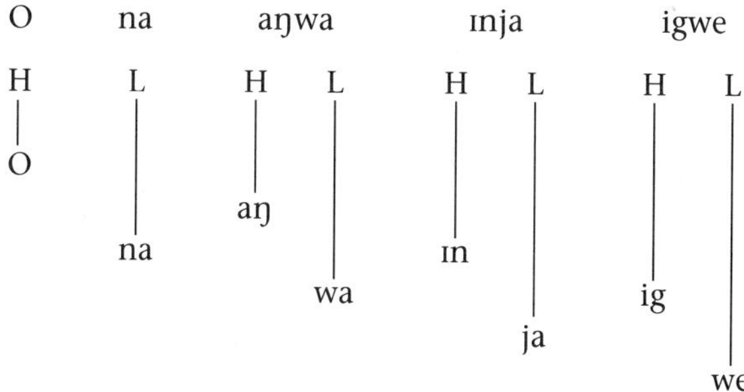

'He is trying to ride a bicycle.'

Figure 2.19 Tone and intonation: downdrift in Igbo

8.2 LENGTH

In many languages there are both vowels and consonants whose articulation takes longer relative to that of other vowels and consonants. This phenomenon, known as length, is widespread in the world's languages. Length is indicated in phonetic transcription by the use of an IPA style colon [ː] (or simply a colon in North American transcription [:]) placed after the segment in question.

Italian, Hungarian, German, Cree, and Finnish are a few of the many languages that have long and short vowels. Yap, a language spoken on the island of Yap in the Western Pacific, shows short and long vowels in pairs of words such as the following.

Table 2.19 Short and long vowels in Yap

[θis]	'to topple'	[θiːs]	'(a) post'
[pul]	'to gather'	[puːl]	'moon'
[ʔer]	'near you'	[ʔeːr]	'part of a lagoon'

Italian shows short and long consonants in pairs of words such as those shown in Table 2.20. Long and short consonants are also found in many other languages, including Finnish, Turkish, and Hungarian.

Table 2.20 Short and long consonants in Italian

fato	[fatɔ]	'fate'	fatto	[fat:ɔ]	'fact'
fano	[fanɔ]	'grove'	fanno	[fan:ɔ]	'they do'
casa	[kasa]	'house'	cassa	[kas:a]	'box'

8.3 STRESS

In any utterance, some vowels are perceived as more prominent than others. In a word such as *telegraphic* [t^h è l ə g r ǽ f ɪ k], the two vowel nuclei that are more prominent than the others are [ɛ] and [æ]. Syllabic segments perceived as relatively more prominent are stressed. **Stress** is a cover term for the combined effects of pitch, loudness, and length—the result of which is prominence. In each language, the effect of these prosodic features varies. In general, English stressed vowels are higher in pitch, longer, and louder than unstressed ones. But this is not always the case. The example word *telegraphic* could just as well be pronounced with the stressed syllables lower than the unstressed ones. The important thing is that they be prominent with respect to the syllables around them, and this is usually accomplished by a relatively large shift in one, two, or all three of the parameters of pitch, loudness, and length.

In some languages, the impression of vowel prominence results from an interaction of the prosodic parameters that is different from that found in English. In Modern Greek, for example, syllables tend to be of equal length. Stress, therefore, is manifested by a change only in pitch and loudness and not in syllable length. Tone languages do not change the pitch level or contour of tones to mark stress. In many of these languages, relative prominence is marked by exaggerating the vowel length or pitch contour.

There are various ways to mark stress in phonetic transcription. North American transcription commonly uses an acute accent [´] placed over the vowel nucleus in question to mark the most prominent or **primary stress**, and a grave accent [`] to mark the second most prominent or **secondary stress** or stresses. (This should not be confused with the use of the same diacritics to mark tone in tone languages.) Stress can also be marked by placing numbers above the stressed vowels, usually for a primary stress and for a secondary stress. The word *telegraphic* is transcribed as either of the following:

2)

                                        2   1
[t^h è l ə g r ǽ f ɪ k]   or   [t^h ɛ l ə g r æ f ɪ k]

The next examples show some differences in English stress placement.

Table 2.21 Differing stress placement in English

(an) éxport	[ɛ́ k s p o r t]	(to) expórt	[ɛ k s p ó r t]
(a) présent	[p r ɛ́ z ə n t]	(to) presént	[p r ij z ɛ́ n t]
télegràph	[t^h ɛ́ l ə g r æ̀ f]		
telégraphy	[t^h ə l ɛ́ g r ə f ij]		
tèlegráphic	[t^h ɛ̀ l ə g r ǽ f ɪ k]		

In the last four examples, you can also see that the quality of certain vowels varies depending on whether they are stressed or unstressed. This phenomenon is common in English, Russian, Palauan, and many other languages, but is not universal.

9 ARTICULATORY PROCESSES

Speech production is not a series of isolated events. The process of articulation is a complex one. The articulatory organs are operating independently of each other, and many fine adjustments are carried out very rapidly as we speak. As a consequence, speech production often results in the articulation of one sound affecting that of another sound. Articulatory adjustments that occur during the production of speech are called **processes**.

9.1 COARTICULATION

Figures 2.5 to 2.7 showed how aspiration results from **coarticulation**. Figure 2.20 shows some more complex aspects of coarticulation. Here, some of the articulatory organs involved in the production of the word *pan* are represented. Reading from top

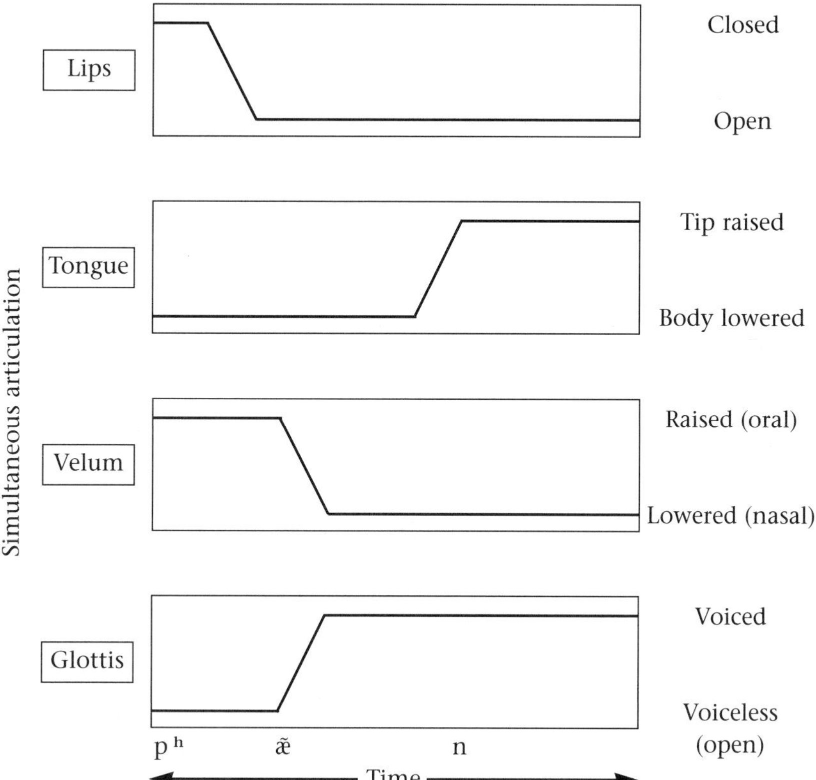

Figure 2.20 Coarticulation among several articulatory parameters of the word *pan*

to bottom, the actions of the lips, tongue, velum, and larynx are shown. The bold black line in each box represents the state of articulation listed to the right of the box.

Lips

The raised line in the upper box indicates that the lips are closed for the articulation of the initial [p] of *pan*. In order to articulate the vowel, the lips are opened—represented by the change in the position of the line—and they stay open during the articulation of the [n].

Tongue

The tongue body is lowered in anticipation of the low front vowel [æ] during articulation of the word-initial consonant. As the vowel articulation ends, the tongue tip is raised to articulate the final [n] of the word.

Velum

You have seen how nasal consonants are produced with the velum lowered to allow air to pass through the nasal cavities. The raising and lowering of the velum is not always precisely co-ordinated with other speech production activity. Speakers often anticipate lowering the velum for nasal consonants and, consequently, produce a nasal vowel before a nasal consonant. Many English speakers do this consistently in fluent speech when they pronounce words like *pan* [pʰæ̃n] or *bank* [bæ̃ŋk] (the tilde [˜] over the vowel indicates nasality). This is reflected in Figure 2.20. The line representing the velum closure changes to the open (lowered) position during the articulation of the vowel, before the tongue tip raises to articulate the word-final [n].

Glottis

You have already seen in Section 5.5 how aspiration results from a delay in voicing after the release of a voiced stop. Aspiration is shown in Figure 2.20 by the black line remaining in the voiceless position even after the lips have opened and the vowel articulation is in place.

Consonant coarticulation with vowels

All speech is characterized by the kind of complex coarticulation among the articulatory organs illustrated in Figure 2.20. Another typical coarticulation phenomenon occurs when we pronounce the sound [k] before the vowel [ij] in English in words such as *keys* and *keel*. The [k] we articulate before [ij] is pronounced with the back of the tongue so far forward it nearly touches the palate (and is transcribed as [k̯]). It is scarcely a velar articulation at all for many speakers. The [k] we pronounce before the vowels [ɑ] and [ow] in words such as *cot* and *cold* is articulated further back, and is a true velar. These adjustments are made in anticipation of the tongue position that will be needed for the vowel in question: front for the [ij] and back for the [ɑ] and [ow]. The [k] pronounced before the vowel [uw] in a word such as *cool* also shows lip rounding in anticipation of the following (back) rounded vowel and is transcribed as [kʷ].

9.2 Processes and efficiency

The cumulative effect of processes often results in making words easier to articulate, and in this sense they are said to make speech more efficient. When speakers of English nasalize the vowel of *bank* they do not delay lowering the velum until the exact moment the nasal consonant articulation is reached. Most English speakers begin lowering the velum for a nasal consonant almost as soon as they articulate the vowel that precedes it.

In a parallel manner, when speakers pronounce [k̂] as more palatal in a word such as *key*, they are speaking more efficiently from the point of view of articulation since they are making a less drastic adjustment in moving from the articulation of a more palatal [k̂] to that of a high front vowel than they would make in moving from a velar [k] to a high front vowel. Even more drastically, a speaker of English who says [pr̥ejd] for *parade* is making a major adjustment that results in a more efficient articulation: the two syllables of a careful pronunciation of *parade* are reduced to one by dropping the unstressed vowel of the first syllable; the tongue position for [r] can be anticipated during pronunciation of the [p]; finally, the voicelessness of the initial stop is carried on through the [r̥].

9.3 Processes and clarity

Some processes appear to make articulation less, not more efficient. For example, English speakers often lengthen consonants and vowels when they are asked to repeat a word that someone has not heard clearly. The following kind of exchange is typical.

3)

"It's Fred."
"Did you say, 'It's red'?"
"No, I said, 'Fffreeed!'"

Lengthening segments results in a greater articulatory effort, but the process results in a form being more distinct and therefore easier to perceive.

Another process that results in more easily perceivable speech adds a segment under certain conditions. When speaking slowly and carefully in a noisy environment, for example, English speakers often insert a vowel inside a group of consonants. This breaks up the sequence of consonants into separate syllables. To judge from the use people often make of this process when they wish to be clearly understood, it may well make words easier to perceive.

4)

"Stop screaming!"
"What?"
"I said, 'Stop sc[ə]reaming.'"

These examples show that there are two basic reasons for the existence of articulatory processes. Some processes result in a more efficient articulation of a series of sounds in that the precise timing and co-ordination of speech is relaxed to various degrees. Other processes result in a more distinct output, which is easier to perceive than fluent or rapid everyday speech. Although these two types of processes might at first appear to be contradictory, each serves a particular end in speech production.

9.4 Types of articulatory processes

Only a finite number of processes operate in language, though their end result is a great deal of linguistic variability. In this section, we survey some of the most common of these processes.

Assimilation

A number of different processes, collectively known as **assimilation**, result from the influence of one segment on another (see Section 1.2). Assimilation always results from a sound becoming more like another nearby sound in terms of one or more of its phonetic characteristics.

Nasalization of a vowel before a nasal consonant is caused by speakers anticipating the lowering of the velum in advance of a nasal segment. The result is that the preceding segment takes on the nasality of the following consonant. This type of assimilation is known as **regressive assimilation**, since the nasalization is, in effect, moving *backwards* to a preceding segment.

The nasalization of vowels following nasal consonants in Scots Gaelic is an example of **progressive assimilation**, since the nasality moves *forward* from the nasal consonant onto the vowel. It results from not immediately raising the velum after the production of a nasal stop.

Table 2.22 Progressive nasalization of vowels in Scots Gaelic

[mõːr]	'big'
[nĩ]	'cattle'
[mũ]	'about'
[nẽːl]	'cloud'

Voicing assimilation is also widespread. For many speakers of English, voiceless liquids and glides occur after voiceless stops in words such as *please* [pl̥ijz], *proud* [pɹ̥awd], and *pure* [pj̊uwr]. These sounds are said to be devoiced in this environment. **Devoicing** is a kind of assimilation. Here, the vocal folds are not set in motion immediately after the release of the voiceless consonant closure. The opposite of devoicing is voicing. In Dutch, voiceless fricatives assimilate to the voicing of the stops that follow them, in anticipation of the voiced consonant. For example, the word *af* [ɑf] 'off, over' is pronounced with a [v] in the words *afbelen* 'to ring off' and *afdeken* 'to cover over'.

Assimilation for place of articulation is also widespread in the world's languages. Nasal consonants are very likely to undergo this type of assimilation, as shown in Table 2.23.

Table 2.23 Assimilation for place of articulation in English

possible	impossible
potent	impotent
tolerable	intolerable
tangible	intangible

The negative form of each of these words is made with either *im* or *in*. In both cases, the form shows a nasal consonant that has the same place of articulation as the stop consonant that follows it: labial in the case of *possible* and *potent*, and alveolar in the case of *tolerable* and *tangible*. In informal speech, many English speakers pronounce words like *inconsequential* and *inconsiderate* with an [ŋ] where the spelling shows *n*. Assimilation can also be heard in pronunciations such as *Va*[ŋ]*couver* and *Ba*[ɱ]*ff* (the symbol [ɱ] represents a labiodental nasal). Assimilation may even cross the boundaries between words. In rapid speech, it is not uncommon to hear people pronounce phrases such as *in code* as [ɪŋkʰowd].

The preceding English example shows regressive assimilation to place of articulation. The following example, taken from German, shows progressive assimilation that again affects nasal consonants. In careful speech, certain German verb forms are pronounced with a final [ən], as in *laden* 'to invite', *loben* 'to praise', and *backen* 'to bake'. In informal speech, the final [ən] is reduced to a syllabic nasal, which takes on the point of articulation of the preceding consonant. The diacritic line under the phonetically transcribed nasals indicates that they are syllabic.

Table 2.24 Progressive assimilation in German

Careful speech		*Informal speech*	
laden	[la:dən]	[la:dn̩]	'to invite'
loben	[lo:bən]	[lo:bm̩]	'to praise'
backen	[bakən]	[bakŋ̩]	'to bake'

Flapping is a process in which a dental or alveolar stop articulation changes to a flap [ɾ] articulation. In English, this process applies to both [t] and [d] and occurs between vowels, the first of which is generally stressed. Flaps are heard in the casual speech pronunciation of words such as *butter, writer, fatter, wader,* and *waiter,* and even in phrases such as *I bought it* [ajbɔ́ɾɪt]. The alveolar flap is always voiced. Flapping is considered a type of assimilation since it changes a noncontinuant segment (a stop) to a continuant segment in the environment of other continuants (vowels). In addition, we may note that voicing assimilation also occurs in the change of the voiceless [t] to the voiced [ɾ].

Dissimilation

Dissimilation, the opposite of assimilation, results in two sounds becoming less alike in articulatory or acoustic terms. The resulting sequence of sounds is easier to articulate and distinguish. It is a much rarer process than assimilation. One commonly heard example of dissimilation in English occurs in words ending with three consecutive fricatives, such as *fifths*. Many speakers dissimilate the final [fθs] sequence to [fts], apparently to break up the sequence of three fricatives with a stop.

Deletion

Deletion is a process that removes a segment from certain phonetic contexts. Deletion occurs in everyday rapid speech in many languages. In English, a schwa [ə] is often deleted when the next vowel in the word is stressed.

Table 2.25 Deletion of [ə] in English

Slow speech	*Rapid speech*	
[pʰəréjd]	[pr̥éjd]	parade
[kʰərówd]	[kr̥ówd]	corrode
[səpʰówz]	[spówz]	suppose

Deletion also occurs as an alternative to dissimilation in words such as *fifths*. Many speakers delete the [θ] of the final consonant cluster and say [fɪfs]. In very rapid speech, both the second [f] and [θ] are sometimes deleted, resulting in [fɪs].

Epenthesis

Epenthesis is a process that inserts a segment within an existing string of segments. For example, in careful speech, the words *warmth* and *something* are pronounced [wɑrmθ] and [sʌ̃mθĩŋ]. It is common in casual speech for speakers to insert a [p] between the *m* and the *th* and pronounce the words [wɑrmpθ] and [sʌ̃mpθĩŋ]. Consonant epenthesis of this type is another example of a coarticulation phenomenon. In English, the articulatory transition from a sonorant consonant to a nonsonorant appears to be eased by the insertion of a consonant that shares properties of both segments. Notice that the epenthesized consonants are all nonsonorant, have the same place of articulation as the sonorant consonant to their left, and have the same voicing as the nonsonorant consonant to their right.

Table 2.26 Some examples of English consonant epenthesis

Word	*Nonepenthesized pronunciation*	*Epenthesized pronunciation*
something	[sʌ̃mθĩŋ]	[sʌ̃mpθĩŋ]
warmth	[wɑrmθ]	[wɑrmpθ]
length	[lɛ̃ŋθ]	[lɛ̃ŋkθ]
prince	[prĩns]	[prĩnts]
tenth	[tɛ̃nθ]	[tɛ̃ntθ]

Vowels may also be epenthesized. In Turkish, a word may not begin with two consonants. When words are borrowed into Turkish, an epenthetic vowel is inserted between certain sequences of two initial consonants, creating a new and permissible sequence. (The reason for the differences among the vowels need not concern us here; note, though, that the vowel is always high; see Section 10.1 for further presentation of these and other unfamiliar symbols.)

Table 2.27 Vowel epenthesis in Turkish

Source word	*Turkish form*
train	tiren
club	kulʏp
sport	sɯpor

Metathesis

Metathesis is a process that reorders a sequence of segments. Metathesis often results in a sequence of phones that is easier to articulate. It is common to hear metathesis in the speech of children, who often cannot pronounce all the consonant sequences that adults can. For example, some English-speaking children pronounce *spaghetti* as *pesghetti* [pəskɛɾij]. In this form, the initial sequence [spə], which is often difficult for children to pronounce, is metathesized to [pəs]. Another example found in many dialects is the form [æks] for [æsk].

The pronunciations of *prescribe* and *prescription* as *perscribe* and *perscription* are often-cited examples of metathesis in adult speech. In these cases, metathesis facilitates the pronunciation of two successive consonant-*r* sequences in each word.

Vowel reduction

In many languages, the articulation of vowels may move to a more central position when the vowels are unstressed. This process is known as **(vowel) reduction**. Typically, the outcome of vowel reduction is a schwa [ə]; this can be observed in pairs of related words that show different stress placement such as *Canada* [kʰǽnədə] versus *Canadian* [kʰənéjdijən]. Note that the first vowel of the words *Canada/Canadian* is [æ] when stressed but a schwa when unstressed, while the second vowel is [ej] when stressed and a schwa when unstressed. Since we cannot predict what vowel a schwa may "turn into" when it is stressed, we assume that [æ] and [ej] are basic to the words in question and are reduced in unstressed position.

10 OTHER VOWELS AND CONSONANTS (ADVANCED)

So far, we have considered only the vowels and consonants of English, many of which are found in other languages. There are also many speech sounds found in the world's languages that are not heard in English. Since phonetic descriptions are universally valid, once the basic articulatory parameters have been mastered it is not too difficult to describe and even to pronounce less familiar sounds. This section presents a number of speech sounds found in other languages.

10.1 Vowels

Front vowels, which in English are always unrounded, can also be rounded. A high front tense rounded vowel is heard in French *pur* 'pure', German *Bücher* 'books', and Turkish *düğme* 'button'. It is transcribed as [y] in IPA transcription, but as [ü] in North America—a difference that sometimes leads to confusion. A rounded high front lax vowel, [ʏ] is heard in Canadian French *lune* 'moon' and *duc* 'duke'. A rounded mid front tense vowel, transcribed [ø] (NA [ö]), is found in French *peu* 'few' and German *schœn* 'beautiful'. A rounded mid front lax vowel, transcribed [œ], is heard in French *oeuf* 'egg' and *peur* 'fear', German *örtlich* 'local', and Turkish *göl* 'lake'. Back vowels may be unrounded; a high back unrounded vowel, transcribed as [ɯ], is heard in Russian words like *byl* 'was', and Rumanian *mînă* 'hand'. These vowels, as well as other 'exotic' ones, are found in many other languages as well. Table 2.28 illustrates the vowels presented in this chapter (UR = unrounded; R = rounded). Note carefully that the tense vowels are presented without glides. This is intentional; whereas English non-low tense vowels are followed by glides, the tense vowels of the languages cited here (and many others) are not.

Table 2.28 Articulatory grid of vowels presented in this chapter

	Front		*Central*		*Back*	
	UR	*R*	*UR*	*R*	*UR*	*R*
High	i	y			ɯ	u tense
	ɪ	ʏ				ʊ lax
Mid	e	ø	ə (reduced)			o tense
	ɛ	œ	ʌ			ɔ lax
Low	æ (lax)		a (lax)		ɑ (tense)	

Nasal vowels

Nasal vowels, like nasal consonants, are produced with a lowered velum. Air passes simultaneously through the oral and nasal cavities. Nasal vowels can be heard in English, French, Portuguese, Hindi, and a wide variety of other languages. They are often transcribed with a tilde [˜] over the vowel symbol.

Table 2.29 Some nasal vowels

English	win	[wĩn]	'win'
French	pain	[pɛ̃]	'bread'
Portuguese	sento	[sẽntu]	'one hundred'
Polish	ząb	[zɔ̃p]	'tooth'

10.2 Consonants

The same consonants found in English are widespread in other languages. A few additional consonants are introduced in this section.

Stops

In many European languages, we find not the alveolar stops [t], [d], and [n], but dental stops [t̪], [d̪], and [n̪]. Although this seems like a very slight difference in articulation, it can be readily observed in the speech of French, Spanish, or Italian speakers.

Other stop positions are common in the world's languages. Retroflex stops [ʈ] and [ɖ], pronounced with the tongue curled back as in English [r], are common in the languages of India. Serbo-Croatian has both a voiceless and a voiced palatal stop in words like *ćaša* 'dish', and *đak* 'pupil'. These are transcribed as [c] and [ɟ], respectively. Inuktitut dialects show a voiceless and voiced uvular stop pair in words like *imaq* 'sea', and *ugsik* 'cow'. These are transcribed as [q] and [G], respectively. A nasal stop is also made at the palatal point of articulation, as in Spanish *año* 'year' (transcribed [ɲ] in IPA and as [ñ] in North America), and at the uvula as well, where it is transcribed as [N].

We now return to the glottal state known as *whispery voice* or *murmur* that was introduced in Section 2.3. In Hindi there is a series of stops sometimes incorrectly referred to as 'voiced aspirated stops' that make use of whispery voice (murmur). These stops are traditionally represented with a following *h*; the double underdots of IPA standard are used here.

In the next table, examples of non-English stop articulations and glottal states are laid out. The distinction between dentals and alveolars is not indicated in the transcription, since most of the world's languages have either dental or alveolar stop articulations, but not both. Sounds found in English are set off in boxes.

Table 2.30 Stops

	Bilabial	*Dental/ alveolar*	*Retroflex*	*Palatal*	*Velar*	*Uvular*	*Glottal*
Voiceless	[p]	[t]	[ʈ]	[c]	[k]	[q]	[ʔ]
Voiced	[b]	[d]	[ɖ]	[ɟ]	[g]	[G]	
Murmured	[b̤]	[d̤]		[ɟ̤]	[g̤]		
Nasal	[m]	[n]	[ɳ]	[ɲ]	[ŋ]	[N]	

Fricatives

Fricatives other than those of English are found in the world's languages. A bilabial fricative, produced by drawing the lips almost together and forcing the airstream through the narrow opening, is found in many languages. The voiceless bilabial fricative [ɸ] is heard word-initially in the Japanese word *Fuji* (the mountain). The voiced bilabial fricative [β] is found in Spanish words like *deber* 'to owe'. A voiceless palatal fricative [ç] is found in Standard German as in the word *ich* 'I'. Velar fricatives are not found in English but are widespread in the world's languages. The voiceless velar fricative [x] is common in German and Russian. (The composer Bach's name, pronounced in German, has this sound.) A voiced velar fricative [ɣ] is commonly heard in Spanish words like *agua* 'water'.

Table 2.31 presents a grid on which some common fricative consonants are ranged according to point and manner of articulation. As in Table 2.30, dentals are not distinguished from alveolars, as most languages have sounds with either one or the other point of articulation, but not both. Sounds found in English are set off in boxes.

Table 2.31 Fricatives

	Bilabial	*Labio-dental*	*Inter-dental*	*Alveolar*	*Alveo-palatal*	*Palatal*	*Velar*	*Glottal*
Voiceless	[ɸ]	[f]	[θ]	[s]	[ʃ]	[ç]	[x]	[h]
Voiced	[β]	[v]	[ð]	[z]	[ʒ]	[ʝ]	[ɣ]	

Affricates

Affricates are found at most points of articulation. In German, a voiceless labiodental affricate, transcribed as [p^f], is heard at the beginning of the word *Pferd* 'horse'. Some New York speakers have voiceless and voiced dental (or alveolar) affricates [ts] and [dz] in words like *time* and *dime*.

Table 2.32 presents a grid including the two English affricates and some others commonly found in other languages. The English sounds are again set off in a box.

Table 2.32 Affricates

	Labiodental	*Alveolar*	*Alveopalatal*	*Velar*
Voiceless	[pf]	[ts]	[tʃ]	[kx]
Voiced	[bv]	[dz]	[ʤ]	[gɣ]

Liquids

As with the stops, laterals may be dental as well as alveolar. Laterals can also be made with the tongue body raised to the palate. Such a sound is called a palatal lateral, and is transcribed with the symbol [ʎ]. It is heard in some pronunciations of the Spanish words *caballo* 'horse' and *calle* 'street', and in the Serbo-Croatian words *dalje* 'farther' and *ljudi* 'people'. The palatal lateral may also be voiceless, in which case it is transcribed as [ʎ̥].

Lateral fricatives are produced when a lateral is made with a narrow enough closure to be classified as a fricative. This sound is transcribed as [ɮ] when voiced and [ɬ] when voiceless. Lateral fricatives can be heard in many American Indian languages, in Welsh, and in the languages spoken in the Caucasus. Table 2.33 shows some examples of voiceless alveolar lateral fricatives from Welsh.

Table 2.33 Voiceless lateral fricatives in Welsh

llan	[ɬan]	'clan'
ambell	[ambɛɬ]	'some'

Other *r*-like sounds are widely heard in the world's languages. A common one is the **trill**, which is made by passing air over the raised tongue tip and allowing it to vibrate. Trills are commonly transcribed as (IPA) [r], but North American [r̃]. They can be heard in the Spanish words *perro* 'dog' and *río* 'river', and the Italian words *carro* 'wagon' and *birra* 'beer'. A similar trilling effect can be made with the uvula, and is called a uvular trill. Its IPA symbol is [ʀ].

A uvular *r* made without trilling is more commonly heard, however. This is the voiced *r* of Standard European French, and is also widespread in German. IPA transcription classifies this sound along with the fricatives. It is transcribed as [χ] when voiceless and as [ʁ] when voiced.

Table 2.34 presents the liquids. As before, sounds found in English are set off in boxes.

Table 2.34 Liquids

		Dental/alveolar	*Palatal*	*Uvular*
Laterals				
	Voiced	[l]	[ʎ]	
	Voiceless	[l̥]	[ʎ̥]	
Lateral fricatives				
	Voiced	[ɮ]		
	Voiceless	[ɬ]		
r's				
	Retroflex	[r]		
	Flap	[ɾ]		
	Trill	[r̃]		[ʀ]

Flaps and trills can be voiceless as well. Voicelessness for these sounds is usually indicated by a small open circle beneath the symbol, as in [r̥̃] or [ʀ̥].

Glides

Other glides are found in the world's languages. A commonly heard one is made with the tongue position of [j] but with the lips rounded. It is transcribed as [ɥ] and can be heard in French words such as [ɥit] *huit* 'eight', [ɥil] *huile* 'oil', and [ɥitχ] *huitre* 'oyster'.

SUMMING UP

The study of the sounds of human language is called *phonetics*. These sounds are widely transcribed by means of the **International Phonetic Alphabet**.

The sounds of language are commonly described in **articulatory** and **acoustic** terms, and fall into two major types: **syllabic sounds** (**vowels**, **syllabic liquids**, and **nasals**) and nonsyllabic sounds (**consonants** and **glides**). Sounds may be **voiced** or **voiceless**, and **oral** or **nasal**. Consonants are produced at various places of articulation: labial, dental, alveolar, alveopalatal, palatal, velar, uvular, glottal, and pharyngeal. At the places of articulation, the airstream is modified by different **manners of articulation** and the resulting sounds are **stops**, **fricatives**, or **affricates**. Vowels are produced with less drastic closure and are described with reference to tongue position (**high**, **low**, **back**, and **front**), tension (**tense** or **lax**), and lip **rounding** (rounded or unrounded). Language also exhibits **suprasegmental** phenomena such as **tone**, **intonation**, and **stress**.

Key terms

acoustic phonetics
affricates
alveolar ridge
alveopalatal (area)
articulatory phonetics
arytenoids
aspiration
assimilation
association line
autosegmental (notation)
back (vowel)
back of tongue
blade of tongue
body of tongue
coarticulation
consonant
continuants
contour tones
cricoid cartilage
deletion
dentals
devoicing
diacritic
diaphragm
diphthong
dissimilation
dorsum
downdrift
epenthesis
feature
flap
flapping
fricatives
front (vowel)
glide
glottals
glottis
high (vowel)
intercostals
interdentals
intonation
IPA
labials
labiodentals
labiovelars
larynx
lateral fricative
laterals
lax vowels
length
loudness
low (vowel)
manners of articulation
metathesis
mid vowels
murmur
nasal (sound)
nasalization
nonterminal (intonation) contour
nucleus
oral (sound)
palatals
palate
pharyngeals
pharynx
phone
phonetics
pitch

place of articulation
primary stress
processes
progressive assimilation
prosodic (properties)
reduced vowel
register tone
regressive assimilation
retroflex
root of tongue
rounding
schwa
secondary stress
segment
sibilants
simple vowels
(sound) classes
speech sounds
stops
stress
stridents
suprasegmental (properties)
syllabic
syllabic liquids
syllabic nasals
syllable
tense vowels
terminal (intonation) contour
thyroid cartilage
tip of tongue
tone
tone language
trachea
trill
uvula
uvulars
velars
velum
vocal folds
vocal tract
voiced
voiceless
voicing assimilation
vowel
vowel reduction
whisper
whispery voice

Sources

Information on the International Phonetic Alphabet can be obtained from the International Phonetic Association, University College, Gower Street, London, WC1E 6BT, England. Sarcee data are taken from E.-D. Cook, "Vowels and Tones in Sarcee" in *Language* 47:164–79; Gaelic data are courtesy of James Galbraith. Bini data are adapted from Ladefoged (cited below). More detailed reading on the phonetics of English and other languages is reported below.

Recommended reading

Catford, J. C. 1977. *Fundamental Problems in Phonetics*. Bloomington, IN: Indiana University Press.
Cruttenden, Alan. 1986. *Intonation*. Cambridge, Eng.: Cambridge University Press.
Fromkin, V. A., ed. 1978. *Tone: A Linguistic Survey*. New York: Academic Press.
Ladefoged, P. 1982. *A Course in Phonetics*. 2nd ed. Toronto: Harcourt Brace Jovanovich.
Pullum, G. K., and W. A. Ladusaw. 1986. *Phonetic Symbol Guide*. Chicago: University of Chicago Press.
Rogers, H. 1991. *Theoretical and Practical Phonetics*. Toronto: Copp Clark Pitman.

earer, William M. 1968. *Illustrated Speech Anatomy.* Springfield, IL: Charles C. Thomas.

ker, Douglas C. 1984. *The Pronunciation of Canadian French.* Ottawa: University of ttawa Press.

Appendix: The International Phonetic Alphabet (condensed)

CONSONANTS

	Bilabial	Labiodental	Dental	Alveolar	Postalveolar	Retroflex	Palatal	Velar	Uvular	Pharyngeal	Glottal
Plosive	p b			t d		ʈ ɖ	c ɟ	k g	q ɢ		ʔ
Nasal	m	ɱ		n		ɳ	ɲ	ŋ	ɴ		
Trill	ʙ			r					ʀ		
Tap or Flap				ɾ		ɽ					
Fricative	ɸ β	f v	θ ð	s z	ʃ ʒ	ʂ ʐ	ç ʝ	x ɣ	χ ʁ	ħ ʕ	h ɦ
Lateral fricative				ɬ ɮ							
Approximant		ʋ		ɹ		ɻ	j	ɰ			
Lateral approximant				l		ɭ	ʎ	ʟ			
Ejective stop	p'			t'		t'	c'	k'	q'		

Where symbols appear in pairs, the one to the right represents a voiced consonant. Shaded areas denote articulations judged impossible.

VOWELS

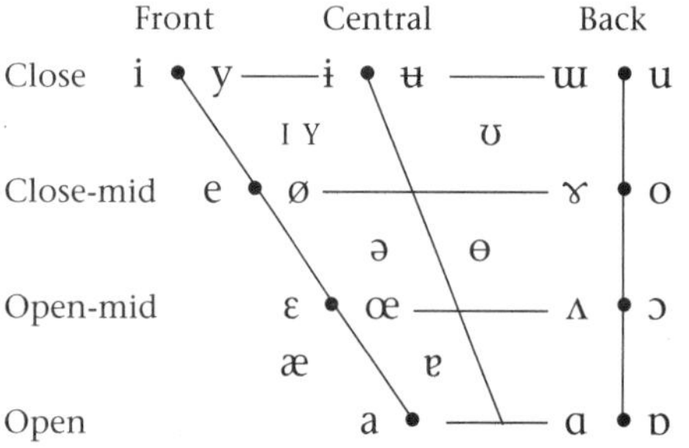

Where symbols appear in pairs, the one to the right represents a rounded vowel. The symbols for vowels used in this book sometimes differ from IPA usage.

QUESTIONS

1. In order to become more aware of the differences between spelling and pronunciation, answer the following questions about English spelling.
   a) Find four words that show four alternate spellings of the sound [f].
   b) Find six words that have the letter 'a' pronounced differently.
   c) Find four words in which different groups of letters represent only one sound.

2. How many segments are there in the following words?

a) at	e) psychology
b) math	f) knowledge
c) cure	g) mailbox
d) hopping	h) awesome

3. Is the first sound in each of the following words voiced or voiceless?

a) though	e) zoom	i) huge	m) when *(may vary)*
b) thought	f) silk	j) choose	n) ghetto
c) form	g) pan	k) judge	o) pneumatic
d) view	h) boat	l) buns	p) winced

4. Using the words presented in question 3, state whether the last sound of each word is voiced or voiceless.

5. For each of the following pairs of sounds, state whether they have the same or a different place of articulation. Then identify the place of articulation for each sound.

a) [s] : [l]	e) [m] : [n]	i) [b] : [f]
b) [k] : [ŋ]	f) [dʒ] : [ʃ]	j) [tʃ] : [dʒ]
c) [p] : [g]	g) [f] : [h]	k) [s] : [v]
d) [l] : [r]	h) [w] : [j]	l) [θ] : [t]

6. For each of the following pairs of sounds, state whether they have the same or different manners of articulation. Then identify the manner of articulation for each sound.

a) [s] : [θ]	e) [l] : [t]	i) [r] : [w]
b) [k] : [g]	f) [ð] : [v]	j) [tʃ] : [dʒ]
c) [w] : [j]	g) [tʃ] : [s]	k) [h] : [ʔ]
d) [f] : [ʃ]	h) [m] : [ŋ]	l) [z] : [dʒ]

7. After each of the following articulatory descriptions, write the sound described and put it in phonetic brackets.

a) voiceless velar stop	e) voiced velar nasal
b) voiced labiodental fricative	f) voiceless interdental fricative
c) voiced alveopalatal affricate	g) high back rounded lax vowel
d) voiced palatal glide	h) low front unrounded vowel

8. Which of the following pairs of words show the same vowel quality? Mark each pair as *same* or *different*. Then transcribe the vowels of each word.

a) back	sat	h) hide	height
b) cot	caught	i) least	heed
c) bid	key	j) drug	cook
d) luck	flick	k) sink	fit
e) ooze	deuce	l) oak	own
f) cot	court	m) pour	port
g) fell	fail	n) mouse	cow

9. Using descriptive terms like sibilant, fricative, and so on, provide a single phonetic characteristic that all the segments in each group share. Try to avoid over-obvious answers such as 'consonant' or 'vowel'.
Example: [b d g œ m j] are all voiced.

a) [p t k g ʔ]	f) [h ʔ]
b) [i e ɛ æ]	g) [u o]
c) [tʃ ʒ ʃ dʒ]	h) [s z tʃ dʒ ʃ ʒ]
d) [p b m f v]	i) [l r m n ŋ j w]
e) [ʌ ə ʊ a]	j) [t d l r n s z]

10. Transcribe the following sets of words. You may use these words to practice transcribing aspiration.

a) tog	i) peel	q) spell
b) kid	j) stun	r) cord
c) attain	k) Oscar	s) accord
d) despise	l) cooler	t) astound
e) elbow	m) sigh	u) pure
f) haul	n) hulk	v) wheeze
g) juice	o) explode	w) remove
h) thimble	p) tube	x) clinical

11. Using H, L, and association lines, transcribe the intonation of the following English phrases. Compare your results with the transcriptions of several classmates. Are they the same? If they aren't, discuss what aspects of intonation (such as emotion or speech context) might account for the differences in transcription.
    a) 'Hi, Alice.'
    b) 'Three people got off the bus at the last stop.'
    c) 'My uncle likes to mountain climb.'

12. Mark primary and secondary (where present) stresses on the following words. It is not necessary to transcribe them.

a) sunny	f) arrive	k) secret
b) banana	g) defy	l) exceed
c) blackboard	h) summary	m) summery
d) Canada	i) Canadian	n) Canadianize
e) (to) reject	j) (a) reject	o) difficult

13. Find a fluent speaker of a language other than English and transcribe phonetically ten words of that language. If you encounter any sounds for which sym-

bols are not found in this chapter, attempt to describe them in phonetic terms and then invent diacritics to help you transcribe them.

14. Using Figure 2.20 as your model, provide coarticulation diagrams for the following words. Be sure that your diagrams capture the movement of the lips, tongue, velum, and glottis as in the model.

    a) had c) please
    b) snap d) dome

15. Compare the careful speech and rapid speech pronunciations of the following English words and phrases. Then, name the process or processes that make the rapid speech pronunciation different from the careful speech. (Stress is omitted here.)

	Careful speech	*Rapid speech*
a) in my room	[ɪn maj ruwm]	[ɪmmajruwm]
b) I see them	[aj sij ðɛm]	[ajsijəm]
c) I see him	[aj sij hɪm]	[ajsijəm]
d) within	[wɪθɪn]	[wɪðɪn]
e) balloons	[bəluwnz]	[bluwnz]
f) popsicle	[p^{h}ɑpsɪkʊl]	[p^{h}ɑpskəl]
g) sit down	[sɪt dawn]	[sɪɾawn]
h) my advice	[maj ədvajs]	[majəvajs]
i) Scotch tape	[skɑtʃ t^{h}ejp]	[k^{h}ɑtʃstejp]
j) protection	[pr̥owt^{h}ɛkʃən]	[pərt^{h}ɛkʃən]
k) hand me that	[hænd mij ðæt]	[hæ̃mijðæt]
l) Pam will miss you	[pæm wɪl mɪs juw]	[pæml̩mɪʃjə]

For the student linguist

DON'T WORRY ABOUT SPELLING

What if you had to choose: either nobody would read and write ever again, or nobody would speak or hear language? This is a total nonchoice for me—I'd pitch out liner notes and lyric sheets in a second, but would be really upset about losing all my Ella Fitzgerald CDs. Not that it would be easy to function without reading and writing. Road signs, for example, are pretty important, and even linguistics textbooks have their uses. But the point is, I think spoken language is more fundamental than reading or writing. Let's assume it is, but let's also assume that writing is pretty important to modern society. The question, then, is how closely writing should resemble speaking.

Current spelling is much closer to the way English *used* to be spoken than the way it's spoken today, and for years various folks have been proposing spelling reforms. Would learning to read be easier if you didn't have to deal with spelling nightmares like *night, though, tough, cough, two, due, who, threw, shoe, through,* or *answer?* Some of these words are already being changed, informally, in advertising, pop music, and casual writing. For example, when my best friend sends me letters, she always writes *nite, tho, tuff, cough, 2, due, who, threw, shoe, thru,* and *anser.* Are these spellings any better? For someone who's learning to read English, it could be hard to figure out that *tho* and *who* aren't supposed to rhyme but *2, due, who, threw, shoe* and *thru* are supposed to rhyme, although there's now a difference in spelling for the nonrhyming *tho* and *tuff.*

Phonetic transcription—using the IPA—is unambiguous about what rhymes with what. For every sound there's exactly one symbol (except for a couple of substitutions for different keyboards), and for every symbol there's exactly one sound. Thus the word list becomes: najt, ðow, tʰʌf, kʰɔf, tuw, duw, huw, θruw, ʃuw, θruw, and ænsər. Making the changeover from standard spelling to IPA would be a nightmare, though. We'd have to reconfigure our keyboards, for starters. Instead of five vowel symbols (and many combinations of them) and twenty-one consonants, we'd have about eighteen vowels and twenty-five consonants.

Imagine all the changeover details could be taken care of (including instantly teaching everyone the IPA). Think about how much richer writing could be if it included all the information you get from hearing someone speak. You'd have information about the writer's regional background and class, plus information about the level of formality of the piece you were reading. Depending on how detailed the writing system was, you would be able to read all sorts of nuances of stress and intonation.

I've transcribed the same piece of dialogue in several different systems below. The first system is probably the hardest to read, and the following systems get progressively easier. Try to figure out the dialogue from the first system, checking the later ones for clarification if you get stuck. Also try to figure out the stylistic differences among the different versions of the dialogue.

1. ʃijləˀejtʰejlardʒpʰʌmpkʰɪnpʰaj ˀəwɛrðæt ˀælənwəzwɑtʃɪŋ o̥:w̥ ˀæ̥l̥ə̥n̥ ʃijsɛdbrɛθɪlij pʰæ̥sm̥i̥j̥ ð̥i̥j̥ w̥ɪ̥ptʰ kʰr̥i̥j̥m̥ ʃijlə hijwajnd ˀajmtʃrajiŋ tʰuwfɪnɪʃgrajndɪŋðijkɔfij
2. ʃijləˀejɾəla:dʒpʰʌmpkʰɪnpʰaj ˀəwɛrðæˀæln̩wəzwɑtʃn̩ o:w ˀælən̩ ʃijsɛˀbrɛθlij pʰæsmijðəwɪpkʰrijm ʃijlə hijwajnd ˀajmtʃrajn̩tʰəfɪnɪʃgrajndn̩ðəkɔfij
3. ʃíjləˀejɾəla:dʒpʰʌmpkʰɪnpʰáj ˀəwɛrðæˀǽln̩wəzwɑ́tʃn̩ o:w ˀǽln̩ ʃijsɛˀbrɛ́θlij pʰæsmijðəwɪpkʰríjm ʃíjlə hijwájnd ˀajmtʃrájn̩tʰəfɪnɪʃgrájndn̩ðəkɔ́fij
4. ʃijlə ejt ej lardʒpʰʌmpkʰɪn pʰaj ˀəwɛr ðæt ˀælən wəz wɑtʃɪŋ o:w ˀælən ʃij sɛd brɛθɪlij pʰæs mij ðij wɪptʰ kʰrijm ʃijlə hij wajnd ˀajm tʃrajiŋ tʰuw fɪnɪʃ grajndɪŋ ðij kɔfij
5. ʃijlə ejt ej lardʒ pʰʌmpkʰɪn pʰaj, ˀəwɛr ðæt ˀælən wəz wɑ tʃɪŋ. "o:w ˀælən," ʃij sɛd brɛθɪlij "pʰæs mij ðij wɪptʰ kʰrijm." "ʃijlə," hij wajnd, "ˀajm tʃrajiŋ tʰuw fɪnɪʃ grajndɪŋ ðij kɔfij."

The downside of this type of writing is that there'd be so much variability. For instance, you might care about the accent or tone of a character in a novel, but do you really need to know where the journalist who wrote this morning's article on the economy was raised? And what if his or her editor were from someplace else? Whose accent would get printed? Not to mention the difficulties of something like a GRE exam or SAT test written in someone else's dialect.

Of course, the degree of variability depends on how extreme the system is. There's a wide gap between standard spelling and the fairly narrow (detailed) transcription system used in examples *1* through *3*. Writing could be more phonetic than it is now, but we don't have to force people to include every minor variation in pronunciation. We could forget about stress marks and anything to show intonation—except for a few simple things like question marks and exclamation points. We could also leave off fairly predictable things like aspiration (you'll discover how predictable aspiration is in the next chapter). Examples *4* and *5* are probably a lot easier to understand than *1* through *3*, since *4* and *5* are not as detailed (broad transcription) and, most importantly, because they have spaces between the words. Putting in spaces makes the writing less like the actual pronunciation, but it also takes away the ambiguity of figuring out whether something like [ʃijla] is supposed to be *she lo . . .* (as in *she locked the door . . .*) or *Sheila.*

In fact, the new writing system could keep punctuation, keep word spaces, and have nothing but the bare minimum to distinguish the way one word sounds from the way other words sound. The trick, then, is to figure out what the bare minimum is. It's a pretty difficult question, and before you can answer it you'll need to read about phonology and morphology. You'll also need to figure out what exactly a word *is,* anyway. So, read the next two chapters and then come back to this section and read it again. Then devise the perfect writing system, use it for your senior thesis, patent it, market it, make a fortune off of it, and retire to a lovely little tropical island (with good food) where they don't speak English.

three

PHONOLOGY: THE FUNCTION AND PATTERNING OF SOUNDS

Michael Dobrovolsky

A person's tongue is a twisty thing, there are plenty of words there of every kind, and the range of words is wide, and their variation.

– HOMER, *The Iliad*, 20

We saw in Chapter 2 that there are a large number of speech sounds that human beings can produce and perceive. No human language exploits all of these possibilities. Furthermore, the sounds of all languages are patterned and organized in such ways that linguists can discover some system that underlies their appearance. Linguists generally assume that speakers have (at least) some subconscious knowledge of this system. For example, we saw in Chapter 1 that English speakers recognize that forms like *slish* and *screnk* are acceptable, while forms like *srish* and *screpk* are not. But speakers can do more than note that certain forms are unnatural in their system; they can also correct such forms to make them acceptable in their own language. Without knowing exactly why, most English speakers would pronounce a form like *srish* as [sərɪʃ] rather than saying [rɪʃ] or [sɪʃ]. It is this largely subconscious knowledge of sound patterns that phonologists are interested in uncovering.

This chapter is about **phonology**, the component of a grammar made up of the elements and principles that determine how sounds vary and pattern in a language. Phonologists attempt to make explicit formal statements about the sound patterns of individual languages in order to discover something about the linguistic knowledge that people must have in order to use these patterns. Even more broadly, the study of phonology attempts to discover general principles that underlie the patterning of sounds in human language.

The existence of patterns in language depends on the organization of certain basic elements or units that combine to make up these patterns. Three major units of analysis will be presented in this chapter. We are already acquainted with the idea that the flow of speech can be divided into segments. In this chapter, we investigate the patterned variation of segments. A second unit of phonological analysis is the **feature**. Features may be thought of as the smallest building blocks of phonological structure, corresponding as they do to articulatory or acoustic categories such as [voice] or [strident]. We will also learn how segments are built up from features and how this fact is connected with phonological patterning. We will also investigate the properties of **syllables** in phonology. A syllable is a unit of linguistic structure that consists of a syllabic element—usually a vowel—and any segments that are associated with it. (The word *segment* itself can be divided into two syllables: *seg* and *ment.*) These units—feature, segment, and syllable—interact with the processes we investigated in the previous chapter and with certain general principles to produce the sound patterns of language.

The existence of patterned elements implies that there must be some principles of organization. Features, segments, and syllables are organized into hierarchical levels; each level is composed of elements at the level beneath it. In Figure 3.1, the word-level unit *segment* is represented by the abbreviation *Wd.* This word consists of two syllables, each of which is represented with the Greek letter σ (*sigma*). Each syllable is made up of a number of segments (the internal structure of syllables is also hierarchical, and is treated in Section 5 of this chapter). Each segment, in turn, is composed of features. A representation of *segment* is given in Figure 3.1. (For purposes of illustration, only a few features are provided for each segment.)

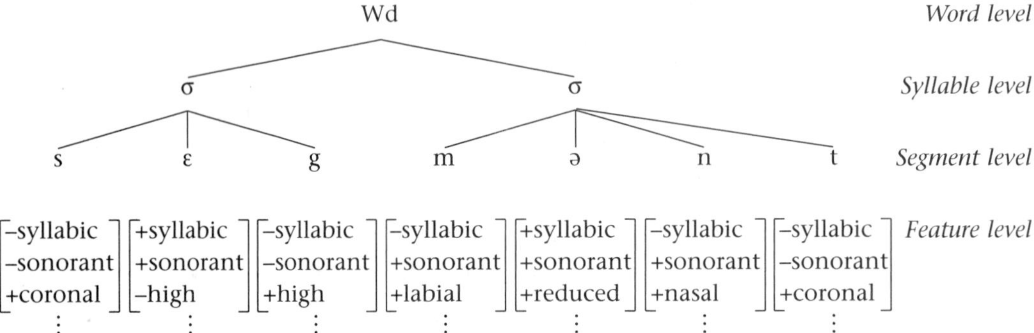

Figure 3.1 Partial phonological representation of *segment*

In the next sections, we look at the phonological knowledge that enables speakers to distinguish among forms and to deal with the considerable phonetic variation found in the pronunciation of speech segments.

1 SEGMENTS IN CONTRAST

All speakers know which segments of their language **contrast**. Segments are said to contrast (or to be distinctive or be in opposition) when their presence alone may distinguish forms with different meanings from each other. The segments [s] and [z] contrast in the words *s̲ip* and *z̲ip*, as do the vowels of *hi̲t*, *ha̲te*, and *ho̲t*.

1.1 Minimal pairs

A **minimal pair** consists of two forms with distinct meanings that differ by only one segment found in the same position in each form. The examples [sɪp] *sip* and [zɪp] *zip* given previously form a minimal pair and show that the sounds [s] and [z] contrast in English.

A number of minimal pairs that demonstrate consonant contrasts for English are given in Table 3.1; remember it is on the basis of sound and not spelling that minimal pairs are established. In displaying contrasts, contrasting words are often placed along the horizontal axis with respect to their place of articulation, reading from left to right (labial, alveolar, and so on), and vertically with respect to manner of articulation, in order to show which places and manners of articulation are exploited by the language in question.

Table 3.1 Contrasts among consonants in English

Labial	*Interdental*	*Alveolar*	*Alveopalatal*	*Velar*	*Glottal*
Stops and affricates (noncontinuants)					
tap [p]		pat [t]	match [tʃ]	pick [k]	
tab [b]		pad [d]	Madge [dʒ]	pig [g]	
Continuants					
leaf [f]	thigh [θ]	sip [s]	mesher [ʃ]		hip [h]
leave [v]	thy [ð]	zip [z]	measure [ʒ]		
Nasals					
sum [m]		sun [n]		sung [ŋ]	
Liquids and glides					
wet [w]			yet [j]		
		leer [l]			
		rear [r]			

The phonetic context in which a sound occurs is called its **environment**. Pairs that show segments in nearly identical environments, such as *azure/assure* or *author/either*, are called **near-minimal pairs**. They help to establish contrasts where no minimal pairs can be found.

You may assume that two segments contrast once a minimal pair or a near-minimal pair has been established. It is in fact rare to find minimal pairs for all distinctive sounds in all environments in a language, since the historical evolution of every language has led to some sounds being utilized more frequently than others, or being eliminated from some environments. For example, you will find no minimal pairs involving [h] and [ŋ] in word-initial or word-final position in English, because there are no words that begin with [ŋ] or end in [h]. It is also difficult to find minimal pairs in English that have the phone [ʒ], which occurs for the most part in words borrowed from French such as *azure* and *mirage*.

Vowel contrasts in English

Contrasts among English vowels can be established with a few sets of examples. For now, we will continue to assume that English vowel-glide sequences like [ij], [uw], [ow], and so on are single vowels. From this perspective, we can say that the vowels [ij] and [ɪ], [ej] and [ɛ], and so on, contrast.

Table 3.2 Vowel contrasts in American English

beet	[bijt]	[ij]
bit	[bɪt]	[ɪ]
bait	[bejt]	[ej]
bet	[bɛt]	[ɛ]
bat	[bæt]	[æ]
cooed	[kʰuwd]	[uw]
could	[kʰʊd]	[ʊ]
code	[kʰowd]	[ow]
caught	[kʰɔt]	[ɔ]
cot	[kʰɑt]	[ɑ]
cut	[kʰʌt]	[ʌ]
lewd	[luwd]	[uw]
loud	[lawd]	[aw]
lied	[lajd]	[aj]
Lloyd	[lojd]	[oj]

1.2 Language-specific contrasts

Contrasts are language-specific; sounds that are distinctive in one language will not necessarily be distinctive in another. For example, the difference between the two vowels [ɛ] and [æ] is crucial to English, as we can see from minimal pairs like *Ben* [bɛn] and *ban* [bæn]. But in Turkish, this difference in pronunciation is not distinctive. A Turkish speaker may pronounce the word for 'I' as [bɛn] or [bæn], and it will make no difference to the meaning.

Table 3.3 Language-specific vowel contrasts: English versus Turkish

English		*Turkish*	
[bɛn]	Ben	[bɛn]	I
[bæn]	ban	[bæn]	I

Conversely, sounds that do not contrast in English, such as long and short vowels, may be distinctive in another language. There are no minimal pairs of the type [hæt]:[hæ:t] or [luws]:[lu:ws] in English. But in Japanese and Finnish, short and long vowels contrast, as the next examples show.

Table 3.4 Short/long vowel contrasts in Japanese and Finnish

Japanese			
[tori]	'bird'	[tori:]	'shrine gate'
[kibo]	'scale'	[kibo:]	'hope'
Finnish			
[tuli]	'fire'	[tu:li]	'wind'
[hætæ]	'distress'	[hæ:tæ:]	'to evict'

Establishing the contrasting segments in a language is a first step in phonological analysis. But in any language, there are many sounds that never contrast. The following section deals with this aspect of phonological analysis.

2 PHONETICALLY CONDITIONED VARIATION: PHONEMES AND ALLOPHONES

Everyday speech contains a great deal of phonetic variation that speakers pay little or no attention to. Some of this variation arises from nonlinguistic factors such as fatigue, excitement, orthodontic work, gum chewing, and the like. This kind of variation is not part of the domain of phonology. But much phonetic variation is systematic. It occurs most often among phonetically similar segments and is conditioned by the phonetic context or environment in which the segments are found. This variation occurs because segments are affected and altered by the phonetic characteristics of neighboring elements or the larger phonological context in which they occur. We rarely notice this kind of variation because every speaker has the ability to factor it out in order to focus attention on only the relevant contrasts of the language.

2.1 Complementary distribution

When first learning phonetic transcription, English speakers are often surprised that all the *l*s they pronounce are not identical. In Table 3.5, the *l*s in column A are voiced, while those in column B are voiceless (indicated here by a subscript ̥). Many speakers of English are unaware that they routinely produce this difference in articulation, which can be heard clearly when the words in column B are pronounced slowly.

Table 3.5 Voiced and voiceless *l* in English

A		*B*	
blue	[bluw]	plow	[pl̥aw]
gleam	[glijm]	clap	[kl̥æp]
slip	[slɪp]	clear	[kl̥ijr]
flog	[flɑg]	play	[pl̥ej]
leaf	[lijf]		

The voicelessness of the *l*s in column B is a consequence of their phonetic environment. Voiced and voiceless *l*s vary systematically in that all of the voiceless [l̥]s occur predictably after the class of voiceless stops. Since no voiced [l] ever occurs in the same phonetic environment as a voiceless one (and vice versa), we say that the two variants of *l* are in **complementary distribution**.

Table 3.6 Complementary distribution of [l] and [l̥] in English

	[l]	[l̥]
After voiceless stops	no	yes
Elsewhere	yes	no

The term *elsewhere* is used in Table 3.6 to indicate the wider distribution (occurrence in a greater number of different phonetic environments) of voiced [l]. It occurs after voiced stops, voiceless fricatives, and in word-initial position.

In spite of these phonetic differences, native speakers consider the two English *l*s to be instances of the same segment, since they are phonetically similar and the differences between them are systematic and predictable. This perception of sameness is supported by the fact that the two *l*s never contrast in English. There are no minimal pairs like [plej] and [pl̥ej]. We can sum up the relationship that the two *l*s bear to each other by stating that, for speakers of English, the two *l*s are *phonetically* different but in the sound system of English, given their phonetic similarity, predictable distribution, and noncontrastiveness, they are *phonologically* the same.

2.2 Phonemes and Allophones

The ability to group phonetically different sounds together into one class is shared by all speakers of all languages. This phonological knowledge is represented formally on a level of phonological representation that is distinct from phonetic representation. Predictable variants of certain segments are grouped together into a contrastive phonological unit called a **phoneme**. These variants, which are referred to as **allophones**, are usually phonetically similar and are frequently found in complementary distribution. A representation of this relationship is shown in Figure 3.2. The phonemic symbol for the class—generally the same symbol as the elsewhere variant—is placed between slashes, and the symbols for allophones are enclosed in phonetic brackets.

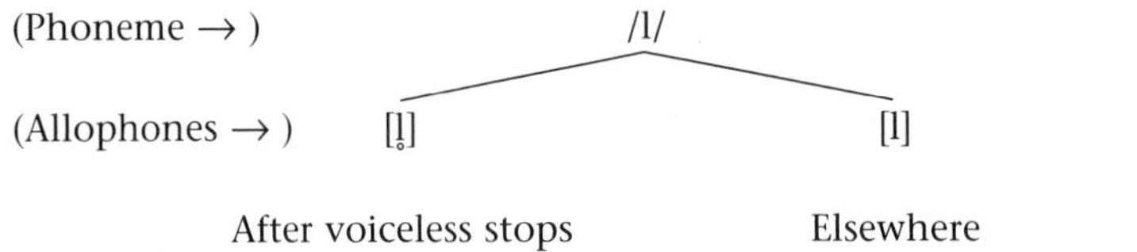

Figure 3.2 The phoneme /l/ and its allophones [l̥] and [l] in English

Allophonic variation is found throughout language. In fact, every speech sound we utter is an allophone of some phoneme and can be grouped together with other phonetically similar sounds into a class that is represented by a phoneme on a phonological level of representation. An important part of phonological analysis deals with discovering the phonemes of languages and accounting for allophonic variation.

Some problematic distributions

At this point, some other considerations in determining phonemes and allophones must be taken into account. So far, we have seen that a minimal pair test is a quick and direct way of establishing that two sounds belong to separate phonemes in a language. If the sounds contrast, they are members of different phonemes. We have also seen that if certain sounds are noncontrastive and in complementary distribution, they may be considered allophones of one phoneme. In some cases, however, we must go beyond these procedures to discover the phonological inventory of a language.

As noted in Section 1.1, certain patterns of distribution prevent some sounds in a language from ever contrasting with each other. In cases like these, we can establish the phonemic status of a sound by default. If the sound cannot be grouped together with any other phonetically similar sounds as an allophone of a phoneme, we may assume it has phonemic status. The following data from English help to illustrate this point.

1)

*[ŋowp]	(does not exist)	[howp]	'hope'
*[ŋejt]	(does not exist)	[hejt]	'hate'

We can see here that [h] and [ŋ] do not contrast in initial position in English. The following examples show that they do not contrast in final position either.

2)

[lɑŋ]	'long'	*[lɑh]	(does not exist)
[sɪŋ]	'sing'	*[sɪh]	(does not exist)
[klæŋ]	'clang'	*[klæh]	(does not exist)

These lists could be extended for pages, but a minimal pair involving [h] and [ŋ] could never be found in English. Additionally, as *1)* and *2)* have shown, [h] and [ŋ] are in complementary distribution. Do these facts taken together not lead us to conclude that [h] and [ŋ] are allophones of one phoneme? No. Since [h] and [ŋ] are so distinct phonetically, we assume that each one is a member of a separate phoneme and that the pattern of distribution is of secondary importance in this instance.

Minimal pairs or near-minimal pairs help us establish which sounds contrast in a language; phonetic similarity and complementary distribution help us decide which sounds are allophones of a particular phoneme. But not all examples of variation among sounds can be dealt with through these approaches.

In some cases, phonetically similar sounds are neither in complementary distribution nor are they found to contrast. It is still possible, nevertheless, to determine which phonemes these sounds belong to. A case in point is the variation in English voiceless stops when they are found in word-final position, as in the word *stop*. Sometimes an English speaker releases the articulation of these sounds rather forcefully. Let us represent this with a diacritic sign [!]. At other times, the same speaker may keep the articulators closed for a moment after the articulation; the diacritic [˺]

can represent this. Some speakers may even coarticulate a glottal closure (represented here with the raised symbol for a glottal stop following the consonant in question) and produce the word as [stɑpˀ]. Thus we can find at least three pronunciations of *stop*: [stɑp!], [stɑp˺], and [stɑpˀ]. Since there is no difference in the meaning of these forms and since the final consonants are phonetically similar, we say that these sounds are in **free variation**, and that they are all allophones of the phoneme /p/. The same pattern holds for the other voiceless stops of English.

2.3 Classes and Generalization in Phonology

Phonological analysis permits us to account for the great amount of phonetic variation in everyday speech. This systematic variation is widely extended within languages. Compare the English data in Table 3.5 with those in Table 3.7.

Table 3.7 Voiced and voiceless allophones of English /r/

A		*B*	
brew	[bruw]	prow	[pr̥aw]
green	[grijn]	trip	[tr̥ɪp]
drip	[drɪp]	creep	[kr̥ijp]
frog	[frɑg]	pray	[pr̥ej]
shrimp	[ʃrɪmp]		

The data show that the allophones of English /r/ pattern like those of English /l/. Based on this information, we can state that there is an /r/ phoneme in English with (at least) two allophones—one voiced, the other voiceless. But if we were to stop there, we would overlook an important point. The phonemes /r/ and /l/ belong to the same class of sounds: both are *liquids*. By taking this information into account, we can state a general fact about English.

3)

In English, liquids show voiceless allophones after voiceless stops and voiced allophones elsewhere.

A major goal of phonological description is the formulation of the most general statements possible about sound patterns. Reference to classes of segments helps accomplish this. Additional data from English illustrate this point.

Table 3.8 Voiced and voiceless allophones of English glides

A		*B*	
beauty	[bjuwɾij]	putrid	[pj̊uwtr̥ɪd]
Duane	[dwejn]	twin	[tw̥ɪn]
Gwen	[gwɛn]	quick	[kw̥ɪk]
view	[vjuw]	cute	[kj̊uwt]
swim	[swɪm]		
thwack	[θwæk]		

These forms demonstrate that the contrasting glides /j/ and /w/ each pattern like the liquids. We can now extend our general statement even further.

4)

In English, liquids and glides have voiceless allophones after voiceless stops, and voiced allophones elsewhere.

Clearly, allophones do not pattern piecemeal, but rather according to their membership in phonetic classes.

2.4 Canadian Raising

In most Canadian and some American dialects, pronunciations like those illustrated in Table 3.9 are common.

Table 3.9 Low and central vowel allophones in raising dialects

[ajz]	eyes	[ʌjs]	ice
[lajz]	lies	[lʌjs]	lice
[tr̥ajd]	tried	[tr̥ʌjt]	trite
[tr̥ajb]	tribe	[tr̥ʌjp]	tripe
[hawz]	(to) house (verb)	[hʌws]	house (noun)
[lawd]	loud	[lʌwt]	lout
[kaw]	cow	[skʌwt]	scout
[flaj]	fly	[flʌjt]	flight

In Table 3.9, the vowels [aj] and [ʌj] are in complementary distribution. The [aj] occurs before the class of voiced consonants or in word-final position, and the [ʌj] occurs before the class of voiceless consonants. The two are allophones of a single phoneme /aj/. The same relationship holds between the vowels [aw] and [ʌw], which are allophones of /aw/.

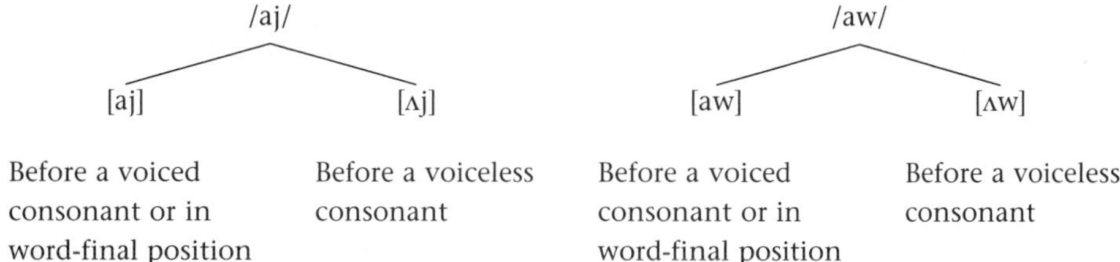

Figure 3.3 Allophones of /aj/ and /aw/ in raising dialects

Again, we see this phonological fact reflected in everyday language use. Most speakers of these dialects find it difficult to distinguish between these allophones, even when the difference is pointed out to them. This is because the difference is not contrastive. On the other hand, many people who speak varieties of English that do not have the [ʌj] or [ʌw] allophones are very much aware of their presence in Canadian English. To them, a Canadian speaker sounds markedly different, even though they may be confused about the nature of the difference.

> *I don't agree he was an American. . . . Where all other English-speaking people pronounce OU as a diphthong, the Canadian . . . makes a separate sound for each letter. The word about, for instance, he pronounces as ab-oh-oot.*
>
> Philip MacDonald, *The List of Adrian Messenger*

This phenomenon is sometimes referred to as Canadian Raising, since the more restricted allophones [ʌj] and [ʌw] have higher vowel components than the elsewhere allophones [aj] and [aw].

2.5 English vowels and glides

A final example of predictable variation that refers to classes of segments is again taken from English. Table 3.2 showed contrasts among English vowels. In English, the nonlow, tense vowels [ij], [ej], [uw], and [ow], always contain one of the two glides [j] and [w]. Note that the labiovelar glide [w] occurs with the back rounded vowels [u] and [o] and the palatal glide [j] occurs with the front unrounded vowels [i] and [e]. Stated in other words, we can say that the back rounded vowels predictably co-occur with the back (labiovelar) glide and the front vowels co-occur with the nonback unrounded glide. These facts are summed up in Table 3.10.

Table 3.10 Tense vowel-glide combinations in English

Vowel	*Glide*			*Vowel*	*Glide*		
(both nonback and unrounded)				*(both back and rounded)*			
i	j	[fijt]	feat	u	w	[buwt]	boot
e	j	[fejt]	fate	o	w	[bowt]	boat

These data show parallels with the **allophonic distribution** we have considered so far: certain elements are predictable under certain systematically stateable phonetic conditions. Here, however, instead of a number of variants of a phoneme, we have two segments whose distribution is predictable: these glides are always found after nonlow tense vowels in English. This predictability is analogous to the predictability of allophonic variants—if certain sounds are predictably found in a given environment, they are not included in the phonemic representation. We can thus draw from the data in Table 3.10 the following generalization about the English vowel system.

5)

The nonlow tense vowels of English are predictably followed by a glide that has the same backness and roundedness as the vowel.

Given the variation in English vowels that we have examined, we are now able to summarize what we have discovered about the English vowel system.

The English vowel system

We have already seen that certain elements of phonemes, such as voicing, vowel height, etc., are not present in phonological representations because they are predictable from the phonetic context in which the allophone is found. Since the presence of the appropriate glides following the class of nonlow tense vowels is predictable, they need not be present in the phonological representation of the English vowels either.

These generalizations enable us to represent the contrasts between words like *heat* and *hit, late* and *let, cooed* and *could* purely as tense versus lax vowel contrasts, and not as contrasts that also involve the presence of glides. We can also represent the vowel found in words like *code* and *snow* without a following glide. Figure 3.4 sums up the differences between phonetic and phonological representations for the vowels of English.

heat	[ij]	/i/				cooed	[uw]	/u/
hit	[ɪ]	/ɪ/				could	[ʊ]	/ʊ/
late	[ej]	/e/	luck	[ʌ]	/ʌ/	code	[ow]	/o/
let	[ɛ]	/ɛ/				caught	[ɔ]	/ɔ/
sat	[æ]	/æ/				cot	[ɑ]	/ɑ/
						boy	[oj]	/oj/
			tide	[aj]	/aj/			
			loud	[aw]	/aw/			

Figure 3.4 Phonetic and phonological representations of English vowels

2.6 Language-specific patterns

Although the phenomenon of allophonic variation is universal, the patterning of phonemes and allophones is language-specific. What we discover for one language may not hold true for another.

Language-specific variation in allophonic nasalization

It is not unusual for nasal vowel allophones to occur near a nasal consonant, but, as Table 3.11 shows, the patterning may vary from language to language.

Table 3.11 Nasal vowels in Scots Gaelic

[mõːr]	'big'
[nĩ]	'cattle'
[nẽːl]	'cloud'
[mũ]	'about'
[rũːn]	'secret'

Scots Gaelic has oral and nasal vowel allophones. Here we can state the following.

6)

Vowels are nasal in Scots Gaelic when preceded or followed by a nasal consonant.

Malay, a language spoken in Malaysia and Singapore, presents another variation on the theme of nasal allophones.

Table 3.12 Nasalization in Malay

[mẽw̃ãh]	'luxurious'
[mãj̃ãŋ]	'stalk'
[mãrah]	'scold'
[nãẽʔ]	'ascend'
[mə̃laraŋ]	'forbid'
[mãkan]	'eat'
[rumãh]	'house'
[kəreta]	'car'

Here, all vowels and glides following a nasal are predictably nasalized until an obstruent, liquid, or glottal ([h], [ʔ]) is reached. For Malay the generalization is as follows.

7)

In Malay, all vowels and glides following a nasal consonant and not separated from it by a non-nasal consonant are nasalized.

Language-specific variation in allophonic distribution

As was shown in Section 1.2, a phonemic contrast in one language may not prove to be a phonemic contrast in another. This means that the relationship of phonemes to allophones may vary. A comparison of the contrasts among stops in English and Khmer (Cambodian) illustrates this point. In both languages, aspirated and unaspirated phones can be heard.

Table 3.13 Stop phones in English and Khmer

English		*Khmer*	
[p]	[pʰ]	[p]	[pʰ]
[t]	[tʰ]	[t]	[tʰ]
[k]	[kʰ]	[k]	[kʰ]

In English, aspirated and unaspirated stops are allophones of their respective phonemes (the distribution is explained in Section 4.5 of this chapter); there are no contrasting forms like [pɪk] and [pʰɪk]. In Khmer, unaspirated and aspirated voiceless stops contrast.

Table 3.14 Khmer contrastive voiceless stops

[pɔːŋ]	'to wish'	[pʰɔːŋ]	'also'
[tɔp]	'to support'	[tʰɔp]	'be suffocated'
[kat]	'to cut'	[kʰat]	'to polish'

The phonological contrasts of the two languages are different, even though the phones are not. These distributions are the same for the other voiceless stops in both languages.

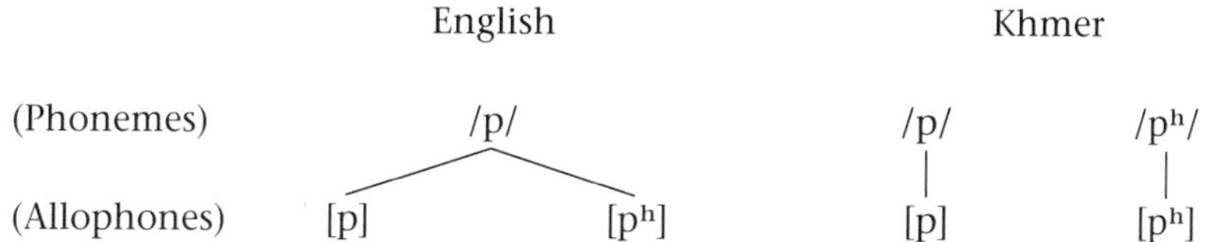

Figure 3.5 English and Khmer voiceless bilabial stop phonemes and allophones

3 PHONETIC AND PHONEMIC TRANSCRIPTION

Having seen how nondistinctive properties of segments are factored out by phonological analysis, we can now compare the type of transcription used for segmental phonological representation with phonetic transcription. The following examples show this difference for the classes of sounds in English that we have examined so far.

Table 3.15 Phonetic and phonemic transcription

Phonetic transcription	*Phonemic transcription*	*Word*	*Predictable property(s) not represented in phonemic transcription*
[pl̥aw]	/plaw/	plow	voicelessness of liquid
[kr̥ijp]	/krip/	creep	voicelessness of liquid; glide after nonlow tense vowel
[kw̥ɪk]	/kwɪk/	quick	voicelessness of liquid
[lejt]	/let/	late	glide after nonlow tense vowel
[lɛt]	/lɛt/	let	—
[tʰajd]	/tajd/	tied	aspiration
[tʰʌjt]	/tajt/	tight	aspiration; Canadian Raising

The contrast between phonetic and phonemic representation is even more striking for the Malay forms given earlier, as is shown in Table 3.16.

Table 3.16 Phonetic and phonemic transcription of Malay nasal vowels

Phonetic transcription	*Phonemic transcription*	*Word*	*Predictable property(s) not represented in phonemic transcription*
[mẽw̃ãh]	/mewah/	'luxurious'	nasalization
[mãj̃ãn]	/majan/	'stalk'	nasalization
[nãɛ̃ʔ]	/naɛʔ/	'ascend'	nasalization

Here, nasalization on all vowel and glide segments is predictable and is therefore omitted from the phonological representation.

4 ABOVE THE SEGMENT: SYLLABLES

We have so far established a segmental unit of phonological analysis called the phoneme. The allophonic variation examined thus far has mostly resulted from conditioning by neighboring segments. The examples of allophonic variation in this section depend on conditioning that involves another level of phonological representation, the **syllable**.

4.1 DEFINING THE SYLLABLE

The syllable is composed of a nucleus (usually a vowel) and its associated nonsyllabic segments. Native speakers of a language demonstrate their awareness of this unit of phonological structure whenever they count syllables in a word. No English speaker would hesitate to say that the word *accident* has three syllables, and most speakers would feel confident that it could be broken up into the syllables /æk.sə.dənt/ (the '.' marks syllable divisions informally). As we will see later on in this chapter, speakers also demonstrate knowledge that syllables have internal structure as well. The organization of a syllable is shown in Figure 3.6 with the monosyllabic English word *sprint*.

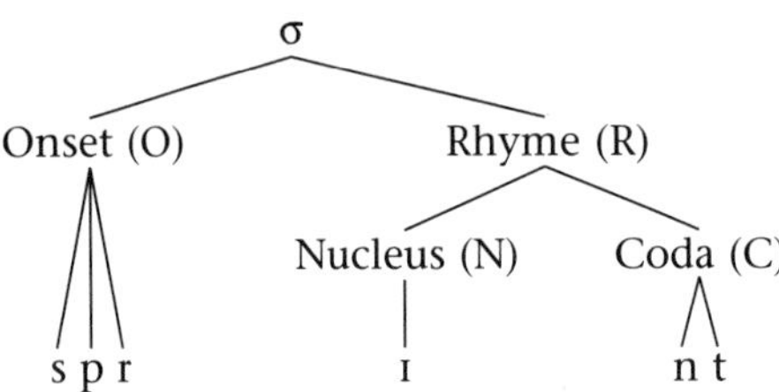

Figure 3.6 Internal structure of a syllable

A complete description of the internal structure of a syllable requires four subsyllabic units. The **nucleus** (abbreviated **N**) is the syllable's only obligatory member; it is a syllabic element that forms the core of a syllable. The **coda** (**C**) consists of those elements that follow the nucleus in the same syllable. The **rhyme** (**R**) is made up of the nucleus and coda. The **onset** (**O**) is made up of those elements that precede the rhyme in the same syllable.

We assume the existence of subsyllabic units for a number of reasons. One of them is the fact that speakers do not syllabify words in random or variable ways. The word *extreme* /ɛkstrim/ would never be syllabified as /ɛ.kstrim/. Instead, syllables comply with certain constraints that prohibit them (in English) from beginning with a sequence like *kstr* and so result in the syllabification /ɛk.strim/.

Table 3.17 Some syllable-initial sequences in English

/ə.plɔd/	applaud
/di.klajn/	decline
/ɛk.splen/	explain
/ɪm.prə.vajz/	improvise

Constraints can be stated for each of the terminal subsyllabic units O, N, and C. To illustrate this, we turn to the constraints that govern the phonological shape of onsets in English.

4.2 Onset constraints and phonotactics

Native speakers of any language intuitively know that certain words that come from other languages sound unusual and they often adjust the segment sequences of these words to conform with the pronunciation requirements of their own language. These intuitions are based on a tacit knowledge of the permissible syllable structures of the speaker's own language. For example, English-speaking students learning Russian have difficulty pronouncing a word like *vprog* [fprɔk] 'value, good', since the sequence /fpr/ is never found in English onsets. Since speakers typically adjust an impermissible sequence by altering it to a permissible one, many English speakers would pronounce the Russian word [fprɔk] as [fəprɔk], or even delete the initial /f/ and say [prɔk] in order to adjust the impermissible sequence /fpr/ to a permissible English onset. **Phonotactics**, the set of constraints on how sequences of segments pattern, forms part of a speaker's knowledge of the phonology of his or her language.

Some English onsets

The following table contains examples of the possible syllable-initial consonant sequences of English that contain a voiceless stop consonant. These sequences are all illustrated in word-initial position to make them easier to pick out. (Stress marking and phonetic details such as liquid-glide devoicing which are not relevant to the present discussion are omitted here.)

Table 3.18 Initial consonant clusters in English containing a voiceless stop

Labial + liquid or glide		*Alveolar + liquid or glide*		*Velar + liquid or glide*	
[pl]	please	[tl]	—	[kl]	clean
[pr]	proud	[tr]	trade	[kr]	cream
[pw]	—	[tw]	twin	[kw]	queen
[pj]	pure	[tj]	tune (British; Southern)	[kj]	cute
[spl]	splat	[stl]	—	[skl]	sclerosis
[spr]	spring	[str]	strip	[skr]	scrap
[spw]	—	[stw]	—	[skw]	squeak
[spj]	spew	[stj]	stew (British; Southern)	[skj]	skewer

The examples in Table 3.18 show that the first segment of a word-initial three-consonant cluster in English is always *s;* the second consonant in the series is always a voiceless stop, and the third is either a liquid or a glide. These sound patterns can be formally represented as follows:

$$\sigma\ [\text{s} \quad \left\{\begin{matrix} \text{p} \\ \text{t} \\ \text{k} \end{matrix}\right. \quad \left\{\begin{matrix} (\text{l}) \\ \text{r} \\ (\text{w}) \\ \text{j} \end{matrix}\right.$$

In this formalization, σ indicates the boundary of a syllable, and the curly braces designate 'either/or'. The sounds in parentheses are not found in all combinations. Although there are twenty-four possible two- and three-consonant syllable-initial sequences in English containing a voiceless stop, not all of these combinations are exploited in the vocabulary of the language.

4.3 Accidental and systematic gaps

Some gaps in the inventory of possible English words include *snool, splick, sklop, fliss, trock*, and *kriff*, although none of these forms violates any constraints on onset combinations found in English. Gaps in a language's inventory of forms that correspond to nonoccurring but possible forms are called **accidental gaps**. Occasionally, an accidental gap will be filled in by the invention of a new word. The word *Kodak* is one such invented word. Borrowed words such as *perestroika* (from Russian), *taco* (from Spanish), and *Zen* (from Japanese) are readily accepted by English speakers as long as their syllable structures conform to the phonotactic patterns of the language.

Table 3.18 has shown which syllable-initial consonant clusters involving voiceless stops are permissible in English. Gaps in the occurring syllable structures of a language that result from the exclusion of certain sequences are called **systematic gaps**. Certain onset sequences like /bz/, /pt/, and /fp/ are systematic gaps in the pattern of English and are outright unacceptable to English speakers. Such sequences will ordinarily be adjusted phonologically when they are pronounced in spontaneous speech. This can be seen in the case of borrowings from other languages into English. Many Greek words beginning with *ps-* and *pt-* have been absorbed into English, as the spellings of *psychology, psoriasis*, and *pterodactyl* attest. In all of them, the impermissible clusters $*_{\sigma}$*ps-* and $*_{\sigma}$*pt-* have been reduced to $_{\sigma}$*s-* or $_{\sigma}$*t-* in onsets. However, when these same forms occur word internally, where their syllabification is different, the 'lost' segments may resurface. For example, the *pter* of *pterodactyl* means 'wing'; both consonants are heard in the word *helicopter*, where English syllabification has resulted in the structure *heli*$_{\sigma}$ *cop*$_{\sigma}$ *ter*$_{\sigma}$.

There are many other words that violate phonotactic conditions but that nonetheless do commonly appear in spoken English, such as *pueblo* [pwɛblow], *Tlingit* [tl̥ɪŋɪt], and Elmer Fudd's *stweet* [stwijt] 'street' (which results from a persistent replacement of /r/ by /w/). The British (and sometimes Southern) pronunciation of 'Tuesday' as [tjuwzdej] is also not difficult for other North American speakers. This appears to be the case because these sequences are not absolutely excluded from the onset phonotactics of English as are such sequences as $*_{\sigma}$*ps-* and $*_{\sigma}$*bz-*. Onsets like $*_{\sigma}$*pw-* and $*_{\sigma}$*stw-* are possibilities that are not exploited due to language-specific restrictions on the sequencing of certain features. For example, a labiovelar glide does not usually occur in an onset after a labial consonant, and an alveolar stop such as /t/ is not followed by /l/; in both cases there is a restriction (in English) on stop-sonorant onset sequences with the same place of articulation. Such restrictions are nonetheless relatively easy to overcome in pronunciation.

Language-specific phonotactics

It is important to emphasize that certain aspects of the particular constraints discussed in the previous section are universal (form part of human linguistic knowledge), whereas others are language-specific. An onset like *pl* is found in many languages besides English (for example, in Russian, Thai, and French), while an onset sequence like *lp* is rarely if ever found. We may therefore say that no restrictions against an onset like *pl* appear to exist as part of human linguistic knowledge, while the virtual nonexistence of onsets like **lp* suggest that something in their phonetic makeup disqualifies them from occurring in language. Language-specific constraints, on the other hand, hold true for individual languages such as English, and they may or may not be found in other languages. Each language has its own set of restrictions on the phonological shapes of its syllable constituents. Speakers of Russian, for example, are quite accustomed to pronouncing onset sequences such as *ps-*, *mgl-*, and *fsl-*, which are not found in English.

Table 3.19 Some onset sequences in Russian

[psa]	'dog's'
[fslux]	'aloud'
[mgla]	'mist'

Phonotactic constraints represent one kind of phonological knowledge. You might wonder what prevents English words like *extreme, applaud, decline, explain,* and *improvise* from being syllabified as /ɛks.trim/, /əp.lɔd/, /dik.lajn/, /ɛks.plen/, and /ɪmp.rəv.ajz/, since these divisions do not violate any phonotactic constraints either. The next section answers this question by providing a procedure for establishing the association of consonants and vowels within syllables.

4.4 Setting up syllables

Each language defines its own syllable structure, although there are universal principles that interact with language-specific factors. The process for setting up syllables in a given language involves the following steps.

- **Step a** Since the syllabic nucleus is the only obligatory constituent of a syllable, it is constructed first. Each vowel segment in a word makes up a syllabic nucleus. To represent this, link a vowel to an N above it by drawing an association line. Above each nucleus symbol, place an R (for rhyme), which is filled out in step c below. Above each R, place a σ symbol; link all with association lines.

Figure 3.7

- **Step b** Onsets before codas: the longest sequence of consonants to the left of each nucleus that does not violate the phonotactic constraints of the language in question is called the **onset** of the syllable. Link these consonants to an O and join it to the same syllable as the vowel to the right. Note that there is no onset in the first syllable of *extreme*.

Figure 3.8

- **Step c** Any remaining consonants to the right of each nucleus form the **coda** and are linked to a C above them. This C is associated with the syllable nucleus to its left in the rhyme. A syllable with a coda is called a **closed syllable**.

Figure 3.9

- **Step d** Syllables that make up a single form (usually a word) branch out from the representation *Wd* (this step is frequently omitted from phonological representations to save space; the complete representation is understood even when *Wd* is not written out).

Figure 3.10

Given this procedure, it is clear why words such as *applaud* and *explain* in Table 3.17 are syllabified the way they are. In accordance with step b 'build onsets before codas', the permissible consonant clusters make up the onset of the second syllable, and not the coda of the first syllable.

Some further syllabification

This procedure is used to syllabify forms in any language. An example from Turkish demonstrates in more detail how this universal syllabification procedure works. Turkish has different syllable structure constraints than English. As in English, onsets are optional in Turkish, but when present, may consist of no more than one segment—clearly not a constraint found in English. A nucleus may consist of a long vowel (which is equivalent to two short vowels in length) or a short vowel. Codas can be no more than two segments long.

The following words can be syllabified in the steps given above (steps c and d have been collapsed here). Note how the procedure leads to different syllabifications of the word *alt* 'bottom' in steps b and c of the examples.

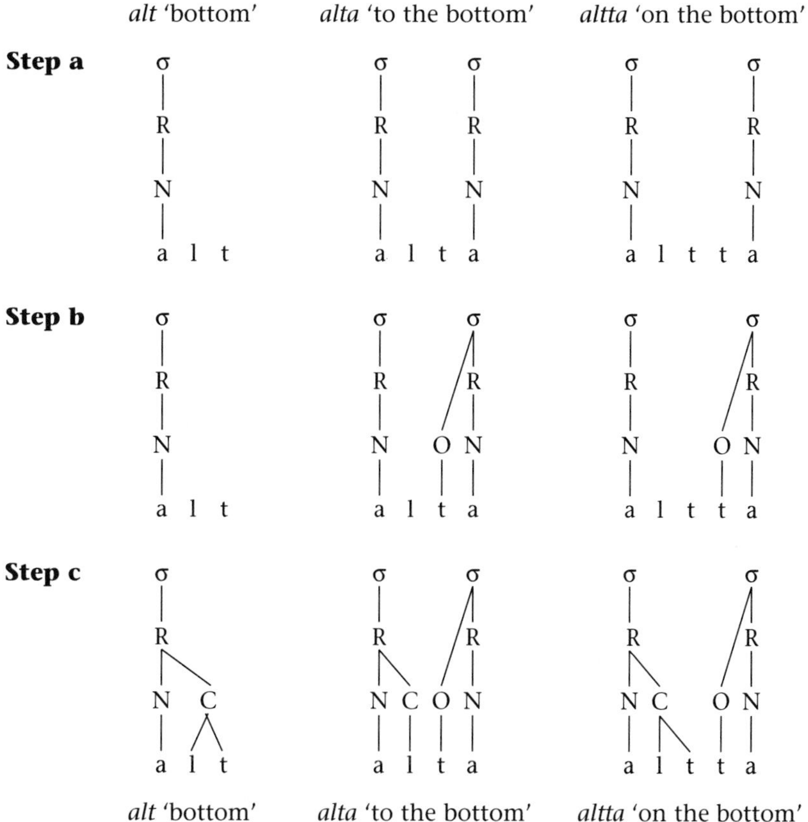

Figure 3.11 Examples of syllabification in Turkish

In these examples, the *t* of *alt* 'bottom' is assigned to the coda of the first syllable, since there is no syllable with an available onset position following it. However, the same phoneme *t* in *alta* 'to the bottom' is assigned to the onset of the second syllable, since onsets are filled first and *t* is available to fill the position. In *altta* 'on the bottom', the two *ts* fill the available coda and onset positions of their respective syllables.

As a final example of the procedure, the following figure demonstrates the syllabification of the English words *slim*, *decline*, and *scrimp*.

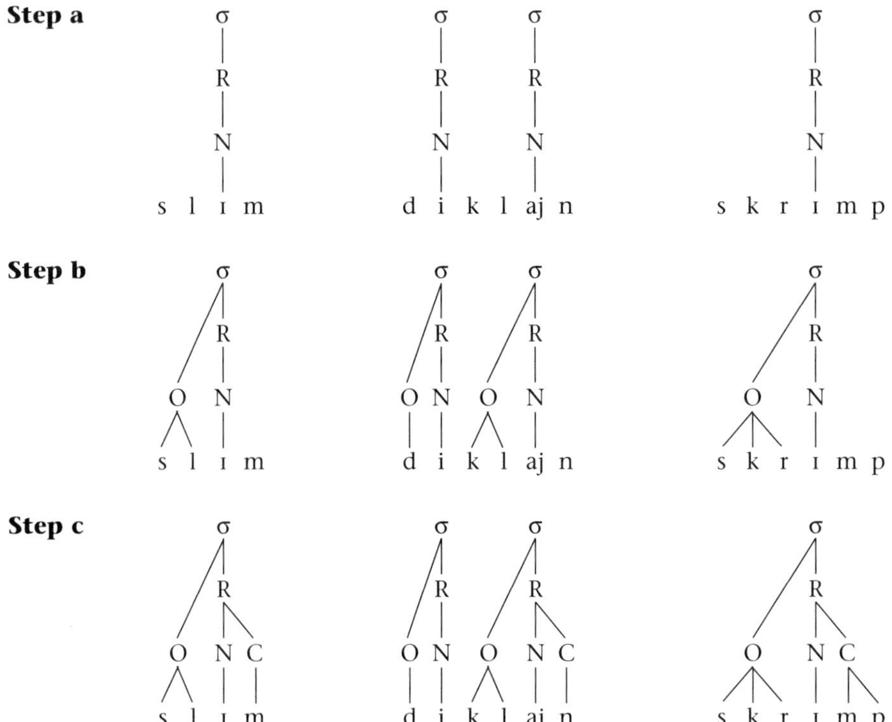

Figure 3.12 Examples of syllabification in English

With this method in mind, we can now consider the relevance of syllables to phonological description.

4.5 Syllabic phonology

One reason that syllables are treated as units of phonological structure is that they are relevant to stating generalizations about the distribution of allophonic features. The next sections provide examples of the role of syllables in phonological analysis.

Aspiration in English

As Table 3.20 shows, the voiceless stops of English each have an aspirated and an unaspirated allophone.

Table 3.20 English aspiration

A		*B*		*C*	
[pʰǽn]	pan	[spǽn]	span	[slǽp]	slap
[pʰéjn]	pain	[spéjn]	Spain	[slɑ́t]	slot
[pʰówk]	poke	[spówk]	spoke	[blɑ́k]	block
[tʰówn]	tone	[stówn]	stone		
[kʰín]	kin	[skín]	skin		
[pʰərspájr]	perspire	[splǽt]	splat		
[tʰəméjɾow]	tomato	[ʌpsɛ́t]	upset		
[kʰənúw]	canoe				
[əpʰɑ́n]	upon				
[ətʰǽk]	attack				
[tʰəkʰíjlə]	tequila				

The distribution of aspiration can be stated generally by referring to syllable structure.

Table 3.21 Distribution of aspirated stops in English

Aspirated stops	*Unaspirated stops*
• syllable-initially	Elsewhere: • in a syllable onset preceded by *s* (whether another C follows or not) • before a consonant

The phonemic representations of the three English stops are unaspirated, since aspiration is predictable. The environments where aspiration occurs can be stated very generally by referring to syllable structure.

8)

English voiceless stops are aspirated syllable-initially.

This statement accounts for all the data in column A of Table 3.20, where voiceless stops appear syllable-initially. No aspiration is found in the forms in columns B and C since the voiceless stops appear either as the second member of the syllable onset (in *span, Spain, spoke, stone,* and *skin*), or in a coda, as in *upset.*

Ambisyllabicity *(Advanced)*

Some English words, such as *upper, happy,* and *walking,* do not show aspiration where it is expected, given that the syllabification procedure results in the following: /ʌ.pər/, /hæ.pi/, and /wɑ.kɪŋ/. This fact is accounted for by assuming that the voiceless stops in these forms are simultaneously in both syllables, a phenomenon known as **ambisyllabicity**. These consonants are all preceded by a stressed syllable; in contrast, the aspirated stops in words like *upon* [ʌpʰɑ́n] and *attack* [ətʰǽk] (Table 3.20, column A) show aspiration, but are all found as the onset of a stressed syllable.

In words with ambisyllabic voiceless stops, it is assumed that the stress 'attracts' the voiceless stop into the preceding syllable. Figure 3.13 shows this process in stages: a shows initial syllabification of the word *happy*; b shows stress placement on the first syllable; in c, the dotted line shows the ambisyllabicity of the voiceless stop that is caused by the stress. The ambisyllabic consonant cannot undergo aspiration since it is (at least partly) in the preceding syllable.

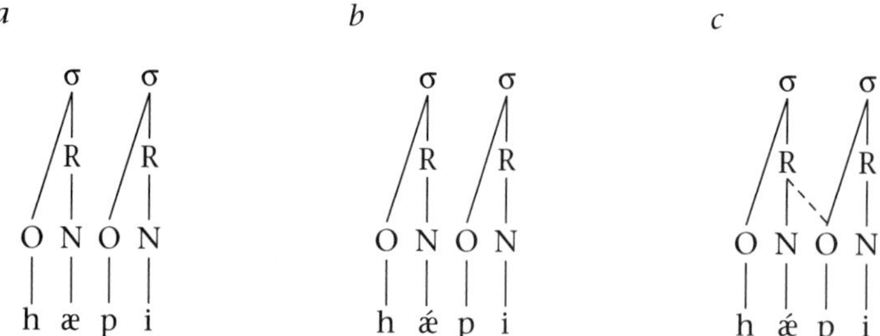

Figure 3.13 Ambisyllabicity in English. *a*: initial syllabification; *b*: stress; *c*: ambisyllabic consonant

Ambisyllabicity is not as arbitrary as it might appear at first. Its presence not only accounts for the lack of aspiration in these forms, but also helps explain why the first syllables of *upper, happy,* and *kicking* might otherwise appear to end in stressed lax vowels, a distribution that is otherwise not frequent in English (except in expressive/onomatopoeic words like *baa* /bæ/). The simultaneous presence of the voiceless stop in the coda of the first syllable and the onset of the second means not only that we do not expect aspiration, but also that the first syllable is closed and so the presence of a lax vowel is normal.

Phonetic length in English vowels

English offers a second example of the phonological relevance of syllables. Phonetic length is predictable in English vowels, as the next examples show.

Table 3.22 Phonetic length in English

A		*B*	
bad	[bæ:d]	bat	[bæt]
Abe	[e:jb]	ape	[ejp]
phase	[fe:jz]	face	[fejs]
leave	[li:jv]	leaf	[lijf]
tag	[tʰæ:g]	tack	[tʰæk]
brogue	[bro:wg]	broke	[browk]
		tame	[tʰẽjm]
		meal	[mijl]
		soar	[sor]
		show	[ʃow]

English vowels are shorter before voiceless consonants, before sonorant consonants, and in word-final position; they are longer before voiced nonsonorant consonants. As the next examples show, this distribution is determined by syllable structure. The first-syllable vowels all precede voiced, nonsonorant consonants, but they are short since the voiced consonant is in the following syllable.

Table 3.23 Short vowels before voiced consonants in English

obey	[ow.bej]	/obe/
redo	[rij.duw]	/ridu/
regard	[rij.gard]	/rigard/
ogre	[ow.gər]	/ogər/

In order for an English vowel to be long, it must be followed by a voiced obstruent in the same syllable. The following generalization can now be made.

9)

English vowels are long when followed by a voiced obstruent in the same syllable.

As the analyses of the distribution of aspiration and vowel length in English have shown, the use of syllabic representations in phonology permits us to make more general statements about certain allophonic patterns in language than if we use only statements that do not make reference to syllable structure.

Syllables and stress in English

English provides a final example of the relevance of syllabic units to phonological analysis. Recall (from Chapter 2, Section 8.3) that stress is defined as the perceived prominence of one or more syllabic elements over others in a word. In some languages—English among them—the structure of individual syllables plays a role in determining which vowel is stressed. Consider the data in the next example.

Table 3.24 English noun stress

A	*B*	*C*
agénda	aróma	cínema
consénsus	Manitóba	cábinet
appéndix	horízon	vénison
synópsis	aréna	América
veránda	Minnesóta	jávelin

The words in columns A and B are all stressed on the next-to-last (penultimate) syllable, while the words in column C are all stressed on the third syllable from the end of the word (the antepenultimate syllable), as the form *America* makes clear. Although the stressing of the words at first may seem arbitrary, reference to syllable structure makes clear that there is some system underlying the assignment of stress here. Words are provided in phonetic transcription.

Syllabifying the words in each column reveals what stress assignment is based on. Figure 3.14 provides the syllabification of one word from each column.

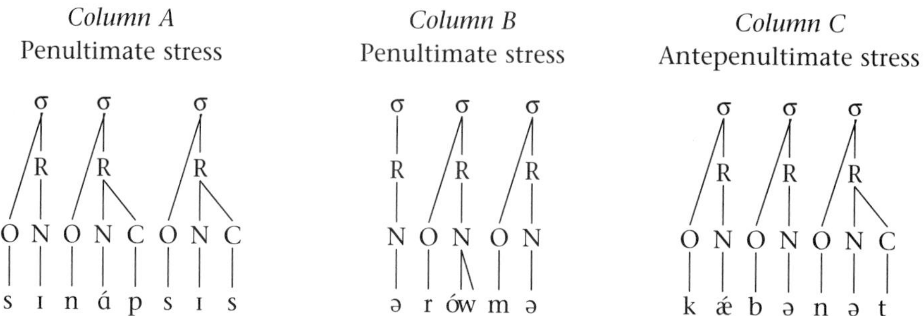

Figure 3.14 Syllable-based stress in English

All the words in column A share a correlation between their syllabification and their stress: the stressed penultimate syllable has a coda (recall that a syllable with a coda is said to be closed). All the words in column B also share a syllabic characteristic: their nucleus contains a tense vowel. Although the syllable is not closed, the nucleus vowel with two elements in it (the vowel-glide sequence) is now represented as branching. Tense vowels, in other words, have the same effect on stress assignment in English as closed syllables. Both closed syllables and syllables with two elements in the nucleus are referred to as heavy syllables. Compare these words with the representative item from column C. We see that the penultimate syllable is not heavy: it is neither closed nor does it contain a branching nucleus. With these facts before us, we can state our generalization. We will be careful to limit it to English *nouns*, that is, words that label or describe some thing or state (see Chapter 5, Section 1).

10)

English nouns are stressed on the penultimate syllable when it is heavy; otherwise, they are stressed on the antepenultimate syllable.

We have limited our generalization to English nouns because the stress pattern of English is rather elaborate. Nevertheless, there is no doubt that syllabification plays a central role in the determining of stress placement in English.

We have one more level of phonological analysis to explore. Although phonetic and phonemic transcription up to this point has employed segments, segmental notation is itself a kind of shorthand, since segments are ultimately composed of features. The next section takes up this aspect of phonology.

5 FEATURES

Current linguistic practice does not assume that segments are the ultimate units of phonological structure. Instead, linguists view segments as composed of smaller elements. This section deals with **features**—the units of phonological structure that make up segments.

5.1 Why we use features

There are a number of reasons why linguists have settled on features as the most basic phonological unit.

Features as independent and coordinated elements

We have already seen in Chapter 1 that speech is produced by a number of coordinated articulatory activities such as voicing, tongue position, lip rounding, and so on. Features such as [voice], [high], [round]—note that features are written in square brackets—directly reflect this activity, in that each feature is rooted in an independently controllable aspect of speech production. The representation of a segment with features can be initially accomplished by placing the features of each segment in an array called a **matrix**. Each feature or group of features defines a specific property of the segment. This representation is in binary terms: [+] means that a feature is present, and [–] means that it is absent. Figure 3.15 shows a feature matrix for the English vowel [ɑ].

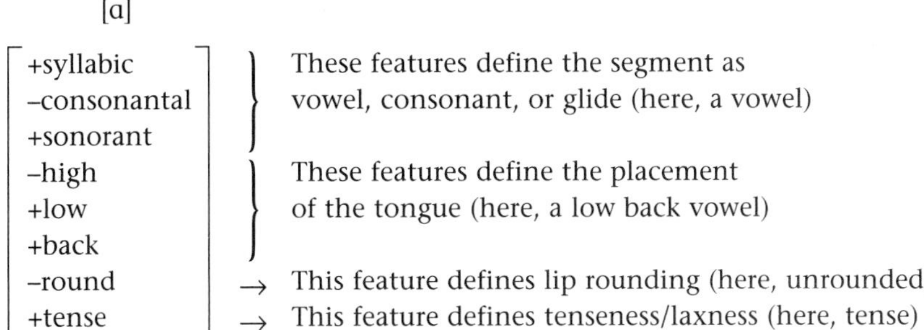

Figure 3.15 Feature matrix for the English vowel /ɑ/

Features and natural classes

A second reason for viewing segments as composed of features is that each feature may represent a phonologically relevant characteristic of segments. To understand what is meant by this, we first examine how features enable us to distinguish among classes of sounds made up of members that vary in one or more articulatory dimensions. For example, the set of sounds /p/, /t/, /k/, /s/, and /ʃ/, all of which differ in place and (in part) in manner of articulation, can be readily distinguished from the equally differing set /b/, /d/, /g/, /z/, and /ʒ/ by the single feature [voice] alone. In phonological terms, features express **natural classes**, which are classes of sounds that share a feature or features, such as voiceless stops, glides, high vowels, nasal consonants, and so on. Any natural class requires fewer features to define it than to define any one of its members. In Table 3.25, for example, fewer features are needed to define the class of English front vowels than to define the vowel /æ/.

Table 3.25 Two natural classes: front and back vowels in English

[–consonantal, +syllabic, +sonorant, –back]	[–consonantal, +syllabic, +sonorant, +back]	[–consonantal, +syllabic, +sonorant, –back, –high, +low, –round]
/i/	/u/	/æ/
/ɪ/	/ʊ/	
/e/	/o/	
/ɛ/	/ʌ/	
/æ/	/ɑ/	

Because features define natural classes, we can now see their relevance to phonological analysis. It is not just individual phonemes such as /p/, /b/, /k/, and /g/ that contrast in English; rather, the entire class of voiced stops contrasts with the class of voiceless stops. It is the feature [voice] that is potentially contrastive, not the individual segments, since we can define the contrast between each pair of segments with otherwise identical articulations as residing in the feature [voice]. Since this single feature is employed in all voiced-voiceless contrasts, we say that [voice] is a **distinctive feature** of English.

Other features provide for other contrasts. For example, we can capture the contrast between /t/ and /s/ in English with the feature [continuant]. Both /t/ and /s/ are voiceless and have an alveolar point of articulation. (The fact that the tongue tip is used in the production of one sound and the tongue blade is used in the other is not relevant to this phonological distinction in English, and can therefore be ignored.) By viewing the relevant distinctive feature as [continuant], we can use the same feature to distinguish between /p/ and /f/, /b/ and /v/, and /d/ and /z/.

Table 3.26 Stop-fricative contrasts as a feature

[–continuant]	[+continuant]
p	f
b	v
t	s
d	z

By systematically examining the phonemic contrasts of a language, we can extract the phonologically distinctive features and state the phonemic inventory in terms of these irreducible linguistic elements.

Features, processes, and allophonic variation

Reference to features also enables us to understand the nature of allophonic variation more exactly. Viewed from the perspective of features, allophonic variation is not simply the substitution of one allophone for another, but rather the environmentally conditioned change or specification of a feature or features. Processes like those presented in Chapter 2 are the primary factors in the changing of features. Liquid-glide devoicing in English, for example, is the change of the value of the feature [voice] from [+voice] to [–voice] after voiceless stop consonants. Vowel nasalization in Malay is the change of the value of the nasal feature from [–nasal] to [+nasal] under the conditions stated in *7*).

Certain features reflect classes of sounds that are not always reflected in traditional descriptive terminology but which are also relevant to phonological patterning. The feature [coronal], for example, refers to the class of sounds made with the tongue tip or blade raised. It turns out that just this feature is required to state the constraint on the selection of consonant sequences in coda position in English presented in Chapter 1: when a vowel is tense and followed by two consonants (*pint*), or when a vowel is lax and followed by three consonants (*next*), the final consonant must always be [+coronal] (t, d, s, z, θ, ð, ʃ, ʒ, tʃ, or dʒ). Features are thus more than phonetic descriptions in a different guise.

Since features are considered to be the ultimate building blocks of phonology, linguists have attempted to state all possible phonological facts about language with the fewest number of features possible. Only a limited number of features—currently around twenty-four—have been proposed. Features thus constitute an important part of a theory of what is possible (and what is not possible) in the phonological behavior of human beings.

The next section presents the features of English. Tables 3.27 and 3.28 present the vowel and consonant segments of English along with the features needed to represent them in matrix form. It is a good idea to look these figures over before going on to read about individual features.

Table 3.27 Feature matrix for English vowels

		i	ɪ	e	ɛ	æ	ʌ	ə	ɑ	u	ʊ	o	ɔ
Major class features	[consonantal]	–	–	–	–	–	–	–	–	–	–	–	–
	[sonorant]	+	+	+	+	+	+	+	+	+	+	+	+
	[syllabic]	+	+	+	+	+	+	+	+	+	+	+	+
Laryngeal features	[voice]	+	+	+	+	+	+	+	+	+	+	+	+
Place features	[round]	–	–	–	–	–	–	–	–	+	+	+	+
Dorsal features	[high]	+	+	–	–	–	–	–	–	+	+	–	–
	[low]	–	–	–	–	+	–	–	+	–	–	–	–
	[back]	–	–	–	–	–	+	+	+	+	+	+	+
	[tense]	+	–	+	–	–	–	–	+	+	–	+	–
	[reduced]	–	–	–	–	–	–	+	–	–	–	–	–
Manner feature	[continuant]	+	+	+	+	+	+	+	+	+	+	+	+

Table 3.28 Feature matrix for English consonants

		p	pʰ	b	t	tʰ	d	k	kʰ	g	f	v	s	z	θ	ð	ʃ	ʒ	tʃ	dʒ	m	n	ŋ	l	r	j	w	ʍ	h	ʔ
Major class	[consonantal]	+	+	+	+	+	+	+	+	+	+	+	+	+	+	+	+	+	+	+	+	+	+	+	+	–	–	–	–	–
features	[sonorant]	–	–	–	–	–	–	–	–	–	–	–	–	–	–	–	–	–	–	–	+	+	+	+	+	+	+	+	–	–
	[syllabic]	–	–	–	–	–	–	–	–	–	–	–	–	–	–	–	–	–	–	–	–	–	–	–	–	–	–	–	–	–
Laryngeal	[voice]	–	–	+	–	–	+	–	–	+	–	+	–	+	–	+	–	+	–	+	+	+	+	+	+	+	+	–	–	–
features	[CG]	–	–	–	–	–	–	–	–	–	–	–	–	–	–	–	–	–	–	–	–	–	–	–	–	–	–	–	–	+
	[SG]	–	+	–	–	+	–	–	+	–	–	–	–	–	–	–	–	–	–	–	–	–	–	–	–	–	–	–	+	–
Place	[labial]	+	+	+	–	–	–	–	–	–	+	+	–	–	–	–	–	–	–	–	+	–	–	–	–	–	+	+	–	–
features	[round]	–	–	–	–	–	–	–	–	–	–	–	–	–	–	–	–	–	–	–	–	–	–	–	–	–	+	+	–	–
	[coronal]	–	–	–	+	+	+	–	–	–	–	–	+	+	+	+	+	+	+	+	–	+	–	+	+	+	–	–	–	–
	[anterior]	+	+	+	+	+	+	–	–	–	+	+	+	+	+	+	–	–	–	–	+	+	–	+	+	–	–	–	–	–
	[strident]	–	–	–	–	–	–	–	–	–	–	–	+	+	–	–	+	+	+	+	–	–	–	–	–	–	–	–	–	–
Dorsal	[high]	–	–	–	–	–	–	+	+	+	–	–	–	–	–	–	–	–	–	–	–	–	+	–	–	+	+	+	–	–
features	[back]	–	–	–	–	–	–	+	+	+	–	–	–	–	–	–	–	–	–	–	–	–	+	–	–	–	+	+	–	–
Manner	[nasal]	–	–	–	–	–	–	–	–	–	–	–	–	–	–	–	–	–	–	–	+	+	+	–	–	–	–	–	–	–
features	[continuant]	–	–	–	–	–	–	–	–	–	+	+	+	+	+	+	+	+	–	–	–	–	–	–	+	+	+	+	+	–
	[lateral]	–	–	–	–	–	–	–	–	–	–	–	–	–	–	–	–	–	–	–	–	–	–	+	–	–	–	–	–	–
	[delayed release]	–	–	–	–	–	–	–	–	–	–	–	–	–	–	–	–	–	–	+	+	–	–	–	–	–	–	–	–	–

5.2 The features of English

Most features have labels that reflect traditional articulatory terms such as [voice], [consonantal], and [nasal]. These features require little further description. A few features have less familiar labels, such as [coronal] and [anterior]. From this point on, features will be used to describe classes of sounds. At the same time, we will continue throughout the book to use time-honored terms such as *consonant, glide,* and *obstruent* (a fricative, affricate, or non-nasal stop) in phonetic description. The traditional terminology will be maintained because it is still widely used in phonetic description.

Features are not ranged haphazardly in a matrix. Rather, they are organized into groups that reflect natural classes. The following headings indicate what these classes are and how the features represent them.

- **Major class features** *Features that represent the classes consonant, obstruent, and sonorant (nasal, liquid, glide, and vowel).*

  [consonantal] Produced with a major obstruction in the vocal tract. All non-sonorant consonants are [+consonantal], but liquids and nasals are also [+consonantal]. Some examples: [p b s z ʃ ʒ l m n ŋ].

  [syllabic] Vowels and syllabic liquids and nasals. Here are some examples: [i ɑ l̩ r̩ m̩ n̩].

  [sonorant] All and only the 'singables': vowels, glides, liquids, and nasals (even when they are voiceless).

Table 3.29 Use of major class features

	Obstruents	*Vowels*	*Glides*	*Liquids*	*Nasals*
[consonantal]	+	–	–	+	+
[syllabic]	–	+	–	–	–
[sonorant]	–	+	+	+	+
Examples:	p b z θ	i ɑ	j w	l r	m n

- **Laryngeal features** *Features that represent states of the larynx.*

  [voice] All voiced sounds are [+voice]; all voiceless sounds are [–voice].

  [spread glottis] (**[SG]**) This feature distinguishes unaspirated from aspirated consonants. Aspirated consonants are [+SG].

  [constricted glottis] (**[CG]**) Made with the glottis closed. In English, only the glottal stop [ʔ] is [+CG].

- **Place features** *Features that represent place of articulation.*

  [labial] Any sound articulated with one or both lips is [+labial]. In English: [p b f v w]. See [round].

  [round] Rounded vowels and the rounded labiovelar glide [w]. Sounds that are [+round] are made by protruding the lips; therefore, all [+round] sounds are also [+labial]. Sounds that are [+labial], however, are not necessarily [+round], since sounds like [p] or [f] can be produced without necessarily rounding the lips.

[coronal] Any sound that is articulated with the tongue tip or blade raised is [+coronal]. Some examples: [t d θ ð s z tʃ dʒ ʃ ʒ n l r].

[anterior] Any sound articulated in front of the alveopalatal region is considered to be [+anterior]. Some examples: [p b t d s z θ ð] .

[strident] The 'noisy' coronal fricatives and affricates only. In English, [s z ʃ ʒ tʃ dʒ] are [+strident].

Table 3.30 Use of place of articulation features

	Labials	*Dentals/ alveolars*	*Alveopalatals*	*Palatals/ velars*
[anterior]	+	+	–	–
[coronal]	–	+	+	–
Examples:	p b m	t d ð θ s z n l r	ʃ ʒ tʃ dʒ	k g ŋ

- **Dorsal features** *Features that represent placement of the body of the tongue.*

  [high] Sounds produced with the tongue body raised are considered [+high]. This applies to both vowels and consonants. Examples: [i u j k g].

  [low] Vowels made with the tongue body distinctly lowered from a central position in the oral cavity are [+low]. Examples: [æ ɑ]; note that [h] and [ʔ] are *not* [+low] since they are not made in the oral cavity.

  [back] Any sound articulated behind the palatal region in the oral cavity. Examples: [u o ɑ k g].

  [tense] Expresses the tense-lax distinctions among vowels.

  [reduced] Only the schwa ([ə]) is [+reduced].

- **Manner features** *Features that represent manner of articulation.*

  [nasal] Any sound made with the velum lowered is [+nasal].

  [continuant] Free or nearly free airflow through the centre of the oral cavity: vowels, fricatives, glides, and the liquid *r*; does not include the lateral liquid *l*. Some examples: [ɛ s j r].

  [lateral] All and only varieties of *l* are [+lateral].

  [delayed release] [DR] All and only affricate consonants such as [tʃ] and [dʒ] are [+delayed release].

Feature notation does not provide a convenient way to distinguish the diphthongs [aj], [aw], and [oj] from the other vowels. These diphthongs may be treated as vowel-glide sequences when using features.

5.3 Representation and the Feature Hierarchy (*Advanced*)

We have seen that segments are composed of smaller elements called features. We have also seen that features are organized into groupings that reflect natural classes. Figure 3.16 presents the grouping of features into a **feature hierarchy**, which is a representation of how features are related to each other.

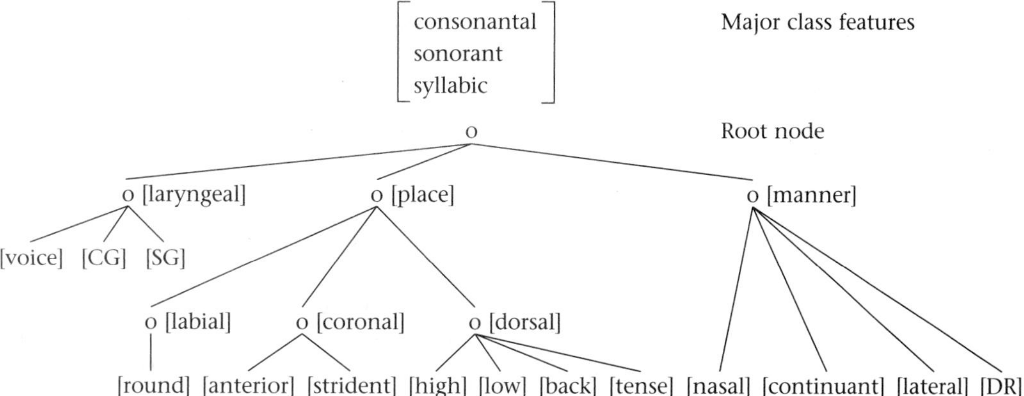

Figure 3.16 The feature hierarchy

Reading the feature hierarchy: nodes and tiers

Each feature grouping in the feature hierarchy is represented by a label called a **class node** or simply **node** (the node symbol is a small circle: o). Beneath each node are grouped the feature or features that make up that subclass.

Nodes and features are ranked on levels or **tiers** that reflect their relation to each other. For example, all major class features are grouped together at the highest node, called the **root node**. The root node thus defines whether a segment in question is a vowel, consonant, or glide.

On the first tier under the root node are placed the nodes and features that specify all the remaining articulatory properties of a segment. From the **laryngeal node** branch out the features that express voicing states. The **place node** branches out into the major place features. The **manner node** branches out into features that relate to general manner of articulation.

Nodes serve a dual purpose in the hierarchy. First, they function as labels for natural classes of features—hence labels like *laryngeal node, place node*, and *manner node*. At the same time, nodes, like features themselves, may be referred to directly when making statements about processes.

While feature representation may at first look more complex and clumsy than strictly segmental representation, it is in the long run very advantageous. Instead of listing individual sets of contrastive phonemes, we express contrasts at the level of the feature as in English, where we can say that the feature [voice] is contrastive. Much allophonic variation can now be represented as the addition, loss, or change of a few features. The influence of the conditioning environment is also made more obvious with this type of representation, as shown in Section 7 of this chapter.

6 DERIVATIONS AND RULE ORDERING

At this point, we have established the existence of three hierarchically related levels of phonological structure. In this model, phonological elements from a lower level are organized and grouped into higher-level elements. Thus, *features* are grouped into (segmental) *phonemes*, which in turn are organized into *syllables*. We have seen how general statements that refer to natural classes and syllable structure account for the presence of noncontrastive elements. Contemporary linguistics also provides a way to link phonological and phonetic representations in a formal manner.

The relationship between phonological and phonetic representation is currently formalized in two ways. In both ways, we assume that the unpredictable features of the phonemic segment are basic or underlying. For our purposes, the terms *phonemic* and *underlying* mean the same thing.

To get from the underlying representations of words—remember that these representations are said to represent our linguistic knowledge—to the spoken (phonetic) forms, we derive the phonetic forms either by the use of **phonological rules** or by showing the process in question as a **representation**. (For now, we will refer to general statements such as *8)*, *9)*, and *10)* as rules; in Section 7 we will see how these statements are formalized). Although underlying and phonetic representations are given in segmental transcription, it is important to keep in mind that all segments are understood to be composed of features.

6.1 DERIVATIONS

Phonetic forms are derived by setting up the underlying representation (also called an **underlying form**) and then allowing the rule or rules in question to operate in those contexts where they are relevant.

The derivation of three phonetic representations (PRs) from underlying representations (URs) is presented in Figure 3.17. Here, the underlying representation is on the top line (the cross hatch # symbolizes a word boundary); reading downward, each rule applies in sequence, and the underlying representation is adjusted as required. Where a rule is not applicable, the form remains unchanged; this information is conveyed by dashes. The resulting output then serves as the input to the following rule. Finally, when all rules relevant to the derivation in question have applied, a phonetic representation is provided. The two rules presented in the following example are aspiration and vowel lengthening (see Section 4.5).

UR	#slæp# 'slap'	#tæp# 'tap'	#pæd# 'pad'
Aspiration	—	#tʰæp#	#pʰæd#
V-length	—	—	#pʰæːd#
PR	[slæp]	[tʰæp]	[pʰæːd]

Figure 3.17 The phonological derivation of three English words

In this example, two rules are applied (since the words being derived are all monosyllabic, the syllable boundaries are equivalent to word boundaries and so are not indicated here). The first accounts for aspiration. Since the initial consonant of the URs #tæp# and #pæd# are voiceless stops found in onset position, they fulfil the conditions under which English stops become aspirated. We therefore indicate that aspiration occurs by providing an intermediate form on a new line.

We have also seen that in English, vowels are predictably long when they occur before a voiced stop in the same syllable. In Figure 3.17, the /æ/'s of *slap* and *tap* occur before voiceless stops and so are not lengthened. The vowel of *pad*, however, occurs in just the environment associated with long vowels and so is predictably lengthened.

The use of such derivations underscores the fact that allophonic variation is the result of processes that apply in the course of language use. Underlying representations express the knowledge that speakers have about the nature of their phonological system, rules reflect the application of allophonic processes, and the phonetic representation reflects the speech output.

6.2 Rule application

We have seen that more than one rule may be employed in a derivation. Consequently, we must now ask how several rules are applied to a given underlying form when these rules interact.

Unordered rule application and feeding

In Figure 3.17, we saw the application of the rules of English aspiration and vowel lengthening, which apply to voiceless stops and vowels, respectively. Note that the environments in which each of these rules apply (onset and pre-coda position, respectively) are entirely different. Therefore, these rules do not interact or affect each other in any way; the order in which they are applied makes no difference to the outcome of a derivation. Figure 3.18 shows the same rules applied in reverse order; there is no difference in the outcome.

UR	#slæp#	'slap'	#tæp#	'tap'	#pæd#	'pad'
V-length	—		—		#pæːd#	
Aspiration	—		#tʰæp#		#pʰæːd#	
PR	[slæp]		[tʰæp]		[pʰæːd]	

Figure 3.18 Unordered rule application

We therefore say that the rules of aspiration and vowel lengthening are *unordered* with respect to each other.

A second type of rule ordering is called **feeding**. Rules are said to be in a feeding order when the application of one rule creates an environment that makes possible the application of another rule that could otherwise not apply. The rules of English schwa-deletion and liquid-glide devoicing, given in example *4)*, are in a feeding relation in the casual speech pronunciation of a word like *parade*. After a schwa has been lost through schwa-deletion, a liquid or glide that follows the schwa in the underlying representation is now directly after a voiceless stop, and therefore subject to liquid-glide devoicing, as the next example shows. The arrows, which are normally not written in derivations, here indicate feeding relationships.

UR	#pəred# 'parade'
Stress	#pəréd#
Schwa deletion	#préd#
Liquid-glide devoicing	#pr̥éd#
Diphthongization	#pr̥éjd#
Vowel lengthening	#pr̥éːjd#
PR	[pr̥éːjd]

Figure 3.19 Feeding order in a derivation

Notice now that no incorrect forms would result if, say, the schwa-deletion rule attempted to apply before the stress rule. Because its environment is not present, the schwa-deletion rule would simply fail to apply. However, once the stress rule was applied, the schwa-deletion rule could then follow in its turn, ultimately leading to a correct phonetic representation. What these facts suggest is that rules in a feeding relation may apply in *free order*, each attempting to apply wherever the required conditions are met. The result will be the desired phonetic output.

6.3 The Form and Notation of Rules

General statements about allophonic distribution are formalized as rules. These rules are written so as to reflect the dynamic nature of processes (Chapter 2, Section 9.4).

Rules

Rules take the following form.

11)

A → B / X ___ Y

In this notation, *A* stands for an element in the underlying representation, *B* for the change it undergoes, and *X* and *Y* for the conditioning environment. Either *X* or *Y* may be absent (null) if the conditioning environment is found only on one side of the allophone. The ___ (focus bar) indicates the position of the segment undergoing the rule. The slash separates the statement of the change from the statement of the conditioning environment. This rule is read as *A becomes B between X and Y*.

As an example of rule writing, we return to the distribution of liquid-glide devoicing in English (Section 2.4): in English, liquids and glides have voiceless allophones after syllable-initial voiceless stops and voiced allophones elsewhere. The rule statement operates on the voiced allophones of liquids and glides as basic (underlying) and changes the feature [+voice] to [–voice] in the appropriate environment. This rule is read as follows.

12)

Liquids and glides become voiceless after syllable-initial voiceless stops.

$$\begin{bmatrix} \text{-syllabic} \\ \text{+sonorant} \\ \text{+voice} \\ \text{-nasal} \end{bmatrix} \rightarrow [\text{-voice}] \,/\, \sigma \begin{bmatrix} \text{-syllabic} \\ \text{+consonantal} \\ \text{-continuant} \\ \text{-voice} \\ \text{-delayed release} \end{bmatrix} \_\_\_\_$$

Figure 3.20 Liquid-glide devoicing in English expressed as a rule

Rule and feature notation formally represents the origin of allophones in phonetic processes that arise in the course of speech. For example, the devoicing of liquids and glides in English is a typical process of **assimilation**. The rule notation in Figure 3.20 shows explicitly how this change of [+voice] to [–voice] occurs in a specific class of sounds following the class of sounds that is [–voice].

Deletion as a rule

We have already seen that English speakers (optionally) drop a schwa [ə] in an open syllable when it is followed by a stressed syllable, as in *police* [pl̥ijs] and *parade* [pr̥ejd]. The rule can be formalized as follows. Here, $C_{\emptyset}$ is an abbreviation for any number of successive consonants from zero on up and the σ represents a syllable boundary.

$$[\text{ə}] \rightarrow \emptyset \,/\, C_{\emptyset} \_\_\_ \sigma\, C_{\emptyset} \underset{[+\text{stress}]}{V}$$

Figure 3.21 Schwa deletion in English

The English schwa deletion rule interacts with the constraint on possible consonant sequences. It automatically fails to apply when an impermissible sequence would result. Since $_{\sigma}$[pʰ and $_{\sigma}$[dl are impermissible onsets in English, there are no forms like *[ptʰéjɾow] *potato* or *[dlíjt] *delete* (except in very, very fast speech).

Epenthesis and alpha rules

Recall that **epenthesis** involves the insertion of a segment (Chapter 2, Section 9.4) into a sequence of other segments. In Section 2.5 we saw that the glides following English tense nonlow vowels are predictable by a general rule: the tense nonlow [–back] vowels /i/ and /e/ are followed by the [–back], glide /j/; the tense nonlow [+back] vowels /u/ and /o/ are followed by the [+back] glide /w/.

In order to represent this epenthesis, we can make use of a type of notation called **alpha notation**. Here, the Greek letter α is a variable (like *x* in algebra) that can stand for either feature value. For example, a feature statement like [α round] can be read as either [+round] or [–round], but the alpha variable or variables used in a rule must match. Whenever the alpha is used in a rule, it must have the same value wherever it occurs. Since alpha notation is used to express two rules, alphas are read twice, once as '+' and once as '–'. When the first alpha is read as '+', all other alphas in the same rule are to be read as '+'; when it is read as '–', all other alphas in the same rule are read as '–'.

With alpha notation, we can express the dual nature of the glide insertion in English as follows.

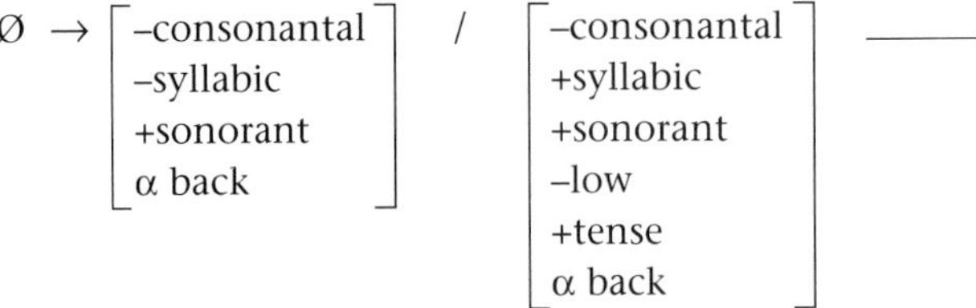

Figure 3.22 Alpha notation in English glide epenthesis

Remember: in reading an alpha, you are reading a rule twice, once with the plus value for the alpha feature, and once with the minus value. The rule in Figure 3.22 states that a [+back] glide is inserted after a [+back] nonlow tense vowel and that a [–back] glide is inserted after a [–back] nonlow tense vowel. Since there are only two glides in the phonological inventory of English, [+back] /w/ and [–back] /j/, the correct glide will be inserted by the rule.

Rules that refer to syllable structure

The rule of vowel lengthening in English makes reference to syllable structure. The boundary of the syllable may be represented by a bracket and a subscript σ. Recall the rule of vowel lengthening in English.

13)

English vowels are long when followed by a voiced obstruent consonant in the same syllable.

The corresponding rule states that an underlying short vowel is lengthened in the appropriate context.

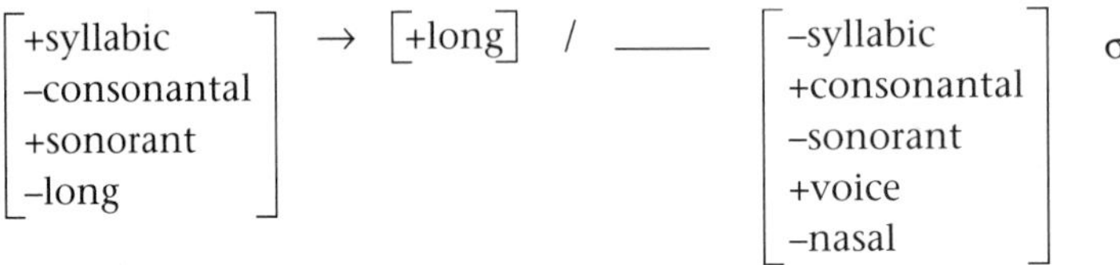

Figure 3.23 Vowel lengthening in English

Notice here that the onset of the syllable is irrelevant to the statement of the rule and so is not included in the formalization.

Vowel epenthesis

Vowel epenthesis is frequently triggered when an impermissible phonotactic structure is encountered in a borrowed word, as in the English pronunciation of the name *Dmitri*. It is also the case that for some speakers of English, a coda consisting of *l* and another consonant is not permitted. For these speakers, *milk* is pronounced [mɪlək] and *film* [fɪləm]. This change can be represented in rule format as follows.

$$\emptyset \rightarrow [\text{ə}] \ / \ [\text{+lateral}] \ \_\_\_ \begin{bmatrix} \text{–syllabic} \\ \text{+consonantal} \end{bmatrix} \sigma$$

Figure 3.24 Schwa epenthesis in English as a rule

A more complete representation of this process requires showing the change of syllable structure, as in Figure 3.25.

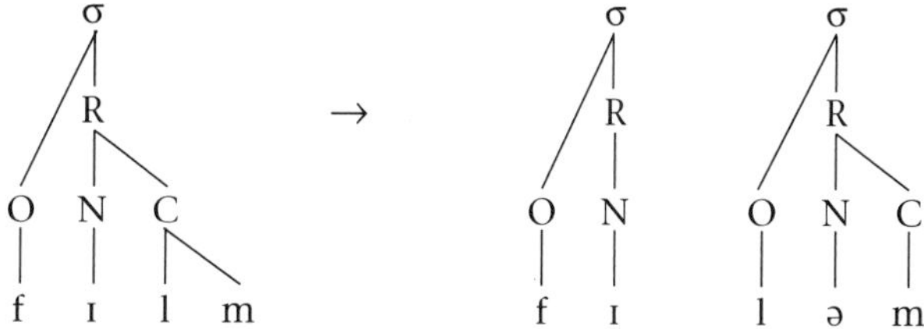

Figure 3.25 Syllabic representation of schwa epenthesis in English

7 REPRESENTATIONS

In recent years, the formalization of rules has become more graphic. This change has taken place because certain types of processes have been viewed as the **spreading** of features from one segment (represented as a feature hierarchy) to another one. It has also been claimed that a simple set of principles governs the way in which features spread.

These graphic presentations of feature changes are referred to as **representations**. The features themselves are referred to as **autosegments**—the label suggests that each feature has a certain autonomy in its operation.

7.1 Assimilation and the feature hierarchy

Assimilation processes are particularly amenable to **autosegmental representation** using the feature hierarchy. This is the case because the overlapping production typical of coarticulation (see Chapter 2, Section 9.1) is neatly represented by the spread of individual features from one 'segment' to another.

Nasal assimilation

In English, a vowel nasalizes when it is immediately followed by a nasal consonant in the same syllable. One or more consonants may follow the nasal consonant. (For some speakers, the vowels must also be stressed.) The words *banks*, *shunted*, and *nimble*, for example, are pronounced [bæ̃ŋks], [ʃʌ̃ntəd], and [nĩmbl̩]. This regressive nasalization in English can be represented as follows (the subscript σ following the square bracket indicates the boundary of the syllable—that is, that the nasal consonant is in the coda; the change undergone by the word *bank* is provided below the representation):

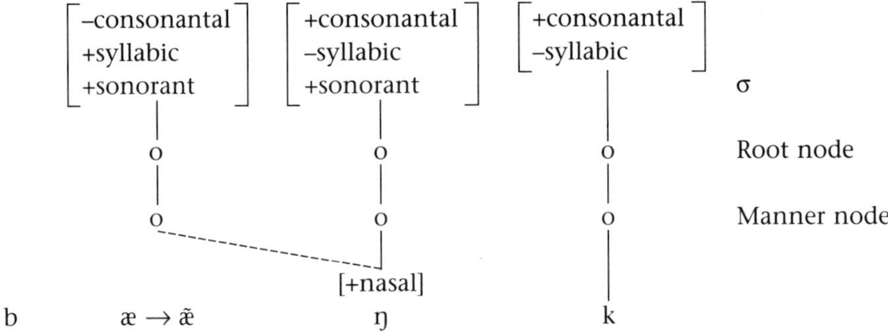

Figure 3.26 Vowel nasalization in English (regressive assimilation)

Note that the English non-nasal vowel is represented as having no feature [nasal]. This fact will be very important in our discussion of representations below. With autosegmental representation, there is no need to list individual segments or even to write a rule. Why not? The next section outlines the principles that govern the spreading of features.

7.2 Autosegmental principles

It is claimed that only three principles account for the many processes that can be represented with autosegmental notation.

- **Association: feature-to-segment** Each autosegment (feature) is associated with at least one segment by an association line.
- **Association: segment-to-feature** Each segment is associated with at least one autosegment (feature) by an association line.
- **Crossing** Association lines do not cross.

Feature spreading

We are now in a position to understand how English nasalization can be viewed as a form of feature spreading. Since English vowels never contrast for the feature [nasal], they can be unspecified for nasality. Our principles note that each feature must be associated with at least one segment, and vice-versa. But nasality is not part of the specification of English vowels. A language-specific rule of English allows leftward spreading. The feature [nasal] on /n/ therefore will 'automatically' spread leftward whenever it finds a vowel that is not specified for nasality. This spreading is not accomplished by a rule, but by a general principle.

Compare nasal spreading in English with nasal spreading in Scots Gaelic. Remember that nasal assimilation in Scots Gaelic can occur progressively. To express this fact autosegmentally, we do not have to write a new rule; we merely state that spreading in Scots Gaelic can operate rightward. The general principles take care of the rest.

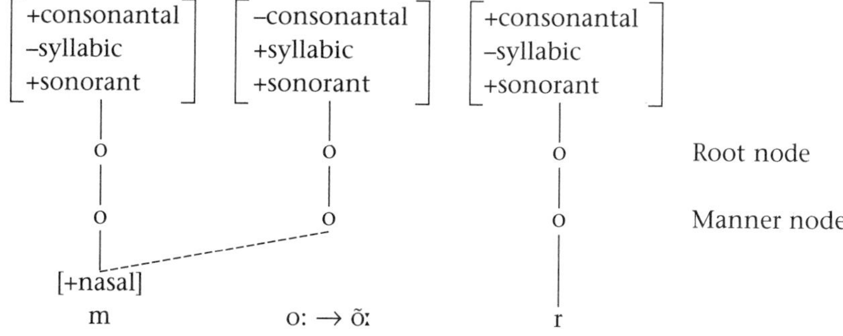

Figure 3.27 Nasal spreading in Scots Gaelic

The spreading of autosegments need not apply only to the feature [nasal]. In theory, just about any feature should follow the same principles. The next section shows how spreading can apply to voicing features.

Laryngeal assimilation: English liquid-glide devoicing revisited

We have already seen (Figure 3.20) how English liquid-glide devoicing is stated in rule format. Since this particular variation is in fact assimilatory, it lends itself well to statement as a representation.

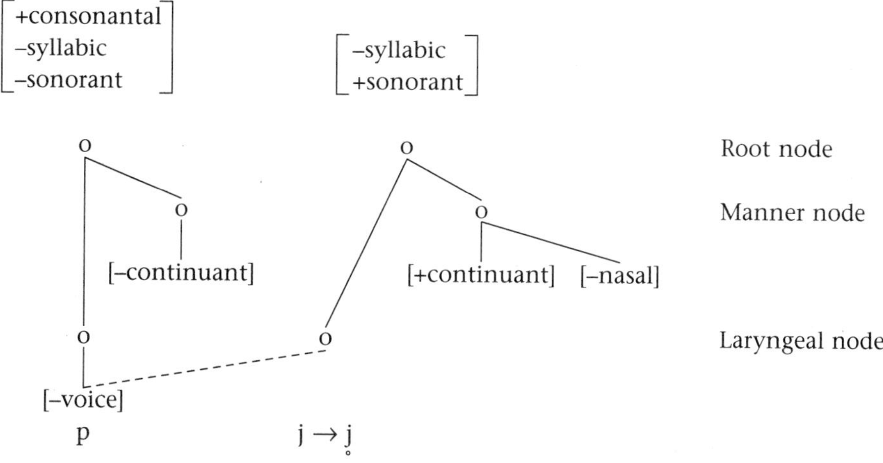

Figure 3.28 Liquid-glide devoicing in English as a representation

The root and manner node features represent the leftmost class as stops and the class to its right as liquids or glides. The place node is not represented since the place of articulation of both the stops and the liquids and glides is irrelevant to the process in question here. The dotted line represents the spreading of the laryngeal node feature [–voice] from the voiceless stop to the liquid or glide.

7.3 Tonal assimilation as a representation

In Chapter 2, you saw how tone is represented on separate levels or tiers of phonological description. Association lines link the tone to the appropriate vowel. A representation of the word *tunko* 'sheep' from Duwai, a language spoken in West Africa, is as follows, where L indicates low tone, and H high tone.

Figure 3.29 Representing tone

This type of representation has the advantage of being able to show explicitly certain facts about tone languages. Tones, like other phonological phenomena, are subject to contextually conditioned variation. A good example of this comes from Duwai. In Duwai, many words show the tonal pattern LH (low-high).

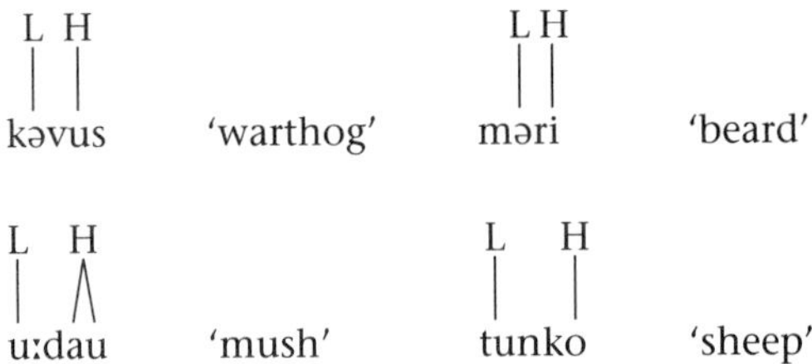

Figure 3.30 Low-high tonal patterns in Duwai

When a word with an LH tonal pattern is followed by a word with an L tone, such as the form *bàì* '(is) not', the H tone of the first word becomes L: *kə̀vús* 'warthog' becomes *kə̀vùs bàì* 'it's not a warthog'; *mə̀rí* 'beard' becomes *mə̀rì bàì* 'it's not a beard', and so on.

This tonal change is a kind of assimilation, and parallels common processes of assimilation of segmental features. This assimilation is viewed as a spreading of the L tone backwards from the word *bàì* to the final vowel of the preceding word, and is represented by drawing a dotted association line (which represents the change in tone) and delinking the original association line from the vowel to the former tone value (the short double lines indicate the loss of association).

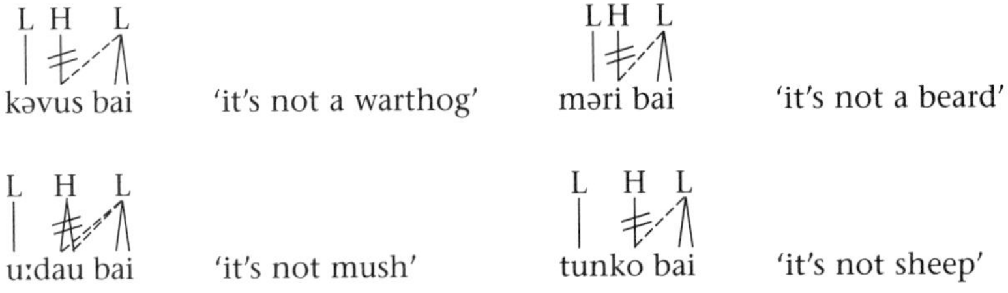

Figure 3.31 Tone assimilation in Duwai

Thus, both features and tonal material are handled by the same type of representation and the same principles.

7.4 Processes, rules, and representations: a last word

The combined use of features and processes in phonological description reflects the dynamic nature of linguistic behavior. First, the use of features reflects a basic level of phonological activity—contrasts take place on the feature level, not on the level where segments are represented. Secondly, the use of process notation and formalization with rules and representations reflects the realities of linguistic production, in which sounds are affected by the context in which they are pronounced as we speak.

Overall, the patterning of phonological units is seen to be based on the interaction of a universal set of features, universal and language specific phonotactic constraints and syllabification procedures, and the use of rules and representations. This current theory of phonology is based on principles that are applicable to the study of any human language.

Summing up

Phonology deals with the sequential and phonetically conditioned patterning of sounds in language. To account for this patterning, three units of phonological representation have been established: the **feature**, the **phoneme**, and the **syllable**. Phonemes are contrastive segmental units composed of distinctive features. Phonetically conditioned variants of phonemes are called **allophones**.

Phonology makes use of **underlying forms**, **derivations**, **phonological rules**, and **representations** in its formal notation. Some rules apply in **free** order. **Autosegments**—features that are autonomous to varying degrees—spread or delete on the basis of a few principles.

Key terms

accidental gaps
allophone
allophonic distribution
allophonic variation
alpha rules
ambisyllabicity
anterior
assimilation
autosegmental representation
autosegmental principles
autosegments
back
class node
closed syllable
coda
complementary distribution
consonantal
constricted glottis
continuant
contrast
coronal
delayed release
deletion
derivations
distinctive feature
dorsal features
environment
epenthesis

feature
feature hierarchy
feeding
free (unordered) rule application
free variation
high
labial
laryngeal features
laryngeal node
lateral
low
major class features
manner features
manner node
matrix
minimal pair
nasal
natural class
node
nucleus
onset
phoneme
phonemic transcription
phonetic transcription
phonetically conditioned variation
phonological rules
phonology
phonotactics
place features
place node
reduced
representations
rhyme
root node
round
sonorant
spread glottis
spreading
strident
syllabic
syllable
systematic gaps
tense
tiers
underlying (form)
voice

Sources

A classic and still valuable presentation of phonemic analysis is found in H. A. Gleason, Jr.'s *An Introduction to Descriptive Linguistics* (Toronto: Holt, Rinehart and Winston, 1961). Tone data on Mende are from W. R. Leben's "The Representation of Tone" and on Duwai from R. G. Schuh's, "Tone Rules," both in *Tone: A Linguistic Survey*, edited by V. A. Fromkin (New York: Academic Press, 1978). Syllabification, tone, and autosegmental analysis are drawn from numerous souces, all summarized recently in Goldsmith (cited below). The Malay data are adapted from M. Kenstowicz and C. Kisseberth, *Generative Phonology* (New York: Academic Press, 1979) with additional examples provided by S. L. Lee (personal communication).

Data sources for problems are as follows: for Inuktitut, B. Harnum (personal communication); for Mokilese, S. Harrison's *Mokilese Reference Grammar* (Honolulu: University of Hawaii Press, 1976); for Tamil, R. Radhakrishnan (personal communication); for Gascon, R. C. Kelly's *A Descriptive Analysis of Gascon* (Amsterdam: Mouton, 1978); for Plains Cree, Y. Carifelle and M. Pepper (personal communication); for Canadian French, D. C. Walker's *The Pronunciation of Canadian French* (Ottawa: University of Ottawa Press, 1984) and A. Teasdale (personal communication); for English fast speech, G. Zhang, *Phonological Representation and Analyses of Fast Speech Phenomena in English*, M.A. thesis, Memorial University of Newfoundland, 1994; for Mende, L. Hyman and D. Pulleyblank, "The Basics of Autosegmental Phonology Applied to Tone"; for Moru, A. N. Tucker, *The Eastern Sudanic Languages* (London: Dawsons, 1967/1940), pp. 112, 271.

Recommended reading

Anderson, Stephen R. 1985. *Phonology in the Twentieth Century*. Chicago: University of Chicago Press.

Carr, Philip. 1993. *Phonology*. London: Macmillan.

Clements, George N., and Samuel Jay Keyser. 1983. *CV Phonology*. Cambridge, MA: MIT Press.

Goldsmith, John. 1990. *Autosegmental and Metrical Phonology*. Cambridge, MA: Blackwell.

Goldsmith, John, ed. 1995. *The Handbook of Phonological Theory*. Cambridge, MA: Blackwell.

Hayes, Bruce. 1995. *Metrical Stress Theory: Principles and Case Studies*. Chicago: University of Chicago Press.

Hyman, Larry M. 1975. *Phonology: Theory and Analysis*. New York: Holt, Rinehart and Winston.

Keating, Patricia. 1988. "The Phonology-Phonetics Interface." In *Linguistics: The Cambridge Survey*. Vol. 1. Edited by F. Newmeyer, 281–302. London: Cambridge University Press.

Kenstowicz, Michael. 1994. *Phonology in Generative Grammar*. Cambridge, MA: Blackwell.

Stampe, David. 1980. *A Dissertation on Natural Phonology*. New York: Garland.

Appendix:
Hints for solving phonology problems

The task of solving a phonology problem is made easier if certain facts presented in this chapter and summarized here are kept in mind.

1. Begin by looking for minimal pairs. These establish which segments are contrastive. For example, in the following data from Tagalog (Philippines), minimal pairs in items a, e and c, f, and the near minimal pair b, d show that the phones [h] and [ʔ] contrast and therefore belong to separate phonemes, /h/ and /ʔ/, respectively.

a)	kahon	'box'	d)	ʔari	'property'
b)	hariʔ	'king'	e)	kaʔon	'to fetch'
c)	ʔumagos	'to flow'	f)	humagos	'to paint'

2. Allophones of a given phoneme are usually phonetically similar. Look for sounds that are phonetically similar, and check to see whether they are in complementary distribution. The best way to do this is to list the environments. In the following data, also from Tagalog, [d] and [r], both voiced alveolars, should be considered as possible allophones. List the environments in which these sounds are found. Are they in complementary distribution?

a) datiŋ	'to arrive'	f) daraʔiŋ	'will complain'
b) dami	'amount'	g) marumi	'dirty'
c) dumi	'dirt'	h) marami	'many'
d) daratiŋ	'will arrive'	i) daʔiŋ	'to complain'
e) mandurukot	'pickpocket'	j) mandukot	'to go pickpocketing'

3. If two potential allophones of one phoneme are in complementary distribution, you can be reasonably sure they are allophones of the same phoneme. Try to make a general statement about their distribution in terms of some natural phonological class. For example:

   Tagalog [d] and [r] are in complementary distribution and are allophones of one phoneme. The allophone [r] occurs between vowels; [d] occurs elsewhere—here, word initially, as in items a), b), c), f), and so on, and after nasal consonants, as in items e) and j).

4. Select one allophone as basic. This is usually the allophone with the widest distribution (the elsewhere variant). It may be helpful to set up a traditional phoneme-allophone diagram (see Figure 3.2).

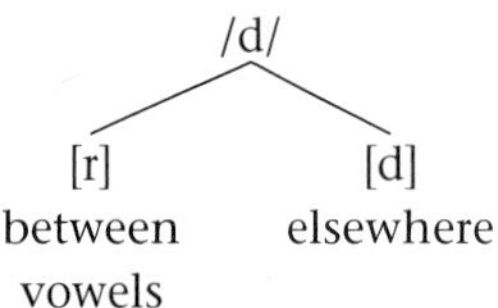

5. Write a phonological rule or provide a representation that accounts for the predictable features of the other allophones. Your rule (or representation) is probably correct if it describes a common linguistic process in terms of natural classes of sounds interacting with neighboring segments and/or syllable structure.

   For example, for the above: $d \rightarrow r\ /\ V\ \_\_\_\ V$

   Here, the process that leads to the allophony is a form of assimilation, in that an underlying stop consonant becomes a continuant when found between two continuants (the vowels).

   You can assume that any segments are phonemic if there are no minimal pairs for them and if they cannot be shown to be allophones of a phoneme. The data simply did not provide minimal pairs.

QUESTIONS

Assume phonetic transcription of the data in all exercises.

1. Inuktitut (Eastern) (Native Canadian)

a) iglumut	'to a house'	h) pinna	'that one up there'
b) ukiaq	'late fall'	i) ani	'female's brother'
c) aiviq	'walrus'	j) iglu	'(snow)house'
d) aniguvit	'if you leave'	k) panna	'that place up there'
e) aglu	'seal's breathing hole'	l) aivuq	'she goes home'
f) iglumit	'from a house'	m) ini	'place, spot'
g) anigavit	'because you leave'	n) ukiuq	'winter'

i) List all the minimal pairs in this data. Based on the minimal pairs you have found, list all the contrastive pairs of vowels.

ii) Using the vowel charts in Figures 2.9 and 2.10 as your models, make a chart of Inuktitut vowel phonemes.

iii) Now consider the data again; here it is transcribed in more phonetic detail. In it, there are phonetically similar segments that are in complementary distribution. Look for them and then answer the question that follows the data.

aa)	iglumut	'to a house'	hh)	pinna	'that one up there'
bb)	ukiaq	'late fall'	ii)	anɪ	'female's brother'
cc)	aivɪq	'walrus'	jj)	iglʊ	'(snow)house'
dd)	aniguvit	'if you leave'	kk)	panna	'that place up there'
ee)	aglʊ	'seal's breathing hole'	ll)	aivʊq	'she goes home'
ff)	iglumit	'from a house'	mm)	inɪ	'place, spot'
gg)	anigavit	'because you leave'	nn)	ukiʊq	'winter'

iv) List the phonetically similar segments that are in complementary distribution. State their distribution in words.

2. Hindi (Hindi is a language of the Indo-European family spoken in India)
Consider the segments [b] and [b̤] in the data below and answer the questions that follow. The segment transcribed [b̤] is a murmured voiced stop; it was presented in Chapter 2, Section 10.2.

a)	[bara]	'large'	f)	[b̤ɛd]	'disagreement'
b)	[b̤ari]	'heavy'	g)	[bais]	'twenty-two'
c)	[bina]	'without'	h)	[b̤əs]	'buffalo'
d)	[b̤ir]	'crowd'	i)	[bap]	'father'
e)	[bori]	'sackcloth'	j)	[b̤ag]	'part'

i) Are the segments [b] and [b̤] allophones of the same phoneme or do they belong to separate phonemes? If you believe they belong to separate phonemes, give evidence from the data to support your analysis. If you believe they are allophones of the same phoneme, list the conditioning environments.

3. Mokilese (Mokilese is an Austronesian language of the South Pacific)
Examine the following data from Mokilese carefully, taking note of where voiceless vowels occur.

a)	pi̥san	'full of leaves'	g)	uduk	'flesh'
b)	tu̥pu̥kta	'bought'	h)	kaskas	'to throw'
c)	pu̥ko	'basket'	i)	poki	'to strike something'
d)	ki̥sa	'we two'	j)	pil	'water'
e)	su̥pwo	'firewood'	k)	apid	'outrigger support'
f)	kamwɔki̥ti	'to move'	l)	ludʒuk	'to tackle'

i) The vowel phonemes of Mokilese are /i e ɛ u o ɔ a/. In Mokilese, [i̥] is an allophone of /i/, and [u̥] is an allophone of /u/. No other vowels have voiceless allophones. State in words the conditioning factors that account for this. Be as general as possible in referring to classes of sounds.

ii) If you have completed the section on rule formalization, write a rule (using features) that accounts for the derived allophones.

4. Gascon (Gascon is spoken in southwest France)
The phones [b], [β], [d], [ð], [g], and [ɣ] are all found in Gascon, as the following examples show. The phone [β] is a voiced bilabial fricative; [ɣ] is a voiced velar fricative (see Chapter 2, Section 10.2).

a) brẽn	'endanger'		n) gat	'cat'
b) bako	'cow'		o) lũŋg	'long'
c) ũmbro	'shadow'		p) saliβo	'saliva'
d) krãmbo	'room'		q) noβi	'husband'
e) dilys	'Monday'		r) aβe	'to have'
f) dũŋko	'until'		s) ʃiβaw	'horse'
g) duso	'sweet'		t) byðɛt	'gut'
h) taldepãn	'leftover bread'		u) eʃaðo	'hoe'
i) pũnde	'to lay eggs'		v) biɣar	'mosquito'
j) dudze	'twelve'		w) riɣut	'he laughed'
k) guteʒa	'flow'		x) agro	'sour'
l) ẽŋgwãn	'this year'		y) ʒuɣɛt	'he played'
m) puðe	'to be able'			

i) Which pairs among the phones [b], [β], [d], [ð], [g], and [ɣ] are the most phonetically similar? Support your claim with phonetic descriptions of the similar pairs.

ii) List the environments in which the phones [b], [β], [d], [ð], [g], and [ɣ] are found. You may ignore word-final position in your consideration.

iii) Is there any evidence for grouping these pairs of sounds into phonemes? State the evidence for each pair.

iv) Make a general statement about the patterning of the phonemes you have established.

v) Following your analysis, write the following forms in phonemic transcription.

a) [puɣo] b) [deðat] c) [ʃiβaw] d) [krãmbo]

5. Plains Cree (Plains Cree is a Native Canadian language of the Algonquian family)
The following data from Plains Cree show a number of different voiced and voiceless consonantal segments.

a) niska	'goose'		l) nisto	'three'
b) kodak	'another'		m) tʃi:gahigan	'axe'
c) asaba:p	'thread'		n) a:dim	'dog'
d) wasko:w	'cloud'		o) mi:bit	'tooth'
e) paskwa:w	'prairie'		p) pime:	'lard'
f) ni:gi	'my house'		q) mide	'heart'
g) ko:gos	'pig'		r) o:gik	'these'
h) tahki	'often'		s) tʃihtʃij	'finger'
i) namwa:tʃ	'not at all'		t) wa:bos	'rabbit'
j) ospwa:gan	'pipe'		u) na:be:w	'man'
k) midʒihtʃij	'hand'		v) mi:dʒiwin	'food'

i) Do [p] and [b] belong to separate phonemes, or are they allophones of one phoneme? If you think they belong to separate phonemes, list data to support your case. If you think they are allophones, first state the conditioning factors in words, and then, using features, write a rule that accounts for their distribution.

ii) Do the same for [t] and [d], [k] and [g], and [tʃ] and [dʒ].

iii) Can you make a general statement about the relationship among all the consonantal pairs whose distribution you have examined?

iv) Using Figure 3.17 as your model, provide complete derivations of the forms for k) *hand,* m) *axe,* and o) *tooth.*

6. There are a number of natural classes in the vowel and consonant data below. Circle three natural classes in each set of data. Indicate which feature or features define the class, as in the example.

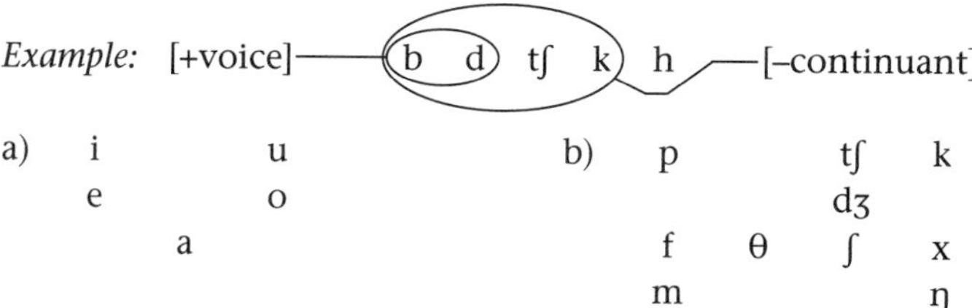

7. Name the single feature that distinguishes the following pairs of sounds.

a) [θ] : [ð]	e) [b] : [m]	i) [ʌ] : [ə]
b) [p] : [f]	f) [s] : [ʃ]	j) [s] : [θ]
c) [u] : [ʊ]	g) [ɪ] : [i]	k) [e] : [ɛ]
d) [i] : [e]	h) [k] : [x]	l) [u] : [o]

8. Complete the feature matrix for each of the sounds indicated. The V abbreviates the features [+syllabic, –consonantal], and the C abbreviates the features [–syllabic, +consonantal].

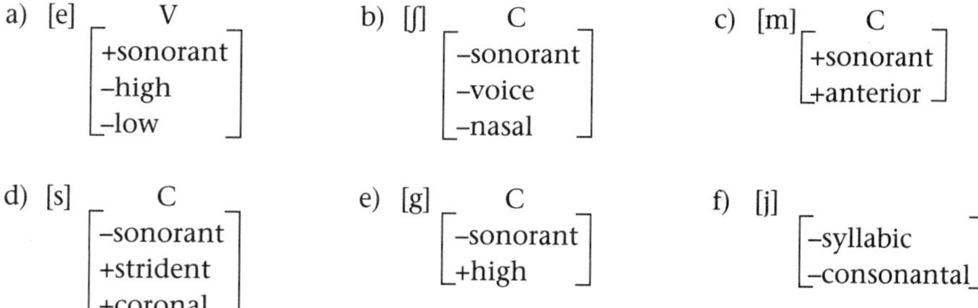

Using the appropriate features, represent each segment on a feature hierarchy tree.

9. English/Korean

As we have seen, phonological adaptation of loanwords may reflect facts about syllable structure. Recently, the Korean automobile name *Hyundai* has been adapted into English in various ways, one of which follows. Given the Korean form and the English adaptation provided, state two reasons based on syllable structure conditions that explain why the English form is pronounced the way it is.

Korean form		*English form*
/hjʌndæ/	→	/hʌnde/ [hʌndej]

10. English

Many speakers of English have two variants of [l]. One, called *clear l*, is transcribed as [l] in the following data. The other, called *dark l*, is transcribed with [ɫ]. Examine the data, and answer the questions that follow.

a) [lajf]	'life'		g) [pʰɪɫ]	'pill'
b) [lijp]	'leap'		h) [fijɫ]	'feel'
c) [luːwz]	'lose'		i) [hɛɫp]	'help'
d) [ijlowp]	'elope'		j) [bʌɫk]	'bulk'
e) [dijlajt]	'delight'		k) [sowɫd]	'sold'
f) [slijp]	'sleep'		l) [fʊɫ]	'full'

Do [l] and [ɫ] belong to separate phonemes or are they allophones of the same phoneme? If you think they belong to separate phonemes, answer question *i)*. If you think they are allophones of the same phoneme, answer questions *ii–iv)*.

i) List the evidence that makes your case for considering [l] and [ɫ] as separate phonemes.
ii) State the distribution of [l] and [ɫ] in words.
iii) Which variant makes the best underlying form? Why?
iv) Can you make reference to syllable structure in your distribution statement? If you can, do so in rule form.

11. Canadian French

For the purposes of this problem, you may assume that syllables in Canadian French have the following structure:

- Maximum number of consonants in an onset: 2. Where there are two onset consonants, the first must be an obstruent, the second a sonorant or a fricative.
- Each vowel forms a syllable nucleus.
- Maximum number of consonants in a coda: 2.

With these stipulations in mind, syllabify the following forms:

a) b u k a n b) e r i t e c) p u d r œ r i d) l i ɔ̃

12. In the following data from Canadian French, each pair of phones is in complementary distribution.

[i] and [ɪ]	are allophones of one phoneme
[y] and [ʏ]	are allophones of a second phoneme
[o] and [ɔ]	are allophones of a third phoneme
[u] and [ʊ]	are allophones of a fourth phoneme

It is possible to make a general statement about the distribution of the vowel allophones that accounts for all four phonemes.

Examine the data and answer the questions that follow.

a) pilʏl	'pill'		i) fyme	'smoke'
b) griʃe	'to crunch'		j) lynɛt	'glasses'
c) grɪʃ	'it crunches'		k) frole	'to skim'
d) pətsi	'little (masc.)'		l) pɔrt	'door'
e) pətsɪt	'little (fem.)'		m) bote	'beauty'
f) vitamɪn	'vitamin'		n) bɔt	'boot'
g) saly	'hi'		o) fo	'false'
h) ʒʏp	'skirt'		p) tɔrdzy	'twisted'

q)	zero	'zero'	aa)	plʏs	'more'
r)	pɔm	'apple'	bb)	fɔl	'crazy (fem.)'
s)	lʏn	'moon'	cc)	ru	'wheel'
t)	pɪp	'pipe'	dd)	rʊt	'road'
u)	grimas	'grimace'	ee)	suvã	'often'
v)	fini	'finished'	ff)	trupo	'herd'
w)	fɪj	'girl'	gg)	sʊp	'flexible'
x)	dzʏr	'hard'	hh)	tʊʃ	'touch'
y)	tryke	'to fake'	ii)	fu	'crazy (masc.)'
z)	fʊl	'(a) crowd'	jj)	trʏk	'(a) trick'

i) Provide a statement of the distribution of [i] and [ɪ], [y] and [ʏ], [o] and [ɔ], [u] and [ʊ] in words. Make your statement as general as possible, but be precise!

ii) If you have completed the section on rule formalization, write a single rule that derives the allophones of each phoneme from the underlying form. Use features! Be sure to give your rule a mnemonic name; use this name in the answer to question *iii)*.

iii) Provide derivations for the following underlying forms.

UR	#	# 'vitamin'	#	# 'glasses'
PR	[vitamɪn]		[lynɛt]	

13. English

The following data contain both careful speech and fast speech forms. Note the differences and answer the questions that follow. Some phonetic detail irrelevant to the question has been omitted from the transcription. Remember that an asterisk before a form indicates that it is not acceptable to (most) native speakers.

Careful speech	*Fast speech*	*Spelled form*
a) [ǽspərən]	k) [ǽsprən]	aspirin
b) [pɔ́rsələn]	l) [pɔ́rslən]	porcelain
c) [nǽʃənəlàjz]	m) [nǽʃnəlàjz]	nationalize
d) [ríjzənəbl̩]	n) [ríjznəbl̩]	reasonable
e) [ɪmǽdʒənətɪv]	o) [ɪmǽdʒnətɪv]	imaginative
f) [sɛ̀pərəbílɪɾij]	p) [sɛ̀prəbílɪɾij]	separability
g) [mɛ́θəd]	q) [mɛ́θəd] *[mɛ́θd]	method
h) [féjməs]	r) [féjməs] *[féjms]	famous
i) [mɛ́məràjz]	s) [mɛ́məràjz] *[mɛ́mràjz]	memorize
j) [kʰənsìdəréjʃən]	t) [kʰənsìdəréjʃən] *[kʰənsìdréjʃən]	consideration

i) The schwa deletion between the careful speech forms and the rapid speech forms in items a–f is systematic. State in words the phonetic conditions that account for the deletion.

ii) The same pattern that occurs between the careful speech forms and the rapid speech forms in items a–f does not occur in items g–j. State in words the phonetic difference between these sets of forms that accounts for the lack of schwa deletion.

iii) Now that you have taken items g–j into account, will you have to change your original statement of the phonetic conditions governing schwa deletion in the fast speech forms? If so, do this in words.

iv) If you have completed the section on rule formalization, convert your statement in *iii)* into formal notation.

14. The English data below provide examples of stress placement on certain verbs.

A	*B*	*C*
appéar	adápt	astónish
collíde	collápse	consíder
eráse	eléct	imágine
caróuse	obsérve	detérmine
corróde	tormént	prómise

i) Describe in words the stress placement on these verbs. Be sure to make reference to syllable structure in your statement.

ii) Provide syllabified representations of the words *collide, elect,* and *consider* in order to illustrate your conclusion about stress placement on these forms.

15. State each of the following rules in English, making reference to natural classes and common linguistic processes.

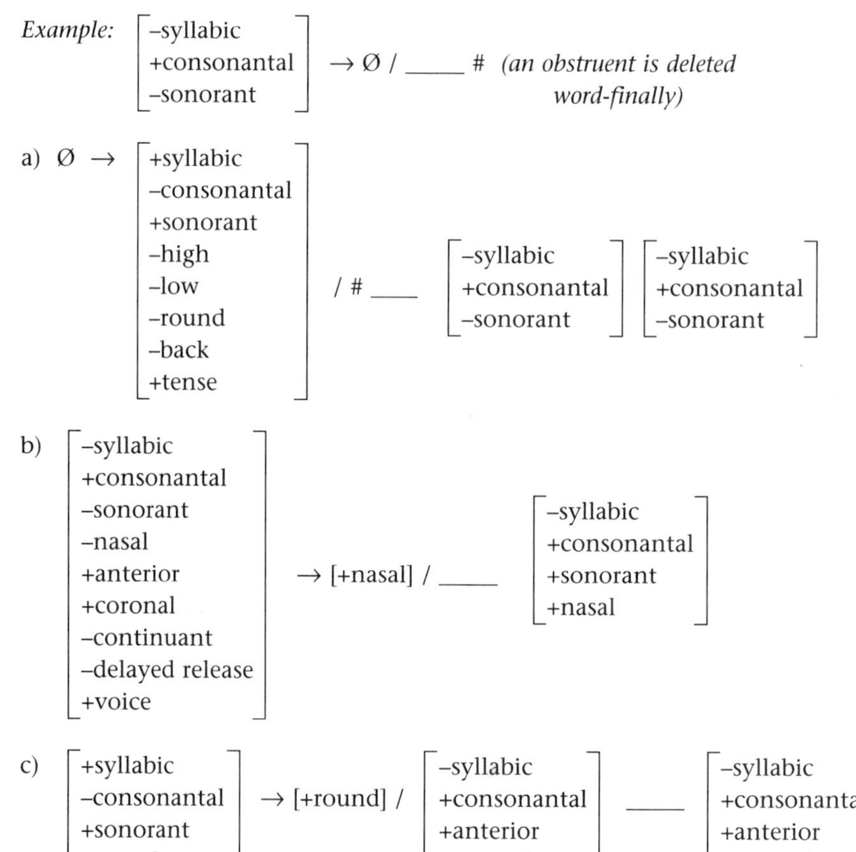

16. Change the following statements into rule notation. Be sure to name the process in question for each case.
    a) Voiceless stops become corresponding fricatives between vowels.
    b) A schwa is inserted between a voiced stop and a word-final voiced fricative.
    c) Low unrounded vowels become rounded before *m*.

17. Tamil (Tamil is a Dravidian language spoken in South India and Sri Lanka)
    In the following Tamil data, some words begin with glides while others do not. The symbol [ɖ] represents a voiced retroflex stop and the diacritic [̪] indicates dentals.

Initial j-glide		*Initial w-glide*		*No initial glide*	
a) jeli	'rat'	f) woɖi	'break'	k) arivu	'knowledge'
b) jiː	'fly'	g) woːlaj	'palm leaf'	l) ain̪t̪u	'five'
c) jilaj	'leaf'	h) wuːsi	'needle'	m) aːsaj	'desire'
d) jeŋgeː	'where'	i) wujir	'life'	n) aːru	'river'
e) jiɖuppu	'waist'	j) woːram	'edge'	o) aːdi	'origin'

i) The occurrence of these glides is predictable. Using your knowledge of natural classes, make a general statement about the distribution of the glides.
ii) Assuming the glides are not present in the underlying representations, name the process that accounts for their presence in the phonetic forms.
iii) Using features, write a rule using alpha notation that formalizes this process. Show the derivation of the forms for *fly* and *break*.

18. Mende (Mende is spoken in Liberia and Sierra Leone)
    In Mende, the forms that mean 'on' (*ma*) and 'in' (*hu*) are suffixes (they are attached to a preceding word; see Chapter 4, Section 1.3). Notice in the data below that suffixes all bear tone, but that the tone varies on different words. In the examples, ´ indicates a high tone, ` a low tone, and ˆ a falling (high-to-low) tone.

a) kɔ́	'war'	kɔ́má	'on war'	kɔ́hú	'in war'
b) pɛ́lɛ́	'house'	pɛ́lɛ́má	'on (the) house'	pɛ́lɛ́hú	'in (the) house'
c) bɛ̀lɛ̀	'trousers'	bɛ̀lɛ̀mà	'on trousers'	bɛ̀lɛ̀hù	'in trousers'
d) ngílà	'dog'	ngílàmà	'on (the) dog'	ngílàhù	'in (the) dog'

i) Can you account for the differences in tone on the suffixes for 'on' and 'in' in Mende? Provide a solution using autosegmental notation. [Hint: assume that the suffixes have no tone to begin with, but that the words to which they are attached do have tone.]
ii) Assuming that you have answered question *i)* successfully, account for the tones of the suffixes meaning 'on' and 'in' in the remaining examples.

e) mbû	'owl'	mbúmà	'on (the) owl'	mbúhù	'in (the) owl'
f) njàhâ	'woman'	njàhámà	'on (the) woman'	njàháhù	'in (the) woman'

19. Moru (Miza dialect; Moru is a Sudanic language)
    In Moru, contour tones are not found on short vowels in underlying representations. However, phonetic forms of combined lexical items do show contour tones. Can you represent this using autosegmental notation? [Hint: a segmental process is involved as well as a typical suprasegmental process and the two

processes must be ordered.] In the data provided, ´ indicates a high tone; ` a low tone; ˆ a falling (high-to-low) tone; and ˇ a rising low-to-high tone. Vowels with no tone mark need not be considered.

a) màá we	→	[mǎ]	'we'
b) ká ùmu he runs	→	[kûmu]	'he runs'
c) ká ɔ̀ŋga he jumps	→	[kɔ̂ŋga]	'he jumps'
d) njá àdì ùzi ja you call who?	→	[njâdùzi ja]	'who are you calling?'

For the student linguist

THE FEATURE PRESENTATION

You've already read that features are the fundamental building blocks of phonemes. By writing rules with features, you can describe simply a change that happens to an entire class of sounds. You also make a stronger statement when you use features in a rule. For example, rule *1* says something about all the stops in a language, but rule *2* only says something about a list of sounds.

1. [– continuant] → [– voice] / ___ #
(stops become voiceless at the end of a word)

2. {p,t,k,b,d,g} → {p,t,k,p,t,k} / ___ #
(p "becomes" p at the end of a word;
b becomes p at the end of a word; etc.)

If you're just listing sounds, nothing requires them to have anything in common with each other. The sounds in the list could be a totally random selection of sounds turning into another totally random selection of sounds, as in rule *3*, and you'd have no way of predicting that *3* should be less common than *2*.

3. {e,t,w,b,n,h} → {ʃ,p,tʃ,g,a,m} / ___ #
(e becomes ʃ at the end of a word; etc.)

If you use features, you can predict that the set of changes described by rule *2* should be common (because once the rule is translated to features, it's merely rule *1*, a delightfully simple rule), but the set of changes described by rule *3* should be weird and unlikely. To describe rule *3* with features you'd have to write six different rules, and each rule would be ugly and complicated. (I'm assuming that the more features you have to include in a rule, the more complicated it is.) For example, the first rule, changing [e] to [ʃ], would be:

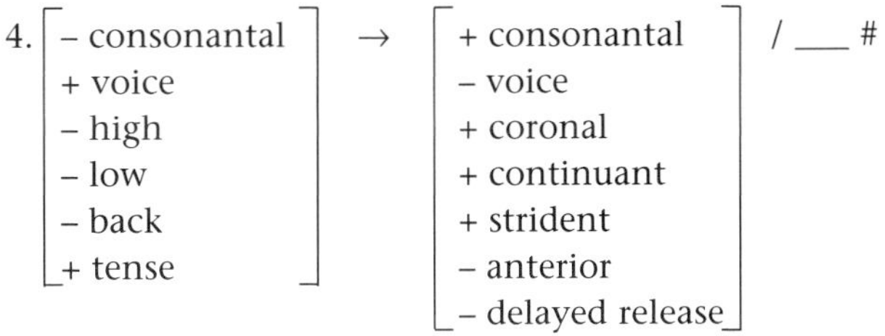

However, you can accept the brilliance of features without buying the idea of using a matrix of binary features (like you've done so far), or a hierarchy of binary features. Features could have only one value (these are called "monovalent" or "privative" features). So instead of, say, [– nasal] and [+ nasal], there'd only be [nasal]. Sounds that had [nasal] in the matrix/representation would be nasal; everything else would be oral. How is that any different from using a binary feature? The difference is that with a binary feature, you can write rules about things that are [– nasal]. You could write a rule like this:

5. [– continuant, – nasal] → [– voice] / ___ #
(oral stops become voiceless at the end of a word).

But if [– nasal] didn't exist, the only rule you could write would be:

6. [– continuant] → [– voice] / ___ #
(all stops, including nasal stops, become voiceless at the end of a word).

If [– nasal] did exist, you could write rule *5 or* rule *6.* Monovalent features, then, give you fewer possible rules. That's great if you can still write all the rules you need for every language, but awful if you can't write every rule you need.

Having fewer possible rules isn't important just because it would make this unit of linguistics easier. It's also important because, theoretically, if there are fewer possible rules in a language, it's easier for a child trying to learn the language to figure out how the sound system in that language works. He or she has fewer options to consider.

What if features could have three values? Or four? Or an infinite number of values? For example, there could be four features for the different laryngeal states: [A laryngeal], for glottal stops; [B laryngeal], for voiced sounds; [C laryngeal], for voiceless unaspirated sounds; and [D laryngeal], for voiceless aspirated sounds. Just like nothing can be both [+ voice] and [– voice] at the same time, nothing could be [A laryngeal] and [B laryngeal] at the same time (or [A laryngeal] and [C laryngeal], etc.). Place of articulation could be handled the same way: [A place] for labials, [B place] for dentals, [C place] for alveolars, etc.

With this type of multivalued system, none of the subgroups (like dentals and alveolars) could be lumped together in a rule. Thus, for the place system I described, you couldn't talk about all of the coronals at once—you could only talk about the dentals or the alveolars or the alveopalatals and so forth. Once again, whether this is good or bad depends on how well it describes actual languages. (You might want to try out a multivalued feature system for place on some of the phonology problems you've already solved for homework or in class discussions, and see if they're harder or easier to do this way than with a binary feature system.)

These are just a couple of the possible variations on feature systems. I haven't even begun to question the merit of these *features*—that is, do we *really* need [voice]? Or [strident]? Or [delayed release]? Think about this as you work on a few phonology problems, and see if you can come up with a better feature system. There's a lot of room for change here.

four

MORPHOLOGY: THE ANALYSIS OF WORD STRUCTURE

William O'Grady
Videa de Guzman
Mark Aronoff

Carve every word before you let it fall.

– OLIVER WENDELL HOLMES, SR.

Part of linguistic competence involves the ability to construct and interpret words in one's native language. The average high school student knows about 60,000 words whose form and meaning are not derived from those of other words. Such words—including *read, language, on, cold,* and *if,* to name but a few—must be learned and stored as separate items in the **lexicon** (or mental dictionary). However, countless other words can be constructed and comprehended by the application of quite general rules to more basic words. For example, any speaker of English who knows the verb *fax* recognizes *faxed* as its past tense form, and can construct and interpret words such as *faxable* (for things that can be faxed) and *fax machine* (for the device that sends and receives faxes).

If we are watching a television program about homelessness in American cities, we may hear that many of the homeless are former mental patients who were released because of a policy of deinstitutionalization. An expert interviewed on the program may advocate reinstitutionalization as the only recourse for many of these people. Even if we have never heard these terms before, we understand quite effortlessly that they refer to the practices of releasing patients from hospitals for the mentally ill (*deinstitutionalization*) and returning them to these institutions (*reinstitutionalization*). We know this because we know what the word *institution* means, and we have an unconscious command of English morphology.

The system of categories and rules involved in word formation and interpretation makes up a language's **morphology**. This chapter presents an introduction to the study of morphology, beginning with the inventory of notions relevant to the analysis of word structure.

1 WORDS AND WORD STRUCTURE

Of all the units of linguistic analysis, the **word** is the most familiar. As literate speakers of English, we rarely have difficulty segmenting a stream of speech sounds into words or deciding where to leave spaces when writing a sentence. It is not easy, however, to define precisely what a word is.

The most reliable defining property of words is that they are the smallest **free forms** found in language. A free form is an element that can occur in isolation or whose position with respect to neighboring categories is not completely fixed. Consider in this regard the elements making up the following sentence.

1)

The birds left.

The plural marker *-s* is not a free form (and therefore not a word) since it never occurs in isolation and cannot be separated from the noun to which it belongs. (Elements that must be attached to another category are written here with a hyphen.)

2)

*The bird left -s.

In contrast, *birds* is a word since it can occur in isolation, as in the following exchange.

3)

Speaker A: What are those things in the tree?
Speaker B: Birds.

Moreover, even when *birds* occurs as part of a larger sentence, it is not attached to anything else. This is why it can appear in different positions within a sentence, as illustrated in *4)*.

4)

a. *birds* occurring in front of a verb:
Birds avoid cats.
b. *birds* occurring after a verb:
Cats chase birds.

Some words, such as *the* in sentence *1)*, do not normally occur in isolation. However, they are still free forms since their positioning with respect to neighboring categories is not entirely fixed. Thus, as shown by the following sentence, *the* does not always have to occur immediately in front of a noun; the two can easily be separated by an intervening word.

5)

The young birds remained in the nest.

1.1 MORPHEMES

Like syllables and sentences, words have an internal structure consisting of smaller units organized with respect to each other in a particular way. The most important component of word structure is the **morpheme**, the smallest unit of language that carries information about meaning or function. The word *builder*, for example, consists of two morphemes: *build* (with the meaning of 'construct') and *-er* (which indicates that the entire word functions as a noun with the meaning 'one who builds'). Similarly, the word *houses* is made up of the morphemes *house* (with the meaning 'dwelling') and *-s* (with the meaning 'more than one').

Some words consist of a single morpheme. For example, the word *train* cannot be divided into smaller parts (say, *tr* and *ain* or *t* and *rain*) that carry information about its meaning or function. Such words are said to be **simple words** and are distinguished from **complex words**, which contain two or more morphemes. It is important to keep in mind that a morpheme is neither a meaning nor a stretch of sound, but a meaning and a stretch of sound joined together. For example, there are at least two morphemes spelled *top* and pronounced /tɑp/ in English, one with the approximate meaning 'upper part or surface' and the other meaning 'a toy designed to be spun.' In each case, the morpheme is not the meaning or the sound, but the two together. Morphemes are usually **arbitrary**: there is no natural connection between their sound and their meaning. So, there is nothing about the sound /kæt/ and the meaning 'domesticated feline' that makes the two go together naturally. We could just as easily call a cat /billi/ as in Hindi, or /neko/ as in Japanese. When we want to distinguish the sound of a morpheme from the entire morpheme, we may use the term **morph**. The English plural and possessive morphemes, for example, may be said to share a single morph, the suffix /-s/.

Table 4.1 Words consisting of one or more morphemes

One	*Two*	*Three*	*More than three*
and			
boy	boy-s		
hunt	hunt-er	hunt-er-s	
magnet	magnet-ize	de-magnet-ize	de-magnet-iz-ation
caliber	calibr-ate	re-calibr-ate	re-calibr-at-ion

Free and bound morphemes

A morpheme whose form can be a word by itself is called a **free morpheme** whereas a morpheme that must be attached to another element is said to be a **bound morpheme**. The morpheme *boy*, for example, is free since it can be used as a word on its own; plural *-s*, on the other hand, is bound.

Concepts that are expressed as free morphemes in English do not necessarily have the same status in other languages. For example, in Hare (an Athapaskan language spoken in Canada's Northwest Territories), morphemes that indicate body parts must always be attached to a morpheme designating a possessor. (The diacritic ´ marks a high tone.)

Table 4.2 Some body part names in Hare

Without a possessor		*With a possessor*	
*fí	'head'	sefí	'my head'
*bé	'belly'	nebé	'your belly'
*dzé	'heart'	ʔedzé	'someone's heart/a heart'

In English, of course, these body part names are free morphemes and do not have to be attached to another element.

Conversely, there are also some bound forms in English whose counterparts in other languages are free. For example, the notion 'past' or 'completed' is expressed by the bound form *-ed* in English, but by the free form *lɛɛw* in Thai. As the following sentence shows, this morpheme can even be separated from the verb by an intervening word. (Tone is not marked here.)

6)

Boon thaan khaaw lɛɛw.
Boon eat rice past
'Boon ate rice.'

Allomorphs

Morphemes do not always have an invariant form. The morpheme used to express indefiniteness in English, for instance, has two forms—*a* and *an*.

7)

an orange	a building
an accent	a car
an eel	a girl

The form *a* is used before words beginning with a consonant and the form *an* before words beginning with a vowel. The variant forms of a morpheme are called its **allomorphs**.

Another example of allomorphic variation is found in the pronunciation of the plural morpheme *-s* in the following words.

8)

cats
dogs
judges

Whereas the plural is /s/ in the first case, it is /z/ in the second, and /əz/ in the third. Here again, selection of the proper allomorph is dependent on phonological facts. We will examine this phenomenon in more detail in Chapter 6.

Other examples of patterns in which a morpheme's form changes when it combines with another element are easy to find in English. The final segment in *assert*, for instance, is realized as /t/ when this morpheme stands alone as a separate word but as /ʃ/ when it combines with the morpheme *-ion* in the word *assertion*. Comparable alternations are found in words such as *permit/permiss-ive*, *include/inclus-ive*, *electric/electric-ity*, *impress/impress-ion*, and so on. In all these cases, we are dealing with variant forms of a single morpheme.

Beginning students can be confused by the changes in spelling that occur in some morphological patterns even when there is no corresponding change in pronunciation. Thus, the final *e* in the words *create* and *ride* is lost when they combine with a morpheme beginning with a vowel (*creat-ive*, *rid-ing*). These spelling modifications do not change a morpheme's identity, of course, and should simply be ignored when doing morphological analysis.

1.2 Representing word structure

In order to represent the internal structure of words, it is necessary not only to identify each of the component morphemes but also to classify these elements in terms of their contribution to the meaning and function of the larger word.

Roots and affixes

Complex words often consist of a **root** and one or more **affixes**. The root morpheme constitutes the core of the word and carries the major component of its meaning. Roots typically belong to a lexical category—usually noun (N), verb (V), and adjective (A). These categories will be discussed in more detail in Chapter 5, Section 1.1. For now it suffices to note that nouns typically refer to concrete and abstract 'things' while verbs (*treat, teach*) tend to denote actions, and adjectives usually name properties (*kind, red*). In general, nouns can occur with *the* (*the car*), verbs with *will* (*will go*), and adjectives with *very* (*very kind*).

Unlike roots, affixes do not belong to a lexical category and are always bound morphemes. A straightforward illustration of this contrast is found in the word *teacher*, which consists of the verb root *teach* and the affix *-er*, a bound morpheme that combines with the root and gives a noun with the meaning 'one who teaches'. The internal structure of this word can be represented in diagram form as follows. (The symbol 'Af' stands for affix.)

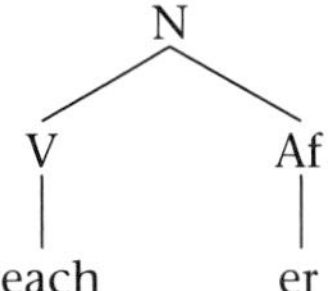

Figure 4.1 The internal structure of the word *teacher*

The internal structure of some other complex words is depicted below.

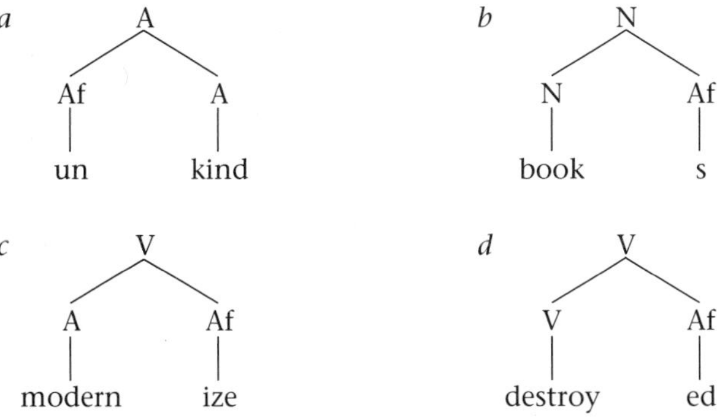

Figure 4.2 Some other words with an internal structure consisting of a root and an affix

These diagrams, which are often called **tree structures**, represent the details of a word's internal organization. Where these details are irrelevant to the point being considered, it is traditional to use a much simpler system of representation that indicates only the location of the morpheme boundaries: *un-kind, modern-ize*, and so on.

Bases

A **base** is the element to which an affix is added. In many cases, the base is also the root. In *books*, for example, the element to which the affix *-s* is added corresponds to the word's root. In other cases, however, an affix can be added to a unit larger than a root. This happens in words such as *blackened*, in which the past tense affix *-ed* is added to the verbal base *blacken*—a unit consisting of the root adjective *black* and the suffix *-en*.

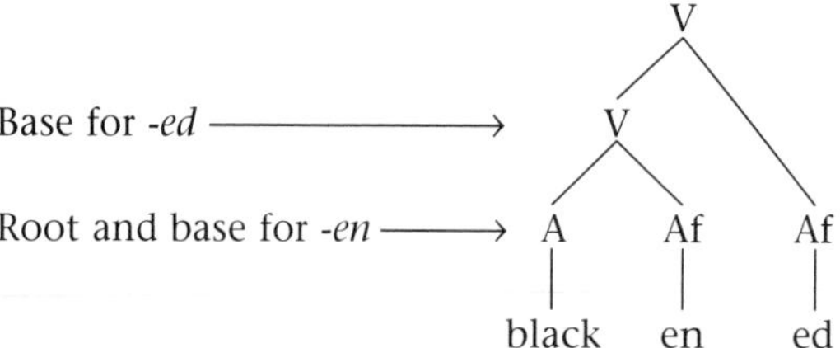

Figure 4.3 A word illustrating the difference between a root and a base

In this case, *black* is not only the root for the entire word but also the base for *-en*. The unit *blacken*, on the other hand, is simply the base for *-ed*.

Problematic cases *(Advanced)*

The majority of complex words in English are built ultimately on roots that are free morphemes. In the words *re-do* and *treat-ment*, for example, the root (*do* and *treat*, respectively) is a V that can appear elsewhere in the language without an affix. This notwithstanding, English contains a significant number of words in which the root is not free. For example, the word *unkempt* seems to consist of the prefix *un-* (with the meaning 'not') and the root *kempt* (meaning 'groomed'), even though *kempt* cannot be used by itself. Other common words of this type include *horr-ify*, *venge-ance*, *in-ept*, and *salv-ation*, to name but a few. We will assign morphemes such as *kempt*, *horr*, *venge*, *ept*, and *salv* to the special category 'bound root' (B), which we will reserve for root morphemes that cannot be used as words and therefore do not belong to a conventional lexical category such as noun or verb.

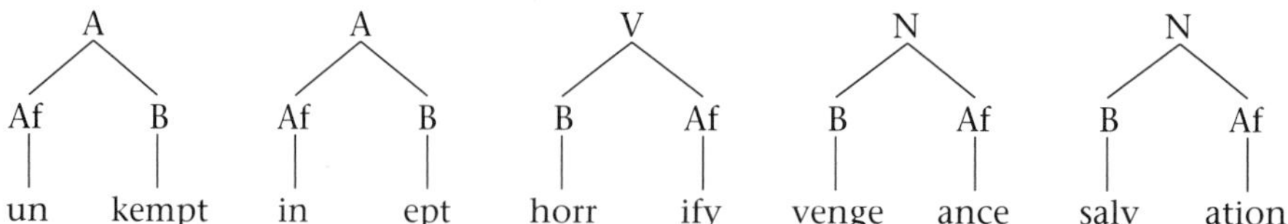

Figure 4.4 The internal structure of words built around a bound root

The origin of most bound roots can be traced to accidents of linguistic history. For example, there was once a word *kempt* in English (with the meaning 'combed'), and it was to this base that the affix *un-* was originally attached. At a later point, however, *kempt* disappeared from the language, leaving behind the word *unkempt* in which an affix appears with a bound root. The remaining examples in Figure 4.4 have a somewhat different history: instead of being formed from words already in the language, they were borrowed into English as whole words. For example, *inept* comes from Latin *ineptus* 'unsuited'; the relationship of its root to the word *apt* may have been evident at one time, but is unknown to most speakers today.

More problematic are words such as *receive, deceive, conceive,* and *perceive* or *permit, submit,* and *commit.* These items were borrowed as whole words into English (many of them from Latin through French). Even at the time of borrowing, the *re-* of *receive* did not have the sense of 'again' that it does in *redo* ('do again') and the *de-* of *deceive* did not express the meaning 'reverse the process' associated with the *de-* in *demystify* or *decertify*. Because the components of words like *receive* and *deceive* carry no identifiable meaning for the average speaker of English (who has no knowledge of Latin), we will not treat them as separate morphemes in this book.[1] Thus, we take the word *receive* to consist of a single morpheme.

1.3 Some common morphological phenomena

Human language makes use of a variety of operations that can modify a word's structure, either by adding some element to it or by making an internal change. This section introduces and illustrates the most common of these processes, including some that are not found in English.

Affixation

An extremely common morphological process in language is **affixation**, the addition of an affix. Normally, linguists distinguish among three types of affixes. An affix that is attached to the front of its base is called a **prefix** whereas an affix that is attached to the end of its base is termed a **suffix**. Both types of affix occur in English, as the following table shows.

Table 4.3 Some English prefixes and suffixes

Prefixes	*Suffixes*
de-activate	vivid-ly
re-play	govern-ment
il-legal	hunt-er
in-accurate	kind-ness

We will consider the nature and properties of English affixes in more detail in Sections 2.1 and 5.

Far less common than prefixes and suffixes are **infixes**, a type of affix that occurs within a base. The following data from the Philippine language Tagalog contain examples of the infixes *-um-* and *-in-*, which are inserted before the first vowel of the base to mark a completed event.

Table 4.4 Some Tagalog infixes

Base		*Infixed form*	
takbuh	'run'	t-um-akbuh	'ran'
lakad	'walk'	l-um-akad	'walked'
pili?	'choose'	p-in-ili?	'chose'

Beginning students sometimes think that a morpheme such as *-ish* in *boy-ish-ness* is an infix since it occurs between two other morphemes (*boy* and *-ness*), but this is not so. To be an infix, an affix must break up its base (as when *-um-* in Tagalog occurs inside *takbuh* 'run'). Nothing of this sort happens in the case of *-ish*, since its base is *boy* not the impossible **boyness*.

A very special type of infixing system is found in Semitic languages such as Arabic, in which a typical root consists simply of three consonants. Affixes consisting of two vowels are then inserted into this root in a manner that intersperses the vowels among the consonants. (In the examples that follow, the segments of the root are written in boldface.)

9)

ka**t**a**b**	**k**u**t**i**b**	a**kt**u**b**	u**kt**a**b**
'write'	'have been written'	'be writing'	'being written'

One way to represent the structure of such words is as follows, with the root and affix assigned to different tiers, or levels of structure, that are put together in the actual pronunciation of the word.

10)

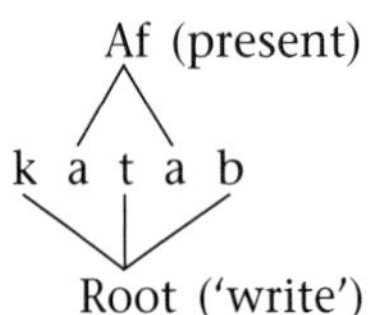

Cliticization

Clitics are short unstressed forms that are pronounced together with another element as if the two were a single unit. A good example of this can be found in English, where certain verb forms have reduced variants (*'m* for *am*, *'s* for *is*, and *'re* for *are*) that cannot stand alone since they no longer constitute a syllable. **Cliticization** occurs, attaching these elements to the preceding word.

11)

a. I'm leaving now.
b. Mary's going to succeed.
c. They're here now.

Cliticization is also common in French, which includes a set of unstressed clitic pronouns that must be attached to the verb. (Although not evident in the written language, the clitic and the verb are pronounced as if they formed a single word.)

12)

Suzanne me voit.
Suzanne me-sees
'Suzanne sees me.'

Clitics that attach to the end of a preceding word (as in the English examples) are called **enclitics**; those that attach to the beginning of a following word (as in the French example) are known as **proclitics**.

The effects of cliticization can bear a superficial resemblance to affixation since in both cases an element that cannot stand alone is attached to another form. The key difference is that, unlike affixes, clitics are members of a lexical category such as verb, noun (or pronoun), or preposition. They often attach to an entire phrase and not to a particular word or word category. In everyday spoken English, the clitic form *'s* of the verb *is* attaches to the last word of the preceding subject phrase (see Chapter 5, Section 1.3), regardless of what category that word belongs to. The word preceding *'s* may be a noun, as in *13a)*, or a preposition, as in *13b)*, or a verb, as in *13c)*.

13)

a. The dog's lying on the couch again.
b. The person you're looking for's not here.
c. The book you want's on the shelf.

Clitics are thus very different from ordinary affixes, which are very selective about what sorts of words they will attach to. The suffix *-ing,* for example, will normally attach to verbs. It may appear to attach to a noun, as in words like *wolfing* or *dogging,* but in almost all such cases, we are dealing with a word that is either a verb or a noun when it stands alone, but that always has the verbal sense when *-ing* is attached to it.

Internal change

Internal change is a process that substitutes one nonmorphemic segment for another to mark a grammatical contrast, as illustrated in the following pairs of words.

Table 4.5 Internal change in English

sing (present)	sang (past)
sink (present)	sank (past)
drive (present)	drove (past)
foot (singular)	feet (plural)
goose (singular)	geese (plural)

Verbs such as *sing, sink,* and *drive* form their past tense by changing the vowel (e.g., from *i* to *a* in the first two examples). The term **ablaut** is often used for vowel alternations that mark grammatical contrasts in this way.

Ablaut can be distinguished from **umlaut**, which involves the fronting of a vowel under the influence of a front vowel in the following syllable. Historically, this is what is responsible for the use of *feet* and *geese* as the plural forms of *foot* and *goose,* respectively: the back vowel in the root (originally /oː/) was fronted in response to the front vowel in an old plural suffix (pronounced /iz/), which was subsequently lost (see Chapter 8, Section 2.1 for further discussion).

The internal changes just considered are not examples of infixing for two reasons. First, there is no reason to think that English has root morphemes such as **ft* (meaning 'lower extremity of the leg') or **sng* (meaning 'produce words in a musical tone'). As shown by the Tagalog examples in Table 4.4, the base into which an infix is inserted must exist as a separate form. Second, there is no independent reason to think that there is a morpheme *oo* in English that means 'singular' or a morpheme *ee* that means 'plural' in the *foot/feet* example any more than there is a morpheme *i* meaning 'present' or a morpheme *a* meaning 'past' in the *sing/sang* case. Since infixes are by definition morphemes, we can conclude that these examples involve internal change (the substitution of nonmorphemic segments) rather than infixing.

Suppletion

Internal change must also be distinguished from **suppletion**, a morphological process that replaces a morph by an entirely different morph in order to indicate a grammatical contrast. An example of this phenomenon in English involves the use of *went* as the past tense form of the verb *go* or *was* and *were* as the past tense forms of *be*.

Table 4.6 Suppletion in other languages

Language	*Basic form*		*Suppletive form*	
French	*avoir*	'to have'	*eu*	'had'
Spanish	*ir*	'to go'	*fue*	'(he) went'
German	*ist*	'is'	*sind*	'are'
Russian	/*xoroʃo*/	'good'	/*lutʃʃe*/	'better' ('more good')

In some cases, it is hard to distinguish between suppletion and internal change. For example, is the past tense of *think* (*thought*) and *seek* (*sought*) an instance of suppletion or internal change? Because the initial phoneme of these verbs remains unchanged and because the phenomenon shows up in several words (see also *catch/caught* and *wreak/wrought*), we will consider this type of alternation to involve an extreme form of internal change rather than true suppletion. (However, the term **partial suppletion** is used by some linguists for these cases.)

Stress and tone placement

Sometimes, a base can undergo a change in the placement of stress or tone to reflect a change in its category. In English, for example, there are pairs of words such as those in Table 4.7 in which the verb has stress on the final syllable while the corresponding noun is stressed on the first syllable. (Stress is represented here by ´.)

Table 4.7 Stress placement in English

Verb	*Noun*
implánt	ímplant
impórt	ímport
presént	présent
subjéct	súbject
contést	cóntest

In the language Mono-Bili (spoken in the African country of Zaire), tone is used to make the distinction between past and future tense. (A high tone is marked by ´ and a low tone by `.)

Table 4.8 Past versus future in Mono-Bili

Past		*Future*	
dá	'spanked'	dà	'will spank'
zɨ́	'ate'	zɨ̀	'will eat'
wó	'killed'	wò	'will kill'

As can easily be observed here, high tone is associated with the past tense and low tone with the future. (The use of tone to mark tense contrasts was also exemplifed in Chapter 2; see Figure 2.14.)

Reduplication

Yet another common morphological process in certain languages (but not English) is **reduplication**, which duplicates all or part of the base to which it applies to mark a grammatical or semantic contrast. **Full reduplication** is the repetition of the entire word, as in the following data from Turkish and Indonesian, respectively.

Table 4.9 Some examples of full reduplication

Base		*Reduplicated form*	
Turkish			
tʃabuk	'quickly'	tʃabuk tʃabuk	'very quickly'
javaʃ	'slowly'	javaʃ javaʃ	'very slowly'
iji	'well'	iji iji	'very well'
gyzel	'beautifully'	gyzel gyzel	'very beautifully'
Indonesian			
oraŋ	'man'	oraŋ oraŋ	'all sorts of men'
anak	'child'	anak anak	'all sorts of children'
maŋga	'mango'	maŋga maŋga	'all sorts of mangoes'

In contrast, **partial reduplication** copies only part of the word. In the following data from Tagalog, for instance, reduplication affects only the first consonant-vowel sequence of the base.

Table 4.10 Reduplication in Tagalog

Base		*Reduplicated form*	
takbuh	'run'	tatakbuh	'will run'
lakad	'walk'	lalakad	'will walk'
piliʔ	'choose'	pipiliʔ	'will choose'

Compounding

A final important morphological process to be considered here involves **compounding**, the combination of lexical categories (nouns, adjectives, verbs, or prepositions) to create a larger word. English includes many compounds such as the following.

Table 4.11 Some examples of English compounds

Noun + Noun	*Adjective + Noun*	*Verb + Noun*	*Preposition + Noun*
streetlight	bluebird	swearword	overlord
campsite	happy hour	washcloth	outhouse
bookcase	high chair	scrub board	in-group

As these examples show, the elements making up a compound can all typically occur as independent words elsewhere in the language.

Of the morphological operations just outlined, two deserve special attention because of the crucial role they play in the formation of new words in English and many other languages—derivation (a type of affixation) and compounding. We will consider these two processes in the next sections of this chapter.

2 DERIVATION

Derivation forms a word with a meaning and/or category distinct from that of its base through the addition of an affix. Table 4.12 contains words formed by adding the suffix *-er* to a verb to form a noun with the meaning 'one who does X'. (Do not confuse this suffix with the *-er* that applies to an N in cases such as *New Yorker* and *islander* or the *-er* that combines with an A in cases such as *taller* and *smarter.*)

Table 4.12 The *-er* affix

Verb base	*Resulting noun*
sell	sell-er
write	writ-er
teach	teach-er
sing	sing-er
discover	discover-er

Once formed, derived words may become independent lexical items that receive their own entry in a speaker's mental dictionary. As time goes by, they often take on a special sense that is not predictable from the component morphemes: *writer* usually refers to someone who writes for a living, *comparable* (with stress on the first syllable) means 'similar' rather than 'able to be compared', *profession* usually denotes a career rather than the act of professing, and so on. The remainder of this section focuses on the role of derivation in English word formation.

2.1 English derivational affixes

Table 4.13 lists some English derivational affixes, along with information about the category of their base (ignoring bound roots) and of the resulting new word. The first entry states that the affix *-able* applies to a verb base and converts it into an adjective. Thus, if we add the affix *-able* to the verb *fix,* we get an adjective (with the meaning 'able to be fixed').

Table 4.13 Some English derivational affixes

Affix	*Change*	*Examples*
Suffixes:		
-able	V → A	fix-able, do-able, understand-able
-ant	V → N	claim-ant, defend-ant
-(at)ion	V → N	realiz-ation, assert-ion, protect-ion
-er	V → N	teach-er, work-er
-ing$_1$	V → N	the shoot-ing, the danc-ing
-ing$_2$	V → A	the sleep-ing giant, a blaz-ing fire
-ive	V → A	assert-ive, impress-ive, restrict-ive
-ment	V → N	adjourn-ment, treat-ment, amaze-ment
-ful	N → A	faith-ful, hope-ful, dread-ful
-(i)al	N → A	president-ial, nation-al
-(i)an	N → A	Arab-ian, Einstein-ian, Minnesot-an
-ic	N → A	cub-ic, optimist-ic, moron-ic
-ize$_1$	N → V	hospital-ize, crystal-ize
-less	N → A	penni-less, brain-less
-ous	N → A	poison-ous, lecher-ous
-ate	A → V	activ-ate, captiv-ate
-en	A → V	dead-en, black-en, hard-en
-ity	A → N	stupid-ity, prior-ity
-ize$_2$	A → V	modern-ize, national-ize
-ly	A → Adv	quiet-ly, slow-ly, careful-ly
-ness	A → N	happi-ness, sad-ness
Prefixes:		
anti-	N → N	anti-abortion, anti-pollution
de-	V → V	de-activate, de-mystify
dis-	V → V	dis-continue, dis-obey
ex-	N → N	ex-president, ex-wife, ex-friend
in-	A → A	in-competent, in-complete
mis-	V → V	mis-identify, mis-place
re-	V → V	re-think, re-do, re-state
un$_1$*-*	A → A	un-happy, un-fair, un-intelligent
un$_2$*-*	V → V	un-tie, un-lock, un-do

Sometimes beginning students have trouble determining the category of the base to which an affix is added. In the case of *worker,* for instance, the base (*work*) is sometimes used as a verb (as in *they work hard*) and sometimes as a noun (as in *the work is time-consuming*). Which category serves as base for the suffix *-er* in the word *worker?* The solution to this problem is to consider the use of *-er* (in the sense of 'one who x's') with bases whose category can be unequivocally determined. In the words *teacher* and *writer,* for instance, we see this affix used with bases that are unequivocally verbs (*teach* and *write*). Moreover, we know that *-er* can combine with the verb *sell* (*seller*) but not the noun *sale* (**saler*). These facts allow us to conclude that the base with which *-er* combines in the word *worker* must be a verb rather than a noun.

2.2 Derivation at work

The information contained in Table 4.13 allows us to build word structures such as the following.

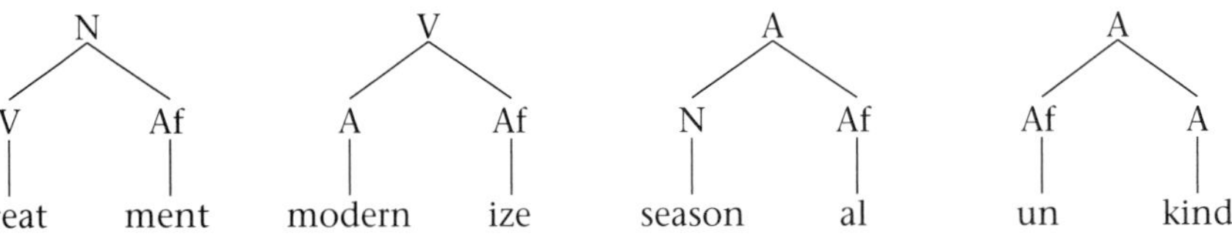

Figure 4.5 Some words formed by derivation

In each of these structures, an affix combines with a base of a particular type to give a new word, in accordance with the properties listed in Table 4.13. In the case of *treatment*, for instance, the affix *-ment* combines with the V *treat* to give the N *treatment*.

These examples illustrate an important property of English complex words: the rightmost morpheme is generally the one that determines the category of the entire word. Thus, the word *unkind* is an adjective because *kind* (the rightmost morpheme) is an adjective. In contrast, the word *treatment* is a noun since the rightmost element is the affix *-ment*, which combines with a V to give an N (see Table 4.13).

In some languages the morpheme that determines the category of the entire word usually appears on the left rather than the right. In the Philippine language Tagalog, for example, the prefix *ma-* combines with a noun base to form an adjective.

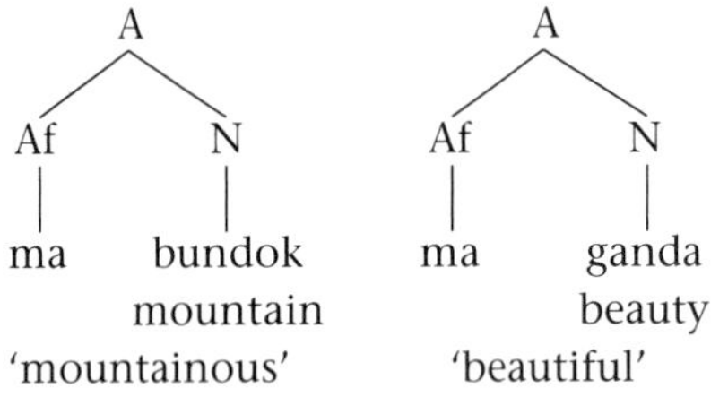

Figure 4.6 Tagalog words with a category-changing prefix

In these examples, it is the prefix that determines that the entire word will be an adjective.

Complex derivations

Since derivation can apply more than once, it is possible to create multiple levels of word structure, as in the following example.

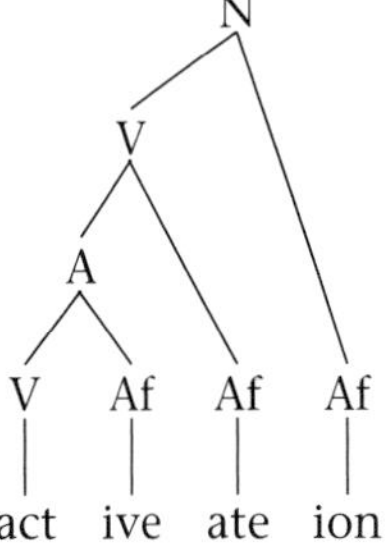

Figure 4.7 A word with a multilayered internal structure

The word *activation* contains several layers, each of which reflects the attachment of an affix to a base of the appropriate type. In the first layer, the affix *-ive* combines with the V base *act* to give an A. (As noted in Table 4.13, *-ive* is the type of affix that converts a V into an A.) In the next layer, the affix *-ate* combines with this A and converts it into a V (*activate*). At this point, the affix *-ion* is added, converting the V into an N and giving the word *activation*.

In some cases, the internal structure of a complex word is not so obvious. The word *unhappiness*, for instance, could apparently be analyzed in either of the ways indicated in Figure 4.8.

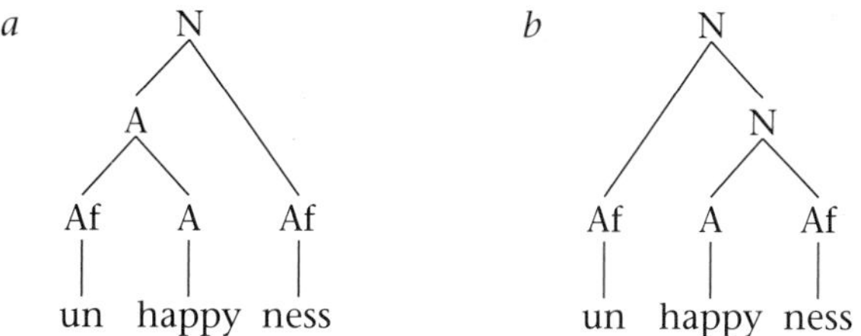

Figure 4.8 Two possible structures for the word *unhappiness*

By considering the properties of the affixes *un-* and *-ness*, however, it is possible to find an argument that favors Figure 4.8a over Figure 4.8b. The key observation is that the prefix *un-* combines quite freely with adjectives, but not with nouns.

Table 4.14 The prefix un-

un + Adj	*un + N*
unable	*unknowledge
unkind	*unhealth
unhurt	*uninjury

This suggests that *un-* must combine with the adjective *happy* before it is converted into a noun by the suffix *-ness*, exactly as depicted in Figure 4.8a.

By contrast, in a word such as *unhealthy*, the prefix *un-* can be attached only *after* the suffix *-y* has been added to the root. Otherwise, there would be no adjective category to which it could attach.

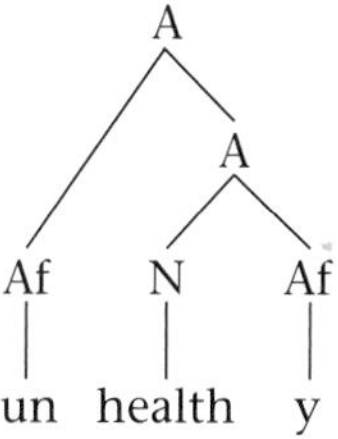

Figure 4.9 The internal structure of the word *unhealthy*

Constraints on derivation

Derivation does not usually apply freely to all members of a given category. For instance, the suffix *-ant* (see Table 4.13) can combine only with bases of Latin origin—as in *defendant, assailant, contestant, servant,* and so forth. This is why it cannot occur with bases such as *fight* and *teach* (**fightant, *teachant*), which are of native English origin.

Sometimes, a derivational affix is able to attach only to bases with particular phonological properties. A good example of this involves the English suffix *-en* (see Table 4.13), which combines with adjectives to create verbs with a causative meaning ('cause to become X'). As the following examples illustrate, however, there are many adjectives with which *-en* cannot combine.

Table 4.15 Restrictions on the use of *-en*

Acceptable	*Unacceptable*
whiten	*abstracten
soften	*bluen
madden	*angryen
quicken	*slowen
liven	*greenen

The suffix *-en* is subject to a phonological constraint. In particular, it can only combine with a monosyllabic base that ends in an obstruent. Hence it can be added to *white,* which is both monosyllabic and ends in an obstruent, but not to *abstract,* which has two syllables, or to *blue,* which does not end in an obstruent.

Two classes of derivational affixes *(Advanced)*

It is common to distinguish between two types of derivational affixes in English. **Class 1** affixes are characterized by the fact that they often trigger changes in the

Table 4.16 Typical effects of Class 1 affixes

Affix	*Sample word*	*Change triggered by affix*
-ity	san-ity	vowel in the base changes from /e/ to /æ/ (cf. *sane*)
	public-ity	final consonant of the base changes from /k/ to /s/, stress shifts to second syllable (cf. *públic* vs *publícity*)
-y	democrac-y	final consonant of the base changes from /t/ to /s/, stress shifts to second syllable (cf. *démocrat* vs *demócracy*)
-ive	product-ive	stress shifts to second syllable (cf. *próduct* vs *prodúctive*)
-(i)al	part-ial	final consonant of the base changes from /t/ to /ʃ/ (cf. *part*)
-ize	public-ize	final consonant of the base changes from /k/ to /s/ (cf. *public*)
-ious	audac-ious	final consonant of the base changes from /s/ to /ʃ/ (cf. *audacity*)
-ion	nat-ion	final consonant of the base changes from /t/ to /ʃ/ (cf. *native*)

consonant or vowel segments of the base and may affect the assignment of stress. (As the final two examples in Table 4.16 help show, Class 1 affixes often combine with bound roots.) In contrast, **Class 2** affixes tend to be phonologically neutral, having no effect on the segmental makeup of the base or on stress assignment.

Table 4.17 Some typical Class 2 affixes

Affix	*Sample word*	*Change triggered by affix*
-ness	prompt-ness	none
-less	hair-less	none
-ful	hope-ful	none
-ly	quiet-ly	none
-er	defend-er	none
-ish	self-ish	none

When Class 1 and Class 2 affixes appear in the same word, the former type of morpheme normally occurs closer to the root than the latter. Moreover, while a Class 1 affix can follow another Class 1 affix and while a Class 2 affix can precede another Class 2 affix, a Class 2 affix usually cannot come before a Class 1 affix. The various possibilities are illustrated below.

14)

relat-ion-al	audac-ious-ness	*fear-less-ity	fear-less-ness
root 1 1	root 1 2	root 2 1	root 2 2

Notice that in the form that is ruled out (**fearlessity*) a Class 1 affix follows a Class 2 affix.

3 COMPOUNDING

Another common way to build words in English involves compounding, the combination of lexical categories (nouns, adjectives, verbs, or prepositions). With very few exceptions, the resulting compound word is a noun, a verb, or an adjective (see Figure 4.10). (Possible examples of compound prepositions include the words *into* and *onto*.) In these and most other compounds of this type, the final component determines the category of the entire word. Thus, *greenhouse* is an N because its rightmost component is an N, *spoonfeed* is a V because *feed* also belongs to this category, and *nationwide* is an A just as *wide* is. The morpheme that determines the category of the entire word is called the **head**.

Once formed, compounds can be combined with other lexical categories to create still larger compounds, as in the following examples in Figure 4.11.

In addition, the word formation processes responsible for derivation and compounding can interact with each other. In Figure 4.12, for instance, a compound is formed by combining a simple word (*debate*) with the derived word *abortion*.

Noun compounds

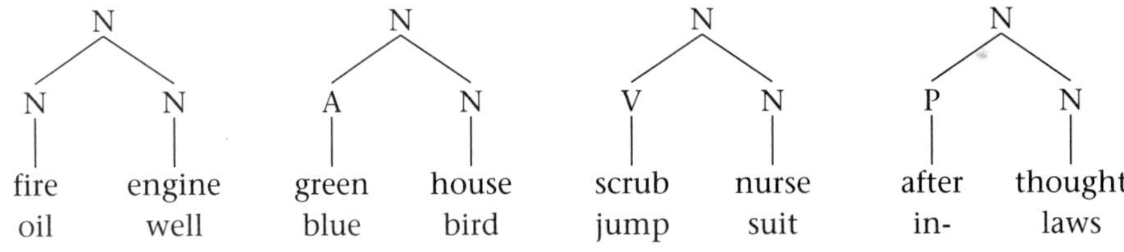

Verb compounds

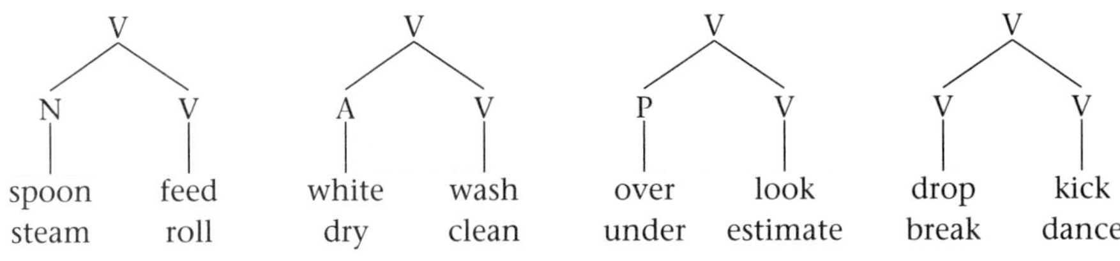

Adjective compounds

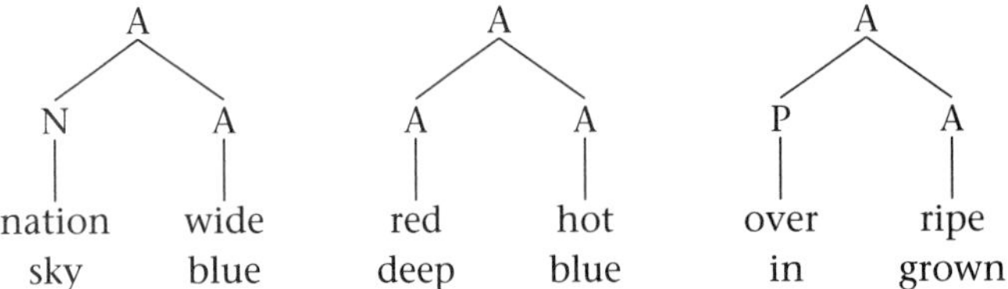

Figure 4.10 Some English compounds

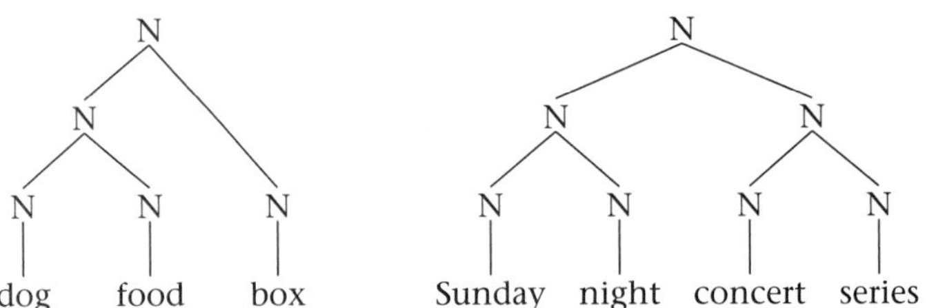

Figure 4.11 Compounds formed from smaller compounds

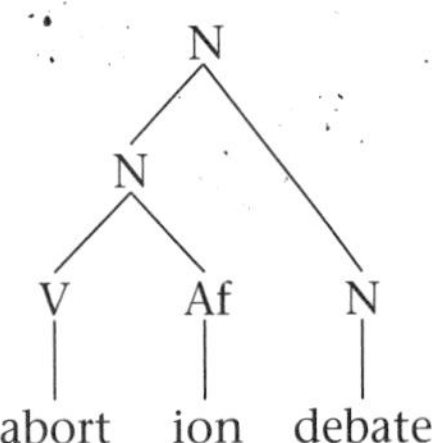

Figure 4.12 The interaction of derivation with compounding

3.1 Properties of compounds

English orthography is not consistent in representing compounds since they are sometimes written as single words, sometimes with an intervening hyphen, and sometimes as separate words. In terms of pronunciation, however, there is an important generalization to be made. In particular, A–N compounds are characterized by a more prominent stress on their first component. In noncompounds consisting of an adjective and a noun, in contrast, the second element is generally stressed.

Table 4.18 Compounds versus noncompounds

Compound word		*Noncompound expression*	
greénhouse	'an indoor garden'	green hoúse	'a house painted green'
bláckboard	'a chalkboard'	black boárd	'a board which is black'
wét suit	'a diver's costume'	wet suít	'a suit that is wet'

A second distinguishing feature of compounds in English is that tense and plural markers can typically not be attached to the first element, although they can be added to the compound as a whole.

15)

tense on the first element in a compound:
*The player [dropped kick] the ball through the goalposts.

tense on the entire compound:
The player [drop kick]ed the ball through the goalposts.

16)

pluralization of the first element in a compound:
*The [foxes hunter] didn't have a licence.

pluralization of the entire compound:
The [fox hunter]s didn't have a licence.

The preceding criteria are especially helpful for identifying compounds whose initial component is a verb or a noun. Compounds whose first element is an adjective (*greenhouse, wet suit*) can be identified with the help of a different test. As illustrated in the following example, the A in a compound cannot be preceded by a word such as *very*.

17)

compound with *very*:
*We live next to a very [greenhouse].

Of course, when it is not part of a compound, an adjective can typically be accompanied by this type of word.

18)

very with an adjective that is not part of a compound:
We live next to a very green fence.

3.2 Types of compounds

Compounds are used to express a wide range of semantic relationships in English. The following table contains examples of just some of the semantic patterns found in N–N compounds.

Table 4.19 Some N–N compounds

Example	*Meaning*
steamboat	'a boat powered by steam'
airplane	'a conveyance that travels through the air'
air hose	'a hose that carries air'
air field	'a field where airplanes land'
fire truck	'a vehicle used to put out fires'
fire drill	'a practice in the event of a fire'
bath tub	'a place in which to bathe'
bath towel	'a towel used after bathing'

In most cases, a compound denotes a subtype of the concept denoted by its head (the rightmost component). Thus *dog food* is a type of food, a *cave man* is a type of man, *sky-blue* is a type of blue, and so on. Such compounds, which include all the examples in Table 4.19, are called **endocentric compounds**. In a smaller number of cases, however, the meaning of the compound does not follow from the meanings of its parts in this way. Thus, a *redhead* is not a type of head; rather, it is a person with red hair. Similarly, a *redneck* is a person and not a type of neck. Such compounds are said to be **exocentric compounds**.

A very striking feature of exocentric compounds shows up in English in those cases where the head of the compound has an irregular plural. Consider in this regard the following examples.

Table 4.20 Pluralization in English compounds

In endocentric compounds	*In exocentric compounds*
oak leaves	Maple Leafs (Toronto's NHL hockey team)
wisdom teeth	saber tooths (extinct species of tiger)
club feet	bigfoots (mythical creatures; 'Sasquatch')
policemen	Walkmans ('a type of portable radio')

Notice that the exocentric compounds permit the plural suffix *-s* for words such as *leaf, tooth, foot,* and *man* even though these forms require an irregular plural when used elsewhere, including in endocentric compounds.

3.3 Compounds in other languages

Although the rules for forming compounds differ from language to language, the practice of combining lexical categories to build a word is very widespread. As the following examples from various languages help illustrate, compound nouns are especially common.

Table 4.21 Noun compounds in various languages

Korean		
kot elum straight ice 'icicle'	isul pi dew rain 'drizzle'	nwun mwul eye water 'tears'
Tagalog		
tanod bayan guard town 'policeman'	anak araw child sun 'albino'	tubig ulan water rain 'rainwater'
German		
Gast-hof guest inn 'hotel'	Wort-bedeutungs-lehre word meaning theory 'semantics'	Fern-seher far seer 'television'
Finnish		
lammas-nahka-turkki sheep skin coat 'sheepskin coat'	elin-keino-tulo-vero-laki life's means income tax law 'income tax law'	
Tzotzil		
piʃ-xól wrap-head 'hat'	méʔ-k'ínobal mother-mist 'rainbow'	ʔóra-tʃón rightaway-snake 'deadly viper'

With the exception of Tagalog, in which compounds are left-headed, these languages all have compounds in which the rightmost element is the head.

A special type of compounding process involves **incorporation**, the combination of a word (usually, but not always, a noun) with a verb to form a compound verb. Although English does not make use of incorporation, the process is common in other languages. The following examples are from Chukchee, spoken in northeastern Siberia, and the Micronesian language Ponapean. (As these examples help illustrate, incorporation often involves phonological adjustments to the noun and/or the verb.)

19)

a. Chukchee

without incorporation:	*with incorporation:*
Tə-pelarkən qoraŋə. I leave reindeer 'I'm leaving the reindeer'	Tə-qora-pelarkən I-reindeer-leave 'I'm in the process of reindeer-leaving.'

b. Ponapean

without incorporation:	*with incorporation:*
I pahn pereki lohs	I pahn perek-los
I will unroll mats	I will unroll-mats
'I will unroll the mats.'	'I will engage in mat unrolling.'

4 OTHER TYPES OF WORD FORMATION

Derivation and compounding are the two most common types of word formation in English, but they are not the only ones. As the examples presented in this section will show, there are various other ways to create new words.

4.1 CONVERSION

Conversion is a process that assigns an already existing word to a new syntactic category. Even though it does not add an affix, conversion is often considered to be a type of derivation because of the change in category and meaning that it brings about. (For this reason, it is sometimes called **zero derivation**.)

Many examples of conversion involving the creation of a new verb from a noun were given in the first chapter of this book (*beach a boat*, *winter in Mexico*, and so on). Table 4.22 contains examples of the three most common types of conversion in English. (As noted in Section 1.3 above, nouns derived from verbs sometimes undergo stress shift, which moves the stress to the initial syllable. The effects of this phenomenon can be seen in the first three examples in the middle column.)

Table 4.22 Some examples of conversion

V derived from N	*N derived from V*	*V derived from A*
ink (a contract)	(a building) pérmit	dirty (a shirt)
butter (the bread)	(an exciting) cóntest	empty (the box)
ship (the package)	(a new) súrvey	better (the old record)
nail (the door shut)	(a brief) report	right (a wrong)
button (the shirt)	(an important) call	total (a car)

Less common types of conversion can yield an N from an A (*the poor*, *a green*) and even a V from a P (*down a beer*, *up the price*).

Conversion is usually restricted to morphologically simple words although there are a few exceptions such as *propos-ition* (noun and verb), *refer-ee* (noun and verb), and *dirt-y* (adjective and verb). In some cases, conversion can even apply to a compound, as when the noun *grandstand* is used as verb (*he likes to grandstand*) in the sense of 'show off'.

4.2 Clipping

Clipping is a process that shortens a polysyllabic word by deleting one or more syllables. Some of the most common products of clipping are names—*Liz, Ron, Rob, Sue,* and so on. Clipping is especially popular in the speech of students, where it has yielded forms like *prof* for *professor, phys-ed* for *physical education, poli-sci* for *political science,* and *burger* for *hamburger.* However, many clipped forms have also been accepted in general usage: *doc, ad, auto, lab, sub, deli, porn, demo,* and *condo.*

In some cases, speakers may not even realize that a particular word is the product of clipping: the word *zoo,* for instance, was formed in this manner from *zoological garden.* A more recent example of this sort that has rapidly become part of general English vocabulary is *fax,* from *facsimile* (meaning 'exact copy or reproduction').

4.3 Blends

Blends are created from nonmorphemic parts of two already existing items. Well-known examples of blends include *brunch* from *breakfast* and *lunch, smog* from *smoke* and *fog, spam* from *spiced* and *ham, telethon* from *telephone* and *marathon, aerobicise* from *aerobics* and *exercise, chunnel* (for the underwater link between Britain and the continent) from *channel* and *tunnel,* and *infomercial* from *information* and *commercial.* As in these examples, a blend is usually formed from the initial part of one word and the final part of a second one.

Some blends have become so integrated into the standard vocabulary of English that speakers are unaware of their status. For example, relatively few people know that blending has produced *chortle* (coined by author Lewis Carroll) from *chuckle* and *snort, motel* from *motor* and *hotel, bit* (in computer jargon) from *binary* and *digit,* and *modem* from *modulator* and *demodulator.*

Sometimes, a word is formed by a process that seems to be on the borderline between compounding and blending in that it combines all of one word with part of another. Examples of this in English include *perma-press* (for *permanent-press*), *workaholic, medicare, guesstimate,* and *threepeat* (used by sports fans to refer to the winning of a championship in three successive years).

4.4 Backformation

Backformation is a process that creates a new word by removing a real or supposed affix from another word in the language. *Resurrect* was originally formed in this way from *resurrection.* Other backformations in English include *enthuse* from *enthusiasm, donate* from *donation, orient* or *orientate* from *orientation,* and *self-destruct* from *self-destruction.* Sometimes, backformation involves an incorrect assumption about a word's form: for example, the word *pea* was derived from the singular noun *pease,* whose final /z/ was incorrectly interpreted as the plural suffix.

A major source of backformations in English has been words that end in *-or* or *-er* and have meanings involving the notion of an agent, such as *editor, peddler, swindler,* and *stoker.* Because hundreds of words like these are the result of affixation, it was assumed that these words too had been formed by adding *-or* or *-er* to a verb. By the process of backformation, the verbs *edit, peddle, swindle,* and *stoke* were formed. A more recent addition is the verb *lase,* produced by backformation from *laser,* which itself had an unusual origin (see Section 4.5).

Backformation continues to produce new words in modern English. For instance, the form *attrit,* from *attrition,* was often used by military officials during the recent Gulf War to refer to the decimation of enemy troops (as in *The enemy is 50 percent attritted*). Among the backformations noticed recently by the authors of this chapter are *liposuct* (from *liposuction,* seen in a magazine article), *orate* (from *oration,* used in a newspaper editorial), and *tuit* (from *intuition,* heard on the radio).

4.5 Acronyms

Acronyms are formed by taking the initial letters of the words in a phrase or title and pronouncing them as a word. This type of word formation is especially common in names of organizations and in military and scientific terminology. Some examples of acronyms include UNICEF for United Nations International Children's Emergency Fund, NASA for National Aeronautics and Space Administration, NATO for North Atlantic Treaty Organization, and AIDS for acquired immune deficiency syndrome.

In some cases, speakers may not know that a word in their vocabulary originated as an acronym. Three commonly used words of this type are *radar* (from radio detecting and ranging), *scuba* (self-contained underwater breathing apparatus), and *laser* (light amplification by simulated emission of radiation). The name of the computer language BASIC is an acronym for Beginner's All-purpose Symbolic Instruction Code.

4.6 Onomatopoeia

All languages have words that have been created to sound like the thing that they name. Examples of such onomatopoeic words in English include *buzz, hiss, sizzle,* and *cuckoo.* Since **onomatopoeic** words are not exact phonetic copies of noises, their form can differ from language to language.

Table 4.23 Onomatopoeia across languages

English	*Japanese*	*Tagalog*
cock-a-doodle-doo	kokekokko	kukaok
meow	nja:	ŋijaw
chirp	pi:-pi:	tiririt
bow-wow	wan-wan	aw-aw

English does not always have an equivalent for the onomatopoeic words found in other languages. The Athapaskan language Slavey, for instance, has the onomatopoeic word *sah sah sah* for 'the sound of a bear walking unseen not far from camp', *ðik* for 'the sound of a knife hitting a tree', and *tɬóòtʃ* for 'the sound of an egg splattering'.

4.7 Other sources

In still other cases a word may be created from scratch. Called **word manufacture** or **coinage**, this phenomenon is especially common in cases where industry requires a new and attractive name for a product. *Kodak, Dacron, Orlon,* and *Teflon* are examples of product names that are the result of word manufacture. (Notice how the *-on* of the final three words makes them more scientific-sounding, perhaps because an affix of this form occurs in various learnèd words of Greek origin such as *phenomenon* and *automaton.*)

Finally, it is sometimes possible to create new words from names. For example, brand names sometimes become so widely used that they are accepted as generic terms (*kleenex* for 'facial tissue' or *xerox* for 'photocopy'). A related practice is exemplified by the words *watt, curie, fahrenheit,* and *boycott,* all of which were derived from the names of individuals (usually the inventors or discoverers) associated with the things to which they refer.

5 INFLECTION

Virtually all languages have contrasts such as singular versus plural, and past versus present. These contrasts are often marked with the help of **inflection**, morphology used to indicate the grammatical subclass to which it belongs. (The base to which an inflectional affix is added is sometimes called a **stem**.) In the case of most English nouns, for instance, inflection marks the plural subclass by adding the affix *-s*. In the case of verbs, inflection can mark a distinction between the past and nonpast subclasses—usually by adding the suffix *-ed* to indicate the past tense.

Table 4.24 Inflection for number and tense

Number		*Tense*	
Singular	*Plural*	*Nonpast*	*Past*
apple	apple-s	work	work-ed
car	car-s	jump	jump-ed
dog	dog-s	hunt	hunt-ed

Because inflection applies after the word formation processes discussed in Sections 2 to 4, the plural affix can be added to the output of derivation and compounding, as well as to a simple noun.

Table 4.25 Inflection of derived and compound nouns

Derived nouns	*Compound nouns*
[worker]-s	[football]-s
[creation]-s	[outlaw]-s
[kingdom]-s	[blackboard]-s

Similarly, tense affixes can be attached to the output of derivation and compounding as well as to simple verbs.

Table 4.26 Inflection of derived and compound verbs

Derived verbs	*Compound verbs*
[hospitalize]-d	[whitewash]-ed
[activate]-d	[backorder]-ed

5.1 INFLECTION VERSUS DERIVATION

As the preceding examples show, inflection is expressed primarily by means of affixation. Thus, in English the plural is marked by the suffix *-s* (barring a few exceptions such as *man/men*) while the past is generally marked by the suffix *-ed* (although a number of verbs use internal change, as in *sink/sank* and *ride/rode*).

Because inflection and derivation are both marked in the same way, the distinction between the two can be a subtle one and it is sometimes unclear which function a particular affix has. Three criteria are commonly used to help distinguish between inflectional and derivational affixes.

Category change

First, inflection does not change either the grammatical category or the type of meaning found in the word to which it applies.

Figure 4.13 The output of inflection: there is no change in either the category of the base or the type of meaning it denotes.

The form produced by adding the plural suffix *-s* in Figure 4.13a is still a noun and has the same type of content or meaning as the base. Even though *books* differs from *book* in referring to several things rather than just one, the type of thing(s) to which it refers remains the same. Similarly, a past tense suffix such as the one in Figure 4.13b indicates that the action took place in the past, but it does not change the word's category (which remains a V), nor does it modify the type of meaning. The verb continues to denote an action regardless of whether the tense is past or nonpast.

In contrast, derivational suffixes characteristically change the category and/or the type of meaning of the form to which they apply and are therefore said to create a new word. Consider the following examples of derivation. As Figure 4.14a shows, *-ize* makes a verb out of an adjective, changing the type of meaning it expresses from a property (*modern*) to an action (*modernize*). Parallel changes in category and type of meaning are brought about by *-ment* (V to N) and *-al* (N to A). Matters are a little

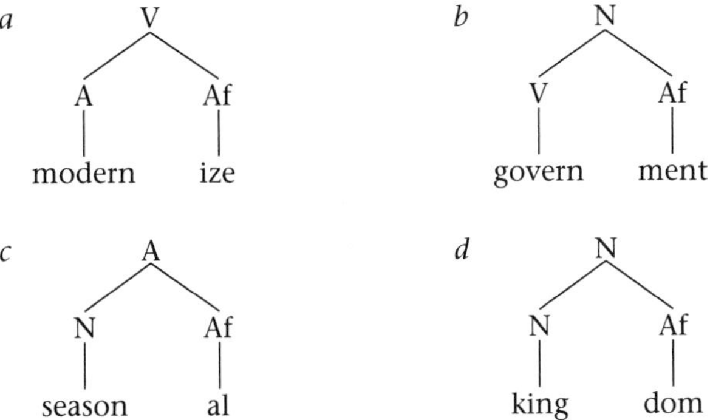

Figure 4.14 The output of derivation: there is a change in the category of the word and/or the type of meaning it denotes.

different in the case of *-dom*, which does not bring about a **category change** in the word *kingdom* (since both the base and the resulting word are Ns). However, *-dom* does modify the type of meaning from 'person' (for *king*) to 'place' (for *kingdom*).

Order

A second property of inflectional affixes has to do with the order in which they are combined with a base relative to derivational affixes. As the following example illustrates, a derivational affix must combine with the base before an inflectional affix does. (IA = inflectional affix; DA = derivational affix)

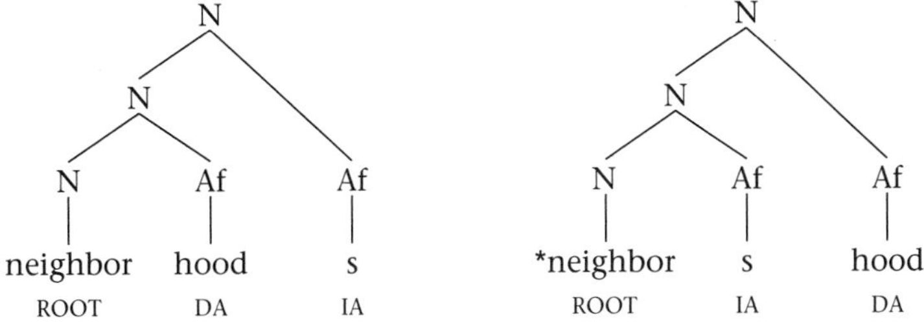

Figure 4.15 The relative positioning of derivational and inflectional affixes: the derivational affix must be closer to the root.

The positioning of inflectional affixes outside derivational affixes in these examples reflects the fact that inflection takes place after derivation.

Productivity

A third criterion for distinguishing between inflectional and derivational affixes is **productivity**, the relative freedom with which they can combine with bases of the appropriate category. Inflectional affixes typically have relatively few exceptions. The suffix *-s*, for example, can combine with virtually any noun that allows a plural form (aside from a few exceptions such as *oxen* and *feet*). In contrast, derivational affixes characteristically apply to restricted classes of bases. Thus, *-ize* can combine with only certain adjectives to form a verb.

20)

modern-ize	*new-ize
legal-ize	*lawful-ize
final-ize	*permanent-ize

In the case of verbs, matters are somewhat more complicated, since many English verbs have irregular past tense forms (*saw*, *left*, *went*, and so on). Nonetheless, the distribution of the inflectional affix *-ed* is still considerably freer than that of a derivational affix such as *-ment*. In Table 4.27, for example, all the verbs can take the regular past tense ending, but only those in the first three rows can take the *-ment* suffix.

Table 4.27 Compatibility of verb bases with inflectional *-ed* and derivational *-ment*

Verb	*With* -ed	*With* -ment
confine	confined	confinement
align	aligned	alignment
treat	treated	treatment
arrest	arrested	*arrestment
straighten	straightened	*straightenment
cure	cured	*curement

5.2 English inflectional affixes

With only eight inflectional affixes (all suffixes), English is not a highly inflected language. Some languages have dozens of inflectional affixes and encode contrasts not represented in English (see Section 6 for some examples). Table 4.28 gives a complete list of English inflectional affixes.

Table 4.28 English inflectional affixes

Nouns	
Plural *-s*	the book<u>s</u>
Possessive *-'s*	John<u>'s</u> book
Verbs	
3rd person sing. nonpast *-s*	John read<u>s</u> well.
Progressive *-ing*	He is work<u>ing</u>.
Past tense *-ed*	He work<u>ed</u>.
Past participle *-en/-ed*	He has eat<u>en</u>/finish<u>ed</u>.
Adjectives	
Comparative *-er*	the small<u>er</u> one
Superlative *-est*	the small<u>est</u> one

Regular versus irregular inflection

Although the majority of inflection in English involves regular affixation, some words mark inflectional contrasts in less regular ways. This is most obvious in the case of verbs, a number of which indicate past tense by internal changes of various sorts and even suppletion: *come-came, see-saw, fall-fell, eat-ate, drink-drank, lose-lost, think-thought, is-was, go-went,* and so on.

There is apparently a fundamental difference in the way in which regular and irregular inflection operates. In particular, it seems that whereas regular inflected forms are constructed as needed in accordance with a general morphological rule (such as 'Add *-ed* to mark the past tense'), irregular forms must be stored permanently in the language user's memory. Some evidence of this difference comes from studies of how long it takes speakers to utter the past tense form of a verb when presented with the base. For irregular forms, there is a correlation between response time and frequency of the verb: thus it takes less time to give the past form of frequent verbs such as *see* and *find* than it does for infrequent verbs such as *stride* and *bid*—presumably because it takes longer to locate infrequently used forms in one's memory. In the case of regular verbs, in contrast, response time is independent of frequency: because the past tense is formed by a regular rule, there is no need to 'look up' the word in the mental dictionary and all verbs can be handled with equal speed.

6 FURTHER EXAMPLES OF INFLECTION *(ADVANCED)*

In this section, we will consider several types of grammatical information that are commonly expressed in human language with the help of inflectional affixes.

6.1 NUMBER

Number is the morphological category that expresses contrasts involving countable quantities. The simplest number contrast consists of a two-way distinction between **singular** (one) and **plural** (more than one). This is the contrast found in English, where a noun usually takes the suffix *-s* if it refers to two or more entities.

Even this basic distinction is not found in all languages, however. In Nancowry (spoken in India's Nicobar Islands), for example, number is not marked on nouns at all. A sentence such as *21)* is therefore ambiguous since *nɔ́t* 'pig' can refer to one or more pigs.

21)

sák nɔ́t ʔin tsiʔə́j.
spear pig the we
'We speared the pig(s).'

In Inuktitut (spoken in northern Canada), on the other hand, there is a three-way number contrast involving singular, dual (two and only two), and plural (more than two).

22)

iglu 'a house'
igluk 'two houses'
iglut 'three or more houses'

6.2 Noun class

Some languages divide nouns into two or more inflectional classes, based on shared phonological and/or semantic properties. The Bantu language SiSwati, for instance, makes use of prefixes to distinguish among more than a dozen noun classes, some of which are given in Table 4.29. (Tone is not represented in these examples.)

Table 4.29 Some noun classes in SiSwati

Prefix	*Description of class*	*Example*	
um(u)-	persons	um-fana	'boy'
li-	body parts, fruit	li-dvolo	'knee'
s(i)-	instruments	si-tja	'plate'
in-	animals	in-ja	'dog'
bu-	abstract properties	bu-bi	'evil'
pha-	locations	pha-ndle	'outside'

The **gender** contrasts of modern French also make up a type of noun classification system. Although the term *gender* is used by linguists to mean 'kind' rather than 'sex', there is a partial correlation between the French gender classes and the sex of the objects to which nouns can refer. Thus *frère* 'brother' is masculine while *soeur* 'sister' is feminine. However, most inanimate nouns are classified more or less arbitrarily: *lune* 'moon' is feminine, but *monde* 'world' is masculine. Even some nouns referring to animate entities seem to be classified arbitrarily: French *victime* 'victim' is feminine regardless of whether the person referred to is male or female and all German words ending in the suffix *-chen*, including *Mädchen* 'young girl', are neuter.

Noun class can be marked in a variety of ways. In some languages, the determiner is inflected to indicate the class of the noun. For example, singular nouns in French take the definite determiner *le* if masculine but *la* if feminine. In other languages, inflectional affixes rather than determiners can be used to indicate the gender class of the noun. Russian, for instance, uses one set of suffixes for nouns in the feminine, animate class and another set for nouns in the masculine, animate class. The following examples show the gender endings for nouns that function as subject of a sentence.

Table 4.30 Gender distinctions in Russian

Class	*Suffix*	*Example*	
Masculine	-Ø	dom	'house'
Feminine	-a	ulits-a	'street'
Neuter	-o	tʃuvstv-o	'sensation'

6.3 Case

Still another type of inflectional contrast associated with nouns in many languages involves **case**—a category that encodes information about an element's grammatical role (subject, direct object, and so on). In Modern English, this information is expressed largely through word order and the use of prepositions.

23)

Bette composed a song on the bus.

In this sentence, the subject *Bette* precedes the verb and the direct object *a song* follows, while the element expressing location (*the bus*) is preceded by the preposition *on*. In many languages, however, these distinctions are marked by inflectional affixes. As an illustration of this, consider the following set of related nominal forms (called a **nominal paradigm** or **declension**) for the Turkish word *ev* 'house'.

Table 4.31 Turkish case

Case	*Form*	*Type of element that it marks*
Nominative	ev-Ø	the subject
Accusative	ev-i	the direct object
Dative	ev-e	the recipient
Genitive	ev-in	the possessor
Locative	ev-de	a place or location
Ablative	ev-den	direction away from somewhere

The following sentences illustrate the use of these case suffixes.

24)

a. Adam-Ø ev-i Ahmed-e göster-di.
Man-Nom house-Ac Ahmed-Dat show-past.
'The man showed the house to Ahmed.'

b. Ev-in rengi-Ø māvidir.
house-Gen color-Nom blue
'The house's color is blue.'

c. Adam-Ø ev-de kaldɨ.
man-Nom house-Loc stayed
'The man stayed in the house.'

d. Adam-Ø ev-den tʃɨktɨ.
man-Nom house-Abl went
'The man went from the house.'

Notice how in the final sentence, for example, *Adam* 'man' bears the zero ending of the nominative to indicate that it is subject while *ev* 'house' bears the ablative suffix indicating the place from which the man went.

The contrasts represented in the Turkish case system are intermediate in complexity compared to Finnish, which has fifteen distinct case categories, and Rumanian, which has only two.

Ergative case marking

Some languages make use of case marking to encode grammatical contrasts quite unlike those found in familiar European languages. In the Australian language Yidin^y, for instance, the case system groups together the subject of an **intransitive verb** and the direct object of a **transitive verb** (both of which receive a zero ending) while using a special marker (*-ngu*) for the subject of a transitive verb. (A verb is transitive if it takes a direct object; otherwise, it is intransitive.)

25)

a. Yidin^y sentence with a transitive verb:
Wagudya-ngu dyugi-Ø gundal.
man-Erg tree-Abs is cutting.
'The man is cutting the tree.'

b. Yidin^y sentence with an intransitive verb:
Wagudya-Ø gundal
man-Abs is cutting
'The man is cutting.'

In this type of system, the case associated with the subject of the transitive verb, *wagudya* 'man' in *25a)*, is called the **ergative**. The case associated with the direct object (*dyugi* 'tree' in the first sentence) and with the subject of an intransitive verb (*wagudya* in the second sentence) is called the **absolutive**.

Ergative case marking is found in a varied set of languages, including Basque (in Spain), Tagalog (in the Philippines), Georgian (in the Caucasus), Inuktitut (in northern Canada and Greenland), and Halkomelem (on the west coast of Canada). Ergative case marking is far less common than the nominative-accusative pattern, which groups together the subjects of transitive and intransitive verbs, distinguishing them from direct objects. This is the pattern found in Turkish (as noted previously), German, Russian, Japanese, Korean, and many other languages.

English nouns and pronouns

At one time, English nouns and determiners (words such as *the*) were inflected for case (see discussion in Chapter 8). In modern English, however, the only remnant of this case system is the genitive suffix *-'s*, used to mark possessors (*the man's book*). Neither nouns nor determiners are inflected to distinguish grammatical relations such as subject and direct object.

26)

a. the man in subject position:
The man left. The man read the book.

b. the man in direct object position:
A noise frightened the man.

However, pronouns exhibit a more elaborate set of contrasts, distinguishing a nominative (*I, they, he*), an accusative (*me, them, him*), and a genitive (*my, their, his*).

27)

Nominative: *He* left. (intransitive verb) *He* read the book. (transitive verb)
Accusative: A noise frightened *him.*
Genitive: Sam took *his* car.

Since the same form of the pronoun is used for the subject of an intransitive verb and the subject of a transitive verb and since this form differs from the one used for direct objects, these contrasts follow the nominative-accusative pattern.

6.4 PERSON AND NUMBER AGREEMENT

A widely attested type of verbal inflection in human language involves **person**—a category that typically distinguishes among the first person (the speaker), the second person (the addressee), and the third person (anyone else). In many languages, the verb is marked for both the person and number (singular or plural) of the subject. When one category is inflected for properties (such as person and number) of another, the first category is said to agree with the second.

Agreement is found in Italian, which exhibits the following contrasts in the present tense. (The set of inflected forms associated with a verb is called a **verbal paradigm** or a **conjugation**.)

Table 4.32 The Italian present tense paradigm

	Singular		*Plural*	
1st person	parl-o	'I speak'	parl-iamo	'we speak'
2nd person	parl-i	'you speak'	parl-ate	'you speak'
3rd person	parl-a	'she, he speaks'	parl-ano	'they speak'

Because the inflectional affixes provide so much information about the person and number of the subject phrase, this element need not be overtly present in Italian. Thus, *parla italiano* 'speaks Italian' can make up a complete sentence. The permissibility of such 'understood subjects' is a common feature of languages with rich verbal inflection.

Modern English has a much more impoverished system of person and number agreement in the verb, and an inflectional affix is used only for the third person singular in the nonpast tense.

Table 4.33 The English verbal paradigm (nonpast forms)

	Singular	*Plural*
1st person	I speak	we speak
2nd person	you speak	you speak
3rd person	she, he, or it speaks	they speak

Except for commands, formal English differs from Italian and other languages with rich verbal inflection in requiring a complete sentence to have an overtly expressed subject.

28)

*Speaks English.

6.5 Tense

Tense is the category that encodes the time of an event with reference to the moment of speaking. Thus, the past tense is used with verbs denoting an event that occurs prior to the moment of speaking.

There are many different types of tense systems in the languages of the world. In terms of inflection, for example, English makes a two-way contrast between past (marked by the inflectional suffix *-ed* in regular verbs) and the nonpast (unmarked). Notice that the nonpast form of the verb can be used for both present and future events.

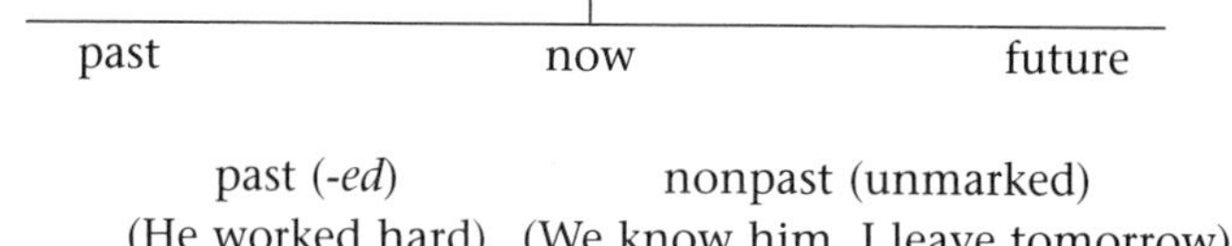

Figure 4.16 Tense in English

In the Australian language Dyirbal, in contrast, there is a two-way distinction between future and nonfuture. As the following examples show, the nonfuture can be used for both present and past events.

29)

a. future:	*b.* nonfuture:
bani-ɲ	bani-ɲu
'will come'	'came, is coming'

In Spanish and Lithuanian, on the other hand, inflectional endings are used to express a three-way contrast involving past, present, and future.

30)

	Spanish	*Lithuanian*
a.	Juan habl-ó bien.	Dirb-au.
	'John spoke well.'	'I worked.'
b.	Juan habl-a bien.	Dirb-u.
	'John speaks well.'	'I work.'
c.	Juan habl-ar-á bien.	Dirb-siu.
	'John will speak well.'	'I will work.'

A still richer system of contrasts is found in the Bantu language ChiBemba, which uses its inflectional system to distinguish degrees of pastness and futurity. (In the following examples, the diacritics mark tone; affixes expressing tense contrasts are underlined.)

Table 4.34 Tense in ChiBemba

Past	*Future*
Remote past (before yesterday) ba-àlí-bomb-ele 'They worked.'	Remote future (after tomorrow) ba-ká-bomba 'They'll work.'
Removed past (yesterday) ba-àlíí-bomba 'They worked.'	Removed future (tomorrow) ba-kà-bomba 'They'll work.'
Near past (earlier today) ba-àcí-bomba 'They worked.'	Near future (later today) ba-léé-bomba 'They'll work.'
Immediate past (just happened) ba-á-bomba 'They worked.'	Immediate future (very soon) ba-áláá-bomba 'They'll work.'

Summing up

This chapter is concerned with the structure and formation of **words** in human language. Many words consist of smaller formative elements, called **morphemes**. These elements can be classified in a variety of ways (**free** versus **bound**, **root** versus **affix**, **prefix** versus **suffix**) and can be combined and modified under various conditions to build words. Operations that can combine and modify morphemes include **affixation**, **cliticization**, **internal change**, **suppletion**, **reduplication**, and **compounding**.

The two basic types of word formation in English are **derivation** and **compounding**. Less common types of word formation include **conversion**, **blending**, **clipping**, and **backformation**. Once formed, words may be inflected to mark grammatical contrasts in **number**, **gender**, **case**, **person**, and **tense**.

Key terms

ablaut
absolutive
acronyms
affixes
affixation
agreement
allomorphs
arbitrariness
backformation
base
blends
bound morpheme
case
category change
Class 1
Class 2
clipping
clitic/cliticization
coinage
complex words
compounding
conjugation

conversion
declension
derivation
enclitic
endocentric compounds
ergative
exocentric compounds
free forms
free morpheme
full reduplication
gender
head
incorporation
infix
inflection
internal change
intransitive verb
lexicon
morph
morpheme
morphology
nominal paradigm
noun class
number
onomatopoeic (words)
partial reduplication
partial suppletion
person
plural
prefix
proclitic
productivity
reduplication
root
simple words
singular
stem
suffix
suppletion
tense
transitive verb
tree structures
umlaut
verbal paradigm
word
word manufacture
zero derivation

Note

[1] An interesting fact about these forms is that although *ceive* and *mit* have no identifiable meaning, they undergo certain alternations that suggest that they have a special status in the language. Thus, the *ceive* in words like *receive* and *deceive* becomes *cept* in *receptive* and *deceptive* while the *mit* in words like *submit* and *permit* becomes *miss* in *submissive* and *permissive*. For further discussion of this point, see *Word Formation in Generative Grammar* by Mark Aronoff (Cambridge, MA: MIT Press, 1976).

Sources

The estimate that the average high school student knows 60,000 'basic' words comes from *The Language Instinct* by Steven Pinker (New York: Morrow), p. 150. The introduction to words and morphemes draws on the classic treatments found in L. Bloomfield's *Language* (New York: Holt, Rinehart and Winston, 1933), Gleason's *An Introduction to Descriptive Linguistics* (cited below), and C. F. Hockett's *A Course in Modern Linguistics* (New York: Macmillan, 1958). The discussion of word formation seeks to portray those aspects of recent and current work that represent widely accepted views and are appropriate for presentation in an introductory textbook. Much of this work is summarized in the books by Jensen, Katamba, and Spencer (cited below) and the many references cited therein.

The Arabic examples in Section 1.3 are from p. 17 of the book by Spencer cited below. The tier-based analysis of Arabic word structure is based on work by John McCarthy, including his article "A Prosodic Theory of Nonconcatenative Morphology," *Linguistic Inquiry* 12:373–418 (1981). The facts concerning the requirement that *-ant* combine with a base of Latin origin (Section 2.2) are noted on p. 71 of the book by Katamba cited below.

The example of Chukchee incorporation in Section 3.3 is from p. 15 of the book by Spencer, cited below. The Ponapean example is from p. 212 of *A Ponapean Reference Grammar* by Kenneth Rehg (Honolulu: University of Hawaii Press, 1981).

The examples of conversion given in Section 4.1 come largely from the discussion in the books by Jensen (pp. 92–93) and Bauer (pp. 229–30) cited below. The data on Slavey onomatopoeia are from "Slavey Expressive Terms" by M. Pepper, *Kansas Working Papers in Linguistics* 10:85–100 (1985).

The definition of *stem* introduced in Section 5 is from the article by S. Anderson cited below (p. 163). The discussion of the difference between regular and irregular inflection draws on information from "Rules of Language" by Steven Pinker, *Science* 253:530–35 (Aug. 1991). The Nancowry example in the section on number was provided by R. Radhakrishnan. The data in the section on tense come principally from "Tense, Aspect and Mood" by S. Chung and A. Timberlake in *Language Typology and Syntactic Description,* Vol. 3, edited by T. Shopen (London: Cambridge University Press, 1985), pp. 202–58.

The questions for this chapter were prepared by Joyce Hildebrand. The data in problem 7 are from *Writing Transformational Grammars* by A. Koutsoudas (New York: McGraw-Hill, 1966).

Recommended reading

Anderson, Stephen. 1988. "Morphological Theory." In *Linguistics: The Cambridge Survey.* Vol. 1. Edited by F. Newmeyer, 146–91. London: Cambridge University Press.

Bauer, L. 1983. *English Word-Formation.* New York: Cambridge University Press.

Carstairs-McCarthy, Andrew. 1992. *Contemporary Morphology.* London: Routledge.

Gleason, H. 1955/1961. *An Introduction to Descriptive Linguistics.* New York: Holt, Rinehart and Winston.

Jensen, John. 1990. *Morphology: Word Structure in Generative Grammar.* Amsterdam: John Benjamins.

Katamba, Francis. 1993. *Morphology*. London: Macmillan.

Spencer, Andrew. 1991. *Morphological Theory.* Cambridge, MA: Blackwell.

Appendix: How to identify morphemes in unfamiliar languages

One part of morphological analysis involves identifying morphemes in unfamiliar languages and determining the nature of the information that they carry. (A number of the problems in the set of exercises that follow this chapter will give you an opportunity to practice this type of analysis.) The key procedure to use in working on this sort of problem can be stated simply as follows:

- Identify recurring strings of sounds and match them with recurring meanings.

Consider in this regard the following small sample of data from Turkish, consisting of four words along with their English translations. (A more realistic data sample would not only be much larger, but would also include sentences in which it might well be unclear where the word boundaries should be placed.)

Table 4.35 Some Turkish words

/mumlar/	'candles'
/toplar/	'guns'
/adamlar/	'men'
/kitaplar/	'books'

As you can probably see, the string of sounds /lar/ occurs in all four items in our sample. From the translations of these items, we can see that there is also a feature of meaning—namely, plurality—that is present in all four cases. Using the procedure just stated, we therefore hypothesize that /lar/ is the morpheme marking plurality in Turkish. Once this has been determined, we can then infer that /mum/ in /mumlar/ is also a morpheme (presumably with the meaning 'candle'), that /top/ in /toplar/ is a morpheme (with the meaning 'gun'), and so on. A larger sampling of Turkish data would confirm the correctness of these inferences.

In doing morphological analysis in unfamiliar languages, there are a number of pitfalls to avoid. For the type of data normally investigated at the introductory level, the following guidelines should prove especially useful.

- Do not assume that the morpheme order in the language you are analyzing is the same as in English. In Korean, for example, morphemes indicating location (the rough equivalent of 'at', 'in', and so forth) follow rather than precede the noun (hence, *hakkyo-eyse* is literally 'school at').

- Do not assume that every semantic contrast expressed in English will also be manifested in the language you are analyzing. In Turkish, for example, there is no equivalent for English *the* and *a*. In Mandarin Chinese, the same pronoun form can be used to refer to a male or a female (there is no *he-she* distinction).

- Do not assume that every contrast expressed in the language you are analyzing is manifested in English. For example, some languages distinguish more than two number categories (Inuktitut distinguishes singular, dual, and plural; see Section 6.1) and some languages make multiple tense contrasts (ChiBemba, discussed in Section 6.5, has an eight-way distinction).

- Remember that a morpheme can have more than one form (allomorph). Just as the English plural suffix can be realized as /s/, /z/, or /əz/ (Section 1.1), so morphemes in other languages can have more than one realization. For example, further study of Turkish would reveal that the plural suffix in this language can also be realized as /ler/, depending on the vowel in the base to which the suffix is attached. (This type of variation is discussed in more detail in Chapter 6.)

Questions

1. Consider the following words and answer the questions below.

a) fly	f) reuse	k) spiteful	p) preplan
b) desks	g) triumphed	l) suite	q) optionality
c) untie	h) delight	m) fastest	r) prettier
d) tree	i) justly	n) deform	s) mistreat
e) dislike	j) payment	o) disobey	t) premature

   i) For each word, determine whether it is simple or complex.
   ii) Circle all of the bound morphemes. Underline all of the roots.

2. All but one of the following Persian words consist of more than one morpheme. (*Note*: *xar* means 'buy' and *-id* designates the past tense.)

a) xaridam	'I bought'
b) xaridi	'you (sg) bought'
c) xarid	'(he) bought'
d) naxaridam	'I did not buy'
e) namixaridand	'they were not buying'
f) naxaridim	'we did not buy'
g) mixarid	'(he) was buying'
h) mixaridid	'you (pl) were buying'

   i) Try to match each of the following notions with a morpheme in the Persian data.

a) I	e) they
b) you (sg)	f) not
c) we	g) was/were + -ing (continuous)
d) you (pl)	

   ii) How would you say the following in Persian?
   a) They were buying.
   b) You (sg) did not buy.
   c) You (sg) were buying.

3. The following Turkish data involve allomorphic variation.

a) lokanta	'a restaurant'	lokantada	'in/at a restaurant'
b) kapɨ	'a door'	kapɨda	'in/at a door'
c) randevu	'an appointment'	randevuda	'in/at an appointment'
d) baʃ	'a head'	baʃta	'in/at a head'
e) kitap	'a book'	kitapta	'in/at a book'
f) koltuk	'an armchair'	koltukta	'in/at an armchair'
g) taraf	'a side'	tarafta	'in/at a side'

   i) Does the Turkish morpheme meaning 'in/at' have more than one allomorph?
   ii) If so, what are the allomorphs? Describe their distribution as generally as possible.

4. Consider the following words.

a) desks	e) triumphed	i) preplan (V)	m) optionality
b) untie	f) ageless	j) fastest	n) prettier
c) invalid (A)	g) justice	k) reuse	o) mistreat
d) dislike (V)	h) payment	l) disobey	p) preview (V)

i) Draw a tree structure for each word.

ii) For the word *optionality*, what is the base for the affix *-ion*? What is the base for the suffix *-ity*? Are either of these bases also the root for the entire word? If so, which one?

5. Each of the following columns illustrates a different morphological process.

Column 1	*Column 2*	*Column 3*
a) mouse/mice	f) go/went	k) récord/recórd
b) dive/dove	g) is/was	l) ímport/impórt
c) take/took	h) good/better	m) cónvict/convíct
d) man/men	i) she/her	n) ímprint/imprínt
e) eat/ate	j) am/are	o) óutrage/outráge

i) What morphological process is at work in column 1? column 2? column 3?

ii) Describe in your own words the difference between the process exemplified in column 1 versus that in column 2.

iii) Think of at least one more English example to add to each column.

6. The following words can be either nouns or verbs.

a) record	f) outline	k) report
b) journey	g) convict	l) assault
c) exchange	h) imprint	m) answer
d) remark	i) reply	n) import
e) surprise	j) retreat	o) cripple

i) For each word, determine whether stress placement can be used to make the distinction between noun and verb.

ii) Think of two more English examples illustrating the process of stress shift to mark a category distinction.

7. The following Samoan data illustrate one of the morphological processes discussed in this chapter.

a) mate	'he dies'	mamate	'they die'
b) nofo	'he stays'	nonofo	'they stay'
c) galue	'he works'	galulue	'they work'
d) tanu	'he buries'	tatanu	'they bury'
e) alofa	'he loves'	alolofa	'they love'
f) taoto	'he lies'	taooto	'they lie'
g) atamaʔi	'he is intelligent'	atamamaʔi	'they are intelligent'

i) What morphological process is illustrated by these data?

ii) Describe the process in your own words.

iii) If 'he is strong' in Samoan is *malosi*, how would you say 'they are strong' in Samoan?

8. The following data from Agta (spoken in the Philippines) illustrate a specific type of affix.

a) dakal	'big'	dumakal	'grow big, grow up'
b) darag	'red'	dumarag	'redden'
c) furaw	'white'	fumuraw	'become white'

i) What is the affix in Agta meaning 'become X'?
ii) What type of affix is it?
iii) Describe its placement.

9. The following words from Chamorro, spoken in Guam and the Mariana Islands, illustrate some of the morphological processes described in this chapter.

I. *Root*		*Derived word*	
a) adda	'mimic'	aadda	'mimicker'
b) kanno	'eat'	kakanno	'eater'
c) tuge	'write'	tutuge	'writer'

II. *Root*		*Derived word*	
d) atan	'look at'	atanon	'nice to look at'
e) sangan	'tell'	sanganon	'tellable'
f) guaija	'love'	guaijajon	'lovable'
g) tulaika	'exchange'	tulaikajon	'exchangeable'
h) chalek	'laugh'	chalekon	'laughable'
i) ngangas	'chew'	ngangason	'chewable'

III. *Root*		*Derived word*	
j) nalang	'hungry'	nalalang	'very hungry'
k) dankolo	'big'	dankololo	'very big'
l) metgot	'strong'	metgogot	'very strong'
m) bunita	'pretty'	bunitata	'very pretty'

i) What morphological process is involved in I? in II? in III?
ii) Do any changes in lexical category take place in I? in II? in III?
iii) Formulate a general statement as to how the derived words in I are formed. Does the same statement apply to the derived words in III? If not, how would you change the statement to account for the forms in III?
iv) Does the affix in II have more than one allomorph? If so, what are the allomorphs? What is their distribution?

10. In this chapter, an argument was presented in favor of the following structure for the word unhappiness.

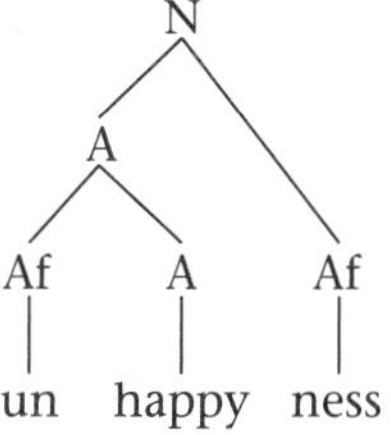

Using the same type of argument, justify tree structures for the words *incomprehensible, redisposal,* and *disestablishment.*

(*Hint:* This will involve determining the type of syntactic category with which the affixes in these words can combine; see Table 4.12.)

11. In English, the suffix *-er* can be added to a place name. Examine the words in the two columns below.

Column 1	*Column 2*
Long Islander	*Denverer
Vermonter	*Philadelphiaer
New Yorker	*San Franciscoer
Newfoundlander	*Torontoer
Londoner	*Miamier

i) In general terms, what does the suffix *-er* mean in these words?
ii) How is this *-er* different in meaning from the *-er* found in the words *skater* and *walker*?
iii) As is shown in Column 2, the distribution of *-er* in the above data is restricted in some way. State the constraint in your own words.
iv) Does this constraint also apply to the type of *-er* used in the word *skater*? (*Hint*: What would you call 'one who discovers' or 'one who ploughs'?)

12. The following words have all been formed by compounding. Draw a tree structure for each word. If you are in doubt as to the lexical category of the compound, remember that the category of the head determines the category of the word.

a) football	i) tree trunk	q) hockey match
b) billboard	j) lead free	r) coffee table
c) sunbath	k) shortstop	s) flower-power
d) in-crowd	l) girlfriend	t) blueprint
e) fast food	m) city center	u) Greenpeace
f) software	n) failsafe	v) space ship
g) freeze-dry	o) potato peel	w) brain dead
h) overbook	p) bitter-sweet	x) kill-joy

13. In this chapter, several ways of identifying compounds were discussed. Using the tests given in the lefthand column, verify the compound status of the forms in the righthand column.

Test	*Compound*
past tense	blow-dry
compatibility with *very*	loudmouth
plural	headlamp
stress	poorhouse

14. Examine the following compounds and answer the questions below.

Column 1	*Column 2*
a) loudmouth	h) cutthroat
b) skinhead	i) pickpocket
c) kill-joy	j) spoilsport
d) bath towel	k) crybaby
e) death blow	l) brain dead
f) bird-brain	m) blow-dry
g) Walkman	n) armchair

i) For each of the compounds in Column 1, determine whether they are endocentric or exocentric.

ii) How do you form the plural of *Walkman* and *loudmouth*?
(*Hint*: see Table 4.20. Also, pay special attention to the pronunciation of *mouth*. Is it any different here than when it is an independent word?)

15. The words in Column 2 have been created from the corresponding word in Column 1. Indicate the word formation process responsible for the creation of each word in Column 2.

	Column 1		*Column 2*
a)	automation	→	automate
b)	humid	→	humidifier
c)	information, entertainment	→	infotainment
d)	love, seat	→	loveseat
e)	(to) reject	→	(a) reject
f)	typographical error	→	typo
g)	aerobics, marathon	→	aerobathon
h)	act	→	deactivate
i)	curve, ball	→	curve ball
j)	methamphetamine	→	meth
k)	(a) comb	→	comb (your hair)
l)	beef, buffalo	→	beefalo
m)	random access memory	→	RAM
n)	megabyte	→	meg
o)	teleprinter, exchange	→	telex
p)	influenza	→	flu
q)	They have finished	→	They've finished

16. Here are five instances where a new word is needed. Create a word for each of these definitions using the word formation process suggested. Fill in the blanks with your new words.
    a) Use an acronym to make a new word for your uncle's second oldest brother.
    "We visited my ____________ at Christmas."
    b) Use onomatopoeia to make a new word for the sound of a coffee percolator at work.
    "I can't concentrate because my perc is ___________ing."
    c) Use conversion to make a new word for wrapping something breakable in bubbles.
    "You'd better ___________ that ornament or else it might break."
    d) Use a compound to make a new word for the annoying string of cheese stretching from a slice of hot pizza to one's mouth.
    "As the _______________ hung precariously from my lips, our eyes met!"
    e) Use backformation to make a new word for the action of backformation.
    "We had to __________________ words in Linguistics today."

17. Create new words for each of the following situations.
    a) Use a product name to make a new word for the act of scrubbing with Ajax.
    "I __________ed the tub after giving Fido a bath."
    b) Use a proper name to make a new word for the act of breaking dishes, which Jonathan does regularly.
    "He's going to _____________ize all of my best dishes."

c) Use clipping to make a new word for a course in ovinology (the study of sheep).
"Have you done your ____________ assignment yet?"
d) Use derivation to make a new word for being able to be contacted.
"The counsellor is not very ______________."
e) Use a blend to make a new word for a hot drink made with milk and nutmeg.
"I'll have a ___________ and two peanut butter cookies, please."

18. Determine whether the words in each of the following groups are related to one another by processes of inflection or derivation.
a) go, goes, going, gone
b) discover, discovery, discoverer, discoverable, discoverability
c) lovely, lovelier, loveliest
d) inventor, inventor's, inventors, inventors'
e) democracy, democrat, democratic, democratize

19. The following sentences contain both derivational and inflectional affixes. Underline all of the derivational affixes and circle the inflectional affixes.
a) The farmer's cows escaped.
b) It was raining.
c) Those socks are inexpensive.
d) Jim needs the newer copy.
e) The strongest rower continued.
f) The pitbull has bitten the cyclist.
g) She quickly closed the book.
h) The alphabetization went well.

For the student linguist

BAMBIFICATION

Well, of course language is productive. You can't possibly read this chapter without being completely convinced of how very easy it is to make up new words. Morphological productivity is mildly interesting when you're creating transparent new words, such as when you have a verb like *fax* and create a new verb like *refax* (fax again) or *speed-fax* (fax fast) or an adjective like *faxable* (can be faxed), but it's not exactly earth-shattering.

What amazes me, though, is running across a new word, knowing it's a perfectly good word in English, knowing exactly how to pronounce it, and not having a clue about what it means. I'm not talking about knowing *frete* could be a word because it doesn't break any phonological rules of English. I'm talking about a word whose meaning remains mysterious even though that word can be broken down into recognizable, meaningful parts. Take the word *Brazilification,* which appears in Douglas Couplan's novel *Generation X. Brazilification* might appear in a sentence like "The recent Brazilification seen in the U.S. will have a large impact on tax reform plans." *Brazilification* could mean "the replacement of forests with cattle ranches," or "the improved quality of coffee," or many other things; it actually means "the widening gulf between the rich and the poor and the accompanying disappearance of the middle classes" (p. 11). From this, the meaning of *Brazilify* is transparent: make the gulf between the rich and the poor wider, thereby causing the disappearance of the middle classes.

Now consider *Bambification,* another morphologically complex word from Coupland's book. It means "make like X", where X is a variable which can be replaced by *Brazil,* or *Bambi,* or some other noun. *Bambification* doesn't mean "make like Bambi's economic system," although theoretically it could. It means "the mental conversion of flesh and blood living creatures into cartoon characters possessing bourgeois Judeo-Christian attitudes and morals" (p. 48).

Morphology is even more interesting when you look at compounds. The four words below, also gleaned from *Generation X,* could each be interpreted in a few ways. For each word, I've given the real definition and my own, made-up definition (Coupland's are made-up too, but his were first, so I count them as the real definitions). I've also given the morphological structure that matches one of the definitions. Your task is to figure out how the structure would be different (if it is) for the other definition.

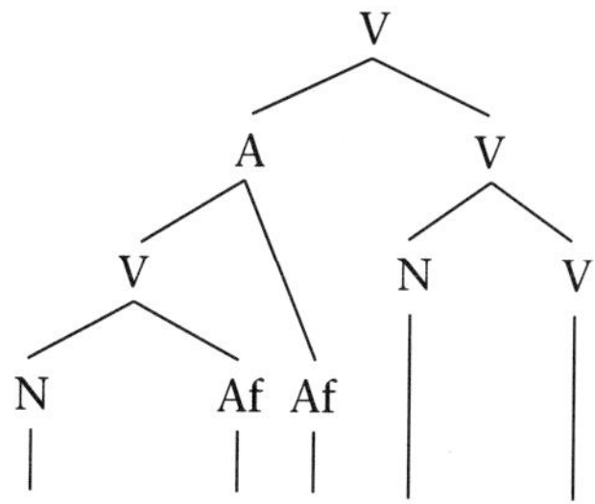

VACCIN ATE D TIME TRAVEL
To fantasize about traveling backward in time, but only with the proper vaccinations. (p. 11)

VACCINATED TIME TRAVEL
To travel freely in time, but only to times and places worth going to.

GREEN DIVISION
Sorting waste into chic recycling bins, showing how environmentally aware you are to all your friends.

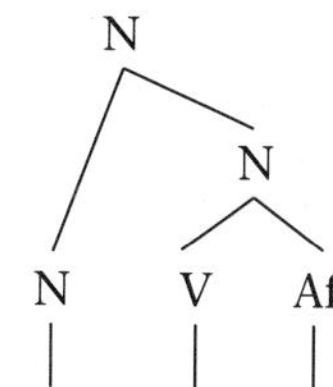

GREEN DIVIS ION
Knowing the difference between envy and jealousy. (p. 150)

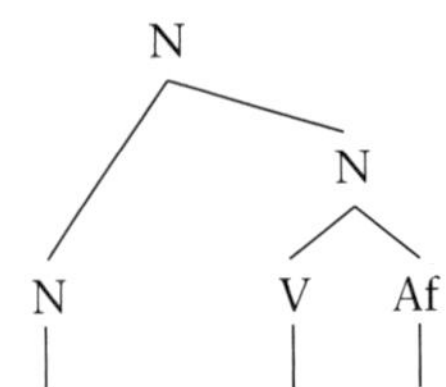

DUMPSTER CLOCK ING
The tendency when looking at objects to guesstimate the amount of time they will take to eventually decompose: *"Ski boots are the worst. Solid plastic. They'll be around till the sun goes supernova."* (p. 162)

DUMPSTER CLOCKING
Reckoning time by the amount and nature of the contents of the dumpster. *"An old couch, three textbooks, and twenty pounds of notebooks beneath a case of empties. Must be late May."*

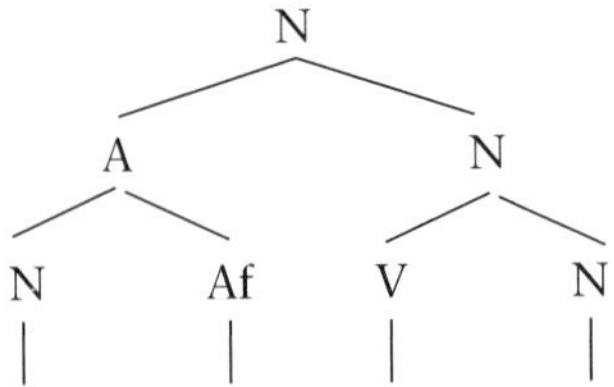

TERMINAL WANDERLUST
The inescapable urge, when seated at a computer, to do *anything* else as long as it involves getting away from the machine. Often involves coffee and cigarettes.

TERMIN AL WANDER LUST
A condition common to people of transient middle-class upbringings. Unable to feel rooted in any one environment, they move continually in the hopes of finding an idealized sense of community in the next location. (p. 171)

five

SYNTAX: THE ANALYSIS OF SENTENCE STRUCTURE

William O'Grady

. . . the game is to say something new with old words . . .

– RALPH WALDO EMERSON, *Journals* (1849)

One of the main themes of this book is that language use involves an intricate system of largely subconscious grammatical knowledge. Nowhere is this more obvious than in the study of how words are combined to form sentences. In this chapter we will consider the system of rules and categories that underlies sentence formation in human language. This component of the grammar is called **syntax**.

Like the other linguistic systems considered in this book, the syntactic component of the grammar is both creative and systematic. As noted in Chapter 1, speakers of a language are able to combine words in novel ways, forming sentences that they have neither heard nor seen before. However, not just any combination of words will give a well-formed sentence. English speakers recognize that the pattern in *1)* is not permissible even though the same words can be combined in a different way to form the acceptable structure in *2)*.

1)

*House painted student a the.

2)

A student painted the house.

We say that an utterance is **grammatical** if speakers judge it to be a possible sentence of their language. Thus, example *2)* is a grammatical sentence of English, but *1)* is not.

This chapter will focus on the 'architecture' of grammatical sentences, with an emphasis on the manner in which words are combined to form various types of structures. Section 1 introduces some of the most common categories of words found in language as well as some simple rules that govern the organization of these categories into larger structural units. Subsequent sections describe other aspects of sentence structure, using examples and phenomena drawn from English and other languages.

Contemporary linguistic research has yet to reach a consensus about precisely how sentence structure should be analyzed and a variety of quite different possibilities are currently being explored. This chapter will introduce a simple version of **transformational syntax**, currently the most popular and best known approach to syntactic analysis. Although many linguists disagree with various features of this approach, it is very widely used in linguistics and other disciplines concerned with language (especially cognitive science). For this reason, it is the usual point of departure for introductions to the study of sentence structure. Section 6 provides a brief discussion of some alternatives to transformational analysis.

1 CATEGORIES AND STRUCTURE

A fundamental fact about words in all human languages is that they can be grouped together into a relatively small number of classes, called **syntactic categories**. This classification reflects a variety of factors, including the type of meaning that words express, the type of affixes that they take, and the type of structures in which they can occur.

1.1 WORD-LEVEL CATEGORIES

Table 5.1 provides examples of the word-level categories that are most central to the study of syntax.

Table 5.1 Syntactic categories

Lexical categories	*Examples*
Noun (N)	Harry, boy, wheat, policy, moisture, bravery
Verb (V)	arrive, discuss, melt, hear, remain, dislike
Adjective (A)	good, tall, old, intelligent, beautiful, fond
Preposition (P)	to, in, on, near, at, by
Adverb (Adv)	silently, slowly, quietly, quickly, now
Non-lexical categories	*Examples*
Determiner (Det)	the, a, this, these
Degree word (Deg)	too, so, very, more, quite
Qualifier (Qual)	always, perhaps, often, never, almost
Auxiliary (Aux)	will, can, may, must, should, could
Conjunction (Con)	and, or, but

The four most studied syntactic categories are **noun (N)**, **verb (V)**, **adjective (A)**, and **preposition (P)**. These elements, which are often called **lexical categories**, play a very important role in sentence formation, as we will soon see. A fifth and less studied lexical category consists of **adverbs (Adv)**, most of which are derived from adjectives.

Languages may also contain **nonlexical** or **functional categories**, including **determiners (Det)**, **auxiliary verbs (Aux)**, **conjunctions (Con)**, and **degree words (Deg)**. Such elements generally have meanings that are harder to define and paraphrase than those of lexical categories. For example, the meaning of the noun *hill* is easier to describe than the meaning of a determiner such as *the* or an auxiliary such as *would*.

A potential source of confusion in the area of word classification stems from the fact that some items can belong to more than one category.

3)

comb used as a noun:
The woman found a comb.

comb used as a verb:
The boy should comb his hair.

4)

near used as a preposition:
The child stood near the fence.

near used as a verb:
The runners neared the finish line.

near used as an adjective:
The end is nearer than you might think.

How, then, can we determine a word's category?

Meaning

One criterion involves meaning. Nouns, for instance, typically name entities such as individuals (*Harry, Sue*) and objects (*book, desk*). Verbs, on the other hand, characteristically designate actions (*run, jump*), sensations (*feel, hurt*), and states (*be, remain*). Consistent with these tendencies, *comb* in *3)* refers to an object when used as a noun but to an action when used as a verb.

The meanings associated with nouns and verbs can be elaborated in various ways. The typical function of an adjective, for instance, is to designate a property or attribute of the entities denoted by nouns. Thus, when we say *That tall building,* we are attributing the property 'tall' to the building designated by the noun.

In a parallel way, adverbs typically denote properties and attributes of the actions, sensations, and states designated by verbs. In the following sentences, for example, the adverb *quickly* indicates the manner of Janet's leaving and the adverb *early* specifies its time.

5)

Janet left quickly.
Janet left early.

Unfortunately, a word's category membership does not always bear such a straightforward relationship to its meaning. For example, there are 'abstract' nouns such as *difficulty*, *truth*, and *likelihood*, which do not name entities in the strict sense. Moreover, even though words that name actions tend to be verbs, some action-naming words can also be used as nouns (*push* and *shove* are nouns in *give someone a push/shove*). Matters are further complicated by the fact that in some cases, words with very similar meanings belong to different categories. For instance, the words *like* and *fond* are very similar in meaning (as in *Mice like/are fond of cheese*), yet *like* is a verb and *fond* an adjective. As we will see later (Section 4.1), this problem becomes even more acute when we consider the fact that languages can differ in terms of how they categorize words with particular types of meanings.

Inflection

Most linguists believe that meaning is only one of several criteria that enter into determining a word's category. A second criterion, compatibility with various types of inflection (see Chapter 4, Section 5), is summarized in Table 5.2.

Table 5.2 Lexical categories and their inflectional affixes

Category	*Inflectional affix*	*Examples*
N	plural *-s*	books, chairs, doctors
	possessive *-'s*	John's, (the) man's
V	past tense *-ed*	hunted, watched, judged
	progressive *-ing*	hunting, watching, judging
A	comparative *-er*	taller, faster, smarter
	superlative *-est*	tallest, fastest, smartest

Although helpful, inflection does not always provide the information needed to determine a word's category. In English, for example, not all adjectives can take the comparative and superlative affixes (**intelligenter*, **beautifulest*) and some nouns do not normally take the plural suffix (*moisture*, *bravery*, *knowledge*).

Distribution

A third and often more reliable criterion for determining a word's category involves the type of elements (especially functional categories) with which it can co-occur (its **distribution**). For example, nouns can typically appear with a determiner, verbs with an auxiliary, and adjectives with a degree word.

Table 5.3 Distributional properties of Ns, Vs, and As

Category	*Distributional property*	*Examples*
Noun	occurrence with a determiner	a car, the wheat
Verb	occurrence with an auxiliary	may go, will stay
Adjective	occurrence with a degree word	very rich, too big

Put another way, a distributional property of nouns is that they can appear with a determiner but not an auxiliary, a distributional property of verbs is that they can appear with an auxiliary but not a determiner, and so forth.

6)

verb with a determiner:
*the destroy

noun with an auxiliary:
*will destruction

Together with information about a word's meaning and its inflectional capabilities, these distributional facts help identify its syntactic category.

1.2 Phrase structure

Sentences are not formed by simply stringing words together like beads on a necklace. Rather, sentences have a hierarchical design in which words are grouped together into successively larger structural units. This section will focus on the nature of the syntactic units built around Ns, Vs, As, and Ps. Such units are called **phrases**.

Heads

Phrases are built around a 'skeleton' consisting of two levels, as depicted below. (The symbol P in the top level stands for 'phrase'.)

Figure 5.1 The organization of phrase structure

Each level of phrase structure can be thought of as a sort of 'hook' (like a hook on a pole) to which elements of different types can be attached.

The lowest level is reserved for the word around which the phrase is built—an N in the case of NPs, a V in the case of VPs, and so on. This element is called the **head** of the phrase. As the following examples show, it is possible to have a phrase in which only the head position is filled. (The material in parentheses provides a context in which these one-word phrases might occur; it is not part of the phrases themselves.)

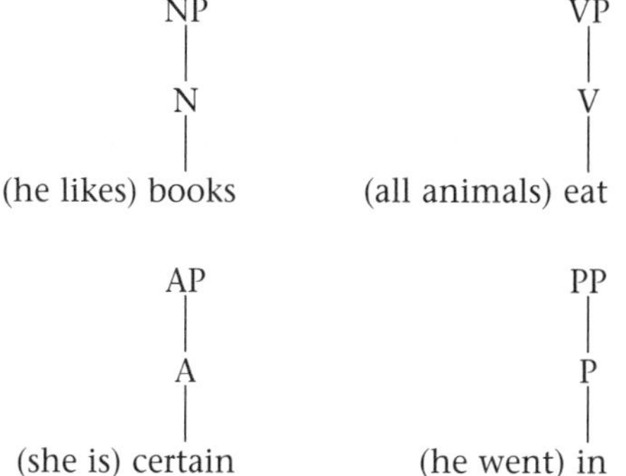

Figure 5.2 Phrases in which only the head position is filled

Although phrases can consist of just one word, they often contain other elements as well. For example:

7)

a. $[_{NP}$ the books]
b. $[_{VP}$ never eat]
c. $[_{AP}$ quite certain]
d. $[_{PP}$ almost in]

In addition to a head (the underlined element), each of these phrases includes a second word that has a special semantic and syntactic role. Such words (determiners such as *the* and *a*, qualifiers such as *never* and *often*, and degree words such as *quite* or *almost*) are said to function as **specifiers**.

Specifiers

Semantically, specifiers help to make more precise the meaning of the head. Hence, the determiner (Det) *the* in *6a)* indicates that the speaker has in mind specific books, the qualifier (Qual) *never* in *6b)* indicates a nonoccurring event, and the degree words (Deg) *quite* and *almost* in *6c, d)* indicate the extent to which a particular property or relation is manifested.

Syntactically, specifiers typically mark a phrase boundary. In English, specifiers occur at the left boundary (the beginning) of their respective phrases. In a tree diagram, they are attached to the top level of phrase structure, to the left of the head. Together, these two elements form the phrase structures depicted in the following tree diagrams.

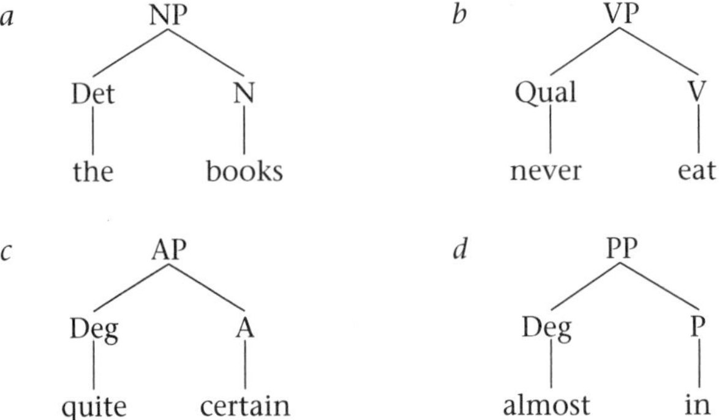

Figure 5.3 Phrases consisting of a head and a specifier

As we will see in Section 4, some languages (Thai, for example) place specifiers at the right boundary (the end) of phrases.

The syntactic category of the specifier differs depending on the category of the head. As the examples in Figure 5.3 help show, determiners serve as the specifiers of Ns while qualifiers typically function as the specifiers of Vs and degree words as the specifiers of As and (some) Ps. Question 3 at the end of the chapter provides practice in identifying specifiers and heads.

Table 5.4 Some specifiers

Category	*Typical function*	*Examples*
Determiner (Det)	specifier of N	the, a, this, those, no
Qualifier (Qual)	specifier of V	never, perhaps, often, always
Degree word (Deg)	specifier of A or P	very, quite, more, almost

Complements

Consider now some examples of slightly more complex phrases.

8)

a. [$_{NP}$ the books about the war]
b. [$_{VP}$ never eat a hamburger]
c. [$_{AP}$ quite certain about Mary]
d. [$_{PP}$ almost in the house]

In addition to a specifier and the underlined head, the phrases in *8)* also contain a **complement**. These elements, which are themselves phrases, provide information about entities and locations whose existence is implied by the meaning of the head. For example, the meaning of *eat* implies an object that is eaten, the meaning of *in* implies a location, and so on.

9)

A vegetarian would never eat [a hamburger].
↑ ↑
head *complement naming the thing eaten*

10)

in [the house]
↑ ↑
head *complement naming a location*

In a tree diagram, complements are attached to the right of the head in English (but to the left in many other languages—see Section 4). Figure 5.4 illustrates the structure of a phrase consisting of a specifier, a head, and a complement. (The NP serving as complement of a V is often called a **direct object**.)

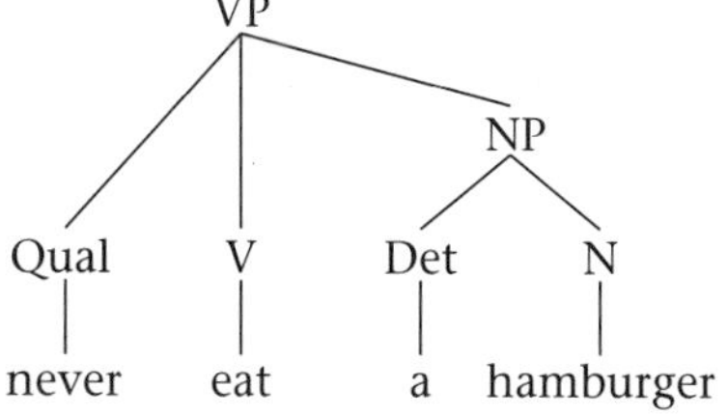

Figure 5.4 A VP consisting of a head, a specifier, and a complement

As noted above, complements are themselves phrases. Thus, the complement of the V *eat* is an NP that itself consists of a determiner (*a*) and a head (*hamburger*). This phrase then combines with the verb and its specifier to form a still larger structural unit.

NPs, APs, and PPs can have a parallel internal structure, as the following examples illustrate. (In order to save space, we do not depict the internal structure of the complement phrases in these examples.)

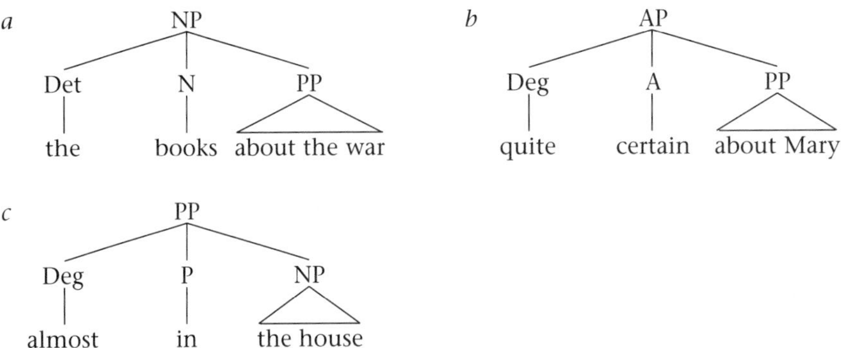

Figure 5.5 Other phrases consisting of a head, a specifier, and a complement

Question 4 at the end of this chapter provides practice in identifying complements.

The rules

How does the grammar ensure that specifiers, heads, and complements occupy the appropriate positions in phrase structure? The arrangement of the elements that make up a phrase is expressed by a special type of grammatical mechanism called a phrase structure rule. The following phrase structure rules stipulate the position of specifiers, heads, and complements in the various types of phrases that we have considered so far. (The arrow can be read as 'consists of' or 'branches into'. The three dots in each rule indicate that other complement options are available; these options will be discussed in Section 2.)

11)

NP → (Det) N (PP) . . .
VP → (Qual) V (NP) . . .
AP → (Deg) A (PP) . . .
PP → (Deg) P (NP) . . .

The first of these rules states that an NP can consist of a determiner, an N head, and a PP complement (as in Figure 5.5a); the second rule captures the fact that a VP can be composed of a qualifier, a V, and an NP complement (as in Figure 5.4); and so on.

As the parentheses in our rules indicate, both specifiers and complements are optional. Thus, a phrase may consist of a specifier, a head, and a complement; a head and a complement; a specifier and a head; or just a head.

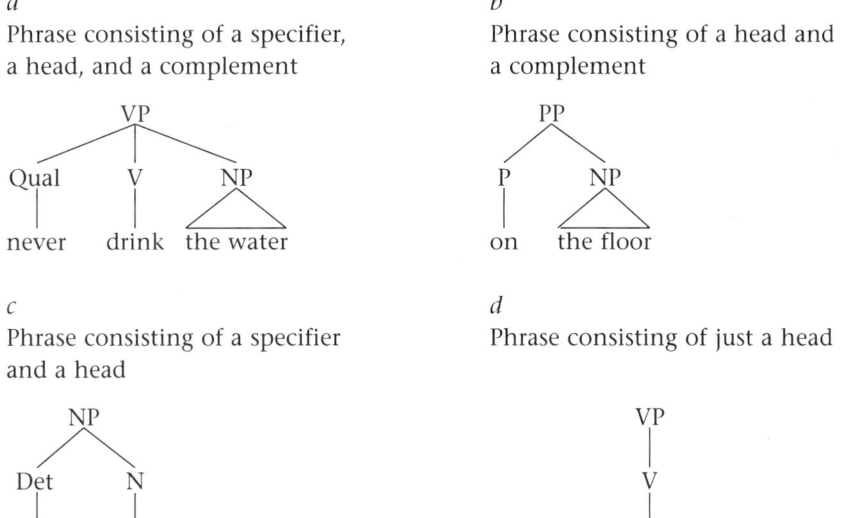

Figure 5.6 Some phrase types. Only the head is present in all patterns.

Generalizing the rules

By now, you will have noticed that there are very obvious structural similarities among the various phrase types exemplified in Figures 5.4 to 5.6. In particular, the specifier precedes the head while the complement follows. These similarities can be summarized with the help of a template, or blueprint, in which X stands for N, V, A, or P.

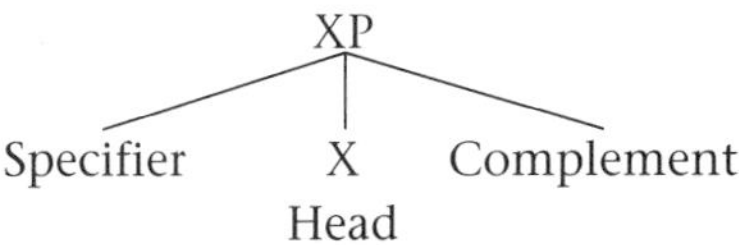

Figure 5.7 The phrase structure template

Instead of having four separate phrase structure rules for the placement of specifiers, heads, and complements, we now can formulate the single general rule in *12)*.

12)

The XP Rule:
XP → (Specifier) X (Complement)

Because the symbol X stands for N, V, A, or P, this rule is an abbreviation for the four separate phrase structure rules given in *11)* above.

The rule in *12)* is more abstract than the four more specific rules that were initially proposed since it makes use of the special symbol X. However, it is also more economical and is able to capture the structural properties shared by the four different phrase types. For these reasons, rules formulated in terms of the X notation are widely used in contemporary syntactic analysis.

1.3 SENTENCES

The largest unit of syntactic analysis is the **sentence** (S). Traditionally, sentences are taken to be the product of the rule in *13)*, which combines an NP (often called the **subject**) with a VP to yield structures such as the one in Figure 5.8.

13)

The S Rule:
S → NP VP

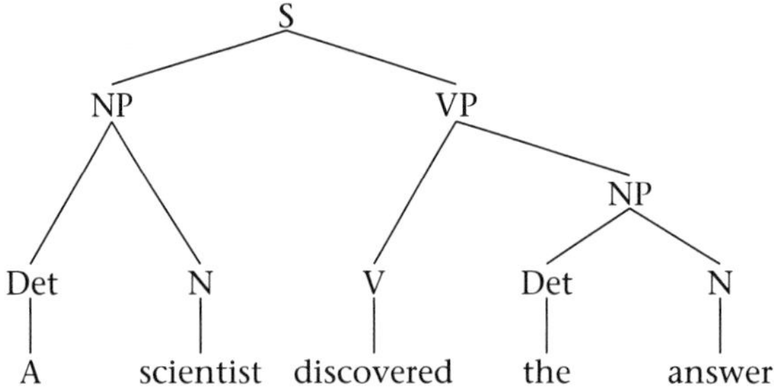

Figure 5.8 The structure of S (traditional view)

This analysis assumes that S is special in not having an internal structure like other phrases (with a head, a complement, and a specifier). However, many linguists now believe that S has the structure depicted in Figure 5.9.

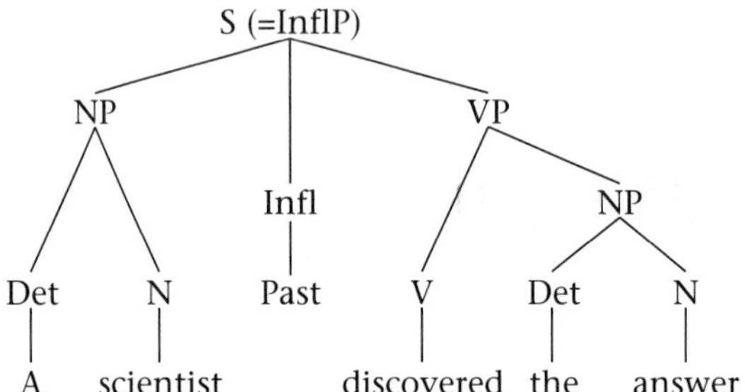

Figure 5.9 The structure of S (popular contemporary view)

According to this idea, sentences have as their head an abstract category dubbed 'Infl', short for 'inflection', which indicates the sentence's tense.[1] Because Infl, like all heads, is obligatory, this automatically accounts for the fact that all sentences of English have tense (e.g., they are either past or nonpast). The rest of sentence structure follows from the fact that Infl takes a VP category as its complement and an NP (the subject) as its specifier. A further advantage of this analysis is that it gives sentences the same internal structure as other phrases and makes them consistent with the XP rule outlined earlier. There is therefore no need for the special S rule in *13).*

Sometimes an actual word can appear in the Infl position. As the next example shows, auxiliary verbs can appear in the head position of sentences and are thus treated as an instance of the Infl category. (Given the long-established meaning of the term *inflection* in morphology, the use of the label 'Infl' by syntacticians to include free forms such as *will* and *can* is unfortunate. However, we will follow this usage here in accordance with the current widespread practice.)

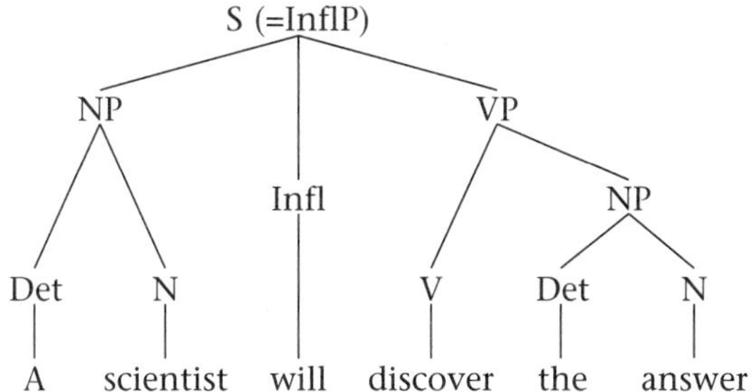

Figure 5.10 An S with an auxiliary in the Infl position

A further justification for treating auxiliaries as a type of Infl is that many words of this type are inherently associated with a particular tense. For example, *will, can,* and *may* are necessarily nonpast, as shown by the unacceptability of patterns such as **He will/can/may work yesterday*. By placing them in the Infl position, we therefore indicate that the sentence is nonpast. (In such cases, it is somewhat redundant to also have a tense label, and we will therefore not include it in our tree structures when an auxiliary is present.)

For the remainder of this chapter, we will adopt the view that sentences have Infl as their head and that this element may be realized as either a tense label (past or nonpast) or an auxiliary.[2] We will continue to use S in this chapter; however, the reader should understand S as an abbreviation for InflP.

The appendix at the end of the chapter outlines a procedure that should help you assign sentences an appropriate tree structure. Question 5 provides an opportunity to practice this procedure.

A look ahead

Thus far in this chapter, we have been concentrating on phrases that consist of specifiers, heads, and complements. However, human language contains other types of syntactic patterns as well. For example, some phrases—called **coordinate structures**—are formed by joining two (or more) elements of the same type with the help of a conjunction such as *and* or *or.*

14)

coordinate structures:

a. [$_{NP}$ a pencil] and [$_{NP}$ a notebook]

b. [$_{N}$ hamburgers] or [$_{N}$ hotdogs]

Still another type of pattern includes a **modifier**, an optional element that describes a property of the head. The most common types of modifiers in English are adjectives (which modify noun heads) and adverbs (which modify verb heads).

15)

a. adjective modifying an N head:
a *good* book

b. adverb modifying a V head:
He slept *soundly.*

We can form sentences containing coordinate structures and modifiers by making relatively small and simple adjustments to our system of phrase structure rules. These adjustments are discussed in Sections 5.1 and 5.2, which can be read now or later at the discretion of the course instructor. We postpone discussion of these matters in favor of some topics in syntactic analysis that go beyond the simple modification of phrase structure rules.

1.4 TESTS FOR PHRASE STRUCTURE

The words that make up a sentence form intermediate structural units called phrases. How do linguists determine which words should be grouped together into phrases? The existence of the syntactic units, or **constituents**, that make up tree structures can be independently verified with the help of special tests. Although we cannot consider all of these tests here, it is possible to give some examples.

The substitution test

Evidence that NPs and VPs are syntactic units comes from the fact that they can often be replaced by an element such as *they, it,* or *do so.* This is illustrated in *16),* where *they* replaces the NP *the citizens* and *do so* replaces the VP *wear ties.* (This is called a **substitution test**.)

16)

a. [$_{NP}$The citizens] rebelled after *they* discovered the truth.
(they = the citizens)

b. The students will [$_{VP}$ wear ties] if the teachers will *do so.*
(do so = wear ties)

The substitution test also confirms that a PP such as *at the corner* is a unit since it can be replaced by a single word in sentences such as *17).*

17)

They stopped [$_{PP}$ at the corner] and we stopped *there* too.
(there = at the corner)

The movement test

A second indication that *at the corner* forms a constituent is that it can be moved as a single unit to a different position within the sentence. (This is called a **movement**

test.) In *18)*, for instance, *at the corner* can be moved from a position after the verb to the beginning of the sentence.

18)

They stopped [$_{PP}$ at the corner] → [$_{PP}$ At the corner], they stopped.

The coordination test

Finally, we can conclude that a group of words forms a constituent if it can be joined to another group of words by a conjunction such as *and*, *or*, or *but*. (This is labelled the **coordination test** since patterns built around a conjunction are called coordinate stuctures; see Section 5.1 below.) Thus, we know that the VP *often sweep the floor* in *19)* is a constituent because it can be joined to another unit by *and* or *but*.

19)

The children [$_{VP}$ often sweep the floor] but [$_{VP}$ never make the bed].

1.5 X' CATEGORIES *(ADVANCED)*

Thus far, we have been assuming that the architecture of phrase structure complies with the blueprint in Figure 5.11, identical to Figure 5.7 above.

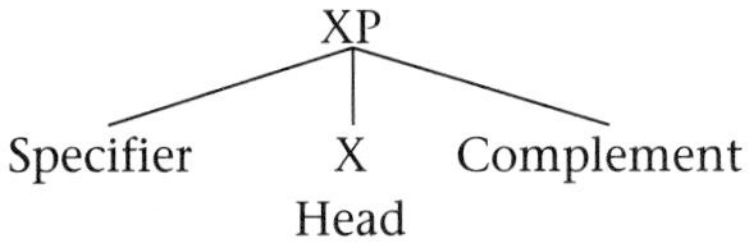

Figure 5.11 The phrase structure template

In fact, however, this is somewhat of a simplification since there is reason to believe that complements and heads may actually be attached to a level of phrase structure midway between the word level and the phrase level, as depicted in Figure 5.12. The intermediate level of structure is represented by the symbol **X'** (pronounced 'X-bar').

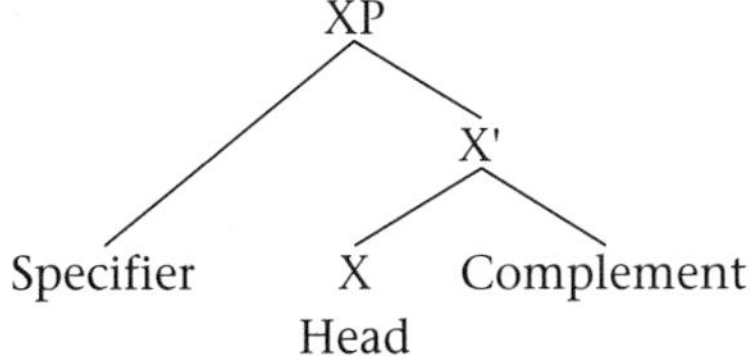

Figure 5.12 The phrase structure template (revised)

According to this viewpoint, then, all phrases have the tri-level structure shown below, in which the head and its complement form an X'-level constituent and the specifier is attached at the higher XP level. (The following example illustrates the internal structure of an S, a VP, and an NP.)

The existence of X' categories can be verified with the help of the same sort of syntactic tests discussed in the previous section. Consider, for example, the V' *educate the public* in Figure 5.13. As the following sentence shows, this unit can be replaced by *do so* and should therefore be a constituent according to the substitution test.

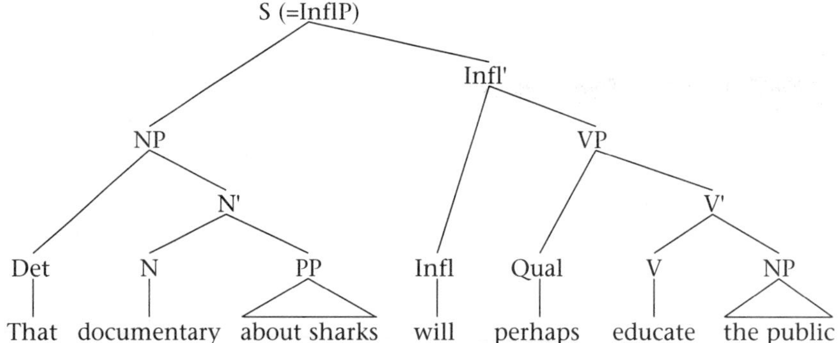

Figure 5.13 Phrase structure with the intermediate X' level

20)

That documentary about sharks will perhaps [$_{V'}$ educate the public], but media reports never *do so*.
(do so = educate the public)

Now consider the N' *documentary about sharks* in Figure 5.13. As the next sentence shows, this unit can be replaced by the element *one.*

21)

That [$_{N'}$ documentary about sharks] is more informative than the previous *one.*
(one = documentary about sharks)

The fact that *one* can replace *documentary about sharks* in this manner confirms that it is a syntactic unit, consistent with the structure in Figure 5.13.

In order to accommodate these new three-level structures, it is necessary to replace our original XP rule by the two phrase structure rules in *22).*

22)

a. XP → (Specifier) X'
b. X' → X (Complement)

The first of these rules stipulates that XP categories such as NP and VP consist of an optional specifier (a determiner, a qualifier, and so forth) and an X'. The second rule then states that an X' (be it an N', a V', or whatever) consists of a head, X, and any complements. Taken together, these two rules form the three-level structure illustrated in Figure 5.13, as desired.

Because three-level structures take up a considerable amount of space and can be tedious to draw, it is common practice to eliminate the intermediate level of phrase structure unless it is absolutely essential to the point being discussed. Since none of the phenomena that we will be considering in this chapter requires an intermediate level of phrase structure, we will not make further use of it here. In order to do more advanced syntactic analysis, though, you will need to be familiar with the X' level.

2 COMPLEMENT OPTIONS

The simple rules outlined in Sections 1.2 and 1.3 can form a very wide variety of phrases and sentences. Much of this variety stems from the fact that human language allows many different complement options.

Information about the complements permitted by a particular word is included in its entry in a speaker's lexicon, or mental dictionary. Thus, the lexicon for English includes an entry for *devour* that indicates its syntactic category (V), its phonological representation, its meaning, and the fact that it must take an NP complement (as in *She devoured the donut*).

23)

devour: category: V
phonological representation: /dəvawr/
meaning: EAT HUNGRILY, . . .
complement: NP

The term **subcategorization** is used to refer to information about a word's complement options.

Subcategorization information interacts with the phrase structure rules to ensure that lexical items appear in the appropriate types of tree structures. Thus, because *devour* belongs to the subcategory of verbs that require an NP complement, it is permitted in the tree structure depicted in Figure 5.14a (where there is an NP complement) but not in the tree structure in Figure 5.14b.

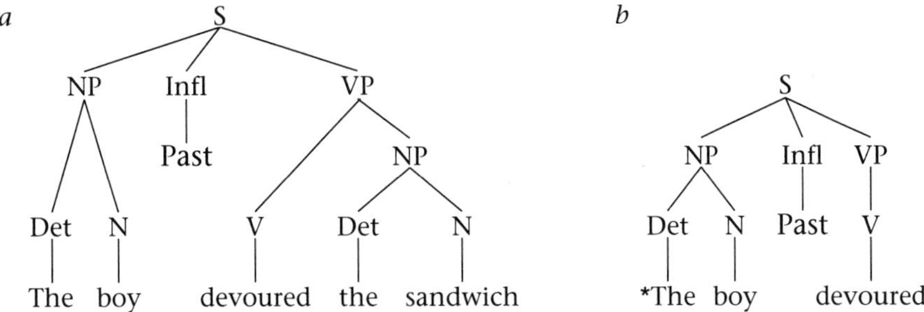

Figure 5.14 Subcategorization determines the type of syntactic structure in which *devour* can occur

Thanks to subcategorization information, heads occur only in tree structures where they have compatible complement phrases.

2.1 COMPLEMENT OPTIONS FOR VERBS

Table 5.5 illustrates some of the more common complement options for verbs in English. The subscripted prepositions indicate the subtype of PP complement, where this is relevant. *Loc* stands for any preposition expressing a location (such as *near, on, under*).

Table 5.5 Some examples of verb complements

Complement option	*Sample heads*	*Example*
Ø	vanish, arrive, die	The child vanished __.
NP	devour, cut, prove	The professor proved $[_{NP}$ *the theorem*].
AP	be, become	The man became $[_{AP}$ *very angry*].
PP_{to}	dash, talk, refer	The dog dashed $[_{PP}$ *to the door*].
NP NP	spare, hand, give	We handed $[_{NP}$ *the man*] $[_{NP}$ *a map*].
NP PP_{to}	hand, give, send	He gave $[_{NP}$ *a diploma*] $[_{PP}$ *to the student*].
NP PP_{for}	buy, cook, reserve	We bought $[_{NP}$ *a hat*] $[_{PP}$ *for Andy*].
NP PP_{loc}	put, place, stand	He put $[_{NP}$ *the muffler*] $[_{PP}$ *on the car*].
PP_{to} PP_{about}	talk, speak	I talked $[_{PP}$ *to a doctor*] $[_{PP}$ *about Sue*].
NP PP_{for} PP_{with}	open, fix	We opened $[_{NP}$ *the door*] $[_{PP}$ *for Andy*] $[_{PP}$ *with a crowbar*].

According to this table, the verbs in the first line (*vanish, arrive,* and *die*) can occur without any complement, those in the second line occur with an NP complement, and so on.

A word can belong to more than one subcategory. The verb *eat,* for example, can occur either with or without an NP complement and therefore belongs to both of the first two subcategories in our table.

24)

After getting home, they ate (the sandwiches).

However, not all verbs exhibit this flexibility. Although *devour* is similar in meaning to *eat,* it requires an explicitly stated complement NP and therefore belongs only to the second subcategory in our table.

25)

a. *devour* without a complement:
*After getting home, they devoured.

b. *devour* with a complement:
After getting home, they devoured the sandwiches.

As the examples in Table 5.5 also show, some heads can take more than one complement. The verb *put* is a case in point, since it requires both an NP complement and a PP complement.

26)

put with an NP complement and a PP complement:
The librarian put [$_{NP}$ the book] [$_{PP}$ on the shelf].

27)

put without an NP complement:
*The librarian put [$_{PP}$ on the shelf].

28)

put without a PP complement:
*The librarian put [$_{NP}$ the book].

The VP *put the book on the shelf* has the structure depicted in Figure 5.15, in which the VP consists of the head *put* and its two complements—the NP *the book* and the PP *on the shelf*.

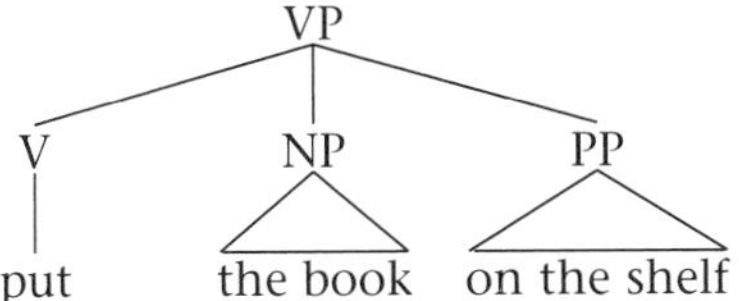

Figure 5.15 A verb with two complements

We can therefore revise our earlier XP rule as follows, using an asterisk after the complement to indicate that one or more of these elements is permitted.

29)

The XP Rule (revised):
XP → (Specifier) X (Complement*)

This rule also captures the simple but important fact that complements (however many there are) follow the head in English.

2.2 Complement options for other categories

Various complement options are also available for Ns, As, and Ps. The following tables provide examples of various possibilities.

Table 5.6 Some examples of noun complements

Complement option	*Sample heads*	*Example*
Ø	car, boy, electricity	the car __
PP_{of}	memory, failure, death	the memory [$_{PP}$ *of a friend*]
PP_{of} PP_{to}	presentation, description, donation	the presentation [$_{PP}$ *of a medal*] [$_{PP}$ *to the winner*]
PP_{with} PP_{about}	argument, discussion, conversation	an argument [$_{PP}$ *with Stella*] [$_{PP}$ *about politics*]

Table 5.7 Some examples of adjective complements

Complement option	*Sample heads*	*Example*
Ø	tall, green, smart	very tall __
PP_{about}	curious, glad, angry	curious [$_{PP}$ *about China*]
PP_{to}	apparent, obvious	obvious [$_{PP}$ *to the student*]
PP_{of}	fond, full, tired	fond [$_{PP}$ *of chocolate*]

Table 5.8 Some examples of preposition complements

Complement option	*Sample heads*	*Example*
Ø	near, away, down	(she got) down __
NP	in, on, by, near	in [$_{NP}$ *the house*]
PP	down, up, out	down [$_{PP}$ *into the cellar*]

Here again, subcategorization ensures that particular heads can appear in tree structures only if there is an appropriate type of complement. Thus, the adjective *curious* (Table 5.7) can occur with an '*about* PP', but the adjective *fond* cannot.

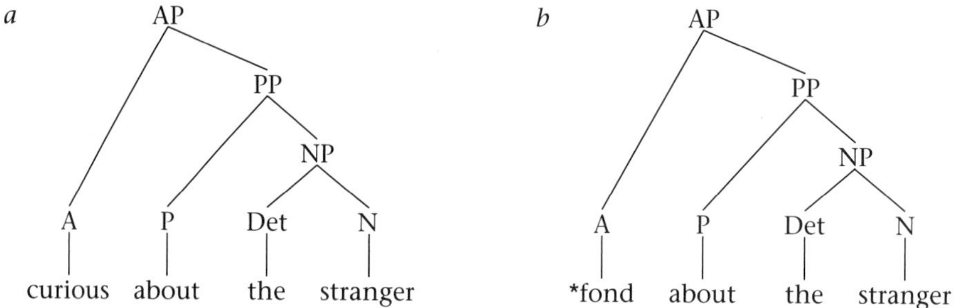

Figure 5.16 Subcategorization permits *curious*, but not *fond*, to take an '*about*-PP' as complement

2.3 Complement clauses

In addition to the complement options considered to this point, languages allow sentence-like constructions to function as complements. A simple example of this from English is given in *30)*.

30)

[The psychic knows [that/whether/if the contestant will win]].

The smaller bracketed phrase in *30)* is called a **complement clause** while the larger phrase in which it is embedded is called the **matrix clause.**

Words such as *that, if,* and *whether* are known as **complementizers** (Cs). They take an S complement, forming the CP (complementizer phrase) structure depicted in Figure 5.17.

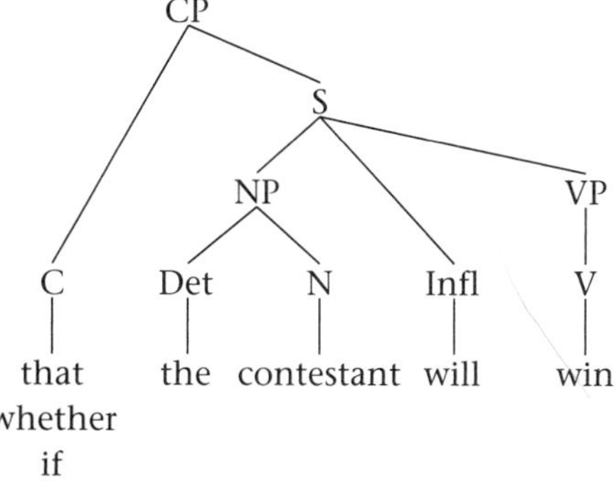

Figure 5.17 The structure of a CP

Although Cs are nonlexical categories, they fit into structures parallel to those found with lexical categories. Thus, the head (C) and its complement (S) together make up an XP category (namely, CP). In Section 3.4, we will see that there is even a type of element that can occur in the specifier position under CP.

When a CP occurs in a sentence such as *30)*, in which it serves as complement of the verb *know*, the entire sentence has the structure in Figure 5.18.

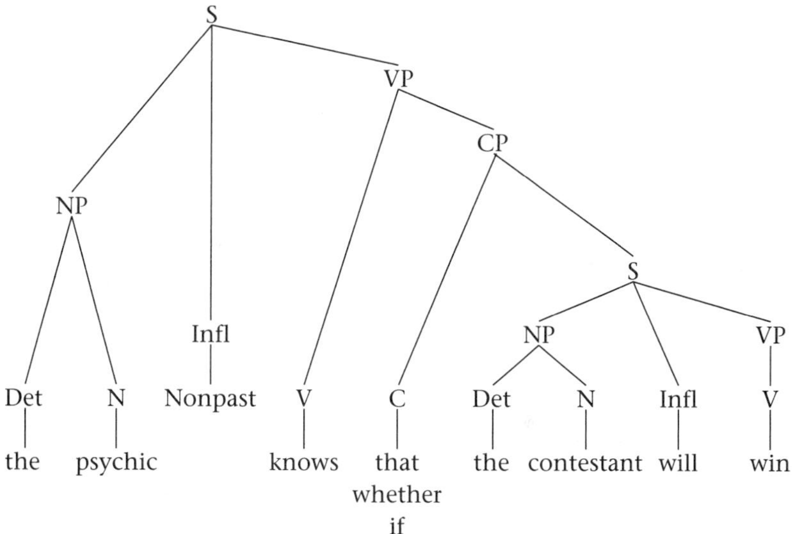

Figure 5.18 The structure of a sentence with an embedded CP

Of course, not all verbs can take a CP complement. Table 5.9 provides examples of some of the verbs that are commonly found with a complement of this type.

There is no limit on the number of embedded clauses that can occur in a sentence, as Figure 5.19 helps to show. This structure is made possible by the fact that each CP complement can contain a verb that itself permits a complement CP. Hence the first clause contains the verb *think*, whose complement clause contains the verb *say*, whose complement clause contains *report*, and so on.

Table 5.9 Some verbs permitting CP complements

Complement(s)	*Sample heads*	*Example*
CP	believe, know, think, remember	They believe [$_{CP}$ *that Mary left*].
NP CP	persuade, tell, convince, promise	They told [$_{NP}$ *Eric*] [$_{CP}$ *that Mary had left*].
PP_{to} CP	concede, admit	They admitted [$_{PP}$ *to Eric*] [$_{CP}$ *that Mary had left*].

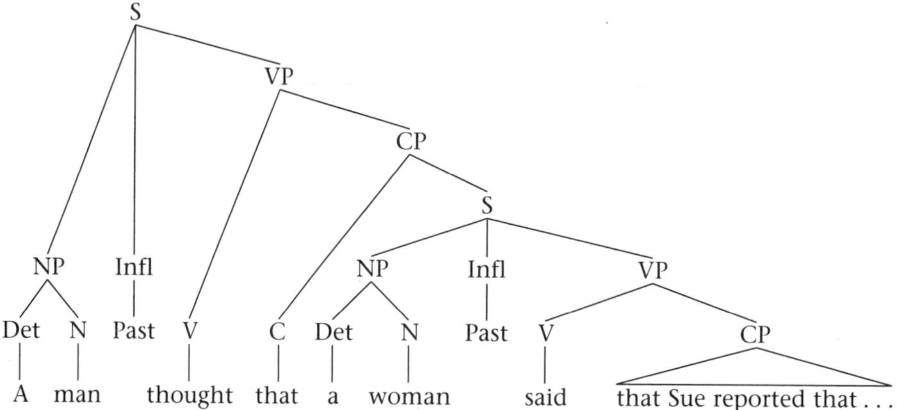

Figure 5.19 The structure of a sentence with more than one embedded CP

Other categories with CP complements *(Advanced)*

As the examples in Figure 5.20 show, a CP may serve as a complement to an N, an A, or a P in addition to a V.

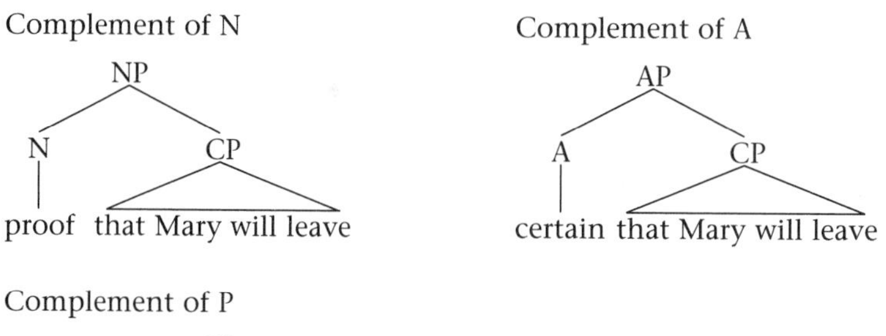

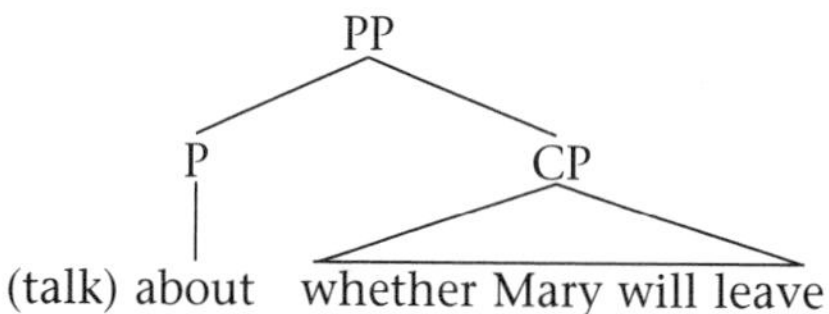

Figure 5.20 N, A, and P with a CP complement

Table 5.10 gives examples of some other adjectives, nouns, and prepositions that can take CP complements.

Table 5.10 Some As, Ns, and Ps permitting CP complements

Items	*Example with CP complement*
Adjectives	
afraid, certain, aware, confident	They are afraid [$_{CP}$ *that Mary left*].
Nouns	
claim, belief, fact, knowledge, proof	They lack proof [$_{CP}$ *that Mary left*].
Prepositions	
over	They argued over [$_{CP}$ *whether Mary had left*].

Although structures of this sort are common in English and other languages, we will restrict our attention in the remainder of this chapter to embedded clauses that are complements of Vs.

3 TRANSFORMATIONS

Even though the phrase structure rule we have been using interacts with the set of complement options permitted by individual heads to form a very wide range of patterns, there are syntactic phenomena that this system cannot describe in an entirely satisfactory way. This section considers two such phenomena and discusses the changes that must be made in order to accommodate them.

3.1 INVERSION IN *YES-NO* QUESTIONS

To begin, let us consider the English *yes-no* questions exemplified in *31)*. (These structures are called *yes-no* questions because the expected response is usually 'yes' or 'no'.)

31)

a. *Will* the girl leave?
b. *Can* the cat climb this tree?

These sentences have an auxiliary verb before the subject, in contrast to the more usual position illustrated in *32)*.

32)

a. The girl *will* leave.
b. The cat *can* climb this tree.

Our XP rule places the auxiliary in the appropriate position in *32)*, but not in *31)*. How does the word order found in *31)* come about?

The question structures that we are considering are built in two steps. In the first step, the usual XP rule is used to form a structure in which the auxiliary occupies its normal position between the subject and the VP.

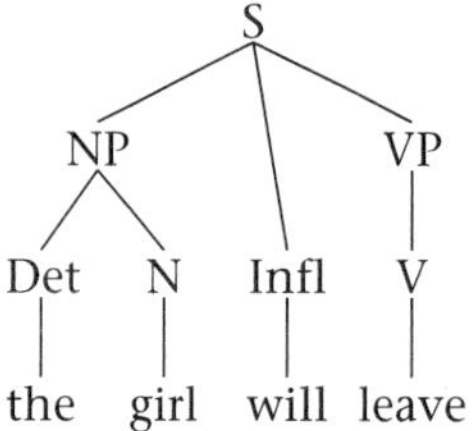

Figure 5.21 *Will* occurring in the head position between the subject (its specifier) and the VP (its complement)

The second step in the formation of question structures requires a **transformation**, a special type of rule that can move an element from one position to another. In the case we are considering, a transformation known as **Inversion** moves the auxiliary from the Infl position to a position in front of the subject. For now, we can formulate this transformation as follows.

33)

Inversion:
Move Infl in front of the subject NP.

Inversion applies to the structure depicted in Figure 5.21, yielding the sentence in *34)* with the auxiliary verb in front of the subject NP—the position appropriate for a question structure. (The arrow shows the movement brought about by Inversion. For now, we will not try to draw a tree diagram for sentences that have undergone a transformation.)

34)

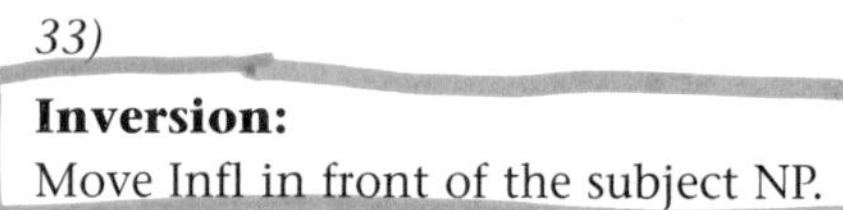

The transformational analysis has at least two advantages. First, we do not have to say that there are two types of auxiliary verbs in English: those that occur at the beginning of the sentence and those that occur in the usual Infl position between the subject and the VP. Rather, we can say that all auxiliaries occur under Infl, consistent with the analysis proposed in Section 1.2. Those sentences that have an auxiliary verb in front of the subject simply undergo an 'extra' process—the Inversion transformation that moves an auxiliary from its original position in order to signal a question.

Second, the transformational analysis automatically captures the fact—known to all speakers of English—that the sentence *Will the girl leave* is the question structure corresponding to *The girl will leave*. According to the analysis presented here, both sentences have exactly the same basic structure. They differ only in that Inversion has applied to move the auxiliary in the question structure.

3.2 Deep structure and surface structure

The preceding examples show that at least some sentences must be analyzed with the help of two distinct types of mechanisms—the XP rule, which determines the internal structure of phrasal categories, and transformations, which can modify these tree structures by moving an element from one position to another. If we think about this in terms of a sentence's architecture, the transformational analysis is claiming that there are two levels of syntactic structure. The first, called **deep structure** (or **D-structure**), is formed by the XP rule in accordance with the head's subcategorization properties. As we will see in the chapter on semantics, deep structure plays a special role in the interpretation of sentences. The second level of syntactic structure corresponds to the final syntactic form of the sentence. Called **surface structure** (or **S-structure**), it results from applying whatever transformations are appropriate for the sentence in question. The deep structure for the question *Will the girl leave?* is given in Figure 5.22.

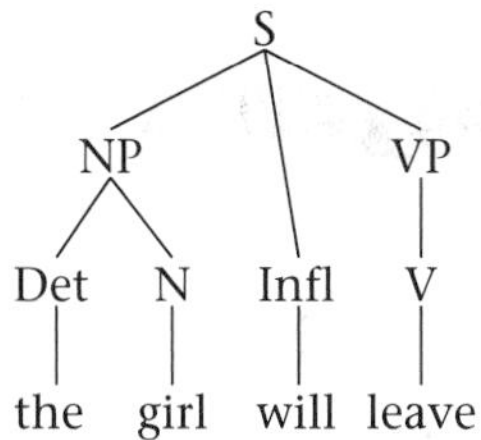

Figure 5.22 The deep structure for the question *Will the girl leave?*

The surface structure for the question pattern is then formed by applying the Inversion transformation, yielding *35)*.

35)

Will the girl __ leave?

The following diagram depicts the organization of the syntactic component of the grammar as it has just been outlined.

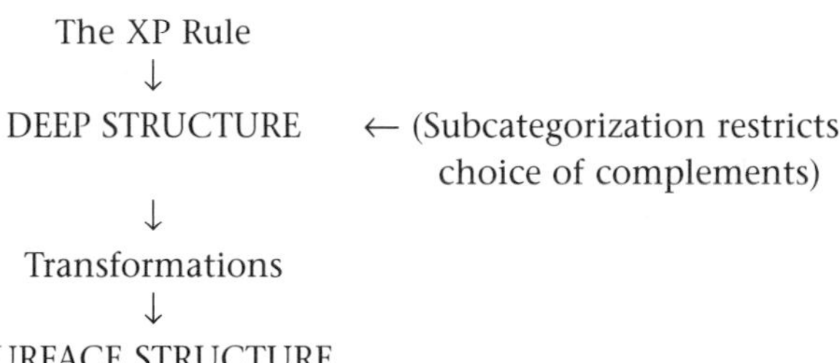

Figure 5.23 The syntactic component of the grammar

As this diagram shows, the grammar makes use of different syntactic mechanisms. Some of these mechanisms are responsible for the architecture of phrases (the XP rule), others for the determination of a head's possible complements (subcategorization), and still others for the movement of categories within syntactic structure (transformations).

3.3 WH MOVEMENT

Consider now the set of question constructions exemplified in *36)*. These sentences are called ***wh* questions** because of the presence of a question word beginning with *wh*.

36)

a. Which car should the man fix?
b. What can the child sit on?

Do the deep structures associated with *36a)* and *36b)* resemble the surface form of these sentences or are they quite different? Within the system of syntactic analysis we are using, the sentences in *36)* have the deep structures illustrated in Figure 5.24. (We treat the *wh* words *who* and *what* as nouns and *which* as a determiner.)

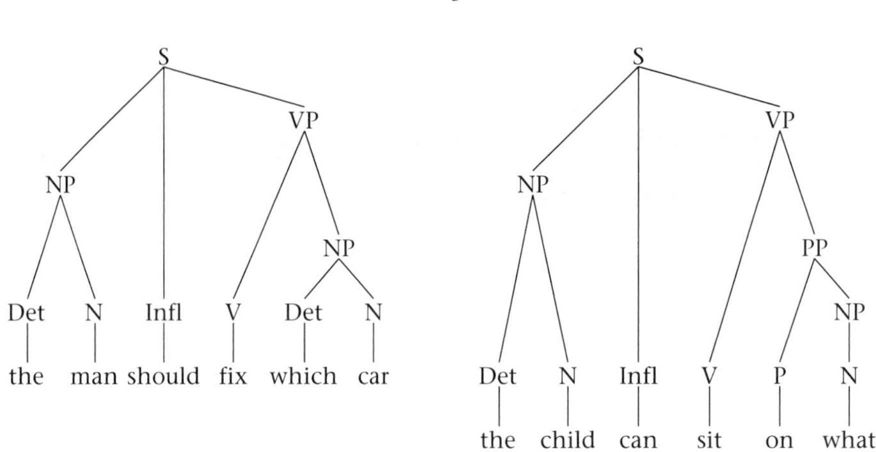

Figure 5.24 The deep structures for two *wh* questions

According to these deep structures, *which car* occurs as complement of the verb *fix* in Figure 5.24a while *what* appears as complement of the preposition *on* in Figure 5.24b. This captures an important fact about the meanings of these sentences since *which car* asks about the thing that was fixed in the first case while *what* asks about the location where the child can sit in the second case.

A second argument in favor of this analysis involves subcategorization. Consider in this regard the following sentences.

37)

a. *The man should fix.
b. *The child can sit on.

Notice that these sentences are somehow incomplete without an NP after *fix* and *on*. However, there is no such problem with the *wh* questions in *36)*, which suggests that the *wh* phrases must be fulfilling the complement function in these sentences. The deep structures in Figure 5.24 express this fact by treating the *wh* phrase as complement of the verb in the first pattern and complement of the preposition in the second.

In order to convert these deep structures into the corresponding surface structures, we need a transformation that will move the *wh* phrase from its position in deep structure to a position at the beginning of the sentence. The transformation in question, called ***Wh* Movement**, can be formulated as follows.

38)

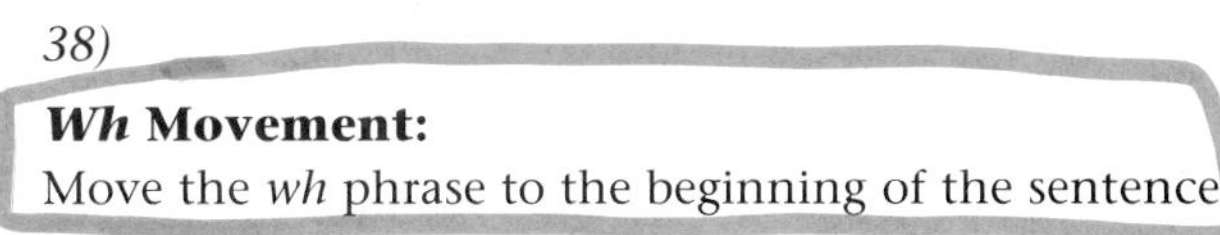

***Wh* Movement:**
Move the *wh* phrase to the beginning of the sentence.

By applying *Wh* Movement and Inversion to the deep structure in Figure 5.24a, we can form the desired question structure.

39)

Which car should the man __ fix __?

Inversion

Wh Movement

Application of the same two transformations to the deep structure in Figure 5.24b yields the *wh* question in *40)*.

40)

What can the child __ sit on __?

3.4 A MORE DETAILED LOOK AT TRANSFORMATIONS (*ADVANCED*)

Up until now, our discussion of transformations has left unsettled an important issue. Reconsider in this regard the simple *yes-no* question exemplified in *41)*.

41)

Will the girl __ leave?

In what position does the auxiliary verb 'land' when it is moved by Inversion in front of the subject? If we assume that sentences such as *41)* are simple Ss, no position is available to the left of the subject, which is the specifier (and hence the first element in the S) according to our analysis.

Another look at Inversion

This problem can be solved if we assume that all Ss occur within larger CPs, as depicted in Figure 5.25.

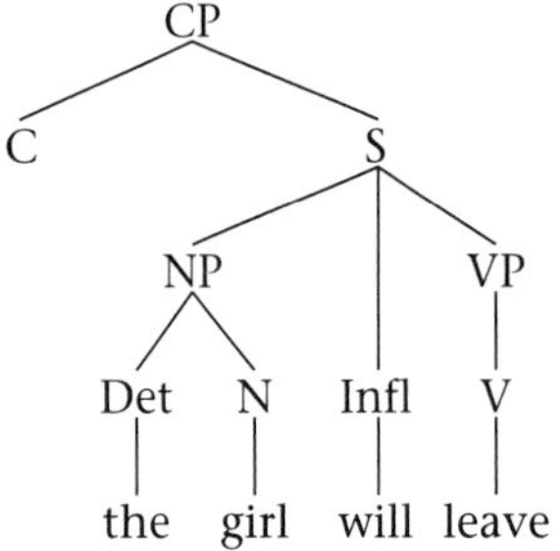

Figure 5.25 An S inside a CP 'shell'

By adopting this structure, we take the position that *all* Ss occur within a CP, whether they are embedded or not. It may help to think of the CP category as a 'shell' that forms an outer layer of structure around an S. When embedded within a larger sentence, the CP can contain an overt complementizer such as *that* or *whether*. Elsewhere, the C position in the CP shell is present but is simply left empty.

It is into this empty position that the auxiliary is moved in *yes-no* questions. Thus, the Inversion transformation can be reformulated as follows.

42)

Inversion (*revised*):
Move Infl to C.

According to this proposal, the sentence *Will the girl leave?* is formed by applying the Inversion transformation to the deep structure in Figure 5.25 above to give the surface structure in Figure 5.26.

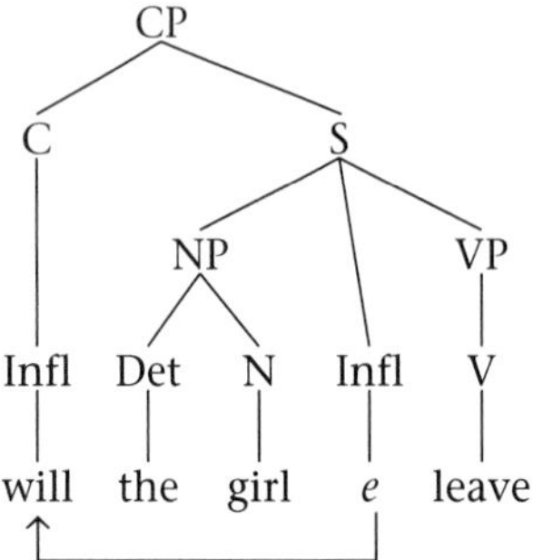

Figure 5.26 Movement of an auxiliary from Infl to C

A transformation can do no more than change an element's position. It does not change the categories of any words and it cannot eliminate any part of the structural configuration created by the phrase structure rules. Thus, *will* retains its Infl label even though it is moved into the C position, and the position that it formerly occupied remains in the tree structure. Marked by the symbol *e* (for 'empty') and called a **trace**, the empty position records the fact that the moved element comes from the head position within S.

Why do we move the auxiliary to the C position rather than some other part of sentence structure? The answer lies in the embedded CPs in sentences such as the following.

43)

a. The coach wonders [$_{CP}$ if the girl should stay].
b. A fan asked [$_{CP}$ whether the team will win].

The underlined elements in these CPs are complementizers and therefore occur in the C position. Assuming that there can be only one element in each position in a tree structure, there should be no room for the moved auxiliary under the C label in the embedded CPs in *43)*. We therefore predict that Inversion should not be able to apply in these cases. The ungrammaticality of the sentences in *44)* shows that this is correct.

44)

Inversion in embedded CPs that include complementizers:
a. *The coach wonders [$_{CP}$ if-should the girl __ stay].
b. *A fan asked [$_{CP}$ whether-will the team __ win].

Interestingly, the acceptability of Inversion in embedded CPs improves quite dramatically when there is no complementizer (and the C position is therefore open to receive the moved auxiliary).

45)

Inversion in embedded CPs that do not have complementizers:
a. The coach wondered [$_{CP}$ should the girl __ stay].
b. A fan asked [$_{CP}$ will the team __ win].

Although many speakers prefer not to apply Inversion in embedded clauses at all (especially in formal speech), even they find the sentences in *45)* to be much more natural than those in *44)*. This is just what we would expect if Inversion must move the auxiliary to an empty C position, as required by our analysis.

To summarize before continuing, we have introduced two changes into the system of syntactic analysis used until now. First, we assume that all Ss occur inside CPs. Second, we assume that the Inversion transformation moves the auxiliary from its position within S to an empty C position in front of the subject NP. This not only gives the correct word order for question structures, it helps explain why Inversion sounds so unnatural when the C position is already filled by another element, as in *44)*.

Do Insertion

As we have just seen, formation of *yes-no* questions in English involves moving the Infl category, and the auxiliary verb that it contains, to the C position. How, then, do we form the questions corresponding to sentences such as those in *46)*, which contain no auxiliary?

46)

a. The students liked the movie.
b. Those birds sing.

Since Infl in these sentences contains only an abstract (i.e., invisible) tense marker, there is nothing for the Inversion transformation to move. English circumvents this problem by adding the special auxiliary verb *do*.

47)

a. *Did* the students like the movie?
b. *Do* those birds sing?

As these examples show, *do* is inserted into sentences that do not already have an auxiliary verb, thereby making Inversion possible. We can capture this fact by formulating an **insertion rule**, an operation that adds an element to a tree structure.

48)

***Do* Insertion:**
Insert interrogative *do* into an empty Infl position.

The sentence in *46b)* can now be analyzed in the following manner.

a Deep structure

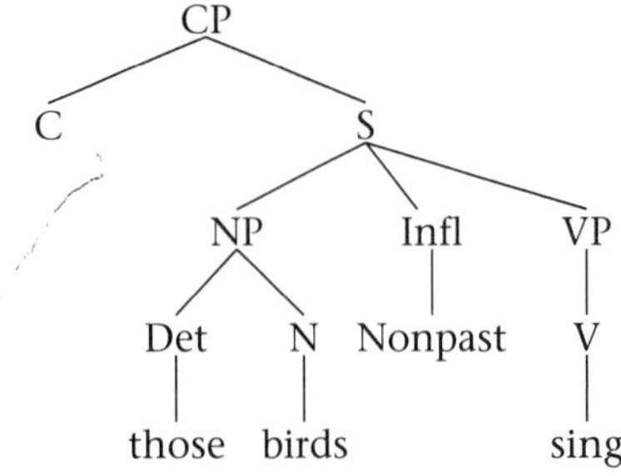

b After *Do* Insertion

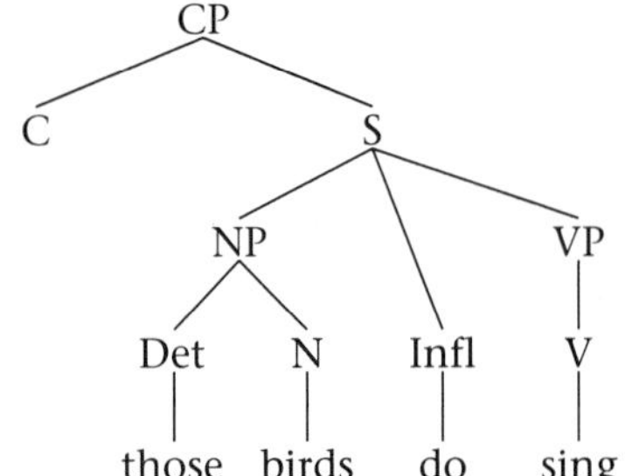

c After Inversion

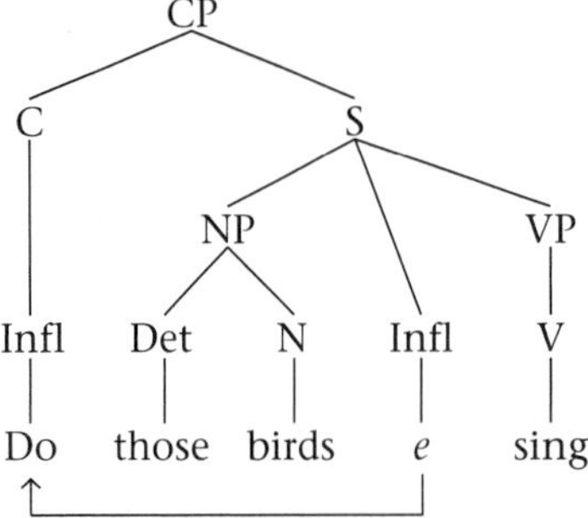

Figure 5.27 A sentence formed with the help of *Do* Insertion

As these tree structures show, the sentence *Do those birds sing?* is built in three steps. In the initial step, the usual XP rule gives the deep structure in Figure 5.27a, which contains no auxiliary verb in the Infl position. The transformation of *Do* Insertion then inserts the special interrogative auxiliary *do* into this position. At this point, Inversion applies, moving interrogative *do* to the C position and giving the desired surface structure.

Another look at *Wh* Movement

Now reconsider the *wh* question pattern in *49)*.

49)

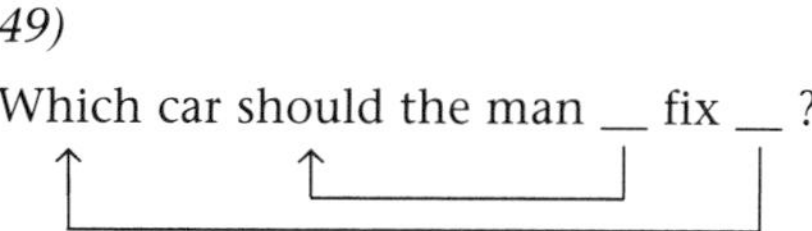

We have already seen that the transformation of *Wh* Movement moves the *wh* phrase to the beginning of the sentence, in front of even the fronted Aux, but we have not attempted to determine its precise place in the tree structure.

Given that the moved auxiliary is located in the C position (see above), it seems reasonable to conclude that the fronted *wh* phrase is in the specifier position of CP (this being the only position to the left of the C). Certainly, we know that this position is available to receive the moved *wh* phrase: because there is no class of words that serves as specifier of C, this position will always be empty in deep structure prior to the application of *Wh* Movement.

We therefore reformulate the *Wh* Movement transformation as follows.

50)

***Wh* Movement** (*revised*):
Move a *wh* phrase to the specifier position under CP.

The sentence *Which car should the man fix?* can now be analyzed in steps, the first of which involves formation of the deep structure depicted in Figure 5.28. Consistent with our earlier assumption, the S here occurs within a CP shell.

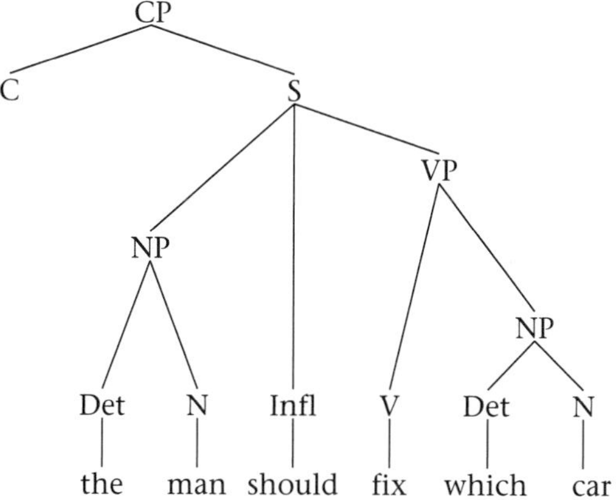

Figure 5.28 Deep structure for *Which car should the man fix?*

Wh Movement and Inversion then apply to this deep structure, yielding the surface structure in Figure 5.29.

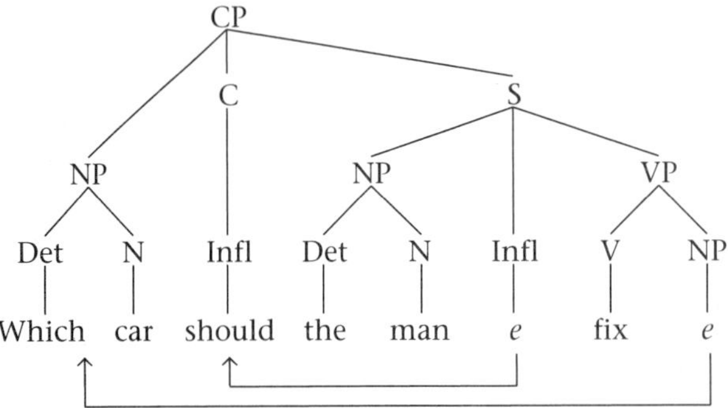

Figure 5.29 Surface structure for *Which car should the man fix?* Infl moves to the C position and the *wh* phrase moves to the specifier position under CP.

Like other transformations, *Wh* Movement cannot eliminate any part of the structural configuration formed by the phrase structure rules. The position occupied by the *wh* phrase in deep structure is therefore not lost. Rather, it remains as a trace (an empty category), indicating that the moved element corresponds to the complement of the verb *fix*.

In the examples considered so far, the *wh* word originates as complement of a verb or preposition. In sentences such as the following, however, the *wh* word is the subject.

51)

Who criticized Maxwell?

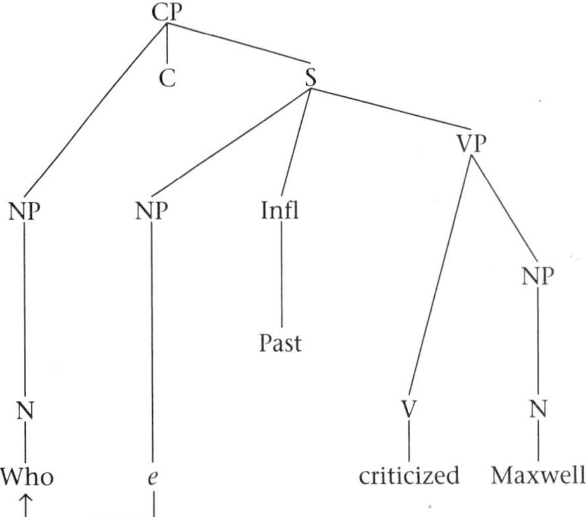

Figure 5.30 Movement of a subject *wh* word. Since there is nothing for the *wh* word to move over in such cases, there is no visible change in word order.

In this sentence, the *wh* word asks about the person who does the criticizing (the subject), not about the person who was criticized (the direct object). In such patterns the *wh* word originates in the subject position and subsequently moves to the specifier position within CP even though the actual order of the words in the sentence does not change as a result of this movement.

3.5 Constraints on transformations (*Advanced*)

Transformations like *Wh* Movement and Inversion are examples of movement rules: they move elements from one position within the sentence to another. Such rules are commonly referred to as instructions to 'Move α', where 'alpha' is a cover term for any element that can be shifted from one location to another.

Movement is not unconstrained. In fact, much of the research undertaken in the field of syntax in recent years has been devoted to determining constraints on movement. It has been shown that only certain categories are targeted by movement rules, that only certain positions can serve as 'landing sites' for moved elements, and that there are limits on how far elements can be moved. For example, Inversion can move an auxiliary from the Infl position only to the nearest C position.

52)

a. movement of an auxiliary to the nearest C position:
$[_{CP}$ $[_{IP}$ Harry should know $[_{CP}$ that the bottle could explode]]]. [Deep structure]
$[_{CP}$ Should $[_{IP}$ Harry __ know $[_{CP}$ that the bottle could explode]]]? [Surface structure]

b. movement of an auxiliary to a more distant C position:
$[_{CP}$ $[_{IP}$ Harry should know $[_{CP}$ that the bottle could explode]]]. [Deep structure]
*$[_{CP}$ Could $[_{IP}$ Harry should know $[_{CP}$ that the bottle __ explode]]]? [Surface structure]

There are also certain contexts in which transformations are unable to operate. As a preliminary illustration of this, consider the following two pairs of sentences.

53)

a. movement of a *wh* word from inside a complement phrase:
Carl should see [a picture of Dracula]. [Deep structure]
Who should Carl see [a picture of __]? [Surface structure]

b. movement of a *wh* word from inside a subject phrase:
[A picture of Dracula] could frighten John. [Deep structure]
*Who could [a picture of __] frighten John? [Surface structure]

In the first example, the *wh* word is extracted from a complement phrase and the result is acceptable. In *53b)*, in contrast, the *wh* word is extracted from the subject NP. The ungrammaticality of the resulting sentence suggests that it is not possible to move an element out of a subject phrase. We can express this fact by formulating the following constraint on transformations.

54)

The Subject Constraint:
No element may be removed from a subject phrase.

A constituent (such as the subject) that does not permit extraction of a component part is called an **island**.

Subject NPs are not the only type of island found in English. As the following examples show, it is also not possible to remove a *wh* word from a coordinate structure. (The coordinate structure is placed in brackets; as Section 5.1 will demonstrate, a coordinate structure is one in which a word such as *and* or *or* joins together categories of the same type.)

55)

a. The author might write [a story or a poem].
b. *What might the author write [a story or __]?

56)

a. Sue will talk [to Tom and to Mary].
b. *Who will Sue talk [to Tom and to __]?

We can account for these facts by formulating the following constraint.

57)

The Coordinate Structure Constraint:
No element may be removed from a coordinate structure.

There are many different types of islands in language, and a good deal of current research focuses on how they should be described, what properties they have in common, and how they differ from language to language. However, since most of this work is too complex to discuss in an introductory textbook, we can do no more than mention this important phenomenon here.

4 UNIVERSAL GRAMMAR AND PARAMETRIC VARIATION

Thus far, our discussion has focused on English. There are many other syntactic phenomena in this language that are worthy of consideration, and we will examine some of them in Section 5. First, though, it is important to extend the scope of our analysis to other languages.

The syntactic devices presented in earlier sections of this chapter are not found only in English. Indeed, recent work suggests that all languages share a small set of syntactic categories and that these categories can be combined to form phrases whose internal structure includes heads, complements, and specifiers. Moreover, it appears that transformational operations are subject to highly similar constraints in all languages. (For example, the prohibition against extraction from coordinate structures discussed in Section 3.5 holds cross-linguistically, so that sentences like *55)* and *56)* in the previous section are not found in any language.) The system of categories, mechanisms, and constraints shared by all human languages is called **Universal Grammar** (**UG**, for short).

The fact that certain syntactic properties are universal does not mean that languages must be alike in all respects. Universal Grammar leaves room for variation, allowing individual languages to differ with respect to certain **parameters**. (You can think of a parameter as the set of options that UG permits for a particular phenomenon.) In this section, we will consider a few examples of parametric variation, beginning with the inventory of syntactic categories. Some additional instances of cross-linguistic differences in syntax are considered in Section 2.3 of Chapter 9.

4.1 Variation in syntactic categories

Of the syntactic categories considered in this chapter, only nouns and verbs are found in all human languages. The adjective category, while very common, is not universal. In many languages (such as Hausa, Korean, Telugu, Hua, and Bemba), there are no true adjectives and no direct translation for English sentences such as *58)*.

58)

The cat is hungry.

Instead, the concept 'hungry' is expressed with the help of a noun in structures such as *59a)* or a verb in structures such as *59b)*.

59)

a. The cat has hunger.
b. The cat hungers.

Some examples of this phenomenon in Korean follow. (Nom = nominative, the subject marker)

60)

use of a noun where English uses an adjective:

a. Ku chayk-i *caymi* issta.
that book-Nom interest exist
'That book is interesting.'

b. Ku pap-i *mas* issta.
that food-Nom taste exist
'That food is tasty.'

61)

use of a verb where English uses an adjective:

a. Ku pap-i *maypta*.
that food-Nom be-spicy
'That food is spicy.'

b. Cip-i *khuta.*
house-Nom be-big
'The house is big.'

Despite their English translation, the words *maypta* 'spicy' and *khuta* 'big' in the latter two examples are a type of verb in Korean, taking tense markers and other types of inflectional endings used for verbs in that language.

Still other languages seem to lack the P category. Where English has a preposition, the Mayan language Jacaltec, for example, either uses no morpheme at all (see *62a)*) or employs a noun (such as *s-wi'* 'head' for 'on', as in *62b)*).

62)

a. Xto naj conob.
went he town
'He went to town.'

b. Aj naj *s-wi'* witz.
is he head hill
'He is on the hill.'

There are even languages that lack both As and Ps. For example, the Nootkan languages of Vancouver Island and northwest Washington State apparently have only two lexical categories—N and V.

The following table summarizes some of the variation in lexical categories found in human language.

Table 5.11 Parametric variation in lexical categories

Language	*Categories used*
Nootkan	N, V
Jacaltec	N, V, A
Korean	N, V, P
English	N, V, A, P

As you can see, the N and V categories are apparently universal, with languages differing from each other in terms of whether they use A and P.

4.2 Variation in Phrase Structure Rules

Even where languages have the same categories, the precise rules for sentence formation may differ. But this variation is not random. For instance, there are significant patterns that recur in language after language in terms of the position of heads within their phrases. To account for these patterns, we can posit a Head Parameter that offers three options—head-initial, head-medial, and head-final. In Japanese, for example, heads consistently occur in the final position within their phrase. Thus, the noun comes at the end of the NP, the verb at the end of the VP, and so on.

Because Ps occur at the end of the PP, they are called **postpositions** rather than prepositions. (Nom = nominative, the subject marker; CP is omitted to save space)

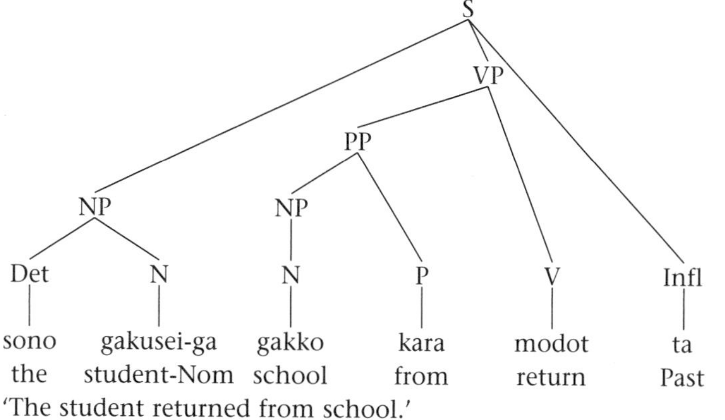

Figure 5.31 Japanese phrase structure: the head is always final.

These word order differences reflect the positioning of heads with respect to the other elements in their phrases, not the presence of an entirely new type of syntactic system. We can account for these facts by formulating the following phrase structure rule for Japanese.

63)

XP → (Specifier) (Complement*) X

As this rule indicates, the head uniformly follows its specifier and complement(s) in Japanese. In English, on the other hand, the head follows its specifier but precedes any complements (the head-medial option).

Matters are not always so simple, however. In Thai, for example, heads precede both specifiers and complements (the head-initial option) within phrases other than S. Thus, Ns appear at the beginning of NPs, Ps at the beginning of PPs, Vs at the beginning of VPs, and so on. (Tones have been omitted here.)

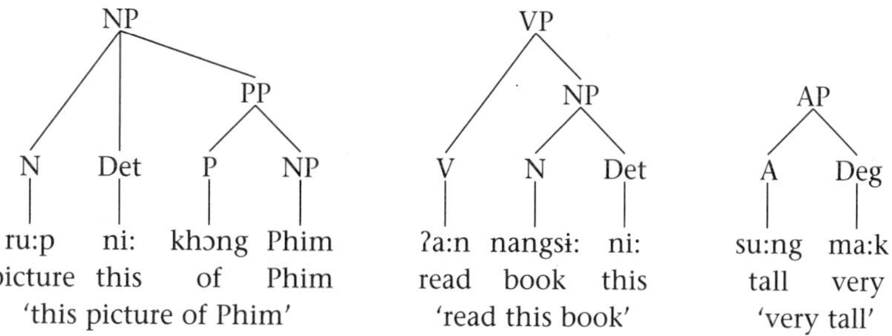

Figure 5.32 Thai phrase structure: the head is initial in phrases other than S.

Within S, however, the specifier (the subject NP) comes first, just as it does in English.

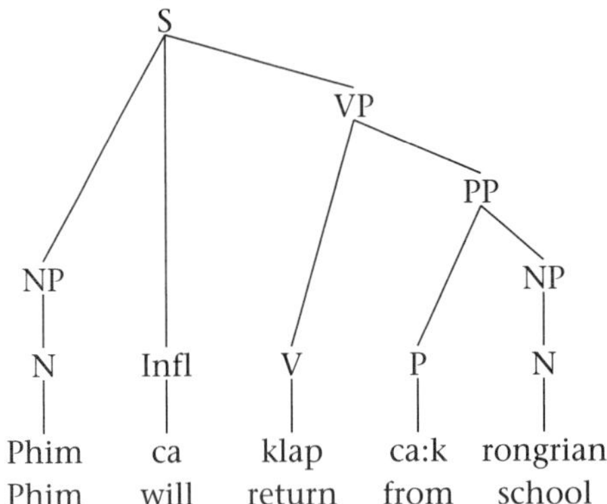

Figure 5.33 Thai sentence structure: the specifier (subject) precedes the head.

Thus, Thai uses one version of the XP rule for S and another version for phrases smaller than S.

64)

XP rule used in Thai for Ss:
XP → (Specifier) X (Complement*)

XP rule used in Thai for phrases smaller than S:
XP → X (Specifier) (Complement*)

The important thing to recognize here is that despite the differences just noted, English, Japanese, and Thai all have phrases and these phrases include a head in addition to optional specifiers and complements. Beneath the obvious word order differences there is a more fundamental similarity in the categories and rule types needed to build syntactic structure.

4.3 Variation in the use of transformations

Languages often differ from each other in the kinds of rules they use to form a particular sentence type. To illustrate this point we will consider three phenomena, two involving question patterns and one involving statements.

Yes-no questions

In Tamil (a language of India), *yes-no* questions are signalled by the presence of the morpheme *-a:* at the end of the sentence, rather than by an Inversion transformation. (The diacritic ̪ indicates a dental point of articulation; ɭ is a retroflex liquid.)

65)

a. Mut̪t̪u paɭam parit̪t̪a:n.
Muttu fruit picked
'Muttu picked the fruit.'

b. Mut̪t̪u paɭam parit̪t̪a:n-a:.
Muttu fruit picked -Ques
'Did Muttu pick the fruit?'

The morpheme *-a:* is treated as a type of complementerizer whose sentence-final position follows from the fact that Tamil is a head-final language. As depicted in Figure 5.34, corresponding to sentence *65b),* the V comes at the end of the VP, Infl at the end of S, and C (containing the question morpheme) at the end of CP.

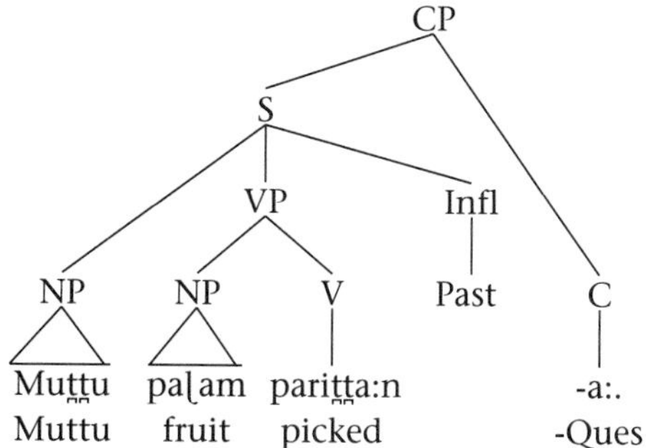

Figure 5.34 A question structure in Tamil

Examples like this show that languages can use very different means to express the same type of meaning. Whereas English can use a movement transformation (Inversion) to form *yes-no* questions, the corresponding sentence type in Tamil is formed by the phrase structure component of the grammar.

Wh questions

Just as some languages form *yes-no* questions without the help of the Inversion transformation, so some languages do not make use of *Wh* Movement in the formation of *wh* questions. Languages of this type include Japanese, Korean, Tamil, Chinese, and Thai. The following example is from Thai.

66)

Khun ʔa:n ʔaray?
you read what
'What did you read?'

Notice that, unlike English, Thai does not front the question word in *wh* questions.

Verb Raising

Consider now the contrast between the following two English sentences.

67)

a. Paul always works.
b. *Paul works always.

This difference is expected since the preverbal qualifier *always* functions as specifier of the verb and therefore should precede it, as in *67a)*. Surprisingly, however, even though specifiers generally precede the head in French, qualifiers such as *toujours* 'always' must follow the verb in that language.

68)

a. *Paul toujours travaille. (= English *67a*)
Paul always works

b. Paul travaille toujours. (= English *67b*)
Paul works always

Why should this be? One possibility that is currently being considered is that French has the **Verb Raising** transformation outlined in *69)*.

69)

Verb Raising:
Move V to Infl

Verb Raising is obligatory in French, applying to the deep structure in Figure 5.35a to give the surface structure in 5.35b.

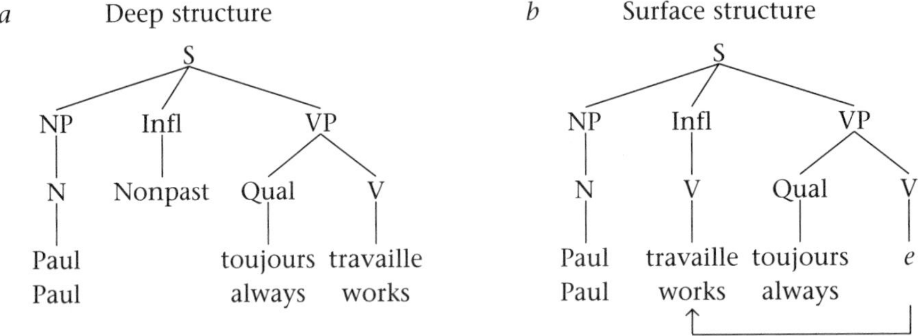

Figure 5.35 Verb Raising in French

By moving the verb to the Infl position in French, the Verb Raising transformation accounts for its occurrence to the left of its specifier in that language.

One piece of independent evidence for this proposal comes from the operation of the Inversion transformation in French. As we have already seen (Section 3.4), this transformation moves Infl to the C position. Now, in English only auxiliary verbs occur under Infl, which explains why only they can undergo Inversion.

70)

a. Inversion of an auxiliary verb in English:
Will you __ know the answer?

b. Inversion of a nonauxiliary verb in English:
*Know you __ the answer?

However, in French, nonauxiliary verbs can also occur under Infl, thanks to the operation of the Verb Raising transformation. This predicts that Inversion should be able to apply to these Vs in French as well as to auxiliaries. This is correct. Like English, French can form a question by moving an auxiliary leftward, as *71)* illustrates.

71)

Inversion of an auxiliary:
As-tu __ essayé?
Have you tried?

However, unlike English, French also allows Inversion of nonauxiliary Vs.

72)

Inversion of a nonauxiliary verb:
Vois-tu __ le livre?
see you the book
'Do you see the book?'

Figure 5.36 depicts the interaction between Verb Raising and Inversion needed to form this sentence. (We treat the pronoun *tu* 'you' as a type of NP.)

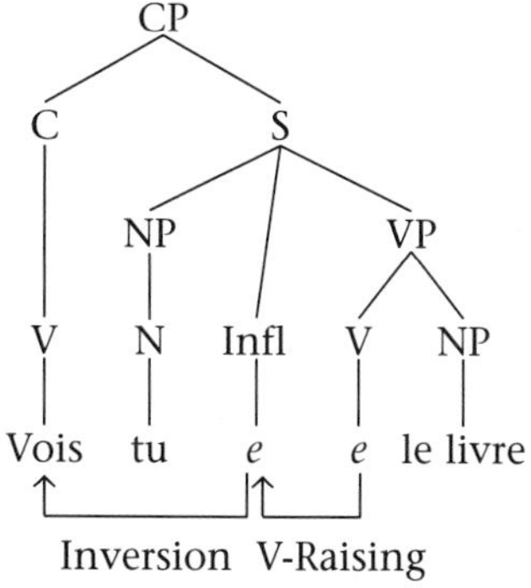

Figure 5.36 The interaction of Verb Raising and Inversion in French

Although English does not use the Verb Raising transformation in general, there is reason to believe that it applies to the 'copula' verb *be* as a special case. As shown by the following example, *be* sounds more natural when it occurs to the left of a qualifier such as *always*, which occurs in the specifier position within VP.

73)

a. *be* to the left of the specifier:
Jane *is* always on time.

b. *be* to the right of the specifier:
?*Jane always *is* on time.

This suggests that *be* can be moved leftward to the Infl position by the Verb Raising transformation.

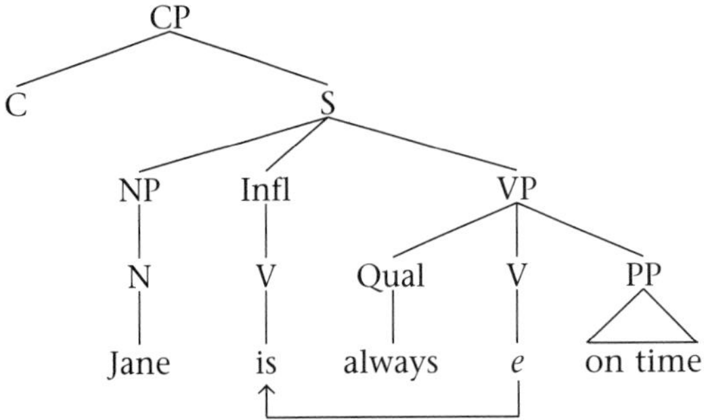

Figure 5.37 Raising of copula *be* in English

As expected, *be* is also able to undergo subsequent movement to the C position (Inversion) in *yes-no* questions, yielding sentences such as *74)*.

74)

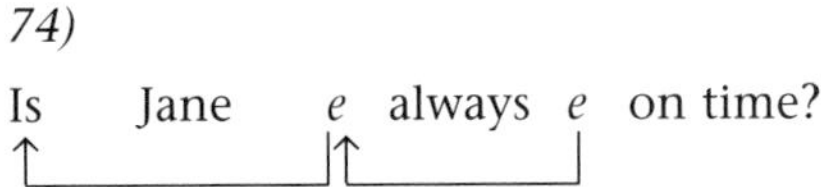

5 SOME EXTENSIONS *(ADVANCED)*

Now that we have considered the basic rule systems used by the syntactic component of the grammar in human language, it is possible to broaden our treatment of English syntax by briefly examining a number of additional structural patterns. We focus in this section on three such patterns—coordinate structures, modifier constructions, and relative clauses.

5.1 COORDINATION

A common syntactic pattern is formed by grouping together two or more categories of the same type with the help of a conjunction such as *and* or *or*. This phenomenon is known as **coordination**.

75)
coordination of NPs:
$[_{NP}$ the man] and $[_{NP}$ a child]

76)
coordination of VPs:
$[_{VP}$ go to the library] and $[_{VP}$ read a book]

77)
coordination of PPs:
$[_{PP}$ down the stairs] and $[_{PP}$ out the door]

78)
coordination of APs:
$[_{AP}$ quite beautiful] and $[_{AP}$ very expensive]

79)

coordination of Ss:
[$_{S}$ The woman entered the building] and [$_{S}$ the man waited in the car].

Coordination exhibits four important properties. First, there is no limit on the number of coordinated categories that can appear prior to the conjunction. Thus, the grammar can form structures such as *80)*, in which the subject NP contains four smaller NPs prior to the underlined conjunction and one after it.

80)

[$_{NP}$ A woman, a boy, a cat, a dog, and a hamster] got into the car.

Second, a category at any level (a head or an entire XP) can be coordinated. The preceding examples illustrate coordination of XPs; following are examples involving word-level categories.

81)

coordination of N:
The [$_{N}$ book] and [$_{N}$ magazine]

coordination of P:
[$_{P}$ up] and [$_{P}$ down] the stairs

coordination of V:
[$_{V}$ repair] and [$_{V}$ paint] the deck.

Third, coordinated categories must be of the same type. Thus, the coordinated categories are both NPs in *75)*, VPs in *76)*, and so on. As *82)* shows, coordination of different category types generally gives a quite unnatural result.

82)

coordination of an NP and a PP:
*She read [$_{NP}$ the book] and [$_{PP}$ in the library]

coordination of an NP and an AP:
*He left [$_{NP}$ the house] and [$_{AP}$ very angry]

Finally, the category type of the coordinate phrase is identical to the category type of the elements being conjoined. Hence, if VPs are coordinated, the coordinate structure is a VP; if NPs are coordinated, the coordinate structure is an NP; and so on.

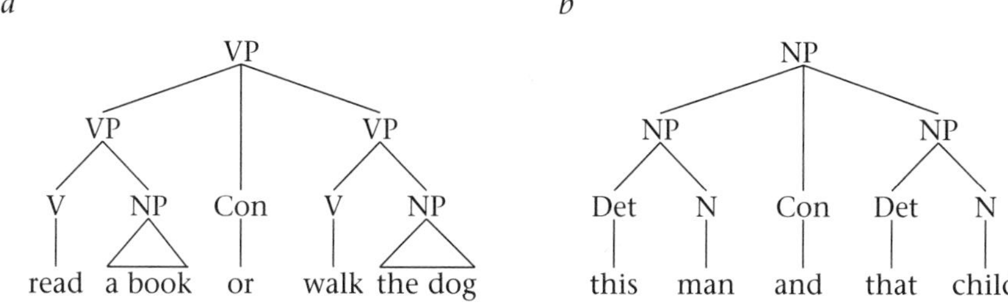

Figure 5.38 Some coordinate structures

How does the grammar form coordinate structures? One possibility is that there is a separate rule for each coordinate structure. For N and NP categories, for example, the following two rules could be formulated. (The * symbol indicates that one or more categories of that type can occur to the left of the conjunction, as in example *80)*; Con = conjunction.)

83)

a. NP → NP* Con NP
b. N → N* Con N

A set of parallel rules for verbal categories could also be formulated.

84)

a. VP → VP* Con VP
b. V → V* Con V

Similar rules can be devised for other categories (S, AP, PP, and so on) as well, but you can probably see that the result will be a rather long list of new rules.

Fortunately, we can avoid these complications by using the 'X notation' to formulate a single general statement that can take the place of the more specific rules exemplified above.

85)

The Coordination Rule:
$X^n \rightarrow X^{n*}$ Con X^n

The symbol X^n in this rule stands for 'a category at any structural level', indicating that either an X or an XP can be coordinated. As before, the asterisk (*) indicates that one or more categories can occur to the left of the conjunction. Thus, we can form not only structures such as *a woman and a boy*, in which just two elements are coordinated, but also structures such as *a woman, a boy, a cat, a dog, and a hamster*, in which a much larger number of items undergoes coordination. By adding just one more rule to the grammar, then, we can form a very broad range of coordinate structures.

5.2 Modifiers

Thus far, our treatment of phrase structure has ignored **modifiers**, a class of elements that encode optionally expressible properties of heads. Although all lexical categories can have modifiers, we will focus here on the types of categories that can modify Ns and Vs.

Adjective phrases (APs) make up the single most commonly used class of modifiers in English. As the following examples show, APs serve as modifiers of Ns. (This is not the only function of APs: they can also be used as complements of verbs such as *become* and *seem*, as in *He became/seemed* [*very angry*]; see Table 5.5.)

86)

APs serving as modifiers of N:
A *very tall* man walked into the room.
She made *exceptional* progress.

The most common modifiers of Vs are adverb phrases (AdvPs) and PPs that describe manner or time.

87)

AdvPs serving as modifiers of V:
describing manner: Ellen proceeded *carefully.*
Ellen *carefully* proceeded.
describing time: We arrived *early.*

88)

PPs serving as modifiers of V:
describing manner: Ellen proceeded *with care.*
describing time: He stayed *for three days.*

As these examples show, English modifiers vary in terms of their position with respect to the head. Thus, APs precede the N while PPs follow the verb. Many AdvPs can occur either before or after the verb that they modify, as the first examples in *87)* illustrate.

Table 5.12 Modifier position in English

Modifier	*Position*
AP	precedes the head
PP	follows the head
AdvP	precedes or follows the head

A rule for modifiers

How do modifiers fit into phrase structure? For the purposes of this introduction to syntax, we will attach modifiers at the XP level of phrase structure, as depicted in Figure 5.39.

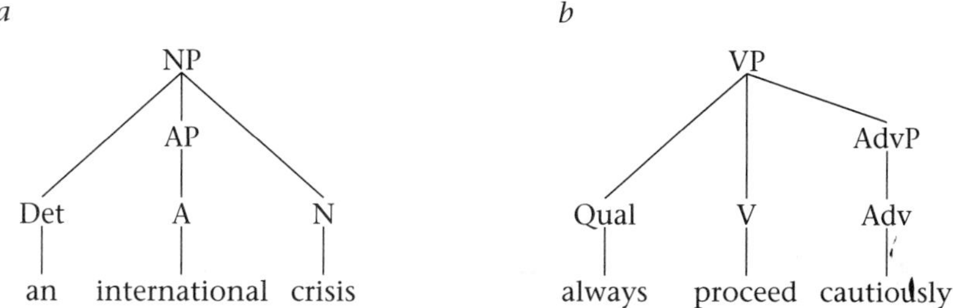

Figure 5.39 Phrases containing modifiers

In order to account for the placement of modifiers, we must expand our original XP rule so that it allows the various options shown in *89)*.

89)

The Expanded XP Rule:
XP → (Spec) (Mod) X (Complement*) (Mod)

This rule allows a modifier to occur either before the head (as in Figure 5.39a) or after it (see Figure 5.39b). Where there is a complement, a modifier that follows the head will normally follow the complement as well. This is illustrated in Figure 5.40.

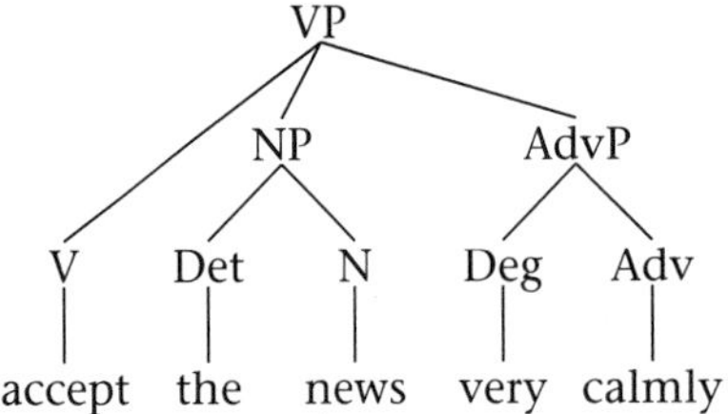

Figure 5.40 A phrase in which both the complement and the modifier follow the head. In such cases, the modifier follows the complement.

In this example, the XP rule gives a phrase consisting of a head (the verb *accept*), a complement (the NP *the news*), and a modifier (the AdvP *very calmly*)—in that order.

5.3 Relative clauses (*Advanced*)

Consider now the structure exemplified in *90)*.

90)

a. Sue may know the man [whom Bob criticized __].
b. Harry visited the village [which Sue walked to __].

The bracketed phrases in *90)* are **relative clauses**, CP-sized modifiers that provide information about the preceding N head. In sentence *90a)*, for example, the relative clause helps identify the man by indicating that he is the person criticized by Bob.

Like other modifiers, relative clauses occur within the same phrase as the head that they modify. Thus, the relative clause in *90a)* should be part of the NP headed by the N *man*. This can be verified with the help of the substitution test illustrated in *91)*, which shows that the sequence *the man whom Bob criticized* is a syntactic unit since it can be replaced by the pronoun *him*.

91)

Sue may know $[_{NP}$ the man $[_{CP}$ whom Bob criticized __]] and I know *him* too.
(him = the man whom Bob criticized)

Wh movement again

Relative clause structures resemble embedded *wh* questions in two respects. First, they begin with a *wh* word such as *who* or *which*. Second, there is an empty position within the sentence from which the *wh* phrase has apparently been moved. In sentences *90a)* and *90b)*, for instance, the NP positions following the transitive verb *criticize* and the preposition *to* are unfilled in surface structure.

The first step in the formation of the relative clause in *90a)* involves the deep structure in Figure 5.41.

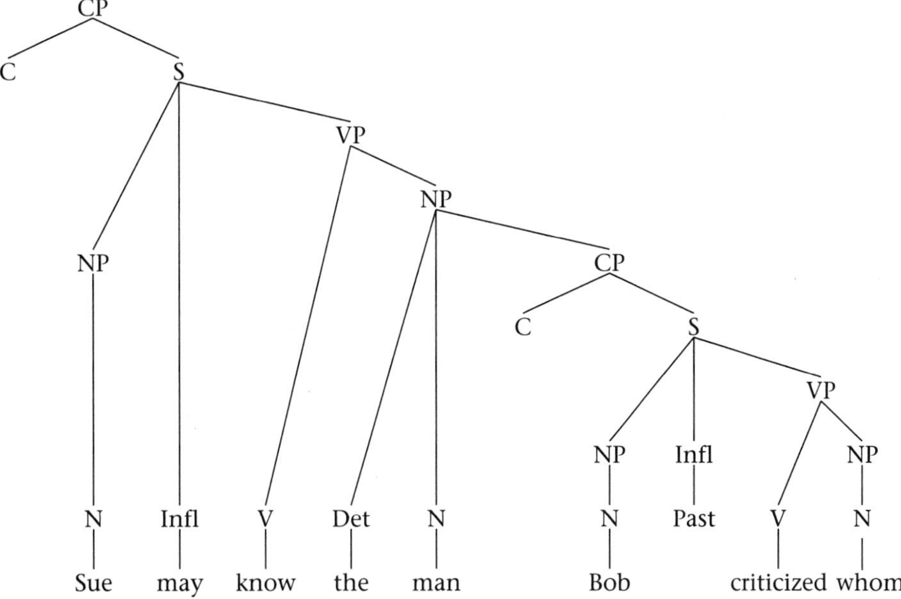

Figure 5.41 The deep structure for a relative clause

Here, the *wh* word *whom* occurs as complement of the verb *criticize* since it corresponds to the person who is criticized. (The relative clause itself is in the usual position for a posthead modifier; see the preceding section.)

The next step involves the application of the *Wh* Movement rule (as outlined in Section 3.4) to give the structure in Figure 5.42.

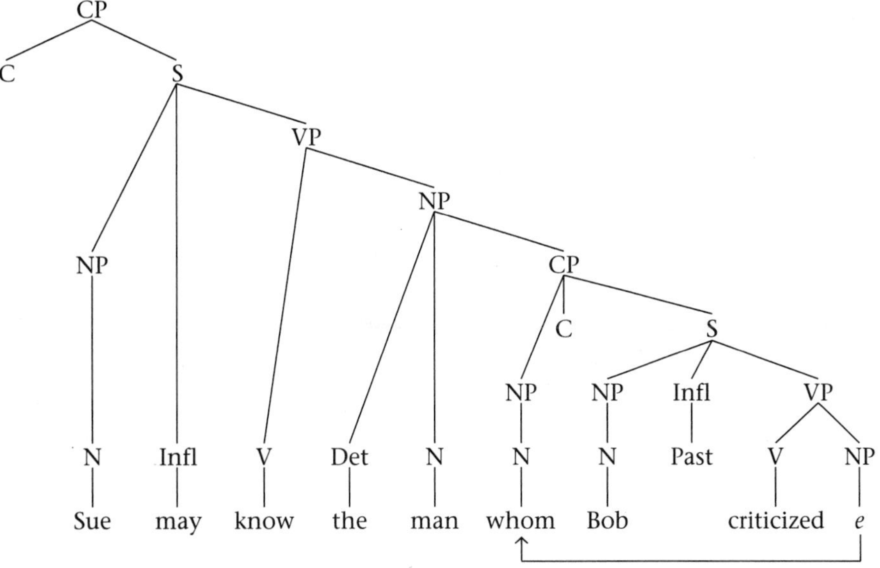

Figure 5.42 The surface structure for a relative clause: the *wh* phrase has moved to the specifier position within CP.

Notice that no new transformations are required to form relative clause structures such as these. Rather, relative clauses can be formed with the help of the same *Wh* Movement transformation that is independently required for *wh* questions.

In the preceding example, the *wh* word originates in the direct object position. But a similar analysis is applicable to other types of relative clause structures, including the one in *92)*, in which the *wh* word originates in the subject position.

92)

Sue may know the man who criticized Bob.

Here *who* corresponds to the person who does the criticizing, not the person who gets criticized, as in the previous example. The deep structure for this sentence therefore corresponds to *93)*, in which the *wh* word appears in the subject position.

93)

Sue may know the man [$_{CP}$ [$_S$ **who** criticized Bob]].

Like other *wh* words, *who* subsequently moves to the specifier position within CP even though the actual order of the words in the sentence does not change as a result of this movement.

94)

Sue may know the man [$_{CP}$ **who** [$_S$ __ criticized Bob]].

6 OTHER TYPES OF SYNTACTIC ANALYSIS

Thus far in this chapter, we have focused our attention on the analysis of sentence structure employed by practitioners of transformational syntax. As mentioned at the outset, however, this is not the only type of syntactic analysis used in contemporary linguistics. In this section, we will briefly consider two other types of syntactic analysis, one focusing on grammatical relations such as subject and direct object, and the other focusing on the way in which syntactic structure is used to communicate information. In order to illustrate how these analyses work, we will make use of a sentence type that has played a very important role in the development of syntactic theory over the last several decades.

6.1 PASSIVE STRUCTURES

Consider the pair of sentences in *95)*, which are virtually identical in meaning despite obvious structural differences.

95)

a. The thieves took the painting.
b. The painting was taken by the thieves.

In order to describe the differences and similarities between these two sentences, it is necessary to distinguish between the **agent** (the doer of the action designated by the verb) and the **theme** (the entity directly affected by that action). (These notions are discussed in more detail in Chapter 7.)

96)

a. active sentence:
The thieves took the painting.
agent *theme*

b. passive sentence:
The painting was taken (by the thieves).
theme *agent*

The *a)* sentence is called **active** because the agent is the subject of the sentence while the *b)* sentence is called **passive** in recognition of the fact that the theme is the subject. There are many other such pairs in English.

97)

a. The dog chased the truck.
b. The truck was chased by the dog.

98)

a. The teacher praised Ginette.
b. Ginette was praised by the teacher.

99)

a. The child broke the dishes.
b. The dishes were broken by the child.

The transformational analysis of passive sentences cannot be adequately discussed until we have considered some issues in the study of semantics (see Section 2.3 of Chapter 7). However, it is possible to consider two other perspectives on the analysis of this important syntactic pattern.

6.2 RELATIONAL ANALYSIS

The key point of **relational analysis** is that at least some syntactic phenomena are best described in terms of grammatical relations such as subject and direct object rather than morphological patterns or the order of words. This can be seen by examining how the passive structure is formed in different languages.

In terms of morphology and word order, the English passive has two distinctive properties. First, a passive sentence contains some form of the auxiliary *be* (*was, is,* and so on) together with a verb in the so-called 'past participle form', which is normally marked by the suffix *-ed* or *-en* (hence *was taken, was chased,* and so on). Second, the relative order of the agent and theme in passive sentences is the reverse of that found in active sentences. Thus, whereas the theme precedes the agent in passive sentences, the opposite order is found in active sentences, as sentence *96)* above demonstrated.

Table 5.13 Properties of the English passive

Morphology	*Word order*
Some form of Aux *be* Past participle form of the V	the theme comes before the agent

The general tendency in human language is to mark passivization both by a change in the relative order of the agent and the theme and by a modification to the form of the verb. The following example from Sre (a Mon-Khmer language spoken in Vietnam) provides another illustration of this.

100)

a. active sentence:
Cal paʔ mpon.
wind open door
'The wind opened the door.'

b. passive sentence:
Mpon gə-paʔ mə cal.
door Pass-open by wind
'The door was opened by the wind.'

However, it seems that passivization is not always signalled in this way. In Tzotzil (a Mayan language of Mexico), for instance, the relative order of the agent and the theme is the same in active and passive constructions. (cmpl = completed action)

101)

a. active sentence:
Lá snákan ti vĩnike ti xpétule.
theme *agent*
cmpl seat the man the Peter
'Peter seated the man.'

b. passive sentence:
Inákanat ti vĩnike yuʔun ti xpétule.
theme *agent*
was-seated the man by the Peter
'The man was seated by Peter.'

Here the passive is signalled by a change in the form of the verb and the appearance of the preposition *yuʔun* 'by' before the agent, but there is no change in the relative order of the agent and theme.

Mandarin Chinese employs yet another option.

102)

a. active sentence:
Zhu laoshi piyue-le wode kaoshi.
agent *theme*
Zhu professor mark cmpl my test
'Professor Zhu marked my test.'

b. passive sentence:
Wode kaoshi bei Zhu laoshi piyue-le.
theme *agent*
my test by Zhu professor mark cmpl.
'My test was marked by Professor Zhu.'

Here, the passive is marked by a change in word order and by the appearance of the preposition *bei* 'by' before the agent, but the verb has exactly the same form in both patterns.

What do the passive sentences of English, Tzotzil, Chinese, and other languages have in common? According to proponents of relational analysis, the crucial facts involve a correspondence between the grammatical relations found in a passive sentence and those in its active counterpart.

103)

a. active sentence*:* The thieves took the painting.

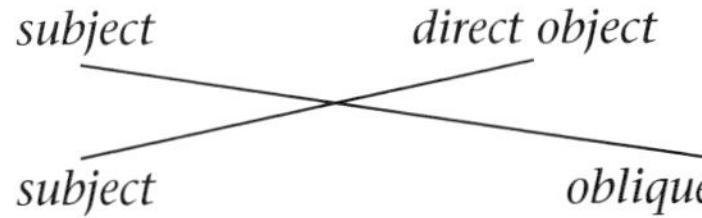

b. passive sentence*:* The painting was taken (by the thieves).

Notice that the direct object in the active *103a)* (*the painting*) is the subject in the passive *103b)* while the subject in *103a)* (*the thieves*) occurs inside a PP in *103b).* (An NP that occurs with a preposition is said to be **oblique**.)

It is now possible to think of passive sentences as the product of the following two changes to the corresponding active pattern.

Table 5.14 Properties of passive structures

Active pattern		*Passive pattern*
Subject	→	oblique
Direct object	→	subject

Since the criteria used to identify subjects and direct objects differ from language to language, these changes are compatible with a variety of different structural effects. In English, where the direct object appears after the verb and the subject before it, a change in an NP's grammatical relation will also involve a change in its linear position. Thus a theme NP that serves as subject (as in the passive) rather than direct object (as in the active) will appear in front of the verb rather than after it.

104)

a. active sentence:
The thieves took the painting.
↑
theme serving as direct object

b. passive sentence:
The painting was taken (by the thieves).
↑
theme serving as subject

In other languages, changes in grammatical relations may be marked by something other than a change in word order. In the Tzotzil passive, for example, addition of the preposition *yuʔun* is enough to indicate that the agent is no longer the subject. Despite these differences, however, passive structures in both English and Tzotzil have in common the pair of relational changes stated in Table 5.14.

Many other syntactic phenomena can be analyzed in terms of processes that affect subjects and direct objects. As our study of passivization illustrates, these concepts are especially useful when comparing syntactic phenomena in languages with different word order and/or morphological patterns. We will see some additional examples of this in Section 2.3 of Chapter 9.

6.3 Functional analysis

Syntactic analysis can also focus on the way in which different syntactic structures are used to communicate information. Such analyses are often called **functional** since they seek to understand syntactic phenomena in terms of their communicative function. The contrast between active and passive sentences is especially instructive in this regard. Although both sentence types have the same basic meaning, they differ from each other in the way in which they present the situation that they describe. Put another way, they differ from each other in the way in which they 'package' the information to be communicated. Two differences can be noted here.

First, passive sentences tend to de-emphasize the role of the agent in the situation being described. In fact, the vast majority of passive sentences do not mention the agent at all. Hence, we can say simply *The painting was taken* or *The dishes were broken*, without attributing responsibility for these events to any particular person.

Second, passive sentences foreground the theme by making it the subject of the sentence. As a result, the situation is presented from the perspective of that individual. (As we will see in Chapter 7, the subject usually introduces the entity that the rest of the sentence is about.) Consider in this regard the following passage.

105)

MacGregor is a pretty lucky guy. Last night, he went out, got drunk, and started rolling around in the street. Before too long, *he was hit by a car.* But he wasn't even injured. In fact, he got up and walked home.

The italicized passive sentence in this passage sounds completely natural since it brings to the foreground the pronoun *he*, which refers to the person (MacGregor) from whose perspective the entire series of events is being described. In contrast, the passive is not nearly so natural in the following context.

106)

MacGregor is a pretty lucky guy. Last night, he went out, got drunk, and started rolling around in the street. Before too long, **a car was hit by him.* But his hand wasn't even injured . . .

Here the passive sentence seems quite out of place. This is because it foregrounds the car even though the rest of the passage is clearly about MacGregor. This in turn creates a discontinuity in the flow of information, making the passage quite unnatural.

In sum, the functional analysis of the passive pattern focuses on the way in which it packages information compared to active sentences. The key claim is that the function of this structure is to de-emphasize the agent (often deleting it entirely) and to draw attention to the theme NP. By analyzing syntactic structures functionally, it is often possible to gain insights into why human language has the particular syntactic patterns that it does and how these patterns contribute to the larger task of communication.

Summing up

In this chapter we have been concerned with some of the fundamental devices involved in the analysis of sentence formation. As we have seen, these devices seem to be of different types: there are **phrase structure rules** (perhaps reducible to a single XP rule) that determine the architecture of a sentence's **deep structure**, **subcategorization** information that ensures a match between **heads** and the **complements** with which they appear in syntactic structure, and **transformations** that can modify deep structure in various ways to produce a **surface structure**. Taken together, these devices make up an important part of our overall linguistic competence in that they provide the means to combine words into sentences in endlessly novel ways.

Although the precise rules for sentence formation differ from language to language, **Universal Grammar** provides all languages with the same general types of devices (syntactic categories, phrase structure rules, and transformations). Many of the differences among languages can be traced to the existence of a small set of **parameters**, each of which makes available a variety of alternatives.

Key terms

active (sentence)
adjective
adverbs
agent
auxiliary verbs
complement
complement clause
complementizers
conjunctions
constituents
coordinate structure constraint
coordinate structures
coordination
Coordination Rule

coordination test
D-structure
deep structure
degree words
determiners
direct object
distribution
do insertion
functional analysis
functional categories
grammatical (sentence)
head
insertion rule
inversion
island
lexical categories
matrix clause
modifier
movement text
nonlexical categories
noun
oblique NP
parameters
passive (sentence)
phrase structure rules
phrases
postpositions
preposition
relational analysis
relative clauses
S rule
S-structure
sentence
specifiers
subcategorization
subject
subject constraint
substitution test
surface structure
syntactic categories
syntax
theme
trace
transformation
transformational syntax
Universal Grammar
verb
Verb Raising
Wh Movement
wh questions
X′ rule
XP rule

NOTES

1 It is commonly assumed that the Infl node also contains information about subject-verb agreement, which—like tense—is often realized as verbal inflection (see Chapter 4, Section 6.4). Thus, the tree in Figure 5.9 would actually look like this, with the features under the Agr(eement) label matching those on the subject.

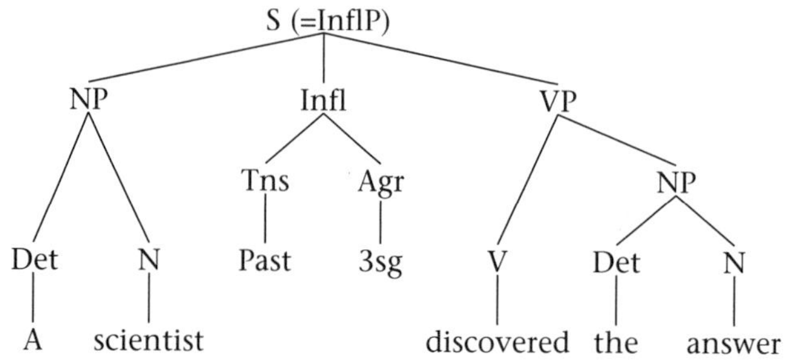

Mechanisms not considered here ensure that the tense and agreement features under Infl are realized appropriately on the verb. In order to keep this introduction to syntax at a relatively simple level, we will not discuss agreement further in this chapter.

2 In this analysis, only the so-called 'modal' auxiliaries mentioned here count as instances of Infl. *Have* and *be* (traditionally called 'aspectual' auxiliaries) are treated as special verbs that take a VP as their complement. For example:

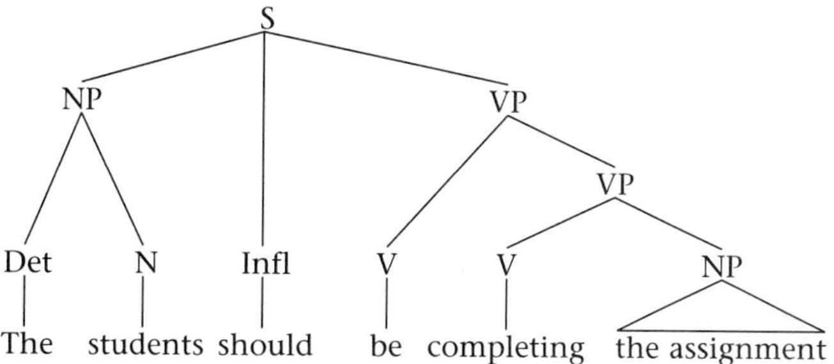

Here, *should* (an instance of Infl) takes as its complement the VP headed by *be*, which in turn takes the VP *completing the assignment* as its complement.

Sources

Transformational syntax is the most popular of the half dozen major syntactic theories used in contemporary linguistics. Traditionally, it is the theory taught in introductory linguistics courses, both because it is so widely used and because many of the other approaches that exist today have developed in response to it. The particular system outlined here involves a variety of simplifications to make it appropriate for presentation in an introductory course.

The treatment of auxiliary verbs involves a simplified version of the system proposed in *Barriers* by N. Chomsky (Cambridge, MA: MIT Press, 1986); see the book by Radford (cited below) for a more detailed introduction. The system of subcategorization employed here is loosely based on the one outlined in *Generalized Phrase Structure Grammar* by G. Gazdar, E. Klein, G. Pullum, and I. Sag (Cambridge, MA: Harvard University Press, 1985), which describes a nontransformational approach to syntax. The theory of transformations presented here is essentially the one employed throughout the 1980s by researchers working within transformational grammar.

The status of adjectives in Universal Grammar is discussed by R. M. W. Dixon in *Where Have All the Adjectives Gone?* (The Hague: Mouton, 1982). The data on Jacaltec (Section 4.1) are from *The Jacaltec Language* by C. Day (Bloomington, IN: Indiana University Press, 1973). The claim that the Nootkan languages have only two lexical categories is based on the discussion in "Noun and Verb in Nootkan" by W. Jacobsen, Jr. in *The Victoria Conference on Northwestern Languages* (Heritage Record No. 4. Vancouver: British Columbia Provincial Museum, 1979), pp. 83–155. A similar system is described for the now extinct Yana by E. Sapir in *Language* (New York: Harcourt Brace, 1921).

The discussion of the relational analysis of passive sentences is intended to be neutral between Lexical Functional Grammar as outlined in *The Mental Representation of Grammatical Relations*, edited by Joan Bresnan (Cambridge, MA: MIT Press, 1982) and Relational Grammar as described in "Toward a Universal Characterization of Passivization" by D. Perlmutter and P. Postal in *Studies in Relational Grammar I*, edited by D. Perlmutter (Chicago: University of Chicago Press, 1983); the Chinese and Tzotzil examples cited in Section 6.2 were taken from this paper. The Sre example is from "Passive in the World's Languages" by E. Keenan in the first volume of the series edited by T. Shopen and recommended below. The functional analysis of passives draws on the discussion in *Functional Syntax* by Susumu Kuno (Chicago: University of Chicago Press, 1987) and *Functional Syntax and Universal Grammar* by W. Foley and R. Van Valin (New York: Cambridge University Press, 1986). The questions for this chapter were prepared by Joyce Hildebrand.

Recommended reading

Blake, Barry. 1990. *Relational Grammar*. New York: Routledge.

Borsley, Robert. 1991. *Syntactic Theory: A Unified Approach*. London: Edward Arnold.

Givón, Talmy. 1984. *Syntax: A Functional Typological Approach*. Vol. 1. Philadelphia: John Benjamins.

Haegeman, Liliane. 1994. *Introduction to Government and Binding Theory*. 2nd ed. Cambridge, MA: Blackwell.

Radford, Andrew. 1988. *Transformational Grammar: A First Course*. New York: Cambridge University Press.

Shopen, Timothy, ed. 1985. *Language Typology and Syntactic Description*. Vols. 1–3. New York: Cambridge University Press.

Appendix: How to build tree structures

Although it is relatively easy to check a tree structure to see if it complies with the XP rule, it is somewhat harder to build a tree structure from scratch when trying to analyze a new phrase or sentence. In such cases, you will probably find it easiest to proceed in steps, working from the bottom up and from right to left. As an illustration, let us first consider the phrase *near the door*.

The first step involves assigning each word to the appropriate lexical category, as depicted in Figure 5.43.

Figure 5.43 The first step: determining the word-level categories

Then, working from right to left, the XP levels are added above each N, V, A, or P. Thus, we first add an NP label above the N *door*. There is clearly no complement here, but there is a specifier (the determiner *the*), which can be attached at the NP level in accordance with the XP rule.

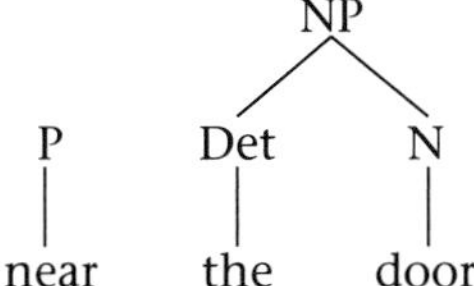

Figure 5.44 Building the NP

Next, we carry out the same procedure for the P *near*, adding the required PP level.

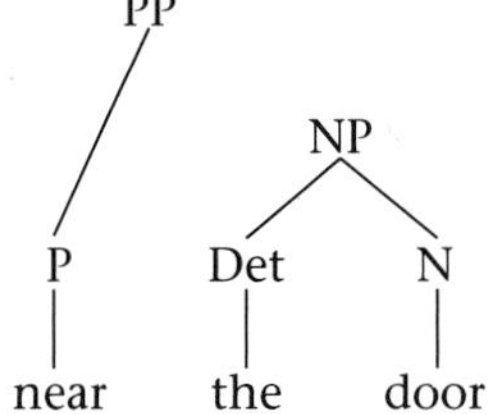

Figure 5.45 Adding the PP level above the P head

The NP to the right of the P clearly functions as its complement (since it names the location entailed by the meaning of *near*). This element is therefore attached at the PP level in accordance with the XP rule, giving the complete structure depicted in Figure 5.46.

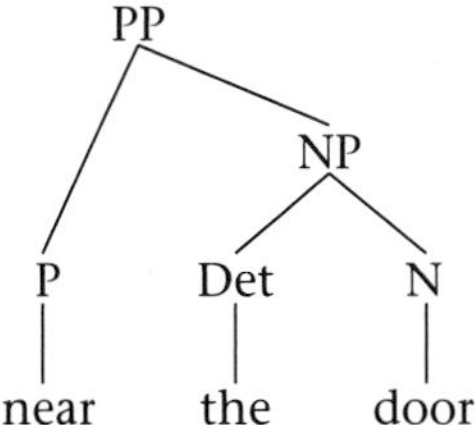

Figure 5.46 The complete PP

A sentential example

Consider now how we proceed in the case of a complete sentence such as *The apple might hit the man*. Assignment of each word to the appropriate lexical category gives the structure depicted in Figure 5.47.

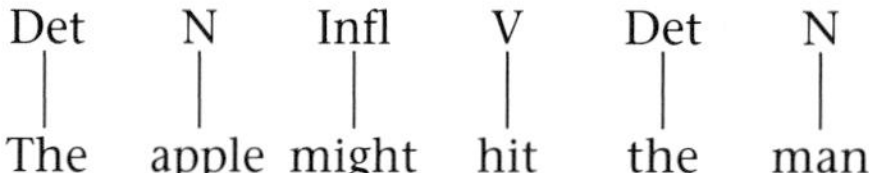

Figure 5.47 The categories for each word in the sentence

Working from right to left, it is easy to see that the noun *man* heads an NP that contains a specifier but no complement.

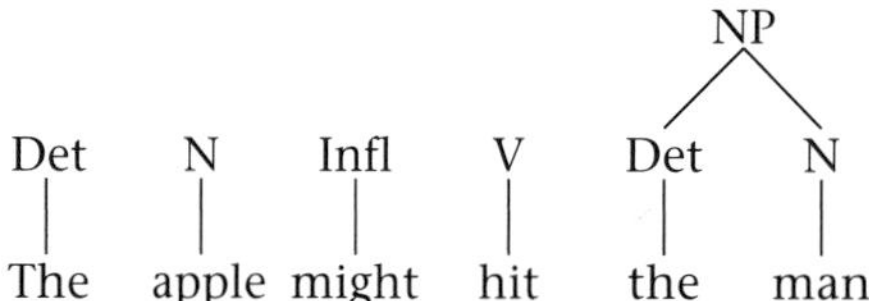

Figure 5.48 The structure of the rightmost NP

Next, we focus on the V *hit*, adding the required VP level and attaching the complement NP *the man*.

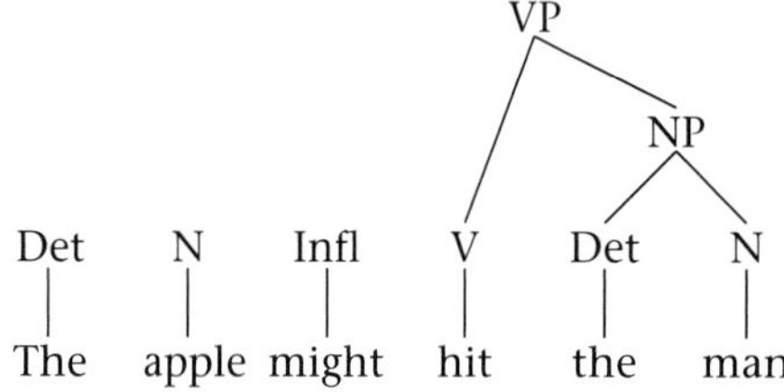

Figure 5.49 Adding the VP level above the V head

As an instance of Infl, the auxiliary *might* is the head of S, with the VP to the right serving as its complement and the NP to the left functioning as its specifier. This yields the complete sentence illustrated in Figure 5.50.

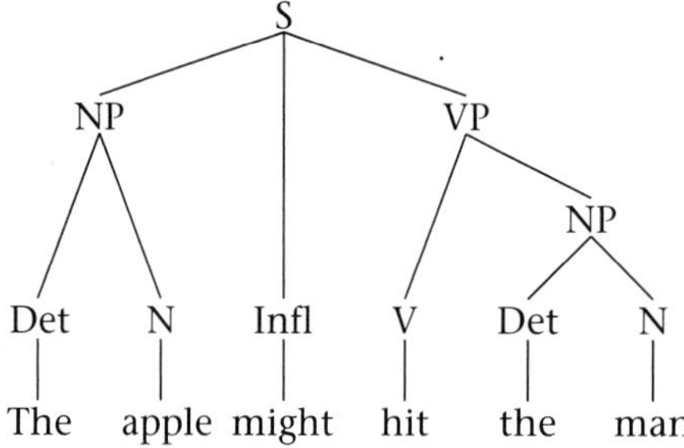

Figure 5.50 The complete sentence

The entire sentence is then embedded in a CP 'shell', giving the tree in Figure 5.51.

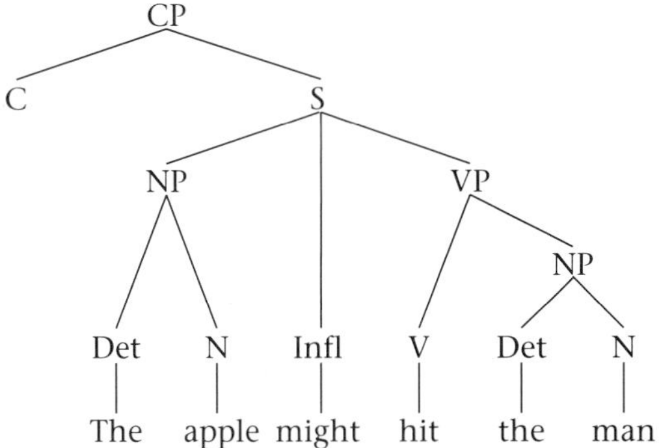

Figure 5.51 The sentence embedded in a CP shell

Transformations

Recognizing that a transformation has applied is relatively simple: if a sentence contains an auxiliary verb to the left of the subject, then Inversion has applied; if it begins with a *wh* word, then *Wh* Movement has applied. In the sentence *What should the farmers plant?*, both of these transformations have applied.

In order to determine the deep structure, we must 'return' the auxiliary verb to its position under Infl and we must determine the position from which the *wh* word has been moved. Since the *wh* word in the sentence *What should the farmers plant?* asks about the complement of the verb (the thing that is planted), we place *what* in the verbal complement position in deep structure. This gives the deep structure depicted in Figure 5.52.

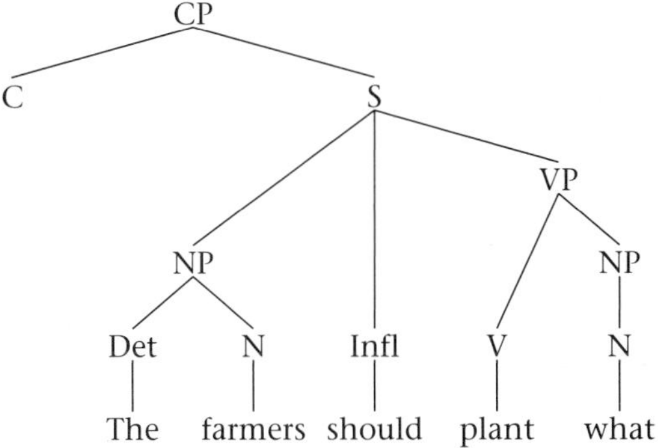

Figure 5.52 The deep structure for the sentence *What should the farmers plant?*

The auxiliary *should* then moves to the C position (Inversion) and *what* to the specifier position under CP (*Wh* Movement), yielding the complete surface structure depicted in Figure 5.53.

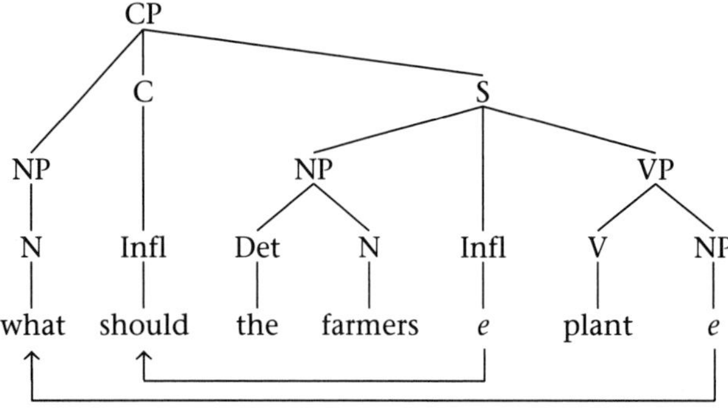

Figure 5.53 The surface structure

QUESTIONS

1. Place an asterisk next to any of the sentences that are ungrammatical for you. Can you figure out what makes these sentences ungrammatical?
   a) The instructor told the students to study.
   b) The instructor suggested the students to study.
   c) The customer asked for a cold beer.
   d) The customer requested for a cold beer.
   e) He gave the Red Cross some blood.
   f) He donated the Red Cross some blood.
   g) The pilot landed the jet.
   h) The jet landed.
   i) A journalist wrote the article.
   j) The article wrote.
   k) Jerome is bored of his job.
   l) Jerome is tired of his job.

2. Indicate the category of each word in the following sentences. (It may help to refer back to Section 1.)
   a) That glass suddenly broke.
   b) A jogger ran toward the end of the lane.
   c) These dead trees might block the road.
   d) The detective hurriedly looked through the records.
   e) The peaches appear quite ripe.
   f) Jeremy will play the trumpet and the drums in the orchestra.

3. Each of the following phrases consists of a specifier and a head. Draw the appropriate tree structure for each example.
   a) the zoo
   b) always try
   c) so witty
   d) perhaps pass
   e) less bleak
   f) this house
   g) very competent
   h) quite cheap
   i) never surrender
   j) those books

4. The following phrases include a head, a complement, and (in some cases) a specifier. Draw the appropriate tree structure for each example. For now, there is no need to depict the internal structure of complements. (See the tree diagrams in Figure 5.5 in the chapter.)
   a) into the house
   b) fixed the telephone
   c) full of mistakes
   d) more towards the window
   e) a film about pollution
   f) always study this material
   g) perhaps earn the money
   h) that argument with Owen
   i) the success of the program

5. After carefully reading the first two sections of the appendix, draw phrase structure trees for each of the following sentences.
   a) Those guests should leave.
   b) Maria never ate a brownie.
   c) That shelf will fall.
   d) The glass broke.
   e) The student lost the debate.
   f) The manager may offer a raise.
   g) The judge often sentences shoplifters.
   h) The teacher often organized a discussion.
   i) A psychic will speak to this group.
   j) Marianne could become quite fond of Larry.

6. Apply the substitution test to determine which of the bracketed sequences in the following sentences form constituents. Rewrite each sentence, replacing the words in brackets with one word. Is the bracketed sequence a constituent?
   a) [The tragedy] upset the entire family.
   b) They hid [in the cave].
   c) The [computer was very] expensive.
   d) [The town square and the civic building] will be rebuilt.
   e) Jane [left town].

7. Apply the movement test to determine which of the bracketed sequences in the following sentences form constituents. Rewrite each sentence so that the bracketed sequence has been moved. Is the sequence a constituent?
   a) We ate our lunch [near the river bank].
   b) Steve looked [up the number] in the book.
   c) The [island has been] flooded.
   d) I love [peanut butter and bacon sandwiches], but not salad.
   e) The environmental [movement is gaining momentum].
   f) The goslings [swam across] the lake.

8. Lexical categories are divided into subcategories on the basis of their complements. For each of the following words, two potential complement options are given. For each of the words:

i) Determine which one of the two options better matches the subcategorization requirements of the verb, noun, or adjective.
ii) Justify your choice by creating a sentence using that complement option.

	Verb	*Options*		*Verb*	*Options*
a)	expire	Ø *or* NP NP	e)	clean	NP PP_{for} *or* NP NP
b)	destroy	NP *or* Ø	f)	mumble	NP *or* NP NP
c)	observe	NP *or* PP_{to} PP_{about}	g)	throw	Ø *or* NP PP_{loc}
d)	discuss	NP *or* Ø	h)	paint	NP PP_{to} *or* NP PP_{for}

	Noun	*Options*
a)	debate	PP_{of} PP_{to} *or* PP_{with} PP_{about}
b)	hammer	Ø *or* PP_{with} PP_{about}
c)	success	PP_{of} PP_{to} *or* PP_{of}
d)	transfer	PP_{with} PP_{about} *or* PP_{of} PP_{to}
e)	sickness	Ø *or* PP_{with} PP_{about}

	Adjective	*Options*
a)	strong	Ø *or* PP_{about}
b)	sick	NP *or* PP_{of}
c)	bored	PP_{with} *or* PP_{of}
d)	knowledgeable	PP_{to} *or* PP_{about}
e)	small	PP_{of} *or* Ø

9. *i)* The following sentences all contain embedded clauses that function as complements of a verb. Draw a tree structure for each sentence.
   a) The reporter said that an accident injured a woman.
   b) The fishermen think that the company polluted the bay.
   c) Bill reported that a student asked whether the eclipse would occur.

   ii) The following sentences all contain embedded clauses that function as complements of an adjective, a preposition, or a noun. Draw a tree structure for each sentence.
   d) The police appeared happy that the criminal would surrender.
   e) That officer was sure that Gerry often speeds down the highway.
   f) Ray wondered about whether the exam would cover that section.
   g) The jury will never believe the claim that the driver totalled the Porsche.

10. The formation of the following sentences involves the Inversion transformation. Draw tree diagrams to show the deep structure and the surface structure for each sentence. (Hint: see the appendix.)
    a) Will the boss hire Hilary?
    b) Can the dog fetch the frisbee?
    c) Should the student report the incident?
    d) Must the musician play that piece of music?
    e) Should that player leave the team?

11. The following sentences involve the rules of *Wh* Movement and Inversion. Draw tree diagrams to show the deep structure and the surface structure for each of these sentences.

a) Who should the director call?
b) Who should call the director?
c) What can Joanne eat?
d) Who will those immigrants live with?
e) What might Terry bake for the party?
f) What can Anne bring to the gathering?

12. The following data are from Igbo, a tone language spoken in Nigeria.

a) Nwáànyì̃ áhù̃	b) ú̃lú̃ à
woman that	house this
'that woman'	'this house'

i) What is the relative order of the determiner and noun in Igbo?
ii) Draw the phrase structure trees for the two Igbo phrases.

13. The following data are from Malagasy, spoken on the island of Madagascar.

a) Entin' kafe Dan.	b) Mankany amin' ny restauranta Dan.
brings coffee Dan	goes to the restaurant Dan
'Dan brings coffee.'	'Dan goes to the restaurant.'

i) Based on this data, what are the phrase structure rules for Malagasy?
ii) Draw the tree structure for each of the Malagasy sentences.

14. Consider the following Selayarese data.

a) La?allei doe? injo i-Baso.
took money the Baso
'Baso took the money.'

b) Nra?bai sapon injo.
collapsed house the
'The house collapsed.'

c) Lataroi doe? injo ri lamari injo i-Baso.
put money the in cupboard the Baso
'Baso put the money in the cupboard.'

i) Write the XP rule required to form these sentences.
ii) How does it differ from the English rule?

15. The following data are from Korean. You may ignore the nominative (subject) and accusative (direct object) markers for the purposes of this question.

a) Terry-ka ku yeca-lul coahanta.
Terry-Nom that girl-Ac likes
'Terry likes that girl.'

b) I noin-i hakkyo ey kassta.
this man-Nom school to went
'This man went to school.'

c) Sue-ka chinkwu eykey chayk-ul ilkessta.
Sue-Nom friend to book-Ac read
'Sue read the book to a friend.'

i) Based on this data, what is the XP rule for Korean?
ii) Draw the tree structure for each of the Korean sentences.

16. The following data illustrate the formation of *yes-no* questions in German.
    a) Das Kind wird die Schwester lehren.
       the child will the sister teach
       'The child will teach the sister.'
    b) Wird das Kind die Schwester lehren?
       will the child the sister teach
       'Will the child teach the sister?'
    c) Der Mann liebt die Frau.
       'The man loves the woman.'
    d) Liebt der Mann die Frau?
       loves the man the woman
       'Does the man love the woman?'

    Assuming that German makes use of the same Inversion transformation as English (i.e., 'Move Infl to the C position'), do the above data tell us whether German employs the Verb Raising transformation? Be sure to include the tree structures for b) and d) in your answer.

17. The following sentences all contain conjoined categories. Draw a tree structure for each of the sentences.
    a) The cyclist drank a gallon of water and a liter of Coke.
    b) The airplane will land at the airport and taxi to the terminal.
    c) The dog went down the stairs and out the door.
    d) Crusoe landed on an island and ate a goat.
    e) Jill should recycle that book and magazine.
    f) Hilary thinks that spring will come and that gardens will flourish.
    g) Mary is fond of dogs but tired of the fleas.

18. The following sentences contain modifiers of various types. For each sentence, first identify the modifier(s), then draw the tree structures.
    a) A large iguana suddenly appeared.
    b) The principal made an important announcement after the class.
    c) An unusual event occurred before the game.
    d) The very hazardous waste seeped into the ground quickly.
    e) A huge moon hung in the black sky.
    f) Timothy drew an enormous map during the afternoon.

19. Each of the following sentences contains a relative clause. Draw the deep structure and the surface structure trees for each of these sentences.
    a) The animals which Sam saw came from Kenya.
    b) Kyle likes the girl whom June befriended.
    c) The woman whom Clyde lives with recycles plastic.
    d) Helen recited the poem which Wordsworth wrote.
    e) The canoe which Crusoe built was too heavy.

20. In the following sentences, indicate above each NP whether it is subject, direct object, or oblique, and indicate below each NP whether it is agent or theme.
    a) Marie purchased a present.
    b) The class was conducted by an expert.
    c) Those books were read by young children.

d) An expert conducted the class.
e) A present was purchased by Marie.

For the Student Linguist

BACKWARDS

Sometimes poetry frustrates me because of all the seemingly nonsensical sentence bits I get after my brain automatically inserts a dramatic pause at the end of each line. Because I'm stuck, waiting for my eyes to get to the next line, as I try to figure out what's so incredibly significant about a line consisting of "Eskimo" or "his amber eyes" or "detritus" and nothing else. But I really like Lesléa Newman's work because the line divisions actually seem meaningful and because she seems to be having so much fun arranging these sentence bits.

Tiff and I*

Tiff and I sit
in Tompkins Square Park
reading poetry
under a sky
full of clapping pigeons.
He calls them flying rats
but I think
the pink and green circles
around their necks
like greasy oil puddles are
beautiful.
Tiff says
all my poems sound better
backwards.

Backwards
all my poems sound better
Tiff says.
Beautiful
like greasy oil puddles
around their necks are
the pink and green circles
but I think
he calls them flying rats.
Full of clapping pigeons
under a sky
reading poetry
in Tompkins Square Park
Tiff and I sit.

If you read the poem as if it were prose, I think the first half sounds pretty bland and the second half is just plain loopy:

> Tiff and I sit in Tompkins Square Park reading poetry under a sky full of clapping pigeons. He calls them flying rats but I think the pink and green circles around their necks like greasy oil puddles are beautiful. Tiff says all my poems sound better backwards.
>
> Backwards all my poems sound better Tiff says. Beautiful like greasy oil puddles around their necks are the pink and green circles but I think he calls them flying rats. Full of clapping pigeons under a sky reading poetry in Tompkins Square Park Tiff and I sit.

In fact, I can't read the second half in prose format without imagining flying poems that have greasy pink and green circles around their necks, a sky that is reading poetry, and two people who've spent the afternoon eating live pigeons.

What is it about the change from prose to poetry that makes this string of words interesting and meaningful? (We've got to drudge through some syntax here, but trust me, it's relatively painless and worth it.) Assume that the first half of the poem has three untransformed sentences, and the second half has sentences that have undergone transformations. Also notice that one word—*are*—gets switched into a different line in the second stanza. It shouldn't be too hard to draw tree structures for the sentences in the first stanza *if* you do it line-by-line (i.e., first draw the tree for "Tiff and I sit," then for "in Tompkins Square Park," etc., and then hook them together).

The sentences in the second stanza will be harder to draw trees for, but if you do the first stanza line by line, those parts will be the same, except for where the word *are* is switched. So all you really need to do is figure out which parts of the trees got moved, and in which order. Actually, that's not even too hard to do, since only constituents can be moved.

You've probably figured out by now why this poem is in the syntax chapter: it does a good job of showing off what constituents are and of showing how the same words, even the same phrases, can have a different meaning when they're moved. However, this poem does more than show off constituents. I also like the rhythm of the poem—the way some of the lines seem to invite me to pause after them, and other lines lead me quickly on to the next line. Take a look at the subcategorizations of the last word of each line. Some of them lead you to expect a complement and others don't. Try reading the poem again and see if the subcategorization frames make a difference in how much emphasis you put on each line.

Finally, look at some other poetry that you love or hate and see what sort of match there is between grouping in lines or stanzas and grouping into constituents. Look at some different types of writing and their phrase structures;

since punctuation is sadly limited in how well it can show pauses or emphasis or any sort of complex tone, the actual structure of the sentence can be crucial if the sentence is to be read with the right emphasis. And look in particular at some of your own writing and at how transformations of sentences could make a difference in their clarity. All of this theory might actually improve your writing.

*Newman, Lesléa (1991) "Tiff and I" in *Sweet Dark Places* HerBooks: Santa Cruz, CA.

six

INTERFACES

Michael Dobrovolsky
William O'Grady

. . . there is always some "leakage" between the hierarchical levels of science . . .

– D. HOFSTADTER

Up to this point, the individual components of a grammar have each been presented in some detail. These components, however, do not function in isolation. Rules in one component may depend on or affect those in another component. In this chapter, we explore some ways in which the different components of a grammar are related to each other. These **interfaces**, as they are called in contemporary linguistics, involve morphology and phonology, phonology and syntax, and morphology and syntax. (A fourth interface, involving syntax and semantics, is considered in the next chapter as part of the discussion of semantics.)

1 MORPHOLOGY AND PHONOLOGY

Chapter 3 of this book dealt with allophonic variation, which is represented by rules that derive allophones from underlying (phonemic) representations. A second type of variation in language involves morphemes and their allomorphs (first introduced in Chapter 4, Section 1.1). An example of allomorphic variation can be seen in the English plural morpheme, which has different allomorphs in the words *cat*[s], *dog*[z], and *match*[əz]. Like allophonic variation, this phenomenon is analyzed with the help of a single **underlying representation** from which the allomorphs can be derived. The rules that account for both allophonic and allomorphic variation make reference to phonetic environments, including syllable structure. There are, however, differences between allophonic and allomorphic variation, two of which are outlined in the following section.

1.1 Morphophonemic rules

Rules that account for alternations among allomorphs (morphophonemic alternations) are called **morphophonemic rules**. The major differences between allophonic and morphophonemic rules can be summed up under two major points.

- Allophonic rules are exceptionless—they apply in the appropriate environment to all classes and forms in a language. There are, for example, no exceptions to a rule such as aspiration in English. In contrast, morphophonemic rules often show exceptions. They may, for example, apply to a limited class of forms, as in the case of the rule that changes final *f* to *v* in the plural of a few English words like *knife* and *thief* (but not in *cough, bluff, whiff, chief,* and so on; we will examine this rule in more detail in Section 1.4).
- Morphophonemic rules often (but do not always) include affix boundaries in their environment. Such boundaries are not found in allophonic rules.

1.2 Deriving allomorphs

We analyze and derive allomorphs in much the same way we derive allophones. An underlying representation (UR) is set up, and rules apply to derive all phonetic variants from the same underlying representation. Often, the underlying representation of the morpheme is the elsewhere allomorph—the one that occurs with the widest distribution.

1.3 Conditioned allomorphs

The allomorphs of the English plural morpheme provide a typical example of phonologically **conditioned allomorphs**.

English plural allomorphs

The plural morpheme in English shows three-way variation in its allomorphs. The three allomorphs, /-s/, /-z/, and /-əz/, are distributed in a systematic manner, as Table 6.1 illustrates.

The phonetic form of these allomorphs is determined by the segment that precedes them. Bases that end in a strident (sibilant) consonant always appear with the /-əz/ allomorph. Bases that end in a vowel or a voiced consonant that is not strident take the /-z/ allomorph, and bases that end in a voiceless consonant that is not strident take the /-s/ allomorph.

A fundamental strategy in selecting the underlying form (UF) of an allomorph is to choose the one with the widest distribution. Since the /-z/ allomorph occurs after all vowels as well as after most voiced consonants, it is chosen as basic. This choice results in underlying representations that show /-z/ after all bases.

Table 6.1 English plural allomorphs

Allomorph: /-s/		*Environment*
tops	/tɑps/	• bases end in a voiceless consonant that is not strident
mitts	/mɪts/	
backs	/bæks/	
puffs	/pʌfs/	
myths	/mɪθs/	
Allomorph: /-z/		*Environment*
cobs	/kɑbz/	• bases end in a vowel or a voiced consonant that is not strident
lids	/lɪdz/	
lads	/lædz/	
doves	/dʌvz/	
lathes	/leðz/	
pins	/pɪnz/	
bums	/bʌmz/	
wings	/wɪŋz/	
teas	/tiz/	
days	/dez/	
Allomorph: /-əz/		*Environment*
hisses	/hɪsəz/	• bases end in a consonant that is strident (s, z, ʃ, ʒ, tʃ, dʒ)
mazes	/mezəz/	
crutches	/krʌtʃəz/	
judges	/dʒʌdʒəz/	
wishes	/wɪʃəz/	

Table 6.2 Underlying representations of some English plurals

tops	/tɑp-z/	cobs	/kɑb-z/	hisses	/hɪs-z/
mitts	/mɪt-z/	lids	/lɪd-z/	buzzes	/bʌz-z/
				judges	/dʒʌdʒ-z/

Derivation

Once the underlying representations have been set up, the phonetic forms can be derived. We can account for the allomorph /əz/ by noting that whenever the underlying /-z/ appears after a base that ends in a strident coronal consonant, a schwa is present. This reflects a phonotactic constraint of English that is expressible with reference to syllable structure: an English word cannot contain a sequence of strident consonants in the same coda. We can see that the reference to syllable structure is a necessary part of this statement by looking at other structures in which sequences of strident consonants occur. Such sequences are found across word boundaries in phrases and compounds, such as *crash site* /kræʃ sajt/ or *buzz saw* /bʌz sɔ/. They may even occur word-internally across syllable boundaries, as in *posture* /pɑstʃər/ (/pɑʃtʃər/ for some speakers). But when a sequence of two coronal stridents occurs in a coda, it is broken up by the epenthesis of a schwa. Since the coda sequence is impossible, a new syllable is created to accommodate it.

$$\text{ø} \rightarrow \begin{bmatrix} \text{+syllabic} \\ \text{+reduced} \end{bmatrix} \; / \; \text{[+strident]} \_\_\_ \text{[+strident]} \; \Big]_{\sigma}$$

Figure 6.1 English coda epenthesis

Given our understanding of this process, we can derive forms such as *matches, judges,* and so on.

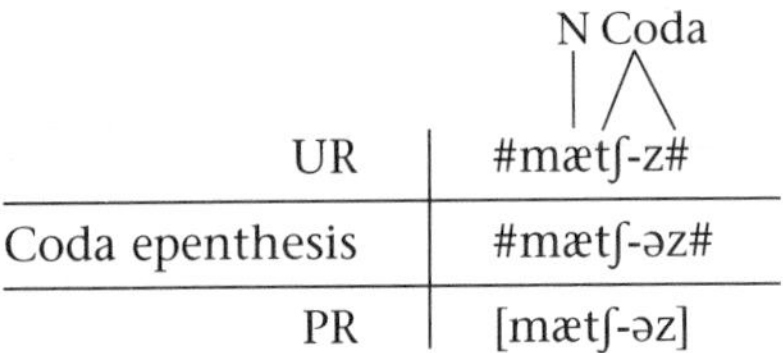

	N Coda
UR	#mætʃ-z#
Coda epenthesis	#mætʃ-əz#
PR	[mætʃ-əz]

Figure 6.2 Derivation of English *matches*

The appearance of [s] after voiceless consonants and [z] elsewhere is now representable as a case of voicing assimilation (laryngeal node spreading).

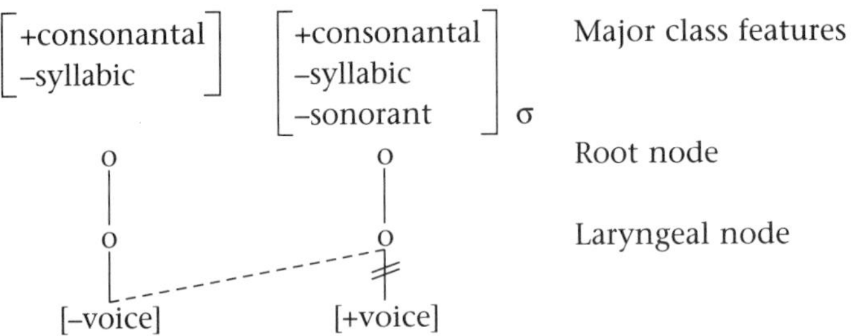

Figure 6.3 English coda voicing assimilation (laryngeal node spreading)

Figure 6.4 shows derivations of all three plural allomorphs. Note that the ordering of the rules is crucial here. If voicing assimilation applied first, the plural ending of forms such as *match* and *hiss* would incorrectly end up as */mætʃ-əs/ and */hɪs-əs/, since the suffix would assimilate in voicing before epenthesis could apply.

UR	#bʊk-z#	#fɪb-z#	#mætʃ-z#
Coda epenthesis	—	—	#mætʃ-əz#
→ Voicing assimilation	#bʊk-s#	—	—
PR	[bʊks]	[fɪbz]	[mætʃəz]

Figure 6.4 Derivations of English plural forms

In the next section we see how these same rules for determining the plural allomorphs of English interact with another type of morphophonemic rule.

1.4 Conditioning by morphological class

A second type of morphophonemic rule refers to a subclass of forms, rather than applying to all members of a class of forms. English plurals again provide the example.

Irregular English plurals

English includes a limited class of words that show an alternating /f/ and /v/ in their plural forms.

Table 6.3 Alternating base-final /f/ and /v/ in English

The /f/-/v/ alternation (irregular forms)		*No alternation (regular forms)*	
wife	wives	whiff	whiffs
thief	thieves	chief	chiefs
leaf	leaves	fife	fifes
knife	knives	laugh	laughs

The alternating class is unproductive; new words with final /f/ entering English will not show this alternation. For example, speakers would pluralize a hypothetical new word *nif* as /nɪfs/, not */nɪvz/. This implies that each word in the alternating class needs to be marked as undergoing a rule that voices its base-final segment when the form is pluralized. Such a rule takes the form shown in Figure 6.5, in which it is labelled *Rule PL* (*PL* stands for plural). Information about rules that a form must undergo is included in its entry in the lexicon. A form that undergoes Rule PL is marked as [+Rule PL]. Forms that are not so marked are automatically assumed to be [–Rule PL].

Rule PL: f → v / ___]-z_{plural}]

Figure 6.5 The f → v alternation rule in English

Following a base-changing rule such as Rule PL, the morphophonemic rule of voicing assimilation introduced in Figure 6.3 applies. Other relevant rules such as glide epenthesis apply as well. (Stress is not shown here.)

UR	#θif-z#$_{\text{[+Rule PL]}}$	#tʃif-z#
Rule PL (f → v)	#θiv-z #	—
Voicing assimilation	—	#tʃif-s#
Other rules	#θi:jv-z#	#tʃijf-s#
PR	[θi:jvz]	[tʃijfs]

Figure 6.6 Derivation of English *thiefs* and *chiefs*

The allophonic rules of vowel lengthening and glide insertion presented in Chapter 3 have also applied here to give the correct form of *thieves*.

The underlying forms presented so far in this chapter are all very much unlike their phonetic representations. The next section takes up the implications of this kind of representation in more detail.

1.5 Abstract underlying representations

Underlying representations generally show some degree of difference from phonetic representations. There are no phonetic forms like [mɪtz], [bʊkz], or [wajfz] in English, although such forms are found as underlying representations. Underlying representations are therefore said to be **abstract** because they are to a greater or lesser degree distinct from their phonetic realizations. The greater the difference between the phonological and the phonetic representations, the more abstract the phonological representation is said to be.

Although the URs that enable us to account for morphophonemic variation can be very abstract, there is an advantage to this kind of representation. Employing abstract underlying representations enables us to make greater generalizations about the relationship among allomorphs. For example, we have just seen how two phonetically distinct forms of the root morpheme *thief* are derived from the same UR.

Abstraction and English bases

In English, we can derive the root of both *electri*[k] and *electri*[s]*ity* from one underlying form. This approach captures the fact that English speakers recognize the two forms as variants of the same morpheme. Assuming that the underlying representation ends in *k*, we can write a morphophonemic rule that changes *k* to *s* before the suffix *-ity*.

k → s / ___ + ɪti

Figure 6.7 English *k* to *s* fronting

The variant of the base that ends in *k* is chosen as underlying for two reasons. First, the base *electri*[k] has a wider distribution than the allomorph *electri*[s]; it occurs in words such as *electrical* as well as in the unsuffixed form. Second, our proposed rule has the advantage of reflecting a natural process of fronting of final /k/ to [s] before the high front vowel of the suffix. It would be more difficult to find phonetic motivation for a rule that changes an /s/ to [k] in final position or before the suffix *-al*.

It is also significant that the rule must include morphological information—the identity of the suffix that triggers the change—since /k/ is not pronounced as [s] every time it appears before the vowel [ɪ] in English. If it were, English speakers would automatically pronounce *kill* as *sill*, and *kick* as *sick*. Since they do not, we assume that the morphological information is a crucial determining factor in this rule.

Derivations of *electric* and *electricity* are given in Figure 6.8. The allophonic rule of flapping and the stress rule are also involved in this derivation but are not formalized here.

UR	#ilɛktrɪk#	#ilɛktrɪk-ɪti#
Stress	#ilɛ́ktrɪk#	#ilɛktrík-ɪti#
k → s rule	—	#ilɛktrís-ɪti#
Flapping	—	#ilɛktrís-ɪɾi#
Other rules	#ijlɛ́ktr̥ɪk#	#ijlɛktr̥ís-ɪɾij#
PR	[ijlɛ́ktr̥ɪk]	[ijlɛktr̥ís-ɪɾij]

Figure 6.8 Derivation of *electric* and *electricity* in English

The underlying form is rather abstract in the case of #ilɛktrɪk-ɪti#, but our rule has allowed us to represent an English speaker's knowledge that the bases *electri*[k] and *electri*[s] are allomorphs of the same morpheme.

The next section examines some interactions between phonology and syntax.

2 PHONOLOGY AND SYNTAX

We saw in the first section of this chapter that some phonological rules include reference to subclasses of words and thus interact with the morphological component of a grammar. There are also rules that depend on certain kinds of syntactic information. Some stress patterns of English, for example, are determined by the syntactic category of the form to which the rules apply.

2.1 English stress

In English, there are pairs such as the following, which show differing stress placement.

Table 6.4 Contrasting stress patterns in English

A: Compounds		*B: Syntactic Phrases*	
gréenhòuse	'a place to grow flowers'	grèen hóuse	'a house that's green'
Whíte Hòuse	'the residence of the U.S. president'	whìte hóuse	'a house that's white'
féatherbèdding	'overemployment'	fèather bédding	'bedding with feathers in it'
bláckbìrd	'the blackbird *Agelaius phoeniceus*'	blàck bírd	'any bird that's black'

In Table 6.4, the words in Column A are compounds; primary stress is assigned to the first word in the compound. The words in Column B, however, are syntactic phrases in which primary stress is assigned to the last word in the phrase.

At the word level, each individual word receives its own stress, as is shown in the upper part of Figure 6.9; thus, *green* and *house* each receive word stress, marked by (x) in the figure. However, when words are grouped together to form compounds or phrases, one of the primary word stresses is more prominent than the others. In compound nouns, additional stress is assigned to the first word in the compound. This is represented by the (x) at the compound level in the lower part of Figure 6.9. In Figure 6.9, the primary stress falls on *green* (two x's), and a secondary stress on *house* (one x): *gréenhòuse*. The rule of stress placement in English noun compounds can be stated as follows:

1)

In an English noun compound, place an additional stress over the first word stress.

Word-level stress

(x) (x) Word level

[green]$_{Adj}$ [house]$_{N}$

Compound stress

(x) Compound level

(x) (x) Word level

[[green]$_{Adj}$ [house]$_{N}$]$_{N}$

(also: Whíte Hòuse, féatherbèdding, and other compounds)

Figure 6.9 Stress assignment in compounds

When words are combined into syntactic phrases, as is the case with the words in Column B in Table 6.4 *(grèen hóuse, whìte hóuse),* the primary stress falls on the last word in the phrase. In Figure 6.10, this is shown by using x's to mark stress at the word level and phrase level.

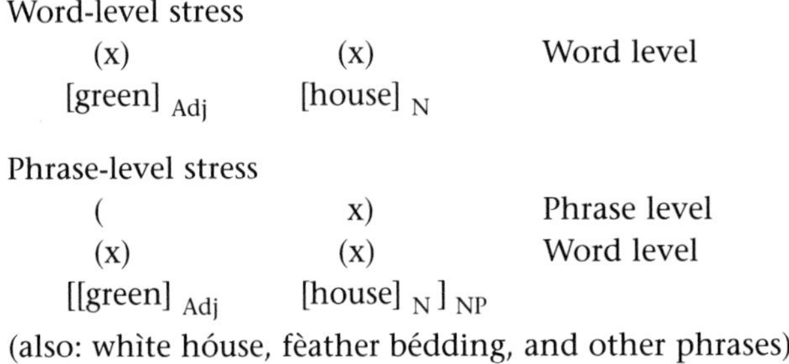

Figure 6.10 Stress assignment in phrases

For syntactic phrases, as for compounds, each word receives its own stress at the word level, as represented by the x's in the upper part of Figure 6.10. At the phrase level in Figure 6.10, unlike the compound level shown in Figure 6.9, the additional x shows that primary stress falls on the *last* word stress of the phrase. The primary stress falls on *hóuse* (two x's), while a secondary stress falls on *grèen* (one x). The rule of stress placement in English syntactic phrases can be stated as follows:

2)

In an English phrase, place an additional stress over the last stress.

2.2 Embedded compound stress

When a compound is embedded in a larger compound, the rule that stresses the first word applies again. For example, if the compound *bláckbìrd* is joined with *nést,* the new compound still shows primary stress on the first element: *bláckbird nèst.* This stress assignment takes place in stages as each part of the compound has stress assigned to it. Another level at which **compound stress** applies is added to the representation. Since the same rule of stressing applies at more than one level, each application is called a **cycle**.

Note that each time a new x is added to a compound at one level, a matching stress must be added to the word(s) outside the parentheses as well (as it is to *nest* here). This procedure assures that the secondary stresses will be correctly placed. The italic *x* indicates the matching stress that must be added to the other word(s) outside the parentheses.

Word-level stress

(x)	(x)	(x)	Word level
[black] $_N$	[bird] $_N$	[nest] $_N$	

Compound stress (first cycle)

(x	)	*x*	Compound level (first cycle)
(x)	(x)	(x)	Word level
[[black] $_N$	[bird] $_N$] $_N$	[nest] $_N$	

Compound stress (second cycle)

(x		)	Compound level (second cycle)
(x	)	x	Compound level (first cycle)
(x)	(x)	(x)	Word level
[[[black] $_N$	[bird] $_N$] $_N$	[nest] $_N$] $_N$	

Figure 6.11 Stress assignment in an embedded compound

Since *bird* did not receive an x at the compound level, its stress, after all stress levels have been assigned, is less than that of *nest*.

3 MORPHOLOGY AND SYNTAX

Many linguistic phenomena reflect the interaction of the morphological and syntactic components of the grammar. An important example of this interaction involves **case**, which indicates an NP's position in syntactic structure. Case is usually marked by inflecting the head of the NP (which will always be a noun or a pronoun).

As noted in Chapter 4, Section 6.3, English has only one case suffix—the ending written as *-'s*. This suffix marks an NP that occupies the specifier position within a larger NP, as depicted in Figure 6.12. (We extend the system of phrase structure presented in Chapter 5 by allowing an NP to serve as specifier of an N.)

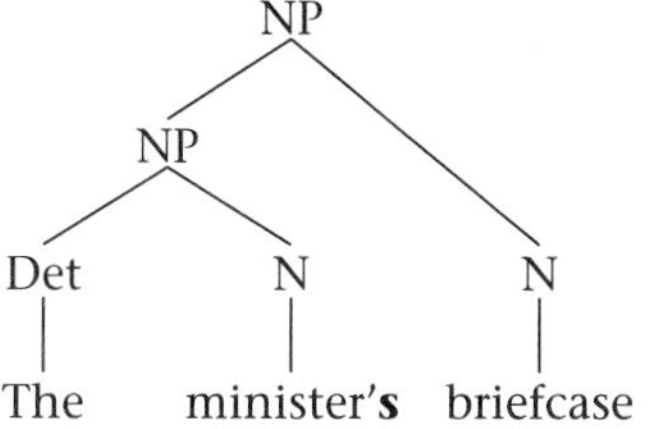

Figure 6.12 The genitive case marks an NP that functions as specifier of an N

As we also noted in Chapter 4, a somewhat richer system of contrasts is found in English pronouns, whose forms reflect a three-way case distinction.

Table 6.5 Case for the third person singular masculine pronoun in English

Form	*Name*	*Function*	*Example*
he	nominative	subject	He left.
his	genitive	specifier of N	his book
him	accusative	complement of V or P	Mary saw him. Mary sat near him.

Japanese also makes a three-way case distinction, with the nominative suffix *-ga* used for a subject, the genitive suffix *-no* for a specifier of N, and the accusative suffix *-o* for a complement of V. (Complements of P do not take a case suffix in Japanese.)

a The nominative and accusative

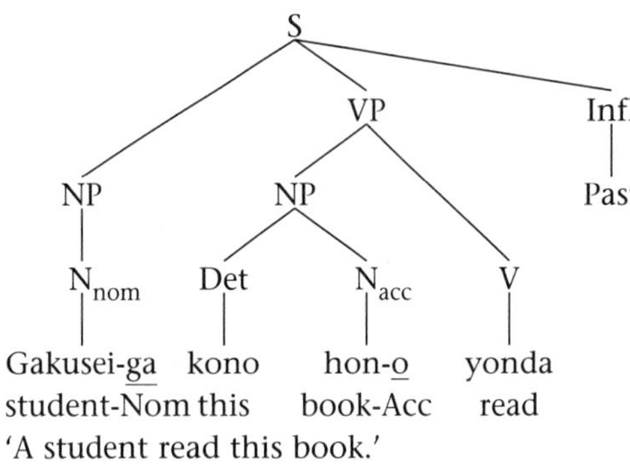

b The genitive

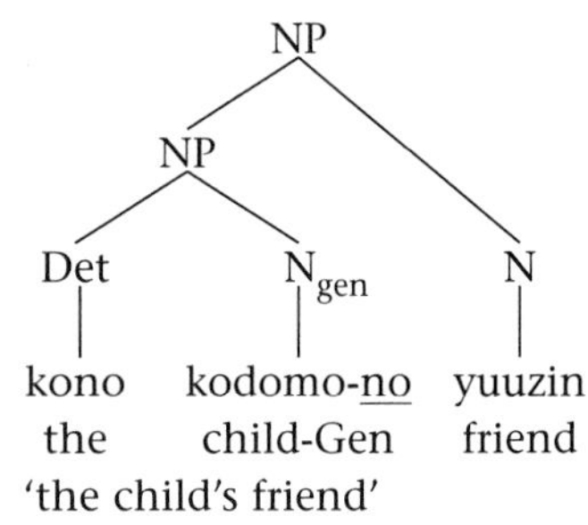

Figure 6.13 Case contrasts in Japanese

The case rules of English

In order to account for the case contrasts found in English nouns and pronouns, the grammar must include a set of rules that associate case with specific syntactic positions. The following rules capture the generalizations about English case noted above.

3)

The Case Rules for English NPs:

a. The complement of V receives accusative case.
b. The complement of P receives accusative case.
c. The specifier of N receives genitive case.
d. The subject receives nominative case.

Let us assume that the lexicon of English includes a list of the various case forms that each word can have. So, the entry for the third person singular masculine pronoun, for example, will include the following information:

4)

Case forms: *he* (nominative)
him (accusative)
his (genitive)

According to the rules in *3)*, then, a sentence such as *Mary saw him* is acceptable since the pronoun in the complement NP is accusative, as required by rule *3a)*.

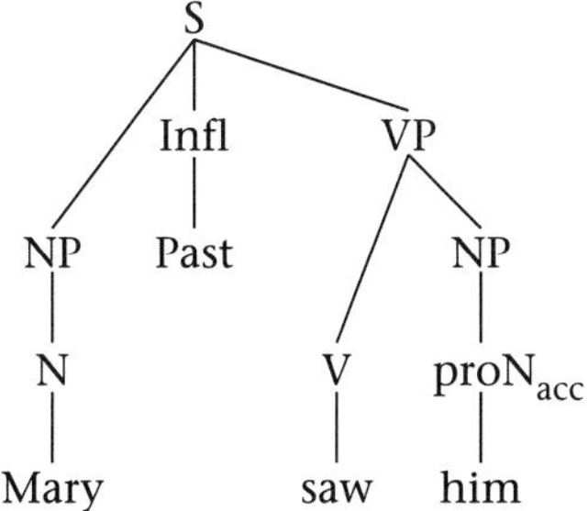

Figure 6.14 An example of case assignment in English

In contrast, a sentence such as **Mary saw he* is ungrammatical since the pronoun in the complement NP has the nominative form, in violation of rule *3a)*.

The Case Filter *(Advanced)*

You may have noticed that the case rules outlined in *3)* do not specify a case form for every imaginable position in syntactic structure. For instance, while the complements of V and P receive accusative case (rules *3a* and *3b*), no rule specifies the case of the complement of an A or N. Interestingly, these latter positions cannot be occupied by an NP.

5)

V with NP complement:
criticize [$_{NP}$ the girl]

P with NP complement:
near [$_{NP}$ the girl]

N with NP complement:
*criticism [$_{NP}$ the girl]

A with NP complement:
*critical [$_{NP}$ the girl]

We account for this by requiring that every NP receive case, regardless of whether the case is overtly expressed through inflection. This requirement is known as the **Case Filter**.

6)

The Case Filter:
Each NP in a grammatical sentence must receive case.

Phrases such as *criticize the girl* and *near the girl* satisfy the Case Filter since the NP *the girl* is in a position to receive accusative case, in accordance with *3a, b)*. (Although nouns have no visible inflection for the accusative case, a pronoun that occurred in this position would have the form *her* rather than *she*, so we know that the accusative case is assigned here.)

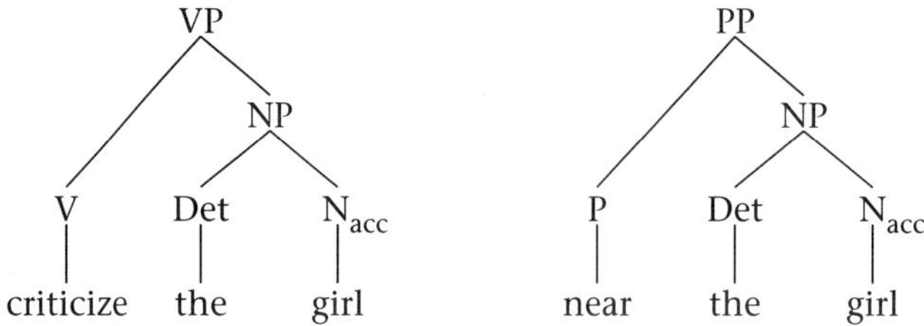

Figure 6.15 Case assignment to the complement of V and P

In contrast, the ill-formed phrases **criticism the girl* and **critical the girl* in *5)* above violate the Case Filter since the NP *the girl* is not in a position to which case is assigned. (Recall that no rule assigns case to the complement of N or A.)

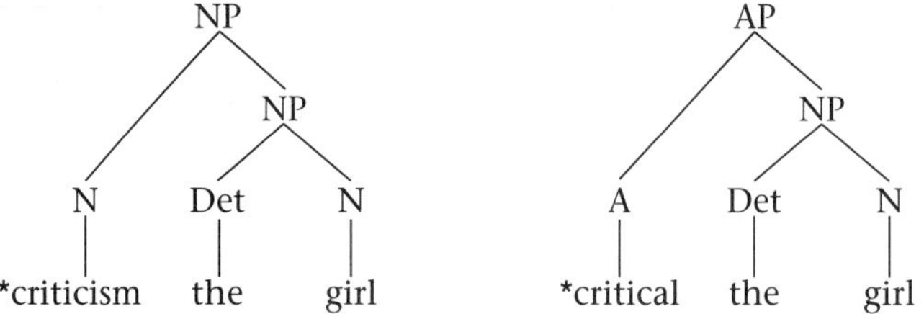

Figure 6.16 The absence of case on the complement of N and A

In order for these phrases to be grammatical, the complement must be realized as a PP.

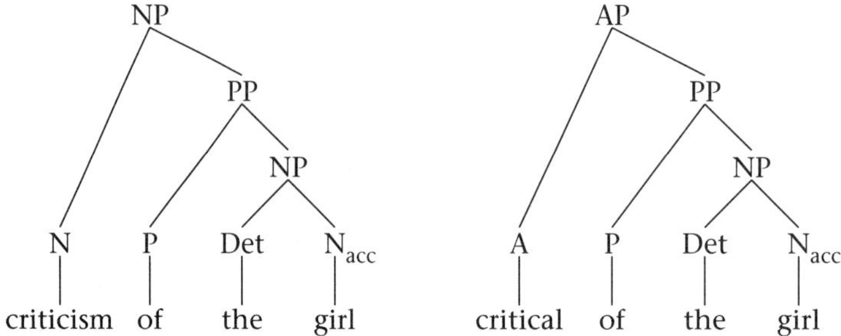

Figure 6.17 Case assignment when the complement of N and A is realized as a PP

As you can see, this structural pattern avoids the problem found in Figure 6.16 since the complement of P receives accusative case according to the rules in *3)*.

Sometimes an NP's case is determined by its position in deep structure rather than surface structure. A good example of this involves *wh* questions, in which the *wh* word appears in a position (the specifier of C) to which no case is assigned. Under such circumstances, the NP's deep structure position determines its case. Direct evidence for this comes from conservative varieties of English, in which *who* is associated with the subject position and the special accusative form *whom* with the direct object position.

7)

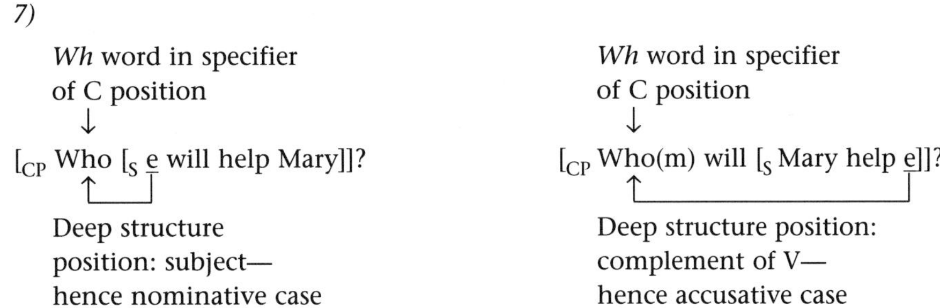

In summary, although case is an inflectional (morphological) category, it encodes syntactic information. This is captured by means of the rules outlined in *3)*, which associate each of the various case forms of English with a different position in syntactic structure (subject, specifier of N, complement of V, and so on). Taking this idea and extending it one step further, the Case Filter then ensures that NPs can only occur in positions to which case is assigned. This explains why an NP may serve as complement of a V or P (Figure 6.15), but not of an N or A (Figure 6.16).

Summing up

This chapter provides a glimpse of the sometimes complex interaction among several components of the grammar. Interaction between the phonological and morphological components is reflected by the presence of allomorphs. The use of underlying representations and derivation by **morphophonemic rules** accounts for these morphophonemic alternations. In some cases, allomorphy is determined by the fact that only certain classes of forms undergo a given morphophonemic rule. Dealing with allomorphy leads to underlying representations which in many cases are **abstract**. The use of a certain amount of abstraction in underlying representations allows allomorphs with distinct phonetic forms to be derived from single underlying forms. This chapter also shows how morphological and syntactic structure play a role in determining stress assignment in compounds and phrases in English. Finally, it demonstrates that **case** marking reflects an interaction between the form of words (**morphology**) and the positions they occupy in syntactic structures (**syntax**).

Key terms

abstract
case
Case Filter
compound stress
conditioned allomorphs
cycle
derivation
interfaces
morphophonemic rules
underlying representation (UR)

Sources

The problem of an underlying form for the plural suffix and of morphophonemic variation in general is discussed in Arnold Zwicky's article "Settling on an Underlying Form: The English Inflectional Endings" in *Testing Linguistic Hypotheses*, edited by D. Cohen and J. Wirth (New York: John Wiley, 1975). For a more detailed discussion of the Case Filter, see *Introduction to Government and Binding Theory*, 2nd edition, by L. Haegeman (Boston: Blackwell, 1994).

Recommended reading

Dressler, W. U. 1985. *Morphonology: The Dynamics of Derivation*. Ann Arbor: Karoma Publishers.

Gleason, Jr., H. A. 1961. *An Introduction to Descriptive Linguistics*. Toronto: Holt, Rinehart and Winston.

Inkelas, Sharon, and Draga Zec, eds. 1990. *The Phonology-Syntax Connection*. Chicago: University of Chicago Press.

Kenstowicz, Michael. 1994. *Phonology in Generative Grammar*. Cambridge, MA: Blackwell.

Pullum, G., and A. Zwicky. 1988. "The Syntax-Phonology Interface." In *Linguistics: The Cambridge Survey*. Vol 1. Edited by F. Newmeyer, 255–80. London: Cambridge University Press.

Questions

1. The following data provide the possible forms of the regular past tense morpheme of English.
   i) List the alternate forms of the past tense morpheme.

a)	walked	/wɔkt/	l)	heaved	/hivd/
b)	cracked	/krækt/	m)	wheezed	/wizd/
c)	flipped	/flɪpt/	n)	fined	/fajnd/
d)	hissed	/hɪst/	o)	flitted	/flɪtəd/
e)	huffed	/hʌft/	p)	butted	/bʌtəd/
f)	hushed	/hʌʃt/	q)	padded	/pædəd/
g)	munched	/mʌntʃt/	r)	loaded	/lodəd/
h)	drubbed	/drʌbd/	s)	collided	/kəlajdəd/
i)	dragged	/drægd/	t)	allowed	/ʌlawd/
j)	jogged	/dʒɑgd/	u)	sowed	/sod/
k)	fudged	/fʌdʒd/			

   ii) Which alternate makes the best underlying form? Why?
   iii) State in words the conditioning factors that account for the presence of the alternate forms of the past tense morpheme.

2. Vowel harmony is a process that results in all vowels of a word sharing a certain feature or features. Morphophonemic rules of vowel harmony are found in many languages.

		Singular	*Plural*
a)	'eye'	gøz	gøzler
b)	'candle'	mum	mumlar
c)	'gun'	top	toplar
d)	'horse'	at	atlar
e)	'sheath'	kɯn	kɯnlar
f)	'thread'	ip	ipler
g)	'rose'	gyl	gyller
h)	'hand'	el	eller
i)	'letter'	mektup	mektuplar
j)	'mother'	anne	anneler
k)	'harbor'	liman	limanlar
l)	'flame'	ʃule	ʃuleler

i) List the allomorphs of the plural morpheme in the preceding data from Turkish.

ii) What phonological feature is shared by the vowels of both allomorphs of the plural?

iii) What phonological feature distinguishes the vowels of the allomorphs?

iv) What feature of the last vowel in the root determines the choice of the plural allomorph?

v) Is it possible in this case to pick one allomorph as the best underlying form?

vi) Choose one allomorph as underlying, and provide a rule using features that derives the other one from it. Provide derivations for the words for 'eye' and 'gun'.

3. Provide derivations for the following English compounds and phrases using the model presented in Figures 6.9 through 6.11. Be careful! Some compounds may contain phrases and some phrases may contain compounds. When assigning stress in a cycle, apply the appropriate rule to the immediately preceding stage without reference to earlier stages.

	Compounds	*Phrases*
a)	basketball net	drive-in movie
b)	night club act	electric pencil sharpener
c)	wetsuit designer	West Hartford Mall

4. The following Russian sentences contain several different forms for the pronoun 'I'—*ja*, *m^{j}en^{j}a*, *mnoj*, and *mn^{j}e* (^{j} is palatalization).

Nominative

a) ja pon^{j}imaju urok
I understand lesson
'I understand the lesson.'

b) ja viʒu joʒika
I see hedgehog
'I see the hedgehog.'

Accusative

c) on uv^{j}id^{j}el m^{j}en^{j}a
he saw me
'He saw me.'

d) on^{j}i vstr^{j}et^{j}il^{j}i m^{j}en^{j}a
they met me
'They met me.'

Instrumental

e) vi poʃl^{j}i sa mnoj
you went with me
'You went with me.'

f) on^{j}i pogovor^{j}il^{j}i sa mnoj
they spoke with me
'They were talking with me.'

Dative

g) on^{j}i poʃl^{j}i k mn^{j}e
they arrived to me
'They came to my place.'

h) on podoʃol k mn^{j}e
he approached to me
'He approached me.'

i) Draw the tree structure for each of these sentences, and make a statement about the context in which each case form occurs.

ii) Does the complement of a preposition receive a special case in Russian?

iii) Is the case assigned to the complement of a preposition the same for the two prepositions used in the data?

seven

Semantics: The Analysis of Meaning

William O'Grady

. . . in every object there is inexhaustible meaning.

– Thomas Carlyle

Up to now, this book has focused on the form of utterances—their sound pattern, morphological structure, and syntactic organization. But there is more to language than just form. In order for language to fulfil its communicative function, utterances must also convey a message; they must have content. Speaking very generally, we can call this message or content the utterance's **meaning**.

This chapter is concerned with **semantics**, the study of meaning in human language. Because some work in this complicated area of linguistic analysis presupposes considerable knowledge of other disciplines (particularly logic, mathematics, and philosophy), not all aspects of contemporary semantics are suitable for presentation in an introductory linguistics textbook. We will restrict our attention here to four major topics in semantics: (1) the nature of meaning, (2) some properties of the conceptual system underlying meaning, (3) the contribution of syntactic structure to the interpretation of sentences, and (4) the role of nongrammatical factors in the understanding of utterances.

1 THE NATURE OF MEANING

Long before linguistics existed as a discipline, thinkers were speculating about the nature of meaning. For thousands of years, this question has been considered central to philosophy. More recently, it has come to be important in other disciplines as well, including psychology and sociology in addition to linguistics. Contributions to semantics have come from a diverse group of scholars, ranging from Plato and Aristotle in ancient Greece to Bertrand Russell in the twentieth century. Our goal in this section will be to consider in a very general way what this research has revealed about meaning in human language. We will begin by considering some of the basic analytic notions used in evaluating the meanings of words and sentences.

1.1 Semantic relations among words

By virtue of their meaning, words and phrases may enter into a variety of semantic relations with other words and phrases in the language. Because these relationships help identify those aspects of meaning relevant to linguistic analysis, they constitute a good starting point for this chapter.

Synonymy

Synonyms are words or expressions that have the same meanings in some or all contexts. The following pairs of words provide plausible examples of synonymy in English.

Table 7.1 Some synonyms in English

youth	adolescent
automobile	car
remember	recall
purchase	buy
filbert	hazelnut
big	large

Although it is easy to think of contexts in which both words in each pair have essentially the same meaning, there are also contexts in which their meanings diverge at least slightly. For example, although *youth* and *adolescent* both refer to people of about the same age, only the latter word has the meaning of 'immature' in a phrase such as *What an adolescent!* Many linguists believe that it would be inefficient for a language to have two words or phrases whose meanings are absolutely identical in all contexts, and that complete synonymy is therefore rare or nonexistent.

Antonymy

Antonyms are words or phrases that are opposites with respect to some component of their meaning. The following pairs of words provide examples of antonymy.

Table 7.2 Some antonyms in English

dark	light
boy	girl
hot	cold
up	down
in	out
come	go

In each of these pairs, the two words contrast with respect to at least one component of their meaning. Thus, the meanings of *boy* and *girl* are opposites with respect to sex, although they are alike with respect to species (both are human). Similarly, *come* and *go* are opposites with respect to direction, although both involve the concept of movement.

Polysemy and homophony

Polysemy occurs where a word has two or more related meanings. The following table contains some examples of polysemous words in English.

Table 7.3 Some polysemy in English

Word	*Meaning a*	*Meaning b*
bright	'shining'	'intelligent'
to glare	'to shine intensely'	'to stare angrily'
a deposit	'minerals in the earth'	'money in the bank'

If you consult a reasonably comprehensive dictionary for any language, you will find numerous examples of polysemy.

Homophony exists where a single form has two or more entirely distinct meanings. In such cases, it is assumed that there are two (or more) separate words with the same pronunciation rather than a single word with different meanings.

Table 7.4 Some homophones in English

Word	*Meaning a*	*Meaning b*
bat	'a mouselike flying mammal'	'a piece of equipment used in baseball'
bank	'a financial institution'	'a small cliff at the edge of a river'
club	'a social organization'	'a blunt weapon'
pen	'a writing instrument'	'a small enclosure'

Polysemy and homophony create **lexical ambiguity** in that a single form has two or more meanings. Thus, a sentence such as *1)* could mean either that Liz purchased an instrument to write with or that she bought a small enclosure.

1)

Liz bought a pen.

Of course, in actual speech the surrounding words and sentences usually make the intended meaning clear. The lexical ambiguity in sentences such as the following therefore normally goes unnoticed.

2)

He got a loan from the *bank*.

3)

Because Liz needed a place to keep her goat, she went downtown and bought a *pen* for $100.

1.2 Semantic relations involving sentences

Like words, sentences have meanings that can be analyzed in terms of their relation to other meanings. We consider three such relations here—paraphrase, entailment, and contradiction.

Paraphrase

Two sentences that can have the same meaning are said to be **paraphrases** of each other. The following pairs of sentences provide examples of paraphrase.

4)

a. The police chased the burglar.
b. The burglar was chased by the police.

5)

a. I gave the summons to Erin.
b. I gave Erin the summons.

6)

a. It is unfortunate that the team lost.
b. Unfortunately, the team lost.

7)

a. Paul bought a car from Sue.
b. Sue sold a car to Paul.

8)

a. The game will begin at 3:00 P.M.
b. At 3:00 P.M., the game will begin.

The *a)* and *b)* sentences in each of the above pairs are obviously very similar in meaning. Indeed, it would be impossible for one sentence in any pair to be true without the other also being true. Thus, if it is true that the police chased the burglar, it must also be true that the burglar was chased by the police. Similarly, if it is false that the police chased the burglar, then it must also be false that the burglar was chased by the police. (Sentences whose meanings are related to each other in this way are said to have the same **truth conditions**.)

For some linguists, this is enough to justify saying that the two sentences have the same meaning. However, you may notice that there are subtle differences in emphasis between the *a)* and *b)* sentences in *4)* to *8)*. For instance, it is natural to interpret *4a)* as a statement about what the police did and *4b)* as a statement about what happened to the burglar. Similarly, *8b)* seems to place more emphasis on the starting time of the game than *8a)* does. As is the case with synonymy, many linguists feel that languages do not permit two or more structures to have absolutely identical meanings and that paraphrases are therefore never perfect.

Entailment

A relation in which the truth of one sentence necessarily implies the truth of another, as happens in examples *4)* to *8)* above, is called **entailment**. In the cases we have been considering, the entailment relation between the *a)* and *b)* sentences is mutual since the truth of either sentence guarantees the truth of the other. In some cases, however, entailment is asymmetrical. The following examples illustrate this.

9)

a. The park wardens killed the bear.
b. The bear is dead.

10)

a. Robin is a man.
b. Robin is human.

The *a)* sentences in *9)* and *10)* entail the *b)* sentences. If it is true that the park wardens killed the bear, then it must also be true that the bear is dead. However, the reverse does not follow since the bear could be dead without the park wardens having killed it. Similarly, if it is true that Robin is a man, then it is also true that Robin is human. Once again though, the reverse does not hold: Even if we know that Robin is a human, we cannot conclude that Robin is a man rather than a woman or a child.

Contradiction

Sometimes, it turns out that if one sentence is true, then another sentence must be false. This is the case with the examples in *11)*.

11)

a. Charles is a bachelor.
b. Charles is married.

If it is true that Charles is a bachelor, then it cannot be true that he is married. When two sentences cannot both be true, we say that there is a **contradiction**.

1.3 What is meaning?

Although it is relatively easy to determine whether two words or sentences have identical or different meanings, it is much more difficult to determine precisely what meaning is in the first place. In fact, despite many centuries of study, we still know very little about the nature of meaning or how it is represented in the human mind. Nonetheless, it is worthwhile to review briefly some of the better known proposals and the problems that they encounter.

Connotation

One notion that is closely linked with the concept of meaning is **connotation**, the set of associations that a word's use can evoke. For most Minnesotans, for example, the word *winter* evokes thoughts of snow, bitter cold, short evenings, frozen fingertips, and the like. These associations make up the word's connotation, but they cannot be its meaning (or at least not its entire meaning). The word *winter* does not become meaningless just because it is a mild year or because one moves to Florida in November. We must therefore look beyond connotation for our understanding of what meaning is.

Denotation

One well-known approach to semantics attempts to equate the meaning of a word or phrase with the entities to which it refers—its **denotation** or **referents**. The denotation of the word *winter*, for example, corresponds to the season around the winter solstice (regardless of whether it is cold and unpleasant). Similarly, the denotation of the word *dog* corresponds to the set of canines, and so on.

Although a word's denotation is clearly connected to its meaning in some way, they cannot be one and the same thing. This is because there are words such as *unicorn* and phrases such as *the present king of France*, which have no referents in the real world even though they are far from meaningless.

A problem of a different sort arises with expressions such as *the Prime Minister of England* and *the leader of the Conservative Party*, both of which refer (in 1996, at least) to John Major. Although these two expressions may have the same referent, it seems wrong to say that they mean the same thing. Thus, we would not say that the phrase *Prime Minister of England* is defined as 'the leader of the Conservative Party' or that the definition of the phrase *leader of the Conservative Party* is 'Prime Minister of England'.

Extension and intension

The impossibility of equating an element's meaning with its referents has led to a distinction between **extension** and **intension**. Whereas an expression's extension corresponds to the set of entities that it picks out in the world (its referents), its intension corresponds to its inherent sense, the concepts that it evokes. Thus, the extension of *woman* is a set of real world entities (women) while its intension involves notions like 'female' and 'human'. Similarly, the phrase *Prime Minister of England* has as its extension an individual (John Major), but its intension involves the concept 'leader of the governing party'.

Table 7.5 Extension versus intension

Phrase	*Extension*	*Intension*
Prime Minister of England	John Major	leader of the governing party
Stanley Cup champions (1995)	New Jersey Devils	winners of the hockey championship
Capital of Missouri	Jefferson City	city containing the state legislature

The distinction between intension and extension does not allow us to resolve the question of what meaning is. It simply permits us to pose it in a new way: What are intensions?

One suggestion is that intensions correspond to mental images. This is an obvious improvement over the referential theory since it is possible to have a mental image of a unicorn or even of the king of France, although there are no such entities in the real world. However, problems arise with the meanings of words such as *dog*, which can be used to refer to animals of many different sizes, shapes, and colors. If the meaning of this word corresponds to a mental image, that image would have to be general enough to include Chihuahuas and St. Bernards, yet still exclude foxes and wolves. If you try to draw a picture that satisfies these requirements, you will see just how hard it is to equate word meanings with images in such cases.

Componential analysis

Still another approach to meaning tries to represent a word's intension by breaking it down into smaller semantic components. Sometimes known as **componential analysis** or **semantic decomposition**, this approach has long been used to analyze the meaning of certain types of nouns in terms of **semantic features**. The following analysis for the words *man, woman, boy,* and *girl* illustrates this. (Nothing depends on the choice of feature names here; the analysis would work just as well with the feature ±FEMALE as ±MALE.)

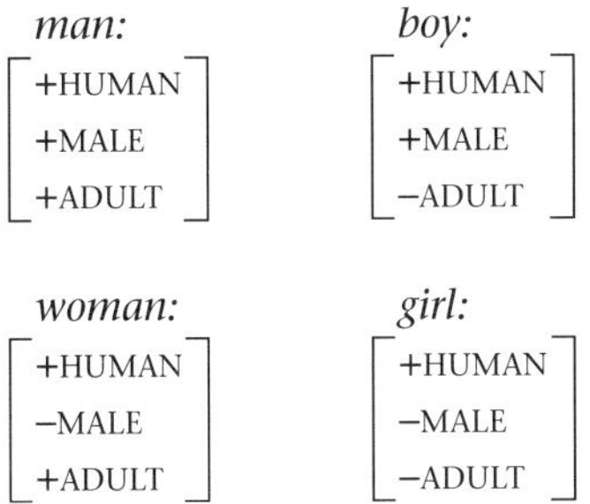

Figure 7.1 Semantic feature composition for *man, woman, boy, girl*

An obvious advantage of this approach is that it allows us to group entities into natural classes (much as we do in phonology). Hence, *man* and *boy* could be grouped together as [+HUMAN, +MALE] while *man* and *woman* could be put in a class defined by the features [+HUMAN, +ADULT].

Componential analysis can also be used to analyze verb meanings, although here the semantic components tend not to be written as binary features. A semantic component that is especially useful for the analysis of verb meaning is GO, which is used to represent change of various sorts. As the following examples help show, the notion of change associated with GO can be manifested in different ways.

12)

manifestations of the concept GO:

a. positional change:
Harvey went from Chicago to Dubuque.

b. possessional change:
The inheritance went to Marla.

c. identificational change:
Max went from being a rational gentleman to being a stark raving lunatic.

This concept is manifested in many verbs other than just *go*. For example, positional GO is present in the meaning of *fly* ('go through the air'), *walk* ('go on foot'), *crawl* ('go on hands and knees'), and so forth. Possessional GO is manifested in the meaning of *give, buy,* and *inherit,* all of which involve a change of possession, while identificational GO shows up in *become* and *turn into* (as in *The caterpillar turned into a butterfly*).

Componential analysis is most useful for uncovering and representing similarities among semantically related words. As illustrated above, a few simple features allow us to express the similarities and differences among subclasses of people—men, women, boys, and girls. Similarly, componential analysis reveals a surprising similarity in the meaning of (for instance) *fly*, *give*, and *become*, all of which incorporate the GO concept (positional in the first case, possessional in the second, and identificational in the third).

However, there are limits on the insights into word meaning offered by componential analysis. What value, for example, is there in characterizing the meaning of *dog* as [+ANIMAL, +CANINE] so long as there is no further analysis of these features? Similarly, do we say that the meaning of *blue* consists of the feature [+COLOR] and something else? If so, what is that other thing? Isn't it blueness? If so, then we still have not broken the meaning of *blue* into smaller components, and we are back where we started.

2 THE CONCEPTUAL SYSTEM

Underlying the use of words and sentences to express meaning in human language is a conceptual system capable of organizing and classifying every imaginable aspect of our experience, from inner feelings and perceptions, to cultural and social phenomena, to the physical world that surrounds us. This section focuses on what the study of this conceptual system reveals about how meaning is expressed through language. We will begin by considering some examples that illustrate the way in which these concepts are structured, extended, and interrelated.

2.1 FUZZY CONCEPTS

We tend to think that the concepts expressed by the words and phrases of our language have precise definitions with clear-cut boundaries that distinguish them from other concepts. Some concepts may indeed be like this. For example, the concept expressed by the word *senator* seems to be clear-cut enough: One is a senator if and only if one is duly elected to a particular legislative body; no other person can be truthfully called a senator.

But are all concepts so straightforward? Consider the concept associated with the word *rich*. How much does one have to be worth to be called rich? Five hundred thousand dollars? Eight hundred thousand? A million? Is there any figure that we can give that would be so precise that a person who was short by just five cents would not be called rich? It seems not. While one could miss out on being a senator by five votes, it does not seem possible to miss out on being rich by just five cents. Moreover, whereas some people clearly qualify as rich and others uncontroversially do not, an indefinitely large number of people fall into the unclear area at the borderline of the concept and it is just not possible to say definitively whether or not they count as rich. This is because the notion of 'richness' does not have clear-cut boundaries; it is what we call a **fuzzy concept**.

Many linguists believe that this type of fuzziness pervades the human conceptual system. Certainly, it is not hard to think of everyday concepts whose boundaries are fuzzy in the same way as the preceding example—*tall, old, athlete, strong, gray-haired, genius, clean, bargain*—the list seems almost endless.

Graded membership

A second important fact about concepts is that their members can be **graded** in terms of their typicality. Consider first a fuzzy concept such as 'figure-skating star'. Even within the set of people who we can agree are figure-skating stars, some provide better examples of this concept than others. At the time of writing, for instance, Nancy Kerrigan is a better example of a skating star than is Michelle Kwan. Although skating fans agree that both are stars, Kerrigan has won more medals, endorsed more products on TV, received more media attention, and so on. This makes her a better example of a star than Michelle Kwan.

Even concepts whose boundaries can be scientifically defined exhibit this type of graded membership. A good example of this involves the concept 'bird'. Even assuming that English speakers all think of birds as 'warm-blooded, egg-laying, feathered vertebrates with forelimbs modified to form wings' (the dictionary definition), they still feel that some of these creatures are more bird-like than others. Thus, robins and magpies, for example, are intuitively better examples of birds than are hummingbirds, ostriches, or penguins.

Examples like these suggest that concepts have an internal structure, with the best or **prototypical** exemplars (Nancy Kerrigan in the case of 'figure skaters', robins in the case of 'birds') close to the core and less typical members arranged in successively more peripheral regions.

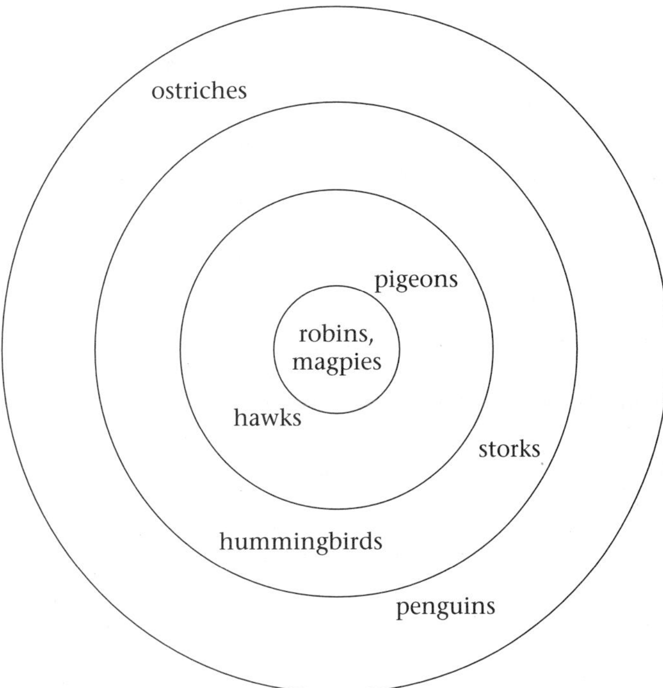

Figure 7.2 Internal structure of the concept 'bird'

The existence of fuzzy concepts and of graded membership in concepts provides important insights into the nature of the human conceptual system. In particular, it seems that many (perhaps even most) concepts expressed in language are not rigid all-or-nothing notions with precise and clear-cut boundaries. Rather, they are characterized by an internal structure that recognizes degrees of typicality as well as by fuzzy boundaries that sometimes overlap with other concepts and make categorization uncertain in some cases.

2.2 Metaphor

The concepts expressed through language are not isolated from each other. Rather, they make up a giant network, with many interconnections and associations among the various subparts. A good example of these interconnections involves **metaphor**, the understanding of one concept in terms of another.

We have a tendency to think of metaphor as a literary device reserved for the use of authors and poets. In fact, however, there is reason to think that it has a prominent place in the conceptual system shared by all human beings. The effects of this prominence are seen in the way in which we use language to talk about various abstract notions.

A simple example of this involves the concept of time, which we analyze metaphorically by treating it as if it were a concrete commodity. Consider in this regard the following sentences, which illustrate how we talk about time.

13)

a. You're *wasting* my time.
b. This gadget will *save* you hours.
c. How do you *spend* your time these days?
d. I have *invested* a lot of time in that project.
e. You need to *budget* your time.
f. Is that *worth* your while?
g. He's living on *borrowed* time.
h. You don't use your time *profitably*.

The words that we use in speaking about time suggest that it is conceptualized as something concrete—a commodity that can be saved, wasted, and invested just like other valuable things can.

What is the basis for the metaphor that determines how we talk about time? There is apparently no objective, inherent similarity between time and commodities such as gold or money. What brings these two concepts together is the *perception*, based in part on culture and in part on feelings that all human beings share, that the passing of time is reminiscent of the passage of valuable commodities from one hand to another.

Spatial metaphor

Another very prevalent metaphor in our language involves the use of words that are primarily associated with spatial orientation to talk about physical and psychological states.

Table 7.6 Metaphorical use of spatial terms

EMOTIONS: HAPPY IS UP; SAD IS DOWN	
I'm feeling *up*.	I'm feeling *down*.
That *boosted* my spirits.	He *fell* into a depression.
My spirits *rose*.	Her spirits *sank*.
You're in *high* spirits.	He's feeling *low*.
the *height* of ecstasy	the *depths* of depression
That gave me a *lift*.	
PHYSICAL HEALTH: HEALTH AND LIFE ARE UP; SICKNESS AND DEATH ARE DOWN	
He's at the *peak* of health	He's *sinking* fast.
Lazarus *rose* from the dead.	He *fell* ill.
He's in *top* shape.	He came *down* with the flu.
	Her health is *declining*.
	She's feeling *under* the weather.

The basis for these metaphors appears to lie in our physical experience. Unhappiness and ill health tend to be associated with lethargy and inactivity, which often involve being on one's back (physically down). In contrast, happiness and good health are often correlated with energy and movement, which involve being on one's feet (physically up).

These few examples illustrate a more general point about language and meaning. The innumerably many concepts that we express through language do not all exist independent of each other. Rather, many concepts are structured and understood metaphorically in terms of notions more basic to our physical and cultural experience. Thus, time is understood in terms of a commodity metaphor, health and happiness in terms of a **spatial metaphor**, and so on. By studying how concepts are represented in language, we can gain valuable insights into the role of experience and metaphor in the human conceptual system.

2.3 THE LEXICALIZATION OF CONCEPTS

Do all human beings share the same conceptual system? Do all languages express concepts in the same way? These are questions that have fascinated and puzzled researchers for many decades. At the present time, there is no reason to believe that human beings in different linguistic communities have different conceptual systems. But there is ample evidence that languages can differ from each other in terms of how they express concepts.

Lexicalization

The classic and frequently distorted example of how languages can differ from each other in the expression of concepts involves the words for 'snow' in Inuktitut. Sometimes estimated in the hundreds by unknowledgeable commentators, the set of simple (one-morpheme) words for 'snow' in Inuktitut is in fact much smaller. For example, one well-known dictionary gives only the following four items (although other dictionaries give several more for at least some varieties of Inuktitut).

Table 7.7 Words for 'snow' in Inuktitut

aput	'snow on the ground'
qana	'falling snow'
piqsirpoq	'drifting snow'
qimuqsuq	'snow drift'

As you can see, there is nothing particularly startling about this list of words. In fact, even in English there is more than just one word to describe snow in its various forms—*snow, slush, blizzard,* and *sleet* come to mind, for example.

The types of differences we are considering involve **lexicalization**, the process whereby concepts are encoded in the words of a language. Thus, Inuktitut lexicalizes the concepts 'falling' and 'snow' in a single word (*qana*) while English uses two separate words. While some lexicalization differences may correlate with cultural factors (the relative importance of types of snow in traditional Inuit culture), this is not always so. For example, English has an unusually rich set of vocabulary items pertaining to the perception of light.

Table 7.8 Some verbs pertaining to light in English

glimmer	glisten
gleam	glow
glitter	flicker
shimmer	shine
flare	glare
flash	sparkle

Although most English speakers know and use the words in this list, it is hard to see how the variety found in this particular area of vocabulary can be correlated with any identifiable feature of our culture or society.

Contrary to popular belief, the lexicalization differences just illustrated are not considered by linguists to have any special importance. As we have tried to emphasize throughout this book, the focus of linguistic analysis is on the *system* of knowledge that makes it possible to speak and understand a language. The fact that a particular language has more words pertaining to snow or light does not in and of itself provide any insight into the nature of the human linguistic system, and therefore does not merit special attention. However, as we will see in the next subsection, there are lexicalization differences whose properties can shed light on how linguistic systems express meaning.

Motion verbs

All languages have words that can describe motion through space (in English, *come, go,* and *move,* among many others). However, recent work suggests that there may be systematic differences in terms of how languages express motion and the concepts related to it. In English, for example, there are many verbs that can simultaneously express both the concept of motion and the manner in which the motion occurs.

Table 7.9 Some verbs expressing motion and manner in English

The rock *rolled* down the hill.
The puck *slid* across the ice.
She *limped* through the house.
The smoke *swirled* through the opening.

Notice how each of these verbs expresses both the fact that something moved and the manner in which it moved (by rolling, sliding, limping, and so on).

Interestingly, Romance languages (descendants of Latin) cannot express motion events in this way. Thus, while Spanish has a verb *rodar* with the meaning 'to roll', it does not use this verb to express both manner and motion as English does.

14)

*La botella rodó en la cueva.
'The bottle rolled into the cave.'

Instead, the motion and its manner have to be expressed separately.

15)

La botella entró en la cueva, rodando.
'The bottle entered the cave, rolling.'

However, Spanish *does* have a series of verbs that jointly express the concept of motion and the path along which it occurs.

Table 7.10 Some verbs expressing motion and path in Spanish

El globo	*bajó*	por la chimenea.
'The balloon moved-down through the chimney'		
El globo	*subió*	por la chimenea.
'The balloon moved-up through the chimney'		
La botella	*volvió*	a la orilla.
'The bottle moved-back to the bank.'		
La botella	*cruzó*	el canal.
'The bottle moved-across the canal.'		
La botella	*salió*	de la cueva.
'The bottle moved-out from the cave.'		

As the English translations show, Spanish verbs of motion express both the concept of movement and the direction of its path—down, up, back, across, out, and so forth. (English too has verbs that can express both motion and path—*descend, ascend, return*, and so on—but these words are not part of its native vocabulary. Rather they were borrowed into English from latinate sources, usually through French.)

Another lexicalization option is found in the Amerindian language Atsugewi (spoken in northern California), in which verbs can express both motion and the type of thing that moves.

Table 7.11 Some verb roots expressing motion and the thing moving in Atsugewi

lup	for movement of a small, shiny spherical object (a hailstone)
t	for movement of a smallish, flat object that can be attached to another (a stamp, a clothing patch, a shingle)
caq	for movement of a slimy, lumpish object (a toad, a cow dropping)
swal	for movement of a limp linear object, suspended by one end (a shirt on a clothesline, a hanging dead rabbit)
qput	for movement of loose, dry dirt
staq	for movement of runny, unpleasant material (manure, guts, chewed gum, rotten tomatoes)

We learn two things from these facts. First, the concept of motion is associated with a number of other concepts, including 'path', 'manner of movement', and 'moving thing'. Second, the way in which these concepts are grouped together for purposes of lexicalization can differ systematically from language to language. Languages such as English have verbs that simultaneously lexicalize motion and manner while other languages have verbs that simultaneously lexicalize motion and path (Spanish) or motion and the type of thing that moves (Atsugewi).

The general picture that is emerging from this type of work is consistent with the key idea underlying componential analysis (Section 1.3). In particular, it seems that at least within certain semantic domains, there may be a small universal set of concepts (motion, manner, path, thing that moves, and so on) and a small set of options for how these concepts can be combined for purposes of lexicalization. Unlike the lexicalization differences involving snow and light discussed earlier, these differences appear to be highly systematic and to reveal some general tendencies about the way in which meaning can be expressed in human language. Further work of this type should provide additional insights into the organization of the human conceptual system as well as the ways in which its component notions can be lexicalized in human language.

2.4 The grammaticization of concepts

Of the indefinitely large set of concepts expressible in human language, a relatively small subset enjoys a special status. These are the concepts that are lexicalized as affixes and nonlexical (functional) categories in one language or another. Some of the concepts that are treated this way in English are listed in Table 7.12. Concepts that are expressed as affixes or nonlexical categories are said to have been **grammaticized**.

Some concepts tend to be highly grammaticizable in that most, if not all, languages lexicalize them as affixes or special nonlexical categories. Negation and conjunction are possible examples of concepts that are grammaticized in all languages. Contrasts involving singular versus plural and past versus nonpast are encoded by special affixes in many languages, but not all. Still other concepts are grammaticized in a smaller number of languages, as the example in Table 7.13 from the Siouan language Hidatsa illustrates.

Table 7.12 Some concepts associated with affixes and nonlexical categories in English

Concept	*Affix*
Past	*-ed*
More than one	*-s*
Again	*re-*
Negation	*in-, un-*
Concept	*Non-lexical category*
Obligation	*must*
Possibility	*may*
Definite, specific	*the*
Indefinite, nonspecific	*a*
Disjunction	*or*
Negation	*not*
Conjunction	*and*

Hidatsa assertion morphemes

In Hidatsa, each statement is accompanied by a morpheme to indicate which of the following five categories it exemplifies. (Still other markers are used for questions, commands, and wishes.)

Table 7.13 Assertion particles in Hidatsa

ski	THE SPEAKER IS CERTAIN OF THE STATEMENT'S TRUTH Waceo iikipi kure heo -ski 'The man (definitely) carried the pipe.'
c	THE SPEAKER BELIEVES THE STATEMENT TO BE TRUE Waceo iikipi kure heo -c. 'The man (supposedly) carried the pipe.'
wareac	THE SPEAKER REGARDS THE STATEMENT TO BE COMMON KNOWLEDGE Waceo iikipi kure heo -wareac. 'The man carried the pipe (they say).'
rahe	THE STATEMENT IS BASED ON AN UNVERIFIED REPORT FROM SOMEONE ELSE Waceo wiira rackci heo -rahe. 'The man roasted the goose (it is rumored).'
toak	THE TRUTH OF THE STATEMENT IS UNKNOWN TO BOTH SPEAKER AND LISTENER Waceo cihpa rakci heo -toak. 'The man roasted the prairie dog (perhaps).'

Choice of the appropriate assertion particle is extremely important in Hidatsa. A speaker who utters a false sentence marked by the particle *-ski* is considered to be a liar. Had he or she used the particle *-c*, on the other hand, it would be assumed that he or she simply made a mistake.

While English has ways of indicating these contrasts (by using expressions such as *perhaps*, *I heard that*, and *I guess*), it does not have a grammatical system of morphemes that obligatorily encodes this information in every sentence. By investigating the grammaticization options found in different languages, it may eventually be possible to identify the factors that determine which concepts are singled out for association with affixes and nonlexical categories.

3 SYNTAX AND SENTENCE INTERPRETATION

The two preceding sections have focused on the meaning conveyed by the individual words and phrases that make up a sentence. In this section, we turn to the problem of sentence interpretation, with an emphasis on how the positioning of words and phrases in syntactic structure helps determine the meaning of the entire sentence, consistent with the following principle.

16)

The Principle of Compositionality:
The meaning of a sentence is determined by the meaning of its component parts and the manner in which they are arranged in syntactic structure.

There are many different ideas about precisely how the meaning of a sentence's component words and their arrangement in syntactic structure determine sentence meaning. For purposes of illustration, we will consider the relevance of syntactic structure to three aspects of sentence interpretation—the representation of structural ambiguity, the assignment of thematic roles, and the interpretation of pronouns.

3.1 Structural ambiguity

Some sentences are **structurally ambiguous** in that the meanings of their component words can be combined in more than one way. A simple example of this is found in the phrase *wealthy men and women*, where 'wealthy' can be seen as a property of both the men and the women or of just the men alone. These two interpretations or **readings** are depicted in Figure 7.3. (Con = conjunction)

Figure 7.3a corresponds to the reading in which *wealthy* modifies both *men* and *women*. This is shown by having the adjective combine with a category that includes both nouns. In Figure 7.3b, on the other hand, the adjective combines only with the N *men*. This structure corresponds to the reading in which 'wealthy' applies only to the men.

Another case of structural ambiguity is found in sentences such as *17)*.

17)

Nicole saw the people with binoculars.

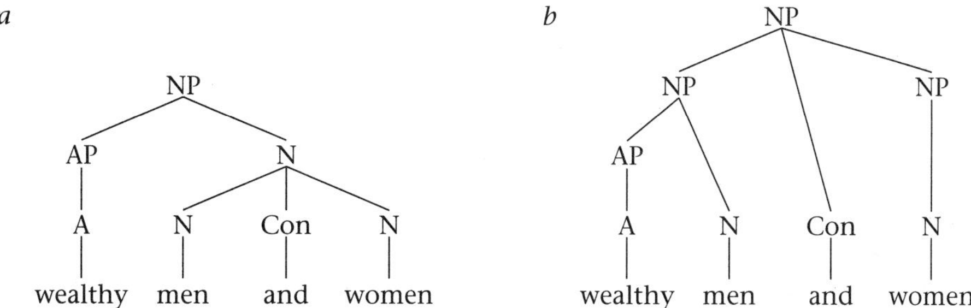

Figure 7.3 An ambiguous phrase. The structure on the left indicates that both the men and the women are wealthy; in the structure on the right, only the men are said to be wealthy.

In one interpretation of *17)*, the people had binoculars when Nicole noticed them (the phrase *with binoculars* modifies the noun *people*) while in the other interpretation Nicole saw the people by using the binoculars (the PP modifies the verb). These two readings can be represented as follows:

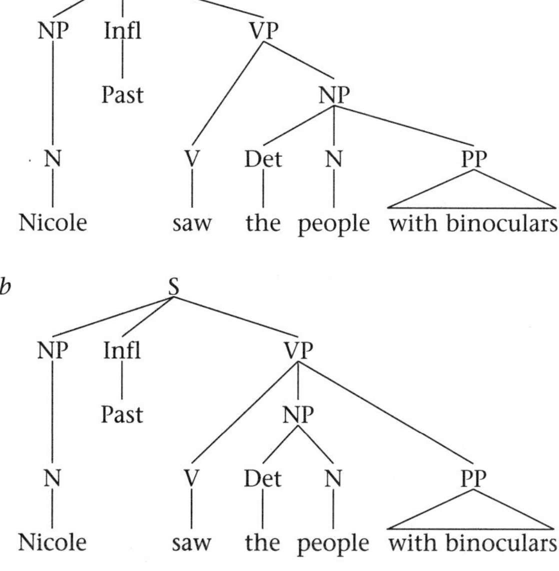

Figure 7.4 An ambiguous sentence. In the first structure, the people have the binoculars; in the second structure, Nicole uses the binoculars to see the people.

In Figure 7.4a, the PP *with binoculars* occurs with the N *people*, reflecting the first reading for this sentence. In Figure 7.4b, on the other hand, the PP occurs with the VP consisting of the verb and its complement. This corresponds to the interpretation in which *with binoculars* describes how Nicole saw the people.

We see, then, that the manner in which words are grouped together in syntactic structure reflects the way in which their meanings are combined by the semantic component of the grammar. It is therefore possible to represent structural ambiguity in language by providing a different tree structure for each interpretation that a particular utterance has.

3.2 Thematic roles

Another aspect of semantic interpretation involves determining the roles that the referents of NPs play in the situations described by sentences. Consider in this regard the sentence in *18)*.

18)

The senator sent the lobster from Boston to Seattle.

It would be impossible to understand this sentence if we could not identify the senator as the person who is responsible for sending something, the lobster as the thing that is sent, and so on. The term **thematic role** is used to describe the part played by a particular entity in an event. In most linguistic analyses, at least the following thematic roles are recognized.

Table 7.14 Thematic roles

Agent	the entity that performs an action
Theme	the entity undergoing an action or a movement
Source	the starting point for a movement
Goal	the end point for a movement
Location	the place where an action occurs

Instances of these thematic roles can be seen in sentences such as the following.

19)

a. The senator sent the lobster from Boston to Seattle.
agent *theme* *source* *goal*

b. The athletes practiced in the Astrodome.
agent *location*

The notion of movement used in the definition of **theme**, **source**, and **goal** is intended to involve not only actual physical motion, but also changes in possession, as in *20)*, and identity, as in *21)*.

20)

Terry gave the skis to Mary.
agent *theme* *goal*

21)

The magician changed the ball into a rabbit.
agent *theme* *goal*

Thematic role assignment

Where do thematic roles come from, and how does the grammar ensure that the appropriate thematic role is associated with each NP in a sentence? Thematic roles originate in word meaning. Thus, if the sentence *Harry hit the ball* contains an **agent** and a theme, it is because the verb *hit* has the type of meaning that implies an entity that does the hitting (an agent) and an entity that gets hit (a theme). Similarly, if we understand *Boston* as a source and *Seattle* as a goal in sentence *18a)*, it is because of the difference in the meaning of the prepositions *from* and *to* that occur with these NPs.

Table 7.15 Some words and the thematic roles implied by their meanings

hit	<agent, theme>
walk	<agent>
to	<goal>
from	<source>
near	<location>

These roles are then assigned to NPs based on their position in syntactic structure, with each NP receiving a single role.

As a first example of this, let us consider the complement of a preposition. In such cases, the process of thematic role assignment can be summarized as follows:

22)

A P assigns a thematic role to its complement NP.

The operation of this convention is illustrated in Figure 7.5.

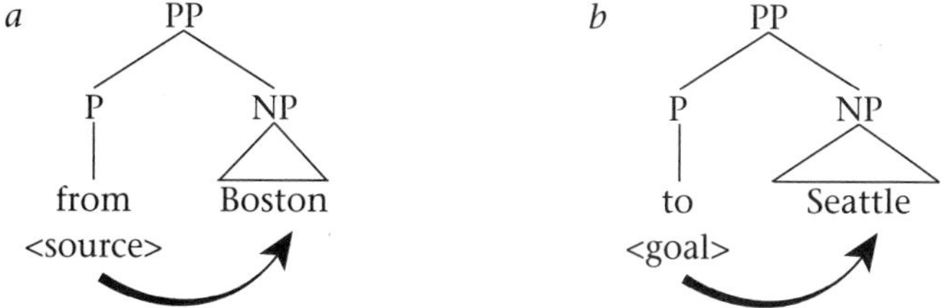

Figure 7.5 Thematic role assignment by prepositions

Matters are slightly more complicated in the case of Vs. Here we must distinguish between the theme role, which is assigned to the V's complement, and the agent role, which is assigned to its subject.

23)

A V assigns a theme role (if it has one) to its complement NP.
A V assigns an agent role (if it has one) to its subject NP.

This is exemplified in the following structures.

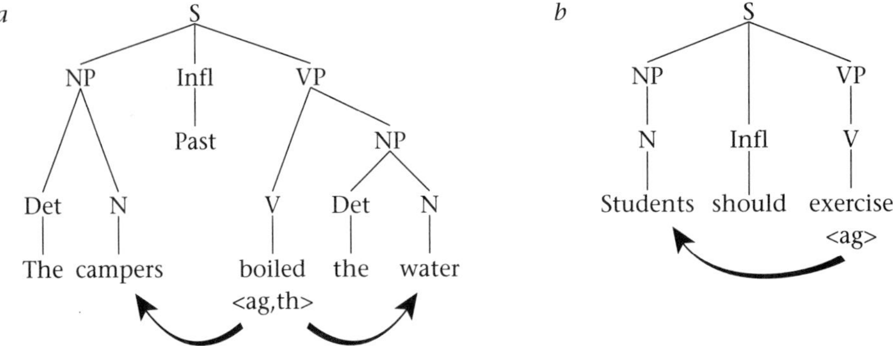

Figure 7.6 Thematic role assignment by verbs

In accordance with *23)*, the theme role (where present) is assigned to the V's NP complement while the agent role is assigned to the subject.

The structure in Figure 7.7 illustrates the assignment of thematic roles in a sentence that contains a P in addition to a V.

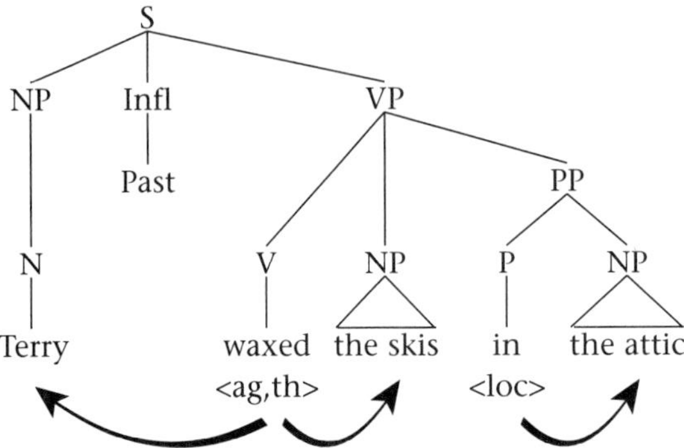

Figure 7.7 Thematic role assignment in a complex sentence

Here, the P *in* assigns its **location** role to its complement NP (*the attic*) while the verb *wax* assigns its theme role to the complement *the skis* and its agent role to the subject *Terry*.

Deep structure and thematic roles

In the examples considered to this point, it is unclear whether an NP receives its thematic role on the basis of its position in deep structure or surface structure. This is because our previous example sentences are all formed without the help of movement transformations, so that each NP occupies the same position in both deep structure and surface structure. But now consider a sentence such as *24)*, which is formed with the help of *Wh* Movement.

24)

What should the man bring?

This sentence has the deep structure depicted in figure 7.8.

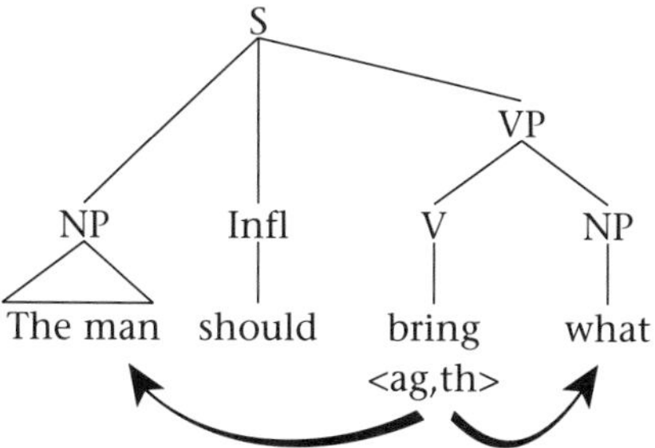

Figure 7.8 Thematic role assignment in a *wh* question

Since the theme role is assigned to the complement of V (see Figure 7.7 above), it follows that the NP *what* in the above example receives this role by virtue of its position in deep structure, not surface structure (where it occurs at the beginning of the sentence). This allows us to draw the following conclusion.

25)

An NP's deep structure position determines its thematic role.

The relevance of deep structure to the assignment of thematic roles is important for two reasons. First, it shows that syntactic structure not only represents the way in which words are organized into phrases, but also is relevant to semantic interpretation. Second, the fact that an NP's position in deep structure determines its thematic role provides additional support for the existence of this underlying level of syntactic structure. This, in turn, lends support to the claim that there must be at least two types of syntactic rules: phrase structure rules, which form the deep structure, and transformations, which convert it into surface structure.

Passives *(Advanced)*

Now let us reconsider the passive structures first discussed in Section 6 of Chapter 5.

26)

The thief was arrested (by the police).
theme *agent*

From the point of view of thematic role assignment, this sentence is strange in two respects. First, the NP that occurs in subject position in this sentence (*the thief*) bears the theme role since it refers to the person who is placed in custody. Yet, as we saw earlier, the theme role should be assigned to the complement of the verb, not its subject. Second, instead of being assigned to the subject position, the agent role (corresponding to the person doing the arresting) is assigned to an NP that occurs in an optional PP headed by the P *by*. How are we to account for these facts?

The first of these facts follows straightforwardly from the type of deep structure assigned to passive sentences. (For the time being, we ignore the PP *by the police*; as indicated in Note 2 of Chapter 5, auxiliary *be* is treated as a V that takes a VP complement.)

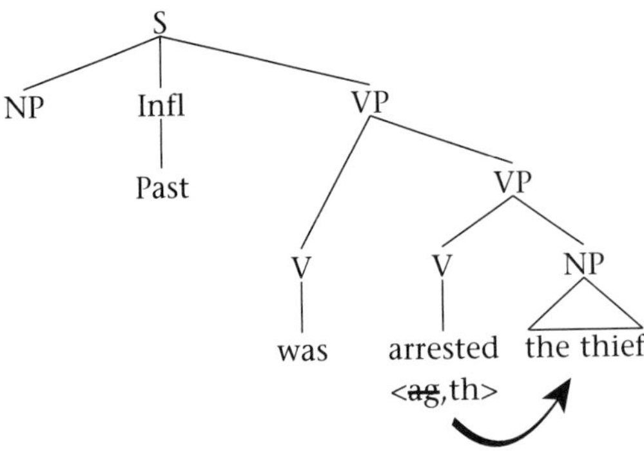

Figure 7.9 The deep structure for *The thief was arrested*; the line through the 'ag' symbol beneath the verb indicates that the agent role is suppressed.

Since the NP *the thief* appears as complement of the verb *arrest* in deep structure and since an NP's deep structure position determines its thematic role, it follows that it will be assigned the theme role, as desired.

But what of the agent role? The crucial assumption is that the passive form of a verb loses the ability to assign an agent role—which is why the 'ag' symbol beneath the verb in Figure 7.9 has a line through it. It is for this reason that passive sentences are perfectly acceptable even when there is no agent NP (for example, *The thief was arrested*). When an NP bearing the agent role does appear, it occurs not in the subject position but rather as complement of the preposition *by*. Because the verb is unable to assign an agent role, some other element must take responsibility for the assignment of this role. *By* is that element, being unique among prepositions in having the type of meaning that assigns an agent role. Thus, the sentence *The thief was arrested by the police* has the deep structure depicted in Figure 7.10. (This *by* should not be confused with the *by* in *He stood by the tree*, which assigns a locative role.)

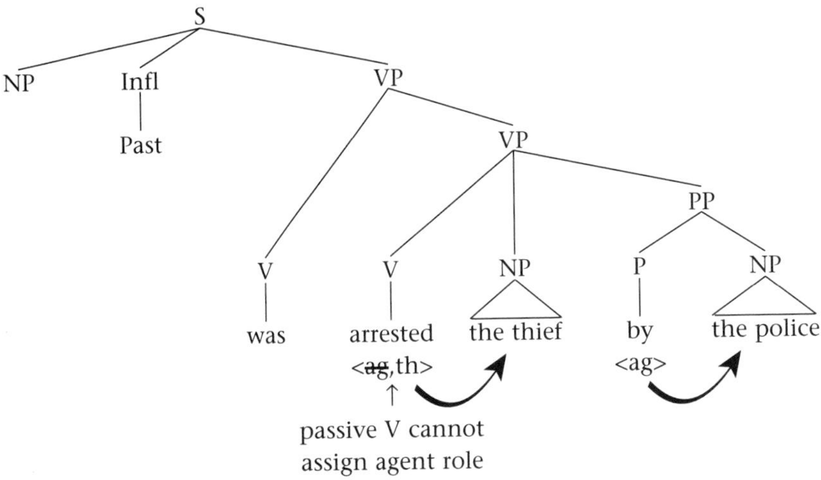

Figure 7.10 Deep structure for *The thief was arrested by the police*

In this structure, the passive verb *(was) arrested* assigns its theme role to its complement (the NP *the thief*) while the special preposition *by* assigns its agent role to its complement (the NP *the police*). This ensures that the sentence has the correct interpretation, with the police doing the arresting and the thief getting arrested.

In order to form the correct surface structure for passive sentences, we need a transformation that will move the NP bearing the theme role from the direct object position to the subject position when the latter is empty.

27)

NP Movement:
Move NP into the subject position.

This transformation applies to the deep structure in Figure 7.10 to give the surface structure depicted in Figure 7.11.

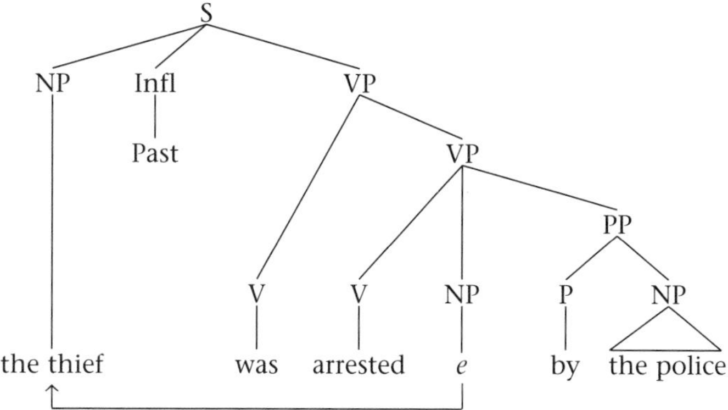

Figure 7.11 Surface structure resulting from NP movement

In sum, then, the transformational analysis of passives makes use of both deep structure and surface structure. In order to account for thematic role assignment, the NP that receives the theme role occurs as complement of the verb in deep structure while the NP that receives the agent role, if present, occurs as complement of the special preposition *by*. A transformation then moves the NP bearing the theme role from its deep structure position to the subject position in surface structure, giving the correct final form of the sentence.

3.3 The interpretation of pronouns *(Advanced)*

The category of **pronouns** includes words such as *he, she, himself,* and *herself*. These words are characterized by the fact that their interpretation can be determined by another element in the same sentence. (This other element is called the **antecedent**.) Consider in this regard the following two sentences.

28)

a. Jim's friends admire *him*.
b. Jim admires *himself*.

In the first of these sentences, the pronoun *him* can have the same referent as the NP *Jim* or can be taken to refer to someone not mentioned in the sentence (say, Jim's father). In the second sentence, in contrast, the pronoun *himself* must have the same referent as *Jim*; no other interpretation is possible. The former type of pronoun is called a **pronominal** and the latter type a **reflexive pronoun**.

The interpretation of pronominals and reflexive pronouns also differs in the following sentences.

29)

a. [$_S$ Clare knew that [$_S$ Alexis trusted *her*]].
b. [$_S$ Clare knew that [$_S$ Alexis trusted *herself*]].

Notice that *her* can refer to either Clare or someone not mentioned in the sentence, but that *herself* refers only to Alexis.

The contrasts illustrated in *28)* and *29)* reflect the fact that the interpretation of reflexive pronouns, but not ordinary pronominals, is subject to the following principle.

30)

A reflexive pronoun must have an antecedent in the smallest S containing it.

Matters are straightforward in *28b)*, where there is only one S. The sentence in *29b)* presents a somewhat more interesting case in that there are two Ss, with *Clare* in the larger one and *Alexis* and *herself* in the smaller one. However, only the NP *Alexis* can serve as antecedent since only it occurs in the smallest S containing the reflexive pronoun.

Principle A

A somewhat more abstract feature of syntactic structure enters into the interpretation of the reflexive pronouns in a sentence such as *31)*, which has the tree structure in Figure 7.12. (Pronouns are treated as N-type categories that head NPs; to save space, some word-level category labels are omitted. As noted in the previous chapter, possessor NPs occur in the specifier position within larger NPs.)

31)

The boy's uncle admired himself.

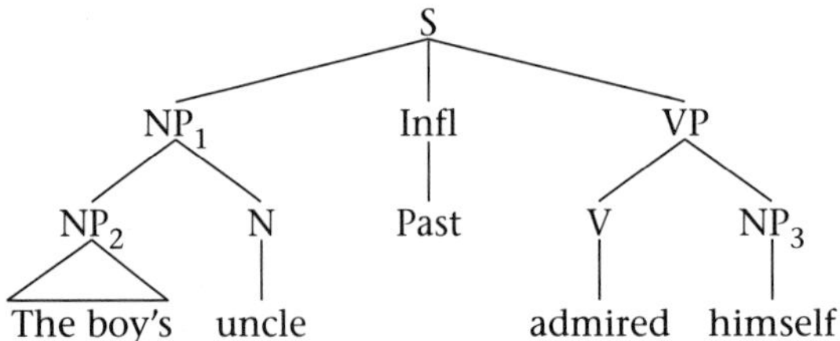

Figure 7.12 Structure containing a reflexive pronoun

Although there are two NPs in the same S as *himself* (*the boy* and *the boy's uncle*), only one (*the boy's uncle*) can serve as antecedent for the reflexive pronoun. Thus, the person who was admired in *31)* must have been the boy's uncle, not the boy.

The principle needed to ensure this interpretation makes use of the notion **c-command**, which is defined as follows.

32)

NP_a c-commands NP_b if the first category above NP_a contains NP_b.

Although c-command might appear to be a rather technical notion, the underlying idea is very simple. Figure 7.13 illustrates the type of configuration in which c-command occurs.

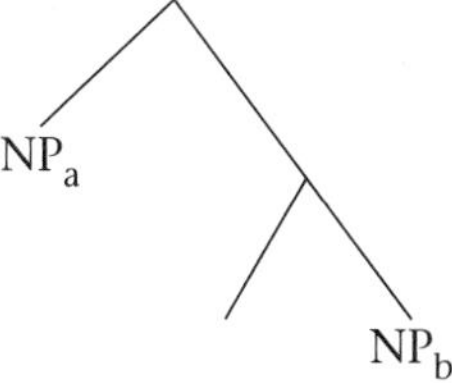

Figure 7.13 The c-command configuration

When trying to determine c-command relations, you can either use the definition in *32)* or apply the template in Figure 7.13 to the tree structure being analyzed.

We can now formulate the constraint on the interpretation of reflexives, called **Principle A**, as follows. In order to keep the discussion at an introductory level, we consider only the version of this principle required for simple, one-clause sentences.

33)

Principle A:
A reflexive pronoun must have an antecedent that c-commands it.

When using Principle A, the key step involves determining whether a potential antecedent c-commands the reflexive pronoun. Compare in this regard the status of the NPs *the boy* and *the boy's uncle* in Figure 7.12.

Since the first category above NP_1 *the boy's uncle* (namely, S) contains the reflexive, this NP c-commands *himself* according to our definition and can therefore serve as its antecedent. As we have already seen, the sentence has this interpretation.

In contrast, the first category above NP_2 (*the boy*) is NP_1, as illustrated in Figure 7.14.

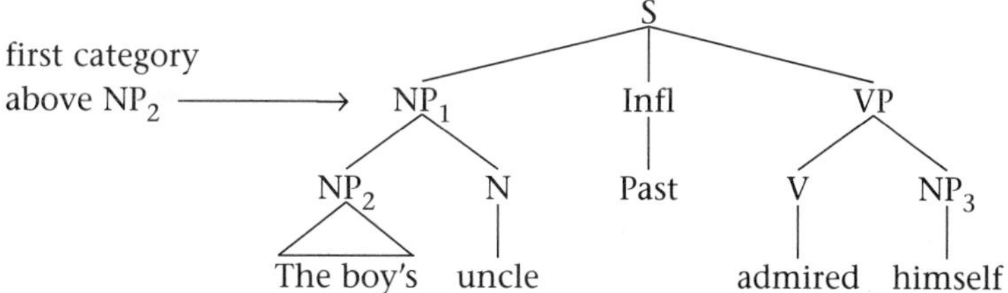

Figure 7.14 Structure illustrating the absence of a c-command relation between NP_2 and NP_3

Since NP_1 does not contain the reflexive, *the boy* does not c-command *himself* according to our definition and therefore cannot serve as its antecedent.

Principle B

Now let us consider the interpretation of pronominals. As the following example shows, the interpretation of the pronominal *him* contrasts sharply with that of the reflexive *himself* in the structure that we have been considering. Thus, *him* can refer to the boy, but not to the boy's uncle—the opposite of what we observed for *himself.*

34)

The boy's uncle admired him.

How are we to account for these facts? The relevant constraint, called **Principle B**, is stated in *35)*. (As with Principle A, we present only the version of this principle relevant to simple one-clause sentences.)

35)

Principle B:
A pronominal must not have an antecedent that c-commands it.

To see how this principle works, consider the following structure.

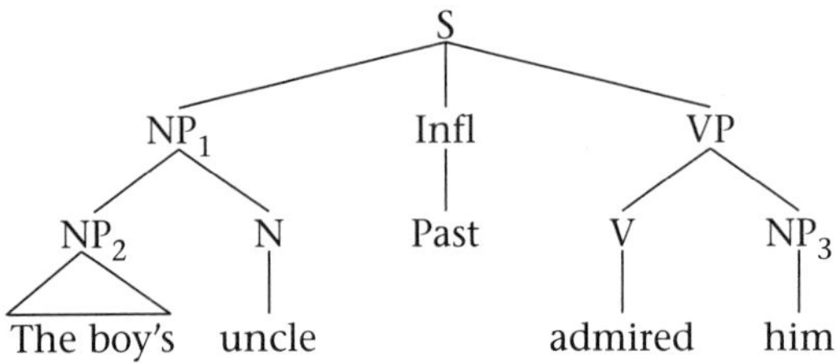

Figure 7.15 Structure containing a pronominal

In this structure, NP_1 (*the boy's uncle*) c-commands *him* since the first category above it (namely, S) also contains *him*. Principle B therefore prevents NP_1 from serving as antecedent for *him*. In contrast, NP_2 (*the boy*) does not c-command *him* since the first category above it (namely, NP_1) does not contain the pronoun. Thus, nothing prevents the interpretation in which *him* and *the boy* refer to the same person.

There is much more that can and should be said about the interpretation of pronouns. A more detailed examination of this very complex phenomenon would reveal the need for even more abstract principles referring to additional properties of syntactic structure. However, the examples we have already considered suffice to illustrate the crucial point in all of this, which is that syntactic structure plays an important role in the interpretation of both pronominals and reflexive pronouns.

4 OTHER FACTORS IN SENTENCE INTERPRETATION

Syntactic structure provides only a part of the information needed to determine the meaning of a sentence. Other necessary information comes from **pragmatics**, which includes the speaker's and addressee's background attitudes and beliefs, their understanding of the context in which a sentence is uttered, and their knowledge of how language can be used to inform, to persuade, to mislead, and so forth. This section focuses on the role of pragmatics in sentence interpretation.

4.1 The role of beliefs and attitudes

As we saw in the preceding section, the grammar includes a structural principle (Principle B) that regulates the interpretation of pronominals such as *he* and *they*. However, as the following sentences show, nonlinguistic knowledge and beliefs can also play an important role in selecting the antecedent for a pronominal.

36)

a. The judge denied the prisoner's request because he was cautious.
b. The judge denied the prisoner's request because he was dangerous.

These two sentences have identical syntactic structures, differing only in the choice of the adjective in the second clause (*cautious* in the first sentence versus *dangerous* in the second). Yet, most people feel that *he* refers to the judge in *36a)* but to the prisoner in *36b)*.

These preferences have nothing to do with structural principles. Rather, the crucial factor involves our beliefs about different groups within society. In particular, since most people believe that a judge is more likely to be cautious and a prisoner more likely to be dangerous, they take the pronoun to refer to the judge in the first sentence but the prisoner in the second.

Presupposition

There are many other ways in which a speaker's beliefs can be reflected in language use. Compare in this regard the following two sentences.

37)

a. Have you stopped exercising regularly?
b. Have you tried exercising regularly?

Use of the verb *stop* implies a belief on the part of the speaker that the listener has been exercising regularly. No such assumption is associated with the verb *try*.

The assumption or belief implied by the use of a particular word or structure is called a **presupposition**. The following two sentences provide another example of this.

38)

a. Nick admitted that the team had lost.
b. Nick said that the team had lost.

Choice of the verb *admit* in *38a)* indicates that the speaker is presupposing the truth of the claim that the team lost. No such presupposition is associated with choice of the verb *say* in *38b)*, where the speaker is simply reporting Nick's statement without taking a position on its accuracy.

Still another type of presupposition is illustrated in *39)*.

39)

a. Abraham Lincoln was assassinated in 1865.
b. Abraham Lincoln was murdered in 1865.

Notice that use of the verb *assassinate* in *39a)* involves the assumption that Abraham Lincoln was a prominent person, but that no such presupposition is associated with the verb *murder*.

4.2 Setting

As noted at the beginning of this section, the pragmatic factors relevant to sentence interpretation can include knowledge of the context in which a sentence is uttered. Two types of contextual information are involved here, the first having to do with the physical environment in which a sentence is uttered (the **setting**) and the second having to do with the other utterances in the speech event (the **discourse**). In this subsection we will consider an example of how information about the setting enters into language use; the role of discourse will be examined in the next subsection. Both these issues are examined from a slightly different perspective in Chapter 14.

Deictics

All languages have forms whose use and interpretation depend on the location of the speaker and/or hearer within a particular setting. Called spatial **deictics**, these forms are exemplified in English by words such as *this* and *here* (proximity to the speaker) versus *that* and *there* (proximity to the hearer and/or distance from the speaker). Thus, if Steve and Brian are sitting across from each other at a table, each would refer to a plate directly in front of him as *this plate* and to a plate in front of the other or a plate distant from both as *that plate*. Without an understanding of how the setting in which a sentence is uttered can influence the choice of words such as *this* and *that*, it would be impossible for speakers of English to use or interpret these forms correctly.

As the preceding examples show, English makes a two-way distinction in its expression of deictic contrasts. However, many languages use a third set of forms in this part of their grammar.

Table 7.16 A three-way deictic distinction

Language	*'this'*	*'that'*	*'that over there'*
Spanish	este	ese	aquel
Korean	i	ku	ce
Japanese	kono	sono	ano
Palauan	tia	tilęcha	se
Turkish	bu	ʃu	o

An even more complex system is found in the Amerindian language Tlingit, which makes a four-way distinction: *yáa* 'this one right here', *héi* 'this one nearby', *wée* 'that one over there', and *yóo* 'that one far off'.

Determiners are not the only type of element whose use and interpretation require reference to features of the setting. In English, for example, deictic contrasts are also crucial to the understanding of such commonly used verbs as *come* and *go*. Notice in this regard the striking difference in perspective found in the following two sentences.

40)

a. The bear is coming into the tent!
b. The bear is going into the tent!

Whereas *come* with a third person subject implies movement towards the speaker or addressee, *go* with the same type of subject suggests movement away from the speaker. Use of *come* with a first person subject (*I*) is different again. Hence the sentence *I'm coming over* implies that the speaker is about to go to where the addressee is. As was the case with deictic determiners, we could not fully understand these sentences without reference to the physical setting in which they are uttered.

4.3 Discourse

Properties of other utterances in the same speech event (the discourse) are also crucial to understanding a sentence. A very simple example of this involves the interpretation of elements such as *he*, *it*, and *there*, whose referent is often determined by a word or phrase in a preceding utterance. Consider in this regard the following passage.

41)

A little girl went for a walk in the park. While *there*, *she* saw a rabbit. Since *it* was injured, *she* took *it* home.

Each of the italicized words in this passage relies for its interpretation on information encoded in a preceding sentence. Thus, we interpret *there* with reference to *in the park*, *she* with reference to *a little girl*, and *it* with reference to *a rabbit*.

Old and new information

One of the most important contrasts in the study of discourse is the distinction between new and old information. **Old** (or **given**) **information** consists of the knowledge that the speaker assumes is available to the addressee at the time of the utterance, either because it is shared by both or because it has already been introduced into the discourse. In contrast, **new information** involves knowledge that is introduced into the discourse for the first time. Consider the contrast between the following two sentences.

42)

a. The man is at the front door.
b. A man is at the front door.

Choice of *the* as the determiner for *man* in *42a)* suggests that the referent of the phrase is someone who has been mentioned in the previous discourse and is therefore already known to the addressee (old information). In contrast, choice of the determiner *a* in *42b)* implies that the referent is being introduced into the discourse for the first time (new information).

Notice that both sentences in *42)* use *the* as the determiner for *front door*. This is because the setting for the conversation presumably includes only one front door, whose identity and location is known to both speaker and addressee. As noted, old information can consist of shared knowledge such as this and need not always be explicitly stated in the previous discourse.

Topics

Another important notion for the study of discourse is that of **topic**, which corresponds to what a sentence or group of sentences is about. Consider the following passage.

43)

Once upon a time there was a merchant with two sons. The older son wanted to be a scholar. He spent his time reading and studying. As for the younger son, he preferred to travel and see the world.

The first sentence in this passage introduces a merchant and his two sons as new information. A topic (the older son) is selected in the second sentence and maintained in the third, in which *he* refers back to *the older son*. The final sentence then switches to a new topic (the younger son), providing some information about him. This switch is facilitated by the expression *as for*, which can be used in English as a marker of new topics.

In English, the subject of the sentence tends also to be the topic. This is why (as mentioned in Section 1.2 above) it is natural to interpret the active sentence in *44a)* as being about the police and the passive sentence in *b)* as being about the burglar (see also Section 6.2 of Chapter 5).

44)

a. The police chased the burglar.
b. The burglar was chased by the police.

In some languages, a special affix is used to identify the topic. The following sentences from Japanese illustrate this phenomenon. (Nom = nominative, the subject marker; Top = topic marker; Ques = question marker)

45)

Speaker A: Dare-ga kimasita-ka?
Who-Nom came -Ques?

Speaker B: John-ga kimasita.
John-Nom came.

Speaker A: John-wa dare-to kimasita-ka?
John-Top who-with came -Ques?
'Who did John come with?'

The topic marker in Japanese (the suffix *-wa*) is distinguished from the subject marker (*-ga*) by its use to mark old or background information. This is why speaker B responds to A's first question by using the subject marker on the NP *John*. Because this NP provides new information here (an answer to A's question), the topic marker would be inappropriate. However, once it has been established that John is the person who came, the corresponding NP can then bear the topic marker. This is precisely what happens in Speaker A's final utterance, wherein the NP *John* (which is now associated with previously established information) is marked by the topic suffix *-wa*.

4.4 Conversational strategies

In addition to background beliefs, the setting, and the discourse context, there is at least one other major type of information that enters into the interpretation of utterances. This information has to do with the 'rules for conversation', our understanding of how language is used in particular situations to convey a message. If, for example, I ask someone, *'Would you like to go to a movie tonight?'* and I receive as a response *'I have to study for an exam'*, I know that the other person is declining my invitation even though there is nothing in the literal meaning of the sentence that says so. Moreover, even though the response does not contain an explicit answer to my invitation, I recognize it as a perfectly appropriate way to respond. (Notice that the same could not be said of a response like *'I have to comb my hair'* or *'I enjoy reading books'*.)

As speakers of a language, we are able to draw inferences about what is meant but not actually said. Information that is conveyed in this way is called a **conversational implicature**. The ease with which we recognize and interpret implicatures stems from our knowledge of how people in our linguistic community use language to communicate with each other.

The general overarching guideline for conversational interactions is often called the **Cooperative Principle**.

46)

The Cooperative Principle:
Make your contribution appropriate to the conversation.

More specific **conversational maxims** or guidelines ensure that conversational interactions actually satisfy the Cooperative Principle.

Table 7.17 Some conversational maxims

The Maxim of Relation:
Be relevant.

The Maxim of Quality:
Try to make your contribution one that is true. (Do not say things that are false or for which you lack adequate evidence.)

The Maxim of Quantity:
Do not make your contribution more or less informative than required.

The Maxim of Manner:
Avoid ambiguity and obscurity; be brief and orderly.

These maxims are responsible for regulating normal conversation but, as we will see directly, each can be suspended under certain circumstances to create particular effects.

Relation

The **Maxim of Relation** is crucial to evaluating the appropriateness of responses to the question *'Would you like to go to a movie tonight?'* (the example given at the beginning of this section). Because we assume that the conversational contributions of others are relevant to the topic at hand, we are able to infer from the response *'I have to study for an exam'* that the speaker is unable or unwilling to go to the movie. Similarly, because it is hard to see a connection between combing one's hair and being able to go to a movie, we judge the response *'I have to comb my hair'* to be irrelevant and hence inappropriate.

Of course, the Maxim of Relation can sometimes be suspended by a speaker who wants to create a particular impression. For example, if someone asks you *'Have you finished that term paper yet?'*, and you respond *'It's been raining a lot lately, hasn't it?'*, you violate the Maxim of Relation by not responding in a relevant way. On the other hand, by giving this response you signal to the other person that you want to change the topic of conversation.

Quality

The **Maxim of Quality** requires that the statements used in conversations have some factual basis. If, for example, I ask *'What's the weather like?'* and someone responds *'It's snowing'*, I will normally assume that this statement provides reliable information about the current weather.

In order to achieve irony or sarcasm, however, it is sometimes possible to abandon the Maxim of Quality and say something that one knows to be false. Thus, if two people live in the middle of a sweltering desert and one person insists on asking every morning *'What's the weather like?'*, it might be appropriate for the other person to respond *'Oh, today it's snowing, as usual'*, perhaps with a particular facial expression or intonation to indicate that the statement was not intended as a true report of the facts.

Quantity

The **Maxim of Quantity** introduces some very subtle guidelines into a conversation. If, for example, someone asks me where a famous American author lives, then the nature of my response will depend in large part on how much information I believe to be appropriate for that point in the conversation. If I know that the other person is simply curious about which part of the country the author lives in, it might suffice to respond *'in Mississippi'*. On the other hand, if I know that the person wants to visit the author, then much more specific information (perhaps even an address) is appropriate.

The Maxim of Quantity can be suspended in order to mislead a conversational partner. For example, if someone asks me where Mary is and I know that Mary does not want to see this person, I might respond by saying *'I think she went downtown or something'* even though I know precisely where she is. In responding in this way, I am not being untruthful since I have said nothing false, but by giving less information than is appropriate I am violating the Maxim of Quantity and hence being misleading.

Manner

The **Maxim of Manner** imposes several constraints on language use, two of which will be exemplified here. First, imagine that I refer to a particular person as *the man who Mary lives with*. A listener would be justified in concluding that the man in question is not Mary's husband. This is because, by the Maxim of Manner, a briefer and less obscure description, *Mary's husband*, would have been used if it could have correctly described Mary's companion.

Second, imagine that I am writing a letter of recommendation to an employer and I say about a former student of mine *'You will be fortunate indeed if you can get Mr. X to work for you'*. By using a sentence that can be interpreted in two dramatically different ways ('You will be glad to have Mr. X on your staff' versus 'It is not easy to get Mr. X to do any work'), I violate the Maxim of Manner by using an ambiguous structure. Since the maxims are violated only for specific purposes (as when the Maxim of Quality is suspended to yield irony), the person to whom the letter is written might be justified in concluding that my choice of language constituted a veiled warning about Mr. X.

The maxims in other societies

The preceding maxims represent constraints on conversation that may well be an integral part of language use in all cultures. This is not to say that the maxims are employed in exactly the same way in all linguistic communities, however. In fact, we know that the circumstances under which it is appropriate to suspend a maxim can differ. A good example of this involves the Maxim of Quantity as it is used in rural areas of the Malagasy Republic (formerly called Madagascar), the large island off the east coast of Africa.

Because rural villages in the Malagasy Republic form small, tightly integrated societies, new information is rare and considerable prestige accrues to its holder. Speakers are therefore often reluctant to impart it to just anyone. When asked about a particular event, then, they may reply evasively, avoiding mention of the information being sought by their conversational partner. Thus, a visit to the market might be described by saying simply *'there were many people there'* rather than giving any specific details. This suggests not only that the Maxim of Quantity can be overridden, but that the conditions under which this happens may be intertwined with the cultural practices of a particular society.

SUMMING UP

The study of **semantics** is concerned with a broad range of phenomena including the nature of **meaning**, the role of syntactic structure in the interpretation of sentences, and the effect of **pragmatics** on the understanding of utterances. Although serious problems and obstacles remain in all these areas, work in recent years has at least begun to identify the type of relations, mechanisms, and principles involved in the understanding of language. These include the notions of **extension** and **intension** in the case of word meaning, **thematic role** assignment in the case of sentence interpretation, and **c-command** in the case of pronoun interpretation. Other factors known to be involved in an utterance's interpretation include the speaker's and hearer's background beliefs (as manifested, for example, in **presuppositions**), the context provided by the **setting** and the **discourse**, and the **maxims** associated with the **Cooperative Principle**.

Key terms

agent
antecedent
antonyms
c-command
componential analysis
connotation
contradiction
(conversational) maxims
conversational implicature
Cooperative Principle
deictics
denotation
discourse
entailment
extension
fuzzy concepts
goal
graded concept
grammaticized (concepts)
homophony
intension
lexical ambiguity
lexicalization
location
Maxim of Manner
Maxim of Quality
Maxim of Quantity
Maxim of Relation
meaning
metaphor
motion verbs
new information
NP movement
old information
paraphrases
polysemy
pragmatics
presupposition
Principle A
Principle B
principle of compositionality
pronominal
pronouns
prototypes
readings
referents
reflexive pronoun
semantic decomposition
semantic features
semantics
setting
source
spatial metaphor
structurally ambiguous
synonyms
thematic role
theme
topic
truth conditions

Sources

Surveys of the nature of word meaning and semantic relations can be found in many sources, including the book by Allen cited below. A prominent advocate of componential analysis is Ray Jackendoff, whose book *Semantic Structures* (Cambridge, MA:

MIT Press, 1991) reviews earlier ideas in addition to offering new proposals. The discussion of fuzzy categories and graded membership in Section 2 draws from Part 1 of *Women, Fire, and Dangerous Things* by G. Lakoff (Chicago: University of Chicago Press, 1987) and the references cited there. The discussion of metaphor takes as its starting point the book *Metaphors We Live By*, cited below. The four Inuktitut words for snow in Table 7.7 are from *The Handbook of American Indian Languages* by F. Boas (Washington: Smithsonian Institute, 1911) and are also cited on p. 123 of the book by Allen referenced below; for a longer list of words for snow, see *Dictionnaire français-eskimau du parler de l'Ungava* (Québec: Presses de l'Université Laval, 1970), brought to my attention by M. Dobrovolsky; see also "The Great Eskimo Vocabulary Hoax" by G. Pullum in *The Great Eskimo Vocabulary Hoax and Other Irreverent Essays on the Study of Language* (Chicago: University of Chicago Press, 1991). The discussion of verbs of motion is based on the paper "Lexicalization Patterns: Semantic Structure in Lexical Form" by L. Talmy in *Language Typology and Syntactic Description*, Vol. 3, edited by T. Shopen (New York: Cambridge University Press, 1985), 57–149. The definition of grammaticization used in Section 2.4 is based on D. Slobin's "Crosslinguistic Evidence for the Language-Making Capacity" in *The Crosslinguistic Study of Language Acquisition*, Vol. 2, edited by D. Slobin (Hillsdale, NJ: Erlbaum, 1985), 1172–73. The data on Hidatsa assertion morphemes in the same section are from *Hidatsa Syntax* by G. H. Matthews (The Hague: Mouton, 1965).

The treatment of structural ambiguity, thematic role assignment, and pronoun interpretation in this chapter presents slightly simplified versions of views widely held within generative grammar in the early 1990s. For a summary of the last two issues, see *Introduction to Government and Binding Theory*, 2nd ed., by L. Haegeman (Cambridge, MA: Blackwell, 1994).

The data used in the discussion of deixis and in question 15 come from "Deixis" by S. Anderson and E. Keenan in *Language Typology and Syntactic Description*, Vol. 3, edited by T. Shopen (New York: Cambridge University Press, 1985), 259–308. The discussion of topicalization draws on the "Major Functions of the Noun Phrase" by A. Andrews in *Language Typology and Syntactic Description*, Vol. 1, edited by T. Shopen (New York: Cambridge University Press, 1985), 62–154. The discussion of the Cooperative Principle and the maxims of conversation is based primarily on "Logic and Conversation" by Paul Grice in *Syntax and Semantics*, Vol. 3, edited by P. Cole and J. Morgan (New York: Academic Press, 1975), 41–58 and the paper by L. Horn cited below. The discussion of Malagasy conversation is based on "The Universality of Conversational Postulates" by E. Ochs in *Language in Society*, 5:67–80 (1976). The questions for this chapter were prepared by Joyce Hildebrand.

Recommended reading

Allen, Keith. 1986. *Linguistic Meaning*. Vols. 1 and 2. New York: Routledge & Kegan Paul.

Horn, Laurence. 1988. "Pragmatic Theory." In *Linguistics: The Cambridge Survey*. Vol. 1. Edited by F. Newmeyer, 113–45. London: Cambridge University Press.

Hurford, James, and Brendan Heasley. 1983. *Semantics: A Coursebook*. New York: Cambridge University Press.

Ladusaw, William. 1988. "Semantic Theory." In *Linguistics: The Cambridge Survey*. Vol. 1. Edited by F. Newmeyer, 89–112. London: Cambridge University Press.

Lakoff, George, and Mark Johnson. 1982. *Metaphors We Live By*. Chicago: University of Chicago Press.

McCawley, James. 1993. *Everything That Linguists Have Always Wanted to Know About Logic*. 2nd edition. Chicago: University of Chicago Press.

Prince, Ellen. 1988. "Discourse Analysis: A Part of the Study of Linguistic Competence." In *Linguistics: The Cambridge Survey*. Vol. 2. Edited by F. Newmeyer, 164–82. New York: Cambridge University Press.

Questions

1. Two relations involving word meanings are antonymy and synonymy. Which relation is illustrated in each of the pairs of words below?
   a) flourish/thrive
   b) intelligent/stupid
   c) casual/informal
   d) young/old
   e) uncle/aunt
   f) intelligent/smart
   g) flog/whip
   h) drunk/sober

2. It was noted in this chapter that a single form can have two or more meanings. Depending on whether these meanings are related to each other, this phenomenon involves polysemy or homophony. Which of these two relations is exemplified by the forms below?
   a) *grass* herbage used for grazing animals; marijuana
   b) *leech* a bloodsucking worm; a hanger-on who seeks advantage
   c) *range* a cooking stove; a series of mountains
   d) *key* an instrument used to apply to a lock; an answer sheet for a test or assignment
   e) *reel* a spool for photographic film; round device at the butt end of a fishing rod for the line
   f) *race* the act of running competitively; people belonging to the same genetic grouping
   g) /flawər/ a blossom; finely ground wheat

3. Three semantic relations among sentences were covered in this chapter: paraphrase, entailment, and contradiction. Which of these relations is exemplified in each of the following pairs of sentences?
   a) I saw Timothy at the anniversary party.
      It was Timothy that I saw at the anniversary party.
   b) Jules is Mary's husband.
      Mary is married.
   c) My pet cobra likes the taste of chocolate fudge.
      My pet cobra finds chocolate fudge tasty.
   d) Vera is an only child.
      Olga is Vera's sister.
   e) It is fifty miles to the nearest service station.
      The nearest service station is fifty miles away.

f) My cousin Bryan teaches at the community college for a living.
My cousin Bryan is a teacher.

4. In discussing the nature of meaning, we noted that it is necessary to distinguish between intension and extension. Describe the intensions and the extensions of each of these phrases.
   a) the President of the United States
   b) the Queen of England
   c) the capital of Canada
   d) women who have walked on the moon
   e) Princess Diana's ex-husband

5. In our discussion of semantic decomposition, we noted that at least some words have meanings that can be represented in terms of smaller semantic features. Four such words are *dog*, *puppy*, *cat*, and *kitten*.
   i) Attempt to provide the semantic features associated with each of these words.
   ii) How are the pairs *dog–puppy* and *cat–kitten* different from *man–boy* and *woman–girl*?
   iii) Try to provide semantic features for the words *circle*, *triangle*, and *quadrangle*. What problems do you encounter?

6. Each of the following words is associated with a concept.

a) island	e) food
b) soft	f) husband
c) white	g) baseball bat
d) wristwatch	h) mountain

   i) Which of these examples are fuzzy concepts?
   ii) Choose one of the fuzzy concepts above. Name one prototypical member of that concept and one member that is closer to the concept boundary.
   iii) Draw a diagram for the concept 'dwelling' similar to that of Figure 7.2 in this chapter. Do the same for the concept 'vehicle'.

7. Examine the following sets of sentences, each of which includes words or phrases used metaphorically.
   a) She gave him an icy stare.
   He gave her the cold shoulder.
   He exudes a lot of warmth towards people.
   They got into a heated argument.
   b) He drops a lot of hints.
   The committee picked up on the issue.
   She dumps all her problems on her friends.
   Although he disagreed, he let it go.
   c) the eye of a needle
   the foot of the bed
   the hands of the clock
   the arm of a chair
   the table legs

d) I'm looking forward to it.
   She can foretell the future.
   I can remember back to when I was two years old.
   He drags up old conflicts.
   You must plan ahead for retirement.

e) This lecture is easy to digest.
   He just eats up the lecturer's words.
   Chew on this thought for a while.
   Listen to this juicy piece of gossip.

For each set of sentences:

i) Identify the words or phrases that are used metaphorically in each sentence.

ii) Determine the basis for each of these metaphor sets.
Use the pattern: 'The metaphors in (x) describe ______ in terms of ______.'
Example: The metaphors in (a) describe human relationships in terms of temperature.

8. The section on lexicalization of concepts discussed how some languages simultaneously express motion and path, motion and movement, and/or motion and thing moving in motion verbs. Can you change the sentence *He moved the goods by truck to the warehouse* so that both movement and the type of vehicle are lexicalized in one verb? What other verbs express a similar combination of concepts?

9. Consider the following Fijian pronouns.

au	1st person singular 'me'
iko	2nd person singular 'you'
koya	3rd person singular 'him/her/it'
kedaru	1st person dual 'you and me'
keirau	1st person dual 'one other (not you) and me'
kemudrau	2nd person dual 'you (two)'
rau	3rd person dual 'them (two)'
kedatou	1st person trial 'two others (including you) and me'
keitou	1st person trial 'two others (excluding you) and me'
kemudou	2nd person trial 'you (three)'
iratou	3rd person trial 'them (three)'
keda	1st person plural 'us (more than three, including you)'
keimami	1st person plural 'us (more than three, excluding you)'
kemuni:	2nd person plural 'you (more than three)'
ira	3rd person plural 'them (more than three)'

i) Identify the concepts that are grammaticized in the Fijian pronoun system but are not grammaticized in the English pronoun system.

ii) Which concept is grammaticized in the English pronoun system but not in the Fijian system?

10. Each NP in the following sentences has a thematic role that represents the part that its referent plays in the situation described by the sentence.

a) The man chased the intruder.
b) The cat jumped from the chair onto the table.

c) Aaron wrote a letter to Marilyn.
d) The governor entertained the guests in the lounge.
e) Henry mailed the manuscript from Atlanta.

Using the terms described in this chapter, label the thematic role of each NP in these sentences and identify the assigner for each thematic role.

Example: Bill wrote a novel in the park.

11. Each of the following sentences has undergone a movement transformation.
    a) What has Larry given to the bride?
    b) Who will Liane kiss?
    c) Which house will the group leave from?
    d) What has Marvin forgotten on the bus?
    e) The necklace was stolen by the burglar.
    f) The ball was thrown to Evan by Louise.

    Write out the deep structure string for each of these sentences and mark all thematic roles and thematic role assigners.

    Example: a) Larry has given what to the bride

12. One of the relations involved in the interpretation of pronouns is that of c-command. Examine the following tree structure for the sentence *Marie's sister gave herself a haircut.*

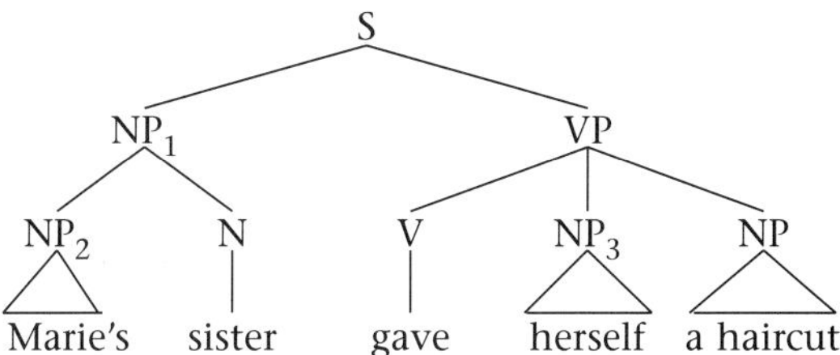

i) Who does *herself* refer to in this sentence?
ii) Does NP_2 c-command NP_3?
iii) How does your answer to *ii)* relate to your answer to *i)*?
iv) Does the antecedent change if you change *herself* to *her*? Why?

13. In the following sentence, the pronoun *she* could, according to Principle B, refer to either *the architect* or *the secretary*.

    The architect gave the secretary a raise after she typed the report.

i) Which interpretation for *she* comes to mind first?
ii) Why?
iii) What happens to the pronoun's interpretation if you change the word *secretary* to *janitor*?

14. In the following pairs of sentences, one of the two sentences contains a presupposition relating to the truth of the complement clause.
    a) John regrets that Maria went to the graduation ceremony.
       John believes that Maria went to the graduation ceremony.
    b) The captain thought that the ship was in danger.
       The captain realized that the ship was in danger.
    c) It is significant that the criminal was sent to prison.
       It is likely that the criminal was sent to prison.

    For each pair:
    i) Identify the sentence that contains this presupposition and state what the presupposition is.
    ii) Locate the word that is responsible for the presupposition.

15. In Malagasy, the use of the deictics *ety* 'here' and *aty* 'there' depends on whether the object in question is visible to the speaker.
    a) Ety ny tranony. 'Here is his house (visible to the speaker)'
    b) Aty ny tranony. 'There is his house (not visible to the speaker)'

    How does this differ from the English use of *here/there*?

16. The syntactic construction *It was* _____ *that* _____ is called a 'cleft construction' and is used in certain discourse contexts. Consider the following conversations involving cleft constructions.
    a) *A*: Did Sally claim that she saw a flying saucer last night?
       B: No, it was a meteorite that Sally claimed she saw last night.
    b) *A*: Did Sally claim that she saw a flying saucer last night?
       B: No, it was Sally that claimed she saw a meteorite last night.
    c) *A*: Did Sally claim that she saw a flying saucer last night?
       B: No, it was last week that Sally claimed she saw a flying saucer.

    i) Is B's response equally acceptable in all three interactions?
    ii) Choose one of the discourses in which B's response is appropriate. How do the underlined parts correspond to new and old information?
    iii) For the discourse in which B's response is unacceptable, can you now explain why it is unacceptable?
    iv) In addition to the cleft construction, identify the way in which new information is marked phonetically in B's responses.

17. Each of the following examples contains a conversational implicature.
    a) *A*: Have you washed the floor and done the dishes?
       B: I've washed the floor.
    b) *A*: Did you get hold of Carl yet?
       B: I tried to call him yesterday.
    c) *A*: What did you think of the movie?
       B: Well, the supporting actor was great.

    What is the implicature for each example?

FOR THE STUDENT LINGUIST

ELVIS'S BIGGEST FAN CLEANS OUT BANK—ACCOMPLICE LAUNDERS THE DOUGH

PEORIA—Blanche VanBuren, an old Elvis fan from Oneida, Illinois, cleaned out the Peoria Institution for Savings yesterday with nothing but a sawed-off broom and old shotgun.

Darrel Apley, the owner of Union Electric and a shocked witness who preferred to remain anonymous said, "Blanche should be at home at this time of the day. Her favorite soap is on the TV."

A teller said, "Someone came in a truck. I heard some screams coming from inside. People were rolling on the floor. Then it was over and I smoked a pack of cigarettes on the way home."

By the time the Bureau had been hauled in, the local pigs had decided someone else had done it. But the tip-off, by Oneida Otters star center Billie Jones, was about her partner. "Everyone thought two people were involved from the beginning," Jones claimed. "But it was when I saw the suds in the record store behind the pizzeria that it all came together."

The King could not be reached for comment by press time.

It's surprisingly easy to write an article in which every sentence is ambiguous. It's much harder—maybe even impossible—to write one that isn't ambiguous, or to write anything that isn't ambiguous. Maybe this explains why legal language is so tedious in its attempt to be unambiguous and why our court system is so clogged (obstructed, that is, not filled with Dutch wooden shoes), and why multiple-choice exams are so awful.

To show that the sentences in this article really are ambiguous, I'll attempt to disambiguate the first couple of paragraphs of Blanche's story in painstaking detail. By the time I'm done, you'll probably be able to see ambiguity everywhere you go.

Blanche VanBuren is an elderly Elvis aficionado who resides in Oneida, Illinois. And she's just plain old, all would agree (see tree *1B*). Or, when considering Elvis fans from Oneida, she's getting up in years (see tree *1A*), but in some other context she'd be considered pretty young (because most of the Elvis fans in Oneida are teenyboppers, whereas Blanche is pushing thirty). Maybe Blanche has been an Elvis fan for a long time. (*1B*). Or maybe, just maybe, most Oneidan Elvis fans are new to their admiration of him (it began with the postage stamp), but Blanche has loved Elvis since 1984, when she encountered him on a spaceship, and is therefore, comparatively speaking, an old Elvis-fan-from-Oneida (tree *1A*). Of course, she could also be a fan of only the *old* Elvis—that is, she liked his Vegas days but hated the early stuff. You can figure out the tree for this reading.

Let's assume Blanche is elderly. And a neat freak, because she washed the Peoria Institution for Savings from top to bottom (taking the shotgun to teach a lesson to litterbugs). Then again, she might be an incredibly compulsive cleaner in her own house and spend so much money on lemon-scented antiseptics that she robbed the P.I.S. and took along that sawed-off broom because she was delirious from inhaling ammonia all day. Let's consider her implements. The shotgun was old. The broom was sawed-off. Was the broom old? We don't know; the story doesn't provide information on its age. Was the shotgun sawed-off? This is a classic case of structural ambiguity, made famous by the example "the old men and women" and the answer should be obvious by now (but see trees *2A* and *2B* for confirmation).

The article does make clear that the event of interest took place yesterday, but I'm wondering whether Blanche habitually cleans out banks, and it just happened to be the P.I.S. yesterday, or if this was an out-of-the-blue cleaning or what. Could be that she cleans the P.I.S. every day, but usually she has more equipment than a broom and a gun.

Then there's the possibility that Blanche is an early model electric cooling device (or an antique paper and balsa wood construction), once owned (and affectionately named) by Elvis, which either: (a) blew all the dirt out of the bank or (b) was brought to life and performed the robbery. You never know.

What about Darrel Apley? If the writer of this article had any ethics, he (Darrel) is not the person who owns Union Electric, nor is he (Darrel) a shocked witness who preferred to remain anonymous. If the writer had ethics there would have to have been three different people who all said "Blanche should be at home . . ." and one of them is Darrel, one's the owner of U.E., and the third is shocked and prefers anonymity (tree *3A*). However, sloppy writing and broken promises are everywhere, and it's quite possible that *the owner of Union Electric* and *a shocked witness who preferred to remain anonymous* are actually intended to describe Darrel (tree *3B*).

"Blanche should be at home at this time of the day." Should? As in, given her normal patterns, the most likely case is that Blanche is at home? Or *should* as in if that lowdown, bank-thieving woman knew what was good for her she'd be at home watching *All My Children*?

"Her favorite soap is on the TV." This one's easy; it's nothing but lexical ambiguity. Her favorite soap could be Ivory Family Size or the aforementioned *All My Children*. If this were spoken instead of written, we'd have to explore the option that her favorite soap is called "On the TV", and actually, considering the doubts you might have about the writer's integrity, that could have been what Darrel (and maybe two others) meant. Of course, "on" is ambiguous between "being broadcast" or "on top of" but enough is enough.

The rest of the article you can disambiguate on your own. It's useful to draw trees for the structurally ambiguous parts and make sure the different interpretations match the trees. Every *written* sentence—every portion of material from one period to another—is ambiguous, but not every *S* in the technical, linguistic sense is ambiguous. Be sure to look for lexical ambiguity, structural ambiguity, and pronouns that could refer to a few different people. Also look carefully at Jones's quote—this one is hard but interesting. Finally, check out your local newspaper. I predict that many of the sentences in it are as ambiguous as the ones in this article. You could even examine the instructions for your next linguistics homework assignment, and (politely) tease your instructor if they're not crystal clear. Be careful, though—he or she might hold you to the same standard in your writing.

TREES:

(1A)

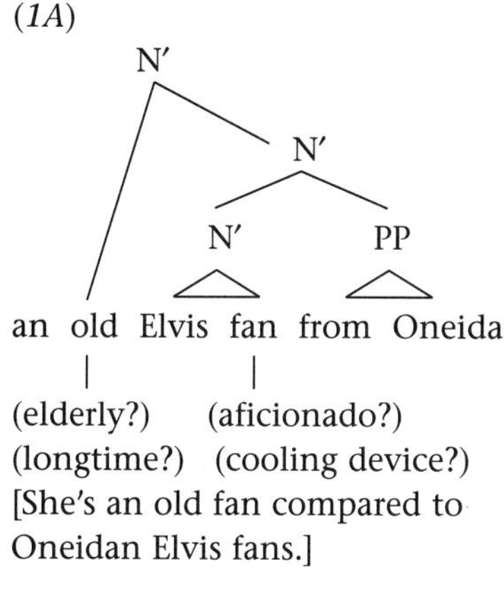

(1B)

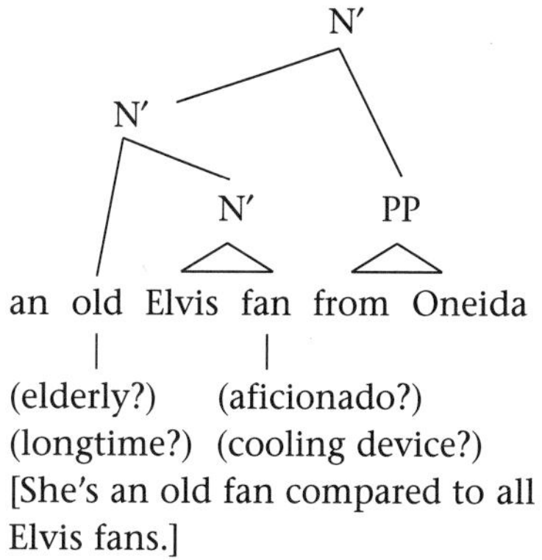

(2A)

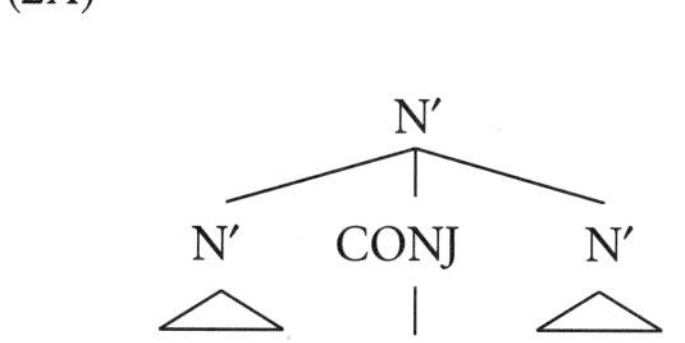

[Only the broom is sawed-off.]

(2B)

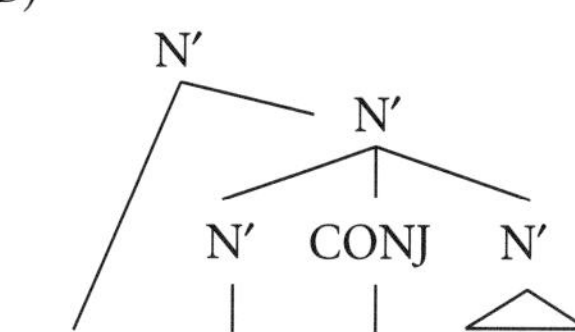

sawed-off broom and old shotgun
[Both the broom and the shotgun are sawed-off.]

(3A)

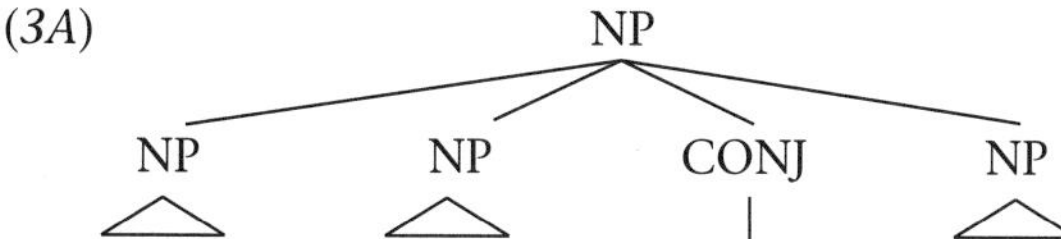

Darrel Apley, the owner of U.E. and a shocked witness . . .
[three different people]

(3B)

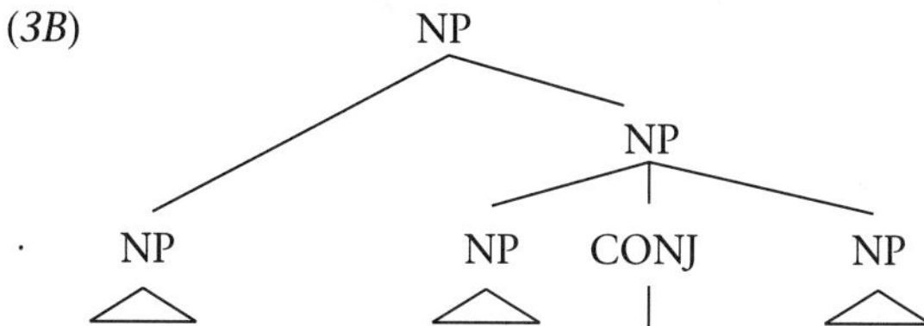

Darrel Apley, the owner of U.E. and a shocked witness . . .
[One person: "Darrell Apley, (who is) the owner . . .", after "who is" has been deleted. Don't worry about the details of this structure.]

eight

HISTORICAL LINGUISTICS: THE STUDY OF LANGUAGE CHANGE

Robert W. Murray

Many men sayn that in sweveninges
Ther nys but fables and lesynges;
But men may some swevenes sene
Whiche hardely that false ne bene,
But afterwarde ben apparaunt.

– CHAUCER, *The Romance of the Rose* (C. 1370)

Language change is both obvious and rather mysterious. The English of the late fourteenth century, for example, is so different from Modern English that without special training it is difficult to understand the opening lines to *The Romance of the Rose* cited above. Not only would these sentences have a foreign sound, but words and structures such as *sweveninges, lesynges,* and *false ne bene* are unfamiliar.[1] The existence of such differences between early and later variants of the same language raises questions as to how and why languages change over time.

Historical linguistics is concerned with both the description and explanation of language change. In this chapter we examine the nature and causes of language change and survey in some detail phonological, morphological, syntactic, lexical, and semantic change. We also explore techniques used to reconstruct linguistic prehistory and briefly discuss interrelated research into language acquisition and linguistic universals.

1 THE NATURE OF LANGUAGE CHANGE

All languages undergo change over time. English has undergone continuous and dramatic change throughout its three major periods: Old English (roughly from 450 to 1100), Middle English (from 1100 to 1500), and Modern English (from 1500 to the present). While Chaucer's Middle English is at least partially comprehensible today, Old English looks like a completely foreign language. The following is an extract from an eighth century Old English document, a translation of Bede's Latin history of England. (The letter *þ*, called 'thorn', represented the phoneme /θ/ in Old English; here and elsewhere in this chapter ¯ marks a long vowel in the orthography.)

1)

and Seaxan þā sige geslōgan.
and Saxons the victory won
'And the Saxons won the victory.'

þā sendan hī hām ǣrenddracan.
then sent they home a messenger
'Then they sent home a messenger.'

These Old English sentences differ from their Modern English counterparts in many respects. In terms of pronunciation, for instance, the Old English word *hām* [haːm] 'home' in the second sentence became [hɔːm] in Middle English, and then [howm] in Modern English. In its morphology, Old English differed significantly from Modern English. The suffix *-an* on the Old English word for 'sent' indicates both past tense and plurality of the subject (*hī* 'they'). Differences in word order are also readily apparent—with the verb following both the subject and the object in the first sentence and preceding both the subject and the object in the second. Neither of these word orders would be acceptable in the Modern English forms of these sentences.

In addition, some Old English words have disappeared from use, as the unfamiliar *ǣrenddracan* 'messenger' and *sige* 'victory' indicate. Still other words have been maintained, but with a change in meaning. For example, the Old English word *geslōgan* (which we translated as 'won') is the past tense of the verb *slēan*, the Old English predecessor of our word *slay*. Although the Modern English meaning of this word in normal usage is restricted to the act of killing, the Old English verb could also mean 'to strike, beat, coin (money), and forge (weapons)'. As these examples imply, all components of the grammar from meaning (semantics) to individual sounds (phonology) are subject to change.

1.1 Systematicity of language change

A striking fact about language change in general is its regularity and systematicity. For example, the development of a fixed subject-verb-direct object (SVO) word order

Table 8.1 Changes affecting Old English [aː]

Old English	*Middle English*	*Modern English*	
[baːt]	[bɔːt]	[bowt]	'boat'
[aːθ]	[ɔːθ]	[owθ]	'oath'
[staːn]	[stɔːn]	[stown]	'stone'

in English did not affect just a few verbs; all verbs in Modern English appear before rather than after the direct object. Similarly, the changes affecting the vowel in the word *hām* did not occur in that word only; they represent the regular development of the Old English vowel *ā* ([aː]) (see Table 8.1).

1.2 Causes of language change

The inevitability of language change is guaranteed by the way in which language is passed on from one generation to the next. Children do not begin with an intact grammar of the language being acquired but rather must construct a grammar on the basis of the available data (see Chapter 12). In such a situation it is hardly surprising that differences will arise, even if only subtle ones, from one generation to the next. Moreover, since all children use the same physiological and cognitive endowment in learning language, it is to be expected that the same patterns of change will be consistently and repeatedly manifested in all languages. Following is a brief overview of the principal causes of language change.

Articulatory simplification

As might be expected, most sound changes have a physiological basis. Since such sound changes typically result in **articulatory simplification**, they have traditionally been related to the idea of 'ease of articulation' (see Chapter 2, Section 9). Although this notion is difficult to define precisely, we can readily identify cases of articulatory simplification in our everyday speech such as the deletion of a consonant in a complex cluster or, in some dialects, the insertion of a vowel to break up a complex cluster.

Table 8.2 Simplification of complex clusters

Deletion of a consonant			
[fɪfθ̲s]	→	[fɪfs]	'fifths'
Insertion of a vowel			
[æθl̲ijt]	→	[æθəlijt]	'athlete'

Spelling pronunciation

Not all changes in pronunciation have a physiological motivation. A minor, but nevertheless important, source of change in English and other languages is **spelling pronunciation**. Since the written form of a word can differ significantly from the way it is pronounced, a new pronunciation can arise which seems to reflect more closely the spelling of the word. A case in point is the word *often*. Although this word was pronounced with a [t] in earlier English, the voiceless stop was subsequently lost resulting in the pronunciation [ɔfən] (compare *soften*). However, since the letter *t* was retained in the spelling, [t] has been reintroduced into many speakers' pronunciation of this word.

Another case in point is the pronunciation of [s] in words such as *assume* and *consume*. Although in earlier English such words were pronounced with [s], **sound change** resulted in a pronunciation with [ʃ] (as in *assure*). Similar to the case of *often* above, a pronunciation with [s] has been reintroduced into many dialects on the basis of the spelling (which remained the same even after the sound change took place). Since spelling tends to remain stable even though sound changes have occurred (English spelling began stabilizing more than three hundred years ago), it can reintroduce a pronunciation that was earlier altered through sound change.

Analogy and reanalysis

Cognitive factors also play a role in change in all components of the grammar. Two sources of change having a cognitive basis are **analogy** and **reanalysis**. Analogy reflects the preference of speakers for regular patterns over irregular ones. It typically involves the extension or generalization of a regularity on the basis of the inference that if elements are alike in some respects, they should be alike in others as well. Both phonological and semantic characteristics can serve as a basis for analogy. For example, on the basis of its phonological similarity with verbs such as *sting/stung* and *swing/swung*, in some dialects *bring* has developed a form *brung*, as in *I('ve) brung it into the house*. Children create forms such as *goed* by analogy with regular past tense forms like *played*. As we will see, analogy plays a very important role in morphological change.

Reanalysis is particularly common in morphological change. Morphological reanalysis typically involves an attempt to attribute an internal structure to a word that formerly was not broken down into component morphemes. A classic example in English is the word *hamburger* which originally referred to a type of meat patty deriving its name from the city of Hamburg in Germany. This word has been reanalyzed as consisting of two components, *ham* + *burger*. The latter morpheme has since appeared in many new forms including *fishburger*, *chickenburger*, and even as a free morpheme *burger*. Note that reanalysis need not be correct (there is usually no ham in a burger!).

Language contact

Another cause of language change is **language contact**. Language contact refers to the situation where speakers of a language frequently interact with the speakers of another language or dialect. As a consequence, extensive **borrowing** can occur, particularly where there are significant numbers of bilinguals or multilinguals. Although borrowing can affect all components of the grammar, the lexicon is typically most affected. English, for example, has borrowed many Amerindian words including *Canada*, *moccasin*, *totem*, *tomahawk*, *pecan*, *moose*, and *skunk*.

Among the effects that borrowing can have on the sound system are the introduction of new phonemes or allophones and changes in their distribution. For example, some English speakers pronounce the name of the classical composer, *Bach*, with the final velar fricative [x] found in the German pronunciation. If there is a significant number of borrowings from another language, the borrowed foreign segment can eventually become a new phoneme. In the early Middle English period, the London dialect had [f] but not [v] in word-initial position. The [v] was later introduced as a result of contact with other English dialects and with French, in which it did occur word-initially. This contact was a factor in the development of a contrast between /f/ and /v/ word-initially, as found in Modern English pairs such as *file* and *vile*.

Language (as well as dialect) contact also results in another minor but nevertheless important source of language change, **hypercorrection**. Hypercorrection occurs when a speaker who is attempting to speak another dialect or language overgeneralizes particular rules. For example, most Americans speak a dialect in which no distinction is made between intervocalic [t] and [d] so that words such as *latter* and *ladder* are both pronounced with an intervocalic flap [ɾ] (see Chapter 2). If a speaker from such a dialect attempts to emulate the pronunciation of a speaker from another dialect who does distinguish the two stops intervocalically, hypercorrection could result in the use of intervocalic [t] in words where [d] should be used; for example, the pronunciation *pro*[t]*igy* for *pro<u>d</u>igy*.

Another example of hypercorrection is the use of *I* in constructions such as *He saw John and I*. This usage is an overgeneralization of the rule that only *I* should be used in subject position, never *me*. According to this rule, *John and I are going* is correct but *John and me/me and John are going* is incorrect. For some speakers, hypercorrection has resulted in the inference that all coordinate phrases with *me* (such as *John and me*) are incorrect even when they serve as direct object (complement) of the verb. Interestingly, even a person who says *He gave it to John and I* would not say *He saw I*.

2 SOUND CHANGE

Although all components of the grammar are susceptible to change over time, some types of change yield more obvious results than others. Variation and change are particularly noticeable in the phonology of a language. Several common types of sound change can be distinguished.

Most sound changes begin as subtle alterations in the sound pattern of a language in particular phonetic environments. The linguistic processes underlying such **phonetically conditioned change** are identical to the ones found in the phonology of currently spoken languages (see Chapter 2, Section 9). The application of such processes usually brings about an articulatory simplification and over time significant changes in the phonology of a language can result.

Although all aspects of a language's phonology (e.g., tone, stress, and syllable structure) are subject to change over time, we will restrict our attention here to change involving segments. Since most sound changes involve sequences of segments, the main focus will be on **sequential change**. However, we will also discuss one common type of **segmental change**, involving the simplification of an affricate. In addition, in order to indicate that more than just articulatory factors play a role in sound change, we will discuss a case of sound change based on auditory factors. All important sound changes discussed in this section and referred to in this chapter are found in the following catalogue.

Table 8.3 Catalogue of sound changes

Sequential change
Assimilation
Place and/or manner of articulation
Palatalization/affrication
Nasalization
Umlaut
Dissimilation
Epenthesis (segment addition)
Metathesis (segment movement)
Weakening and deletion
Vowels
Vowel reduction
Syncope
Apocope
Consonants
Degemination
Voicing
Frication
Rhotacism
Deletion
Consonant strengthening
Glide strengthening
Segmental change
Deaffrication
Auditorily based change
Substitution

2.1 Sequential change

Assimilation

The most common type of sequential change is **assimilation**, which has the effect of increasing the efficiency of articulation through a simplification of articulatory movements. We will focus here on the four main types indicated in the catalogue.

Partial assimilation involving place or manner of articulation is a very common change which, over time, can result in **total assimilation**. In the Spanish and Latin examples in Table 8.4, the nasal took on the place of articulation of the following consonant.

Table 8.4 Assimilation (place of articulation) in Spanish and Latin[2]

Old Spanish	semda	Modern Spanish	senda	'path'
Early Latin	inpossibilis	Later Latin	impossibilis	'impossible'

The first of the Old English examples in Table 8.5 shows voicing assimilation and the second shows assimilation involving nasality.

Table 8.5 Assimilation in voicing and nasality in Old English

Early Old English	*Later Old English*	
slǣpde	slǣpte	'slept'
stefn	stemn	'stem (of a tree)'

In the Italian examples in Table 8.6, a stop assimilates totally to a following stop.

Table 8.6 Total assimilation in Italian

Latin	*Italian*	
octo (*c* = [k])	otto	'eight'
septem	sette	'seven'
damnum	danno	'damage'

Another type of assimilation is **palatalization**—the effect that front vowels and the palatal glide [j] typically have on velar, alveolar, and dental stops, making their place of articulation more palatal. If you compare your pronunciation of *keep* as opposed to *cot*, you will notice that the pronunciation of [k] in *keep* is much more palatal than in *cot* due to the influence of [i]. Palatalization is often the first step in **affrication**, a change in which palatalized stops become affricates, either [ts] or [ʧ] if the original stop was voiceless or [dz] or [ʤ] if the original stop was voiced.

Table 8.7 Palatalization/affrication induced by front vowels and [j]

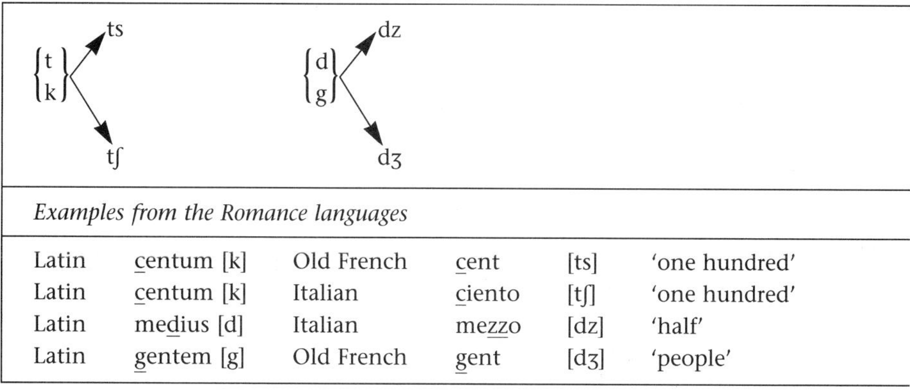

Examples from the Romance languages					
Latin	centum [k]	Old French	cent	[ts]	'one hundred'
Latin	centum [k]	Italian	ciento	[tʃ]	'one hundred'
Latin	medius [d]	Italian	mezzo	[dz]	'half'
Latin	gentem [g]	Old French	gent	[dʒ]	'people'

Nasalization refers to the nasalizing effect that a nasal consonant can have on an adjacent vowel. This change occurred in both French and Portuguese, with the subsequent loss of the nasal consonant. (The pronunciation of the vowels in our examples underwent additional changes in height and backness in French.)

Table 8.8 Nasalization in Portuguese and French

Latin	*Portuguese*	*French*	
bon-	bon [bõ]	bon [bɔ̃]	'good'
un-	um [ũ]	un [œ̃]	'one'

Although assimilation is probably most common in the case of adjacent segments, it can also apply at a distance. A case in point is **umlaut**, the effect a vowel or sometimes a glide in one syllable can have on the vowel of another syllable, usually a preceding one. Umlaut (resulting in front rounded vowels [y] and [ø]) played an important role in Old English and is the source of irregular plurals such as *goose/geese* and *mouse/mice* in Modern English. For example, the plural of the pre-Old English words *gōs* 'goose' and *mūs* 'mouse' was formed by adding a suffix -[i]. As a result, umlaut of the vowel in the preceding syllable occurred in the plural forms (see pre-Old English stages 1 and 2) but not in the singular forms. By early Old English, the suffix -[i] had been lost in a separate change leaving the umlauted vowel as the marker of the plural form. (Subsequent changes included the derounding of the umlauted vowels [ø̄] and [ȳ] to [ē] and [ī] respectively in Middle English as well as the Great Vowel Shift as described in Section 2.4 below.)

Table 8.9 Umlaut in English

Pre-Old English 1		*Pre-OE 2*		*Early OE*		*Subsequent changes*	
[gōs]	>	[gōs]	>	[gōs]	>	[guws]	'goose'
[gōsi]	>	[gø̄si]	>	[gø̄s]	>	[gijs]	'geese'
[mūs]	>	[mūs]	>	[mūs]	>	[maws]	'mouse'
[mūsi]	>	[mȳsi]	>	[mȳs]	>	[majs]	'mice'

Dissimilation

Dissimilation, the process whereby one segment is made less like another segment in its environment, is much less frequent than assimilation. This type of change typically occurs when it would be difficult to articulate or perceive two similar sounds in close proximity. The word *anma* 'soul' in Late Latin, for example, was modified to *alma* in Spanish, thereby avoiding two consecutive nasal consonants. Like assimilation, dissimilation can also operate at a distance to affect nonadjacent segments. For instance, the Latin word *arbor* 'tree' became *arbol* in Spanish and *alboro* in Italian, thereby avoiding two instances of [r] in adjacent syllables. (By contrast, dissimilation did not occur in French where *arbre* has retained both instances of /r/.)

Epenthesis

Another common sound change, **epenthesis**, involves the insertion of a consonant or vowel into a particular environment. In some cases, epenthesis results from the anticipation of an upcoming sound.

Table 8.10 Epenthesis in Old English

Earlier form	*Change*	*Later form*	
ganra	VnrV > VndrV	gandra	'gander'
simle	VmlV > VmblV	simble	'always'
ǣmtig	VmtV > VmptV	ǣmptig	'empty'

In these examples, the epenthetic [b], [d], or [p] has the same place of articulation as the preceding nasal but agrees with the following segment in terms of voice and nasality. The epenthetic segment therefore serves as a bridge for the transition between the segments on either side.

Table 8.11 The nature of epenthesis

[m]	*[b]*	*[l]*	*[m]*	*[p]*	*[t]*
labial	labial	nonlabial	labial	labial	nonlabial
nasal	nonnasal	nonnasal	nasal	nonnasal	nonnasal
voiced	voiced	voiced	voiced	voiceless	voiceless

In other cases, vowel epenthesis serves to break up a sequence of sounds that would otherwise be difficult to pronounce or even inconsistent with the phonotactic patterns of the language. As mentioned above, some English speakers avoid [θl] clusters by inserting an epenthetic [ə] in their pronunciation of words such as *athlete* as *ath*[ə]*lete*. In the history of Spanish, word-initial [sk] clusters were avoided by adding an initial vowel.

Table 8.12 Examples of epenthesis in Spanish

Latin	schola [sk]	Spanish	escuela [esk]	'school'
Latin	scrībere [sk]	Spanish	escribir [esk]	'write'

Metathesis

Metathesis involves a change in the positioning of segments. This change, like assimilation and dissimilation, can affect adjacent segments or segments at a distance.

Table 8.13 Metathesis of adjacent segments in Old English

Earlier form	*Later form*	
wæps	wæsp	'wasp'
þridda	þirdda	'third'

Metathesis at a distance is found in the change from Latin *mīrāculum* 'miracle' to Spanish *milagro*, in which [r] and [l] have changed places although they were not adjacent.

Figure 8.1 Metathesis of nonadjacent segments in Spanish

Weakening and deletion

Both vowels and consonants are also susceptible to outright **deletion** as well as to various **weakening** processes. We will first treat the effects of these processes on vowels and then turn to their effects on consonants.

Vowel deletion may involve a word-final vowel (**apocope**) or a word-internal vowel (**syncope**). A vowel in an unstressed syllable is particularly susceptible to deletion, especially when a nearby neighboring syllable is stressed.

Table 8.14 Vowel deletion in French

Apocope		
Latin	*French*	
cū́ra̱	cure [kyʁ]	'cure'
ōrnā́re̱	orner	'decorate'
Syncope		
Latin	*French*	
pḗrde̱re	perdre	'lose'
vī́:ve̱re	vivre	'live'

The effects of syncope are also apparent in the loss of the medial vowel in Modern English words such as *vege̱table* and *fami̱ly*, which are frequently pronounced as [vɛ́ʤtəbl̩] and [fǽmlij].

Vowel deletion is commonly preceded by **vowel reduction**, in which a full vowel is reduced to a schwa-like (i.e., short, lax [ə]) vowel. Vowel reduction typically affects short vowels in unstressed syllables and may affect all or only a subset of the full vowels.

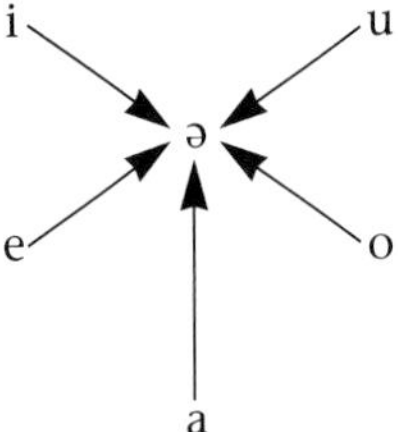

Figure 8.2 Vowel reduction

Vowel reduction with subsequent deletion (syncope and apocope) occurred in Middle English and Early Modern English.

Table 8.15 Vowel reduction and deletion in English

Syncope					
Old English		*Middle English (vowel reduction)*		*Early Modern English (vowel deletion)*	
stan<u>a</u>s	[a]	ston<u>e</u>s	[ə]	ston<u>e</u>s	Ø
stan<u>e</u>s	[e]	ston<u>e</u>s	[ə]	ston<u>e</u>'s	Ø
Apocope					
Old English		*Middle English (vowel reduction)*		*Early Modern English (apocope)*	
nam<u>a</u>	[a]	nam<u>e</u>	[ə]	nam<u>e</u>	Ø
tal<u>u</u>	[u]	tal<u>e</u>	[ə]	tal<u>e</u>	Ø

Consonant deletion is also a very common sound change. For example, the word-initial cluster [kn] was found in Old and Middle English, as the spelling of such words as *knight*, *knit*, *knot*, and *knee* implies, but the [k] was subsequently lost, giving us our modern pronunciation. The loss of word-final consonants has played a major role in the evolution of Modern French. The final letters in the written forms of the following words reflect consonants that were actually pronounced at an earlier stage of the language.

Table 8.16 Consonant loss in French

French spelling (masculine form)	*Current pronunciation*	
gros	[gro]	'large'
chaud	[ʃo]	'warm'
vert	[vɛʁ]	'green'

Just as vowel reduction can be identified as a weakening process since it represents an intermediate step on the pathway from a full vowel to deletion of the vowel, so too can pathways of **consonant weakening** be identified. The following scale of **consonantal strength** is helpful in identifying cases of weakening.

Consonantal strength
stronger ↑ voiceless stops
voiceless fricatives, voiced stops
voiced fricatives
nasals
liquids
weaker ↓ glides

Note: Geminate (long) consonants are stronger than their nongeminate counterparts.

Figure 8.3 Scale of consonantal strength

Accordingly, geminates weaken to nongeminates (**degemination**), stops weaken to fricatives (**frication**), and voiceless stops or voiceless fricatives weaken to voiced stops or voiced fricatives respectively (**voicing**).[3] Weakening can ultimately result in the deletion of the consonant. Following is a typical pathway of weakening.

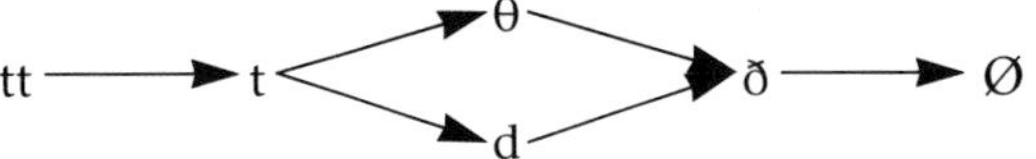

Figure 8.4 Typical pathway of consonant weakening

Consonants are particularly subject to weakening in an intervocalic environment. Parts of the pathway of consonantal weakening are exemplified with developments from the Romance languages shown in Table 8.17.

Table 8.17 Consonantal weakening in Romance

Degemination (tt > t)	Latin	mittere	Spanish	meter	'to put'
Voicing (t > d)	Latin	mātūrus	Old Spanish	maduro	'ripe'
Frication (d > ð)	Old Spanish	maduro	Spanish	maduro [ð]	'ripe'
Deletion (ð > Ø)	Old French	[maðyr]	French	mûr	'ripe'

Rhotacism is a relatively common type of weakening that typically involves the change of [z] to [r]. Often rhotacism is preceded by a stage involving the voicing of [s] to [z]. Within the Germanic family of languages for instance, [s] first became [z] in a particular intervocalic environment. This [z] remained in Gothic but became [r] in other Germanic languages such as in English, German, and Swedish. The effects of the latter part of this change can be seen in the standard spellings of the following words.

Table 8.18 Rhotacism in English, German, and Swedish

Gothic	*English*	*German*	*Swedish*
maiza	more	mehr	mera
diuzam	deer	Tier	djur
huzd	hoard	Hort	—

In Modern English, rhotacism is the source of the alternation between [z] and [r] in *was* and *were*. The [r] resulted from earlier [z], which was originally intervocalic.

Consonantal strengthening

Just as consonants weaken, they can also strengthen. **Glide strengthening** (the strengthening of a glide to an affricate) is particularly common, especially in word-initial position. In the following Italian examples, the glide [j] has been strengthened to [ʤ].

Table 8.19 Glide strengthening in Italian

Latin	iūdicium	[j]	Italian	giudizio	[ʤ]	'justice'
Latin	iuvenis	[j]	Italian	giovane	[ʤ]	'young'

2.2 Segmental change

Segments such as affricates are considered phonologically complex because they represent the fusing of a stop plus a fricative into a single segment, [ʤ] or [ts]. Such complex segments are commonly subject to simplification. A very common type of segmental simplification is **deaffrication**, which has the effect of turning affricates into fricatives by eliminating the stop portion of the affricate.

Table 8.20 Deaffrication in French

Old French	cent [ts]	French	cent [s]	'one hundred'
Old French	gent [ʤ]	French	gent [ʒ]	'people, tribe'

Since deaffrication of [ʧ] (as well as of [ʤ]) has not occurred in English, early borrowings from French maintain the affricate, while later borrowings have a fricative.

Table 8.21 Borrowing from French

Early borrowing (before deaffrication occurred in French)	
Old French [ʧ]	*English* [ʧ]
chaiere	chair
chaine	chain
(*Note:* Compare Modern French [ʃ] in chaire 'throne, seat' and chaîne 'chain'.)	
Later borrowings (after deaffrication occurred in French)	
Modern French [ʃ]	*English* [ʃ]
chandelier	chandelier
chauffeur	chauffeur

2.3 Auditorily based change

Although articulatory factors (particularly relating to 'ease of articulation') are of central importance in sound change as indicated in the discussion above, auditory factors also play a role. **Substitution** is a type of auditorily based change involving the replacement of one segment with another similar sounding segment. A common type of substitution involves [f] replacing either [x] or [θ]. Earlier in the history of English, [f] replaced [x] in some words in standard varieties of English while [f] replaced [θ] in Cockney, a nonstandard dialect spoken in London.

Table 8.22 Auditorily based substitution

[x] > [f]	Middle English	laugh [x]	Modern English	laugh [f]
[θ] > [f]	Standard English	thin [θ]	Cockney	[fɪn]

So far we have treated sound changes without consideration of their effect on the sound pattern of the particular language as a whole. All of the foregoing sound changes can lead both to new types of allophonic variation and to the addition or loss of phonemic contrasts. Examples of such cases are presented in the next section.

2.4 Phonetic versus phonological change

The sound changes outlined in the previous sections can affect the overall sound pattern (phonology) of a language in different ways. Commonly, the first stage of a sound change results in the creation of a new allophone of an already existing phoneme. The term **phonetic sound change** can be used to refer to this stage.

A good example of phonetic sound change involves the laxing of short high vowels that has developed in Canadian French. This change can be seen in closed word-final syllables, among other environments.

Table 8.23 Vowel laxing in Canadian French

European French	*Canadian French*	
Closed syllable		
[vit]	[vɪt]	'quick'
[libʁ]	[lɪb]	'free'
[ekut]	[ekʊt]	'listen'
[pus]	[pʊs]	'thumb'
Open syllable		
[vi]	[vi]	'life'
[li]	[li]	'bed'
[vu]	[vu]	'you'
[lu]	[lu]	'wolf'

Whereas Canadian French has the lax vowels [ɪ] and [ʊ] in closed final syllables, European French has kept the tense vowels [i] and [u]. Both dialects of French retain [i] and [u] in open syllables. This suggests that Canadian French has developed the following rule.

$$\underset{\begin{bmatrix}\text{+high}\\ \text{–long}\end{bmatrix}}{\text{V}} \rightarrow [\text{–tense}] \; / \; \_\_ \; \text{C}]_\sigma$$

Figure 8.5 Vowel laxing rule in Canadian French

While this rule did introduce an allophone not present in European French, it did not create any new phonemes since the difference between lax vowels and their tense counterparts in Canadian French is not contrastive (i.e., it does not play a role in distinguishing minimal pairs; see Chapter 3, question 12.

Splits

Sometimes sound change can lead to changes in a language's phonological system by adding, eliminating, or rearranging phonemes. Such **phonological change** can involve **splits**, **mergers**, or **shifts**.

In a phonological split, allophones of the same phoneme come to contrast with each other due to the loss of the conditioning environment, with the result that one or more new phonemes are created. The English phoneme /ŋ/ was the result of a phonological split. Originally, [ŋ] was simply the allophone of /n/ that appeared before a velar consonant. During Middle English, consonant deletion resulted in the loss of [g] in word-final position after a nasal consonant, leaving [ŋ] as the final sound in words such as *sing*.

Table 8.24 Phonological split resulting in /ŋ/

Original phonemic form	/sɪng/
Original phonetic form	[sɪŋg]
Deletion of [g]	[sɪŋg] > [sɪŋ]
New phonemic form	/sɪŋ/

The loss of the word-final [g] created minimal pairs such as *sin* (/sɪn/) and *sing* (/sɪŋ/), in which there is a contrast between /n/ and /ŋ/. This example represents a typical phonological split. When the conditioning environment of an allophonic variant of a phoneme is lost through sound change, the allophone is no longer predictable and thus itself becomes phonemic. The original phoneme (in our example /n/) splits into two phonemes (/n/ and /ŋ/).

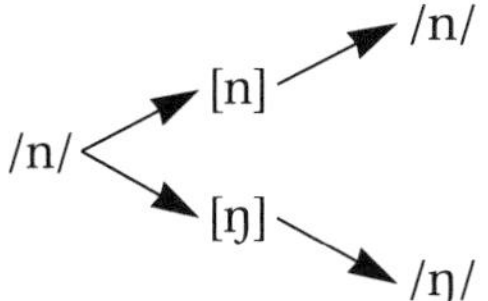

Figure 8.6 A phonological split

Mergers

In a phonological merger, two or more phonemes collapse into a single one, thereby reducing the number of phonemes in the language. The case of auditorily based substitution discussed above has this effect in Cockney English, where all instances of the interdental fricative /θ/ have become /f/. Consequently, the phonemes /θ/ and /f/ have merged into one (/f/), and words such as *thin* and *fin* have the same phonological form (/fɪn/). Similarly, /v/ and /ð/ have merged (e.g., /smuv/ for *smooth*).

Figure 8.7 A phonological merger

Shifts

A phonological shift is a change in which a series of phonemes is systematically modified so that their organization with respect to each other is altered. A well-known example of such a change is called the **Great English Vowel Shift**. Beginning in the Middle English period and continuing into the eighteenth century, the language underwent a series of modifications in the long vowels.

Table 8.25 The Great English Vowel Shift

Middle English	*Great Vowel Shift*			*Modern English*	
[ti:d]	[i:]	>	[aj]	/tajd/	'tide'
[lu:d]	[u:]	>	[aw]	/lawd/	'loud'
[ge:s]	[e:]	>	[i:]	/gis/	'geese'
[sɛ]	[ɛ:]	>	[i:]	/si/	'sea'
[go:s]	[o:]	>	[u:]	/gus/	'goose'
[brɔ:kən]	[ɔ:]	>	[o:]	/brokən/	'broken'
[na:mə]	[a:]	>	[e:]	/nem/	'name'

Figure 8.8 illustrates the changes that gradually affected the English long vowels.

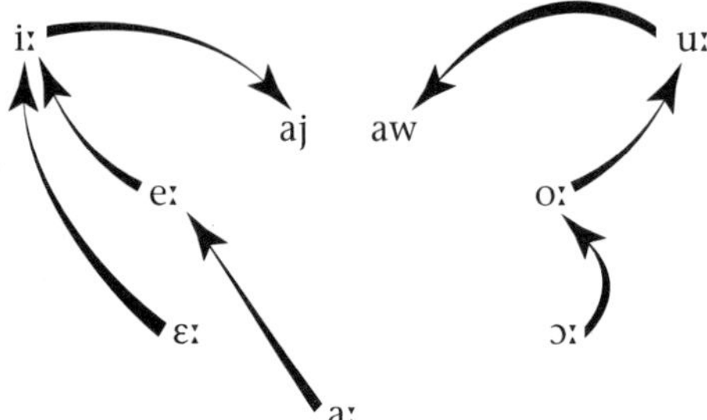

Figure 8.8 Changes brought about by the Great English Vowel Shift

2.5 Explaining phonological shift

The causes and even the details of the Great English Vowel Shift still remain unclear. In fact, the causes of phonological shift in general are not well understood. A possible motivation in some cases appears to involve the phonemic system itself, where the notion of phonological space plays a role. As in the case of 'ease of articulation', phonological space is difficult to define precisely. For our purposes and focusing on vowels only, we can consider the vowel quadrangle (a schematicization of the oral cavity) as the phonological space that vowels must occupy. Although the vowel systems of languages can be arranged in various ways (see Chapter 9), there is a tendency for languages to maximize the use of space in the quadrangle. Accordingly, if a language has only three vowels, they will likely be [i], [a], and [o] or [u], not (for example) [i], [e], [ɛ]. Similarly, if a language has five vowels, they will be distributed throughout the phonological space typically as [i], [e], [a], [o], [u] rather than [u], [ʊ], [a], [o], [ɔ], for example.

Languages with seven (or more) vowels (the case in English at the starting point of the Great English Vowel Shift in Figure 8.8) often undergo **diphthongization**. This can be seen as a reaction to the overcrowding of the phonological space. Its

a Typical distribution of vowels in phonological space

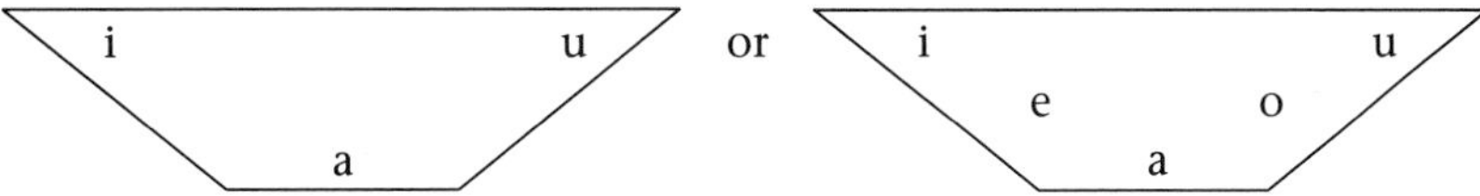

b Atypical distribution of vowels in phonological space

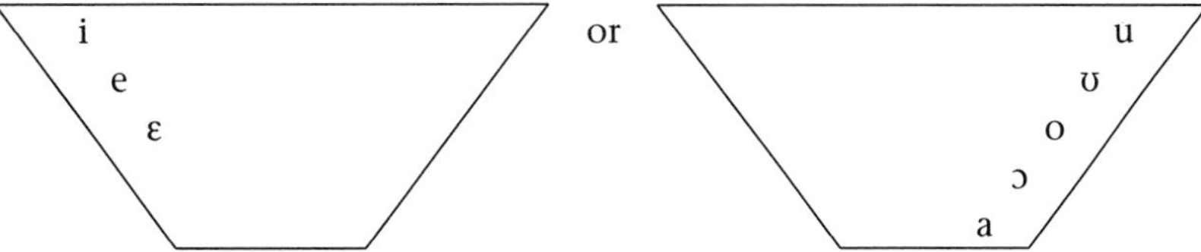

Figure 8.9 Vowel distribution

effect is to reduce the seven vowel system to a five vowel system. (Think of the two diphthongs as not infringing on the space of the simple vowels.)

Overcrowding appears to have resulted in diphthongization in many languages, including Old High German and Spanish.

Table 8.26 Diphthongization in Old High German and Spanish

Old High German diphthongization			*Spanish diphthongization*		
iː	uː		i		u
iaː	uaː		e	je we	o
eː ↗	↖ oː		ɛ ↗	↖ ɔ	
ɛː	ɔː			a	
aː					
Old High German			*Latin*	*Spanish*	
Earlier	*Later*				
heːr	hiar	'here'	petra	piedra	'stone'
floːt	fluat	'flood'	mortem	muerte	'death'

The diphthongization in these two languages differs from that of the Great English Vowel Shift in two ways. The mid vowels and not the high vowels are affected, and different sets of diphthongs result. Nevertheless, in terms of phonological space, all these cases of diphthongization achieve the same result: namely, the reduction of an overcrowded seven vowel system to a five vowel system. (Of course, the Great English Vowel Shift is further complicated by other developments.)

2.6 Sound change and rule ordering

In describing language change, it is often crucial to identify the relative chronology, or times at which different changes have occurred. Three important changes in the history of English can be given as the following (somewhat simplified) rules.

1. Voicing
   C → [+voice] / [+voice] ___ [+voice]

2. Syncope
   V → Ø / ___ C #
   [–stress]

3. Assimilation
   C → [+voice] / C + ___
   [+voice]

Figure 8.10 Three rules in the history of English

These changes have played an important role in the evolution of English plural forms such as *hooves* (versus *hoof*) and *wolves* (versus *wolf*). Of the possible orderings of these three rules, only one will derive the contemporary pronunciation from the earlier (Old English) phonemic form. Two of the possible orderings are given below.

Table 8.27 Rule ordering in the history of English

Hypothesis A	
Original phonemic form	wulfas
Voicing	wulvas
Syncope	wulvs
Assimilation	wulvz
Hypothesis B	
Original phonemic form	wulfas
Voicing	wulvas
Assimilation	(cannot apply)
Syncope	wulvs (incorrect)

If we assume hypothesis A with the ordering voicing, syncope, and assimilation, we can account for the [vz] in the modern pronunciation of a word such as *wolves*. By contrast, the ordering proposed in hypothesis B would not account for the present pronunciation.

3 MORPHOLOGICAL CHANGE

In this section we discuss morphological changes resulting from analogy and reanalysis as well as changes involving the addition or loss of affixes.

3.1 ADDITION OF AFFIXES

Borrowing has been a very important source of new affixes in English. During the Middle English period, many French words containing the suffix *-ment* (e.g., *accomplishment, commencement*) made their way into the language. Eventually, *-ment* established itself as a productive suffix in English and was used with bases that were not of French origin (e.g., *acknowledgment, merriment*). The ending *-able*, which converts a verb into an adjective (e.g., *readable, lovable*, etc.), followed a similar pattern. Although words with this ending (e.g., *favorable, conceivable*) were initially borrowed into English as whole units, eventually the suffix became productive and was used with new bases.

Not all new affixes are the result of borrowing. Lexical forms can become grammatical forms over time through a process called **grammaticalization** (see Chapter 7, Section 2.4). In the case where two words are frequently adjacent, over time they can become fused together to form a single unit consisting of a base and an affix. **Fusion** refers to the specific type of grammaticalization where words develop into affixes (either prefixes or suffixes).

Table 8.28 Fusion

word word	>	base + affix (suffixation)
word word	>	affix + base (prefixation)

A number of Modern English suffixes are derived from earlier words by means of fusion.

Table 8.29 English suffixes resulting from fusion

Suffix	*Old English word*	
-hood (childhood)	hād	'state, condition, rank'
-dom (freedom)	dōm	'condition, power'
-ly (fatherly)	(ge-)līc	'similar, equal, like'

Another case of fusion is the development of the future tense affixes in Italian that are derived from various forms of the Latin word *habere* 'to have'.

Table 8.30 Fusion resulting in a future tense affix in Italian

Latin	*Italian*	
amāre + habēo	amerò	'I will love'
amāre + habēmus	ameremo	'we will love'

3.2 Loss of affixes

Just as affixes can be added to the grammar, they can also be lost. Sometimes affixes simply fall into disuse for no apparent reason. For example, a number of Old English derivational affixes, including *-bǣre* and *-bora*, are no longer used.

Table 8.31 Affixes no longer found in English

N + bǣre	→	A	(e.g., lustbǣre 'pleasant, agreeable' from *lust* 'pleasure')
N + bora	→	N	(e.g., mundbora 'protector' from *mund* 'protection')

It is also very common for affixes to be lost through sound change. For example, Old English had a complex system of affixes marking case and gender. Nouns were divided into three gender classes—masculine, neuter, and feminine. Assignment to a class was not based on sex (natural gender) but on grammatical gender; for example, the word for *stone* (Old English *stān*) and even a word for *woman* (*wīfmann*) were masculine, the word for *sun* (*sunne*) was feminine, and another word for *woman* (*wīf*) was neuter. Each gender class was associated with a different set of case endings (see Table 8.32).

The following Old English sentence contains all four case categories.

2)

Se cniht	geaf	gief-e	þæs hierd-es	sun-e
the youth-Nom	gave	gift-Acc	the shepherd-Gen	son-Dat

'The youth gave a gift to the shepherd's son.'

Table 8.32 Old English case affixes

	Masculine		*Neuter*		*Feminine*	
Singular						
	hund	'dog'	dēor	'animal'	gief	'gift'
Nominative	hund		dēor		gief-u	
Accusative	hund		dēor		gief-e	
Genitive	hund-es		dēor-es		gief-e	
Dative	hund-e		dēor-e		gief-e	
Plural						
Nominative	hund-as		dēor		gief-a	
Accusative	hund-as		dēor		gief-a	
Genitive	hund-a		dēor-a		gief-a	
Dative	hund-um		dēor-um		gief-um	

Table 8.33 The loss of case affixes through sound change (in English *hound*)

	Old English	*Middle English (e = [ə])*	*Modern English*
Singular			
Nominative	hund	hund	hound
Accusative	hund	hund	hound
Genitive	hund-es	hund-(e)s	hound's
Dative	hund-e	hund-(e)	hound
Plural			
Nominative	hund-as	hund-(e)s	hounds
Accusative	hund-as	hund-(e)s	hounds
Genitive	hund-a	hund-(e)	hounds'
Dative	hund-um	hund-(e)	hounds

By the fifteenth century, English case endings had changed radically. Consonant deletion resulted in the loss of the earlier [m] of the dative plural suffix and through vowel reduction all the unstressed vowels of the case endings were reduced to the short, lax vowel [ə] (which was later lost through vowel deletion). Consequently, many of the earlier case and gender distinctions were obliterated. (The examples in Table 8.33 also include changes to the base-internal vowels as the result of various processes, including the Great English Vowel Shift.)

Whereas Old English had five distinct case affixes, Middle English had only two suffixes, *-e* and *-es*. With the loss of schwa, they were ultimately reduced to the single suffix *-s*, still used in Modern English for the plural and the possessive. This represents a typical example of how sound change can result in modification to the morphological component of the grammar.

3.3 From synthetic to analytic to synthetic

Since languages vary greatly in the complexity of their morphology, linguists often make a distinction between **analytic** and **synthetic** languages (see Chapter 9). Whereas analytic languages have very few inflectional affixes (for example, Modern English), synthetic languages have many (for example, Latin, Old English).

Even in the absence of borrowing, sound change and fusion ensure that there is constant flux in the morphology of a language over time. Due to the loss of case endings through sound change, English has developed from a synthetic language with many inflectional affixes to an analytic one with very few, as the above discussion of nouns such as *hound* indicates.

By contrast, fusion ensures the rise of new synthetic forms. Fusion can be observed in some Modern English dialects in forms such as *coulda* (e.g., *I coulda won*), which represents the fusion of *could* and *have*. For many speakers, the *-a* is treated as a suffix that is no longer related to *have*, as evident in spellings such as *could of*, which result from confusion over how to represent the pronunciation of *coulda* in written English. Through fusion, a language with an analytic morphology can become more synthetic over time.

3.4 Analogy

The drastic effects that sound change can have on the morphology of a language are often alleviated through **analogy**. For example, the plural of Old English *hand* 'hand' was *handa*. Vowel reduction and apocope applying to *handa* would have yielded a Modern English plural form identical to the singular form, namely *hand*.

Table 8.34 Sound changes applied to Old English *handa* 'hands'

handa	
handə	vowel reduction
hand	apocope

Obviously, then, the Modern English plural *hands* cannot be the consequence of sound change. Rather, it is the result of earlier analogy with words such as Middle English *hund* 'hound' (see Table 8.33), which did form the plural with the suffix *-s*.

This suffix, whose earlier form *-as* was predominant even in Old English, was extended by analogy to all English nouns with a few exceptions (*oxen, men, geese,* etc.). Other plural forms besides *hands* that were created on the basis of analogy include *eyes* (*eyen* in Middle English) and *shoes* (formerly *shooen*).

Continuing analogy along these lines is responsible for the development of the plural form *youse* (from *you*) in some English dialects. Each generation of English-speaking children temporarily extends the analogy still further by producing forms such as *sheeps, gooses,* and *mouses*. To date, however, these particular innovations have not been accepted by adult speakers of Standard English and are eventually abandoned by young language learners.

3.5 Reanalysis

As we mentioned in Section 1.2, reanalysis can result in a new morphological structure for a word. It can affect both borrowed words and, particularly in cases where the morphological structure of the word is no longer transparent, native words. Reanalysis can result in new productive patterns—as in the case of *(-)burger*—or it can remain quite isolated affecting perhaps only one word. Since the type of reanalysis exemplified by *hamburger* is not based on a correct analysis of a word (at least from a historical perspective) and does not usually involve a conscious or detailed study of the word on the part of the speaker, it is often called **folk etymology**.

Although in the case of *hamburger*, the only evidence of folk etymology is the productive use of *(-)burger* (e.g., as an independent word and in compounds of the type *fishburger*), folk etymology commonly involves changes in pronunciation reflecting the new morphological analysis. For example, our word *earwig* derives from Old English *ēarwicga* [ǽərwiʤa], a compound consisting of 'ear' and 'insect'. Taking into consideration sound change alone, the expected Modern English pronunciation of this word would be *earwidge* [irwɪʤ]. However, the second part of the compound was lost as an independent word by Middle English, so speakers could no longer associate it with the meaning of 'insect'. Subsequently, reanalysis related the second part of the compound to the verb 'wiggle' resulting in Middle English *arwygyll* (literally 'ear + wiggle'). The end result is Modern English *-wig* and not *-widge*. More examples of folk etymology are found in the following table.

Table 8.35 Folk etymology in English (native words and borrowings)

Modern word	*Source*
belfry	Middle English *berfrey* 'bell tower' (unrelated to bell)
bridegroom	Middle English *bridegome* (unrelated to groom) (compare Old English *brȳd* 'bride' and *guma* 'man')
muskrat	Algonquian *musquash* (unrelated to either *musk* or *rat*)
woodchuck	Algonquian *otchek* (unrelated to either *wood* or *chuck*)

Although reanalysis of individual words is common, affixes can also be affected, sometimes with new productive morphological rules developing as a result. This is the case of the Modern English adverbial suffix *-ly*, developing from Old English *-lic(e)*. In Old English, adjectives could be derived from nouns by adding the suffix

-lic. Adverbs, in turn, could be derived by adding the suffix *-e* to adjectives (including those derived with *-lic*).

Table 8.36 The derivation of Old English adjectives and adverbs

Formation of an adjective from a noun			
$[\text{dæg}]_N$	+ lic →	$[\text{dæglic}]_A$	'daily' (as in, e.g., 'daily schedule')
Formation of an adverb from an adjective			
$[\text{dēop}]_A$	+ e →	$[\text{dēope}]_{Adv}$	'deeply'
Formation of an adverb from a derived adjective with -lic			
$[\text{dæg+lic}]_A$	+ e →	$[\text{dæglice}]_{Adv}$	'daily' (as in, e.g., 'she ran daily')

At some point, the entire complex suffix *-lic+e* was reanalyzed as an adverbial suffix (rather than as an adjectival suffix *-lic* plus an adverbial suffix *-e*). It was then used by analogy to derive adverbs from adjectives in forms where it was not used before, resulting in Modern English *deeply* and other such words.

4 SYNTACTIC CHANGE

Like other components of the grammar, syntax is also subject to change over time. Syntactic change can involve modifications to phrase structure rules or transformations, as the following examples illustrate.

4.1 WORD ORDER

All languages make a distinction between the subject and direct object. This contrast is typically represented through case marking or word order. Since Old English had an extensive system of case marking, it is not surprising that its word order was somewhat more variable than that of Modern English. In unembedded clauses, Old English placed the verb in second position (much like Modern German). Thus we find subject-verb-object order in simple transitive sentences such as the following.

3)

S	V	O	
Hē	geseah	þone	mann.
'He	saw	the	man.'

When the clause began with an element such as *þa* 'then' or *ne* 'not', the verb was still in second position, but now preceded the subject as in the following example.

4)

	V	S	O
þa	sende	sē cyning	þone disc
then	sent	the king	the dish

'Then the king sent the dish.'

Although this word order is still found in Modern English, its use is very limited and subject to special restrictions, unlike the situation in Old English.

5)

	V	S	O
Rarely	has	he ever deceived	me.

When the direct object was a pronoun, the subject-object-verb order was typical.

6)

S	O	V
Hēo	hine	lǣrde.
She	him	advised

'She advised him.'

The subject-object-verb order also prevailed in embedded clauses, even when the direct object was not a pronoun.

7)

	S	O	V	
þa	hē	þone cyning	sōhte,	hē bēotode.
when	he	the king	visited,	he boasted

'When he visited the king, he boasted.'

Since case markings were lost during the Middle English period through sound change, fixed subject-verb-object order became the means of marking grammatical relations. As Table 8.37 shows, a major change in word order took place between 1300 and 1400, with the verb-object order becoming dominant.

Table 8.37 Word order patterns in Middle English

Year	*1000*	*1200*	*1300*	*1400*	*1500*
Direct object before the verb (%)	53	53	40	14	2
Direct object after the verb (%)	47	47	60	86	98

From SOV to SVO

Just as languages can be classified in terms of their morphology, languages can also be grouped on the basis of the relative order of subject (S), object (O), and verb (V) in basic sentences (see Chapter 9, Section 2.3). Almost all languages of the world fall into one of three types: SOV, SVO, or VSO, with the majority of languages being one of the first two types. Just as languages change through time from one morphological type to another, they can also change from one syntactic type to another. A case in point is found in the history of English, which shows the development from SOV to SVO syntax.

Evidence indicates that the earliest form of Germanic from which English descended was an SOV language. One of the earliest recorded Germanic sentences, for example, has this word order. The sentence in *8)* was inscribed on a golden horn (now called the Golden Horn of Gallehus) about sixteen hundred years ago.

8)

Horn of Gallehus

S		O	V
ek HlewagastiR	HoltijaR	horna	tawido
I Hlewagastir	of Holt	horn	made

'I, Hlewagastir of Holt, made the horn.'

Another type of evidence for an earlier SOV order is found in compounding. Since compounding depends on frequently occurring syntactic patterns, it can sometimes serve as an indicator of earlier syntax. The OV compound, very common in Old English (as well as in Modern English), likely reflects an earlier stage of OV word order.

Table 8.38 Old English compounds with OV structure

manslæht	'man' + 'strike'	'manslaughter, murder'
æppelbǣre	'apple' + 'bear'	'apple-bearing'

If the earliest Germanic was SOV and Modern English is firmly SVO, then Old English represents a transitional syntactic type. In developing from SOV syntax to SVO syntax, languages seem to follow similar pathways. For example, Modern German, which developed from the same Germanic SOV source as English, shares two of Old English's distinguishing characteristics. First, the verb is typically placed in the second position of the sentence in main clauses, preceded by the subject or some other element (such as an adverb). Secondly, the SOV order is employed for embedded clauses.

9)

Modern German word order

a. verb in second position in unembedded clauses:
(Compare the Old English sentences in *4)*.)

	V	S	O
Gestern	hatte	ich	keine Zeit.
yesterday	had	I	no time

'I had no time yesterday'

b. SOV in embedded clauses:
(Compare the Old English sentences in *7)*.)

	S	O	V
Als	er	den Mann	sah . . .
when	he	the man	saw

'When he saw the man . . .'

The change from SOV to SVO is not restricted to English and other Germanic languages. The same change is evident, for example, in completely unrelated languages such as those of the Bantu family of Africa. Since linguists are still not sure why languages change from one syntactic type to another, the causes of such change will undoubtedly remain an important area of investigation, especially since the relative order of verb and object (OV versus VO) has been closely linked with other word order patterns (see Chapter 9).

4.2 Inversion in the history of English

In Old and Middle English the inversion transformation (see Chapter 5) involved in the formation of *yes-no* questions could apply to all verbs, not just auxiliaries, yielding forms that would be unacceptable in Modern English.

10)

Speak they the truth?

During the sixteenth and seventeenth centuries, the Inversion rule was changed to apply solely to auxiliary verbs.

11)

Inversion (old form):	Inversion (new form):
The V moves in front of the subject.	The Aux moves in front of the subject.
They speak → Speak they?	They speak → *Speak they?
They can speak → Can they speak?	They can speak → Can they speak?

With this change, structures such as *Speak they the truth?* were no longer possible. The corresponding question came to be formed with the auxiliary *do* as in *Do they speak the truth?*

5 LEXICAL AND SEMANTIC CHANGE

Another obvious type of language change involves modifications to the lexicon. Since we have already dealt with some changes relating to derivational and inflectional morphology in Section 3, the main focus here will be on lexical change involving entire words. Simply stated, there are two possible types of lexical change, addition and loss. The addition or loss of words often reflects cultural changes that introduce novel objects and notions, and that eliminate outmoded ones.

5.1 Addition of lexical items

Addition is frequently the result of technological innovations or contact with other cultures. Such developments result in **lexical gaps** that can be filled by adding new words to the lexicon. New words are added either through the word formation processes available to the language or through borrowing.

Word formation

The most important word formation processes are compounding and derivation, although other types including conversion, blends, backformation, clipping, and acronyms (see Chapter 4) can play a significant role.

Compounding and derivation have always been available to English speakers for the creation of new words. In fact, much of the compounding and derivation in Old English seems very familiar.

Table 8.39 Compounding and derivation in Old English

Noun compounds			
N + N	sunbēam		'sunbeam'
A + N	middelniht		'midnight'
Adjective compounds			
N + A	blōdrēad		'blood-red'
A + A	dēadboren		'stillborn'
Derived nouns			
[bæc] ere	→	bæcere	'baker'
$[\text{frēond}]_N$ + scipe	→	frēondscipe	'friendship'
Derived adjectives			
$[\text{wundor}]_N$ + full	→	wundorfull	'wonderful'
$[\text{cild}]_N$ + isc	→	cildisc	'childish'

Just as speakers of Modern English can use compounding and derivational rules to create new words (e.g., the N + N compound *airhead*) so could Old English speakers create new words such as the poetic N + N compound *hwælweg*, literally 'whale' + 'path' to mean 'sea'.

Note, however, that even though many Old English compounding and derivational patterns have been maintained in Modern English, words which were acceptable in Old English are not necessarily still in use in Modern English, even though many of them are quite understandable.

Table 8.40 Old English compound and derived words that are no longer used

Noun compounds			
N + N	bōccræft ('book' + 'craft')		'literature' (compare *witchcraft*)
A + N	dimhūs ('dim' + 'house')		'prison'
Adjective compounds			
N + A	ælfscīene ('elf' + 'beautiful')		'beautiful as a fairy'
A + A	eallgōd ('all' + 'good')		'perfectly good'
Derived nouns			
sēam_V + ere	→	sēamere	'tailor' (compare *seamster, seamstress*)
$[\text{man}]_N$ + scipe	→	manscipe	'humanity' (compare 'friendship')
Derived adjectives			
$[\text{word}]_N$ + full	→	wordfull	'wordy' (compare *wonderful*)
$[\text{heofon}]_N$ + isc	→	heofonisc	'heavenly' (compare *childish*)

However, not all word formation processes available to Modern English speakers were found in Old English. For example, conversion (such as in Modern English $[\text{summer}]_N \rightarrow [\text{summer}]_V$) was not possible in Old English. In fact, conversion is typically not available to (synthetic) inflectional languages such as Old English since change in a word category in such languages is usually indicated morphologically and conversion, by definition, does not involve the use of affixes.

Borrowing

As discussed in Section 1.2, language contact over time can result in an important source of new words, borrowing. Depending on the cultural relationship holding between languages, three types of influence of one language on the other are traditionally identified: **substratum**, **adstratum**, and **superstratum influence**.

Substratum influence is the effect of a politically or culturally nondominant language on a dominant language in the area. Both American and Canadian English and Canadian French, for instance, have borrowed vocabulary items from Amerindian languages (see examples in Section 1.2). From a much earlier period in the history of English, the influence of a Celtic substratum is also evident, particularly in place names such as *Thames*, *London*, and *Dover*. Substratum influence does not usually have a major impact on the lexicon of the borrowing language. Borrowed words are usually restricted to place names and unfamiliar items or concepts. This situation reflects the fact that it is usually the speakers of the substratum language who inhabited the area first.

Superstratum influence is the effect of a politically or culturally dominant language on another language or languages in the area. For example, the Athapaskan language Gwich'in (Loucheux) (spoken in Canada's Northwest Territories), has borrowed a number of governmental terms and expressions from English, including *bureaucratic*, *constituents*, *program*, *business*, *development*, and *political*.

In the case of English, Norman French had a superstratum influence. The major impact of French on the vocabulary of English is related to a historical event—the conquest of England by French-speaking Normans in 1066. As the conquerors and their descendants gradually learned English over the next decades, they retained French terms for political, judicial, and cultural notions. These words were in turn borrowed by native English speakers who, in trying to gain a place in the upper middle class, were eager to imitate the speech of their social superiors. Not surprisingly, borrowing was especially heavy in the vocabulary areas pertaining to officialdom:

Table 8.41 Some French loanwords in English

Government	tax, revenue, government, royal, state, parliament, authority, prince, duke, slave, peasant
Religion	prayer, sermon, religion, chaplain, friar
Judiciary	judge, defendant, jury, evidence, jail, verdict, crime
Science	medicine, physician
Culture	art, sculpture, fashion, satin, fur, ruby
Warfare	army, navy, battle, soldier, enemy, captain

government, the judiciary, and religion. Other areas of heavy borrowing include science, culture, and warfare.

In some cases, French loanwords were used in conjunction with native English words to convey distinctions of various sorts. For a minor crime, for example, the English word *theft* was employed, but for a more serious breach of the law the French word *larceny* was used. The English also kept their own words for domesticated animals, but adopted the French words for the meat from those creatures.

Table 8.42 French loanwords used in conjunction with native English words

English origin	*French origin*
cow	beef
calf	veal
sheep	mutton
pig	pork

Adstratum influence refers to the situation where two languages are in contact and neither one is clearly politically or culturally dominant. In a city such as Montreal with its large number of bilingual speakers, English and French inevitably influence each other.

Table 8.43 French influence on Montreal English

Montreal English	
subvention	'subsidy'
metro	'subway'
autoroute	'highway'

Earlier in the history of English, when the Scandinavians settled part of England beginning in 800 AD, there was substantial contact between the speakers of English and Scandinavian, resulting in an adstratum relationship. As evident in the examples in Table 8.43 and below in Table 8.44, adstratum contact usually results in the borrowing of common, everyday words. In fact, without consulting a dictionary, most English speakers could not distinguish between borrowings from Scandinavian and native English words.

Table 8.44 Some loanwords from Scandinavian

anger, cake, call, egg, fellow, gear, get, hit, husband, low, lump, raise, root, score, seat, skill, skin, take, their, they thrust, ugly, window, wing

Borrowed words from many other languages attest to various types of cultural contact and serve often to fill the lexical gaps such contact may bring.

Table 8.45 Some lexical borrowings into English

Italian	motto, artichoke, balcony, casino, pizza, malaria
Spanish	comrade, tornado, cannibal, mosquito, guitar, vigilante, marijuana
German	poodle, kindergarten, seminar, noodle, pretzel
Dutch	sloop, cole slaw, smuggle, gin, cookie, boom
Slavic languages	czar, tundra, polka, intelligentsia, robot
Amerindian languages	toboggan, opposum, wigwam, chipmunk, Chicago, Missouri
Hindi	thug, punch (drink), shampoo, chintz

Although borrowing has been a very rich source of new words in English, it is noteworthy that loanwords are least common among the most frequently used vocabulary items. This reflects a general tendency for highly frequent words to be relatively resistant to loss or substitution.

Table 8.46 Origin of the 5,000 most frequent words in English

Degree of frequency	*Source language (%)*			
	English	*French*	*Latin*	*Other*
First 1,000	83	11	2	4
Second 1,000	34	46	11	9
Third 1,000	29	46	14	11
Fourth 1,000	27	45	17	11
Fifth 1,000	27	47	17	9

5.2 Loss of lexical items

Just as words can be added to the lexicon, they can also be lost. Changes in society play an important role in the loss of words since words are often lost because the object or notion they refer to has become obsolete.

Table 8.47 Some Old English words lost through cultural change

dolgbōt	'compensation for wounding'
þeox	'hunting spear'
eafor	'tenant obligation to the king to convey goods'
flȳtme	'a bloodletting instrument'

5.3 Semantic change

Although changes in word meaning take place continually in all languages, words rarely jump from one meaning to an unrelated one. Typically, the changes are step by step and involve one of the following phenomena.

Semantic broadening is the process in which the meaning of a word becomes more general or more inclusive than its historically earlier form.

Table 8.48 Semantic broadening

Word	*Old meaning*	*New meaning*
bird	'small fowl'	'any winged and feathered creature'
barn	'place to store barley'	'any agricultural building'
aunt	'father's sister'	'father or mother's sister'

Semantic narrowing is the process in which the meaning of a word becomes less general or less inclusive than its historically earlier meaning.

Table 8.49 Semantic narrowing

Word	*Old meaning*	*New meaning*
hound	'any dog'	'a hunting breed'
meat	'any type of food'	'flesh of an animal'
fowl	'any bird'	'a domesticated bird'
disease	'any unfavorable state'	'an illness'

In **amelioration** the meaning of a word becomes more positive or favorable. The opposite change, **pejoration**, also occurs.

Table 8.50 Amelioration

Word	*Old meaning*	*New meaning*
pretty	'tricky, sly, cunning'	'attractive'
knight	'boy'	'a special title or position'

Table 8.51 Pejoration

Word	*Old meaning*	*New meaning*
silly	'happy, prosperous'	'foolish'
wench	'girl'	'wanton woman, prostitute'

Given the propensity of human beings to exaggerate, it is not surprising that the **weakening** of meaning frequently occurs. For example, our word *soon* used to mean 'immediately' but now simply means 'in the near future'. Other examples include the following.

Table 8.52 Weakening

Word	*Old meaning*	*New meaning*
wreak	'avenge, punish'	'to cause, inflict'
quell	'kill, murder'	'to put down, pacify'

Semantic shift is a process in which a word loses its former meaning and takes on a new, but often related, meaning.

Table 8.53 Semantic shift

Word	*Old meaning*	*New meaning*
immoral	'not customary'	'unethical'
bead	'prayer'	'prayer bead, bead'

Sometimes a series of semantic shifts occurs over an extended period of time, resulting in a meaning that is completely unrelated to the original sense of a word. The word *hearse*, for example, originally referred to a triangular harrow. Later, it denoted a triangular frame for church candles and later still was used to refer to the device that held candles over a coffin. In a subsequent shift it came to refer to the framework on which curtains were hung over a coffin or tomb. Still later, *hearse* was used to refer to the coffin itself before finally taking on its current sense of the vehicle used to transport a coffin.

One of the most striking types of semantic change is triggered by **metaphor**, a figure of speech based on a perceived similarity between distinct objects or actions. (See Chapter 7 for a discussion of metaphor.) Metaphorical change usually involves a word with a concrete meaning taking on a more abstract sense, although the word's original meaning is not lost. The meanings of many English words have been extended through metaphor.

Table 8.54 Some examples of metaphor in English

Word	*Metaphorical meaning*
grasp	'understand'
yarn	'story'
high	'on drugs'

6 THE SPREAD OF CHANGE

Up to this point, we have been concerned with the causes and description of linguistic change. Still to be dealt with is the question of how linguistic innovations spread. This section focuses on two types of spread, one involving the way in which an innovation is extended through the vocabulary of a language and the other the way in which it spreads through the population.

6.1 DIFFUSION THROUGH THE LANGUAGE

Some linguistic change first manifests itself in a few words and then gradually spreads through the vocabulary of the language. This type of change is called **lexical diffusion**. A well-attested example in English involves an ongoing change in the stress pattern of words such as *convert*, which can be used as either a noun or a verb. Although the stress originally fell on the second syllable regardless of lexical category, in the latter half of the sixteenth century three such words, *rebel*, *outlaw*, and *record*, came to be pronounced with the stress on the first syllable when used as nouns. As the following figure illustrates, this stress shift was extended to an increasing number of words over the next decades.

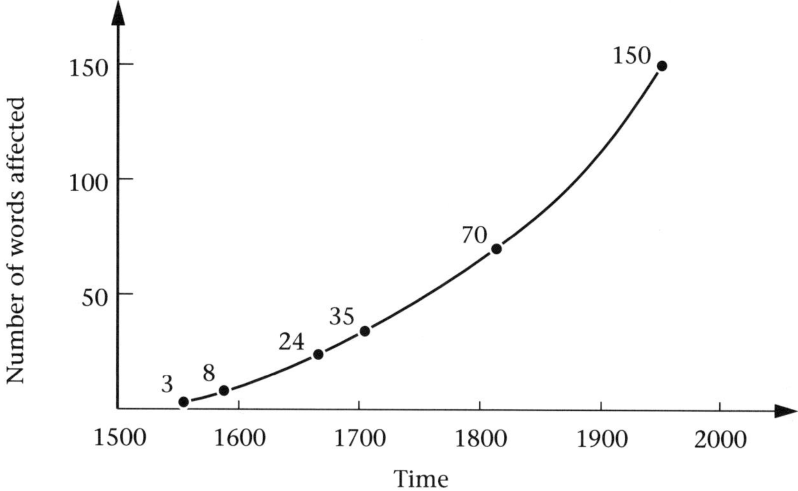

Figure 8.11 Diffusion of stress shift in English

This change has still not diffused through the entire vocabulary of English. There are about a thousand nouns of the relevant sort that still place the stress on the second syllable (e.g., *report, mistake*, and *support*). The following table illustrates the spread of this change to date.

Table 8.55 Stress shift in English (nouns)

Before the 16th century	*During the 16th century*	*During the 18th century*	*Today*
rebél	rébel	rébel	rébel
affíx	affíx	áffix	áffix
recéss	recéss	recéss	récess
mistáke	mistáke	mistáke	mistáke

This ongoing change can be observed in progress today. The noun *address*, for example, is pronounced by many people with stress on the first syllable as [ǽdrɛs], although the older pronunciation [ədrɛ́s] is still heard. Some speakers alternate between the two pronunciations. This change may continue to work its way through the language until all nouns in the class we have been considering are stressed on the first syllable.

The changes discussed in the section on analogy also spread word by word. For example, the transition of strong (irregular) verbs (the *sing/sang/sung* type) to the weak verb class (regular verbs with past tense *-ed*) is an ongoing change. Both strong and weak past tense forms of original strong verbs such as *shine* are heard in current English: *shone/shined.*

However, not all linguistic change involves gradual diffusion through the vocabulary of a language. Sound changes typically affect all instances of the segment(s) involved. For example, in some dialects of Spanish (such as Cuban) the consonantal weakening of [s] to [h] in syllable-final position affects all instances of *s* in those positions. The relevant rule can be stated as follows.

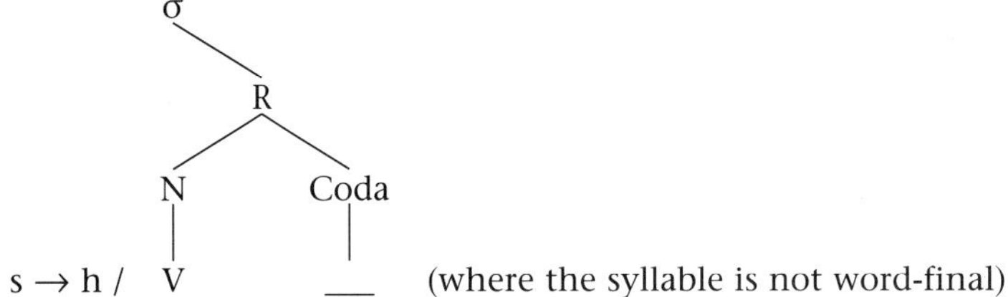

Figure 8.12 Consonant weakening of [s] to [h] in certain Spanish dialects

This rule has resulted in changes such as those exemplified in Table 8.56.

Table 8.56 The effects of the [s] to [h] change in Spanish dialects

Standard pronunciation	*New pronunciation*	
[felismente]	[felihmente]	'happily'
[estilo]	[ehtilo]	'type'
[espaɲa]	[ehpaɲa]	'Spain'

This change is entirely regular, affecting all instances of syllable-final [s] in the speech of individuals who adopt it.

Accordingly, two types of language change can be identified. One, exemplified by the stress shifts in disyllabic English nouns of the type we have discussed, affects individual words one at a time and gradually spreads through the vocabulary of the language. The other, exemplified by the consonant weakening of syllable-final [s] to [h] in some dialects of Spanish, involves an across the board change that applies without exception to all words.

6.2 Spread through the population

For a language change to take place, the particular innovation must be accepted by the linguistic community as a whole. Although as mentioned, for example, children acquiring English sometimes form the past tense of *go* as *goed* instead of *went*, *goed* has never received widespread acceptance. Doubtless the verb form in *he throve on fame* would be equally unacceptable to most speakers today. In earlier English, however, *throve* was the past tense form of *thrive* (compare *drive/drove*). At some point in the past then, the novel form *thrived* did receive general acceptance.

Just as change sometimes begins with a small number of words, often effects of a change only appear first in the speech of a small number of people. Social pressures often play an important role in whether a particular innovation will spread through the entire linguistic community. Since speakers can consciously or unconsciously alter the way they speak to approximate what they perceive to be a more prestigious or socially acceptable variety of speech, once a change has taken hold in the speech of a high prestige group it may gradually spread to other speakers and ultimately affect the entire linguistic community.

There have been numerous examples of this in the history of English, notably the loss of postvocalic [r] along the east coast of the United States. This change, which resulted in an '*r*-less' pronunciation of words such as *far* as [faː], originated in parts of England in the seventeenth and eighteenth century. At that time, postvocalic [r] was still pronounced throughout English-speaking settlements in North America. Two factors accounted for its loss in parts of this continent. First, the children of the New England gentry picked up the new pronunciation in British schools and subsequently brought it back to the colony. Second, the speech of newly arrived immigrants, including colonial administrators and church officials who enjoyed high social status in the colony, typically lacked the postvocalic [r]. As a result, the innovation was widely imitated and ultimately spread along much of the east coast and into the south.

Social pressures were also involved in limiting the spread of this innovation. It did not penetrate Pennsylvania or the other Midland states since the most prestigious group of settlers there were Quakers from northern England, an area that retained the postvocalic [r]. Similarly, in Canada, the influence of Scottish and Irish settlers, whose dialects did not undergo the change in question, helped ensure the survival of postvocalic /r/ in all but a few areas where contact with New England was strongest, most notably in parts of Nova Scotia and in some areas of New Brunswick. More recently the '*r*-less' pronunciation has become stigmatized, and we now see a trend toward restoration of [r] in environments where it had been deleted.

7 LANGUAGE RECONSTRUCTION

When we compare the vocabulary items of various languages, we cannot help but notice the strong resemblance certain words bear to each other. By systematically comparing languages, we can establish whether two or more languages descended from a common parent and are therefore **genetically related** (see Chapter 9). The comparative method refers to the procedure used to reconstruct earlier forms on the basis of a comparison of later forms. By means of such **comparative reconstruction**, we can infer properties of the parent language with a great degree of certainty.

7.1 Comparative reconstruction

The most reliable sign of family relationships is the existence of **systematic phonetic correspondences** in the vocabulary items of different languages. Many such correspondences can be found in the following sample of vocabulary items from English, Dutch, German, Danish, and Swedish, all of which are members of the Germanic family of languages.

Table 8.57 Some Germanic cognates

English	*Dutch*	*German*	*Danish*	*Swedish*
man	man	Mann	mand	man
hand	hand	Hand	hånd	hand
foot	voet	Fuß (ß=[s])	fod	fot
bring	brengen	bringen	bringe	bringa
summer	zomer	Sommer	sommer	sommar

Since the relationship between the phonological form and meaning of a word is mostly arbitrary, the existence of systematic phonetic correspondences in the forms of two or more languages must point toward a common source. Conversely, where languages are not related, their vocabulary items fail to show systematic similarities. This can be seen by comparing words from Turkish, which is not related to the Germanic languages, with their counterparts in the languages cited in Table 8.58.

Table 8.58 Some words in Turkish, a non-Germanic language (phonemic transcription)

adam	'man'
el	'hand'
ajak	'foot'
getir	'bring'
jaz	'summer'

Words that have descended from a common source (as shown by systematic phonetic correspondences and, usually, semantic similarities) are called **cognates**. Cognates are not always as obvious as the Germanic examples in Table 8.57. Where languages from the same family are only distantly related, the systematic correspondences may be considerably less striking. This is exemplified in the following data from English, Russian, and Hindi, all of which are distantly related to each other. Forms from the unrelated Turkish are included to emphasize the similarities among the first three languages.

Table 8.59 Some distantly related cognates compared to nonrelated Turkish

English	*Russian*	*Hindi*	*Turkish (phonemic transcription)*
two	dva	dō	iki
three	tri	tīn	ytʃ
brother	brat	bhāī	kardeʃ
nose	nos	nahī̃	burun

Once the existence of a relationship between two or more languages has been established, an attempt can be made to reconstruct the common source. This reconstructed language, or **proto-language**, is made up of **proto-forms**, which are written with a preceding * (e.g., **hand*) to indicate their hypothetical character as reconstructions of earlier forms that have not been recorded or are not directly observable. (This use of an asterisk therefore does not indicate that a form is unacceptable, in contrast to the practice adopted in other chapters of this book.)

7.2 Techniques of reconstruction

Reconstruction can be undertaken with some confidence because (as discussed in the previous sections) the processes underlying language change are systematic. Once the processes are uncovered by linguists, they can be reversed, allowing us to infer earlier forms of the language. Although it is possible to reconstruct all components of a proto-language (its phonology, morphology, syntax, lexicon, and semantics), we will focus in the following on phonological reconstruction, the area in which linguists have made the most progress.

Reconstruction strategies

Reconstruction of a proto-form makes use of two general strategies. The most important one is the **phonetic plausibility strategy**, which requires that any changes posited to account for differences between the proto-forms and later forms must be phonetically plausible. Secondarily, the **majority rules strategy** stipulates that if no phonetically plausible change can account for the observed differences, then the segment found in the majority of cognates should be assumed. It is important to note that the first strategy always takes precedence over the second; the second strategy is a last resort.

Consider the following cognates (somewhat simplified) from members of the Romance family.

Table 8.60 Romance cognates

French	*Italian*	*Rumanian*	*Spanish*	
si	si	ʃi	si	'yes'

The data exemplify a correspondence between [s] and [ʃ] before the vowel [i]. To account for this, we could assume either that Rumanian underwent a change that converted [s] to [ʃ] before [i] or that the other three languages underwent a change converting [ʃ] to [s] before [i].

Hypothesis A
Proto-form: *si
Sound change (Rumanian only): *s > ʃ / __ i

Hypothesis B
Proto-form: *ʃi
Sound change (French, Italian, and Spanish): *ʃ > s / __ i

Figure 8.13 Romance cognates

Both reconstruction strategies favor Hypothesis A. Most importantly, the phonetic change needed to account for the Rumanian pronunciation involves palatalization before [i]. Since palatalization in this context is a very common phenomenon in human language, it is reasonable to assume that it occurred in Rumanian. It would be much more difficult to argue that the proto-language contained [ʃ] before [i] and that three languages underwent the change posited by Hypothesis B since depalatalization before [i] would be an unusual phonetic process. (The reconstructed *s posited in Hypothesis A is also compatible with the majority rules strategy since three of the four languages in the data have [s] before [i].)

Reconstruction and the catalogue of sound changes

Although there are factors that can confound our attempt to determine the relative plausibility of various sound changes, the changes listed in the catalogue in Table 8.3 can generally be considered highly plausible. The following table lists some plausible versus less plausible or even implausible changes based on that catalogue.

Table 8.61 Different rules in terms of their plausibility based on the catalogue of sound changes

Rule	*Name of sound change in the catalogue*
High probability	
t > tʃ / __ i	palatalization
n > m / __ b	assimilation (place of articulation)
t > d / V __ V	voicing
k > Ø / V __ st	consonant deletion
Low probability	
tʃ > t / __ i	(does not correspond to any listed change)
m > n / __ b	(does not correspond to any listed change)
d > t / V __ V	(does not correspond to any listed change)
Ø > k / V __ st	(does not correspond to any listed change)

Reconstructing Proto-Romance

Consider now a slightly more complex example involving data from several languages of the Romance family.

Table 8.62 Some Romance cognates

Spanish	*Sardinian*	*French*	*Portuguese*	*Rumanian*	*Original meaning*
riba [ß]	ripa	rive [ʁiv]	riba	rîpă	'embankment'
amiga [ɣ]	amica	amie [ami]	amiga	—	'female friend'
copa	cuppa	coupe [kup]	copa	cupă	'cup, goblet'
gota	gutta	goutte [gut]	gota	gută	'drop'

(*Note*: Orthographic *c* represents [k] in all the above examples and Rumanian ă represents [ə]. [ß] is a voiced bilabial fricative and [ɣ] a voiced velar fricative. Some details of vowel quality have been ignored.)

Our goal here is to reconstruct the proto-forms for these words in Proto-Romance, the parent language of the Modern Romance languages, which stands very close to Latin.

Let us first consider the reconstruction of the Proto-Romance form for 'embankment'. Since the first two segments are the same in all the cognate languages, we can reconstruct Proto-Romance **r* and **i* on the basis of the majority rules strategy. In the case of the second consonant, however, there are differences between the cognates.

Table 8.63 Systematic correspondences in the second consonant of the cognates for 'embankment'

Spanish	*Sardinian*	*French*	*Portuguese*	*Rumanian*
-ß-	-p-	-v	-b-	-p-

It is most important that we first think in terms of phonetic plausibility. In the absence of evidence to the contrary, we will assume that one of the segments found in the cognates ([p], [b], [v], or [ß]) should be reconstructed for Proto-Romance. Logically possible changes ranked with respect to their phonetic plausibility are found in the following table.

Table 8.64 Changes based on phonetic plausibility

Change in V_V	*Name of change based on catalogue*	*Phonetic plausibility*
p > b	voicing	high
p > v	voicing (p > b) and frication (b > v)	high
p > ß	voicing (p > b) and frication (b > ß)	high
b > p	—	low
ß > p	—	low
v > p	—	low

In terms of plausibility, the only possible reconstruction for Proto-Romance is **p*. Proto-Romance **p* undergoes no change in Sardinian and Rumanian, but in Portuguese it underwent intervocalic voicing and in Spanish it underwent both voicing and frication (that is, weakening). (We assume that voicing preceded frication since Portuguese shows voicing but no frication.) If we assume that the final vowel of the proto-form was still present in French when the consonant changes took place, we can conclude that voicing and frication occurred in this language as well. (In its written form, *rive* retains a sign of the earlier reduced vowel [ə].) These changes are phonetically plausible and thus expected.

Table 8.65 Summary of the changes affecting Proto-Romance **p*

*p > p /V_V	no change in Sardinian or Rumanian
*p > b /V_V	voicing in Portuguese
*p > b > ß /V_V	voicing and frication in Spanish
*p > b > v /V_V	voicing and frication in French

Turning now to the final vowel, we note that three languages have full vowels, Rumanian has [ə], and French has no vowel. Since vowel reduction and apocope are identified as phonetically plausible changes in the catalogue, it is appropriate to posit a full vowel for the proto-language. Furthermore, since the three languages with a full vowel all have [a] we can posit this vowel on the basis of the majority rules strategy. Accordingly, the reconstructed proto-form is **ripa*.

Table 8.66 Summary of the changes affecting Proto-Romance **a*

Language	*Change (word-final)*	*Name of change(s)*
Rumanian	*a > ə	vowel reduction
French	*a > ə > Ø	vowel reduction and deletion

We can now outline the evolution of the word in French, which has the most complicated development of the six languages.

Table 8.67 Evolution of French *rive* from **ripa*

Change	**ripa*	*Name of change*
p > b / V__ V	riba	voicing
b > v / V __ V	riva	frication
a > ə / __ #	rivə	vowel reduction
ə > Ø / __ #	riv	apocope

In the case of the cognates for 'female friend' (the second row of Table 8.62), the first three segments are the same in all the languages in the data. According to the majority rules strategy we can reconstruct the first three segments as **ami-*. In the reconstruction of the second consonant, however, we must appeal to our strategy of phonetic plausibility.

Table 8.68 Systematic correspondences in the second consonant of the cognates for 'female friend'

Spanish	*Sardinian*	*French*	*Portuguese*	*Rumanian*
-ɣ-	-k-	-Ø	-g-	—

Once again, since intervocalic voicing, frication, and deletion are phonetically plausible changes, it is most appropriate to posit **k* for the proto-form.

Table 8.69 Summary of the changes affecting Proto-Romance **k*

Language	*Change (in V_V)*	*Name of change(s)*
Portuguese	*k > g	voicing
Spanish	*k > g > ɣ	voicing and frication
French	*k > g > ɣ > Ø	voicing, frication, and deletion

In the case of the final vowel, we have the same situation we had in the previous form. The full vowel is found in Spanish, Sardinian, and Portuguese, but there is no vowel in French. We can therefore assume the full vowel **a* for the proto-form, with subsequent vowel reduction and apocope in French. Consequently, we arrive at the proto-form **amika*.

Finally, applying the same procedure to the cognates in the final two rows of Table 8.62 yields the proto-forms **kuppa* 'cup' and **gutta* 'drop'. All the languages in the data retain the initial consonant of both proto-forms. The vowel **u* is reconstructed on the basis of the majority rules strategy, since we have no phonetic grounds for choosing either [u] or [o] as the older vowel. The systematic correspondences involving the intervocalic consonants are given in the following table.

Table 8.70 Systematic correspondences of the medial consonants of **kuppa* and **gutta*

Spanish	*Sardinian*	*French*	*Portuguese*	*Rumanian*
-p-	-pp-	-p	-p-	-p-
-t-	-tt-	-t	-t-	-t-

Regardless of whether we are dealing with original **pp* or **tt,* the same pattern is evident in the case of both geminate types. There is a geminate stop consonant in Sardinian and a single consonant in Spanish, French, Portuguese, and Rumanian. Since degemination is an expected sound change (see the catalogue in Table 8.3), we assume that the proto-forms contained geminate consonants that underwent degemination except in Sardinian. This is an example of a case where the phonetic plausibility strategy overrules the majority rules strategy (since four of the five languages have [p]/[t] whereas only one language has [pp]/[tt]). As far as the final vowels are concerned, the same pattern found in the previous examples is once again evident. Proto-Romance **a* was retained in Spanish, Sardinian, and Portuguese, reduced to [ə] in Rumanian, and deleted in French (see Table 8.66).

Of the languages exemplified here, Sardinian is considered the most **conservative** since it has retained more of the earlier consonants and vowels. (In fact, the Sardinian words in the examples happen to be identical with the proto-forms, but this degree of resemblance would not be maintained in a broader range of data.) In the case of the other Romance languages and changes we have discussed, the most to least conservative are: Portuguese (degemination and voicing) and Rumanian (degemination, vowel reduction); Spanish (degemination, voicing, and frication); and French (degemination, voicing, frication, consonant deletion, vowel reduction, apocope).

Although there is no reason to expect Proto-Romance to be identical with Classical Latin, close similarity is expected. Accordingly, the fact that our reconstructions are so close to the Latin words gives us confidence in our methods of reconstruction.

Notice that it is sometimes not possible to reconstruct all characteristics of the proto-language. For example, on the basis of our data we were not able to reconstruct

Table 8.71 Comparison of Latin and Proto-Romance forms

Latin	*Proto-Romance form*
rīpa	*ripa
amīca	*amika
cuppa (c = [k])	*kuppa
gutta	*gutta

vowel length (Latin had a distinction between long and short vowels) since there was no evidence of this characteristic in the cognate forms.

It is also worth noting that we are not always so fortunate as to have written records of a language we expect to be very close to our reconstructed language. In the case of the Germanic languages, for example, there is no ancient written language equivalent to Latin. We must rely completely on our reconstruction of Proto-Germanic to determine the properties of the language from which the modern-day Germanic languages descended. Furthermore, for many languages of the world we have no written historical records at all and for other languages, such as the Amerindian languages of North America, it is only very recently that we have written records.

In summary, when the forms of two or more languages appear to be related, we can, through a consideration of systematic phonetic correspondences among cognates, reconstruct the common form from which all the forms can be derived by means of phonetically plausible sound changes. Genetically related lexical forms of different languages are called **cognates**, while the reconstructed forms are known as **proto-forms**, and a reconstructed language is called a **proto-language**.

7.3 Internal reconstruction

Sometimes it is possible to reconstruct the earlier form of a language even without reference to comparative data. This technique, known as **internal reconstruction**, relies on the analysis of morphophonemic variation within a single language. The key point is that the sound changes that create allomorphic and allophonic variation can be identified and then used to infer an earlier form of the morpheme. The following data are from French; because of borrowing, English exhibits a parallel set of contrasts involving [k] and [ʃ].

Table 8.72 [k] / [s] correspondence in French

maʒik	'magic'	maʒis-jɛ̃	'magician'
lɔʒik	'logic'	lɔʒis-jɛ̃	'logician'
myzik	'music	myzis-jɛ̃	'musician'

The root morpheme in each row exhibits two forms, one ending in [k], the other ending in [s]. The same methods and principles used in comparative reconstruction can be applied here to reconstruct the historically earlier form of the root morpheme. If a root ending in *s* is posited, no phonetically plausible change can account for the [k] in the left-hand column. By contrast, if a root-final *k* is posited, the [s] can be accounted for by assuming that the *k* was fronted under the influence of the high front vowel of the suffix (palatalization) and became an affricate [ts] (affrication), which was later simplified to a fricative [s] (deaffrication). All of these changes are phonetically plausible and listed in the catalogue in Table 8.3. Accordingly, internal reconstruction indicates that at an earlier point in the development of French, the root morphemes in Table 8.72 contained the consonant **k*.

7.4 The discovery of Indo-European

The late eighteenth century discovery that Sanskrit (the ancient language of India) was related to Latin, Greek, Germanic, and Celtic revolutionized European linguistic studies. Sir William Jones, a British judge and scholar working in India, summed up the nature and implications of the findings in his 1786 address to the Royal Asiatic Society, a part of which follows:

> The Sanskrit language, whatever be its antiquity, is of a wonderful structure; more perfect than the Greek, more copious [having more cases] than the Latin, and more exquisitely refined than either, yet bearing to both of them a stronger affinity, both in the roots of the verbs and in the forms of the grammar, than could possibly have been produced by accident; so strong indeed, that no philologer could examine them all three, without believing them to have sprung from some common source, which, perhaps, no longer exists; there is a similar reason . . . for supposing that both the Gothic and the Celtic . . . had the same origin with the Sanskrit; and the old Persian might be added to the same family.

This discovery led to several decades of intensive historical-comparative work and to important advances in historical linguistics during the nineteenth century. By studying phonetic correspondences from an ever increasing number of languages, linguists eventually ascertained that most of the languages of Europe, Persia (Iran), and the northern part of India belong to a single family, now called Indo-European. By applying the techniques of the comparative method, they began reconstructing the grammar of the proto-language from which these languages evolved, **Proto-Indo-European (PIE)**.

A number of individuals advanced this research. In 1814, the Danish linguist Rasmus Rask carefully documented the relationships among cognates in a number of Indo-European languages, and at the same time established the methods that would govern the emerging science of historical-comparative linguistics. He wrote:

> When agreement is found in [the most essential] words in two languages, and so frequently that rules may be drawn up for the shift in letters [sounds] from one to the other, then there is a fundamental relationship between the two languages; especially when similarities in the inflectional system and in the general make-up of the languages correspond with them.

Rask worked without access to Sanskrit. The first comparative linguistic analysis of Sanskrit, Greek, Persian, and the Germanic languages was done by the German scholar Franz Bopp in 1816. In 1822, another German, Jakob Grimm, extended Rask's observations and became the first person to explain the relationships among the cognates noted by Rask in terms of a **sound shift,** the systematic modification of a series of phonemes. Some of the correspondences on which he based his work are given in Table 8.73.

Table 8.73 Some Indo-European phonetic correspondences

Greek	*Latin*	*English*
patḗr	pater	father
treîs	trēs	three
hekatón	centum	hundred

The crucial observation is that where English has [f], [θ], and [h] (here, in word-initial position), Greek and Latin have [p], [t], and [k]. Grimm tabulated a series of consonant shifts for Proto-Germanic that differentiated it from other Indo-European languages. **Grimm's Law** is the name given to the consonant shifts that took place between Proto-Indo-European and Proto-Germanic.

Table 8.74 The sound shifts underlying Grimm's Law

Proto-Indo-European	p	t	k	b	d	g	bh	dh	gh
Germanic	f	θ	x	p	t	k	b	d	g

Some additional examples of the relationships captured by these shifts are given below in Table 8.75. The Proto-Indo-European consonants were either maintained in Sanskrit, Greek, and Latin or in some cases underwent changes different from those found in Germanic.

Table 8.75 Some examples of the consonant shifts underlying Grimm's Law

Shift in Germanic	*Sanskrit*	*Greek*	*Latin*	*English*
p > f	pād-	pod-	ped-	foot
t > θ	tanu-	tanaós	tenuis	thin
k > x	çatam	hekatón	centum	hundred
b > p	—	—	lūbricus	slippery
d > t	daça	déka	decem	ten
g > k	ajras	agrós	ager	acre
bh > b	bhrātā	phrā́tēr	frāter	brother
dh > d	vidhavā	ēítheos	vidua	widow
gh > g	hansas	khḗn	(h)ānser	goose

Although there appeared to be exceptions to Grimm's Law, they turned out to be systematic and could be traced to specific environments. For example, voiceless stops were not subject to Grimm's Law when they were immediately preceded by *s*.

Table 8.76 A systematic exception to Grimm's Law

Original s + voiceless stop			
Latin	stāre	English	stand [st] (not [sθ])

A particularly important discovery was made by Karl Verner, who traced a group of exceptions to Grimm's Law to the original accentual pattern of Proto-Indo-European. In a generalization that came to be known as **Verner's Law**, he proposed that a voiceless fricative resulting from Grimm's Law underwent voicing if the original Proto-Indo-European accent did not immediately precede it. Since stress came to be fixed on the root syllable in Germanic subsequent to the changes covered by Verner's Law, the original environment was obscured. However, Sanskrit provides very direct evidence for Verner's claim since Sanskrit was very conservative in its maintenance of the original Proto-Indo-European accent. Although the English forms are complicated by other developments, the effects of Verner's Law are apparent in the following Gothic examples. In the Gothic word for *brother*, PIE **t* becomes [θ] according to Grimm's Law, whereas in the word for *father* it becomes [ð] in accordance with both Grimm's and Verner's Law.

Table 8.77 Verner's Law

PIE	*Sanskrit*	*Grimm's Law*	*Verner's Law*	*Gothic*	
*t	bhrā́tā	*t > θ	—	[bro:θar]	'brother'
*t	pitā́	*t > θ	θ > ð	[faðar]	'father'

It should also be noted here that borrowing is an important factor which must be taken into consideration when comparative reconstruction is being carried out. For example, English has many words that do not show the effects of Grimm's law.

Table 8.78 English words not showing the effects of Grimm's law

Expected by Grimm's Law	*Latin*	*English*
p > f	ped-	pedestrian
t > θ	tenuis	tenuous
k > h	canalis	canal

The apparent failure of Grimm's Law here stems from the fact that the English words were borrowed directly from Latin or French many centuries after the sound shifts described by Grimm's Law had taken place. The task of reconstruction can often be complicated by such borrowings.

Subsequent developments

By the middle of the nineteenth century, the study of language had made great strides, especially in the field of phonetics, which opened the way for the detailed comparison of linguistic forms. One influential hypothesis at that time was that sound laws operated without exception. A group of linguists known as the Neogrammarians adopted this idea and made many important contributions to the fledgling science of linguistics by applying it to new and more complicated data. Although such factors as lexical diffusion and social pressures were more or less ignored by the Neogrammarians, their hypothesis represented an important and daring advance in the scientific study of language.

The nineteenth century also saw major advances in the classification of languages. A German scholar, August Schleicher, developed a classification for the Indo-European languages in the form of a genealogical tree. This type of genetic classification is discussed in much more detail in the chapter on language typology that follows.

Work in comparative reconstruction is far from finished. In particular, linguists are now considering the possibility of superfamilies. One such proposed family is Nostratic, which includes Indo-European, Afro-Asiatic (e.g., Arabic, Hebrew), Altaic (e.g., Japanese, Korean, Turkic), and Uralic (e.g., Finnish, Hungarian). (See Chapter 9 for further discussion.) Comparative reconstruction is also playing an important role in determining the genetic relationships of the hundreds of North American indigenous languages, a topic that still remains highly controversial.

7.5 Reconstruction and Typology

Since the 1800s when the reconstruction of Proto-Indo-European was carried out, linguists have accumulated vast amounts of information on thousands of languages. This is in part because of the explosion of studies in the field of linguistic typology, which is concerned with the investigation of structural similarities among languages that are not genetically related. Even languages that do not belong to the same family can have striking similarities. For example, in addition to shared word order patterns (see Section 2.3 in Chapter 9), SOV languages commonly exhibit a strong tendency toward agglutinating morphology (a type of complex affixation; see Chapter 9) and vowel harmony. Typological studies play an important role in the linguist's search for universals of language—statements that are true for all languages.

The extensive information on the languages of the world available to modern linguists was, of course, not available at the time the original reconstruction of Proto-Indo-European was undertaken. Modern linguists involved in comparative reconstruction now take a keen interest in typological studies and the role of **typological plausibility** in reconstruction has become an important topic. For example, a linguist would be very reluctant to propose a reconstruction that violated a universal property of language or that had no parallel in any known language.

Some linguists have argued that the traditional reconstruction of the PIE consonant system (given in Table 8.79) should be rejected on the basis of typological plausibility.

Table 8.79 The traditional reconstruction of the Proto-Indo-European consonants

p	t	ḱ	k	k^w	(voiceless stops)
(b)	d	ǵ	g	g^w	(voiced stops)
bh	dh	ǵh	gh	g^wh	(voiced aspirated stops)
	s				

(*Note: ḱ, ǵ,* and *ǵh* are palatal stops and ^{w} indicates a labialized consonant.)

This reconstruction is typologically questionable in at least two respects. First, reconstructed forms with PIE **b* are extremely rare, almost as if there were a gap in the labial system. Such a gap is very uncommon in the languages of the world. Typically if there is a missing labial stop, it is the voiceless stop that is missing, not the voiced counterpart. Second, the traditional reconstruction posits a series of voiced aspirated stops but no corresponding series of voiceless aspirated stops, even though some typologists have argued that all languages which have a voiced series also have the voiceless one.

Such facts have led some linguists to propose what they believe is a more typologically plausible reconstruction of Proto-Indo-European involving a voiceless stop series, an ejective series,[4] and a voiced stop series (as well as **s* as in the traditional reconstruction).

Table 8.80 A recent reconstruction of the Proto-Indo-European consonants

p	t	ḱ	k	k^w	(voiceless stops)
(p')	t'	ḱ'	k'	k'^w	(ejectives)
b	d	ǵ	g	g^w	(voiced stops)
	s				

Not only does this reconstruction avoid the problem with aspirates, it is also common for languages with an ejective series to lack the labial. From this perspective, this reconstruction seems much more plausible than the traditional one.

Both reconstructions have their supporters. In fact, however, it is difficult to come to a definitive decision on the basis of typological considerations since it is common for a proposed universal to have exceptions. For example, a few languages have been found with the characteristics attributed to Proto-Indo-European by the traditional reconstruction. These languages have labial gaps in the voiced series (e.g., Amerindian languages of the Athapaskan and Caddoan families) and a voiced aspirate series but no voiceless counterpart (Madurese, an Indonesian language). Accordingly, as long as the traditional reconstruction is linguistically possible, it would not seem right to reject it simply because the phonological system proposed would be a rare one.

Typological plausibility will likely continue to play a secondary role in reconstruction until linguists can draw a clear line between what is linguistically possible and what is not. Nevertheless, as our knowledge and understanding of language universals continues to be improved, it is certain that linguists involved in the reconstruction of proto-languages will maintain an interest in typological plausibility.

8 LANGUAGE CHANGE AND NATURALNESS

A striking fact about language change is that the same patterns of change occur repeatedly, not only within the same language at different periods in its history but also across languages. Both the similarity of changes across languages as well as the directionality of language change suggest that some changes are more natural than others. This notion of **naturalness** is implicit in the phonetic plausibility strategy introduced in the section on comparative reconstruction.

If naturalness is a factor in language change, its manifestations should also be found in the language acquisition process and in language universals. This does seem to be the case. As a specific example, let us consider the frequently made claim that the CV syllable is the most natural of all syllable types. At least three different kinds of evidence can be brought forth in support of this claim.

First, in terms of universals, all languages of the world have CV syllables in their syllable type inventory. Second, a variety of sound changes have the effect of reducing less natural syllable types to the more natural CV type.

Table 8.81 Sound changes yielding CV syllables

Deletion							
CCV	>	CV	Old English	cnēow	English	knee	/ni/
CVC	>	CV	Old Spanish	non	Spanish	no	
Vowel epenthesis							
CCVCV	>	CVCVCV	Italian	croce	Sicilian	kiruci	'cross'

By contrast, note that such changes rarely if ever apply to a CV syllable to yield a different syllable type. Deletion of the C in a word-initial CV syllable is extremely rare, as is vowel epenthesis in a CV syllable or a sequence of CVCV syllables.

Third, in terms of language acquisition the CV syllable type is one of the first syllable types to be acquired and many phonetic processes found in child language have the effect of yielding CV syllables, just like the sound changes in Table 8.81 (see Chapter 12 on language acquisition).

Table 8.82 Phonetic processes in language acquisition yielding CV syllables

CCV → CV	tree → [tij]	(simplification of consonant clusters)
CVC → CV	dog → [dɑ]	(deletion of final consonants)

It is clear, however, that it is inappropriate to take a simplistic view of linguistic naturalness. For example, some sound changes produce less natural syllables. Thus, syncope has the effect of reducing a sequence of CVCVCV syllables to the less natural CVCCV. Usually in such cases, a different motivation can be identified, such as the preference for shorter phonological forms over longer forms. But given the complexity of human language, not to mention human behavior in general, it should not be surprising that there are many different parameters of linguistic naturalness and that these can, in turn, lead to apparently conflicting changes in language over time. It remains an important task of the linguist to identify, rank, and ultimately explain relations of linguistic naturalness. The study of language change will continue to make an important contribution to this area.

Summing up

Historical linguistics studies the nature and causes of language change. The causes of language change find their roots in the physiological and cognitive makeup of human beings. Sound changes usually involve articulatory simplification as in the case of the most common type, **assimilation**. **Analogy** and **reanalysis** are particularly important factors in morphological change. **Language contact** resulting in **borrowing** is another important source of language change. All components of the grammar, from phonology to semantics, are subject to change over time. A change can simultanteously affect all instances of a particular sound or form, or it can spread through the language word by word by means of **lexical diffusion**. Social factors can play an important role in determining whether or not a linguistic innovation is ultimately adopted by the linguistic community at large. Since language change is systematic, it is possible, by identifying the changes that a particular language or dialect has undergone, to reconstruct linguistic history and thereby posit the earlier forms from which later forms have evolved. Using sets of **cognates**, **comparative reconstruction** allows us to reconstruct the properties of the parent or **proto-language** on the basis of **systematic phonetic correspondences**.

Studies in historical linguistics can provide valuable insights into relationships among languages and shed light on prehistoric developments. Furthermore, historical studies of language are of great importance to our understanding of human linguistic competence. In fact, it has often been stated that language change provides one of the most direct windows into the workings of the human mind. Furthermore, the study of language change contributes to our understanding of how social, cultural, and psychological factors interact to shape language. Finally, the integration of studies on language change, language acquisition, and language universals remains one of the most important challenges facing linguists today.

Key terms

adstratum influence
affrication
amelioration
analogy
analytic (languages)
apocope
articulatory simplification
assimilation
borrowing
cognates
comparative reconstruction
conservative (language)
consonant deletion
consonant strength
consonant weakening
deaffrication
degemination
deletion
diphthongization
dissimilation
epenthesis
folk etymology
frication
fusion
genetically related (languages)
glide strengthening
grammaticalization
Great English Vowel Shift
Grimm's Law
historical linguistics

hypercorrection
internal reconstruction
language contact
lexical diffusion
lexical gaps
majority rules strategy
mergers
metaphor
metathesis
nasalization
naturalness
palatalization
partial assimilation
pejoration
phonetic plausibility strategy
phonetic sound change
phonetically conditioned change
phonological change
proto-form
Proto-Indo-European (PIE)
proto-language
reanalysis
rhotacism
segmental change
semantic broadening
semantic narrowing
semantic shift
sequential change
shifts
sound change
sound shift
spelling pronunciation
splits
substitution
substratum influence
superstratum influence
syncope
synthetic (languages)
systematic phonetic correspondence
total assimilation
typological plausibility
umlaut
Verner's Law
voicing
vowel reduction
weakening (phonetic)
weakening (semantic)

Notes

[1] The translation for these lines is as follows:
Many men say that in dreams
There is nothing but talk and lies
But men may see some dreams
Which are scarcely false
But afterward come true.

[2] In these and other examples throughout this chapter, orthographic forms are given where these clearly reflect the sound change(s) in question. If required, partial or full phonetic transcriptions are provided.

[3] Since voicing commonly occurs between voiced segments, it can also be considered a type of assimilation. It is treated here as a weakening since it is often part of a larger pattern of change involving various weakening processes.

[4] Ejectives are produced by a closing of the glottis and raising of the larynx.

Sources

The advanced textbooks (cited below under Recommended Reading) by Anttila, Hock, and Labov provide much more detailed discussions of most of the major topics in this chapter. They are also excellent sources for references relating to particular topics. Hock is particularly important for detailed discussions of syntactic change and the role of typology in reconstruction.

Overviews of historical linguistics as it applies to the development of English are presented in the books by Williams, Pyles and Algeo, Baugh and Cable, and Millward cited below under Recommended Reading.

The catalogue of sound changes is adapted from catalogues proposed by Theo Vennemann in an article "Linguistic Typologies in Historical Linguistics" in *Società di linguistica italiana* 23:87–91 (1985) and a book entitled *Preference Laws for Syllable Structure and the Explanation of Sound Change* (Amsterdam: Mouton· de Gruyter, 1988). Section 2 has also benefited from unpublished material (particularly the manuscript *Linguistic Change*) kindly made available by Theo Vennemann (University of Munich) to the author during his stay in Munich from 1980–85.

The data on vowel laxing in Canadian French are from Douglas C. Walker's book *The Pronunciation of Canadian French* (Ottawa: University of Ottawa Press, 1984). The data on the origin of English vocabulary and word order in Old and Middle English come from the book by Joseph Williams cited below. The examples of English loanwords in Gwich'in (Loucheux) are given in *Dene Yati* 1 (1): (1985), published by the Dene Language Terminology Committee, Yellowknife, The Northwest Territories. The discussion of borrowing and semantic change in English draws on materials in the book by Williams.

The table depicting lexical diffusion of the stress change in English nouns derived from verbs is taken from the book by Jean Aitchison cited below. Aitchison's remarks are based on the article by M. Chen and W. Wang, "Sound Change: Actuation and Implementation" in *Language* 51:255–81 (1975). The data on the realization of [s] as [h] in Spanish were provided by Herbert Izzo of the University of Calgary.

The Germanic cognates used to illustrate family relationships are based on Leonard Bloomfield's classic work, *Language* (New York: Holt, Rinehart and Winston, 1933). The data on sound change in Muskogean come from Mary Haas's book *The Prehistory of Languages* (Amsterdam: Mouton, 1969). Some of the Romance cognates in this section come from *Proto-Romance Phonology* by Robert A. Hall, Jr. (New York: Elsevier, 1976). The quotation from Sir William Jones is taken from *A Reader in Nineteenth-Century Historical Indo-European Linguistics*, edited and translated by Winfred P. Lehmann (Bloomington, IN: Indiana University Press, 1967) and the quotation from Rasmus Rask is taken from Holger Pedersen's book *The Discovery of Language: Linguistic Science in the Nineteenth Century* (Bloomington, IN: Indiana University Press, 1959).

Question 2 is based on data provided by Dr. George Patterson. The data for questions 3 and 4 are from F. Columbus's *Introductory Workbook in Historical Phonology* (Cambridge, MA: Slavica Publishers, 1974). Question 10 is based on data provided by David Bellusci. The data for question 18 are drawn from *Source Book for Linguistics* by W. Cowan and J. Rakusan (Philadelphia: John Benjamins, 1987).

Recommended reading

Aitchison, Jean. 1985. *Language Change: Progress or Decay?* New York: Universe Books.

Anttila, Raimo. 1989. *Historical and Comparative Linguistics.* New York: John Benjamins.

Arlotto, Anthony. 1972. *Introduction to Historical Linguistics*. Lanham, MD: University Press of America.

Baugh, Albert C., and Thomas Cable. 1978. *A History of the English Language*. Englewood Cliffs, NJ: Prentice-Hall.

Hock, Hans Henrich. 1992. *Principles of Historical Linguistics*. Amsterdam: Mouton de Gruyter.

Hopper, Paul J., and Elizabeth Closs Traugott. 1993. *Grammaticalization*. Cambridge: Cambridge University Press.

Jeffers, Robert J., and Ilse Lehiste. 1979. *Principles and Methods for Historical Linguistics*. Cambridge, MA: MIT Press.

Labov, William. 1994. *Principles of Linguistic Change: Internal Factors*. Oxford: Blackwell.

Lehmann, Winfred P. 1992. *Historical Linguistics*. London: Routledge.

Millward, C. M. 1989. *A Biography of the English Language*. New York: Holt, Rinehart and Winston.

Pyles, Thomas, and John Algeo. 1982. *The Origins and Development of the English Language*. 3rd ed. New York: Harcourt Brace Jovanovich.

Williams, Joseph. 1975. *Origins of the English Language: A Social and Linguistic History*. New York: Free Press.

Questions

1. Identify the following sound changes with reference to the catalogue of sound changes provided in Table 8.3. In each pair of examples, focus on the segment(s) in bold only. The form on the left indicates the original segment(s) before the change and the form on the right indicates the segment(s) after the change. (Note that * stands for a hypothetical representation.)

a)	Sanskrit	**sn**eha	Pali	**sin**eha	'friendship'
b)	Old English	**hl**āf	English	**l**oaf	
c)	Latin	**i**uvenis [j]	Italian	**gi**ovane [ʤ]	'young'
d)	English	tria**thl**on	dialect	tria**th[ə]l**on	
e)	Latin	vi**du**a [dw]	Spanish	vi**ud**a[wd]	'widow'
f)	Sanskrit	sa**pt**a	Pali	sa**tt**a	'seven'
g)	Latin	tur**tur**	English	tur**tl**e	
h)		*ve**nr**é	Spanish	ve**ndr**é	'I will come'
i)	Italian	mu**nd**o	Sicilian	mu**nn**u	'world'
j)	Old French	**c**ire [t^s]	French	**c**ire [s]	'wax'
k)	Latin	p**ān**-	French	p**ain** [ɛ̃]	'bread'
l)	Latin	**mul**gēre	Italian	**mun**gere	'to milk'
m)	Latin	pa**c**āre [k]	Italian	pa**g**are	'to pay'
n)	Old Spanish	ma**d**uro	Spanish	ma**d**uro [ð]	'mature'
o)	Latin	pe**cc**ātum [kk]	Spanish	pe**c**ado [k]	'sin'
p)		*honō**s**is	Latin	honō**r**is	'honor (gen sg)'
q)	English	ra**ge**	French	ra**ge** [ʒ]	'rage'
r)	English	co**ff**ee	Chipewyan	[ka**θ**i]	
s)	Latin	mar**e**	Portuguese	mar	'sea'

t)	Latin	vīcīn**it**ās	Spanish	vecindad	'neighborhood'
u)	Gothic	**þ**liuhan [θ]	English	**f**lee	
v)	Old English	(ic) sing**e**	English	(I) sing	
w)	Latin	su**mm**a	Spanish	su**m**a	'sum, gist'
x)	Latin	ōrn**ā**mentum	Old French	orn**e**ment [ə]	'ornament'
y)		*l**ū**si	Old English	l**ȳ**s [yː]	'lice'

2. a) Describe the difference between the two French dialects in the following data. Assume that the data are in phonetic transcription.
   b) What sound change would you posit here? Why?
   c) State the sound change in the form of a rule.

	Standard French	*Acadian French*	
i)	okyn	oʧyn	'none'
ii)	kør	ʧør	'heart'
iii)	ke	ʧe	'wharf'
iv)	kɛ̃ːz	ʧɛ̃ːz	'fifteen'
v)	akyze	aʧyze	'accuse'
vi)	ki	tʃi	'who'
vii)	kav	kav	'cave'
viii)	kɔr	kɔr	'body'
ix)	kurir	kurir	'run'
x)	ɑ̃kɔːr	ɑ̃kɔːr	'again'

3. a) What sound changes differentiate Guaraní from its parent language, Proto-Tupí-Guaraní, in the following data?
   b) State these changes in rule form.

	Proto-Tupí-Guaraní	*Guaraní*	
i)	jukɨr	jukɨ	'salt'
ii)	moajan	moajã	'push'
iii)	puʔam	puʔã	'wet'
iv)	meʔeŋ	meʔẽ	'give'
v)	tiŋ	ʧĩ	'white'
vi)	potiʔa	poʧiʔa	'chest'
vii)	tatatiŋ	tataʧĩ	'smoke'
viii)	kɨb	kɨ	'louse'
ix)	men	mẽ	'husband'

4. a) Describe the three changes that took place between Proto-Slavic and Bulgarian in the following data. (The symbol ˘ over a vowel indicates that it is short.)
   b) State these changes as rules and indicate, as far as possible, the order in which they must have applied.
   c) Apply these rules to the Proto-Slavic word for 'adroit' to show how the Bulgarian form evolved.

	Proto-Slavic	*Bulgarian*	
i)	gladŭka	glatkə	'smooth'
ii)	kratŭka	kratkə	'short'

iii) blizŭka	bliskə	'near'
iv) ʒeʒĭka	ʒeʃkə	'scorching'
v) lovŭka	lofkə	'adroit'
vi) gorĭka	gorkə	'bitter'

5. For each word, list all the sound changes required to derive the later form from the proto-form. Where necessary, give the chronology of the sound changes.

a) *feminam	Old French	femme (final e =[ə])	'woman'
b) *lumine	Spanish	lumbre	'fire'
c) *tremulare	Spanish	temblar	'tremble'
d) *stuppam	Spanish	estopa	'tow'
e) *populu	Rumanian	plop	'poplar'

6. Taking into consideration the Great Vowel Shift, give all the changes necessary to derive each of the Modern English forms from the Old English forms. (*Note:* Assume, simplifying somewhat, that the Old English forms were pronounced as they are written.)

Old English	*Modern English*	
a) brōde (sg acc)	brood	[bruwd]
b) cnotta (c = [k])	knot	[nɑt]
c) wīse	wise	[wajz]
d) hlǣfdige	lady	[lejdij]

7. Place names are often subject to spelling pronunciation. Transcribe your pronunciation of the following words and then compare your pronunciation with that recommended by a good dictionary. Do you think any of your pronunciations qualify as spelling pronunciations?
   a) Worcestershire
   b) Thames
   c) Edinburgh (Scotland; compare Edinburgh, Texas)
   d) Cannes (France)
   e) Newfoundland

8. Compare the Old English singular and plural forms:

Singular	*Plural*	
bōc	bēc	'book(s)'
āc	ǣc	'oak(s)'

   Although the Old English words have an umlaut plural (as in Old English gōs/gēs 'goose/geese'), the Modern English forms do not. Explain how the change in plural formation could have come about.

9. As evident in the following sentence, Shona, a modern Bantu language, has SVO word order. (*Note*: The morpheme *ano-* marks present tense.)

mwana	anotengesa	miriwo
child	sells	vegetables

   'The child sells vegetables'

   By contrast, Shona's morphology reflects a different pattern, as is evident in the following examples.

mwana ano**mu***ona*
child **him**+*see*
'The child sees him'

mukadzi ano**va***batsira*
woman **them**+*help*
'The woman helps them'

What do these examples indicate about earlier Shona or possibly Proto-Bantu word order?

10. All of the following English words at one time had meanings that are quite different from their current ones. Identify each of these semantic changes as an instance of narrowing, broadening, amelioration, pejoration, weakening, or shift.

Word	*Earlier meaning*
a) moody	'brave'
b) uncouth	'unknown'
c) girl	'young person'
d) butcher	'one who slaughters goats'
e) witch	'male or female sorcerer'
f) sly	'skillful'
g) accident	'an event'
h) argue	'make clear'
i) carry	'transport by cart'
j) grumble	'murmur, make low sounds'
k) shrewd	'depraved, wicked'
l) praise	'set a value on'
m) ordeal	'trial by torture'
n) picture	'a painted likeness'
o) seduce	'persuade someone to desert his or her duty'
p) box	'a small container made of boxwood'
q) baggage	'a worthless person'
r) virtue	'qualities one expected of a man'
s) myth	'story'
t) undertaker	'one who undertakes'
u) hussy	'housewife'
v) astonish	'strike by thunder'
w) write	'scratch'
x) quell	'kill'

11. Look up the following words in a good dictionary. What semantic changes have affected the underscored portions since Old English? Do you think speakers of Modern English have reanalyzed any of these forms in terms of folk etymology?
    a) wed<u>lock</u>
    b) witch<u>craft</u>
    c) stead<u>fast</u>
    d) after<u>ward</u>

12. The following line is from *Troilus and Criseyde V* by Geoffrey Chaucer.

    His lighte goost ful blisfully is went.
    [hɪs liçtə gɔːst fʊl blɪsfʊlli ɪs wɛnt] ([ç] is a voiceless palatal fricative).
    'His light spirit has gone very blissfully.'

    a) How has the meaning of the word *ghost* changed since Chaucer's time?
    b) Describe the changes that have taken place in the pronunciation of *light* and *ghost*.

13. Consider the following lyrics from the Middle English song "Sumer Is I-cumen In." Compare the Middle English lyrics with the Modern English translation and answer the questions that follow.

Original text	*Transcription*
Sumer is i-cumen in;	[sʊmər ɪs ɪkʊmən ɪn
Lhude sing, cuccu!	luːdə sɪŋg kʊkku
Grōweþ sēd, and blōweþ mēd,	grɔːwəθ seːd and blɔːwəθ meːd
And springþ þe wude nū.	and sprɪŋgθ ðə wʊdə nuː]

    Translation
    'Summer has come in;
    Loudly sing, cuckoo!
    Seed grows and meadow blooms
    And the wood grows now.'

    a) What affix converted the adjective *loud* into an adverb in Middle English?
    b) What accounts for the difference between the Middle English and Modern English pronunciation of the vowel in *loud*?
    c) What other words in this poem reflect this general shift?
    d) How has the relative ordering of the subject and verb changed since this was written?
    e) How has the third person singular present tense suffix changed since Middle English?

14. The following Cree words were borrowed from French as the result of contact between the two groups on the Canadian prairies. (Notice that the French determiner was not treated as a separate morpheme and was carried along with the borrowed word.) What types of considerations could one plausibly assume played a role in the borrowing of these words into Cree?

	Cree	*French*	
a)	labutōn	le bouton	'button'
b)	lībot	les bottes	'boots'
c)	lamilās	la mélasse	'molasses'
d)	lapwīl	la poêle	'frying pan'
e)	litī	le thé	'tea'

15. The following Latin roots are found in words that have been borrowed into English. Since these words were borrowed after Grimm's Law had applied, they do not show its effects. All of these roots, however, do have Germanic cognates that did undergo Grimm's Law. On the basis of your knowledge of this law and

the meaning of the borrowing, try to determine the Modern English (Germanic) cognate for each root. Consult a good dictionary if you need help. (*Note:* Focus on the portion of the Latin word in bold only; vowel changes must also be taken into consideration.)

Latin root	*Related borrowing*	*English cognate*
a) **ped**is	pedestrian	foot
b) **nep**os	nepotism	______
c) **pisc**is	piscine	______
d) **ten**uis	tenuous	______
e) **corn**u	cornucopia	______
f) **duo**	dual	______
g) **ed**ere	edible	______
h) **gen**us	genocide	______
i) **ager**	agriculture	______

16. Assume that the Proto-Germanic form for each pair of cognates is the same as the Gothic. Focusing on the vowels, describe the changes that affected the Old English forms. (*Note:* y = [y], œ= [ø], and j = [j].)

	Gothic	*Old English*	
a)	kuni	cyn	'kin'
b)	badi	bed	'bed'
c)	dōmjan	dœ̄man	'to judge'
d)	sōkjan	sœ̄can	'to seek'
e)	bugjan	bycgan	'to buy'
f)	nati	net	'net'

17. Reconstruct the Proto-Romance form for each set of cognates. Give all the changes necessary to derive each of the modern forms from the proto-forms. If you are not sure how to proceed, return to Section 7. (*Note*: The Spanish and Rumanian spelling 'ie' represents the sequence /je/, and the Rumanian spelling 'ia' represents the sequence /ja/.)

	Spanish	*Sardinian*	*Rumanian*	
a)	vida	bita	vită (ă = [ə])	'life'
b)	sí	si	şi (ş = [ʃ])	'yes'
c)	riso	rizu	rīs	'laugh'
d)	miel	mele	miere	'honey'
e)	hierro	ferru	fier	'iron'
f)	piedra	pedra	piatră (ă = [ə])	'stone'
g)	hierba	erva	iarbă (ă = [ə])	'grass'
h)	oso	ursu	urs	'bear'
i)	roto	ruttu	rupt	'broken'
j)	lecho	lettu	—	'bed'

nine

The Classification of Languages

Aleksandra Steinbergs

Everything it is possible for us to analyze depends on a clear method which distinguishes the similar from the not similar.

– Linneus, *Genera Plantarum* (1754)

In the world today there are thousands of different languages, each with its own sound patterns, grammar, and vocabulary. Regardless of how different these languages are, they have important similarities that allow linguists to group them into a fairly small number of families and types. This chapter describes the methods of classification linguists use, and some of the findings that have resulted from this type of research.

1 SOME PRELIMINARIES

We will begin by considering two topics—the problem of distinguishing between a language and a **dialect**, and the chief methods of language classification used in linguistics today.

1.1 Dialect and language

It is often difficult to determine whether two linguistic communities speak different languages or merely different dialects of the same language. One test that linguists use to decide this involves the criterion of **mutual intelligibility**. Mutually intelligible varieties of the same language can be understood by speakers of each variety. According to this criterion, the English of Toronto, the English of Milwaukee, and the English of London qualify as dialects of the same language. On the other hand, if two speakers cannot understand one another, then linguists normally conclude that they are speaking different languages. The Italian of Florence and the French of Paris are examples of varieties of speech that are not mutually intelligible.

Political, cultural, social, historical, and religious factors frequently interfere when determining linguistic boundaries. For example, Serbs and Croatians often claim that they speak different languages. However, even though their history, religion, and spelling systems differ, Serbian and Croatian are actually mutually intelligible dialects of the same language, which linguists call Serbo-Croatian. In contrast, we often speak of Chinese as if it were a single language, even though it is actually a number of separate, mutually unintelligible languages (Cantonese, Mandarin, Hakka, and so on), each with a multitude of dialects of its own.

In addition to the problems presented by these nonlinguistic considerations, complications also arise when we try to divide a continuum of mutually intelligible dialects whose two end points are not intelligible. Dutch and German, for example, are mutually intelligible around the border area between Germany and Holland; however, the Dutch of Amsterdam and the German of Munich are not. Similarly, Palestinian Arabic and Syrian Arabic are mutually intelligible, but Moroccan Arabic and Iraqi Arabic are not.

Taking these considerations into account, how many languages are there in the world today? The best available estimate places the current figure at about six thousand. However, many of these languages have only a few hundred speakers and many others are in grave danger of demise as indigenous peoples throughout the world lose their traditional cultures and homelands. Indeed, according to one estimate, only around three hundred of the world's languages have a secure future.

Section 3 of this chapter presents an overview of a few hundred languages and the families to which they belong. First, however, we will turn our attention to some of the procedures that are used for classifying languages into a manageable number of types.

1.2 Types of classification

Within the field of linguistics, three different approaches to language classification are used.

Genetic classification categorizes languages according to their descent. Languages that developed historically from the same ancestor language are grouped together and are said to be **genetically related**. This ancestor may be attested (that is, texts written in this language have been discovered or preserved, as in the case of Latin), or it may be a reconstructed proto-language for which no original texts exist (as is the case for Indo-European). Genetic classification is discussed further in Section 3.

Although genetically related languages often share structural characteristics, they do not necessarily bear a close resemblance. For example, Latvian and English are genetically related (both are descended from Indo-European), but their morphological structure is quite different. An English sentence like *It has to be figured out* can be expressed in Latvian by a single word.

1)

ja:izgudro
(one) must out figure (it)
'It has to be figured out.'

Of course, Latvian and English are very distantly related, and languages that are more closely related will typically share a larger number of similarities. On the other hand, it is also necessary to recognize that even languages that are totally unrelated may share some structural similarities. Thus, English and Swahili, which are unrelated, both employ Subject-Verb-Object word order in simple declarative sentences.

2)

Maria anapenda Anna
'Maria likes Anna.'

For this reason, another approach to language classification is useful. Known as **linguistic typology**, it classifies languages only according to their structural characteristics, without regard for genetic relationships. Thus typologists might group together languages with similar sound patterns or, alternatively, those with similar grammatical structures. Typological studies also endeavor to identify **linguistic universals**, that is, structural characteristics that occur in all or most languages. We discuss linguistic typology further in Section 2.

Finally, **areal classification** identifies characteristics shared by languages that are in geographical contact. Languages in contact often borrow words, sounds, morphemes, and even syntactic patterns from one another. As a result, neighboring languages can come to resemble each other, even though they may not be genetically related. Due to space considerations, this chapter will not deal with areal classification specifically; however, borrowing is discussed in Sections 1.2 and 5.1 of Chapter 8.

2 TYPOLOGICAL CLASSIFICATION

As already noted, the classification of languages according to their structural characteristics is known as linguistic typology. Typological studies group together languages on the basis of similarities in their syntactic patterns, morphological structure, and/or phonological systems. An important area of research within the study of linguistic typology is the search for linguistic universals. Structural patterns and traits that occur in all languages are called **absolute universals**, while those that simply occur in most languages are known as **universal tendencies**.

Many typological generalizations involve **implicational universals**, which specify that the presence of one trait implies the presence of another (but not vice versa). For instance, languages with fricative phonemes (such as /f/ and /s/) will also have stop phonemes (such as /p/ and /t/), although the reverse is not necessarily true.

Another way to analyze linguistic universals is through **markedness theory**. Within this theory, **marked** traits are considered to be more complex and/or universally rarer than **unmarked** characteristics. In addition, a marked trait is usually found in a particular language only if its unmarked counterpart also occurs. Thus, markedness theory is closely related to the study of implicational universals.

An example can provide some clarification of these terms. Nasalized vowels are said to be marked, while nonnasalized (oral) ones are said to be unmarked. Phonologically, oral vowels can be considered less complex: Oral vowels allow the airstream to exit only through the mouth, while nasalized vowels allow air to escape from both the mouth and the nose. Cross-linguistically, we find that all languages have oral vowels, while only some languages have nasalized vowels. Even in the languages which have both, there are usually fewer nasalized vowels than oral ones. Thus, nasalized vowels (which are considered to be marked) are both rarer and phonologically more complex than (unmarked) oral vowels.

The following sections present some of the typological generalizations and universals that have been proposed in the areas of phonology, morphology, and syntax.

2.1 Phonology

In this section, we represent all vowel and consonant systems phonemically. This simplifies their presentation; note, however, that the exact phonetic realization of these systems may vary in the individual languages.

Vowel systems

Languages are often classified according to the size and pattern of their vowel systems. The most common vowel system has five phonemes—two high vowels, two mid vowels, and one low vowel. The front vowels are unrounded, as is the low vowel, and the back vowels are rounded.

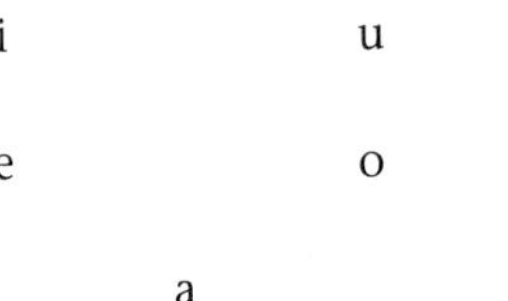

Figure 9.1 The most common vowel system

About half the world's languages, including Basque, Hawaiian, Spanish, and Swahili, have such a system.

The majority of the world's languages have vowel systems with three to nine different vowels (disregarding contrasts based on length or nasalization, which can double or triple the number of phonemic vowels). Languages with fewer than three or more than nine distinctive vowels are rare. Some typical vowel systems are presented in Figure 9.2.

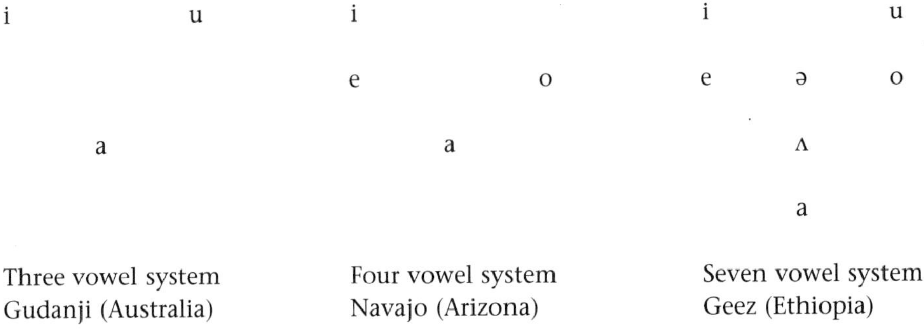

Figure 9.2 Common vowel systems

Analysis of many languages has led to the discovery of a number of universal tendencies pertaining to vowel systems. Some of these tendencies are listed here, along with a description of the most commonly occurring vowels.

- The most commonly occurring vowel phoneme is /a/, which is found in almost all of the languages of the world. The vowels /i/ and /u/ are almost as common as /a/.
- Front vowel phonemes (/i, e, ɛ, æ/) are generally unrounded, while nonlow back vowel phonemes (/ɔ, o, u/) are generally rounded.
- Low vowels (/æ, a, ɑ/) are generally unrounded.

Although English has an above-average number of vowels, they all conform to the above tendencies. In American English, for instance, all the front vowels and all the low vowels are unrounded, whereas all of the back, nonlow vowels are rounded. This vowel system can be represented as follows:

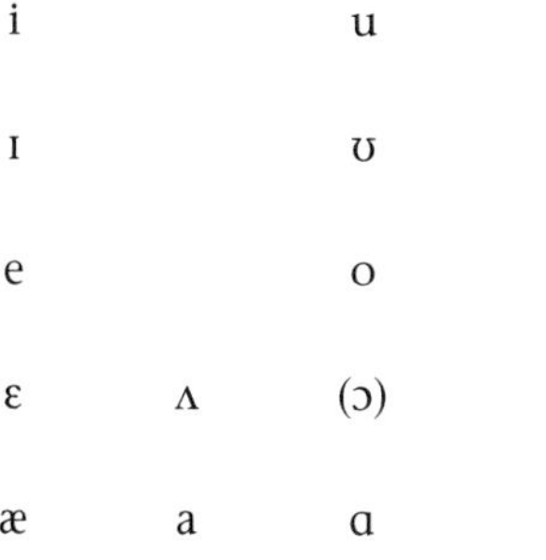

Figure 9.3 The English vowel system

The relationship between contrasting vowel types (such as oral versus nasal, and long versus short) can also be expressed in terms of implicational universals, since the presence of one vowel phoneme type implies the presence of another (but not vice versa).

- If a language has contrastive nasal vowels, then it will also have contrastive oral vowels. For example, French contrasts different nasal vowels (/lɔ̃/ 'long' and /lã/ 'slow'), and contrasts oral vowels with nasal vowels (/la/ 'weary' and /lã/ 'slow'). Predictably, French also contrasts different oral vowels, as in /klo/ 'shut' and /klu/ 'nail'. English shows contrasts among oral vowels but does not contrast nasal vowels with oral vowels. There are no contrasts in English like /bɑt/ and /bɑ̃t/.
- If a language has contrasting long vowels, then it will also have contrasting short vowels. For example, Finnish shows contrasting long vowels, and, predictably, contrasting short vowels. The reverse is not necessarily the case. English shows contrasting short vowels (/bɪt/ versus /bɛt/) but does not contrast long vowels with short ones.

Table 9.1 Finnish vowel contrasts

Long versus long	/vi:li/	'junket'	/va:li/	'election'
Short versus short	/suka/	'bristle'	/suku/	'family'
Short versus long	/tuli/	'fire'	/tu:li/	'wind'

Consonant systems

It is not particularly useful to classify languages according to the number of consonants that they contain, since languages may have as few as eight consonant phonemes (as in Hawaiian), or more than ninety. (!Kung, a language spoken in Namibia, has ninety-six consonant phonemes.) Nevertheless, typological analysis of consonant systems has produced a number of well-substantiated universals:

- All languages have stops.
- The most common stop phonemes are /p, t, k/. Very few languages lack any one of these, and there are no languages that lack all three. If any one of these three stops is missing, it will probably be /p/; for example, Aleut, Nubian, and Witchita have no /p/ phoneme. The most commonly occurring phoneme of the three is /t/.
- The most commonly occurring fricative phoneme is /s/; few languages lack it. If a language has only one fricative, it is most likely to be /s/. It is the only fricative found in Nandi (a language of Kenya) and Weri (a language of New Guinea). The next most common fricative is /f/.
- Almost every known language has at least one nasal phoneme. In cases where a language has only one nasal phoneme, that phoneme is usually /n/ (as in Arapaho, spoken in Wyoming). If there are two contrasting nasals, they are normally /m/ and /n/.
- The majority of languages have at least one phonemic liquid. However, a small number of languages have none at all; e.g., Blackfoot, Dakota, Efik (spoken in Nigeria), and Siona (found in Ecuador). English, of course, has two: /l/ and /r/.

Consonant phonemes are also subject to various implicational universals:

- If a language has voiced obstruent phonemes (stops, fricatives, or affricates), then it will also have voiceless obstruent phonemes. The reverse is not necessarily true; for example, Ainu (a language of northern Japan) has only voiceless obstruent phonemes: /p, t, k, tʃ, s/.
- Sonorant consonants are generally voiced. Very few languages have voiceless sonorants; those that do always have voiced sonorants as well. For example, Burmese contrasts voiced and voiceless nasals and laterals.
- If a language has fricative phonemes, then it will also have stop phonemes. There are no languages that lack stops; however, there are some languages that lack fricatives. For example, Gilbertese (Gilbert Islands), Kitabal (eastern Australia), and Nuer (southeastern Sudan) have no fricatives.

- Languages that have affricates will also have fricatives and stops. This is not surprising, since an affricate is, in essence, a sequence of a stop followed by a fricative. However, many languages lack affricates altogether. Note that while French, for example, has fricatives and stops, but no affricates, English has all three.

Suprasegmental systems

Languages can also be classified according to their prosodic, or suprasegmental type. Languages which use pitch to make meaning distinctions between words are called tone languages. (The phonetics and phonology of tone were introduced in Chapters 2 and 3.)

A great many of the world's languages are tone languages. Mandarin Chinese, for instance, has four contrastive tones.

Table 9.2 Tone contrasts in Mandarin Chinese

High tone	dā	'build'
Mid rising tone	dá	'achieve'
Falling rising tone	dǎ	'hit'
High falling tone	dà	'big'

The other Chinese languages, as well as many languages of Southeast Asia, Africa, and the Americas are also tone languages. A few tone languages are also found in Europe; for example, in one of the dialects of Latvian a three-way tonal distinction is made.

Table 9.3 Tone contrasts in Latvian

Falling tone	loks	[lùoks]	'arch, bow'
Level (high) tone	loks	[lūoks]	'green onion'
Rising-falling (broken) tone	loks	[lûoks]	'window'

As noted in the chapter on phonetics, there are two types of tones: *level* tones and *contour* tones. Tone languages most often contrast only two tone levels (usually high and low). However, contrasts involving three tone levels (such as high, low, and mid tones) are also relatively common. Five or more levels of tonal contrast are practically unknown.

Tone systems, too, exhibit various universal tendencies:

- If a language has contour tones (such as rising tone or falling tone) then it will also have level tones (such as high, mid, or low tone). Burmese, Crow, Latvian, and Mandarin are examples of languages that fit this pattern. The reverse pattern (languages with contour tones but no level tones) is extremely rare (although Dafla, spoken in northern India, has such a system).

- If a language has complex contour tones (such as rising-falling, or falling-rising), then it will also have simple contour tones (like rising or falling). Both the Mandarin and Latvian examples fit this pattern.

Differences in stress, discussed in Chapter 2, are also useful in classifying languages. **Fixed stress** languages are those in which the position of stress on a word is predictable. For example, in Mayan, stress always falls on the last syllable of a word; in Polish, Swahili, and Samoan, stress falls on the penultimate (second-to-last) syllable of a word, while in Czech, Finnish, and Hungarian, the stressed syllable is always the first syllable of a word. In **free stress** languages, the position of stress is not predictable and must be learned for each word. Free stress is also called phonemic stress because of its role in distinguishing between words. Russian is an example of a language with free stress.

Table 9.4 Stress contrasts in Russian

múka	'torture'	muká	'flour'
zámok	'castle'	zamók	'lock'
rúki	'hands'	rukí	'hand's' (genitive singular)

Syllable structure

All languages permit V and CV syllable structures (where V normally stands for a vowel, and C for a consonant). These syllable types are unmarked, in the sense that they are permitted in all languages. They are also simpler than most other syllable structures, such as CVC or VCC. VC is apparently as simple as CV, but only the latter is universally permitted. The presence of an onset (as in a CV syllable) is apparently more valued than the presence of a coda (as in a VC syllable).

In any given language, onsets may be structured differently from codas. For example, in English, a nasal + stop sequence is permitted in the coda (in a word like *hand*), but not in the onset (there are no English words that begin with the sequence *nd*). However, Swahili has precisely the opposite restrictions: The *nd* sequence is permitted in onset position (in words like *ndizi* 'banana'), but not in coda position. In fact, Swahili syllables are coda-less—they can only end in vowels.

Differing syllable structure constraints can have interesting consequences when languages come in contact. For example, in Hawaiian only V and CV syllables are permitted. Thus, when a word is borrowed from a language like English, which allows more complicated syllable structures, vowels are inserted to produce the only allowed syllable structures. For example, when the phrase *Merry Christmas* was borrowed into Hawaiian, it was reformulated as follows: *mele kalikimaka*. (Of course, some consonant changes were made as well, since Hawaiian lacks /r/ and /s/ phonemes.)

Two examples of implicational universals for syllable structure are presented here. Both deal with the complexity of onsets as opposed to codas.

- If a language permits sequences of consonants in the onset, then it will also permit single consonants or zero consonants in the onset.

- If a language permits sequences of consonants in the coda, then it will also permit single consonants or zero consonants in the coda.

2.2 Morphology

Words and morphemes are both cross-linguistically legitimate categories. However, there are clear differences in the ways in which individual languages combine morphemes to form words. Four types of systems can be distinguished.

The isolating type

If a language is purely **isolating** or **analytic**, its words consist of a single (root) morpheme. In such a language there are no affixes, and categories such as number and tense therefore have to be expressed by a separate word. In Mandarin Chinese, which is primarily an isolating language, the morpheme *le* is often used to indicate a past or completed action. Although this morpheme is thus semantically similar to a past tense, it acts just like an independent word since its position in the sentence may vary:

3)

Ta chi fan *le*.
he eat meal past
'He ate the meal.'

Ta chi *le* fan.
he eat past meal
'He ate the meal.'

Other languages that are primarily isolating include Cantonese, Vietnamese, Laotian, and Cambodian.

The polysynthetic type

In a **polysynthetic** language, single words can consist of long strings of roots and affixes that often express meanings associated with entire sentences in other languages. The following word from Inuktitut illustrates this.

4)

Qasuiirsarvigssarsingitluinarnarpuq.

Qasu	-iir	-sar	-vig	-ssar	-si	-ngit	-luinar	-nar	-puq
tired	not	cause-to-be	place-for	suitable	find	not	completely	someone	3/sg.

'Someone did not find a completely suitable resting place.'

Polysynthetic structures can be found in many native languages of North America, including Inuktitut, Cree, and Sarcee.

The terms *isolating* and *polysynthetic* refer to two extremes: words consisting only of single morphemes versus words that can be complete sentences. Few if any languages are either purely isolating or purely polysynthetic. Rather, the vast majority of languages fall somewhere in between. Such languages, which are sometimes called **synthetic**, can be divided into two types.

The agglutinating type

An **agglutinating** language has words which can contain several morphemes, but the words are easily divided into their component parts (normally a root and affixes). In such languages, each affix is clearly identifiable and typically represents only a single grammatical category or meaning.

Table 9.5 Affixes in Turkish

köy	'village' (singular)
köy-ler	'villages' (plural)
köy-ler-in	'of the villages' (genitive plural)

Turkish words can have a complex morphological structure, but each morpheme has a single, clearly identifiable function. In Table 9.5, for instance, *-ler* marks plurality and *-in* marks the genitive case (which is used to indicate the possessor).

The fusional type

Words in a **fusional** or **inflectional language** can also consist of several morphemes. However, in contrast to agglutinating systems, the affixes in fusional languages often mark several grammatical categories simultaneously. In Russian, for example, a single inflectional affix simultaneously marks the noun's gender class (masculine, feminine, or neuter), its number (singular or plural), and its grammatical role (subject, direct object, and so on). The suffix *-u*, for instance, can be used to indicate that a noun belongs to the feminine gender class, is singular, and functions as the direct object.

5)

mi vid^{j}im ruk-u
we see hand-fem/sg/Acc
'We see a/the hand.'

This situation is typical of the entire Russian case system.

The distinction between agglutinating and fusional is sensitive to the number of semantic 'bits' of information normally packed into an affix; in an agglutinating language, each affix normally carries only one piece of grammatical information, while in a fusional language, affixes often have several simultaneous functions.

Mixed types

Most languages do not belong exclusively to any of the four categories just outlined. For example, English employs isolating patterns in many verbal constructions, where each notion is expressed by a separate word. The future, for instance, is indicated by the free morpheme *will* (rather than an affix) in structures such as *I will leave*. On the other hand, English also exhibits considerable agglutination in derived words, such as *re-en-act-ment*, which consist of a series of clearly identifiable morphemes, each with its own unique meaning and function. However, the English pronoun system is largely fusional, since a single form can be used to indicate person, number, gender, and case. The word *him*, for instance, is used to express a third person, singular, masculine direct object.

Since most of the world's languages exhibit mixed patterns of this type, it has been suggested that terms like *isolating, agglutinating,* and *fusional* should be used to refer not to a language as a whole, but to particular structures within a language. It is also important to recognize that these classifications ignore morphological processes such as compounding (e.g., English *greenhouse*), reduplication (e.g., Tagalog *sulat* 'write' versus *susulat* 'will write'), grammatical use of stress or tone (e.g., the noun *présent* versus the verb *presént* in English), and internal word change (e.g., vowel ablaut, as in English *run* versus *ran*). As these examples help demonstrate, much remains to be done in the area of typological classification.

Implicational universals: morphology

A variety of generalizations can be made about word structure in human language.

- If a language has inflectional affixes, it will also have derivational affixes. For example, English not only has inflectional affixes such as the past tense *-ed* and possessive *-'s*, but it also contains derivational affixes like *un-* (*unhappy, unwanted*) and *-ly* (*quickly, slowly*).
- If a word has both a derivational and an inflectional affix, the derivational affix is closer to the root. (DA = derivational affix; IA = inflectional affix)

Table 9.6 The ordering of derivational and inflectional affixes

English					
friend-ship-s			*friend-s-ship		
Root	DA	IA	Root	IA	DA
Turkish					
iʃ	-tʃi	-ler	*iʃ	-ler	-tʤi
work	-er	-pl	work	-pl	-er
Root	DA	IA	Root	IA	DA

- If a language has only suffixes, it will also have only postpositions. (As noted in Chapter 5, postpositions are the equivalent of prepositions in languages that place the head at the end of the phrase.) Turkish, for example, has only suffixes; as expected, it also has postpositions rather than prepositions. This is illustrated in the following sentence.

6)

Ahmet Ajʃe *itʃin* kitab-ɨ al-dɨ.
Ahmet Ayshe for book-Acc bought
'Ahmet bought a book for Ayshe.'

2.3 Syntax

Because we lack detailed descriptions for most of the world's languages, much of the work on syntactic universals has been restricted to the study of word order in simple declarative sentences such as *The men built the house*. Patterns are classified in terms of the order of the subject (S), direct object (O), and verb (V). The three most common word orders (in descending order of frequency) are SOV, SVO, and VSO. Over 95 percent of the world's languages use one of these patterns as their basic word order.

7)

SOV (Turkish):
Hasan öküz-ü al-dɨ.
Hasan ox-Acc bought
'Hasan bought the ox.'

8)

SVO (English):
The athlete broke the record.

9)

VSO (Welsh):
Lladdodd y ddraig y dyn.
killed the dragon the man
'The dragon killed the man.'

SOV, SVO, and VSO patterns all have one common trait: the subject appears before the direct object. This S-O pattern may be so prevalent because of the fact that the subject usually coincides with the topic of the sentence (i.e., what the sentence is about; see Chapter 7, Section 4.3), and therefore is most useful at an early point in the utterance.

Although an overwhelming majority of the world's languages place the subject before the direct object in their basic word order, this pattern is not universal. There are a small number of VOS languages, the best-known example of which is Malagasy.

10)

VOS (Malagasy):
Nahita ny mpianatra ny vehivavy.
saw the student the woman
'The woman saw the student.'

As well, there are a very few OVS and OSV languages, all of which seem to be spoken in South America:

11)

OVS (Hixkaryana):
Kana yanɨmno bɨryekomo
fish caught boy
'The boy caught a fish'

12)

OSV (Apurinã):
Anana nota apa
pineapple I fetch
'I fetch a pineapple'

Word order universals

Sometimes, the order of elements within one kind of structure has implications for the order of elements in other structures. Many of these implications concern the relationship between the verb and its (direct) object.

- If a language has VO word order, then it will have prepositions rather than postpositions. Languages of this type include Berber (spoken in Morocco), Hebrew, Maori (spoken in New Zealand), Maasai (spoken in Kenya), Welsh, and Irish Gaelic.

13) Irish Gaelic

a. VSO pattern:
Chonaic mé mo mháthair
saw I my mother
'I saw my mother.'

b. preposition pattern:
sa teach
in house
'in the house'

- If a language has OV word order, then it will probably have postpositions rather than prepositions. Languages with this structural pattern include Basque, Burmese, Hindi, Japanese, Korean, Quechua, Turkish, and Guugu Yimidhirr, an aboriginal language of Australia.

14) Guugu Yimidhirr

a. S-OV pattern:
Gudaa-ngun yarrga dyinday.
dog-Erg boy bit
'The dog bit the boy'

b. postposition pattern:
yuwaal nganh
beach from
'from the beach'

- PPs almost always precede the verb in OV languages, and usually follow the verb in VO languages.

15) Japanese

a. S-OV pattern:
Gakusei-ga hon-o yonda
student-Nom book-Acc read
'The student read a book'

b. PP precedes verb:
Taroo-ga [$_{PP}$ nitiyoobi ni] tsuita.
Taroo-Nom Sunday on arrived
'Taroo arrived on Sunday.'

16) English

a. S-VO pattern:
I like candy.

b. PP follows verb:
George left [$_{PP}$ on Sunday].

- Manner adverbs overwhelmingly precede the verb in OV languages and generally follow the verb in VO languages.

17) Japanese (S-OV pattern, as seen in *15a)*)
manner adverb precedes verb:
hayaku hasiru
fast run

18) English (S-VO pattern, as seen in *16a)*)
manner adverb follows verb:
John runs fast.

- With respect to possessive structures, there is an overwhelming preference for Genitive + N order in OV languages, and a (somewhat weaker) preference for N + Genitive order in VO languages.

19) Japanese (S-OV pattern, as seen in *15a)*)
genitive structure precedes head N:
Taroo-no hon
Taroo-Gen book
'Taroo's book'

20) French

a. S-VO pattern:
Pierre aime Marie.
'Pierre likes Marie.'

b. genitive structure follows head N:
la maison de Marie
the house of (Gen) Marie
'Marie's house'

English, although an SVO language, exhibits both Gen + N and N + Gen patterns:

21)

a. Gen + N pattern:
Mary's friend

b. N + Gen pattern:
a friend of Mary

Examples like these do not invalidate the universals we have presented, since these universals are intended to capture tendencies only.

Grammatical hierarchies

Implicational universals are often stated in terms of **hierarchies** of categories or relations. One of the most important hierarchies of this type refers to the grammatical relations of subject and direct object (see Chapter 5).

Hierarchies represent degrees of markedness, with the least marked option at the top and the most marked at the bottom. According to the hierarchy in Figure 9.4, a process that applies only to subjects is less marked than a process that applies to direct objects, and so on. Given the definition of markedness outlined at the begin-

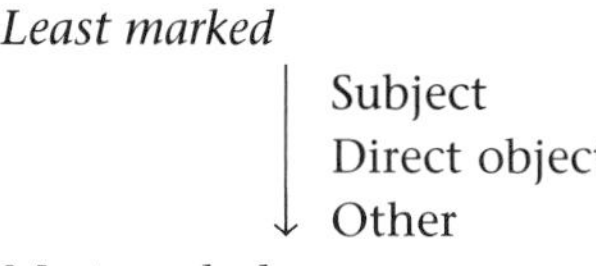

Figure 9.4 Hierarchy of grammatical relations

ning of Section 2, it follows that if a particular phenomenon applies to direct objects, it should also apply to subjects. The opposite, however, need not be true: It would not be surprising to find a process that applies to subjects but not direct objects.

Among the many typological phenomena that conform to this hierarchy is verb agreement, first mentioned in Chapter 4 (Section 6.4). As the following examples show, there are languages in which the verb agrees only with the subject, and there are languages in which the verb agrees with both the subject and the direct object. (3 = 3rd person, sg = singular, pl = plural, pst = past)

22)

agreement with subject only (Spanish):

Subject
Juan parti-ó
Juan leave-3/sg/pst
'Juan left.'

23)

agreement with subject and direct object (Swahili):

Subject *Direct object*
Juma a- li- wa- piga watoto
Juma 3/sg pst 3/pl hit children
'Juma hit the children.'

However, as predicted by the hierarchy, there are no languages in which the verb agrees only with the direct object.

2.4 Explaining universals

Linguists are still uncertain about how to explain the existence of many linguistic universals. Nonetheless, a number of interesting proposals have been made, and it is worthwhile to consider some of them here.

Phonology

Perceptual factors play a role in shaping phonological universals. For example, the fact that /s/ is the most commonly occurring fricative may have to do with its acoustic prominence: Varieties of /s/ are inherently louder than other kinds of fricatives.

Vowel systems (discussed in Section 2.1) develop so as to keep vowel phonemes as different from each other as possible. A three vowel system such as the following allows for plenty of 'space' around each vowel, which probably makes each vowel easier to distinguish from the others.

i u

a

Figure 9.5 A three vowel system

The same holds true for the distribution of stop phonemes. It may be that /p/, /t/, and /k/ are the three most common stops because they occur at three maximally distant places of articulation within the supralaryngeal vocal tract. These three stops are perceptually much easier to distinguish from each other than a sequence of dental, alveolar and palatal stops, for example, all of which are produced in the central region of the oral cavity (i.e., the center of the mouth).

It has been recently suggested that consonant systems in general respond to the articulatory pressures that give rise to unmarked sounds and systems. Articulatorily basic obstruents such as [p], [t], and [k] are found much more commonly than more complex articulations such as [tɬ] and [qʷ]. Table 9.7 shows the set of obstruents that is most widely used cross-linguistically.

Table 9.7 Obstruents found cross-linguistically

p	t	k	ʔ
b	d	g	
f	s		h
	tʃ		

Languages tend to have consonant systems that consist of about 70 percent obstruents and 30 percent sonorants no matter what the total size of their consonant inventories may be. These figures reflect the articulatory possibilities available for contrast: More distinctions can be made among obstruents than among sonorants. There are, for example, no nasal fricative sonorants, because the air pressure needed to force air through a narrow opening (which is necessary for the production of fricatives) cannot be built up when so much air is flowing through the nasal passage at the same time. For reasons such as this, the number of obstruent consonants in any language is potentially much larger than the number of possible sonorant consonants. This is just one example of how considerations involving articulation can play a role in the shaping of consonant systems.

Morphology

Other types of explanations are pertinent for morphological universals. For example, the fact that languages with suffixes but no prefixes always have postpositions (Section 2.2) may have a historical explanation. In these languages, some postpositions became attached to a preceding word and were thereby converted into suffixes. Because suffixes in such languages have evolved from postpositions, the link between the two elements can be traced to their common origin.

The requirement that derivational affixes occur closer to the root than inflectional affixes has another type of explanation. As noted in the morphology chapter, derivation typically forms new words, while inflection marks the subclass (for example, plural for Ns, past tense for Vs) to which a word belongs. Given that a word must be formed before its subclass can be determined, it follows that derivational processes will precede inflection. This is reflected in word structure, where derivational affixes appear closer to the root than inflectional markers. In Figure 9.6, for instance, the verbal root *treat* is converted into a noun by the affix *-ment* before the plural inflectional marker is added.

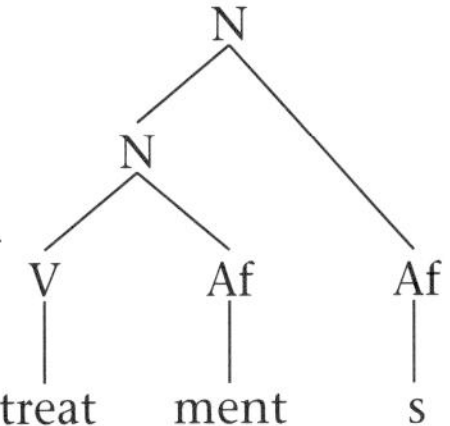

Figure 9.6 The structure of a word containing a derivational affix and an inflectional affix

Syntax

At least some syntactic universals may be explained in terms of the way that the human brain processes sentence structure. Consider the following summary of word order patterns, which is based on the implicational universals discussed in Section 2.3.

Table 9.8 Word order patterns

Constituents	*Order in VO language*	*Order in OV language*
P & NP	preposition-NP	NP-postposition
V & PP	Verb-PP	PP-Verb
V & manner Adv	verb-manner Adv	manner Adv-verb
Gen & N	noun-Genitive	Genitive-noun

One recent explanation as to why the word order properties in the second and third columns cluster together involves the contrast between right-branching and left-branching languages. In right-branching languages, the more elaborate part of a phrase's structure occurs on its right branch; in left-branching languages, it occurs on the left. Thus, a verb-object pattern is right-branching since a phrasal constituent (an XP) appears on its right branch, but an object-verb pattern is left-branching:

a Right-branching (VO) *b* Left-branching (OV)

Figure 9.7 Right-branching and left-branching patterns

As you can easily determine for yourselves, the P-NP, V-PP, V-Adv, and N-Gen patterns commonly associated with VO languages are also all right-branching (both genitives and adverbials are a type of phrase). In contrast, the NP-P, PP-V, Adv-V, and Gen-N patterns typically found in OV languages are all left-branching. In other words, it seems that languages are fairly consistent in using one or the other type of branching structure. This sort of uniformity may make it easier for speakers and hearers to process syntactic structure. Thus, just as some human beings are right-handed and others left-handed, it appears that some languages prefer to use consistently right-branching systems, while others prefer consistently left-branching systems.

3 GENETIC CLASSIFICATION

The world's languages can be grouped into a relatively small number of language families. However, genetic classification is sometimes difficult for a number of reasons. Perhaps the biggest problem is simply the amount of data that must be collected before linguists can be confident about the status of a group of languages. It is only in the last two or three decades, for example, that enough information has been accumulated to propose a detailed classification of the languages of Africa. Many of the languages of South America, New Guinea, and Australia are still relatively unknown.

In many cases, linguists face the problem of establishing the tests or criteria to be used in proposing genetic relationships. There is some disagreement over the degree of similarity that should exist among languages before a genetic relationship can be proposed. This issue arises because unrelated languages are often typologically similar (that is, share some structural characteristics). This is particularly likely if languages have been in contact long enough to have borrowed a large number of words, sounds, morphemes, or syntactic structures from one another.

Additional difficulties stem from the fact that genetically related languages need not be typologically similar. This is especially true if the relationship is a distant one, as is the case with English and Russian. Russian has numerous inflectional affixes, an extensive case system, and fairly free word order, while English has relatively few inflectional affixes, virtually no case marking, and fixed word order. Yet, both belong to the **Indo-European family**.

To complicate matters even further, linguists also disagree as to the number of cognates that must be uncovered before a genetic relationship between languages can be established. The more distant the genetic relationship between languages, the less likely it is that a large number of obvious cognates will be found. Sound changes, for example, can obscure similarities between cognate words. English and Latin are related (though distantly), but the similarity between cognates like Latin *unda*, meaning 'wave', and English *water* is certainly not striking.

Research is hampered, as well, by the fact that words which may be excellent indicators of a genetic relationship can drop out of the lexicon. For example, Old English had a word *leax* ('salmon'), which was cognate with German *Lachs* and Yiddish *lox*, but this lexical item has since been lost from the native English lexicon (although *lox* has, of course, been borrowed back into some varieties of English as the name for smoked salmon). Since word loss is a common historical event, linguists prefer to use the oldest available form of a language for their research; thus, our knowledge of

Proto-Indo-European is heavily based on Old English, Sanskrit, and Latin rather than English, Hindi-Urdu, French, and their other modern descendants. Of course, languages which are genetically related do share many similarities, particularly if their common ancestor is not too distant.

Some language families contain many hundreds of languages; in other cases, only one language may remain to represent a family; in still other cases, families have become extinct. The following sections present some information about the makeup and membership of a few of the language families represented in the world today.

3.1 The Indo-European family

With only about a hundred languages, Indo-European is not a large family in terms of the total number of languages. However, it is the largest language family in the world in terms of the total number of speakers: There are about 1.7 billion native speakers of an Indo-European language. Living Indo-European languages can be assigned to one of the nine branches illustrated in Table 9.9.

Table 9.9 Main branches of the Indo-European family

Germanic	Armenian
Celtic	Baltic
Italic	Slavic
Hellenic	Indo-Iranian
Albanian	

Germanic

The Germanic branch of Indo-European can be divided into three sub-branches. The East Germanic branch included Gothic, the oldest Germanic language for which written texts exist (dating from the fourth century AD). Gothic and any other languages belonging to this branch of Germanic have long been extinct. The North Germanic (or Scandinavian) branch originally included Old Norse (also known as Old Icelandic), a dialect of which was spoken by the Vikings. From it descended Icelandic, Norwegian, and Faroese (spoken on the Faroe islands, north of Scotland); the other North Germanic languages are Swedish and Danish.

The West Germanic branch includes German, Flemish (spoken in Belgium), Dutch, Afrikaans, Frisian, and English. Afrikaans is descended from the Dutch spoken by seventeenth-century settlers in South Africa (the Boers). Frisian is spoken on the north coast of Holland, and on the Frisian islands just off the coast, as well as on the northwestern coast of Germany. English descended from the speech of the Angles, Saxons, and Jutes, Germanic tribes who lived in northern Germany and southern Denmark (in an area just east of the Frisians) before invading England in 449 AD and settling there.

The organization of the Germanic family of languages is illustrated in Table 9.10. (In this and other tables, parentheses are used to indicate languages that no longer have any native speakers. The tables are intended to illustrate the membership and organization of the families; they do not necessarily provide a complete list of the languages in each family.)

Table 9.10 The Germanic family

(East Germanic)	*North Germanic*	*West Germanic*
(Gothic)	Icelandic	German
	Faroese	Dutch
	Norwegian	Frisian
	Danish	English
	Swedish	Afrikaans
		Yiddish

Celtic

The Celtic branch of Indo-European (see Table 9.11) has two main sub-branches: Insular and Continental (now extinct). Gaulish, a member of the Continental branch, was once spoken in France (the Gauls were the tribe Julius Caesar defeated), but it has long been extinct. The Insular sub-branch can be subdivided into two groups of languages: Brythonic and Goidelic. Brythonic languages include Welsh and Breton (which is spoken in northwestern France) as well as Cornish, which was formerly spoken in southwest Britain but is now extinct. The Goidelic branch contains Irish (or Irish Gaelic), which is still spoken natively in the western parts of Ireland, and Scots Gaelic, which is native to some of the northwestern parts of Scotland (especially the Hebrides Islands).

Table 9.11 The Celtic family

Insular		*Continental*
Brythonic	*Goidelic*	
Welsh	Irish [= Irish Gaelic]	(Gaulish)
Breton	Scots Gaelic	
(Cornish)		

Italic

The Italic family originally incorporated a variety of languages spoken in the area corresponding roughly to modern-day Italy. The Italic languages that are presently spoken are all descended from Latin, the language of the Roman Empire, and, therefore, are called Romance languages. They can be divided into an Eastern group (consisting of Italian and Rumanian), and a Western group, containing all of the other Romance languages with the exception of Sardinian (which stands alone). The Western group is further divided into Ibero-Romance (Spanish, Portuguese, and

Catalan—the latter is spoken in northeastern Spain, around Barcelona) and Gallo-Romance, which includes French, Occitan (spoken in southern France), and Romansch (one of the four official languages of Switzerland). These divisions are illustrated in Table 9.12.

Table 9.12 The Romance family

Eastern	*Western*		
	Ibero-Romance	*Gallo-Romance*	
Italian Rumanian	Spanish Portuguese Catalan	French Occitan Romansch	Sardinian

Hellenic

The Hellenic branch of Indo-European has only one living member, Greek. All modern Greek dialects are descended from the classical dialect known as Attic Greek, which was the speech of Athens during the Golden Age of Greek culture (approximately 500 to 300 BC). Hellenic Greek, which was used in subsequent centuries, was the language of commerce throughout the Middle East. (Hellenic Greek was also Cleopatra's native language; Egyptian was long extinct by her time.)

Albanian

The Albanian branch of Indo-European has only one member, Albanian, which is spoken not only in Albania, but also in parts of the former Yugoslavia, Greece, and Italy.

Armenian

The Armenian branch also has only one member, Armenian. This language is centered in Armenia (located between the Black Sea and the Caspian Sea, in the area known as the Caucasus).

Baltic

The Baltic branch contains only two surviving languages, Latvian and Lithuanian. They are spoken in Latvia and Lithuania (located just west of Russia and northeast of Poland). Lithuanian has an elaborate case system that resembles the one proposed for Proto-Indo-European.

Slavic

The Slavic branch of Indo-European can be divided into three sub-branches: East, West, and South. The East Slavic branch is made up of Russian (also called Great Russian), Ukrainian, and Byelorussian (or White Russian); the latter is spoken in Byelorussia, which is just east of northern Poland. The West Slavic branch includes Czech, Slovak, and Polish.

The South Slavic branch consists of Bulgarian, Macedonian, Serbo-Croatian, and Slovenian. Note that although Alexander the Great was king of Macedonia, he spoke Hellenic Greek, not (Slavic) Macedonian; Slavic-speaking tribes did not move into that area until several centuries later. The organization of the Slavic group of languages is represented in Table 9.13.

Table 9.13 The Slavic family

East Slavic	*South Slavic*	*West Slavic*
Russian	Slovenian	Czech
Ukrainian	Serbo-Croatian	Slovak
Byelorussian	Macedonian	Polish
	Bulgarian	

Indo-Iranian

The Indo-Iranian branch of Indo-European is divided into the Iranian and Indic sub-branches. The Iranian sub-branch contains about two dozen different languages, including Modern Persian (also called Farsi, spoken in Iran), Pashto (the principal language of Afghanistan), and Kurdish (found in Iran, Iraq, Turkey, and Syria). Other Iranian languages are spoken in Pakistan, southern parts of the former USSR, and China.

There are about thirty-five different Indic languages. Most of the languages spoken in northern India, Pakistan, and Bangladesh belong to this branch of Indo-European. Some of the most widespread (in terms of number of speakers) are Hindi-Urdu, Bengali, Punjabi, Marathi, and Gujarati. Although speakers of Hindi and Urdu can understand each other, the languages have totally different writing systems and are associated with different cultures; Urdu is spoken principally in Pakistan by Muslims while Hindi is spoken primarily in India by Hindus.

Less well known as an Indic language is Romany, or Gypsy. It is believed that the Gypsies were an entertainment caste in India who were invited to perform in the Middle East sometime in the Middle Ages. They never returned to India, but travelled instead to Turkey and, eventually, Europe. Romany contains many borrowed words—particularly from Greek, which was spoken in Turkey at the time of their stay. Table 9.14 depicts the organization of Indo-Iranian.

Table 9.14 The Indo-Iranian family

Iranian	*Indic*
Persian [= Farsi]	Hindi-Urdu
Pashto	Bengali
Kurdish	Punjabi
	Marathi
	Gujarati
	Romany [= Gypsy]

The following map illustrates the geographic location of the Indo-European families identified in this chapter.

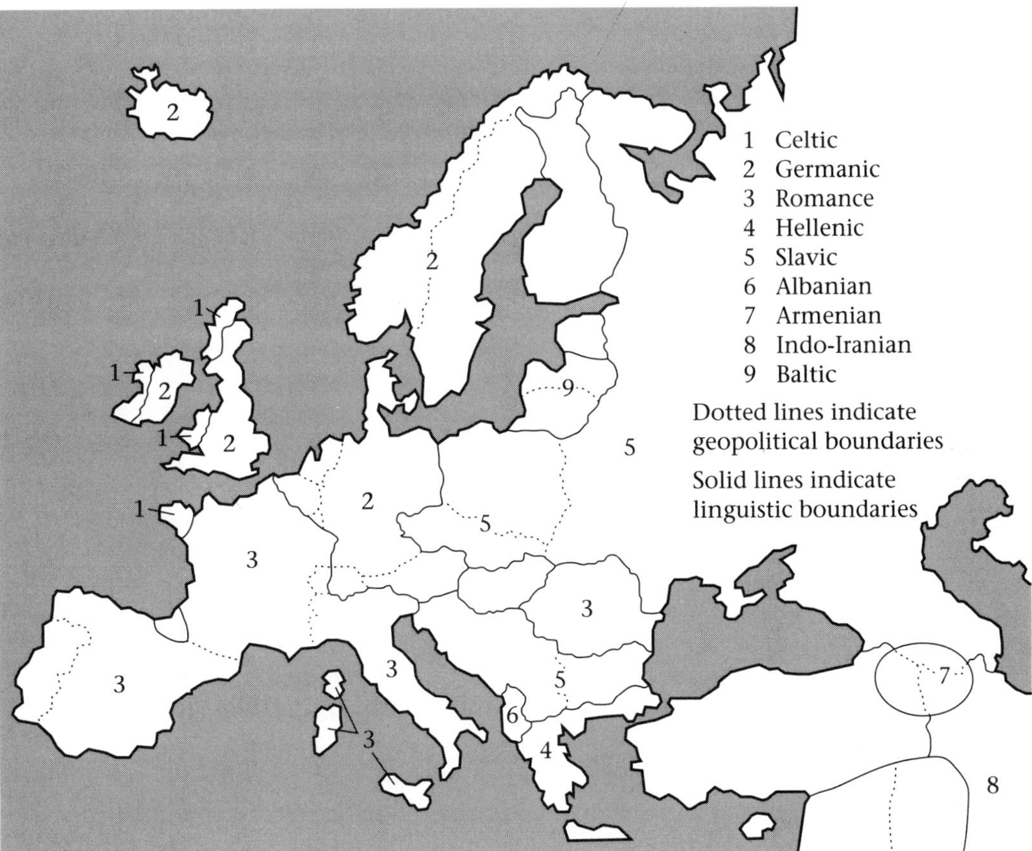

Figure 9.8 Location of Indo-European languages

3.2 Some other families

Although no introductory text could hope to present a complete survey of all of the world's language families, some further discussion of this topic is worthwhile in order to illustrate the extraordinary variety of human language.

Uralic

The Uralic family (see Table 9.15) contains about twenty languages and has approximately twenty-two million speakers. Uralic languages are spoken in a band across the northern part of Europe, all the way from northern Norway to Siberia. Uralic has two major branches: Samoyed and Finno-Ugric. The Samoyed branch contains a handful of languages spoken in northern Russia, particularly in areas around the Ural mountains, and also in Siberia.

The most widely spoken Finno-Ugric language is Hungarian. Other Finno-Ugric languages are Finnish, Sami (or Lapp, spoken in northern Scandinavia and northwestern Russia), Estonian (Estonia), Livonian (Latvia), Karelian (eastern Finland and northwestern Russia), and Mordvin (or Mordva, spoken in parts of Russia).

Table 9.15 The Uralic family

Finno-Ugric		*Samoyed*
Finnic	*Ugric*	
Finnish	Hungarian	Nganasan
Estonian	Ostyak	Selkup
Sami/Lapp	Vogul	Nenets
Karelian		Enets
Livonian		
Vepsian		
Vodian		
Mordvin/Mordva		
Mari (Cheremis)		
Votyak		
Komi		

Uralic languages are primarily agglutinating and most have postpositions with SOV or SVO word order. The nouns often have many cases (Finnish has fifteen), which appear to have developed historically from postpositions that became attached to nouns as suffixes.

Altaic

Languages belonging to the Altaic family are spoken in a continuum from Turkey to Siberia, China and, possibly, Korea and Japan. The membership of the Altaic family (see Table 9.16) is still very much in dispute, but it probably includes at least three branches: Turkic, Mongolian, and Tungusic. Recent scholarship has collected substantial evidence that Korean and Japanese are also members of the Altaic family. However, dissenting scholars argue that the similarities between Japanese, Korean, and the other languages in this proposed family are primarily typological, and that there are few reliable cognates encompassing the complete spectrum of the proposed Altaic family.

The best-known Turkic language is Turkish, which is spoken by over forty million people. Turkish accounts for about 40 percent of the speakers of Turkic languages. Other Turkic languages (most of which are spoken in central Asia) include Uzbek (Uzbekistan), Azerbaijani (Azerbaijan Republic and Iran), Tatar (Tataristan and Kazakhstan), Uighur (China and Kazakhstan), Kazakh (Kazakhstan, China, and Mongolia), and Saxa (Yakut) (northern Siberia).

The Mongolian languages are spoken by around ten million people, primarily in Mongolia and China, while the Tungusic languages are found in central Siberia and Mongolia. The number of speakers of Tungusic languages probably does not exceed one million people.

Altaic languages are usually agglutinating, often with several suffixes in the same word. They normally employ SOV word order and typically use postpositions rather than prepositions. Many Altaic languages have vowel harmony, a phonological phenomenon in which all vowels of a word share certain features, such as [round] or [back].

Table 9.16 The Altaic family

Turkic	*Mongolian*	*Tungusic*		
Turkish	Khalkha	Evenki	Korean	Japanese
Uzbek	Buriat	Chakar		
Azerbaijani				
Tatar [= Tartar]				
Uighur				
Kazakh				
Saxa (Yakut)				

Caucasian

The languages that are normally grouped together as Caucasian have not yet been assigned to families in a definitive way. These languages are primarily spoken in northeastern Turkey and between the Black Sea and the Caspian Sea, in and around the Caucasus Mountains. The best evidence so far points to three distinct language families—Northwest Caucasian, Northeast Caucasian, and South Caucasian (see Table 9.17). South Caucasian (sometimes called Kartvelian) consists of Georgian, Svan, and Laz-Mingrelian. Northwest Caucasian contains Circassian (or Kabardian) and Abhkaz, whereas Northeast Caucasian consists of about two dozen languages; of these Chechen, Lezghian, and Avar have the largest number of speakers. Altogether

Table 9 .17 The Caucasian languages

The South Caucasian (Kartvelian) family
Georgian Svan Laz-Mingrelian
The Northwest Caucasian family
Kabardian [= Circassian] Abkhaz
The Northeast Caucasian family
Chechen Lezghian Avar

there are about thirty-five languages in the three separate families, with a total of approximately five million speakers.

Although no genetic relationship has been proven to exist among these three families, they do seem to share a number of features (probably brought about through mutual borrowing): many Caucasian languages have glottalized consonants, complex consonant clusters, a large consonantal inventory, and very few vowel phonemes.

Recent claims have been made that would assign the Northwest and Northeast Caucasian languages to one single family. However, this grouping is not yet widely accepted among Caucasianists.

Dravidian

There are twenty-five Dravidian languages, which are primarily found in the southern half of India, but also in Sri Lanka, Pakistan, and Nepal (see Table 9.18). About a hundred and seventy-five million people are native speakers of a Dravidian language. The most widely spoken languages in this family are Telugu, Tamil, Kannada, and Malayalam. Dravidian languages are normally SOV. They are agglutinating and nontonal, and usually have initial stress.

Table 9.18 The Dravidian family

North	*Central*	*South-Central*	*South*
Kurux	Kolami	Telugu	Tamil
Malto	Naiki	Savara	Malayalam
Brahui	Parji	Konda	Kannada
	Gadaba	Gondi	Tulu

Sino-Tibetan

In terms of numbers of speakers, the Sino-Tibetan family (see Table 9.19) is the largest language family after Indo-European. There are about three hundred Sino-Tibetan languages, with well over a billion native speakers. There are two major branches: Tibeto-Burman and Sinitic. To the first branch belong the Tibetan languages, Burmese, and many other languages spoken in northeastern India, Nepal, Burma, and Tibet.

Table 9.19 The Sino-Tibetan family

Tibeto-Burman	*Sinitic*				
	Mandarin	*Wu*	*Min*	*Yue*	*Hakka*
Burmese	Mandarin	Wu	Taiwanese	Cantonese	Hakka
Tibetan			Amoy		
Sharpa			Hokian		
Newari			Fukian		

The Sinitic branch contains the languages that we call 'Chinese'. From a linguistic point of view Chinese consists of several different, mutually unintelligible languages. They are often called 'dialects' by nonlinguists, primarily because the same writing system is used across China and can be understood by speakers of different Chinese languages (see Chapter 14, Section 3.1). However, the Sinitic branch contains several different languages (each of which may have many different dialects). Mandarin Chinese has dialects spoken in Peking (Beijing), Szechuan, Nanking, and Taiwan. The other major Sinitic languages are Wu (with dialects in Shanghai and Suchow), Min (which includes Taiwanese, Amoy, and Fukian), Cantonese, and Hakka.

The Sino-Tibetan languages typically have SVO or SOV word order. The Sinitic languages are all tonal (as are many of the Tibeto Burman languages) and are predominantly isolating. Morphemes generally consist of a single CV(C) syllable.

Austroasiatic

The Austroasiatic family of languages (see Table 9.20) consists of about a hundred and fifty languages with approximately eighty million speakers. The Munda branch of Austroasiatic includes languages spoken in central and northeastern India, such as Santali and Mundari. Mon-Khmer is the largest branch of Austroasiatic and contains Vietnamese, Cambodian (also called Khmer) and many other languages of Cambodia, Vietnam, Burma, and southern China. Other Austroasiatic languages are spoken in Malaysia and on the Nicobar Islands (northwest of Sumatra). Some Austroasiatic languages are tonal (for example, Vietnamese) and some are characterized by large and complex vowel systems. Word order is generally SVO or SOV.

Table 9.20 The Austroasiatic family

Munda	*Nicobarese*	*Aslian*	*Mon-Khmer*
Santali	Car	Jahai	Vietnamese
Mundari	Nancowry	Semai	Cambodian [= Khmer]
Ho		Semelai	Mon
			Khasi
			Bahnar

Austronesian

The Austronesian family (see Table 9.21) contains over nine hundred languages (according to some estimates more than twelve hundred), which are spoken from the island of Madagascar halfway across the world to Southeast Asia, Hawaii, Easter Island, and New Zealand. Some of the languages of Taiwan also belong to this family; however, Taiwanese, which is spoken by most of the island's residents, is a Sinitic language (see above).

The largest branch within the Austronesian family contains the Malayo-Polynesian languages. They include Malagasy (spoken on Madagascar), Malay (and the mutually comprehensible Indonesian), Tagalog (the basis for Pilipino, the official language of the Philippines), Javanese, and hundreds of other languages spoken in the Philippines, Malaysia, Vietnam, Cambodia, and the islands of Indonesia. The

Polynesians were intrepid ocean travellers and colonized Hawaii, Easter Island, and New Zealand, sometime between 200 and 1000 AD. Well-known Malayo-Polynesian languages in the Pacific include Fijian, Tongan, Samoan, Tahitian, Maori, and Hawaiian (which now has fewer than one thousand native speakers).

Table 9.21 The Austronesian family

Formosan	*Malayo-Polynesian*		
	Western	*Central*	*Eastern*
Amis	Tagalog	Soboyo	Samoan
Bunun	Malay	Manggarai	Tongan
Paiwan	Javanese	Ngadha	Fijian
Puyuma	Malagasy	Tetum	Tahitian
Rukai	Sundanese		Hawaiian
Seediq	Balinese		Maori

Some recent research has confirmed earlier attempts to link the Austronesian family with Austroasiatic, and this relationship is now widely accepted.

One feature characteristic of Austronesian languages is the use of reduplication. As well, many of these languages use infixes, which are extremely rare in other language families. Word order is usually SVO, although VSO is more prevalent in Taiwan, the Philippines, and Polynesia.

Indo-Pacific

Indo-Pacific (or Papuan) languages are all spoken on the island of New Guinea, on nearby islands such as New Britain or Bougainville, or on the Andaman Islands (just southwest of Burma). Little is known about many of these languages, but they appear to be about seven hundred in number, with just under three million speakers. Two languages with relatively large speaker populations are Enga (a hundred and sixty-five thousand speakers, spoken in the western highlands of New Guinea) and Bunak (fifty thousand speakers, spoken on the island of Timor, west of New Guinea).

Indo-Pacific languages are normally tone languages. Nouns are often marked for case, but not always for number. Word order is usually SOV.

Australian

Recent studies have established that all of the aboriginal languages of Australia belong to the same family. There are about one hundred and seventy such languages, but many have very few speakers. There are currently only about thirty thousand speakers of aboriginal Australian languages.

The majority of Australian languages are spoken in Arnhem Land (north central Australia) and the northern part of Western Australia. The languages with the largest number of speakers are Mabuiag (seven thousand speakers on the Torres Straits Islands, north of Australia) and the Western Desert Language (five thousand speakers in Western Australia).

Australian languages are characterized by simple vowel systems. Nouns are normally marked for case, sometimes in unusual and intricate ways, and word order can be very free.

Afroasiatic

Afroasiatic languages (see Table 9.22) are spoken primarily in a band across the northern half of Africa and in the Middle East. There are about two hundred and fifty Afroasiatic languages and a hundred and seventy-five million speakers of these languages. Afroasiatic has five main branches, one of which—Egyptian—no longer contains any living languages. Although Old Egyptian was spoken from 3000 BC onward (including during the life of Rameses II, who was Pharaoh at the time of Moses), it has long been extinct. Its descendant, Coptic, is now used only as the liturgical language of the Coptic church.

A second branch of Afroasiatic is Cushitic, whose member languages are spoken in the Sudan, Ethiopia, Somalia, and Kenya. A third branch, Berber, includes several languages of Algeria, Morocco, and Niger, such as Tuareg and Tamazight. Still another branch, Chadic, contains many of the languages of Chad and Nigeria, such as Hausa. Unlike other Afroasiatic languages, Chadic languages are tonal.

The fifth and largest branch of Afroasiatic (in terms of number of speakers) is the Semitic branch. Many (now extinct) languages mentioned in the Bible were of Semitic origin, such as Babylonian, Assyrian, Moabite, Classical Hebrew, and Biblical Aramaic. Biblical (or Palestinian) Aramaic was the language spoken in Palestine at the time of Jesus, and was probably his native language.

Classical Hebrew has not been spoken as a native language for millennia, although it has been maintained as a religious language by Jews. Modern Hebrew (or Israeli) is not directly descended from Classical Hebrew; rather, it was recreated at the beginning of this century by regularizing some aspects of Classical Hebrew and adding new vocabulary. Modern Hebrew has only had a community of native speakers for the past few decades.

Still another Semitic language, Arabic, has various dialects (not all of which are mutually intelligible) spoken all across North Africa and throughout the Middle East. All of these are descended from Classical Arabic, which was the language of Muhammad, the founder of Islam, and is the language of the Koran, the holy book of Islam.

The Semitic languages are characterized by a system of consonantal roots. Most roots consist of three (sometimes two) consonants with vowels being inserted to

Table 9.22 The Afroasiatic family

(Egyptian)	*Cushitic*	*Berber*	*Chadic*	*Semitic*
(Coptic)	Somali	Tuareg	Hausa	(Babylonian)
	Oromo	Tamazight		Aramaic
		Shilha		Modern Hebrew
		Kabyle		Arabic
		Zenaga		Amharic

indicate various morphological categories (see Chapter 4, Section 1.3). For example, Arabic has the root *k-t-b* (denoting the concept of writing) from which a variety of words can be formed, including *kitaabun* 'book', *kaatibun* 'writer', *kataba* 'he had written', and *yaktubu* 'he will write'. The Semitic languages frequently have complex consonant clusters and pharyngeal or pharyngealized consonants.

Niger-Congo

Most of the languages spoken in Subsaharan Africa belong to the Niger-Congo family of languages (see Table 9.23). In all, this family contains over nine hundred languages, with a total of (approximately) one hundred and eighty million speakers. It can be divided into nine major subfamilies: Mande, Kordofanian, Atlantic, Ijoid, Kru, Gur, Adamawa-Ubangi, Kwa, and Benue-Congo.

Table 9.23 The Niger-Congo family

Kordofanian	*Atlantic*	*Ijoid*	*Mande*	*Gur*	*Kwa*	*Adamawa-Ubangi*	*Benue-Congo*	*Kru*
Koalib	Fula	Ijo	Bambara	Mooré	Twi	Banda	Yoruba	Grebo
Katla	Wolof	Defaka	Mende	Dagaari	Fante	Ngbandi	Igbo	Guéré
	Temne		Maninka		Ewe	Ngbaka	Efik	Bassa
	Drola					Zande	Bemba	Klao
	Manjaku						Shona	
							Zulu	
							Swahili	
							Xhosa	

The Atlantic branch of Niger-Congo contains west coast languages such as Wolof (Senegal) and Fula (Guinea). The Mande branch also contains many West African languages, such as Mende, Bambara, and Maninka (Alex Hailey's famous African ancestor, described in the novel *Roots*, was probably a speaker of Maninka). The Benue-Congo subfamily constitutes the largest branch within Niger-Congo. It includes the Bantu group of languages, which number over a hundred and have more than sixty million speakers. Some of the principal Bantu languages are Swahili (Tanzania and Kenya), Zulu (South Africa), Ganda (Uganda), Shona (Zimbabwe), and Kongo (Zaire).

Niger-Congo languages are typically SVO and usually have tone systems (with the notable exception of Swahili). The Bantu languages are usually agglutinating with verb-subject and verb-direct object agreement. Languages in the Bantu group also exhibit a complex system of noun classes, each of which is marked by a distinctive set of prefixes.

Nilo-Saharan

The Nilo-Saharan family is found primarily in eastern and central Africa and includes approximately one hundred and twenty languages, with about thirty million speakers. Some of the languages in this family are Maasai, Luo (both spoken in Kenya), Nubian (Sudan), Kanuri (Nigeria), and Songhai (Niger and Mali). Nilo-Saharan languages generally have tonal systems, and nouns are usually marked for case.

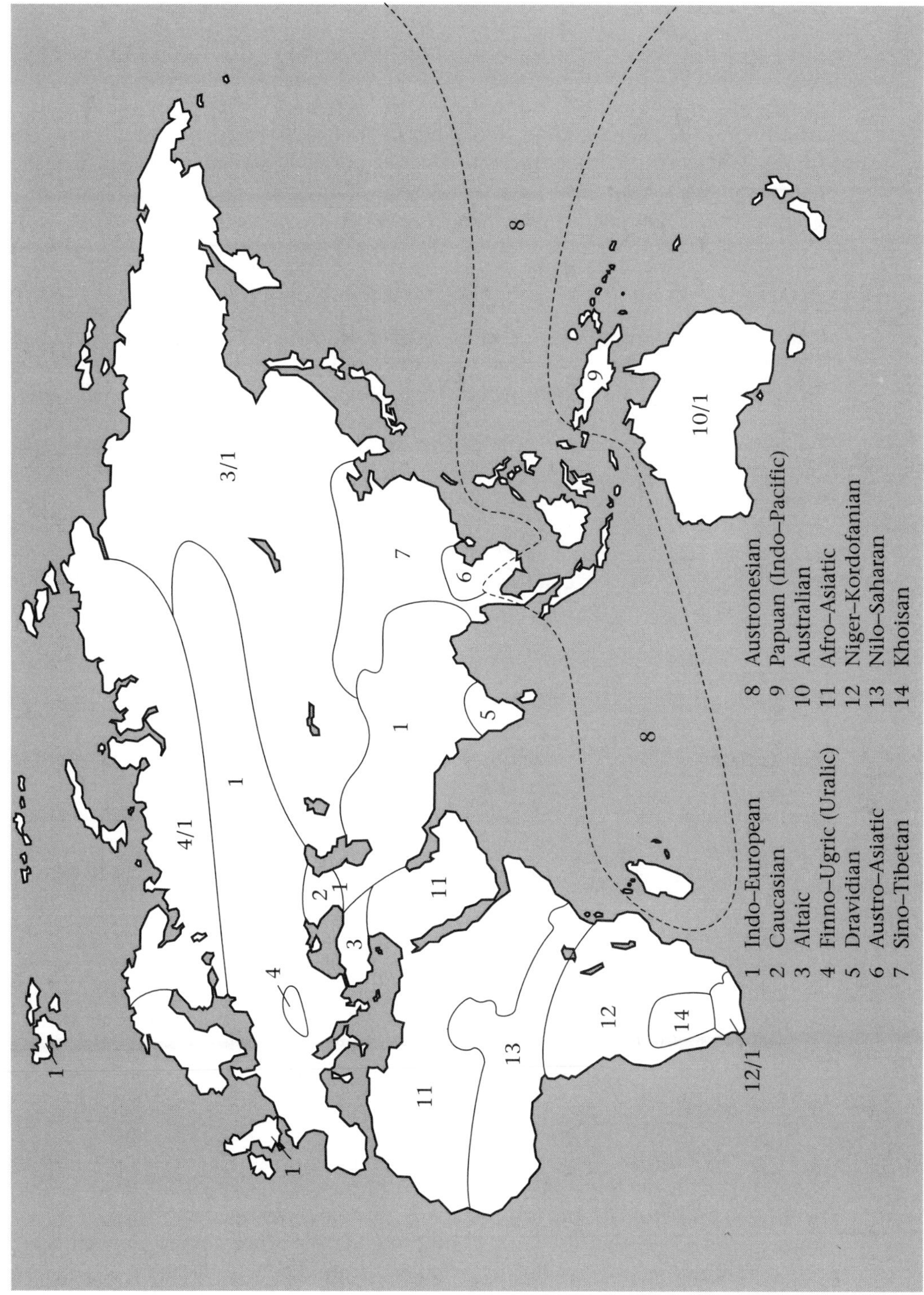

Figure 9.9 Location of some major language families

Khoisan

The Khoisan family is quite small, containing only about thirty languages, spoken by a hundred and twenty thousand speakers. The majority of Khoisan languages are spoken in the southern and southwestern areas of Africa. Some Khoisan languages are Hottentot (= Nama), !Kung, and Sandawe (one of only two Khoisan languages spoken in east Africa). Khoisan languages have unusual click sounds in their consonantal systems. These clicks have been borrowed by a few neighboring Bantu languages, such as Zulu and Xhosa.

3.3 North, Central, and South America

Contrary to popular belief, not all native American Indian (usually called **Amerindian**) languages belong to the same family. Although many of the genetic relationships are still unclear, it appears that there are several different language families in the Americas. Figure 9.10 shows the location of groups found in North and Central America.

Table 9.24 North, Central, and South American families

Language family	*Some member languages*
Eskimo-Aleut	Inuktitut, Yupik
Athapaskan	Navajo, Apache, Chipewayan, Dogrib
Algonquian	Cheyenne, Shawnee, Cree, Ojibwa (Mohican)
Siouan	Crow, Winnebago, Omaha, Lakhota
Iroquoian	Seneca, Mohawk, Oneida, Cherokee
Caddoan	Caddo, Witchita, Pawnee
Wakashan	Makah, Nootka, Nitinat
Salish	Flathead, Spokan, Kalispel, Coeur d'Alene
Klamath-Sahaptin	Nez Perce, Sahaptin, Klamath
Penutian	Patwin, Wintu, Nomlaki, Zuni
Muskogean	Choctaw, Koasati, Mikasuki
Hokan	Diegueño, Yuma, Mohave
Coahuiltecan	Comecrudo, Cotoname, Pakawa, Carrizo
Uto-Aztecan	Northern Paiute, Snake, Comanche, Pima/Papago
Otomian-Pame	Otomi, Pame, Pirinda, Mazahua
Mayan	Huastecan, Cholan, Maya, Tzeltal, Tojolabal
Andean-Equatorial	Quechua, Aymara, Arawak, Guaraní
Ge-Pano-Carib	Carib, Bororo, Witoto, Mataco
Macro-Chibchan	Cuna, Cayapa, Epera, Warao, Talamanca

The study of North American languages has made a number of significant contributions to the development of linguistics. In practically every book that the student of linguistics reads, the impact of work in this area is evident. It would be no exaggeration to say that the lasting and profound influence of such eminent pioneers of linguistics as Franz Boas, Edward Sapir, and Leonard Bloomfield is due in large part to the seminal work they did on structurally diverse Amerindian languages.

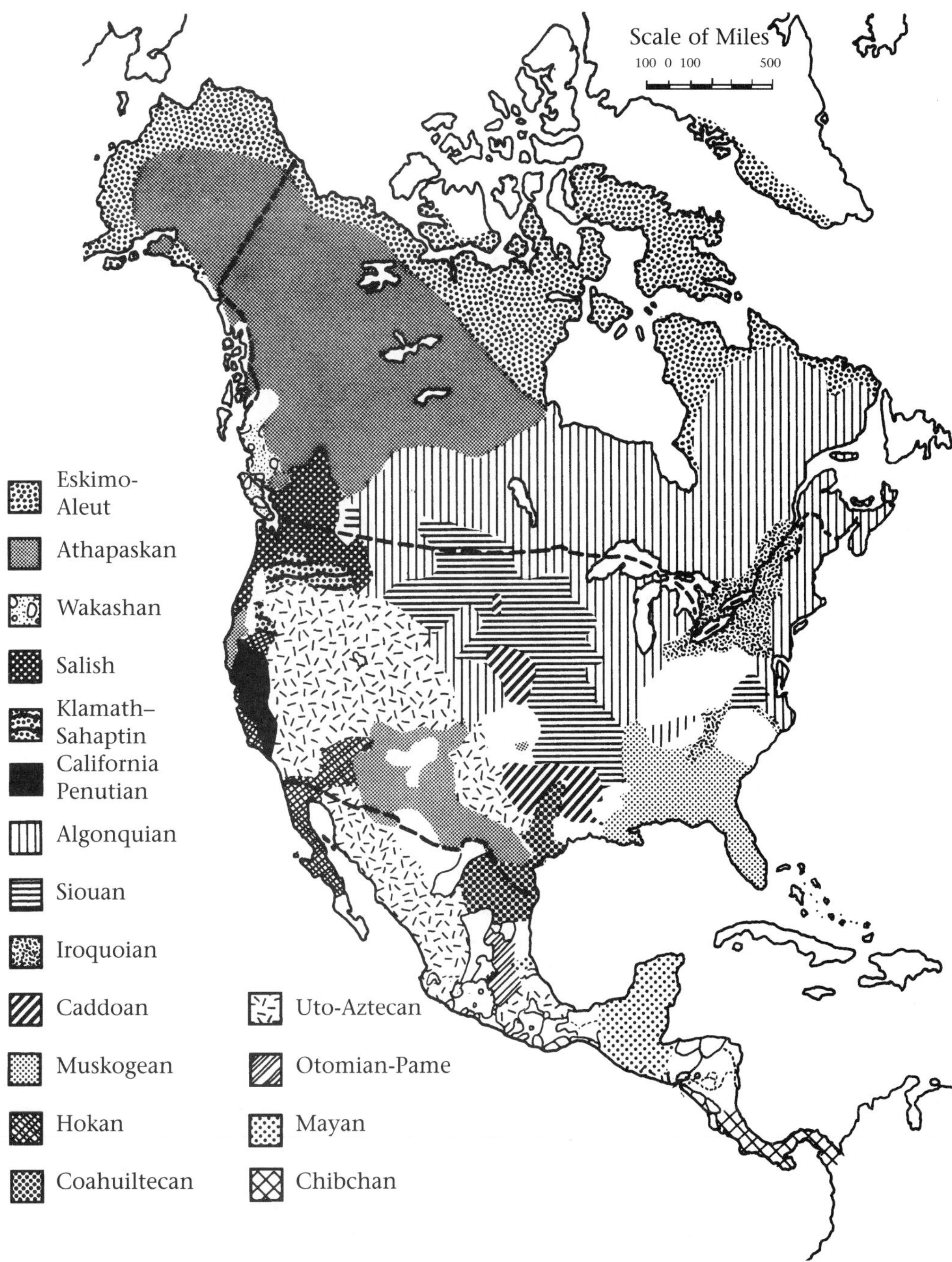

Figure 9.10 North and Central American language groups

When the European settlers arrived in North America, hundreds of distinct languages were spoken by the indigenous people. In the intervening centuries, many of these languages have disappeared under the pressure of English and European culture. In the 1990 U.S. census, in answer to the question "Do you speak a language other than English at home? If so, list it," approximately 140 Native American languages were named. Of these, the ten with the largest number of speakers are listed in Table 9.25. Among language families of Canada and the United States, Algonquian, Athapaskan, Eskimo-Aleut, Iroquoian, Muskogean, and Siouan are the most robust. Unfortunately, the outlook for these languages is not good: more and more Native American children are growing up to be monolingual speakers of English.

Table 9.25 The ten largest Native American languages in the United States (1990)

Language	*Language family*	*Where spoken*	*Number of speakers*
Navajo	Athapaskan	Arizona, New Mexico	148,530
Dakota/Lakhota	Siouan	Montana, North and South Dakota, Nebraska	15,355
Yupik	Eskimo-Aleut	Alaska	13,150
Apache	Athapaskan	Arizona, New Mexico	12,390
Cherokee	Iroquoian	North Carolina, Oklahoma	11,905
Pima/Papago	Uto-Aztecan	Arizona	11,819
Choctaw/ Chickasaw	Muskogean	Oklahoma	9,211
Keres	isolate	New Mexico	8,722
Zuni	Penutian	New Mexico	6,413
Muskogee/Creek	Muskogean	Oklahoma, Alabama	6,213

There are at least six hundred different Amerindian languages spoken in South America, by about eleven million people. However, our knowledge of these languages is often minimal, and some linguists estimate that there may be over a thousand South American Amerindian languages. Most of these languages belong to one of three families: Andean-Equatorial, Ge-Pano-Carib, and Macro-Chibchan.

The Andean-Equatorial family contains languages that are found throughout South America, and may have as many as ten million speakers all together. The principal language in this family is Quechua, which has over six million speakers. Dialects of Quechua are spoken in Peru, Ecuador, and Bolivia. This was the language of the Inca empire, which reached its height in the sixteenth century AD, before being destroyed by the Spanish conquistadors. Other languages belonging to this family are Aymara (Peru), Arawak (Surinam), and Guaraní (the major language of Paraguay). One of the interesting typological features of Andean-Equatorial languages is that some of them have no lateral consonants whatsoever.

The Ge-Pano-Carib family is also spread over much of South America. Some of the languages belonging to this family are Carib (Surinam), Bororo (Brazil), Witotu (Peru), and Mataco (Argentina). Languages of the Ge-Pano-Carib family also often lack laterals; the dominant word order in these languages is usually SOV.

Languages of the Macro-Chibchan family are found in Central America and the northwestern part of South America. Some languages belonging to this family are Cuna (Panama), Cayapa (Ecuador), Epera (Colombia), and Warao (Venezuela). Macro-Chibchan languages generally have SOV word order.

3.4 Language phyla

In recent years attempts have been made to group many of the language families presented in Sections 3.1, 3.2, and 3.3 into even larger groupings called **phyla** (singular phylum) or **macrofamilies**. These attempts are, as yet, extremely controversial, as they challenge established modes of thought within linguistics. However, they also afford a number of intriguing possibilities. In this section we will attempt to provide a balanced view of these ventures into long-range comparison.

One of the best known of the proposed phyla is Nostratic (also called Eurasiatic by some). It includes Indo-European, Uralic, Altaic, and (depending on the linguist) various other languages and language families. A number of reconstructed forms have been proposed for this phylum; two of the most convincing are the reconstructed first and second person singular pronouns: **m-* 'I' and **t-* 'you (sg)'. These forms are particularly persuasive, since pronoun systems are normally extremely stable, and thus are among the most likely forms to have remained constant for the extended period of time (about 20,000 years) since the existence of Proto-Nostratic.

Another proposed phylum is Dene-Caucasian. It includes Sino-Tibetan, Na-Dene, North Caucasian, and a number of other individual languages. A third proposal for a phylum is Austric, which would include Austroasiatic, Austronesian, Daic (the family to which Thai belongs), and the Miao-Yao group of languages.

To take this approach still further, some linguists have gone so far as to reconstruct a single, common ancestor for all human languages, which has been called Proto-World or Proto-Sapiens. This ancestor language would have been spoken approximately 60,000 to 70,000 years ago. For the sake of interest, we provide a (simplified) example of one of the more than two dozen Proto-World etymologies that have been reconstructed to date. (It must be acknowledged that the semantic correspondences among the proposed cognates are rather loose.)

- **Proto-World **mena* 'to think (about)'** Proposed cognates: Latin *men(s)* 'mind'; Basque *munak* (pl.) 'brains'; Hungarian *mon(-d)* 'say'; Telugu *manavi* 'prayer, humble request'; Shawnee *menw* 'prefer, like'; Bambara *mɛ* 'know'; Tumale *aiman* 'think'; Songhai *ma* 'understand'; Masa *min* 'wish'.

It is certainly possible that all human languages descended from a single ancestor language. It is generally agreed that all human beings are closely biologically related; indeed, recent genetic studies have proposed that all living human beings are descended from a particular woman of the species *Homo sapiens sapiens* who lived in Africa some 200,000 years ago.

Most linguists would probably agree that all human languages must have descended from a small number of languages, if not a single mother language. However, many argue that the tools that are used for reconstruction (the historical-comparative method) are not able to provide any linguistic evidence for long-range comparisons that go back more than about 8,000 or 10,000 years. There are a number of reasons for this.

First, it is argued, the pronunciation and meaning of words can change radically over even a much shorter period of time, rendering cognates completely unrecognizable. Thus, Latin *aqua* [akwa] 'water' developed into French *eau* [o] 'water' in less than 2,000 years, Proto-Indo-European (PIE) **dwo* 'two' developed into Armenian *erku* 'two' in 5,000 to 8,000 years; and Old English *hūswīf* 'housewife' radically changed its meaning, to become *hussy* 'a strumpet, or trollop' in less than 1,500 years. Of course, as noted in Section 3 above, languages also lose words altogether, which can make it all the more difficult to uncover the cognates needed to establish a genetic relationship.

Another argument against long-range comparison has to do with the complications introduced by borrowings. For instance, for many years Thai was thought to be a Sino-Tibetan language, because it contained so many Chinese loanwords. However, painstaking research has finally made it clear that Thai is not Sinitic, but that it belongs to the Daic family.

A further difficulty arises when words that appear to be cognates may have evolved independently as instances of onomatopoeia. Since onomatopoeic words (e.g., *cuckoo, vroom*) are intended to sound like real world noises, it would not be surprising to find that such words would be similar even in unrelated languages.

Another argument against long-range comparison is that certain cross-linguistic similarities among sounds may stem from the fact that all human beings have the same vocal tract configuration. Thus, the presence of universally common sounds like / p t k s i a u / in suspected cognates may be due not to a shared ancestor, but rather to the fact that these sounds have articulatory and acoustic properties that favor their frequent use.

In defense of their endeavor, supporters of long-range comparison claim that loanwords and onomatopoeic words are easily identifiable by the experienced researcher, and can thus be easily discounted. Furthermore, they note, language change need not affect all of the words of a language; some words retain a similar meaning and pronunciation for thousands of years. Thus, Old English *fisc* [fɪʃ] apparently had the same pronunciation and the same meaning as modern English *fish* [fɪʃ], despite a lapse of 1,500 years; Latin *aqua* [akwa] 'water' did not change its meaning or pronunciation in Italian *acqua* [akwa] (2,000 years); PIE **dwo* changed very little in pronunciation in Latin *duo* (about 6,000 years); and PIE **nepōt* 'nephew, grandson' had a meaning and pronunciation almost identical to those of its descendant *nepot* 'nephew, grandson' in modern Rumanian (about 8,000 years).

Supporters of long-range comparison claim that both anthropological and biological evidence show the relationship of all human beings and that it is therefore plausible to believe that all human languages must be related as well. It only remains, they claim, for linguists to determine the degree of relationship between individual families.

This controversy is far from resolved, and it is fair to say that most linguists remain very skeptical about the evidence and conclusions associated with comparative research involving a time depth greater than 10,000 years. Nonetheless, the debate has presented new and intriguing possibilities in the study of linguistic classification.

Summing up

The focus of this chapter is on the criteria that linguists use to classify languages, and on the enormous variety of languages found throughout the world. Linguists sometimes attempt to classify languages solely in terms of their structural similarities and differences (that is, in terms of their **linguistic typology**). Analysis of cross-linguistic data has identified a number of linguistic **universals**, indicating the most common characteristics of human language. The other major type of classificatory work in linguistics is concerned with **genetic relationships**—establishing language families whose members are descended from a common ancestor. While research in this area is hampered both by the large number of languages involved and the scarcity of the available data, a sizable portion of the world's several thousand languages have been placed in families. Finally, we present the controversial work recently done on linguistic **phyla** or **macrofamilies**. Research in these areas can shed light on the nature of language change, as well as the movement of peoples throughout the world.

Key terms

absolute universals
agglutinating (languages)
Amerindian (languages)
analytic (languages)
areal classification
dialect
fixed stress
free stress
fusional (languages)
genetic classification
genetically related (languages)
(grammatical) hierarchies
implicational universals
Indo-European family
inflectional languages
isolating (languages)
linguistic typology
linguistic universals
macrofamilies
marked (traits)
markedness theory
mixed types (of languages)
mutual intelligibility
phyla
polysynthetic (languages)
synthetic (languages)
universal tendencies

Sources

The estimate that approximately six thousand languages are spoken in the world today comes from *Ethnologue: Languages of the World*, 11th ed., edited by B. Grimes (Dallas: Summer Institute of Linguistics, 1988). The suggestion that only three hundred of these languages have a secure future is due to K. Hale, professor of linguistics at MIT, cited in *Time* magazine (September 23, 1991, p. 48). For further discussion, see "Endangered Languages" by K. Hale et al., *Language* 68:1–42 (1992).

The section on linguistic typology draws on data from the books by B. Comrie and J. Greenberg cited below as Recommended Reading. Other material for this section comes from *Tone: A Linguistic Survey*, edited by V. Fromkin (New York: Academic Press, 1978); J. Hawkins' article "On Implicational and Distributional

Universals of Word Order" in *Journal of Linguistics* 16:193–235 (1980); M. Dryer's article "The Greenbergian Word Order Correlations" in *Language* 68:81–138 (1992); *Patterns of Sounds* by I. Maddieson (Cambridge, Eng.: Cambridge University Press, 1984); M. Ruhlen's book *A Guide to the Languages of the World* (Language Universals Project: Stanford University, 1976); *The World's Major Languages*, edited by B. Comrie (Oxford: Oxford University Press, 1990), and the four-volume series *Universals of Human Language*, edited by J. Greenberg (Stanford, CA: Stanford University Press, 1978).

The discussion of morphological typology draws on information presented in B. Comrie's book recommended below; examples *7)* to *10)* are from this same source (p. 87). The estimate of the relative frequency of languages in which the subject precedes the direct object is based on information in the book by W. Croft recommended below. The data on OVS and OSV languages are from "Object-Initial Languages" by D. Derbyshire and G. Pullum, *International Journal of American Linguistics* 47:192–214 (1981). The discussion of consonant systems in Section 2.4 is based on "Phonetic Universals in Consonant Systems" by B. Lindblom and I. Maddieson in *Language, Speech and Mind: Studies in Honor of Victoria Fromkin*, edited by L. Hyman and C. Li (New York: Routledge & Kegan Paul, 1988), pp. 62–78.

The section on language families is based on B. Comrie's book *The Languages of the Soviet Union* (London: Cambridge University Press, 1981); J. Greenberg's *The Languages of Africa* (Bloomington, IN: Indiana University Press, 1966); the book by M. Ruhlen cited previously, another book by Ruhlen entitled *A Guide to the World's Languages*, Vol. 1, *Classification* (Stanford, CA: Stanford University Press, 1987), and C. F. and F. M. Voegelin's *Classification and Index of the World's Languages* (cited below). The maps used to illustrate the geographic location of language families are adapted from *Problems in the Origins and Development of the English Language*, 3rd ed. by John Algeo, copyright © 1982 by Harcourt Brace & Company, reprinted by permission of the publisher.

The information on numbers of speakers of North American Native languages is drawn from "1990 Census Figures for Speakers of American Indian Languages" by George Aaron Broadwell, *International Journal of American Linguistics* 61: 145–49 (1995).

The section on language phyla is based on the book by M. Ruhlen cited below as Recommended Reading, and on *Sprung from Some Common Source*, edited by S. Lamb and E. Mitchell (Stanford, CA: Stanford University Press, 1991).

The data for questions 1 to 3 are found in *A Guide to the Languages of the World* by M. Ruhlen, cited above.

Recommended reading

Comrie, Bernard. 1989. *Language Universals and Linguistic Typology*. 2nd ed. Oxford: Blackwell.

Croft, William. 1990. *Typology and Universals*. New York: Cambridge University Press.

Greenberg, Joseph, ed. 1966. *Universals of Language*. 2nd ed. Cambridge, MA: MIT Press.

Hawkins, Peter. 1984. *Introducing Phonology*. London: Hutchinson.

Ruhlen, Merritt. 1994. *On the Origin of Languages*. Stanford, CA: Stanford University Press.

Voegelin, C. F., and F. M. Voegelin. 1977. *Classification and Index of the World's Languages*. New York: Elsevier.

QUESTIONS

1. Which tendencies and universals are manifested in the following two vowel systems? (Hint: Look at the pattern of the vowel system and at rounding.)

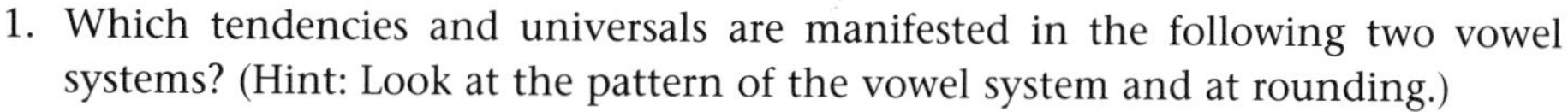

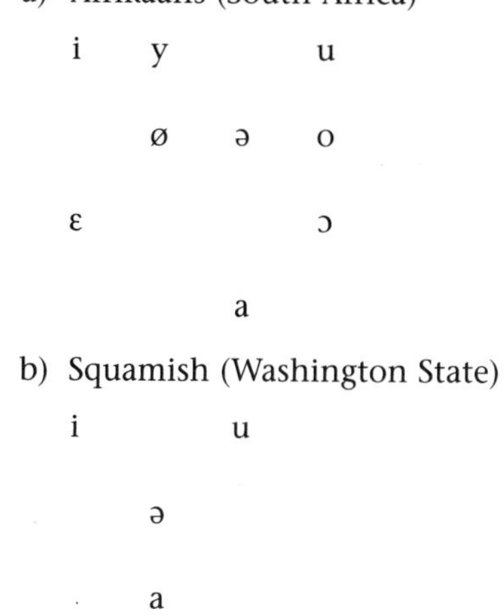

a) Afrikaans (South Africa)

b) Squamish (Washington State)

2. As noted in Section 2.1, the presence of long and nasal vowel phonemes is governed by implicational universals. In what ways do the vowel systems below comply with the implicational universals that make reference to length and nasality?

a) Maltese Arabic

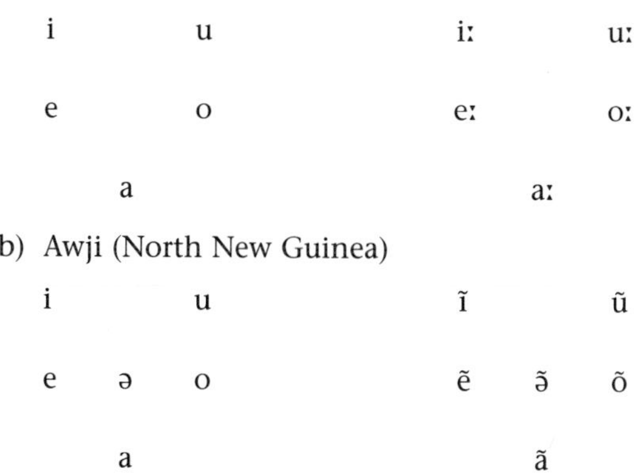

b) Awji (North New Guinea)

3. Consider the following consonant systems. Do these consonant systems comply with the implicational universals mentioned in this chapter? Explain your answer.

a) Tahitian (Tahiti)

p	t	ʔ
f		h
v	r	
m	n	

b) Palauan (Palau Islands)

	t	k	ʔ
b			
	ð		
	s		
m		ŋ	
	l, r		

c) Nengone (Loyalty Islands, South Pacific)—Stop and nasal system only

p^h	t^h	$ʈ^h$		k^h	ʔ
b	d	ɖ		g	
m	n		ɲ	ŋ	
m̥	n̥			ŋ̊	

(*Note:* [ʈ] and [ɖ] are retroflex consonants; [̥] marks a voiceless nasal; [ɲ] represents a palatal nasal.)

d) Mixe (South Mexico)

p	t		k	ʔ
	d		g	
	ts	tʃ		
	s		x	h
v			ɣ	
m	n			

4. Morphological phenomena can be classified into four types: analytic, polysynthetic, agglutinating, and fusional. Which type does each of the following

languages belong to? (recip = reciprocal; caus = causative; indic = indicative statement)

a) Swahili

ha-	tu-	ku-	wa-	pat-	an-	ish-	a
neg	1pl	pst	3pl	get	recip	caus	indic

'We didn't get them to agree with each other.'

b) Latvian

las-u	las-ām	rakst-u	rakst-ām
read-1sg/pres	read-1pl/pres	write-1sg/pres	write-1pl/pres
'I read'	'we read'	'I write'	'we write'

c) Japanese

gakusei-wa	homer-are-na- i
student-Topic	praise-pass-neg-pres

'The student is not praised.'

5. Do a morphological analysis of the following data from Latvian. Single out each morpheme and identify its meaning. After you have segmented and identified the morphemes, describe how the data reflect the implicational universals in Section 2.2 (j=[j]).
   a) lidotājs — 'aviator (nominative)'
   b) lidotāju — 'aviator (accusative)'
   c) lidotājam — 'to the aviator (dative)'
   d) lidot — 'to fly'
   e) rakstītājs — 'writer (nominative)'
   f) rakstītāja — 'writer's (genitive)'
   g) rakstīt — 'to write'

6. Note the following data from Malagasy, an Austronesian language spoken on the island of Madagascar. Does Malagasy comply with the word order tendencies mentioned earlier in Section 2.3?
   a) amin' ny restauranta
      'to the restaurant'
   b) Enti' ny labiera ny mpiasa.
      brings the beer the waiter
      'The waiter brings the beer.'

7. To which families do the following languages belong?

a) Gujarati	j) Yuma
b) Hakka	k) Korean
c) Lapp	l) Kabardian
d) Uzbek	m) Koasati
e) Sandawe	n) Aramaic
f) Huastecan	o) Flathead
g) Faroese	p) Telugu
h) Twi	q) Javanese
i) Santali	r) Navajo

8. Make a list of up to fifteen languages spoken by friends and acquaintances and identify the language family to which each belongs.

ten

PSYCHOLINGUISTICS: THE STUDY OF LANGUAGE PROCESSING

Gary Libben

He is the very pineapple of politeness.

– "Mrs. Malaprop," SHERIDAN, *The Rivals* (1775)

We engage in language processing every day of our lives. This processing takes place when we watch television, listen to the radio, read a passing billboard, write a letter, or have a conversation. Usually these language activities are carried out with great ease and in a completely subconscious manner. We might sometimes be aware that we are searching for a word, composing a sentence, or straining to understand someone else, but we are never aware of the actual mechanisms and operations involved in producing and understanding language.

Psycholinguistics is the study of exactly these language processing mechanisms. Psycholinguists study how word, sentence, and discourse meaning is represented and computed in the mind. They study how complex words and sentences are composed in speech and how they are broken down into their constituent parts during listening and reading. In short, psycholinguists seek to understand *how language is done.*

This chapter introduces the field of psycholinguistics by first discussing some methods used by psycholinguists to probe language representation and processing in the mind. This is followed by a summary of recent research on language processing in the domains of phonetics, phonology, morphology, and syntax. Finally, we will discuss how these various aspects of linguistic processing work together to make the everyday acts of speaking, listening, and reading appear so simple and effortless.

1 METHODS OF PSYCHOLINGUISTIC RESEARCH

As was noted, language users are unaware of the details of language processing. Just paying attention to what they are doing will not provide reliable insights into how they access words or build sentences. Perhaps the reason for this is that, in normal use, language processing must occur very quickly. By shielding mental linguistic operations from the conscious mind, it is possible that the language processing system is maximizing its ability to operate with speed and efficiency.

In order to get a sense for the extent to which language processing is subconscious, you might try the following exercise: Give a friend a page of text to read silently and sit opposite him or her. Carefully observe your friend's eyes as they move across the text. You will notice that the eyes do not move smoothly from left to right but rather proceed in a series of jerks called **saccades**. Like most of us, your friend probably has the subjective impression that his or her eyes are moving very evenly across the page. But that subjective impression is incorrect. As humans, it seems that we are simply not constructed to be able to monitor many of our automatic activities, including language processing.

A substantial additional challenge for the psycholinguistic researcher is presented by the fact that most language processing does not involve observable physical events such as eye movement, but rather involves mental events that cannot be observed directly. Research therefore requires that language processing events in the mind be inferred from observable behavior. Consequently, a large part of psycholinguistic research is concerned with the development of new (and often very clever) techniques to uncover how language processing is accomplished. Some of these techniques are presented in the following sections.

1.1 Slips of the Tongue

Some of the earliest and most influential studies of language processing examined the spontaneous slips of the tongue produced during speech. **Spoonerisms** are slips of the tongue named after the Reverend William A. Spooner who was head of New College Oxford between 1903 and 1924. Reverend Spooner was famous for producing a great many, often humorous, speech errors. Some of his more well-known mistakes are provided below.

1) What he intended: "You have missed all my history lectures".
What he said: "You have hissed all my mystery lectures".

2) What he intended: "Noble sons of toil".
What he said: "Noble tons of soil".

3) What he intended: "You have wasted the whole term".
What he said: "You have tasted the whole worm".

4) What he intended: "The dear old Queen".
What he said: "The queer old dean".

Beginning in the 1960s, Victoria Fromkin began to study these and other naturally occurring slips of the tongue and noted that they can be very revealing of the manner in which sentences are created in speech. For example, as can be seen in the preceding examples, the characteristic pattern in Reverend Spooner's errors is a tendency to exchange the initial consonants of words in the utterance. When this creates new words (as opposed to nonwords as in "fire and brimstone → bire and frimstone"), the result is often humorous. But here's the important psycholinguistic point: In order for these exchanges to occur, there must be considerable preplanning before an utterance is actually produced. Otherwise, how would it be possible in example *1)* for the first segment of the sixth word 'history' to be transported backwards so that it becomes the first segment of the third word (missed → hissed)?

Another important observation that Fromkin made was that speech errors also often involve 'mixing and matching' morphemes within words. Consider the following slips of the tongue:

5) Intended: "rules of word formation".
Produced: "words of rule formation".
6) Intended: "I'd forgotten about that".
Produced: "I'd forgot aboutten that".
7) Intended: "easily enough".
Produced: "easy enoughly".

All these errors involve morphemes being exchanged within an utterance. As is the case for sound exchange errors, these slips of the tongue provide evidence that a sentence must be planned out before speech begins. They also provide evidence that the morpheme, rather than the word, is the fundamental building block of English sentence production. Note how in example *5)*, although the nouns *rule* and *word* are exchanged in the sentence, the inflectional suffix *-s* remains in its original position. In examples *6)* and *7)*, it is the suffixes that move while the stems remain in their original positions. These examples all suggest that morphological components of words can function independently during sentence production (and of course also in sentence *mis-production*).

As can be seen from these examples, slips of the tongue can offer fascinating insights into the mechanisms involved in language production and the role that linguistic units such as phonemes and morphemes play in that production. But because slips of the tongue are naturally occurring events, the researcher has no control over when and where they will happen and must simply wait for them. In this way, the analysis of slips of the tongue is a **field technique** and differs from the **experimental paradigms** discussed in the following sections. In these experimental paradigms the researcher takes an active role in controlling the circumstances under which language is processed, the stimuli to which the experimental subjects are exposed, and the ways in which subjects may respond to these stimuli.

1.2 Experimental methods: Words in the mind

One of the most intense areas of psycholinguistic research has been the investigation of how words are organized in the mind. We are all in possession of a vocabulary that forms the backbone of our ability to communicate in a language. In many ways, this vocabulary must be used just as a normal dictionary is used. It is consulted to determine what words mean, how they are spelled, and what they sound like. But the dictionary in our minds—our mental lexicon—must also be substantially different from a desktop dictionary. It must be much more flexible, accommodating with ease the new words that we learn. It must be organized so that words can be looked up extremely quickly—word recognition takes less that one-third of a second and the average adult reads at a rate of about 250 words per minute. It must allow access to entries in terms of a wide variety of characteristics. The 'tip-of-the-tongue' phenomenon, in which we are temporarily unable to access a word, is particularly revealing of how flexible access to the mental lexicon can be. We have all experienced episodes in which we eventually retrieve words on the basis of their meaning, sound, spelling, first letter, or even what they rhyme with.

Many psycholinguists conceive of the mental lexicon as a collection of individual units as in Figure 10.1. In this figure, the lexicon is shown as a space in which entries of different types are stored and linked together. The main questions that are asked about the mental lexicon are: (1) How are entries linked? (2) How are entries accessed? (3) What information is contained in an entry?

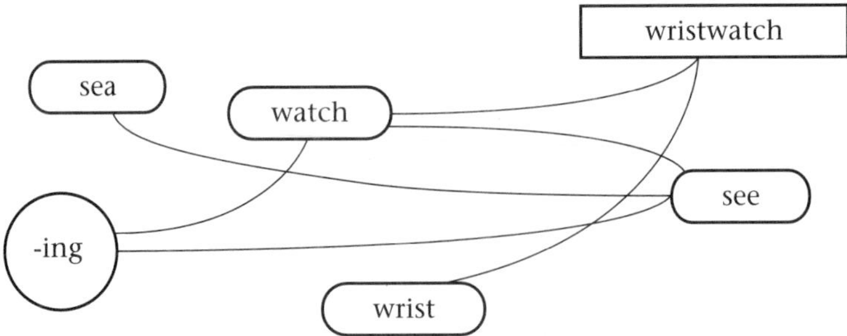

Figure 10.1 Units in the mental lexicon

Although these questions are simple and straightforward, there is no way to answer them directly because the human mental lexicon cannot be observed. So the psycholinguist must use experimental methods that are indirect to understand how words are organized, accessed, and represented in the mind. We will briefly discuss the two most common of these methods—**lexical decision** and **priming**.

Lexical decision

In the lexical decision paradigm, the experimental subject (in this example, a native speaker of English) is seated in front of a computer screen. A word appears in the middle of the screen and the subject must judge as quickly as possible whether or not the word is a real English word by pressing a button labelled yes or a button labelled no (see Figure 10.2).

This task is very easy for subjects to carry out. They typically see and judge hundreds of words in a single fifteen-minute lexical decision experiment. In most lexical decision experiments there are two **dependent variables**, that is, things that are being measured: the time that it takes for a subject to respond (**response latency**) and whether or not the subject's judgment is correct (**response accuracy**). A response is judged as correct if a subject responds yes to a real word such as *glove* or *sadness* and no to a nonword such as *blove* or *sadding*.

Lexical decision experiments usually involve comparing a subject's performance on one set of stimuli (e.g., nouns) to his or her performance on another set of stimuli (e.g., verbs). The key to the importance of the experimental paradigm is that in order for a subject to respond no to a stimulus such as *blove* or yes to a real word such as *glove*, the subject's **mental lexicon** must be accessed. The lexical decision task can therefore be used to measure the speed and accuracy with which words in

Figure 10.2 A lexical decision experiment

the mental lexicon are accessed. It has been found in many experiments, for example, that subjects take about half a second (500 milliseconds) to press the yes button for frequently used words such as *free*, but almost three-quarters of a second to press the yes button for less common words such as *fret*. This finding has been called the **frequency effect**. Assuming that longer response times reflect processing that is more difficult or complex, this finding suggests that our mental dictionaries are organized so that words we typically need more often (the frequent words) are more easily and quickly available to us.

Another way in which the lexical decision task can be used to explore language representation and processing is to investigate the speed and accuracy with which subjects press the no button for different types of stimuli. It has been found, for example, that pronounceable nonwords, such as *plib*, show slower no response times than unpronounceable nonwords, such as *nlib*. Thus subjects' lexical decisions seem to take into account the phonotactic constraints of the language. It has also been found that nonwords that sound like real words (e.g., *blud, phocks*) take longer to reject than stimuli that are nonwords both visually and phonologically. Again this tells us that aspects of phonology are automatically activated during word reading (although in the lexical decision task, the subject never has to pronounce the word).

The priming paradigm

The priming paradigm very often involves the lexical decision task and can be considered an extension of it. Recall that in lexical decision tasks different categories of stimuli (e.g., concrete versus abstract words) are compared in terms of subjects' response latency and accuracy. Priming experiments typically involve the same procedure as the lexical decision task except that the word to be judged (now called the **target**) is preceded by another stimulus (called the **prime**). What is measured is the extent to which the prime influences the subject's lexical decision performance on the target stimulus.

The priming paradigm is an excellent technique for probing how words are related in the mind. One of the first experiments using this paradigm showed that response time is faster when a target is preceded by a semantically related prime (e.g., *cat-dog)* as compared to when it is preceded by an unrelated prime (e.g., *cat-pen*). Results of this sort lead us to the view that words are related in the mind in terms of networks. On the basis of evidence from these priming experiments, psycholinguists reason that when a word such as *cat* is seen, its image is activated in the mind and that activation spreads to other words in the lexical network that are semantically related (e.g., *dog*). Now, because the mental representation for *dog* has already been activated through the prime, it is in a sense 'warmed up' so that when the subject later sees it on the screen as the target, response time is faster than it otherwise would have been. This is called the **priming effect**.

In recent years, the priming paradigm has been used to explore many aspects of the representation of words in the mind, and researchers have explored many types of priming in addition to the semantic priming above. For example, priming effects have been found for orthographically related words (e.g., *couch, touch*) and phonologically related words (e.g., *light, bite*); they are also found between word roots and complex forms (e.g., *legal, illegality*). This last finding suggests that words are represented in the mind in terms of their constituent morphemes. This will be discussed further in Section 2.2.

1.3 Experimental methods: sentence processing

The lexical decision and priming paradigms offer interesting insights into how words are processed, but are of limited use in exploring the processing of sentences. The main reason for this is that the types of questions asked about sentence processing tend to be different from those asked about the mental lexicon. The majority of the sentences that we hear are unique events. Therefore, sentence processing must be fundamentally a process that relies on a particular type of computation (as opposed to a particular type of storage in the case of words in the mind). It is presumed that in sentence processing (i.e., in reading or listening) a sentence is understood through the analysis of the meanings of its words and through the analysis of its syntactic structure. Psycholinguists refer to this type of subconscious automatic analysis as **parsing**. Much of the research on sentence processing is concerned with the principles and steps involved in sentence parsing, the speed of parsing, and the manner and conditions under which parsing can break down. In this section, we review two groups of experimental paradigms that have been used extensively to study sentence processing. These are timed-reading experiments and eye-movement experiments.

Timed-reading experiments

Timed-reading experiments begin with the assumption that the more difficult sentence processing is, the longer it should take. Therefore, by timing how long it takes subjects to read particular sentence types or parts of sentences, we can study the determinants of sentence-processing difficulty.

One of the more common and revealing timed-reading experimental paradigms is the *bar-pressing paradigm* in which subjects are seated in front of a computer screen and read a sentence one word at a time. The subject begins by seeing the first word of the sentence in the upper left-hand corner of the screen. When the subject presses a bar on the keyboard, the first word disappears and the second word of the sentence appears in its place. This process continues until the subject has read all the words in the sentence. The dependent variable in these experiments is the amount of time it takes subjects to press the bar after seeing a particular word (i.e., the amount of time they need to process that word in the sentence).

Bar-pressing experiments can be very revealing of the manner in which sentence processing occurs. Subjects do not show equal bar-pressing times across a sentence, but rather a pattern that reflects the syntactic structure of the sentence. An example of such a pattern is shown in Figure 10.3, which displays bar-pressing times for the sentence *The Chinese, who used to produce kites, used them in order to carry ropes across the rivers.*

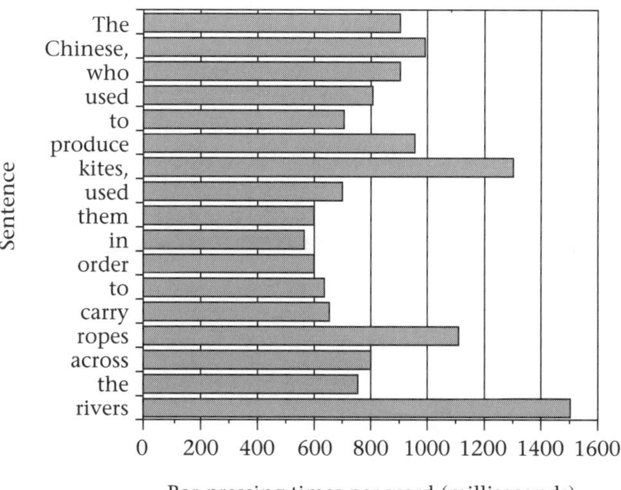

Figure 10.3 Bar-pressing times in sentence reading (adapted from Stine 1990)

As can be seen in Figure 10.3, subjects show longer bar-pressing times for processing most nouns and verbs and relatively less time for function words such as determiners, conjunctions, and prepositions. What is particularly interesting is how subjects pause at the end of clause boundaries. This increased processing time is interpreted as reflecting the extra amount of time required to integrate preceding information into a complete clause structure. Thus the greatest bar-pressing time is required for *rivers*, the final noun in the sentence, and the second greatest for *kites*, which is the last word in the embedded relative clause that modifies Chinese.

8)

$[_{CP}$ The Chinese $[_{CP}$ who used to produce *kites*] used them in order to carry ropes across the *rivers*]

Eye movements

We have already noted that sentence reading involves a series of jerky eye movements called saccades. A number of events occur during these jerky movements. When the eyes are at rest they take a 'snapshot' of two or three words. These snapshots usually last from 200 to 250 milliseconds. While the snapshot is being taken, the language-processing system calculates where to jump to next. During a jump to the next fixation location (usually about eight letters to the right), the subject is essentially blind.

The details of eye movements in sentence reading are studied with sophisticated laboratory procedures in which a subject is seated in front of a computer screen on which text is displayed. A low-intensity infra-red beam of light is bounced off the subject's eyeball and registered on a video camera. The image from the video camera is fed to a computer, which is also controlling the display of text on the screen. The computer calculates where on the screen the subject is currently fixating.

This technique has revealed that fixation times are typically longer for less frequent words, and the points of fixation are typically centred on content words such as nouns and verbs rather than on function words such as determiners and conjunctions. Difficult sentence structures create longer fixation times as well as many more regressive (backward) saccades. **Regressive saccades** are backward jumps in a sentence and are usually associated with mis-parsing or miscomprehension. On average, backward saccades make up 10 to 15 percent of the saccades in sentence reading, but syntactically complex sentences and semantically anomalous sentences (e.g., *The pizza was too hot to drink*) create many more regressive saccades. It has also been found that poor readers jump back and forth through sentences much more often than good readers do.

1.4 Brain activity: event-related potentials

Perhaps the most exciting new technique to be used in psycholinguistic research is the study of **event-related potentials (ERPs)** produced by the brain during language processing. As a research technique, the ERP paradigm has the same basic advantage as eye-movement studies. The subject simply sits in front of a computer screen and reads. This is a relatively natural language processing activity that, unlike lexical decision or bar pressing, is similar to what subjects do in normal language processing situations.

ERP experiments measure electrical activity in the brain. Electrodes are placed on a subject's scalp and recordings are made of voltage fluctuations resulting from the brain's electrical activity. The difference between ERP recordings and the more familiar EEG (electroencephalogram) recordings is that, in the EEG, all the electrical activity of the brain is recorded. This electrical activity results from a very large number of background brain activities that are always going on. The advantage of the ERP approach is that it uses a computer to calculate what part of the electrical brain activity is related to a stimulus event (in our case, words or sentences on a screen). This is done by a process of averaging. The computer records the instant at which a stimulus is presented and compares the voltage fluctuation immediately following the stimulus presentation to the random background 'noise' of the ongoing EEG. By repeating this process many times with stimuli of a particular type, random voltage fluctuations are averaged out and the electrical potentials related to that stimulus type can be extracted. The resulting waveforms are called the event-related potentials.

The ERP pattern is typically illustrated in terms of a line graph in which time is shown from left to right and voltage is shown on the vertical axis with negative values on top and positive values on the bottom. An example of an ERP graph is provided in Figure 10.4 which shows responses to the sentences in 9).

9)

a. The pizza was too hot to eat.
b. The pizza was too hot to drink.
c. The pizza was too hot to cry.

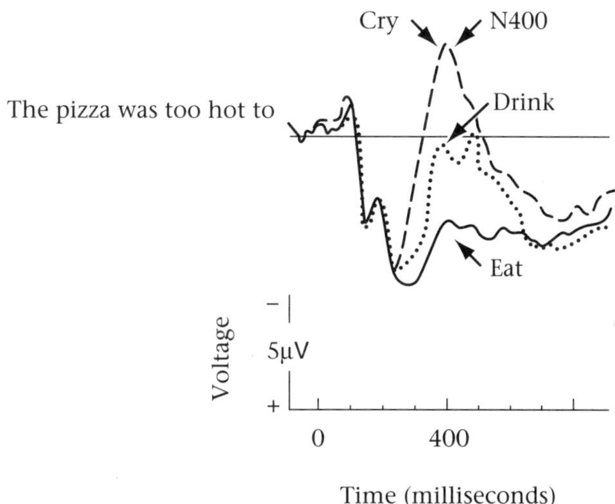

Figure 10.4 ERPs elicited by sentence-final words that are congruent, incongruent, and very incongruent with the sentence context

Figure 10.4 also displays one of the most interesting psycholinguistic findings using ERPs. It turns out that in the processing of sentences, the brain displays a characteristic ERP sign of surprise. The sentences in *9)* are arranged in order of semantic plausibility. In the first case, the last word fits in perfectly well with the sentence and would typically be expected by the reader. As can be seen in Figure 10.4, the ERP for this sentence shows a positive voltage associated with the last word. In the case of *9b)*, however, in which the last word does not make sense (people do not drink pizza), the ERP is much more negative. As is shown in the horizontal axis, this negative spike occurs 400 milliseconds after the onset of the word. For this reason this signal of semantic anomaly is called the N400 (negative spike at 400 milliseconds after stimulus presentation). Note how the N400 is even stronger in the case of sentence *9c)*, which is less congruent with the sentence context (*drink* is at least associated with food).

The N400 effect can be obtained not only at the ends of sentences but also in any sentence position. This fact suggests that sentence processing is immediate and online. When reading a sentence we do not wait until the entire string is complete, but are rather constantly building interpretations of the sentence as it unfolds. Whenever what we see or hear contradicts our expectations based on our ongoing interpretative processes, a N400 ERP spike is observed.

2 LANGUAGE PROCESSING AND LINGUISTICS

In the preceding sections we discussed some of the methods that psycholinguists use to investigate the manner in which language is processed. One of the most important results of such psycholinguistic investigations has been that many of the concepts and principles used by linguists to describe and understand the structure of language in terms of phonetics, phonology, morphology, and syntax have been found to also play an important role in the understanding of how language is produced and comprehended during activities such as speaking, listening, reading, and writing. In this section we will focus on these points of contact between theoretical linguistics and psycholinguistics. In doing so we will also highlight the correspondence between the study of language processing and the concepts discussed in Chapters 1 to 6 of this book.

2.1 PHONETICS AND PHONOLOGY

The study of phonetics and phonology reveals that the sound system of language is richly structured into many different levels of representation. Thus, as is discussed in Chapters 2 and 3, individual segments can be characterized in terms of place and manner of articulation or with respect to a hierarchy of phonological features. Sequences of sounds can be grouped into syllabic structures, and allophonic variation can be described in terms of underlying phonemes and surface allophones. How much of this structure plays a role in language processing?

The simple answer to this question is: "All of it!" The more complex answer—and, of course, also the more accurate answer—is that language processing shows evidence that features, phonemes, and syllable structure all capture some aspects of the way in which we process language, but that speech production and perception is a complex activity that involves much more than these phonetic and phonological representations.

To see why this is the case, consider what might occur when you hear the sentence *The dog bit the cat.* Because the utterance unfolds in time, you will first hear the segment /ð/ and then the segment /ə/. (In fact, you do not hear these segments separately but rather you create them out of a continuous sound stream.) As soon as these segments are identified you have already accessed the representation for the word *the* in your mental lexicon. When the next segment comes up in the sound stream, you already know that it is the beginning of a new word and you also know that this word is likely to be a noun. The phonetic analysis that follows identifies the segments /dɔg/ and the corresponding lexical entry. Now come the first segments of the word *bit.* In principle, the first two phonemes /b ɪ/ could be the first two segments of the word *built,* but you are not likely to consider this possibility because your developing interpretation of the sentence is biasing you toward the word *bit,* which is associated in your mind with *dog.*

As can be appreciated from this example, language processing involves the interplay of information that develops simultaneously at many different levels of analysis. The person hearing the sentence *The dog bit the cat* is performing phonetic analysis to isolate phonemes and word boundaries, and to relate these to representations in the mental lexicon. This inductive analysis is referred to as **bottom-up processing**. But we do not wait until we have analyzed all the phonemes in a sentence before we begin to try to understand it. Rather, we begin interpretation of a sentence spontaneously and automatically on the basis of whatever information is available to us. For this reason, by the time we get to the word *bit* in the sentence, we are not only recognizing it using bottom-up processing but we are also employing a set of expectations to guide phonetic processing and word recognition. This is called **top-down processing**. In normal language use we are always engaged in both bottom-up and top-down activities. We never process just features, or phonemes, or syllables. We process language for the purposes of understanding each other.

In Section 3, we will discuss how phonetic and phonological analysis fits into other processes involved in speaking and listening. For now, however, we will concentrate on three levels of linguistic structure that seem fundamental to phonetic and phonological representation: features, phonemes, and syllables.

Features

In both linguistics and psycholinguistics, the term *feature* is used to refer to the most basic level of representation. It is always associated with bottom-up processing in language. In the processing of sound, it refers to characteristics of individual phonemes (e.g., ± voice ± continuant, etc.). The most straightforward evidence concerning the role of such features comes from the analysis of slips of the tongue. Some examples of these slips are presented in Table 10.1.

The errors in Table 10.1 follow a pattern, but that pattern can only be understood with reference to a system of phonological features. In all three examples, the errors

Table 10.1 The role of features in speech errors

Intended	Actually produced
a) big and fat	pig and vat
b) Is Pat a girl?	Is bat a curl?
c) Cedars of Lebanon	Cedars of Lemmanon

involve a *phonological feature*. In example (a) the feature [voice] has been exchanged between the words *big* and *fat* to create the new words *pig* and *vat* (the phoneme pairs /b-p/ and /f-v/ only differ in the feature [voice]). This same pattern of the exchange of the feature [voice] can be seen in example (b) where *Pat* becomes *bat* and *girl* becomes *curl*. Finally, the error in (c) is particularly intriguing because we normally think of /b/ and /m/ as completely different phonemes. In fact, however, they are both voiced bilabial stops that only differ in terms of the feature [±nasal]. Changing the /b/ in *Lebanon* from [–nasal] to [+nasal] creates the error *Lemmanon*. These examples offer evidence that language production makes use of the individual feature components of phonemes and that the phonemes that we produce in speech may actually be put together 'on the fly' out of bundles of such features.

Phonemes

We have seen in Section 1.1 that spoonerisms show evidence of entire phonemes being misplaced during sentence planning. The phonemic unit of representation also plays a central role in psycholinguistic models of speech processing, such as the **cohort model**. This model states that, in word comprehension, words are analyzed by hearers from beginning to end. So, for example, when we hear the word *glass*, we initially consider all the words that begin with the sound [g]. When the next sound [l] is recognized, the number of possible words (the cohort) is reduced to those words that begin with [gl]. This process continues until the cohort of possible words is reduced to one—the word that is being recognized. Evidence in favor of the cohort model comes from a number of experiments in which it has been found that the beginnings of words play a more important role in word recognition than the middle or end portions. The cohort model has also been supported by experiments that found that the beginning-to-end analysis of spoken words proceeds one phoneme at a time, rather than one cluster or one syllable at a time.

Syllables

Although in the *cohort model*, the phoneme rather than the syllable seems to be the fundamental unit of auditory word recognition, there is other evidence that the syllable plays an important role in speech perception. In one study, subjects were presented with disyllabic words (e.g., *bullet*) and disyllabic nonwords (e.g., *sullet*) and were asked to press a button if a particular target unit was in the stimulus. The target units were either syllables (e.g., *let*) or segments (e.g., *t*). It was found both for words and nonwords that subjects were significantly faster at identifying syllable targets than at identifying single segment targets. It was concluded that syllable identification was faster because, in normal auditory analysis, subjects first break down stimuli into syllables and then into individual segments as the situation demands.

Another source of evidence on the role of the syllable in language processing comes from observing subjects' performance on word games. For example, subjects are given two words such as *bug* and *cat*. In this game, subjects are required to blend the words together to make a new word. Now, what sounds better: (*bug* + *cat* = *bat*) or (*bug* + *cat* = *but*)? The difference between these two possibilities is that the first one takes the onset of the first syllable and combines it with the rhyme of the second syllable. The other possibility does not split the words in a natural point of English syllable structure. As you might expect, subjects are much better at creating word blends that correspond to the syllable structure of their language and prefer such blends when presented with a choice. The fact that English speakers find such onset-rhyme divisions easier and more natural suggests that the sound of words is represented in speakers' minds in terms of their syllables and syllable constituents (e.g., Onset and Rhyme).

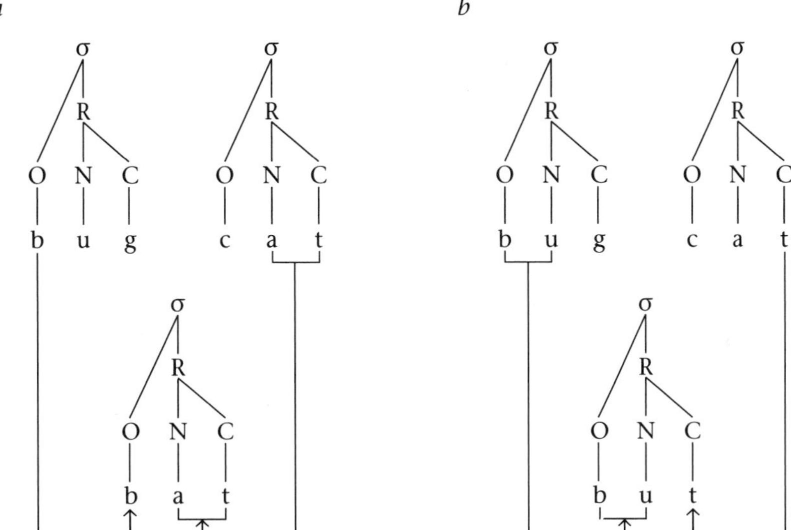

Figure 10.5 Speakers of English find the word blend in *a* easier and more natural than the word blend in *b* because the former involves breaking the words at natural syllable-structure boundaries.

2.2 Morphological processing

The linguistic study of morphology is the study of word structure. It seeks to characterize the system of categories and rules involved in word formation and interpretation. The psycholinguistic study of morphological processing seeks to understand how this word structure plays a role in language processing. In the following sections, we will summarize some psycholinguistic research that reveals how morphological structures and principles play a substantial role in the representation of words in the mind and in word recognition.

Morpheme activation

Words such as *blackboard*, *happiness*, and *watched* are made up of two morphemes. In the case of the compound *blackboard*, both these morphemes are roots. In the case of *happiness*, one morpheme is a root and the other is a derivational suffix. Finally in the case of *watched*, one morpheme is a root and the other is an inflectional affix. The first question we will address is whether the individual morphological components of words play a role in processing.

The answer to this question seems to be a straightforward yes. For most multimorphemic words, individual morphemes are automatically activated during word recognition. One source of evidence for this conclusion comes from priming experiments in which it is found that words like *happiness* will prime their constituents and vice versa in a lexical decision experiment. When a subject is exposed to a multimorphemic word such as *happiness*, the activation of that word in the mind automatically activates the lexical entry for its root *happy*, which results in its showing a faster response time as the target in a lexical decision task.

Another source of evidence for this view comes from semantic priming in lexical decision experiments involving compounds. For example, it was found that presentation of a compound such as *crowbar* will produce a priming effect for the subsequent lexical decision time for a word such as *bird*. For this priming effect to take place, the morpheme *crow* would have to be individually activated during word recognition because as a whole, the compound *crowbar* has nothing to do with birds.

Selectional restrictions

As is discussed in Chapter 4, one of the properties of English morphology is that not all affixes can attach to all stems. So, for example, the suffix *-ize* attaches to adjectives or nouns to form verbs. For this reason, English morphological constraints would not allow a word such as **understandize* because *understand* is already a verb. Now the question for psycholinguistic research is: Do these formal restrictions play a role in the way in which native speakers of English process new words? In a recent experiment in morphological processing, subjects were presented with nonsense roots (e.g., *birm*) that had prefixes and suffixes attached to them. Because they contained nonsense roots, none of these words made much sense (e.g., *re-birm-able*, *re-birm-ize*, *re-birm-ity*). Notice that as is shown in Figure 10.6, however, that *re-birm-able* and *re-birm-ize* are morphologically legal whereas *re-birm-ity* violates a morphological constraint—the prefix *re-* must attach to a verb and the suffix *-ity* must attach to an adjective. The construction is illegal because the nonsense root *birm* cannot be both an adjective and a verb at the same time. In experiments with these sorts of

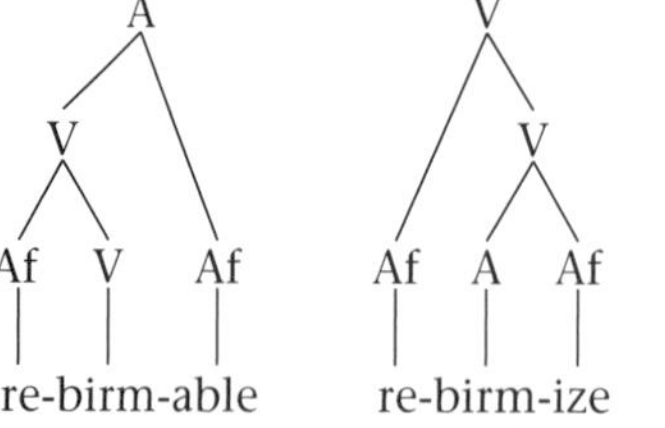

Figure 10.6 Morphologically legal and illegal affixed nonsense roots

stimuli, it was found that response times were significantly longer for the illegal nonsense words than for the morphologically legal words. These results suggest that knowledge of the selectional restrictions of affixes does indeed form part of the word-processing system.

Hierarchical structure

In Figure 10.6, trimorphemic words are represented in terms of a tree diagram in which constituent morphemes are arranged in a hierarchy. The last question we will consider in our discussion of morphological processing is whether there is evidence that the representation of multimorphemic words in the mind includes a representation of hierarchical structure.

This question has been investigated in priming experiments that use lexical decision response times as the dependent variable. These experiments compare stimuli such as *refillable*, which have a left-branching structure, to stimuli such as *unbearable*, which have a right-branching structure (see Figure 10.7). This means that for the word *refillable*, the substring *fillable* is not a morphological component of the tree structure (even though it is a real word of English). However, because the word *unbearable* is right-branching, its final two morphemes (*bear* and *-able*) make up a component of the morphological tree.

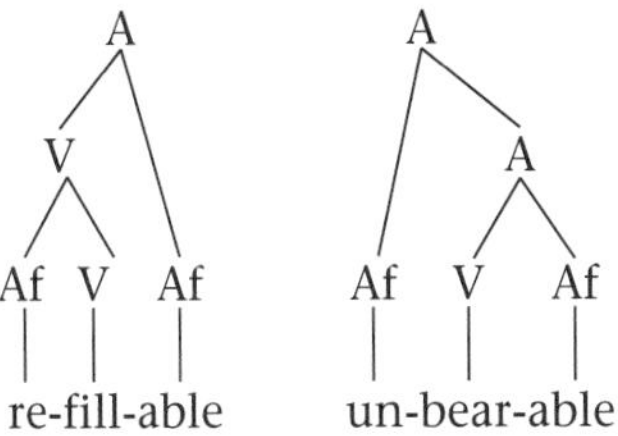

Figure 10.7 Left-branching and right-branching trimorphemic words

In the priming experiments, subjects were first shown the right substrings, such as *fillable*, and then the full trimorphemic word, such as *re-fill-able*. Priming effects were measured in terms of the lexical decision response times for the full word. It was found that those substrings that were real morphological constituents produced a significantly larger priming effect than those that were not.

Note that if hierarchical structure were not part of the representation of multimorphemic words in the mind, that is, if these words were simply strings of morphemes (e.g., *re + fill + able)*, then there should be no difference between the priming effects for right-branching versus left-branching stimuli. The fact that such priming effects were observed is evidence that our representation of complex words is organized in terms of hierarchical morphological structure.

2.3 SYNTAX

Syntax is the system of rules and categories that underlies sentence formation in human language. Sentences are unique events—virtually all of the sentences you read in this chapter are sentences that you have never encountered before. They are typically made up of familiar words, but the arrangement of those words into a syntactic structure is unique to each sentence. The question that we will consider in this section is: How are these syntactic structures created during sentence processing?

The syntax module

One very simple possibility for how sentences are processed is that production and comprehension employ the system of rules that are used by linguists to describe sentence structure. This possibility suggests that speakers would begin with deep structure representations and employ a series of transformations to derive the surface structure characteristics of a sentence. Many psycholinguistic experiments examined this possibility by testing, for example, whether sentences with many transformations take longer to process than sentences with fewer transformations. It turned out that the number of transformations in a sentence did not predict processing time. Researchers concluded that there is at least some difference between the rules that native speakers use to generate and comprehend sentences and the rules that linguists use to characterize the linguistic knowledge of native speakers.

As a result, it was necessary to postulate a special module for sentence processing and another for grammatical knowledge. The processing module is called the **syntactic parser**. This parser is understood to be the system that makes use of grammatical knowledge but also contains special procedures and principles that guide the order in which elements of a sentence are processed and the manner in which syntactic structure is built up. Because our parsing ability is based in part on our grammatical knowledge of our language, there is usually a close correspondence between sentence parsing and grammatical structure. However, because the parsing module has its own set of principles, sentences that are grammatically complex are not necessarily difficult to parse and sentences with relatively simple syntactic structure can be.

It should be noted that in discussing how processing takes place, the term **module** has a special meaning. It refers to a unit of processing that is relatively autonomous from other processing units. The idea of processing modules has been very important and controversial in many domains of human information processing. To get a sense for how processing may involve the coordination of separate modules, consider what occurs when you watch a movie. The movie director, in order to obtain a variety of effects, tries to manipulate how the audience will respond by relying on processing modularity. The director knows that when an airplane on the screen goes into a dive or when a canoe goes over the falls you, the viewer, will experience a physical sensation of falling. The director knows that you cannot stop this from happening even though you are aware that you are sitting in a chair that is not moving. Similarly, you will be frightened by the sudden appearance of a monster, even though you know that you are really in no danger. All these effects result from processing modularity. The bottom-up information that comes from processing modules cannot be turned off by the top-down information that you are seated in a stationary and safe movie theatre environment.

Psycholinguistic studies have investigated whether this same sort of modularity is present in syntactic processing—in other words, whether syntactic parsing operates in an automatic and obligatory manner that is relatively independent of the activity of other processing systems. Two sources of evidence have been very important in the exploration of the principles of modularity of sentence processing. These are **garden path sentences** and **sentence ambiguity**.

Garden path sentences

Some sentences are extraordinarily difficult to understand even though they are not very complex syntactically. These sentences are called garden path sentences because they lead the syntactic parser down the garden path to the wrong analysis. Perhaps the most famous garden path sentence is the one given in *10)*:

10)

The horse raced past the barn fell.

This sentence is perfectly grammatical, but almost impossible to understand. The reason for this is that as we read the sentence, we build up a syntactic structure in which *The horse* is the subject of the sentence and *raced past the barn* is the main VP of the sentence. When we get to the word *fell*, we are surprised because the sentence we have built up has no room for an extra VP. In the correct interpretation for the sentence, *fell* is the head of the main VP and *raced past the barn* is a clause that attaches to the NP *the horse* (see Figure 10.8; for expository convenience, *Infl* is not represented here).

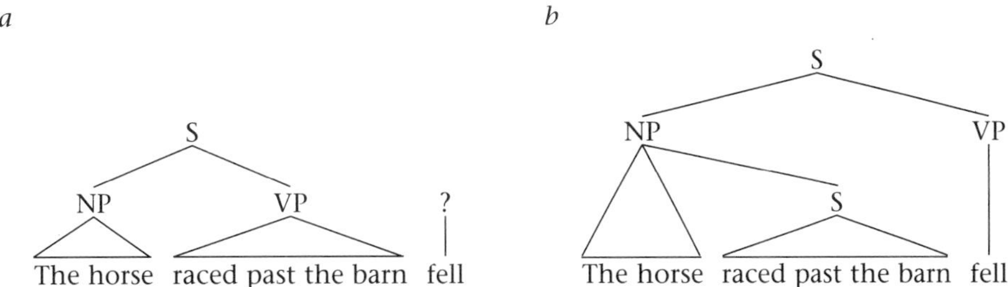

Figure 10.8 A garden path sentence. The garden path effect is shown in *a*. The correct interpretation is represented in *b*.

The ways in which native speakers misunderstand garden path sentences reveal how the parser might work. It seems that we construct syntactic representations from the beginning of the sentences to the end and that our sentence parsers are organized so that we make a number of assumptions about how a sentence will proceed. This can be seen by considering the garden path sentence in *11)*:

11)

Since Jay always walks a mile seems like a short distance to him.

This sentence is not as difficult to process as the one in *10)*, but you probably noticed yourself having to backtrack after an initial mis-analysis. Your parser is inclined to build a single VP out of the string *walks a mile*, when in fact *walk* and *a mile* belong to different clauses. This tendency has been extensively studied by psycholinguists. The backtracking that you might have noticed in your own reading shows up significantly in eye-movement studies in which it is found that subjects show more regressive saccades for these sentences as well as longer fixation times. It has been claimed that the garden path effect results from two principles of parsing. These are **minimal attachment** and **late closure**. The principle of minimal attachment states that we do not postulate new syntactic nodes (like the extra embedded S in Figure 10.8b), unless it is clear that we absolutely have to. The principle of late closure states that we prefer to attach new words to the clause currently being processed as we proceed through a sentence from beginning to end. The result of late closure is shown in Figure 10.8a) where we are inclined to continuously add words to the VP until we arrive at the last word *fell*, which cannot be integrated into the syntactic structure that is being created.

Now, there is one last point to be made concerning what garden path sentences can tell us about how people process sentences. Try reading the sentence in *11)* again. You should find that although you now know the correct analysis for the sentence, you misread it the second time just as you did the first time. This suggests that the parsing system is in fact a module that operates automatically and independently of top-down knowledge.

Sentence ambiguity

Another important clue to how syntactic processing is accomplished comes from the study of ambiguity. Consider the sentence in *12)*.

12)

They all rose.

In fact the last word in *12)* is ambiguous. The word *rose* can either be related to *stand* or related to *flower*. The sentence context, however, leads us clearly to favor the *stand* version of the word. Does the sentence context therefore inhibit activation of the other meaning of *rose?* This question was investigated in a lexical decision experiment in which the sentence in *12)* served as the prime. After seeing the sentence, subjects were presented with either the word *flower* or *stand*. The researchers found that the sentence facilitated lexical decision response times to both words; that is, both meanings for the word *rose* in the sentence were activated, even though the sentence clearly presented a bias in favor of one reading over the other.

This experimental finding is one of many that reveal a fundamental property of human language processing. We create all representations possible and then discard the ones that are either incorrect or unnecessary. This last characteristic was found in a follow-up priming experiment which was identical to the one just described except that there was a pause of several hundred milliseconds between the prime and the target. When the pause was present, the priming effect disappeared for the meaning that was unrelated to the sentence context (i.e., *flower*). This suggests that, in fact, sentence processing proceeds in two stages: In the first stage, all possible representations and structures are computed. In the second stage, one of these structures is selected and all others are abandoned. Of course, all this happens very quickly and subconsciously so that as native speakers of a language we are never aware that for a sentence such as *13)*, we compute two possible interpretations.

13)

The tuna can hit the boat.

In reading this sentence, you ended up imagining either:

a. tuna meat that is packed in a small round can; or
b. a large fish swimming toward a boat.

The point of the psycholinguistic experiments just described is this: No matter which interpretation you arrived at (a or b), you probably considered both of them, chose one, discarded the other, and forgot about the whole thing in less than a second.

3 PUTTING IT ALL TOGETHER: PSYCHOLINGUISTIC MODELING

Up to this point, our discussion of psycholinguistic research has examined characteristics of phonetic, phonological, morphological, and syntactic processing as well as the relation between the concepts used in theoretical linguistics and in psycholinguistics. It is important to note, however, that research in language processing seeks not only to discover which types of representations play a role in language processing, but also how these representations and processes fit together to make activities such as speaking, listening, reading, and writing possible.

Psycholinguistic researchers present their ideas of how *language is done* in terms of models. These models very often take the form of flow charts made up of boxes and arrows. A **psycholinguistic model** incorporates the results of experiments into a proposal of how processing takes place. It is a statement of *what happens when.*

Suppose, for example, we wished to present the finding discussed in Section 2.3 that a sentence such as *They all rose* will prime both the words *flower* and *stand.* The model might look like Figure 10.9.

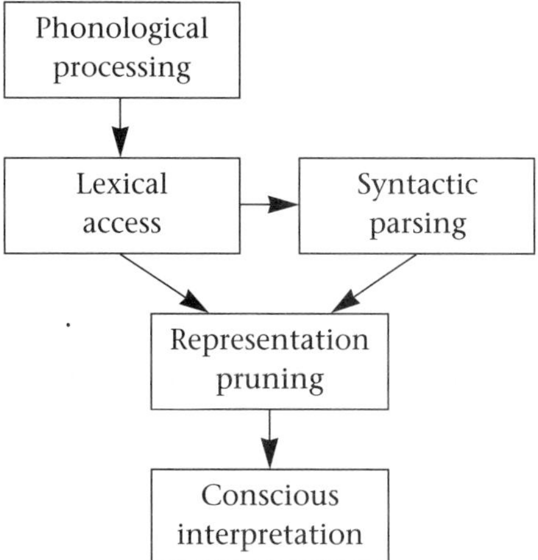

Figure 10.9 A psycholinguistic model

For our present purposes, it is not important whether this model is actually correct. The purpose of the model is simply to illustrate how psycholinguistic statements can be represented as flow chart models. The model in Figure 10.9 'says' that we first perform phonological processing. So, at this stage the input is processed into a representation such as /ðe ɑl roz/. At the lexical access stage, units of the mental lexicon corresponding to *rose* (meaning 1), *rose* (meaning 2), *they*, and *all* are activated. Information from lexical access 'feeds' the syntactic parsing module which might produce a representation such as $[_S[_{NP}$They all$][_{VP}$rose$]]$. The model also claims that information from both the lexical access module and the syntactic parsing module are fed to the representation pruning module (the module that discards extra/unneeded representations). So, this module is the one that would determine that *rose* is related to standing and not related to flower. Finally, the model states that interpretation only becomes conscious in the final stage of analysis and that information flows to conscious interpretation along a 'one-way street' (the conscious mind cannot 'peek' at how things are going).

You will note that in creating this model we have taken two kinds of shortcuts: First, we have created a novel name (e.g., representation pruning) to describe an operation that has been deduced from the results of psycholinguistic experimentation. Second, our model uses the box notation as a shorthand for a constellation of processes. Thus, it is understood that as the model becomes more elaborated, each one of the boxes in Figure 10.9 would be expanded into a flow chart of its own.

As you inspect the model in Figure 10.9 you should find that it is really very inadequate. It is missing much important detail, it seems to characterize only one aspect of sentence processing, and it avoids any mention of how meaning is accessed or how sentence interpretation actually takes place. To be a model of any real value, it would have to be much more elaborate.

Indeed, the types of psycholinguistic models that have been proposed in recent years are very elaborate. This is a good thing. We want models to be as detailed and comprehensive as possible, to take a great deal of experimentation into account and, perhaps most importantly, to show how linguistic and nonlinguistic operations work together in the processing of language.

In Figure 10.10, a real psycholinguistic model is presented. This model is a proposal about how speech is produced and is fairly complex. In principle, however, it is no different from the 'pretend' model in Figure 10.9. It contains boxes that stand for constellations of activities. These boxes are given creative names (e.g., formulator) to give an indication of the action they perform. The boxes are connected by arrows that indicate what takes place first, second, and so on. Finally, the boxes are arranged in space so as to show what activities may take place simultaneously.

The model presented in Figure 10.10 is currently the most influential model of speech production and is based on a wide array of psycholinguistic results. It states that speech production begins in the conceptualizer (in which a message is formed). The message is then given linguistic form in the formulator. This formulator contains grammatical and phonological processes and draws upon the lexicon, which includes lexical entries (such as *walk*) and the forms they can take (e.g. *walks, walking, walked*), represented in the center of the model. From the formulator, information is passed to the articulator, which actually produces the utterance.

Note that in this model, information does not flow in one direction only. Rather there is feedback so that while producing language, a speaker monitors through the

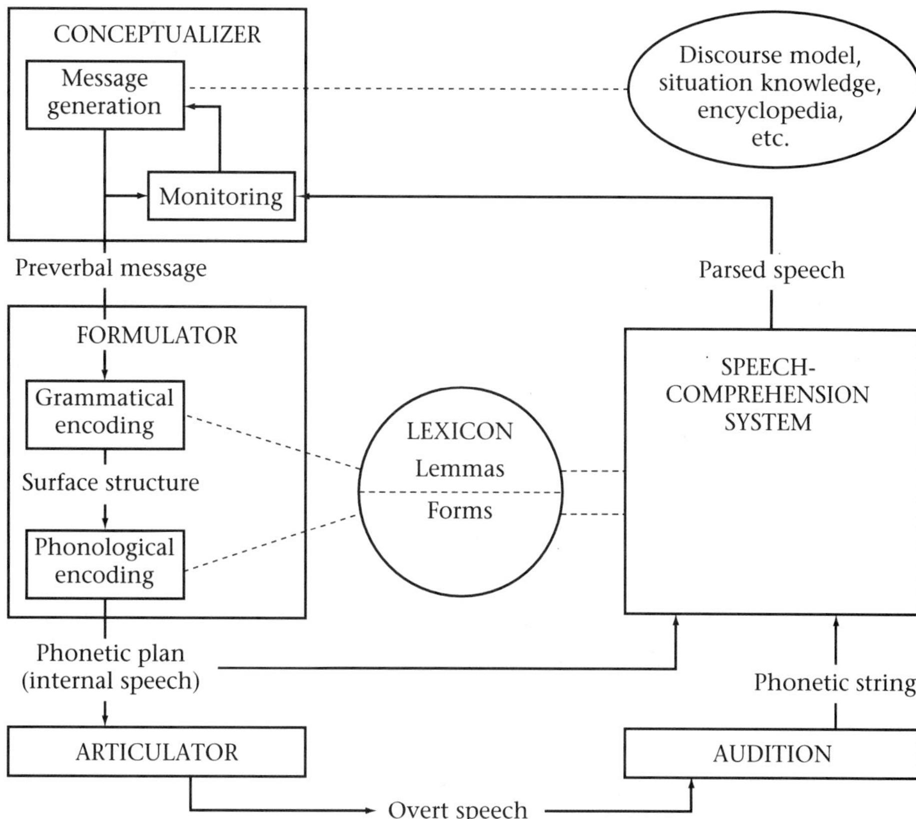

Figure 10.10 Levelt's model of speech production

comprehension system whether the utterance makes sense. This is represented as an arrow that feeds back to the conceptualizer.

Although **Levelt's model of speech production** might look quite complex, it is clear that the model, as presented in Figure 10.10, is a great simplification of what might actually occur in the mind during language processing. The more we think about the details of language processing, the more we realize that the study of *how people do language* is still in its infancy. The fundamental mystery remains: What mechanisms allow a task so complex to be accomplished with such ease? This is a question worth pondering the next time you are listening to a lecture, writing notes, and overhearing a whispered conversation close to you all at the same time.

Summing up

Psycholinguistics is the study of language processing. Psycholinguists study how people perform the functions of language comprehension and production. They seek to discover the nature of the mental representations that serve these functions and the nature of the cognitive operations and computations that are employed when we understand and produce language.

Since language processing involves computations and representations that cannot be observed and measured directly, psycholinguists have devised special experimental techniques to investigate language processing. Some of these techniques, such as **lexical decision** and **priming**, measure a subject's response time and response accuracy to linguistic stimuli. Other techniques measure eye movement while subjects are reading silently and yet others measure electrical activity in the brain during language processing.

Language processing involves many processing **modules** that are specialized for a particular language-processing task and that interact with other modules in restricted ways. Thus language processing involves a constant interplay between **bottom-up** and **top-down** processing. We process phonetic features, phonemes, and words all at the same time. We construct syllable representations, morphological representations and syntactic representations in a spontaneous and automatic manner. As conscious beings, we are aware of the results of our processing but not of the processing itself.

In general, psycholinguistic studies have revealed that many of the concepts employed in the analysis of sound structure, word structure, and sentence structure also play a role in language processing. An account of language processing, however, also requires that we postulate additional processing units such as a **parser**, as well as the nonlinguistic components of models of language processing. These language-processing models are often presented in flow chart form and seek to provide explicit accounts of how particular language tasks are accomplished.

Key terms

bottom-up processing
cohort model
dependent variables
event-related potentials (ERPs)
experimental paradigms
field technique
frequency effect
garden path sentences
late closure
Levelt's model of speech production
lexical decision
mental lexicon
minimal attachment
module
parsing
prime
priming
priming effect
psycholinguistic model
psycholinguistics
regressive saccades
response accuracy
response latency
saccades
sentence ambiguity
Spoonerisms
syntactic parser
target
top-down processing

Sources

In recent years, many new books on psycholinguistics have appeared. These include *Psycholinguistics* by Joseph Kess (Philadelphia: John Benjamins, 1992) and *Psycho-*

linguistics by Jean Berko Gleason and Nan Bernstein Ratner (Philadelphia: Harcourt Brace, 1993). Another excellent source is the 1994 *Handbook of Psycholinguisics* edited by Morton Ann Gernsbacher (New York: Academic Press, 1994).

Some of the 'slip of the tongue' material in Section 1.1 is drawn from Victoria Fromkin's chapter on speech production (pp. 272–300) in the Berko Gleason and Ratner volume cited above. Levelt's model of speech production is also taken from this chapter. Copyright © 1993 by Holt, Rinehart and Winston Inc., reproduced by permission of the publisher.

The experiment in which bar-pressing times were found to correspond to clause boundaries was originally reported by E. A. Stine in an article titled "On-Line Processing of Written Text by Younger and Older Adults" in *Psychology and Aging* 5:68–78 (1990). Copyright © (1990) by the American Psychological Association. Adapted with permission. It is discussed in Arthur Wingfield's chapter "Sentence Processing" in the Berko Gleason and Ratner text.

The discussion of eye-movement data in psycholinguistics was based on the article by K. Rayner and S. Sereno, "Eye Movements in Reading" in the *Handbook of Psycholinguistics*, edited by M. A. Gernsbacher, as well as in the book by K. Rayner and A. Pollatsek, *The Psychology of Reading* (Englewood Cliffs, NJ: Prentice-Hall, 1989).

The material on event-related potentials is discussed in an article by Marta Kutas and Cyma Van Petten in the *Handbook of Psycholinguistics* cited earlier. The syllable-processing experiment cited in the syllable section was reported in an article by J. Segui, U. Frauenfelder, and J. Mehler, "Phoneme Monitoring, Syllable Monitoring, and Lexical Access" in the *British Journal of Psychology* 72:471–77 and is discussed in R. E. Remez's article "On the Perception of Speech" in the *Handbook of Psycholinguistics*.

The word-blending studies are reported in a series of studies conducted by Rebecca Treiman, e.g., "The Structure of Spoken Syllables: Evidence from Novel Word Games," in *Cognition* 15:49–74 (1983). A cross-linguistic study using a forced-choice version of these word games is reported in G. E. Wiebe and B. L. Derwing's article, "A Forced-Choice Blending Task for Testing Intra-syllabic Break Points in English, Korean, and Taiwanese" in the *Twenty-First LACUS Forum* (Chapel Hill, NC: LACUS, 1994).

The morphological priming experiments are summarized in an article by William Marslen-Wilson, Lorraine Komisarjevsky Tyler, Rachelle Waksler, and Lianne Older, "Morphology and Meaning in the English Mental Lexicon" in *Psychological Review* 101 (1): 3–33 (1994). The experiments on selectional restrictions are reported in G. Libben's "Are Morphological Structures Computed During Word Recognition" in *Journal of Psycholinguistic Research* 22 (5): 535–44.

The section on the processing of garden path sentences is taken from Lynn Frazier's article, "Sentence Processing: A Tutorial Review" in *Attention and Performance*, Vol. 12, *The Psychology of Reading*, edited by M. Coltheart (London: Lawrence Erlbaum, 1987), pp. 559–96. These sentence types are also discussed in David Caplan's book *Language: Structure, Processing and Disorders* (Cambridge, MA: MIT Press, 1994).

The study of sentence ambiguity is reported in M. K. Tannenhaus, G. N. Carlson, and M. S. Seidenberg, "Do Listeners Compute Linguistic Representations?" in *Natural Language Parsing*, edited by D. R. Dowty, L. Karttunen, and A. M. Zwicky (Cambridge: Cambridge University Press, 1985).

RECOMMENDED READING

Berko Gleason, J., and Nan Bernstein Ratner. 1993. *Psycholinguistics*. Philadelphia: Harcourt Brace.

Gernsbacher, M. A. 1994. *Handbook of Psycholinguistics*. New York: Academic Press.

Kess, J. 1992. *Psycholinguistics*. Philadelphia: John Benjamins.

QUESTIONS

1. How do psycholinguistic investigations of language differ from theoretical linguistic investigations?

2. Consider the following slips of the tongue. What does each reveal about the process of language production?
   a) They *laked* across the *swim*.
   b) The spy was *gound* and *bagged*.
   c) I will *zee* you in the *bark*.

3. Imagine that you read that a psycholinguist has reported an experiment in which a priming effect was found for morphological roots on suffixed past tense forms in a lexical decision task.
   a) State the dependent variable in the experiment.
   b) Give an example of a prime stimulus.
   c) Give an example of a target stimulus.

4. Imagine that ERP researchers find that a positive spike is consistently observed half a second after the presentation of a particular sentence type. What do you think this new ERP spike would be called?

5. Complete the following sentences by filling in the blanks. In each case, what type of top-down processing and bottom-up processing guided your decision?
   a) The children ____ running in the park.
   b) All ___ movies I like have happy endings.
   c) He tends to see everything as ____ and white.

6. Recall that according to the cohort model a word is recognized from beginning to end, one phoneme at a time. According to the cohort model, how many phonemes of each of the following words would have to be processed before a hearer would be sure which word had been spoken?
   a) giraffe
   b) splat
   c) computerize

7. Write the garden path sentences in examples *10)* and *11)* of this chapter on separate index cards. Take a few other cards and write a normal sentence on each of them. Now, have some friends try to read aloud the sentences on the cards. What evidence, if any, do they show that the garden path sentences are more difficult to process?

8. What is a processing model? Try to describe the process of reading single words in terms of a processing model that contains specific modules.

9. In this chapter, parsing has been discussed in the context of sentence processing. The notion of parsing, however, can also be used to describe how morphologically complex words are parsed. Describe, in terms of parsing, how you think the following multimorphemic words would be processed.
   a) bookmark
   b) unredoable
   c) overbearing

10. Imagine yourself as a psycholinguist trying to devise experiments to investigate how people do language. What experiments would you make up to address the following questions? Be as specific as possible about how you would interpret the question and about what you would do to try to find an answer through a psycholinguistic experiment.
    a) Are semantically abstract words easier to process than semantically concrete ones?
    b) Are simple clauses more difficult to understand than conjoined clauses?
    c) Do people read words from beginning to end?
    d) Do people with different degrees of education process language in fundamentally different ways?
    e) Does the way you parse a sentence depend on what language you speak?

eleven

BRAIN AND LANGUAGE

Gary Libben

The goal of neurology is to understand humanity.

– WILDER PENFIELD

In this chapter we will be concerned with the branch of neuroscience that has as its goal the understanding of how language is represented and processed in the brain. This field of study is called **neurolinguistics**. Although the study of the relationship between brain and language is still in its infancy, much has already been learned about which parts of the brain are involved in various aspects of language production and comprehension. The field of neurolinguistics has also done much to deepen the way we think about the nature of linguistic competence.

The chapter provides a brief survey of brain structure and the methods that are currently available to study the brain. This is followed by a discussion of the different types of language disturbance that result from brain damage and by a discussion of how phonology, morphology, syntax, and semantics may be represented in the brain. The chapter concludes by reviewing the current answers to the important neurolinguistic question: Where is language?

1 THE HUMAN BRAIN

Contained within your skull is about 1,400 grams of pinkish-white matter. It may be the most complex 1,400 grams in the galaxy. For most of human history, however, the role of the brain as the center of mental life remained completely unknown. Even the Greek philosopher Aristotle believed that its primary function was to cool the blood.

We now know much more about the structure and functioning of the brain. But in many ways we are still quite like Aristotle, finding it hard to believe that this wrinkled mass of nerve cells could be the stuff that dreams, fears, and knowledge are made of. Nevertheless it is, and the task of brain science (or **neuroscience**) is to understand how the breadth and depth of human experience is coded in brain matter.

The brain is composed of nerve cells or **neurons** that are the basic information processing units of the nervous system. The human brain contains about 10 billion neurons that are organized into networks of almost unimaginable complexity. This complexity results from the fact that each neuron can be directly linked with up to 10 thousand other neurons. But the brain is not simply a mass of interconnected neurons. It is composed of structures that seem to play specific roles in the integrated functioning of the brain. The following sections provide a brief overview of these structures.

1.1 The cerebral cortex

The brain encompasses all the neurological structures above the spinal cord and appears to have evolved from the bottom up. The lower brain structures are shared by almost all animals. These structures are responsible for the maintenance of functions such as respiration, heart rate, and muscle coordination that are essential to the survival of all animals. As we move farther away from the spinal cord, however, we begin to find structures that have developed differently in different species. At the highest level of the brain, the **cerebral cortex**, the differences are most pronounced. Reptiles and amphibians have no cortex at all, and the progression from lower to higher mammals is marked by dramatic increases in the proportion of cortex to total amount of brain tissue. The human brain has the greatest proportion of cortex to brain mass of all animals.

In humans, the cortex is a grey wrinkled mass that sits like a cap over the rest of the brain. The wrinkled appearance results from the cortex being folded in upon itself. This folding allows a great amount of cortical matter to be compressed into the limited space provided by the human skull (in much the same way as the folding of a handkerchief allows it to fit into a jacket pocket). It has been estimated that up to 65 percent of the cortex is hidden within its folds.

It is the human cortex that accounts for our distinctness in the animal world and it is within the human cortex that the secrets of language representation and processing are to be found. The remainder of our discussion of brain structure, therefore, will focus on the features of the cerebral cortex.

1.2 The cerebral hemispheres

The most important orientation points in mapping the cortex are the folds on its surface. The folds of the cortex have two parts: sulci (pronounced /sʊlsaj/; singular: **sulcus**), which are areas where the cortex is folded in, and gyri (singular: **gyrus**), which are areas where the cortex is folded out toward the surface.

Figure 11.1 shows a human brain as seen from above, illustrating the many sulci and gyri of the cortex. A very prominent feature is the deep sulcus (in this case called a **fissure** because of its size) which extends from the front of the brain to the back. This fissure is known as the **longitudinal fissure**. It separates the left and right

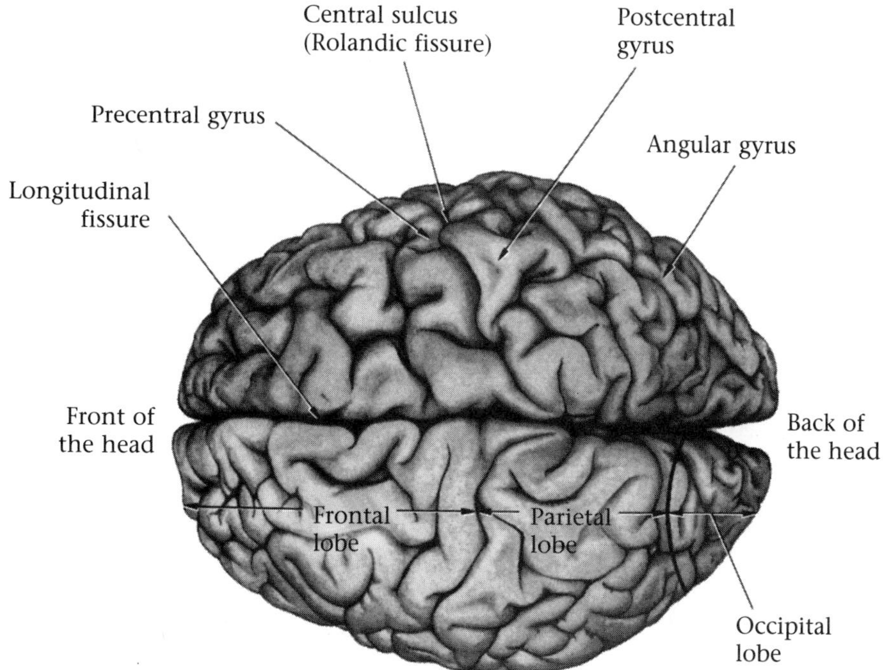

Figure 11.1 The cerebral hemispheres seen from above the head. Note the many fissures and gyri of the cortex and the prominence of the longitudinal fissure that separates the left and right hemispheres.

cerebral hemispheres. In many ways, the cerebral hemispheres can be considered to be separate brains and indeed are often referred to as the left brain and the right brain. There are two main reasons for this: the first reason is that the hemispheres are almost completely anatomically separate. The main connection between them is a bundle of nerve fibres known as the **corpus callosum**, whose primary function is to allow the two hemispheres to communicate with one another.

The other reason for considering the hemispheres to be separate brains is that they show considerable functional distinctness. In terms of muscle movement and sensation, each hemisphere is responsible for half the body—oddly enough, the opposite half. Thus the left hemisphere controls the right side of the body and the right hemisphere controls the left side of the body. These **contralateral** (contra = opposite, lateral = side) responsibilities of the cerebral hemispheres account for the fact that people who suffer damage to one hemisphere of the brain (as a result of a stroke or accident) will exhibit paralysis on the opposite side of the body.

The hemispheres also show functional distinctness with respect to higher cognitive functions. In general, the left hemisphere seems to excel in analytic tasks such as arithmetic, whereas the right hemisphere excels in tasks that require an overall appreciation of complex patterns such as the recognition of familiar faces and melodies.

Despite the fact that the hemispheres show such specialization, we should be cautioned against sweeping generalizations about left brain versus right brain abilities or strategies. In all probability, complex mental activities involve the coordinated functioning of both hemispheres. The representation of language in the brain provides a useful example of this.

Most right-handed individuals have language represented in the left cerebral hemisphere and are therefore said to be left **lateralized** for language. But not every aspect of language is represented in the left hemisphere of right-handers. Adults who have had their left cerebral hemispheres surgically removed lose most, but not all, of their linguistic competence. They typically lose the ability to speak and process complex syntactic patterns but retain some language comprehension ability. Clearly, it must be the right hemisphere that is responsible for whatever language processing ability remains.

It has also been reported that right-handed patients who suffer damage to the right cerebral hemisphere exhibit difficulty in understanding jokes and metaphors in everyday conversation. These patients are able to provide only a literal or concrete interpretation of figurative sentences such as *He was wearing a loud tie.* They frequently misunderstand people because they cannot use loudness and intonation as cues to whether a speaker is angry, excited, or merely joking. Thus the right hemisphere has a distinct role to play in normal language use.

Finally, consideration of language representation in the brains of left-handers makes matters even more complex. Contrary to what might be expected, few left-handers have a mirror image representation for language (that is, language localization in the right hemisphere). Rather, they tend to show significant language representation in both hemispheres. Thus left-handers are generally less lateralized for language.

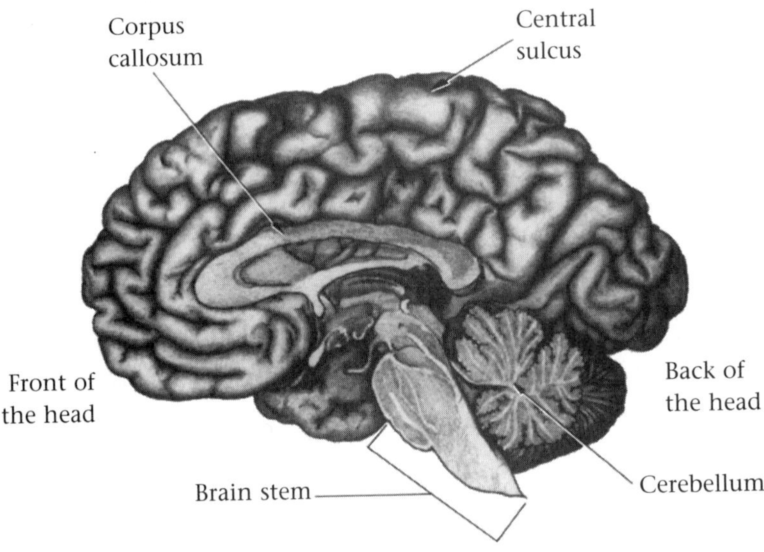

Figure 11.2 The right hemisphere seen from the inside. In this picture the corpus callosum has been cut so that one hemisphere may be separated from the other. Note how the grey cortex caps the lower structures (the brain stem and cerebellum), which are whitish in color.

To sum up, although the left and right hemispheres have different abilities and different responsibilities, complex skills such as language do not always fall neatly into one hemisphere or the other. Research into why this is the case constitutes an important part of neuroscience. This research promises to reveal much about the cerebral hemispheres and about the individual representations and processes that comprise language.

1.3 The lobes of the cortex

We have seen that the cerebral hemispheres make distinct contributions to the overall functioning of the brain. In addition, each hemisphere contains substructures that appear to have distinct responsibilities. The substructures of the cortex in each hemisphere are called **lobes**. Like the hemispheres, the lobes of the cortex can be located with reference to prominent fissures, sulci, and gyri, which are useful as orientation points in much the same way that rivers and mountain ranges are useful in finding particular locations on a map. As can be seen in Figure 11.3, the **central sulcus** (also called the fissure of Rolando) extends from the top of the cortex to another groove known as the **lateral fissure** (also called the Sylvian fissure). These two features are important in the delineation of the cerebral lobes. The **frontal lobe** lies in front of the central sulcus and the **parietal lobe** lies behind it. The **temporal lobe** is the area beneath the lateral fissure. The fourth lobe, the **occipital lobe**, is not clearly marked by an infolding of the cortex, but can be identified as the area

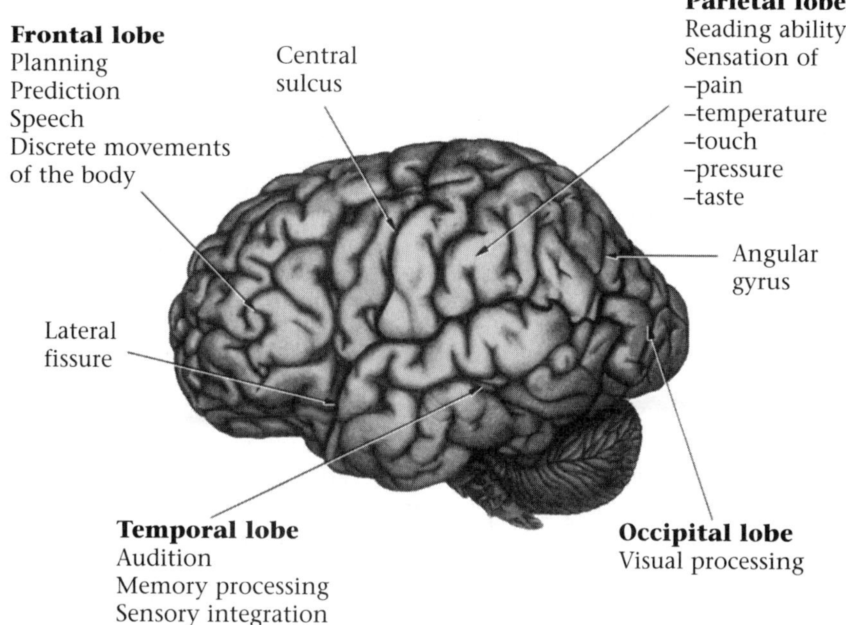

Figure 11.3 The left hemisphere seen from the outside

to the rear of the **angular gyrus** (which has been found to play an important role in reading).

Figure 11.3 shows the left hemisphere of the brain. It indicates the location of each lobe and its specialized functions. Assuming that this is the brain of a right-hander, it is also possible to identify those areas of the cortex that have a particular role to play in language processing, as we will see.

2 INVESTIGATING THE BRAIN

Imagine that you could open the top of a living human being's skull and observe the brain while the individual is engaged in activities such as reading, writing, watching a football game, or having a heated argument. What would you see? The answer is—nothing! To the outside observer, the working brain shows no evidence of its activity. This is clearly a problem for the field of neurolinguistics, which requires the use of special investigative techniques to uncover the secrets of where and how language is processed in the brain. In addition, these special techniques must meet the ethical requirements of research with human subjects. While other neuroscientists are able to do much of their research using animal subjects, this option is not available to neurolinguists.

Imposing as they may be, the problems of investigating the processing of language in the brain are not insurmountable. Recent decades have seen a number of technological advances that have greatly facilitated the investigation of the question: What is going on in the brain when people are engaged in language behavior? In the following sections, we discuss some of the techniques of neurolinguistic investigation.

2.1 AUTOPSY STUDIES

Until recently the only way to study the brain was through **autopsy studies**. This technique was most often carried out with patients who were admitted to the hospital displaying a neurological disorder. Careful observations were made of a patient's behavior, and after his or her death, the brain was examined to determine which areas were damaged. By comparing the area of brain damage and the type of disorder the patient displayed while alive, neurologists could develop theories about the role of the damaged brain parts in normal brain functioning.

A famous example of this type of analysis comes from the work of Paul Broca, a nineteenth-century French neurologist. In 1860, Broca observed a patient who had been hospitalized for over twenty years in Paris. For most of his hospitalization, the patient was almost completely unable to speak, but appeared to understand everything that was said to him. Toward the end of his life (he died at age 57) the patient also developed a paralysis of the right arm and leg. Immediately after his death (as a result of an unrelated infection) Broca examined his brain. It showed severe damage (called a **lesion**) in the lower rear area of the left frontal lobe. Broca concluded that because the patient was unable to speak, this part of the frontal lobe must normally be responsible for speech production. Since that time, many other autopsy studies have supported Broca's conclusions. This lower rear portion of the left frontal lobe is now called **Broca's area** (see Figure 11.4, which shows this and other language processing areas of the left hemisphere). As will be discussed in Section 3.1, the impairment of the ability to speak as a result of brain damage is called **Broca's aphasia**.

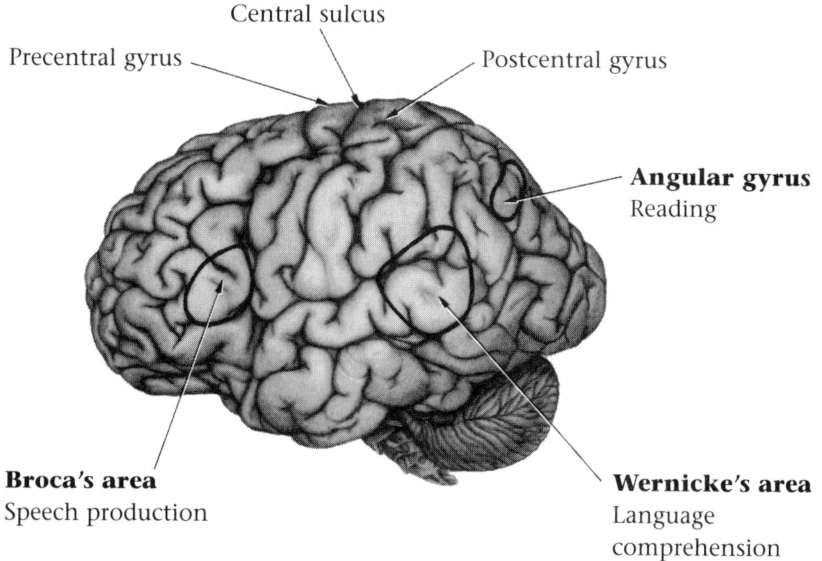

Figure 11.4 Language processes in the left hemisphere. Damage to Broca's area is usually associated with nonfluent speech and difficulty processing complex syntactic patterns. Damage to Wernicke's area is usually associated with comprehension disturbances. Damage to the area around the angular gyrus results in reading impairment.

2.2 Images of the Living Brain

Autopsy analysis has been and continues to be an important tool in the understanding of the brain. But an autopsy can only be carried out after the patient's death. Therefore, whatever information it reveals about the nature and extent of the patient's brain damage can no longer be of any use in treating the patient.

Computerized Axial Tomography (also called **CT scanning**) is a relatively new technique that uses a narrow beam of X-rays to create brain images that take the form of a series of brain slices. CT scans have offered neuroscientists their first opportunity to look inside a living brain. However, like autopsy, CT scanning provides a static image of the brain. It is most useful in identifying brain lesions and tumors.

Recently a number of new techniques have emerged that also make it possible to study the brain in action. One such technique is **Positron Emission Tomography** (also called PET). The technique capitalizes on one of the brain's many interesting properties—it is extremely hungry for glucose and oxygen.

Although the brain accounts for only about 2 percent of total body weight, it consumes about 20 percent of the oxygen the body uses while at rest. This oxygen is, of course, carried to the brain by the blood.

In the PET technique, positron emitting isotopes, which function as radioactive tracers, are injected into the arteries in combination with glucose. The rate at which the radioactive glucose is used by specific regions of the brain is recorded while the subject is engaged in various sorts of cognitive activities. These recordings are used to produce maps of areas of high brain activity associated with particular cognitive functions. Examples of such PET maps are represented in Figure 11.5.

PET studies have greatly increased our knowledge of where language processing takes place in the brain. It has been found, for example, that when subjects speak, much blood flows to the left hemisphere of the cortex and to Broca's area in particular. When subjects read, much blood flows to the occipital lobe (because it is responsible for visual processing), to the angular gyrus (which has a special role to play in reading), and to other areas of the left hemisphere. These observations support the view that the left hemisphere is primarily responsible for language and that there are specific language areas within the left hemisphere.

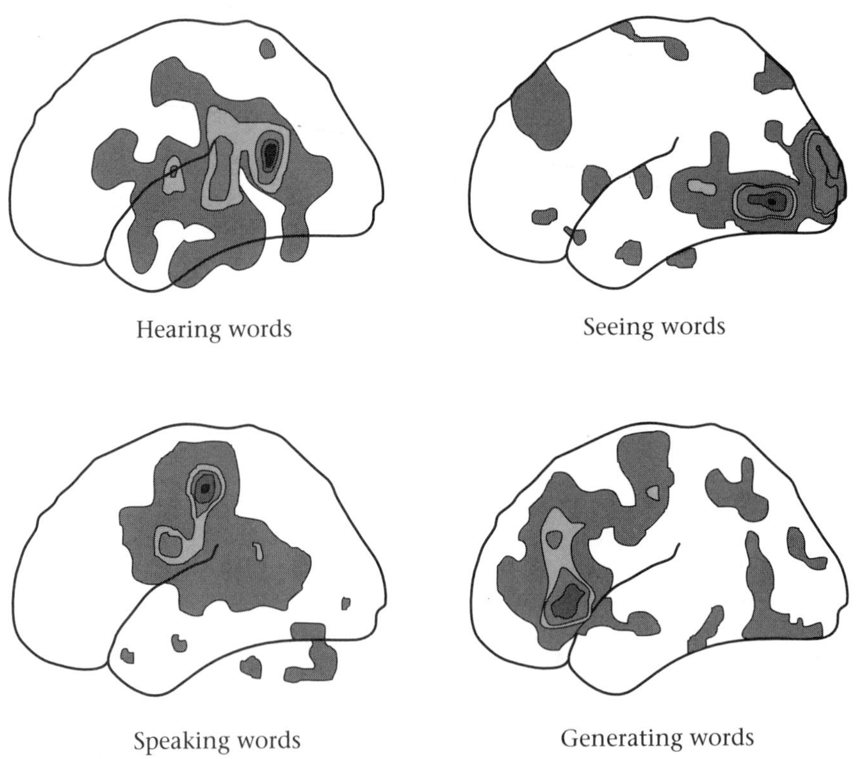

Figure 11.5 Pet scans show how blood flow to the brain shifts to different locations depending on which task is being performed.

2.3 Learning from hemispheric connections and disconnections

In the techniques that have been described, information about language representation in the brain is gained through an investigation of the brain itself. In this section, we review an alternate approach—one which examines behavior that can be associated with a particular brain hemisphere.

Dichotic listening studies

Dichotic listening studies have been extremely important in the accumulation of the knowledge we possess about the specialization of the cerebral hemispheres. The technique capitalizes on the property of the brain that we have discussed in Section 1.2—namely, that each hemisphere is primarily wired to the opposite side of the body (including the head). So, most of the input to your right ear goes to the left hemisphere of your brain. Now, if the left cerebral hemisphere is indeed specialized for language processing in right-handers, these individuals should process language better through the right ear.

If you are right-handed, you will most probably be able to verify this by observing the difference between holding a telephone receiver to your right ear and holding it to your left ear during a conversation. When the receiver is held to the right ear, it will appear that the speech is louder and clearer. This phenomenon is known as the **right ear advantage (REA)**. In the laboratory technique, stereo earphones are used and different types of stimuli are presented to each ear. In general, the right ear shows an advantage for words, numbers, and Morse code, whereas the left ear shows an advantage for the perception of melodies and environmental sounds such as bird songs.

Split brain studies

If the left hemisphere is wired to the right ear, why is it possible to understand speech presented to the left ear? There are two reasons for this. The first is that the auditory pathways to the brain are not completely crossed—there are also secondary links between each hemisphere and the ear on the same side of the body. The second is that after the right hemisphere receives information from the left ear, that information can be transferred to the left hemisphere via the corpus callosum—the bundle of fibres that connects the two hemispheres.

Evidence concerning the crucial role that the corpus callosum plays in normal brain functioning comes from the study of patients who have had this pathway surgically severed. Studies that have investigated the effects of this surgery on cognition are referred to as **split brain experiments**. They have provided dramatic illustrations of what happens when the hemispheres cannot communicate with one another.

It appears from the behavior of split brain patients that although the right hemisphere does show some language understanding, it is mute. In one of the many split brain experiments, a patient is blindfolded and an object (e.g., a key) is placed in one hand. When the key is held in the right hand, the patient can easily name it, because the right hand is connected to the left hemisphere, which can compute speech output. However, when the key is placed in the left hand, the patient cannot say what it is. The right hemisphere, which receives information from the left hand, knows what is there, but it can neither put this into words nor transfer the information across the severed corpus callosum to the left brain.

Split brain experiments have presented new and important knowledge about the functioning of the brain. In terms of overall investigative methodology, however, they are not quite as exotic as they seem. In fact, the logic of split brain experiments is identical to the logic employed by Broca in 1860. In both cases, the researcher endeavors to learn how the normal brain works by examining which functions are lost as a result of the brain damage. In the case of split brain studies, the damage is surgically induced. In the case of Broca's patient, disease caused an experiment in nature. In the following section, we return to these experiments in nature and examine what they reveal about language representation in the brain.

3 APHASIA

Occasionally, humans suffer damage to particular parts of their brains. The most common cause of such brain damage is a **stroke** (also called a **cerebrovascular accident**). A language deficit caused by damage to the brain is called **aphasia**. The study of aphasia is by far the most important tool in the investigation of language in the brain. By observing and documenting the varieties of aphasic symptoms, neurolinguists have the best chance of identifying the major components of language in the brain.

In general, the amount and type of aphasic disturbance that a patient will exhibit depends on how much the brain is damaged and where it is damaged. There are many varieties of aphasia. In the following sections, we will describe some of the more important types.

C. S. Moss was a psychologist who became aphasic subsequent to a stroke. He later wrote a book about the experience entitled *Recovering with Aphasia*. The following is an excerpt from that book:

> I recollect trying to read the headlines of the *Chicago Tribune* but they didn't make any sense to me at all. I didn't have any difficulty focusing; it was simply that the words, individually or in combination, didn't have meaning, and even more amazing, I was only a trifle bothered by that fact. . . .
>
> The second week I ran into a colleague who happened to mention that it must be very frustrating for me to be aphasic since prior to that I had been so verbally facile. [I] later found myself wondering why it was not. I think part of the explanation was relatively simple. If I had lost the ability to converse with others, I had also lost the ability to engage in self-talk. In other words, I did not have the ability to think about the future—to worry, to anticipate or perceive it—at least not with words.
>
> It took a great deal of effort to keep an abstraction in mind. For example, in talking with the speech therapist I would begin to give a definition of an abstract concern, but as I held it in mind it would sort of fade, and chances were that I would end up giving a simplified version rather than the one at the original level of conception. It was as

> though giving an abstraction required so much of my added intelligence that halfway through the definition I would run out of energy available to me and regress to a more concrete answer.

A consideration of Moss's recollections leads to some provocative questions about the relationship between language and thought. Is it possible that the ability to think about the future is dependent on language? Does language support abstract thought?

The type of aphasia that Moss reports involves a mixture of deficits—speaking, listening, reading, and writing. Some other forms of aphasia, however, are much more specific. In these more specific forms, particular skills are lost, and others remain intact. The study of the specific aphasias can tell us much about the building blocks of language in the brain. Sections 3.1 and 3.2 discuss the two most important specific aphasias.

3.1 Nonfluent aphasia

Nonfluent aphasia (also called **motor aphasia**) results from damage to parts of the brain in front of the central sulcus. Recall that an important part of the frontal lobe is concerned with motor activity and that the bottom rear portion of the frontal lobe (Broca's area) is responsible for the articulation of speech (see Figure 11.4). Not surprisingly, therefore, nonfluent patients show slow effortful speech production (hence the term *nonfluent*). The most severe form of nonfluent aphasia is **global aphasia**. In this type of aphasia, the patient is completely mute. Of the less severe forms, **Broca's aphasia** is the most important.

The speech of Broca's aphasics is very halting. Patients have great difficulty in accurately producing the sounds needed to say a word. For example, a patient who wishes to produce the sentence in *1a)* would be likely to produce the utterance in *1b)*.

1)

a. "It's hard to eat with a spoon"
b. /. . . har it . . . wɪt . . . pun/

The ellipsis dots (. . .) between the words in *1b)* indicate periods of silence in the production of the utterance. Sentences produced at this slow rate tend to also lack normal sentence intonation. This is a common characteristic of the speech of Broca's aphasics and is called **dysprosody**. Note how the patient simplifies the consonant clusters in the words *hard* and *spoon* and changes the /θ/ to /t/ in the word *with*. The speech errors that result from these sorts of phonemic errors are called **phonemic paraphasias**.

It is tempting to think that the impairment of speech production in Broca's aphasia is caused by the fact that Broca's area is adjacent to the motor strip that controls movement of the facial muscles. The problem with this hypothesis is that damage to Broca's area usually only produces mild weakness of the muscles on the opposite side of the face and no permanent damage. Yet, for some reason, even people who can still control the muscles used in speech cannot use language properly after damage to Broca's area. This suggests that Broca's area has a language-specific responsibility.

Broca's aphasia as a syntactic disorder

Returning to the utterance in *1b)*, note that the patient also omits a number of words that would normally be used in this utterance. The words that are omitted are: *it, is, to, a*—the sorts of words that we too would be likely to omit if we were writing a telegram (e.g., *I will meet you in the airport lounge → Meet you in airport lounge)*. These 'little words' are often called **function words** and their omission in the speech of Broca's aphasics has been referred to as **telegraphic speech**. (We will return in Section 5 to the problem of determining which items belong to the set of function words.)

One possible account of the speech of Broca's aphasics is that it results from an economy of effort. Speech production is very effortful for these patients so they use as few words as possible because, like telegram writers, they are 'paying' by the word. But there are other characteristics of their linguistic abilities that point to a deeper cause—the disturbance of syntactic competence.

In addition to omitting function words, Broca's aphasics tend to omit inflectional affixes such as *-ing, -ed,* and *-en* in words such as *running, chased,* and *broken*. They also show difficulty judging the grammaticality of sentences. For example, given sentences such as the ones in *2)*, Broca's aphasics will not always be able to determine which ones are grammatical and which ones are not.

2)

a. The boy ate it up.
b. *The boy ate up it.
c. *Boy ate it up.
d. The boy ate up the cake.

Finally, a close examination of the comprehension of Broca's aphasics offers further support to the view that there is a syntactic component to the disorder.

3)

a. The mouse was chased by the cat.
b. The dog was chased by the cat.
c. The cat was chased by the mouse.

Broca's aphasics tend to interpret sentences such as *3a)* correctly. In a sentence such as this, knowledge about the behavior of cats and mice helps the patient to guess correctly at the meaning of the sentence. For sentences such as *3b)*, however, in which knowledge of the world is not a reliable guide to comprehension, patients are unsure about the meaning. Finally, Broca's aphasics tend to interpret a sentence such as *3c)* as though it had the same meaning as *3a)*. When we read a sentence like *3c)*, we recognize it as describing an unlikely event, but our interpretation is driven by the syntax of the sentence, not by our knowledge of the world. Many Broca's aphasics appear not to have this ability.

These sorts of observations have led many neurolinguists to reconsider the traditional view that Broca's aphasia is simply a production deficit. The possibility that Broca's aphasia also involves some central disturbance of syntactic competence is intriguing and may lead to a deeper understanding of how syntactic knowledge is represented in the brain. We will return to this question in Section 4.

A final point about Broca's aphasia is of a less technical nature but of great importance to the understanding of the syndrome as a whole. Unlike patients such as C. S. Moss, Broca's aphasics are acutely aware of their language deficit and are typically very frustrated by it. It is as though they have complete understanding of what they should say, but to their constant dismay, find themselves unable to say it. This plight of Broca's aphasics is consistent with our understanding of the role of the frontal lobe, which is usually the site of the lesion in the syndrome. Broca's area of the frontal lobe plays an extremely important role in language; however, it does not seem to be involved in the semantic relationships between words and the relationship between units of language and units of thought. The neurological basis of these meaning relationships remains almost entirely unknown. From the analysis of nonfluent aphasia in general and Broca's aphasia in particular, however, we suspect that these semantic relationships are the responsibility of areas of the brain that lie behind the central sulcus—in the temporal and parietal lobes of the brain (see Figure 11.3). This suspicion is supported by the type of language deficits associated with damage to the temporal-parietal lobes.

3.2 Fluent aphasia

The type of aphasia that results from damage to parts of the left cortex behind the central sulcus is referred to as **fluent aphasia** (or **sensory aphasia**). This type of aphasia stands in sharp contrast to nonfluent aphasia. Fluent aphasics have no difficulty producing language, but have a great deal of difficulty selecting, organizing, and monitoring their language production.

The most important type of fluent aphasia is called **Wernicke's aphasia**. The syndrome is named after the German physiologist Carl Wernicke, who, in 1874, published a now famous report of a kind of aphasia that was almost the complete opposite of Broca's aphasia. It was determined from autopsy data that this type of aphasia was associated with a lesion in the temporal lobe just below the most posterior (rear) portion of the lateral fissure. In severe cases, the lesion could also extend upward into the lower portion of the parietal lobe. This area of the brain is now known as **Wernicke's area** (see Figure 11.4).

In contrast to Broca's aphasics, Wernicke's aphasics are generally unaware of their deficit. Their speech typically sounds very good: there are no long pauses; sentence intonation is normal; function words are used appropriately; word order is usually syntactically correct. The problem is that the patient rarely makes any sense. The following is a conversation between an examiner (E) and a Wernicke's patient (P).

4)

E: How are you today, Mrs. A?
P: Yes.
E: Have I ever tested you before?
P: No. I mean I haven't.
E: Can you tell me what your name is?
P: No, I don't I . . . right I'm right now here.

E: What is your address?
P: I cud /kʌd/ if I can help these this like you know . . . to make it.
We are seeing for him. That is my father.

The patient in this conversation produces a number of errors, but note that most of these errors are different in kind from the errors of Broca's aphasia. While the patient is able to produce some well-formed structures (e.g., no, I don't), these structures appear intermittently amidst various unrelated fragments. Not only are these constructions unrelated to each other, but they are also unrelated to the examiner's questions. It appears that the patient has no understanding of the questions being asked.

This patient displays a significant but not severe form of Wernicke's aphasia. Her speech appears to result from a semi-random selection of words and short phrases. In very severe cases of this syndrome, phonemes are also randomly selected and the result is speech that has the intonational characteristics of English but actually contains very few real words of the language. This is termed **jargonaphasia**.

The type of deficit found in Wernicke's aphasia leads us to a greater understanding of the role of the temporal-parietal area of the brain known as Wernicke's area and to a deeper consideration of the nature of language comprehension. Wernicke's aphasia is primarily a comprehension deficit. But as we have seen, when comprehension breaks down, most of what we call language ability breaks down with it. Patients cannot express themselves because they cannot understand what they have just said and use that understanding in the planning of what to say next. In a very real sense, these patients have lost contact with themselves (and therefore with the rest of the world). Wernicke's patients can't have coherent trains of thought—the brain damage does not allow the elements of the train to be connected.

In summary, our discussion of fluent and nonfluent aphasia has demonstrated how normal language use is a marriage of content and form. In the case of nonfluent aphasia, form is compromised but the content of language remains relatively intact. In contrast, fluent aphasia is characterized by a rapid flow of form with little content.

4 ACQUIRED DYSLEXIA AND DYSGRAPHIA

Reading and writing involve a complex array of perceptual and motor skills. In this section we will consider impairments of reading and writing that are caused by damage to the brain. The impairment of reading ability is called **acquired dyslexia** (or acquired alexia). The impairment of writing ability is called **acquired dysgraphia** (or acquired agraphia). In both cases the term *acquired* indicates that the patient possessed normal reading and/or writing ability prior to brain damage and distinguishes the syndromes from developmental dyslexia and developmental dysgraphia, which deal with disturbances of reading and writing development in children.

4.1 Reading and writing disturbances in aphasia

Acquired dyslexia and dysgraphia typically accompany the aphasic syndromes that we considered in Section 3. Most Broca's aphasics show writing disturbances that are comparable to their speaking deficits. In other words, a patient who cannot pronounce the word *spoon* will also not be able to write it correctly. The resulting error in writing (e.g., *poon*) is called a **paragraphia**. In spontaneous writing, Broca's aphasics also tend to omit function words and inflectional affixes. Finally, while the silent reading of Broca's aphasics is very good, their reading aloud shows the same telegraphic style as their spontaneous speech. These observations reinforce the view that the deficit in Broca's aphasia is much more than a speech articulation deficit. It is a production deficit at a very deep level of language planning.

Wernicke's aphasics also show reading and writing deficits that match their deficits in speaking and listening. The writing of Wernicke's aphasics is formally very good. They typically retain good spelling and handwriting. What they write, however, like their speaking, makes little sense. Reading comprehension is also severely impaired in Wernicke's aphasia. Like C. S. Moss, patients can see the letters and words, but cannot make any sense of them. Again the conclusion to be drawn is that Wernicke's aphasia, like Broca's aphasia, is a central disturbance of language competence—the knowledge that underlies language functioning. In such cases of central language disturbance, whatever impairment the patient has in listening and speaking will be matched in reading and writing.

4.2 Acquired dyslexia as the dominant language deficit

In addition to the reading and writing deficits that accompany aphasia, there are many cases in which the disruption of reading and writing ability is the dominant symptom. This typically follows damage in and around the angular gyrus of the parietal lobe. An analysis of these types of disabilities have led to some very interesting theories about the nature of reading (at least in English).

Before we proceed to discuss two contrasting types of acquired dyslexia, it might be worthwhile to reflect on the abilities involved in the reading of words. Up to this point in the chapter you have read over five thousand words. Some of these words (such as the function words) are very familiar to you and you probably recognized them as wholes. But others, such as *angular gyrus* are words that you probably read for the first time. How then could you know how to pronounce them? Many theorists believe that readers maintain a set of spelling-to-sound rules that enables them to read new words aloud. These rules are important in the development of reading ability and in the addition of new words to our reading vocabulary.

Phonological dyslexia is a type of acquired dyslexia in which the patient seems to have lost the ability to use spelling-to-sound rules. Phonological dyslexics can only read words that they have seen before. Asked to read a word such as *blug* aloud, they either say nothing or produce a known word that is visually similar to the target (e.g., *blue* or *bug*).

Surface dyslexia is the opposite of phonological dyslexia. Surface dyslexics seem unable to recognize words as wholes. Instead they must process all words through a set of spelling-to-sound rules. This is shown by the kinds of errors they make. Surface dyslexics do not have difficulty reading words such as *bat* that are spelled regularly. They read irregularly spelled words such as *yacht*, however, by applying regular rules and thus producing /jɑʧt/. The most interesting aspect of surface dyslexics' reading ability is that they understand what they produce, not what they see. For example, a surface dyslexic would be likely to read the word *worm* as /warm/ (and not /wərm/). When asked what the word means, the patient would answer: the opposite of cold.

Data from acquired dyslexia allow researchers to build models that specify the components of normal reading ability and their relationship to each other. Clearly, this type of analysis plays a very important role in the development of our understanding of language, the mind, and the brain.

5 LINGUISTIC THEORY AND APHASIA

Looking at aphasia in terms of linguistic theory gives us a new perspective on language in the brain. Linguistic theory has been traditionally concerned with the structure of language, not with how it is used in the processes of listening, speaking, reading, and writing. In contrast, the traditional way of looking at aphasia has been in terms of what the patient can and cannot do. The involvement of theoretical linguists in the study of aphasia has caused a revolution in the field. Aphasia researchers have begun to think about the deficit in terms of the loss of knowledge representations such as semantic features, phonological rules, and perhaps syntactic tree structures. Theoretical linguists have also found that the study of aphasia offers an important area for testing theoretical distinctions such as the one between derivational suffixes and inflectional suffixes. In this section, we will look at some of the areas in which the marriage of theoretical linguistics and neurolinguistics has been most fruitful. This fruitfulness has usually meant an increase in the sophistication of the questions that are asked about aphasia. It has also meant the discovery of new and often bizarre aphasic phenomena.

5.1 Features, rules, and underlying forms

In the area of phonology, we have found that the phonemic paraphasias of Broca's aphasics usually differ from the target phoneme by only one distinctive feature—recall Section 3.1, example *1)*: 'with' → 'wɪt'—and can therefore be easily described by phonological rules. Observations such as these lead us to believe that phonological features and rules might be good tools to characterize how language is represented and produced.

In the area of morphology, the study of aphasia has offered empirical support for the theoretical distinction between inflection and derivation. As we have discussed, Broca's aphasics show a sensitivity to this distinction in their omission of affixes in speech. Inflectional affixes are commonly dropped, but derivational affixes are usually retained. Perhaps most interesting is the tendency of some aphasics to produce underlying forms of morphemes in reading and repetition. Asked to repeat the word *illegal,* for example, some aphasics will produce *inlegal,* using the underlying form of the negative prefix rather than the allomorph that should occur before a base beginning with /l/. Again, errors such as these point to the possibility that phonological processes such as nasal assimilation and the notion of underlying form are not only an elegant way to represent linguistic competence but are also relevant to the processing of language in the brain.

The study of aphasia also stands to shed light on the nature of semantic representations. Most of the work in this area has concentrated on the many subvarieties of acquired dyslexia. In a syndrome known as **deep dyslexia,** patients produce reading errors that are systematically related to the word which they are asked to read (in the sense that they share some semantic features but not others). Given the word *mother,* for example, a deep dyslexic may read *father.* This suggests that semantically associated words are mentally represented in a manner that makes them easily confused and mis-selected.

The detailed study of semantic deficits associated with brain damage has also led to some very surprising discoveries. Most aphasics and dyslexics find abstract words much more difficult to process than concrete words. But there have been reports of concrete word dyslexia in which the patient shows exactly the opposite problem (having difficulty with concrete words such as *table*). There has even been a report of a patient who shows a selective inability to read words that refer to fruits and vegetables.

5.2 Agrammatism

In Section 3.1 we observed that many theorists now believe that Broca's aphasia involves a central syntactic deficit. The syndrome that is characterized by telegraphic speech has been given the name **agrammatism**—to indicate that grammatical ability has been lost. Agrammatism is the aphasic disturbance that has been most studied by linguists. As was discussed in Section 3.1, it is characterized by the omission of function words such as *it, is, to,* and *a,* the omission of inflectional affixes, and by comprehension deficits in cases where the correct interpretation of a sentence is dependent on syntax alone.

In recent years, many linguists have become involved in the problems of characterizing the agrammatic deficit. These problems have raised both specific questions such as: What exactly is a function word? and general questions such as: Is it possible to lose syntax? The involvement of linguists has also generated cross-linguistic studies of agrammatism that provide interesting insights into the interaction between characteristics of the syndrome and characteristics of particular languages.

5.3 Function words

Intuitively, function words can be distinguished from content words such as nouns, verbs, and adjectives. In terms of formal syntax, however, they are quite heterogeneous. They include pronouns, auxiliaries, determiners, and prepositions—items that do not fall into any single syntactic category. Much of the recent work in this area by linguists has concentrated on working out what exactly the so-called function words have in common. Some researchers have suggested that they form a phonological group—they are all words that do not normally take stress. Others have pointed to the fact that function words do not normally take affixes and therefore form a morphological group. Still others have suggested that syntactic theory should be modified so that all the words that are lost in agrammatism fall under the heading *functional category* (this would involve changing the status of prepositions, which are currently treated as lexical categories—see Chapter 5).

Whatever the outcome of this debate, it is clear that neurolinguistic evidence has presented a new set of challenges to the field of formal linguistics. One of these challenges is to build bridges between normal and pathological linguistic competence by finding units of analysis that are appropriate to both.

5.4 The loss of syntactic competence

Another, much more general, challenge is to define what it means to possess syntactic competence such that we can speak of its loss. This challenge has forced researchers to address the question: What is the essence of syntactic knowledge? Is it the hierarchical arrangement of elements? Is it the representation of abstract entities such as syntactic categories and traces?

Some researchers have suggested that agrammatism involves the loss of the ability to form hierarchical representations. They claim that agrammatics interpret sentences as strings of content words and assign thematic roles to nouns (as opposed to NPs) according to a default strategy such as: The first noun is the agent. This strategy works reasonably well for simple sentences in which the first noun can be assigned the thematic role of agent and the second noun can be assigned the role of theme as in sentence *5a)*. It results in miscomprehension, however, for sentences such as *5b)* and *5c)*, where the first NP does not have the role of agent.

5)

a. The girl kissed the boy.
b. The girl was kissed.
c. It was the girl that the boy kissed.

Other researchers have argued that agrammatism does not involve the loss of syntactic competence, but rather an alteration of that competence. They have claimed that agrammatics show hierarchical arrangements of elements but can no longer represent the traces that indicate an NP's position in deep structure. As a result, they are unable to recognize that the subject NP bears the theme role since they do not realize that it is the complement of the verb in deep structure (see Section 3 of Chapter 7).

5.5 Agrammatism in other languages

Data from other languages has suggested that the original characterization of agrammatism as a syndrome in which function words and inflectional affixes are lost may not reflect the true nature of this deficit, but rather reflects the fact that such deletions are possible in English.

In English, affixes are typically attached to a base that is itself a free form. The past form of the verb *watch,* for example, is created by the addition of *-ed*; the third person singular is created by the addition of *-s*. However, not all languages work this way. In Semitic languages, such as Hebrew, the base is typically a string of three consonants, which is unpronounceable in its uninflected form. Inflections are produced by inserting vowels into this triconsonantal 'skeleton'. For example, the Hebrew root for the verb to write is /ktv/. The masculine third person present form of the verb is /kɔtɛv/ and the masculine third person past form is /katav/. If Hebrew agrammatics simply 'lose' inflectional affixes the way they do in English, they should not be able to produce any verbs. As it turns out, Hebrew agrammatics do produce verbs, but instead of dropping inflectional forms, they choose randomly among them. This sort of evidence has provided a convincing argument against the view that agrammatic language results from a simple economy of effort. Rather, it seems that it is a linguistic deficit that involves the mis-selection of linguistic forms. It is only in languages such as English, where the base is also a legal free form, that the agrammatism is characterized by affix omission.

6 WHERE IS LANGUAGE?

In this chapter we have outlined some important findings that have greatly increased our understanding of the types of language disturbances that result from damage to the brain, as well as our understanding of the association between specific areas of the brain and particular language functions. We have seen that Broca's area plays a crucial role in the articulation of speech and in the ability to create syntactic representations. Wernicke's area plays a key role in language comprehension, and the area surrounding the angular gyrus plays a special role in reading.

On the other hand, we have seen that, in an important sense, normal language use involves the integrated functioning of the entire cortex. Even right-handers who are strongly left lateralized for language show some language deficit in cases of damage to the right hemisphere. Finally, virtually all forms of aphasia are accompanied by word-finding difficulties. This observation suggests that the storage and retrieval of word forms may be diffusely represented in the brain.

There is, therefore, no simple answer to the question: Where is language? Even if there were, the task of neurolinguistics would be far from done, for the truly important question concerning language in the brain is not Where is it? but What is it? Indeed, the answer to the first question may have little to do with the answer to the second question. Consider, by analogy, the goal of understanding the American Congress: To what extent does the knowledge that Congress is to be found in Washington advance the understanding of how it works?

Ultimately, the goal of neurolinguistics is to understand, in neurological terms, what language is. The field of neurolinguistics is still a long way from being able to specify how syntax is coded in brain matter, or even how a word is represented. Nevertheless, as our discussion of agrammatism has revealed, recent work by neurolinguists has resulted in important new perspectives on the nature of language competence.

SUMMING UP

This chapter is concerned with how language is represented and processed in the human brain. **Dichotic listening** studies and **split brain** studies have shown that the left hemisphere of the brain carries most of the responsibility for language processing in right-handed individuals. Neuroscientists have also used **autopsy studies**, **computerized axial tomography**, and **cerebral blood flow studies** to determine the relationship between particular areas of the left hemisphere and specific language functions. It has been found that **Broca's area** is primarily responsible for speech production, **Wernicke's area** is primarily responsible for language comprehension, and the area surrounding the **angular gyrus** plays an important role in reading. Most of our knowledge concerning language representation in the brain comes from the study of **aphasia**—language disturbance resulting from damage to the brain. Neurolinguists, trained in both linguistics and neuroscience, carefully examine the manner in which linguistic competence is affected by brain damage. Their goal is to increase our understanding of how linguistic knowledge is coded in brain matter and how this knowledge is used in the processes of language comprehension and production.

KEY TERMS

acquired dysgraphia
acquired dyslexia
agrammatism
angular gyrus
aphasia
autopsy studies
Broca's aphasia
Broca's area
central sulcus
cerebral blood flow studies
cerebral cortex
cerebral hemispheres
cerebrovascular accident
Computerized Axial Tomography
contralateral
corpus callosum
deep dyslexia
dichotic listening
dysprosody
fissure
fluent aphasia
frontal lobe
function words
global aphasia
gyrus
jargonaphasia
lateral fissure
lateralization
lesion
lobes
longitudinal fissure
motor aphasia
neurolinguistics
neurons
neuroscience
nonfluent aphasia
occipital lobe
paragraphia
parietal lobe
phonemic paraphasias
phonological dyslexia
Positron Emission Tomography
right ear advantage
sensory aphasia
split brain experiments
stroke
sulcus
surface dyslexia
telegraphic speech
temporal lobe
Wernicke's aphasia
Wernicke's area

Sources

David Caplan's 1987 book *Neurolinguistics and Linguistic Aphasiology: An Introduction* is an excellent introduction to neurolinguistics. A more practical approach to aphasia and its treatment is to be found in the Rosenbek et al. book *Aphasia: A Clinical Approach.*

The discussion of agrammatism was drawn from the rich literature that includes M-L. Kean's edited volume *Agrammatism* (New York: Academic Press, 1985) and Yosef Grodzinsky's challenging proposals in *Theoretical Perspectives on Language Deficits* (Cambridge, MA: MIT Press, 1990). An alternative approach to Grodzinsky's is well represented in David Caplan and Nancy Hildebrandt's book *Disorders of Syntactic Comprehension* (Cambridge, MA: MIT Press, 1988).

C. S. Moss's autobiographical account of his aphasic experience is to be found in *Recovery with Aphasia* (Urbana, IL: University of Illinois Press, 1972). Another book that offers an experiential perspective on aphasic disturbance is Howard Gardner's *The Shattered Mind* (New York: Knopf, 1975).

The material on acquired dyslexia is drawn from the volumes *Deep Dyslexia and Surface Dyslexia* (see Recommended Reading), as well as Y. Zotterman's book *Dyslexia: Neuronal, Cognitive and Linguistic Aspects* (Oxford: Pergamon Press, 1982).

Figure 11.5 is adapted from Gerald D. Fischbach, "Mind and Brain," *Scientific American* (September 1992).

Recommended reading

Caplan, D. 1987. *Neurolinguistics and Linguistic Aphasiology.* New York: Cambridge University Press.

Coltheart, M., J. Patterson, and J. C. Marshall, eds. 1980. *Deep Dyslexia.* London: Routledge & Kegan Paul.

Patterson, K. E., J. C. Marshall, and M. Coltheart, eds. 1986. *Surface Dyslexia.* Hillsdale, NJ: Erlbaum.

Rosenbek, J. C., L. L. Lapointe, and R. T. Wertz. 1989. *Aphasia: A Clinical Approach.* Boston: College-Hill Press.

Segalowitz, S. 1983. *Two Sides of the Brain.* Engelwood Cliffs, NJ: Prentice-Hall.

Questions

1. What distinguishes the human brain from a nonhuman brain?

2. In what ways can the cerebral hemispheres be considered to be two separate brains?

3. What are the relative advantages and disadvantages of the various techniques used to investigate the brain? Consider ethics, cost, intrusiveness, and type of information yielded.

4. Below is an unlabelled diagram of the left hemisphere. Choose four contrasting colors and color each lobe of the cortex. Use arrows to point to the central sulcus, the lateral fissure, and the angular gyrus. Finally, use a pencil to indicate

areas of lesion that would result in Broca's aphasia, Wernicke's aphasia, and acquired dyslexia. Label these lesions.

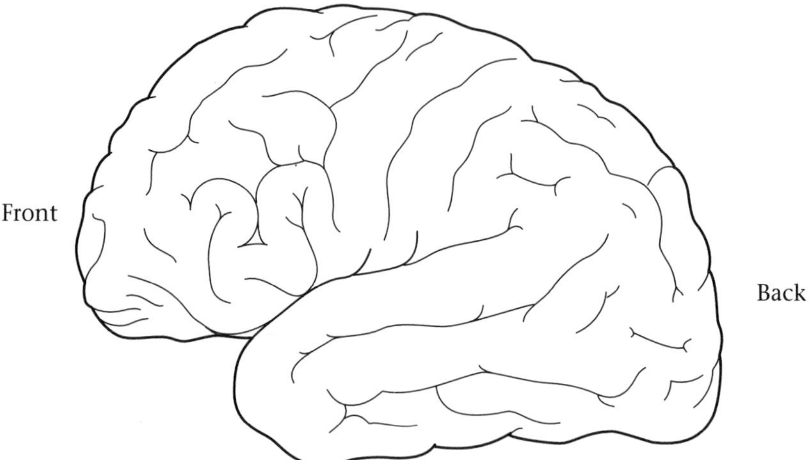

5. What do dichotic listening tests tell us about the specialization of the cerebral hemispheres? Can you think of types of stimuli that would be interesting to present dichotically?
6. Do you think it is possible to learn how the normal brain functions by studying brain-damaged patients? What can the study of aphasia tell us about normal language competence?
7. Contrast the differences in behavior between fluent and nonfluent aphasics? What could explain these differences?.
8. Describe the differences between phonological and surface dyslexia.
9. Reread the introduction to Section 3. What do you think Moss's account tells us about the relationship between language and thought?
10. Many researchers have claimed that agrammatism involves a loss of syntactic knowledge. Imagine a type of aphasia that involves a loss of phonological knowledge. How would patients with this type of aphasia behave?

twelve

LANGUAGE ACQUISITION: THE EMERGENCE OF A GRAMMAR

Sook Whan Cho
William O'Grady

Human brains are so constructed that one brain responds in much the same way to a given trigger as does another brain, all things being equal. This is why a baby can learn any language; it responds to triggers in the same way as any other baby.

– D. HOFSTADTER

One of the most intriguing phenomena studied by linguists is children's acquisition of language. So rapid and commonplace that it is taken for granted by most people, language acquisition is in fact a major intellectual achievement. In recent decades, an increasingly large amount of linguistic research has focused on the question of how children the world over are able to master the complexities of human language in the space of a few short years.

This chapter deals with some of the major findings of research into the nature of the language acquisition process. We will begin by considering the research strategies used by linguists and psychologists in the study of linguistic development. We will then describe some of the major findings concerning children's acquisition of the phonological, morphological, syntactic, and semantic systems of their language. The chapter concludes with a brief examination of the contribution of the linguistic environment to language acquisition, the relationship between the emergence of language and cognitive development, and the possible existence of inborn linguistic knowledge.

1 THE STUDY OF LANGUAGE ACQUISITION

Although we commonly refer to the phenomenon of linguistic development as 'language acquisition', the end result of this process is actually a *grammar*—the mental system that allows people to speak and understand a language. There are at least two reasons for believing that the development of linguistic skills must involve the acquisition of a grammar.

First, as noted in Chapter 1, mature language users are able to produce and understand an unlimited number of novel sentences. This can only happen if, as children, they have acquired a system of productive grammatical rules that are applicable to novel cases. Simple memorization of a fixed inventory of words and sentences would not equip the language learner to deal with previously unheard utterances—a basic requisite of normal language use.

A second indication that children acquire grammatical rules is found in their own utterances. For example, rather than simply memorizing all the regular and exceptional past tense forms for English verbs, children formulate a general rule that adds *-ed* to the verb stem. This rule sometimes produces forms such as **doed*, **leaved*, and **goed* in addition to *washed*, *walked*, and so forth. Such errors provide clear signs of children's attempts to construct grammatical rules.

Because language acquisition involves the emergence of a grammar, its study is closely tied to the type of linguistic analysis with which we have been concerned in preceding chapters. Indeed, linguists and psychologists studying language acquisition must often look to the study of phonology, syntax, and other components of the grammar for help in identifying and describing the rules and categories that children acquire during the first years of life.

1.1 Methods

A good deal of research on the acquisition of language focuses on children's early utterances, the order in which they emerge, and the kinds of errors they contain. The study of these phenomena not only contributes to a description of the language acquisition process, but also provides valuable clues about the nature of the mental mechanisms involved in linguistic development.

Investigators concerned with these problems draw on two basic methods—naturalistic observation and experimentation. Although both methods provide valuable information about the nature of the language acquisition process, they do so in different ways.

The naturalistic approach

In the **naturalistic approach**, investigators observe and record children's spontaneous verbal behavior. One type of naturalistic investigation is the so-called **diary study**, in which a researcher (often a parent) keeps daily notes on a child's linguistic progress. Alternatively, a researcher may visit individual children on a regular basis and record (or videotape) a sample of utterances (perhaps one hour every second week over a period of five months). In both cases, attention is paid to the context in which children's speech occurs, the toys they are playing with, the pictures they are looking at, and the like.

The experimental approach

In **experimental** studies, researchers typically make use of specially designed tasks to elicit linguistic activity relevant to the phenomenon that they wish to study. The child's performance is then used to test hypotheses about the type of grammatical system acquired at that point in time.

Experimental research is typically **cross-sectional** in that it investigates and compares children (or groups of children) of different ages. A typical cross-sectional study might involve conducting a single experiment with a group of two year olds, a group of four year olds, and a group of six year olds—taking each of these groups to be representative of a particular stage or 'cross-section' of the developmental process. In contrast, naturalistic studies tend to be longitudinal in that they examine language development in a particular child or group over an extended period of time (sometimes as long as several years). As the name suggests, longitudinal studies take a long time to conduct, but unlike cross-sectional studies they have the advantage of permitting researchers to observe development as an ongoing process in individual children.

Experimental studies usually employ tasks that test children's comprehension, production, and imitation skills. One widely used method for testing children's comprehension makes use of a picture selection format. For example, in order to test the interpretation of reflexive pronouns, an experimenter might show children a picture of Big Bird scratching himself as Cookie Monster looks on and a picture of Big Bird scratching Cookie Monster, and then ask which picture goes with the sentence *Big Bird is scratching himself.* A second method involves supplying children with an appropriate set of toys and then asking them to act out the meaning of a sentence—perhaps a passive structure such as *The truck was bumped by the car.* Children's responses can provide valuable clues about the type of grammatical rules being used to interpret sentences at particular stages of development.

In a typical production task, the child is shown a picture and asked to describe it. Although production tasks can be useful for assessing certain types of linguistic knowledge, there are many structures (such as passives) which are hard to elicit even from adults since they are used only in special contexts. Moreover, because children's ability to comprehend language is often more advanced than their ability to produce sentences of their own, production tasks can provide an overly conservative view of linguistic development unless they are accompanied by other types of tests.

Both comprehension and production tests are often used in conjunction with imitation tasks. Although one might think that imitation would be excessively easy, it has been found that children's ability to repeat structures reflects the state of their current grammatical knowledge and that a form that has not been mastered will probably not be correctly repeated. Thus, a child who has not yet acquired auxiliary verbs will repeat the sentence *Mommy is talking* as *Mommy talking.*

By using naturalistic observation together with experimental techniques, linguists and psychologists have made significant progress in the study of the language acquisition process. Much of this chapter is devoted to a survey of this progress, beginning with the development of speech sounds.

2 PHONOLOGICAL DEVELOPMENT

From birth, children are exposed to a variety of noises in their environment. Before they can begin to acquire language, they must first separate nonspeech noise from speech sounds. The rudiments of this ability seem to be present at birth, since newborns respond differently to human voices than to other sounds and can recognize their mother's voice within a matter of weeks.

From around one month of age, children exhibit the ability to distinguish among certain speech sounds. In one experiment, infants were presented with a series of identical [ba] syllables. These were followed by an occurrence of the syllable [pa]. A change in the children's sucking rate (the normal reaction to a new stimulus) indicated that they perceived the difference between the two syllables, and were therefore able to distinguish between [p] and [b].

Despite this early sensitivity to contrasts among speech sounds, children initially cannot distinguish between meaningful words. The emergence of this ability has been examined in a task in which children are presented with two toy animals named *bok* and *pok* and are asked to respond to sentences such as *Show me pok*. To respond correctly, children must not only hear the difference between [p] and [b] but also recognize that this difference is linguistically significant—that it is used to distinguish between words in their language. Children under eighteen months have little success in this type of task.

2.1 Babbling

Even before children master the phonemic contrasts of their language, they begin to develop the articulatory movements needed to produce these distinctions in speech. Although there is considerable variation in the pattern of phonological development, a number of general trends can be identified.

The emergence of articulatory skills begins around six months of age, with the onset of **babbling**. It is likely that babbling provides children with the opportunity to experiment with and begin to gain control over their vocal apparatus—an important prerequisite for later speech. Children who are unable to babble for medical reasons can subsequently acquire normal pronunciation, but their speech development is significantly delayed.

Despite obvious differences among the languages to which they are exposed, children from different linguistic communities exhibit significant similarities in their babbling. The tendencies in Table 12.1 are based on data from fifteen different languages, including English, Thai, Japanese, Arabic, Hindi, and Mayan. (We focus here on consonant sounds, for which the data are somewhat more reliable than for vowels.)

Such cross-linguistic similarities suggest that early babbling is at least partly independent of the particular language to which children are exposed. In fact, even deaf children babble, although their articulatory activity is somewhat less varied than that of hearing children.

Table 12.1 Cross-linguistic similarities in babbling

Frequently found consonants	*Infrequently found consonants*
p b m	f v θ ð
t d ṅ	ʃ ʒ tʃ dʒ
k g	l r ŋ
s h w j	

2.2 The developmental order

Babbling increases in frequency until the age of about twelve months, at which time children start to produce their first understandable words. Babbling may overlap with the production of real words for several weeks before dying out. By the time children have acquired fifty words or so, they begin to adopt fairly regular patterns of pronunciation.

Language acquisition researchers have expended a good deal of effort trying to determine the order in which speech sounds are mastered in production and perception. Although this work has been hindered by difficulties in determining precisely when a contrast has been acquired and by a shortage of reliable data from a sufficiently broad range of languages, some general trends seem to exist.

- As a group, vowels are generally acquired before consonants (by age three).
- Stops tend to be acquired before other consonants.
- In terms of place of articulation, labials are often acquired first followed (with some variation) by alveolars, velars, and alveopalatals. Interdentals (such as [θ] and [ð]) are acquired last.
- New phonemic contrasts manifest themselves first in word-initial position. Thus, the /p/-/b/ contrast, for instance, will be manifested in pairs such as *pat-bat* before *mop-mob*.

By age two, a typical English-speaking child might have the following inventory of consonant phonemes.

Table 12.2 Typical consonant inventory at age two

Stops	*Fricatives*	*Other*
p b m	f	w
t d n	s	
k g		

By age four, this inventory is considerably larger and typically includes the following sounds.

Table 12.3 Typical consonant inventory at age four

Stops	*Fricatives*	*Affricates*	*Other*
p b m	f v	tʃ dʒ	w j
t d n	s z		l r
k g ŋ	ʃ		

Still to be acquired at this age are the interdental fricatives [θ] and [ð] and the voiced alveopalatal fricative [ʒ].

In general, the relative order in which sounds are acquired during the language acquisition process reflects their distribution in languages of the world. The sounds that are acquired early are generally found most widely in the world's languages while the sounds that are acquired late tend to be less common across languages.

2.3 EARLY PHONETIC PROCESSES

The sound patterns found in child language are quite different from those used by adults in terms of both the segments they contain and the phonotactic combinations they allow. These differences are the product of a limited number of universal phonetic processes that replace certain sounds with others that children find easier to produce and/or perceive. In discussing examples of these processes, we will assume that children's mental representation of a word's pronunciation is close to that of an adult even though its spoken form may be quite different.

Syllable simplification

One frequent process in children's speech involves the systematic deletion of certain sounds in order to simplify syllable structure. In the following data, typical of the speech of two- and three-year-old children, consonant clusters are reduced by deleting one or more segments.

Table 12.4 Reduction of consonant clusters

[s] + stop (strategy: delete [s])
stop → [tɑp]
small → [mɑ]
desk → [dɛk]
stop + liquid (strategy: delete liquid)
try → [taj]
crumb → [gʌm]
bring → [bɪŋ]
fricative + liquid (strategy: delete liquid)
from → [fʌm]
sleep → [sijp]
nasal + voiceless stop (strategy: delete nasal)
bump → [bʌp]
tent → [dɛt]

Another common deletion process in early child language involves the elimination of final consonants. Initial consonants, in contrast, are typically retained if they precede a vowel.

1)

dog → [dɑ]
bus → [bʌ]
boot → [buw]

Both the reduction of consonant clusters and the deletion of final consonants have the effect of simplifying syllable structure, bringing it closer to the CV pattern that is universally favored by children and that is the most widely found pattern in human language in general.

Substitution

One of the most widespread phonetic processes in early language involves substitution—the systematic replacement of one sound by an alternative that the child finds easier to articulate. Common substitution processes include **stopping**, the replacement of a fricative by a corresponding stop; **fronting**, the moving forward of a sound's place of articulation; **gliding**, the replacement of a liquid by a glide; and **denasalization**, the replacement of a nasal stop by a nonnasal counterpart. These processes are illustrated with the help of English examples in Table 12.5.

Table 12.5 Substitution in early speech

Process	*Example*	*Change*
Stopping	sing → [tɪŋ]	s → t
(continuant → stop)	sea → [tij]	s → t
	zebra → [dijbrə]	z → d
	thing → [tɪŋ]	θ → t
	this → [dɪt]	ð → d, s → t
	shoes → [tuwd]	ʃ → t, z → d
Fronting	ship → [sɪp]	ʃ → s
	jump → [dzʌmp]	dʒ → dz
	chalk → [tsɔk]	tʃ → ts
	go → [dou]	g → d
Gliding	lion → [jajn]	l → j
	laughing → [jæfɪŋ]	l → j
	look → [wʊk]	l → w
	rock → [wɑk]	r → w
	story → [stowij]	r → w
Denasalization	spoon → [buwd]	n → d
	jam → [dæb]	m → b
	room → [wuwb]	m → b

Assimilation

Still another widespread phonetic process in child language is assimilation—the modification of one or more features of a segment under the influence of neighboring sounds. In the following examples, initial consonants have been voiced in anticipation of the following vowel.

2)

tell	[dɛl]
pig	[bɪg]
push	[bʌs]
soup	[zuwp]

Assimilation is also observed in children's tendency to maintain the same place of articulation for all of the consonants or vowels in a word. This can lead to the pronunciation of *doggy* as [gɑgij] (with two velar stops) or as [dɑdij] (with two alveolar stops). Other examples of this include [fɛlf] for *self* (with identical consonants) and [bibi] for *baby* (with identical vowels in both syllables).

2.4 Production versus Perception

As noted at the beginning of Section 2, children are initially unable to use phonemic contrasts to distinguish between words in their language. Do children develop the ability to perceive the phonemic contrasts of their language at the same time as they learn how to produce them, or do perceptual skills emerge first? According to one study, a young boy who could not produce a distinction in his own speech between *mouse* and *mouth, cart* and *card,* or *jug* and *duck* was nonetheless able to point to pictures of the correct objects in a comprehension task. Evidently, this child's ability to perceive the phonemic contrasts in question exceeded his ability to produce them.

Another indication that children's perceptual abilities are more advanced than their articulatory skills comes from their reaction to adult speech that fails to respect the normal phonemic contrasts. The following report describes one such incident.

> One of us, for instance, spoke to a child who called his inflated plastic fish a *fis*. In imitation of the child's pronunciation, the observer said: "This is your *fis*?" "No," said the child, "my *fis*." He continued to reject the adult's imitation until he was told, "That is your fish." "Yes," he said, "my fis."

The child's reaction to the adult's initial pronunciation of *fish* shows that he could perceive the difference between [s] and [ʃ] even though he could not yet produce it himself.

3 MORPHOLOGICAL DEVELOPMENT

As is the case with the sound pattern of language, the details of morphological structure emerge over a period of several years. Initially, the words of English-speaking children seem to lack any internal morphological structure. Affixes are entirely absent and most words consist of a single root morpheme. Gradually, inflectional and derivational morphemes appear, marking an increased capacity for word formation.

In a language such as English, which has many examples of irregular inflection (*men* as the plural of *man, ran* as the past of *run*), children often begin by simply memorizing forms on a case-by-case basis without regard for general patterns or rules. Thus, they may initially produce the correct plural form for *man* and the correct past tense for *run*. When they subsequently observe the generality of *-s* as a plural marker and *-ed* as a past tense marker around age 2;6 (two years, six months), they sometimes incorrectly use these suffixes for the irregular forms—producing words such as **mans* and **runned*. (Errors that result from the overly broad application of a rule are called **overgeneralizations** or **overregularizations**.) Even occasional mixed forms such as *felled*, a blend of *fell* and *falled*, may be used.

Recent work has shown that inflectional overgeneralization, which can last into the school years, is much less frequent than traditionally thought: Preschool chil-

Table 12.6 The development of affixes

Stage 1	case-by-case learning
Stage 2	overuse of general rule
Stage 3	mastery of exceptions to the general rule

dren seem to overregularize irregular verbs less than 25 percent of the time at any point in development. This suggests that the overgeneralization errors observed in early speech reflect lapses in accessing the appropriate irregular form from the lexicon rather than the failure to learn irregular forms per se.

3.1 A DEVELOPMENTAL SEQUENCE

An important result of child language research during the 1970s was the discovery that the development of bound morphemes and functional categories (such as determiners and auxiliaries) takes place in an orderly sequence with relatively little variation from child to child. In a pioneering study of three children between the ages of twenty and thirty-six months, the following **developmental sequence** was found to be typical.

Table 12.7 Typical developmental sequence for nonlexical morphemes

1. *-ing*
2. plural *-s*
3. possessive *-'s*
4. *the, a*
5. past tense *-ed*
6. third person singular *-s*
7. auxiliary *be*

An interesting feature of this developmental sequence is that it seems to be largely unrelated to the frequency of the different morphemes in the speech heard by children. For example, as Table 12.8 shows, the determiners *the* and *a* are the most frequent nonlexical morphemes in the children's environments even though they are acquired relatively late.

Table 12.8 Typical relative frequency of morphemes in parental speech

1. *the, a*
2. *-ing*
3. plural *-s*
4. auxiliary *be*
5. possessive *-'s*
6. third person singular *-s*
7. past tense *-ed*

This shows that frequency by itself cannot explain the relative developmental order for nonlexical morphemes, although it may have some role to play in conjunction with other factors.

Determining factors

What, then, determines the order of acquisition of nonlexical categories and bound morphemes? Research on a variety of languages suggests that several factors are involved.

1. *Frequent occurrence in utterance-final position* Children show a greater tendency to notice and remember elements that occur at the end of the utterance than those found in any other position.
2. *Syllabicity* Children seem to take greater notice of morphemes such as *-ing*, which can constitute syllables on their own, than the plural or possessive suffix, whose principal allomorphs (/s/ and /z/) are single consonants.
3. *A straightforward relation between form and meaning* Whereas the word *the* functions only as a determiner in English, the verbal suffix *-s* simultaneously represents three linguistic categories: person (third), number (singular), and tense (nonpast). This latter type of morpheme is more difficult for children to acquire.
4. *Few or no exceptions in the way it is used* Whereas all singular nouns form the possessive with *-'s*, not all verbs use *-ed* to mark the past tense (*saw, read, drove*). Such exceptions hinder the language acquisition process.
5. *Allomorphic invariance* Whereas the affix *-ing* has the same form for all verbs, the past tense ending *-ed* has three major allomorphs—/t/ for verbs such as *chase*, /d/ for forms such as *crave*, and /əd/ for verbs such as *recite*. This type of allomorphic variation, which also occurs with the plural, possessive, and third person singular affixes in English, slows morphological development.
6. *Clearly discernable semantic function* Whereas morphemes such as plural *-s* express easily identifiable meanings, some morphemes (such as the third person singular *-s*) make no obvious contribution to the meaning of the sentence. Acquisition of this latter type of morpheme is relatively slow.

The status of the English morphemes whose developmental order we have been considering is indicated in Table 12.9; as before, morphemes are listed in order of emergence. (The numbers 1–6 in the table refer to the determining factors listed above. The ± symbol in the second column indicates that the morphemes in question have both syllabic and nonsyllabic allomorphs. The plural suffix, for example, is realized as /s/ in some contexts but as /əz/ in others.)

Table 12.9 Factors affecting development

	Determining Factors					
Morphemes	*1*	*2*	*3*	*4*	*5*	*6*
-ing	+	+	+	+	+	+
plural *-s*	+	±	+	+	–	+
possessive *-'s*	–	±	+	+	–	+
the, a	–	+	+	+	–	–
past tense *-ed*	+	±	+	–	–	+
third person singular *-s*	–	±	–	+	–	–
auxiliary *be*	–	±	–	+	–	–

As Table 12.9 helps show, the morphemes that are acquired first generally exhibit more of the properties just outlined than those that emerge at a later point.

3.2 Allomorphic rules

As children's productive and perceptual abilities improve, they start to follow the rules regulating the sort of allomorphic variation associated with the English plural (/s/ in *hats*, /z/ in *pens*, /əz/ in *judges*) and the past tense (/t/ in *taped*, /d/ in *played*, /əd/ in *hunted*). Initially, though, even allomorphic variation as straightforward as the *a/an* alternation in English can cause difficulty for language learners, and it is not unusual to hear children aged two to three produce utterances such as **a apple*.

A well-known technique for studying the development of morphophonemic rules involves presenting children with nonsense words and then asking them to form plurals or past tense forms. If the children have mastered productive rules for allomorphic variation, they ought to be able to add appropriate endings even to words they have never heard before. In a classic experiment, children were shown a picture of a strange creature and told, "This is a wug." A second picture was then presented and the children were given the following type of question.

3)

Now, there's another wug. There are two of them.
Now, there are two. . . ?

Children who knew the plural formation rule were able to respond with the form /wʌgz/. Table 12.10 indicates the average scores attained by preschoolers (aged four to five) and first graders (aged five and a half to seven) on specific nonsense words in this experiment.

Table 12.10 Percentage of correct responses on wug test

Allomorph	*Nonsense word*	*Preschoolers (%)*	*First graders (%)*
/s/	heafs	79	80
/z/	wugs	76	97
	luns	68	92
	tors	73	90
	cras	58	86
/əz/	tasses	28	39
	gutches	28	38
	kashes	25	36
	nizzes	14	33

These results suggest that the various allomorphs of the plural are acquired at different times. Particularly problematic is the /əz/ allomorph, which is needed in the last four items in Table 12.10. Even first grade children fail to produce the correct form of the plural here in well over half the cases studied, perhaps because /əz/ is the least frequent of the plural allomorphs and occurs in the most restrictive context (after a strident; see Chapter 6, Section 1.2).

3.3 Word formation rules

Like inflectional morphemes, derivational affixes and compounding appear to be acquired in a more or less fixed order. In one experiment, children were given sentence frames that required the formation of a new word from a real or made-up root. For the agentive *-er*, for example, a typical frame would be *A person who niches is called a* ___. As Table 12.11 shows, not all word formation processes were equally easy for the children.

Table 12.11 Percentage correct for made-up roots

Construction	*Preschool (%)*	*Early school (%)*	*Middle school (%)*
Agentive *-er*	7	63	80
Compound	47	50	65
Adjectival *-y*	0	30	55
Instrumental *-er*	7	35	45
Adverbial *-ly*	0	13	20

The crucial factor in determining the order of emergence of these word formation processes seems to be productivity. The two processes that apply most freely in English (the formation of a noun by the addition of the agentive affix *-er* to a verb and compounding) were the first to emerge. On the other hand, morphemes that can apply to only a restricted set of roots (e.g., *-ly*, which can combine with *quick* but not *fast*) seem to be mastered at a much later age. This supports the earlier suggestion that the relative lack of exceptions facilitates morphological development (factor 4 in the list given in Section 3.1).

Even subtle properties of word formation may be acquired in the preschool years. One such property, first discussed in Section 3.1 of Chapter 4, involves the fact that an inflectional suffix such as the plural cannot occur inside compounds (compare **dogs catcher* with *dog catcher*). In one study, children as young as three years of age produced compounds that obeyed this constraint. Thus, when asked a question such as 'What do you call someone who eats cookies?', they responded by saying *cookie eater* rather than **cookies eater*.

Of course, the acquisition of word formation processes is not entirely error-free. Three- and four-year-old children, for example, have been observed to make word order errors in compounds, producing forms such as **breaker bottle* (for *bottle breaker*) and **builder wall* (for *wall builder*). However, such errors typically disappear by age five.

4 SYNTACTIC DEVELOPMENT

Like phonological and morphological development, the emergence of syntactic rules takes place in an orderly sequence. Beginning with the production of one-word utterances near the end of the first year of life, children gradually master the rules for sentence formation in their language. Some of the milestones in this developmental process are considered here.

4.1 The one-word stage

As noted earlier, children begin to produce one-word utterances between the ages of twelve and eighteen months. A basic property of these one-word utterances is that they can be used to express the type of meaning that would be associated with an entire sentence in adult speech. Thus, a child might use the word *dada* to assert 'I see Daddy', *more* to mean 'Give me more candy', and *up* to mean 'I want up'. Such utterances are called **holophrases** (literally 'whole sentences').

In forming holophrastic utterances, children seem to choose the most informative word that applies to the situation at hand. A child who wanted a candy, for example, would say *candy* rather than *want* since the former word is more informative in this situation. Similarly, a child who notices a new doll would be more likely to say *doll* than *see*, thereby referring to the most novel feature of the situation he or she is trying to describe.

Table 12.12 lists some of the semantic relations that children commonly try to express during the **one-word stage**.

Table 12.12 Semantic relations in children's one-word utterances

Semantic relation	*Utterance*	*Situation*
Agent of an action	*dada*	as father enters the room
Action or state	*down*	as child sits down
Theme	*door*	as father closes the door
Location	*here*	as child points
Recipient	*mama*	as child gives mother something
Recurrence	*again*	as child watches lighting of a match

4.2 The two-word stage

Within a few months of their first one-word utterances, children begin to produce two-word 'mini-sentences'. Table 12.13 provides a sampling of these utterances and the types of meaning they are commonly used to express. (Although these examples are from English, similar patterns are found in the early development of all languages.)

Table 12.13 Some patterns in children's two-word speech

Utterance	*Intended meaning*	*Semantic relation*
Baby chair	'The baby is sitting on the chair.'	agent-location
Doggie bark	'The dog is barking.'	agent-action
Ken water	'Ken is drinking water.'	agent-theme
Hit doggie	'I hit the doggie.'	action-theme
Daddy hat	'Daddy's hat'	possessor-possessed

As these examples help illustrate, the vast majority of two-word utterances employ an appropriate word order, suggesting a very early sensitivity to this feature of sentence structure. It is somewhat less clear whether children have acquired syntactic categories such as noun, verb, and adjective at this point in their development. This is because the inflectional affixes that help distinguish among syntactic categories in adult English (such as the plural and the past tense) are absent during this period. To complicate matters still further, the relative shortness of the utterances produced during the **two-word stage** means that the positional differences associated with category distinctions in adult speech are often not manifested. Thus, words such as *busy* (an adjective in adult speech) and *push* (a verb) may appear in identical patterns.

4)

Mommy busy.
Mommy push.

While this does not show that children lack syntactic categories, it makes it very difficult to demonstrate that they possess them. For this reason, linguists and psychologists are split over whether to describe children's utterances in terms of the semantic relations that they express (as in Table 12.13) or the syntactic categories of adult speech.

4.3 The telegraphic stage

After a period of several months, during which their speech is limited to one- and two-word utterances, children begin to produce longer and more complex grammatical structures. Some representative utterances from the first part of this period follow.

5)

Chair broken.
Daddy like book.
What her name?
Man ride bus today.
Car make noise.
Me wanna show Mommy.
I good boy.

At first, these utterances lack bound morphemes and most nonlexical categories. Because of their resemblance to the style of language found in telegrams, this acquisitional stage is often dubbed telegraphic. Over a period of several months, affixes, determiners, and auxiliary verbs emerge in accordance with the developmental sequence discussed in Section 3.

A noteworthy feature of the **telegraphic stage** is that despite the emergence of complex new syntactic structures, children make virtually no word order errors. As the previous examples illustrate, adult word order patterns are employed even though individual words may not have the appropriate endings. In languages with variable word order (such as Korean and Russian), children use the various word order patterns with roughly the same relative frequency as adults do.

Language development from age two onward is rapid. As the examples in the following table help illustrate, children move from relatively primitive two- and three-word utterances at the beginning of the telegraphic stage to a broad range of syntactically intricate sentence types in the space of just a few months.

Table 12.14 Sample utterances from a child's speech over a 12-month period

Age	*Sample utterances*
28 mos	Play checkers. Big drum. I got horn. A bunny-rabbit walk.
30 mos	Write a piece a paper. What that egg doing? I lost a shoe. No, I don't want to sit seat.
32 mos	Let me get down with the boots on. Don't be afraid a horses. How tiger be so healthy and fly like kite? Joshua throw like penguin.
34 mos	Look at that train Urusula brought. I simply don't want put in chair. Don't have paper. Do you want little bit, Cromer? I can't wear it tomorrow.
36 mos	I going come in fourteen minutes. I going wear that to wedding. I see what happens. I have to save them now. Those are not strong mens. They are going sleep in wintertime. You dress me up like a baby elephant.
38 mos	So it can't be cleaned? I broke my racing car. Do you know the lights went off? What happened to the bridge? Can I put my head in the mailbox so the mailman can know where I are and put me in the mailbox?

Because of the diversity and sophistication of the utterances produced during the telegraphic stage, there is general agreement that this period is characterized by the emergence of powerful grammatical devices. Foremost among these are the phrase structure rules, which regulate the order and composition of syntactic units. If you reconsider the examples in *5)* above, you will see evidence for the rule that forms phrases consisting of a head (especially a V) and a complement (*like book, ride bus, show mommy*). Modifiers, including adjectives like *good* and adverbs like *today*, also exist during this period. (The place of modifiers in phrase structure is discussed in Section 5.2 of Chapter 5.) As already noted, determiners and other nonlexical categories are conspicuously absent from the telegraphic stage.

Table 12.15 summarizes the development of phrase structure.

Table 12.15 The development of phrase structure

Stage	*Approx. age*	*Developments*
Holophrastic	1–1.5 yrs	single word utterances; no structure
Two-word	1.5–2 yrs	early word combinations; presence of syntactic categories unclear
Telegraphic	2–2.5 yrs	emergence of phrase structure, especially head-complement and subject-VP patterns
Later	2.5 yrs up	emergence of nonlexical categories (Det, Aux)

4.4 Later development

In the years following the telegraphic stage, children continue to acquire the complex grammar that underlies adult linguistic competence, including the system of transformational rules outlined in Chapter 5. Some highlights of this period of development are reviewed in this section.

Inversion

In the very early stages of language acquisition, children signal *yes-no* questions by means of rising intonation alone. (Recall that auxiliary verbs are a relatively late development.)

6)

See hole?
I ride train?
Ball go?
Sit chair?

Even after individual auxiliary verbs appear in child language, there is often a delay of a few months before they undergo Inversion and appear at the beginning of the sentence in *yes-no* questions. In one study, for example, a young boy began using the auxiliary verb *can* at age two years, five months, but did not invert it in questions until six months later.

An interesting error in children's early use of inversion in both *yes-no* and *wh* questions is exemplified in *7)*.

7)

Can he *can* look?
What *shall* we *shall* have?
Did you *did* came home?

In these sentences, the auxiliary verb occurs twice—once to the left of the subject (in the position that it occupies after Inversion) and once to the right (in the position it occupies in deep structure). It has been suggested that this pattern reflects an error in the application of the Inversion transformation in that a copy of the moved auxiliary is left behind in its original position.

Experimental work has shown that this type of error is more likely in a sentence such as *8)*, which has a complex subject NP.

8)

[The girl who is crying] should leave →
*Should [the girl who is crying] should leave?

This presumably happens because the subject NP stands directly between the auxiliary's deep structure position and the position to which it is moved in surface structure. As such, its complexity can interfere with the Inversion operation.

Wh questions

Wh questions emerge gradually between the ages of two and four. For many children, the following three stages are involved.

Stage 1 Children produce both *yes-no* questions and *wh* questions, but Inversion is not possible since auxiliary verbs are not yet acquired. The first *wh* words to be acquired are typically *what* and *where*, followed by *who, how,* and *why; when, which,* and *whose* are relatively late acquisitions.

9)

Where that?
What me think?
Why you smiling?
Why not me drink it?

Stage 2 Auxiliary verbs make their appearance and undergo Inversion, but more frequently in *yes-no* questions than in *Wh* questions.

10)

Yes-no questions (with Inversion):
Did Mommy pinch her finger?
Can't you fix it?
Do I have it?
Is Mommy talking to Robin's grandmother?

11)

Wh questions (no Inversion):
What I did yesterday?
Why Kitty can't stand up?
Where I should put it?
Where I should sleep?
Why you are smiling?

Stage 3 Inversion is common in *wh* questions as well as *yes-no* questions.

12)

Where did my mitten go?
Where should I sleep?
Why are you smiling?

For some children, Inversion in *wh* questions develops in two substages, appearing later in negated sentences. In these cases, children who are able to produce the constructions in *12)* still use ill-formed negated sentences such as the following:

13)

Why you can't sit down?
Why Kitty can't stand up?

5 SEMANTIC DEVELOPMENT

By age eighteen months or so, the average child has a vocabulary of fifty words or more. Common items include the words listed in Table 12.16.

Table 12.16 Common items in the first fifty words

Entities
Names for people: *daddy, mommy,* etc. Words referring to humans: *baby* food/drink: *juice, milk, cookie, water, toast, apple, cake* animals: *dog, cat, duck, horse* clothes: *shoes, hat* toys: *ball, blocks* vehicles: *car, boat, truck* other: *bottle, key, book*
Properties
hot, allgone, more, dirty, cold, here, there
Actions
up, sit, see, eat, go, down
Personal-social
hi, bye, no, yes, please, thank-you

As Table 12.16 shows, noun-like words make up the single largest class in the child's early vocabulary, with verb- and adjective-like words being the next most frequent category types. Among the most frequent individual words are expressions for displeasure or rejection (such as *no*) and various types of social interaction (such as *please* and *bye*). Over the next months children's vocabulary grows rapidly, sometimes by as much as ten or twelve words a day. By age six, most children have mastered about thirteen thousand words.

Children seem to differ somewhat in the types of words that they focus on, especially in the early stages of language acquisition. One of these differences is reflected in the number of nouns in early vocabulary. Whereas some children have a relatively high proportion of such words (75 percent or more) by age two, other learners exhibit a much lower percentage of nouns (50 percent or less). Making up for the smaller number of nouns is a larger vocabulary in the area of socially useful expressions such as *bye, go-away, stop-it, thank-you, I-want-it,* and so on. (Hyphens are used here to indicate that these expressions are not yet segmented into their component words.)

5.1 The Acquisition of Word Meaning

A major factor in lexical development is the child's ability to make use of contextual clues to draw inferences about the category and meaning of new words. For instance, from early in the language acquisition process, children can use the presence or absence of determiners to distinguish between names and ordinary nouns. Two-year-old children who are told that a new doll is *a dax* will apply this label to similar-looking dolls as well. However, if they are told that the new doll is *Dax,* they will restrict use of the new word to the doll they have actually been shown. Like adults, these children treat *dax* as an ordinary noun when it is preceded by *a,* but as a name when there is no determiner.

Children are also able to use the meaning of other words in the sentence and their understanding of the nonlinguistic context to form hypotheses about new words. In one experiment, for example, three- and four-year-old children were asked to act out the meaning of sentences such as 'Make it so there is *tiv* to drink in this glass (of water)'. The only clues to the interpretation of the nonsense word *tiv* come from the meaning of the rest of the sentence and from the child's understanding of the types of changes that can be made to a glass of water. Not only did more than half the children respond by either adding or removing water, some even remembered what *tiv* 'meant' two weeks later!

The meanings that children associate with their early words sometimes correspond closely to the meanings employed by adults. In many cases, however, the match is less than perfect. The two most typical semantic errors involve overextension and underextension.

Overextension

In cases of **overextension**, the meaning of the child's word is more general or inclusive than that of the corresponding adult form. The word *dog,* for example, is frequently overextended to include horses, cows, and other four-legged animals. Similarly, *ball* is sometimes used for any round object, including a balloon, an Easter egg, a small stone, and so on. Following are some additional examples of overextension.

Table 12.17 Examples of overextension

Word	*First referent*	*Subsequent extensions*
tick tock	watch	clocks, gas-meter, fire hose on a spool, scale with round dial
fly	fly	specks of dirt, dust, small insects, child's toes, crumbs of bread
quack	duck	all birds and insects, flies, coins (with an eagle on the face)
candy	candy	cherries, anything sweet
apple	apples	balls, tomatoes, cherries, onions, biscuits
turtle	turtles	fish, seals
cookie	cookies	crackers, any dessert
kitty	cats	rabbits, any small furry animal
box	boxes	elevators
belt	belts	watchstrap

The basis for overextension

An important issue in the study of language acquisition has to do with whether children's overextensions are the result of similarities in the appearance (shape, size, texture) or the function of the objects to which the overextended word refers. The evidence collected to date suggests that perceptual properties are the critical factor in children's first hypotheses about word meanings. As a result, children often overextend a word to include a set of perceptually similar objects that they know to have diverse functions. For example, one child used the word *moon* for the moon, grapefruit halves, and a crescent-shaped car light. Another child used the word *money* for a set of objects ranging from pennies to buttons and beads. If you reconsider the examples of overextension given in Table 12.17, you will see that they too are more plausibly explained in terms of perceptual similarities than a shared function.

Children seem to overextend more in their production than in their comprehension. A child who overextends the word *dog* in his or her own speech, for example, may well point only to the appropriate animal when asked by an adult to find a dog in a picture. This suggests that children sometimes deliberately overextend words in production to compensate for their limited vocabulary.

Underextension

While overextensions are the most frequent type of word-meaning error in early language (about one-third of children's words are overextended at the fifty-word stage of vocabulary development), children also frequently employ **underextension** by using lexical items in an overly restrictive fashion. Thus, *kitty* might be used to refer to the family pet, but not to any other cats. Or the word *dog* might be used for collies, spaniels, and beagles, but not for chihuahuas.

Underextension errors often reflect children's propensity to focus on prototypical or core members of a category. As noted in Section 1.3 of Chapter 7, the potential referents of many words differ in terms of how well they exemplify the properties associated with a particular concept. Thus, among the potential referents of the word *dog*, collies and spaniels have more of the properties associated with the concept 'dog' (long hair, relative size, type of bark, and so on) than do chihuahuas. While the preference for a prototype can be overruled by factors such as the presence of a nontypical category member in the child's everyday experience (e.g., a chihuahua as a family pet), it is clear that the internal structure of concepts can have an important influence on semantic development.

5.2 Spatial and dimensional terms

English has many words that are used to express spatial relations (such as *in*, *on*, and *behind*). Although syntactically similar (most are prepositions), these words differ from each other in terms of their semantic complexity. Notice, for example, that the relation expressed by *on* and *in* does not depend on the speaker's viewpoint: If two marbles are on a box, then they are on it no matter where the speaker is standing. However, matters are more complicated in the case of the relations expressed by *behind* and *in front of* since we would say that the marbles are behind the box only if the box is between us and the marbles. If we stand on the opposite side of the box, the marbles would then appear to be in front of the box. Matters are slightly simpler when the object with respect to which the marbles are situated has an inherent front and back (such as a television). In this case, we can ignore our own position and focus on the marbles' location with respect to the front part of the television.

These considerations seem to be directly reflected in the order in which words expressing spatial relations are acquired.

Table 12.18 Order of acquisition for words expressing spatial relations

Step	*Words*	*Description*
1	*in, on, under, beside*	independent of speaker's perspective
2	*behind, in front of*	used with objects with inherent fronts and backs
3	*behind, in front of*	used with objects without inherent fronts or backs

Interestingly, a comparable developmental order has been observed in a number of languages (Italian, Turkish, and Serbo-Croatian) other than English. This suggests that the considerations that determine the semantic complexity of spatial words are universal and therefore are manifested in the acquisition of all languages.

Dimensional terms

Like words referring to spatial relations, terms describing size and dimensions are also acquired in a relatively fixed order, depending on their generality. The first dimensional adjectives to be acquired, *big* and *small*, are the most general in that they can be used for talking about any aspect of size (height, area, volume, and so on). In contrast, the second group of adjectives to emerge—*tall*, *long*, *short*, *high*, and *low*—can only be used for a single dimension (height/length). The remaining modifiers (*thick-thin*, *wide-narrow*, and *deep-shallow*) are still more restricted in their use since they describe the secondary or less extended dimension of an object. For instance, the dimension of a stick that we describe in terms of width or thickness is almost always less extended than the dimension that we describe in terms of height or length, which tends also to be perceptually more salient.

Table 12.19 Order of acquisition for dimensional adjectives

Step	*Words*	*What they describe*
1	*big-small*	any aspect of size
2	*tall-short, long-short, high-low*	a single dimension
3	*thick-thin, wide-narrow, deep-shallow*	a secondary dimension

The importance of the salient dimension in the development of adjectives is underlined by a peculiar error that has been observed in children's early use of the modifier *big*. When asked to choose which of the following two figures is the 'big one', children between the ages of three and five tend to choose Figure 12.1b over 12.1a.

Figure 12.1

Although figure *a* is larger in overall area, figure *b* is greater on the vertical dimension. The fact that children take b to be bigger suggests that height is more salient to them than is overall area.

5.3 The interpretation of sentence structure (*Advanced*)

As noted in Chapter 7, the interpretation of sentences draws heavily on information about how words are hierarchically organized to form phrase structure. In this section we will briefly consider some aspects of the acquisition of two interpretive phenomena that rely on information about syntactic structure.

Thematic roles

In Chapter 7, we saw that thematic roles are assigned to particular (deep structure) positions in accordance with the following generalizations.

14)

A P assigns its role (location, source, or goal) to an NP complement.
A V assigns its theme role to an NP complement.
A V assigns its agent role to the subject.

Children learning English are able to associate thematic roles with particular structural positions at a very early point in the acquisition process. By the time their average utterance length is two words, they are able to respond correctly about 75 percent of the time to comprehension tests involving simple active sentences such as *15)*, in which the truck is the agent and the car is the theme.

15)

The truck bumped the car.

However, children find it much harder to interpret passive sentences correctly. This is especially true for passive sentences such as the one in *16)*, which contains no semantic clues about which NP is agent and which one is theme. (Note that it makes just as much sense for the car to bump the truck as it does for the truck to bump the car. Such sentences are said to be 'reversible'.)

16)

The car was bumped by the truck.

Although children produce passive sentences in their own speech from around age three, they have continuing difficulty responding appropriately to passive constructions in comprehension tests.

Table 12.20 Comprehension of reversible passive constructions

Group	*Percentage correct*
Nursery school	20
Kindergarten	35
Grade 1	48
Grade 2	63
Grade 3	88

Why should this be so? Thematic role assignment in passive structures is complicated by the fact that the NP bearing the theme role occurs in the subject position while the agent (marked by the preposition *by*) appears after the verb.

17)

Passive sentence: The car was bumped by the truck
theme *agent*

Active sentence: The truck bumped the car.
agent *theme*

Thus, passive sentences are almost mirror images of their active counterparts in that the agent occurs after the verb and the theme before it rather than vice versa. Significantly, the most common error made by children is to assume that the first NP in passive sentences is the agent and the second NP the theme. This suggests that they tend to overgeneralize the thematic role pattern found in active sentences, thereby systematically erring on passive patterns.

As the data in Table 12.20 show, children begin to apply this strategy randomly around age six, suggesting that they are starting to realize that it is not always appropriate. A year or so later, their scores start to rise dramatically, indicating that they recognize the special properties associated with thematic role assignment in the passive construction.

Pronominals and reflexives

In Chapter 7, we saw that a reflexive pronoun (*himself, herself,* and so on) must have a 'higher' (i.e., c-commanding) antecedent in the minimal clause containing it. Thus, *himself* must refer to Gary in the following sentence.

18)

Sam said that [$_S$ Gary slapped *himself* on the wrist].

In contrast, a pronominal (*him, her*) in this position can refer only to Sam or to someone not mentioned in the sentence.

19)

Sam said that [$_S$ Gary slapped *him* on the wrist].

In terms of language acquisition, there is some reason to believe that children are able to interpret reflexives correctly before pronominals. Thus, children between the ages of three and five correctly interpret *himself* as Gary. However, they often misinterpret *him* as if it were a reflexive, allowing it to refer to Gary in *19)*. It is not until age seven or so that language learners are able to uniformly give the correct interpretation for pronouns in this type of structure.

6 DETERMINANTS OF LANGUAGE ACQUISITION

In the preceding sections, we have seen that children acquire the grammar of their language over a period of several years. While it is relatively easy to describe the order in which children acquire various phonemic contrasts, morphemes, and syntactic rules, it is much more difficult to explain *how* they do this. The sections that follow outline some of the factors that may help children discover the categories and rules that make up the grammar of their language.

6.1 THE ROLE OF IMITATION AND CORRECTION

At one time, it was widely believed that children learn language by simply imitating the speech of those around them. We now know that this cannot be true, since many utterance types produced by children do not closely resemble structures found in adult speech. Plural forms such as *foots* and question structures such as *Why the sun shining* are obvious examples of patterns that are unique to child language. As noted earlier, such utterances reflect children's attempts to formulate grammatical rules, not the imitation of adult speech.

The importance of imitation to language acquisition is placed in further doubt by the fact that children are typically unable to imitate structures that they have not yet learned. For instance, a child who has not yet acquired the Inversion rule for *wh* questions will imitate sentence *20a)* by producing *20b)*.

20)

a. What can you see? (*model*)
b. What you can see? (*child's imitation*)

Findings like these suggest that children rely on their current grammatical rules to process the speech they hear and that they are therefore not able to imitate sentences exactly as they are produced by adults.

This is not to say that imitation plays no role in language learning. While many children rarely attempt to repeat utterances, some language learners do seem to make selective use of imitation. They imitate new words in constructions they have already learned and repeat novel constructions that contain words already familiar to them. Thus, they might imitate the new word *computer* in a familiar subject-verb-object pattern (such as *Daddy bought a computer*). Similarly, they might imitate a new structure such as the passive if it contained familiar words (*Daddy was called by Mommy*). But they would not imitate a sentence whose structure and vocabulary were both new to them. Such selective imitation suggests that children do not blindly mimic adult speech, but rather exploit it in very restricted ways to improve their linguistic skills.

Correction

Another classic attempt to explain language development is based on the assumption that parents provide children with direct linguistic training by correcting ill-formed utterances. However, such an assumption has not been supported by studies of actual interactions between parents and children. Instead, it has been found that parents evaluate the truth of children's utterances rather than their grammaticality. In one case, a parent even reacted to the utterance *Mama isn't boy, he's a girl* by responding *That's right.*

Even when adults do attempt to correct children's grammatical errors, their efforts seem to have little effect. The following exchange between a child and his mother is typical in this regard.

21)

Child: Nobody don't like me.
Mother: No, say "Nobody likes me."
Child: Nobody don't like me.
[*Exchange is repeated eight times.*]
Mother: No, now listen carefully; say "Nobody likes me."
Child: Oh! Nobody don't LIKES me.

A more subtle form of correction occurs when adults repeat a child's utterance, making adjustments to its form and/or content.

22)

Child: Daddy here.
Mother: Yes, Daddy is here.

Child: Boy chasing dog.
Mother: Yes, the boy is chasing the dog.

Child: Him go.
Mother: Yes, he is going.

Child: The dog is barking.
Mother: Yes, he is barking at the kitty.

A study of upper-middle-class families in the United States suggests that mothers of two-year-old children exhibit a slightly greater tendency to revise ungrammatical utterances than grammatical utterances (26 percent versus 14 percent). (No such tendency was found in response to the speech of older children.) However, no mothers revised all ungrammatical utterances produced by their children and even grammatical utterances were often revised (the fourth example in *22)*). The mothers' responses therefore apparently do not provide reliable information about whether the children's utterances are well formed.

6.2 The role of adult speech

Linguistic development obviously depends in crucial ways on the child's linguistic experience. Children who are exposed to English learn to speak English, those exposed to Cree learn Cree, and so on. Moreover, children who are not exposed to language do not develop linguistic skills beyond the babbling stage.

A good deal of recent work has been devoted to the search for a possible relationship between language acquisition and the type of speech that is typically addressed to young language learners. Such speech is often called **motherese** or **caregiver speech**. A valuable product of this research has been the discovery that speech addressed to young children has special properties that could well heighten its comprehensibility. Phonologically, for example, motherese is known to consist of clearly articulated utterances with pauses between phrases and exaggerated intonation contours to signal questions, imperatives, and statements. Maternal speech also tends to concentrate on the here and now, consisting primarily of statements relating to the child's current surroundings, activities, and needs. The following examples help illustrate this.

Table 12.21 Some examples of maternal speech

Mother's utterance	*Context*
That's right, pick up the blocks.	the child is picking up a box of building blocks
That's a puppy.	the child is looking at a young dog
The puppy's in the basket.	the child is examining a puppy in a basket

It seems reasonable to suppose that exposure to this type of language makes it easier for children to match forms (morphemes, words, and phrases) with meanings, and thereby to acquire the vocabulary and structure of their language. Table 12.22 lists some features commonly found in the speech of middle-class English-speaking mothers to their children.

Table 12.22 Some features of English motherese

Phonetic
Slower speech Higher pitch Exaggerated intonation and stress Longer pauses
Lexical and semantic
More restricted vocabulary Concrete reference to here and now
Syntactic
Few incomplete sentences Short sentences More imperatives and questions
Conversational
More repetitions Few utterances per conversational turn

Although potentially helpful, it is not clear that these phenomena are actually crucial to the language acquisition process. In some cultures, for instance, children are not considered to be potential conversational partners until they are fluent speakers. Little speech is addressed directly to them, although they do spend a lot of time with their mothers and are exposed to a good deal of conversation among adults. The fact that these children seem to learn language in a normal fashion indicates that exposure to the speech style typical of middle-class mothers in North American society is not necessary for language acquisition.

We also know that maternal speech has highly selective effects on child language. In one widely cited study, the speech of fifteen mothers to their daughters (aged one year to two years and three months) was analyzed. It was found that there were correlations between only some aspects of motherese and child speech. For instance, the number of *yes-no* questions in maternal speech was correlated with the rate at which auxiliary verbs developed. This was presumably because auxiliaries occur in the salient sentence-initial position in *yes-no* questions (*Can Jennifer go?*). However, many other features of maternal speech seem not to influence child language. As we saw earlier (Section 3.1), for example, the relative frequency of bound morphemes and nonlexical categories in maternal speech apparently does not determine their order of acquisition.

In and of itself, maternal speech cannot explain how language acquisition occurs. However, research into motherese may contribute to this goal in less direct ways by helping determine the types of linguistic experience that are most valuable to children. This in turn should help identify the types of mechanisms and strategies involved in language acquisition.

6.3 The role of cognitive development

Cognitive development is the name given to the emergence of the various mental abilities and skills that make up the human intellect. Because there are dramatic changes in both linguistic and nonlinguistic abilities during the first years of life, it is tempting to think that the two are somehow linked. Indeed, prominent psychologists have suggested both that general cognitive development shapes language acquisition (a view put forward by the Swiss psychologist Jean Piaget) and that language acquisition is crucial to other aspects of cognitive development (a position associated with the Russian pyschologist Lev Vygotsky).

There are many suggestive similarities between language acquisition and cognitive development. During the first two years of life, for example, several cognitive advances that could facilitate language acquisition take place. One of these involves the development of **object permanence**, the ability to recognize that objects have an existence independent of one's interaction with them. Prior to the development of this ability, children seem to assume that an object ceases to exist when it moves out of sight, and that it is a different entity when it reappears. They therefore do not know where to look for an object that they observe being hidden; from their perspective, it has apparently simply ceased to exist. Object permanence emerges around age eighteen months, just prior to a period of rapid growth in the child's vocabulary. The relative timing of these two events suggests a possible connection: Children's ability to learn the names for objects increases dramatically once they understand that those objects have an independent existence.

During the first twenty-four months of their lives, children also acquire the ability to classify objects and actions. They seem to understand that certain things are eaten, others can be sat upon, still others serve as toys, and so on. It is conceivable that these classification skills also play a role in dividing words into linguistic categories such as noun and verb on the basis of their semantic, morphological, and syntactic properties. It has also been suggested that a general ability to arrange and order elements with respect to each other is manifested in children's attempts to organize words into sentences.

Still another link between cognitive development and language acquisition involves seriation, the ability to arrange elements (such as sticks) in order of increasing or decreasing size. Children who are unable to perform this type of task typically describe the objects on which they are working simply as *long* or *short*. In contrast, children who are capable of seriation (age five and older) use comparative terms such as *longer* and *shorter*. Here again, there is an apparent connection between an aspect of language (the comparative form for adjectives) and a more general cognitive skill (seriation).

Just as cognitive development may influence language acquisition, so the emergence of linguistic skills may have an effect on cognition. At the very least, language seems to provide its users with an enhanced capacity for complex reasoning. It is also conceivable that language may help draw children's attention to certain conceptual distinctions that would otherwise develop more slowly. For instance, in the course of learning words such as *father, mother, brother,* and so on, children may make discoveries about family relationships that would otherwise develop more slowly.

Special cases

Considerations such as these notwithstanding, there is reason to think that language acquisition and other types of cognitive development are to a very significant degree independent of each other. A rich source of evidence for this conclusion comes from the study of children with particular types of mental deficits, including those whose general cognitive development is deficient but whose language is highly developed.

One important study of this type focused on Rick, a severely retarded fifteen year old whose performance on a variety of nonlinguistic tasks suggests that his general cognitive level is that of a preschool child. Yet, as the following examples illustrate, Rick's speech shows signs of syntactic and morphological sophistication—with appropriate use of affixes, nonlexical categories, and word order.

23)

She must've got me up and thrown me out of bed.
She keeps both of the ribbons on her hair.
If they get in trouble, they'd have a pillow fight.
She's the one that walks back and forth to school.
I wanna hear one more just for a change.

Case studies such as this suggest that certain aspects of language (in particular, morphology and syntax) are independent of nonlinguistic types of cognitive development. This in turn implies that the mental mechanisms responsible for the acquisition of those parts of the grammar are relatively autonomous and that their operation neither follows from nor guarantees general cognitive development.

6.4 THE ROLE OF INBORN KNOWLEDGE

Although both cognitive development and exposure to the speech of others are clearly crucial to language acquisition, other factors must also be involved. Apes have many of the cognitive skills of two-year-old children, but they do not acquire language even when they are exposed to speech (see Chapter 16). This suggests that there is something about the human mind that equips it to acquire language.

A very influential view among linguists is that children are born with prior knowledge of the type of categories and rules that are found in the grammar of any human language. They therefore know, for example, that the words in the language they are acquiring will belong to a small set of syntactic categories (N, V, and so on) and that there will be rules of a certain sort to create larger phrases (NP, VP, S). The set of inborn categories and principles common to all human languages makes up **Universal Grammar (UG)**, first mentioned in Chapter 5.

Of course, not every feature of a language's grammar can be inborn. In the case of phrase structure, for example, UG stipulates that an XP constituent can include a head X and its complements, but it does not specify the relative order of these elements. This differs from language to language, so that a child acquiring English must learn that Vs and Ps precede their complements while a child acquiring Japanese must learn that heads follow their complements. As noted in Section 4 of Chapter 5, Universal Grammar includes a parameter (set of options) for word order.

As Table 12.23 illustrates, these options include head-initial order versus head-final order. (We ignore the positioning of specifiers for the purposes of this illustration.)

Table 12.23 The word order parameter

Stipulated by UG	*Resulting options*
XP → X, Complement	XP → X Complement [head-initial] XP → Complement X [head-final]

The view that certain grammatical knowledge is inborn is known as **nativism**. Although nativism has roots in philosophy that date back thousands of years, its popularity in linguistics is due largely to the theories of Noam Chomsky. Chomsky's basic claim is that the grammars for human language are too complex and abstract to be learned on the basis of the type of experience to which children have access. Therefore, he argues, significant components of the grammar must be inborn. To illustrate this, we must consider a relatively complex example involving the notion of c-command introduced in Chapter 7 (Section 3.3).

Principle A *(Advanced)*

As you may recall, c-command is defined as follows.

24)

NP_a c-commands NP_b if the first category above NP_a contains NP_b.

The c-command relation plays a crucial role in the statement of **Principle A**, which restricts the interpretation of reflexive pronouns (in English, pronouns ending in *self* or *selves*).

25)

Principle A:
A reflexive pronoun must have an antecedent that c-commands it.

Principle A is responsible for the fact that *himself* in Figure 12.2 takes *the boy's father* as its antecedent, but not *the boy*. That is, the sentence must be taken to mean that the father of the boy is the person who was hurt. (As mentioned in Chapter 7, a possessor NP can occur in the specifier position within a larger NP.)

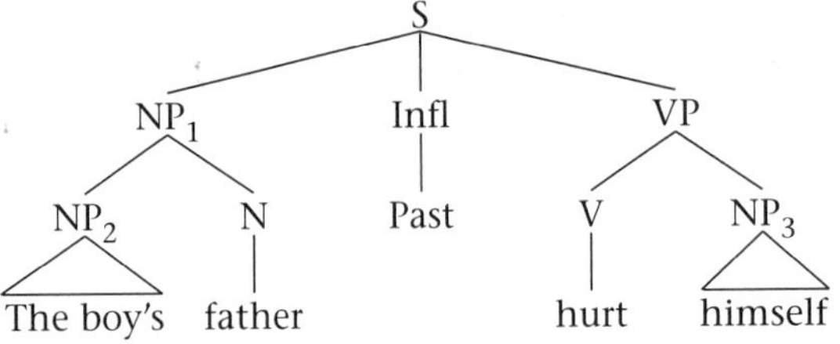

Figure 12.2 The reflexive pronoun takes the c-commanding NP_1 as its antecedent

In Figure 12.2, there is only one category above the NP *the boy's father*—namely S. Since this category contains the reflexive pronoun, NP_1 c-commands *himself* according to our definition and can therefore serve as its antecedent in accordance with Principle A. The same is not true of *the boy* (NP_2) since the first category above it is NP_1, which does not contain the reflexive. This means that NP_2 does not c-command the reflexive and cannot serve as its antecedent.

There are two major reasons for believing that Principle A must be inborn. First, the notion of c-command is quite abstract. It is not the type of concept that we would expect young children to discover simply by listening to sentences. Since we also know that no one teaches them about c-command, it makes sense to think that this notion is inborn and therefore does not have to be discovered or taught.

Second, the c-command component of Principle A seems to be universal. Thus, there appear to be no languages in which the equivalent of English *himself* can refer to the boy rather than the boy's father in structures such as the one in Figure 12.2. The universality of this restriction would be explained if it were innate and hence part of the inborn linguistic knowledge of all human beings.

The claim that children are born with abstract linguistic principles is controversial, and research on alternatives continues. However, the hypothesis that the grammar is genetically structured is an exciting and imporant development in linguistics. It is one of the many areas in the field of language acquisition where important breakthroughs remain to be made.

6.5 Is there a critical period?

One of the most intriguing issues in the study of language acquisition has to do with the possibility that normal linguistic development is possible only if children are exposed to language during a particular time frame or **critical period**. Evidence for the existence of such a period comes from the study of individuals who do not experience language during the early part of their lives.

One such individual is the much discussed Genie, who was kept in a small room with virtually no opportunity to hear human speech from around age two to age thirteen. After many years of therapy and care, Genie's nonlinguistic cognitive functioning was described as 'relatively normal' and her lexical and semantic abilities as 'good'. In terms of syntax and morphology, however, many problems remained, as evidenced in the following sample utterances.

Table 12.24 Some of Genie's utterances

Utterance	*Meaning*
Applesauce buy store	'Buy applesauce at the store.'
Man motorcycle have	'The man has a motorcycle.'
Want go ride Miss F. car	'I want to go ride in Miss F.'s car.'
Genie have full stomach	'I have a full stomach.'
Mama have baby grow up	'Mama has a baby who grew up.'

As these examples show, Genie makes word order errors (the second example above) and her speech does not contain nonlexical categories or affixes.

Another revealing case study involves Chelsea, a deaf child who was misdiagnosed as retarded and emotionally disturbed. Chelsea grew up without language and was not exposed to speech until the age of 31, when she was finally fitted with hearing aids. After intensive therapy, she is able to hold a job and to live independently. However, her vocabulary consists of only two thousand words and her sentences are badly ill-formed, as the following examples help show.

26)

The woman is bus the going
Combing hair the boy.
Orange Tim car in.
The girl is cone the ice cream shopping buying the man.

It is now widely believed that the ability to acquire a first language in an effortless and ultimately successful way begins to decline from age six and is severely compromised by the onset of puberty.

Summing up

This chapter has been concerned with the problem of how children acquire the grammar of their first language. Research in this area deals with two major issues: the nature of the **developmental sequence** leading to the emergence of mature linguistic competence and the factors that make it possible for children to acquire complex grammatical rules. We have seen that over a period of several years children gradually acquire different subsystems of the grammar (**phonology**, **morphology**, **syntax**, and **semantics**). In many cases, acquisition of a rule will involve a number of intermediate stages, each of which marks a successively closer approximation to the adult grammar. A number of factors may contribute to the child's acquisition of language, including the properties of maternal speech (**motherese**), the effects of general cognitive development, and (possibly) inborn linguistic knowledge. We look to future research for deeper insights into the precise role of these and other factors.

Key terms

babbling
caregiver speech
cognitive development
critical period
cross-sectional (research)
denasalization
developmental sequence
diary study
experimental approach
fronting
gliding
holophrases
motherese
nativism
naturalistic approach
object permanence
one-word stage
overextension

overgeneralizations	telegraphic stage
overregularizations	two-word stage
Principle A	underextension
stopping	Universal Grammar (UG)

SOURCES

Pioneering work on infant perception is reported in "Developmental Studies of Speech Perception" by P. Eimas in *Infant Perception*, edited by L. Cohen and P. Salapatek (New York: Academic Press, 1975); the ability to use phonetic contrasts to distinguish between words is examined in "Perception and Production in Child Phonology: The Testing of Four Hypotheses" by M. Edwards in *Journal of Child Language* 1:205–19 (1974). The cross-linguistic data on babbling are summarized and discussed on pp. 9–11 of *Phonological Acquisition and Change* by J. Locke (cited below); see also "Adaptation to Language: Evidence from Babbling and First Words in Four Languages" by B. de Boysson-Bardies and M. Vihman in *Language* 67:297–319 (1991). For a recent discussion of the relevance of babbling to the development of control over the vocal tract, see S. Pinker's *The Language Instinct* (New York: Morrow, 1994), p. 266. Differences between children's production and perception of speech sounds are outlined in *The Acquisition of Phonology: A Case Study* by N. Smith (New York: Cambridge University Press, 1973); the "*fis* phenomenon" is reported in "Psycholinguistic Research Methods" by J. Berko and R. Brown in *Handbook of Research Methods in Child Development*, edited by P. Mussen (New York: John Wiley, 1960). David Ingram's *Phonological Disability in Children* (London: Edward Arnold, 1976) contains many useful examples of early phonetic processes. The data on developmental order for speech sounds come from Chapter 8 of *First Language Acquisition* by D. Ingram, cited below.

The remarks on inflectional overgeneralization are based in part on *Overregularization in Language Acquisition* by G. Marcus, S. Pinker, M. Ullman, M. Hollander, T. Rosen, and F. Xu (*Monographs of the Society for Research in Child Development*, Serial No. 228, Vol. 57, No. 4, 1992). The pioneering work on the developmental order for English bound morphemes and lexical categories was done by R. Brown and reported in his book *A First Language: The Early Stages* (Cambridge, MA: Harvard University Press, 1973). The cross-linguistic data on the factors determining morphological development come from "Universal and Particular in the Acquisition of Language" by D. Slobin in *Language Acquisition: The State of the Art*, edited by E. Wanner and L. Gleitman (New York: Cambridge University Press, 1982). The original "*wug* test" was done by J. Berko and is reported in her article "The Child's Learning of English Morphology" in *Word* 14:150–77 (1958). The work on the development of derivational affixes and compounding in English is from "Recent Research on the Acquisition of English Morphology" by B. Derwing and W. Baker in *Language Acquisition*, edited by P. Fletcher and M. Garman (New York: Cambridge University Press, 1979).

The data on the acquisition of the prohibition against inflection within compounds are from "Level-Ordering in Lexical Development" by P. Gordon in *Cognition* 21:73–93 (1985). Word order errors within compounds are reported in "Coining

Complex Compounds in English: Affixes and Word Order in Acquisition" by E. Clark, B. Hecht, and R. Mulford in *Linguistics* 24:7–29 (1986).

The data in Table 12.14 in Section 4.3 are taken from S. Pinker, *The Language Instinct* (New York: Morrow, 1994), pp. 269–70. The data on the development of question structures are based on the classic article by E. Klima and U. Bellugi, "Syntactic Regularities in the Speech of Children" in *Psycholinguistic Papers*, edited by J. Lyons and R. Wales (Edinburgh: Edinburgh University Press, 1966). The auxiliary copying error in question structures is the subject of an experiment reported by M. Nakayama, "Performance Factors in Subject-Auxiliary Inversion," *Journal of Child Language* 14:113–26 (1987). The developmental order for *Wh* words is documented by L. Bloom, S. Merkin, and J. Wootten, "*Wh* Questions: Linguistic Factors that Contribute to the Sequence of Acquisition," *Child Development* 53:1084–92 (1982). Other descriptions confirming the main points of this account can be found in Chapter 9 of the book by Ingram cited below.

The sample fifty-word vocabulary in Section 5 is from p. 149 of the book by Ingram, cited below. The estimate that children know 13,000 words by age six is from S. Pinker, *The Language Instinct* (New York: Morrow, 1994), p. 151. The differences in the type of words in children's early vocabulary were first noted by K. Nelson "Structure and Strategy in Learning to Talk" in *Monographs of the Society for Research in Child Development*, Vol. 38, No. 149, 1973. The '*dax* experiment' on proper and common nouns is reported by N. Katz, E. Baker, and J. Macnamara in their article "What's in a Name? A Study of How Children Learn Common and Proper Nouns" in *Child Development* 45:469–73 (1974); the '*tiv* experiment' is from "The Child as Word Learner" by S. Carey in *Linguistic Theory and Psychological Reality*, edited by M. Halle, J. Bresnan, and G. Miller (Cambridge, MA: MIT Press, 1978). The contrast between overextension in production and comprehension is described on pp. 152–53 of the book by Ingram cited below; see also "Overextensions in Production and Comprehension Revisited" by L. Naigles and S. Gelman in *Journal of Child Language* 22:19–46 (1995). The literature on spatial and dimensional terms is reviewed both in the book by Ingram and in "Cognitive Prerequisites: The Evidence from Children Learning English" by J. Johnston in *The Crosslinguistic Study of Language Acquisition*, Vol. 2, edited by D. Slobin (Hillsdale, NJ: Erlbaum, 1985), pp. 961–1004.

The data on the acquisition of passive structures come from a study by E. Turner and R. Rommetveit, reported in their article "The Acquisition of Sentence Voice and Reversibility" in *Child Development* 38:650–60 (1967).

The role of correction in language development is examined in "Derivational Complexity and the Order of Acquisition in Child Speech" by R. Brown and C. Hanlon in *Cognition and the Development of Language*, edited by J. Hayes (New York: John Wiley, 1970). The data on mothers' reactions to children's ungrammatical and grammatical utterances come from "Brown and Hanlon Revisited: Mothers' Sensitivity to Ungrammatical Forms" by K. Hirsh-Pasek, R. Treiman, and M. Schneiderman in *Journal of Child Language* 11:81–88 (1984). The relationship between *yes-no* questions in maternal speech and the development of auxiliaries is discussed by E. Newport, H. Gleitman, and L. Gleitman in their article, "Mother, I'd Rather Do It Myself: Some Effects and Noneffects of Maternal Speech Style" in *Talking to Children*, edited by C. Snow and C. Ferguson (New York: Cambridge

University Press, 1977). General reviews of the role of the cognitive development in language acquisition can be found in the article by J. Johnston (cited above) and the book by D. Ingram (below). The description of Genie and of Rick is based on "Abnormal Language Acquisition and the Modularity of Language" by S. Curtiss in *Linguistics: The Cambridge Survey,* Vol. 2, edited by F. Newmeyer (New York: Cambridge University Press, 1988), pp. 96–116. Chelsea's case is discussed by S. Curtiss in "The Independence and Task-Specificity of Language" in *Interaction in Human Development,* edited by A. Bornstein and J. Bruner (Hillsdale, NJ: Erlbaum, 1989). The questions for this chapter were prepared by Joyce Hildebrand.

Recommended Reading

De Villiers, Jill, and Peter de Villiers. 1985. "The Acquisition of English." In *The Crosslinguistic Study of Language Acquisition.* Vol. 1. Edited by D. Slobin. Hillsdale, NJ: Erlbaum.

Goodluck, Helen. 1991. *Language Acquisition.* Cambridge, MA: Blackwell.

Ingram, David. 1989. *First Language Acquisition: Method, Description and Explanation.* New York: Cambridge University Press.

Locke, John. 1983. *Phonological Acquisition and Change.* New York: Academic Press.

O'Grady, William. 1997. *Syntactic Development.* Chicago: University of Chicago Press.

Piattelli-Palmarini, Massimo, ed. 1980. *Language and Learning: The Debate Between Jean Piaget and Noam Chomsky.* Cambridge, MA: Harvard University Press.

Questions

1. One piece of evidence that children acquire a grammar is their production of forms like *doed, leaved,* and *goed.* From recollections of your experience with children, what are some other forms (not related to the past tense rule) that children produce that indicate they are acquiring and overusing grammatical rules?

2. In one naturalistic study, a search for passive structures in a sample of 18,000 utterances from sixty children yielded only nineteen examples produced by twelve of the children.
   a) Is this evidence that the other forty-eight children had not yet mastered the passive structure? Why or why not?
   b) How are the disadvantages of the naturalistic method exemplified here?

3. The following transcriptions represent the pronunciation of a two-year-old child. Indicate which phonetic processes have applied in each case.

a) skin	[kɪd]	h) tent	[dɛt]
b) spoon	[buwn]	i) teddy	[dɛdij]
c) zoo	[duw]	j) brush	[bʌt]
d) John	[dɑn]	k) bump	[bʌp]
e) bath	[bæt]	l) play	[pwej]
f) other	[ʌdə]	m) breakfast	[brɛkpəst]
g) Smith	[mɪt]	n) cheese	[tʃijs]

4. Drawing on the phonetic processes posited for the preceding exercise, predict one or more plausible immature pronunciations for each of the following words.

a) show	e) juice
b) please	f) thumb
c) spit	g) zebra
d) under	h) ring

5. Based on the discussion in Section 3.1 about the developmental sequence of morpheme acquisition, consider the acquisition in other languages of the morphemes listed in Table 12.7. Would you predict that these morphemes would be acquired in exactly the same order as their English equivalents? Why or why not?

6. Considering children's tendency to overuse morphological rules, what might we expect a young child to use in the place of the following adult words? Justify your choice in each case.
   a) fish (plural)
   b) went
   c) mice
   d) ate
   e) has
   f) geese
   g) brought
   h) hit (past tense)
   i) himself
   j) women

7. Each of the following utterances is from the speech of a child in the two-word stage. Identify the semantic relation expressed by each of these utterances.

Intended meaning	*Child's utterance*
a) Jimmy is swimming.	Jimmy swim.
b) Ken's book	Ken book
c) Daddy is at work.	Daddy work
d) You push the baby.	push baby
e) Mommy is reading.	Mommy read

8. Consider the following data from Jordie, a two-and-a-half-year-old child, in light of the list of morphemes in Table 12.7.

Intended meaning	*Jordie's utterance*
a) Where's my blanket?	Where my blanket?
b) Does it go right here, Mommy?	Go right here, Mommy?
c) It's running over.	Running over.
d) Here, it goes here.	Here, go here.
e) No, that's mine.	No, that mine.
f) Dinosaurs say gronk.	Dinosaur say gronk.
g) There's more.	There more.

i) Which of the morphemes in Table 12.7 are missing in Jordie's sentences but present in the equivalent adult utterance?

ii) List the morphemes that are present in both the adult interpretations and in Jordie's speech. How do they differ from the missing morphemes?

9. Now consider the following utterances from a child named Krista.

	Intended meaning	*Krista's utterance*
a)	My name is Krista.	Mine name Krista.
b)	My last name is Pegit.	Last name Pegit.
c)	The tape is right there.	Tape right there.
d)	Daddy's book	Daddy book.
e)	I've got a book.	I'm got a book
f)	Read me a story.	Read me story.
g)	I'll do it.	I'm do it.
h)	He went outside.	He went outside.
i)	Open the gate, please.	Open a gate, please.
j)	Gramma's house.	Gramma's house.
k)	Smell the flowers.	Smell flowers.
l)	Shoes on.	Shoes on.
m)	The wee boy fell down.	Wee boy fell down.
n)	That's my ball.	That's mines ball.

i) Which morphemes are missing in Krista's speech, but present in the adult interpretations?
ii) Krista uses the past tense twice in the above utterances. Do you think this is evidence that she has acquired the past tense morpheme? Why or why not?
iii) Comment on Krista's difficulty with possessive pronouns.
iv) Do you think she has acquired possessive *-'s*? Why or why not?

10. The allomorphic variation associated with the 3rd person singular verbal ending *-s* is identical to that found with plural *-s*.
   a) Make up a test parallel to the one discussed in Section 3.2 .
   b) If possible, give your test to children between the ages of three and seven. Are your results similar to the ones discussed in the chapter?

11. The following utterances were produced spontaneously by Holly, age three years.
   a) I learned about loving moms.
   b) Put him in the bathtub.
   c) We eated gummy snakes.
   d) Thank you for giving these books us.
   e) I don't know.
   f) He bited my finger. (when corrected, she said: He bitted my finger.)
   g) I runned in the water.
   h) I rided on a elephant.

   i) Has Holly acquired the past tense morpheme? How do you know?
   ii) What is the evidence that words such as *bathtub, books,* and *water* are nouns for Holly and that words such as *eat, know,* and *ride* are verbs?
   iii) What is the evidence in Holly's speech that she has learned the XP rule?

12. Consider the following speech sample from a child.
    a) What Evan will read?
    b) What he can ride in?
    c) Will you help me?
    d) Can I have a piece of paper?

    i) Determine the stage of development of this child in terms of his acquisition of question structures.
    ii) What do we expect to happen next?

13. Consider the following examples of overextensions, all of which have actually been observed in children's speech. What is the basis for each of these overextensions?

	Word	*First referent*	*Overextensions*
a)	sch	sound of a train	music, noise of wheels, sound of rain
b)	bow-wow	dog	sheep, rabbit fur, puppet
c)	baby	baby	people in pictures
d)	sizo	scissors	nail file, knife, screwdriver, spoon
e)	policeman	policeman	mailman, sailor, doctor
f)	strawberry	strawberry	grapes, raspberry
g)	fireworks	fireworks	matches, light, cigarette
h)	Batman	Batman logo on a T-shirt	any logo on a T-shirt

14. Since children have a tendency to focus on the prototypical members of categories in the acquisition of words, how might you expect children to underextend the following words? What members of the category might you expect children not to include?
    a) car
    b) tree
    c) ball

15. As mentioned in this chapter, children acquire certain spatial terms like *behind* and *in front of* relatively late. They also acquire words like *those, this, here,* and *there* relatively late. What do all of these words have in common that delays their acquisition?

16. It has been reported that hearing children growing up in homes with non-speaking deaf parents cannot learn language from radio or even television (see p. 278 of *The Language Instinct* by S. Pinker).
    i) Can you think of any reasons for this?
    ii) What are the implications of these findings for our understanding of the type of experience that is required for language acquisition?

thirteen

Second Language Acquisition

John Archibald

When we talk about acquisition in SLA research, we are not talking about acquisition in the sense that one acquires polo ponies, Lladró figurines, or CBS, but rather in the sense that one acquires vicious habits, a taste for Brie, or a potbelly.

– Kevin R. Gregg,
"Second Language Acquisition Theory" (1989)

The field of **second language acquisition (SLA)** research investigates how people attain proficiency in a language which is not their mother tongue. So, whether we are looking at someone learning to read Greek in college, or someone becoming fluent in a fifth language in their forties, or a child acquiring a new language after moving to a new country, we call the process second language acquisition. The interesting phenomenon of children simultaneously acquiring two languages is generally investigated in the field known as **bilingualism**. In this chapter, we will primarily be concerned with second language acquisition in adults.

Over the years, the study of second language acquisition has been undertaken from a variety of different perspectives. In the 1950s and 60s the primary objective was pedagogic. Researchers were interested in trying to improve the way in which second languages were taught. We went from looking at how teachers taught to how learners learned. From the 1970s on, the focus shifted from the teacher to the learner.

The reason for this has something to do with what was going on in linguistics, psychology, and first language acquisition research. All three of these areas shifted focus from the external to the internal in the 1960s. Linguistics became concerned with the mental grammar of the speaker, not just the description of the linguistic structures of a given language. Psychology shifted from behaviorism (which denied the importance of mental representations) to cognitive psychology. And research on first language acquisition focused on children's internal grammars. Linguistics, psychology, and first language acquisition are also crucial to the study of SLA. Linguistics gives us a sophisticated and accurate description of what learners are trying to learn (the second language) and what they already know (the first language). Psychology can provide us with a learning theory to account for how people acquire knowledge. The field of first language acquisition, which has been around longer than the field of second language acquisition, offers various findings that can be productively applied to SLA. For example, we know that children who are acquiring their first language (L1) have grammars that are systematic and that their utterances are not just bad imitations of the adult language. As we will see, second language learners, too, are developing a grammar that is systematic even if it is not nativelike.

1 THE STUDY OF SECOND LANGUAGE ACQUISITION

In the case of first language acquisition, we may ascribe the difference between child and adult grammars to either cognitive or biological immaturity in the child. In the case of second language learning by adults, however, we cannot say that the learners are either cognitively or biologically immature. Rather, they are subject to an influence that is absent from the child's situation: the first language grammar. Let us diagram the situation as follows:

L1 ⟶ Interlanguage grammar ⟵ L2

Figure 13.1 Influences on an interlanguage grammar

This diagram illustrates the fact that second language learners have a systematic **interlanguage (IL)** grammar—so-called because it is influenced by both the first and the second language and has features of each.

1.1 THE ROLE OF THE FIRST LANGUAGE

One of the most easily recognizable traits of a second language learner's speech is that it bears a certain resemblance to the first language. Thus, someone whose first language is French is likely to sound different from someone whose first language is German when they both speak English. Consider in this regard the following typical pronunciation of the English word *have* by speakers of French and German.

Table 13.1 Phonological transfer

English target	*French speaker*	*German speaker*
have [hæv]	[æv]	[hæf]

The form produced by the French speakers reflects the fact that French lacks the phoneme /h/ while the pronunciation associated with German speakers can be traced to the fact that German includes a rule of Syllable Final Obstruent Devoicing (which changes the [v] to a [f]). The term **transfer** is used to describe the process whereby a feature or rule from a learner's first language is carried over to the IL grammar. Other examples can be seen in Table 13.2.

Table 13.2 More phonological transfer

L1	*L2*	*Example*	*Comment*
Spanish	English	I espeak Espanish.	Spanish does not allow s + consonant sequences word-initially.
English	French	[ty] (you) → [tu]	English does not have the front, rounded vowel [y]. The English speaker substitutes the [u] sound.
Quebec French	English	Over dere.	The [ð] sound is replaced by [d].
European French	English	Over zere.	The [ð] sound is replaced by [z].
English	Spanish	[paɾa] 'for' → [para]	As English does not have the tapped [ɾ] as an allophone of /r/, [r] is substituted.

1.2 The role of the second language

The first language is not the only influence on the interlanguage grammar, since some properties of the IL can be traced to aspects of the L2. In the case of a German speaker who is learning English, for example, the IL grammar will contain some features of both German and English. Consider how a German speaker learning Canadian English might pronounce the word *eyes*.

Table 13.3 One possible pronunciation of the English word *eyes* by a German-speaking learner

Target form	*Result of Final Obstruent Devoicing*	*Result of Canadian Vowel Raising*
/ajz/	[ajs]	[ʌjs]

Here, the learner first applies the rule of Syllable Final Obstruent Devoicing (transferred from German), changing /ayz/ to [ays]. But the learner also has acquired some knowledge of the target language—in this case, the rule of Canadian Vowel Raising (discussed in Chapter 3), which states that [aj] becomes [ʌj] before a voiceless consonant in the same syllable. Thanks to application of the Syllable Final Obstruent

Devoicing Rule, the input form now ends in a voiceless consonant ([s]) which triggers Canadian Raising. This example serves to show us something about the nature of an interlanguage: it contains features of both the L1 and the L2.

1.3 THE NATURE OF AN INTERLANGUAGE

The dual nature of IL grammars is captured in the **Ontogeny Model** of second language acquisition. According to this model, there are two types of error in an IL grammar: **transfer errors** and **developmental errors**. As we have seen, the former type of error reflects transfer from the L1. In contrast, developmental errors involve the same sort of mistakes that children make in acquiring their L1. For example, as we saw in Chapter 12, children learning English as a first language sometimes produce forms like *goed* and *breaked*, apparently overgeneralizing the regular rule for past tense formation. A similar developmental error is observed in second language learners, who also overgeneralize rules as they acquire a grammar.

It is possible that the processes of transfer and overgeneralization in L2 learning are the result of a single cognitive strategy that could be informally stated as "use what you know" or "go with what you have". This predicts that the kind of errors made by second language learners will be dependent on their level of proficiency. Beginning learners may have nothing to draw on but their L1. More advanced learners, however, have acquired a certain amount of knowledge about the L2 and this knowledge becomes a potential source of errors. This is illustrated in Table 13.4.

Table 13.4 Error patterns in L2 acquisition

Level of proficiency	*Transfer errors*	*Developmental errors*
Beginner	high	low
Intermediate	medium	high
Advanced	low	low

The predictions of the Ontogeny Model are illustrated in Figure 13.2. The number of transfer errors should decrease over time, whereas the number of developmental errors should be small initially but then should increase before finally decreasing.

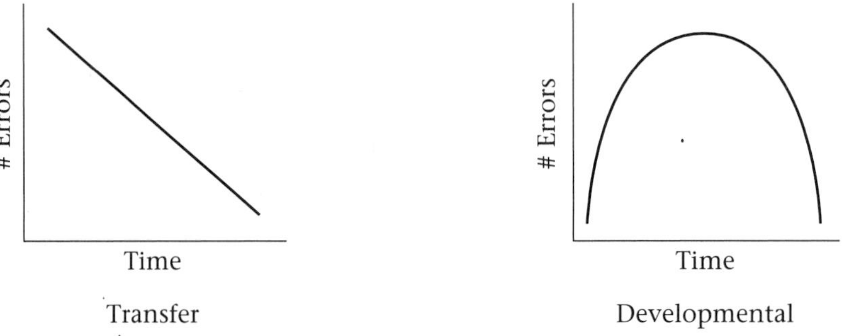

Figure 13.2 Error patterns predicted by the Ontogeny Model

The IL grammar, then, is influenced by both the L1 and the L2, though the proportion of influence is dependent on the learner's level of overall proficiency. Note that advanced learners have low numbers of both transfer and developmental errors. Not all learners, however, reach this advanced stage. It is common in second language acquisition for learners to reach a plateau in their development. For example, even after many years of exposure to English, a second language learner may still produce sentences like *I don't know what should I do* (meaning 'I don't know what I should do') in spite of hearing the grammatical version from native speakers and perhaps being corrected. When the interlanguage grammar stops changing, it is said to have **fossilized**.

Second language learners can exhibit nonnativelike characteristics in any linguistic domain, as can be seen in Table 13.5.

Table 13.5 Types of errors found in the acquisition of English

L1	*Example*	*Error type*	*Comment*
Spanish	My wife is embarrassed. (meaning 'pregnant')	lexical	Spanish *embarasada* = 'pregnant'
Various	I live in a two bedroom department.	lexical	Sometimes the wrong word can be chosen.
Various	I didn't took the car.	morphological	English does not mark the past tense on both auxiliary and main verbs.
Various	She get ups late.	morphological	The speaker adds the agreement marker to the particle not the verb.
French	He drinks frequently beer.	syntactic	French places the verb before the adverb.
Various (e.g., Turkish, Arabic)	There's the man that I saw him.	syntactic	Some languages allow pronouns in this position in a relative clause.

1.4 The final state

So far we have been talking about the characteristics of the intermediate grammar. But a discussion of what an IL grammar looks like must consider the **target**, that is, what is to be acquired. The field of SLA, then, must address the issue of actual proficiency or **communicative competence**. While knowledge of a language's grammar allows us to distinguish between grammatical and ungrammatical sentences, successful communication requires much more than this. The learner must also be able to use the language in a way that is appropriate to the situation or context. As the following figure helps illustrate, both grammatical accuracy and communicative ability are part of communicative competence. We will briefly consider each of the major subparts of the model.

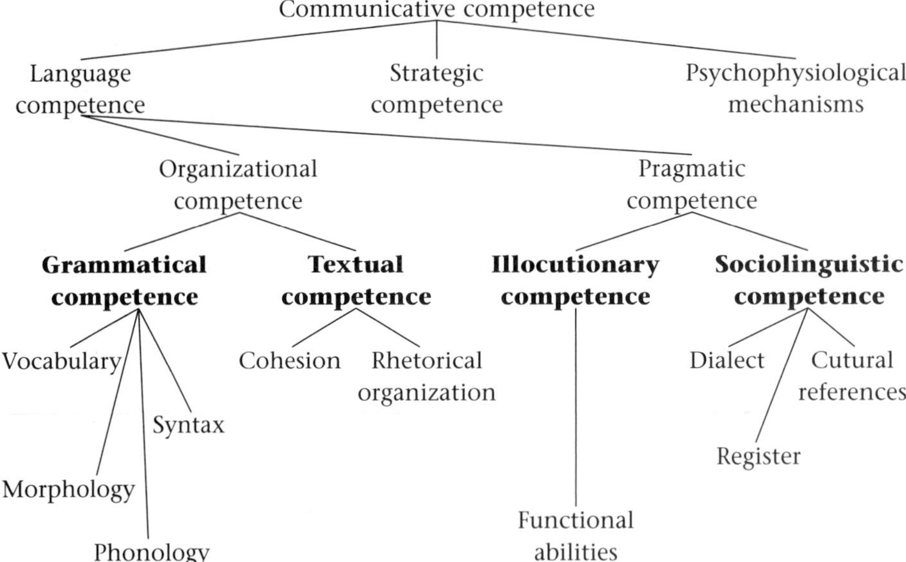

Figure 13.3 A model of communicative competence

Grammatical competence

Grammatical competence has to do with knowledge of the core components of the grammar: phonetics, phonology, morphology, syntax, and semantics. We will address these areas in detail in Section 2.

Textual competence

As the following examples show, a text is not just a sequence of grammatical utterances. **Textual competence** involves knowledge of the rules that string sentences together to make a well-formed **text** in the spoken or written language.

1)

MGs can be very tempermental. MGs won't start if they are wet. When they work, MGs are fun to drive. They do not work often.

2)

Like most sports cars, MGs can be very temperamental. For example, they won't start if they are wet. However, on the rare days when they work, they are fun to drive.

The difference between the two texts does not involve the grammaticality of individual sentences, but rather relates to differences in the use of intersentential links such as *like, for example,* and *however.* To be proficient, second language learners have to acquire the ability to organize and link sentences in this way.

Illocutionary competence

The meaning of an utterance is not always directly reflected in its surface structure. For example, when uttering the sentence *Have you ever considered professional help?*, a speaker could have in mind a variety of intended meanings. He or she might mean 'I can't help you, but maybe somebody else could' or 'I think you are a truly disturbed individual; get help.' The speaker's intent in producing an utterance is referred to as **illocutionary force**. **Illocutionary competence**, then, refers to the ability to comprehend a speaker's intent, and to produce a variety of syntactic structures to convey a particular intent in various circumstances (e.g., *Are you cold?, Could I close the window?, Why on earth is the window open?*). This, too, is something that second language learners need to acquire.

Sociolinguistic competence

As we will see in Chapter 14, language use can vary according to the context. For example, we use a different style of language in informal situations than we do in formal ones. This can affect phonology, syntax, and lexical choice, as can be seen in the following two utterances.

3)

I assume we will be working late again this evening? What a shame!

4)

Workin' late again! Dammit!

In order to be **sociolinguistically competent**, second language learners need to be able to comprehend and produce a variety of social dialects appropriately.

In sum, communicative competence is a model of proficiency that allows us to measure second language knowledge and ability, to construct second language proficiency tests, and to design balanced second language courses.

1.5 Variation in performance

An important goal of L2 research is to integrate the study of competence (linguistic knowledge) and **performance** (actual language use in particular situations). One of the characteristics of the output of second language learners is that it is quite inconsistent. For example, a learner might well produce the following sentence:

5)

I **didn't** like **th**at movie so I told her I **no** want to go **d**ere.

In this (hypothetical) example, the learner is inconsistent, getting one of the two negatives right and correctly pronouncing one of the interdental fricatives. The question that intrigues researchers has to do with what causes this sort of variation. We usually think of knowledge as fairly stable within an individual. So, for example, if you make a mistake while speaking in your native language, you tend not to question your competence in that language, but rather to assume that you made some kind of performance error. So how do we account for learners who behave as if they know how to negate a verb or pronounce [ð] on some occasions, but not others? Do they have the knowledge or don't they?

It is difficult to answer this question, in part because of considerations involving error frequency. If a second language learner gets something wrong 10 percent of the time, is it the same (in terms of competence) as getting it wrong 60 percent of the time? We would probably say that a nonnative speaker who gets the English past tense correct 10 percent of the time doesn't know it, and that someone who gets it right 90 percent of the time does. But what of someone who gets it right somewhere between those two scores? This is a complex research question. The (admittedly simplistic) view adopted in this chapter is that variation of this sort falls into the realm of linguistic performance.

Linguistic performance clearly involves the interaction of a number of cognitive systems and has much in common with other skills. An important notion for the study of how skills develop involves the distinction between controlled and automatic processing. When acquiring a new skill (e.g., playing golf) we begin by having to devote a lot of conscious or controlled processing to the activity. Feet apart, head down, elbow straight, white shoes, etc. Once we become proficient, we 'just' hit the ball; the activity has become automatic.

We need to shift processing from controlled to automatic because, as humans, we have a fixed processing capacity. We can't consciously process everything at once. Shifting some material into automatic processing frees up space for more controlled processing. Consider an example from reading. When we first learn how to read, we devote much of our cognitive processing to determining what the written symbols stand for. When we are focusing on decoding the letters, we do not have the processing capacity to deal with things like reading for prejudice or bias. After a time, though, letter recognition happens automatically in our first language and learners can devote more of their cognitive capacity to higher-level skills.

That native speakers do this kind of thing automatically can be seen by the difficulty we have in proofreading. It is hard to suppress the information we're getting from the context since the mind tries to make sense of what it's reading. Conversely, when we are forced by exceptional circumstances to devote a lot of energy to decoding the print (e.g., a bad photocopy or fax), our higher-level processing slows down; we can't focus as much on the message when we are focusing on the form.

All this is relevant to second language acquisition in that it can help explain the variable performance of L2 learners. When learners are focusing on the form of the L2 utterance, they may be able to produce it accurately. When there are extra demands, however, such as trying to communicate a complex thought or carry on a conversation in a noisy room, errors may occur. This suggests that the learner has a mental representation of the form in question (say a negated verb or a [ð]) but can have difficulty implementing or accessing it under certain conditions.

2 INTERLANGUAGE GRAMMARS

Let us turn now to a discussion of the specifics of what is acquired when learning the phonology, morphology, and syntax of a second language. The general question we are trying to answer here is "What is the structure of an interlanguage?" Second language learners are acquiring grammars, and those grammars involve mental representations. Therefore we can investigate the nature of those representations within the various subdomains of linguistic theory. We begin with phonology.

2.1 L2 PHONOLOGY

Let us consider what is to be acquired in the domain of phonology. Broadly speaking, we can distinguish between segmental and prosodic phonology. Segmental phonology has to do with the characteristics of phonological segments, like consonants and vowels. Prosodic phonology, on the other hand, has to do with phonological phenomena that affect more than a single segment (e.g., syllables and stress).

Segmental phonology

As we saw in Chapter 3, languages vary in terms of the sounds in their segmental inventory. There is thus a good chance that a second language learner will have to learn to produce and perceive some new sounds when acquiring a second language.

One of the most obvious characteristics of adult second language speech is that it is 'accented' as the result of phonological and phonetic transfer from the native language. This is why native speakers of English can usually distinguish French-accented English from German-accented English. Consider the following examples.

Table 13.6 French- and German-accented English

English target		*Quebec French speaker*	*German speaker*
[ðə]	'the'	[də]	[zə]

As both French and German lack the interdental fricative [ð], native speakers of those languages substitute a sound from their L1 where English has that sound. Generally, the learners substitute a sound that shares some features with the target sound. In the example in Table 13.6, the French speaker substituted a voiced alveolar (coronal) stop, while the German speaker substituted a voiced alveolar (coronal) fricative for the English voiced, interdental (coronal) fricative. Particularly at a beginning level of proficiency, L2 learners pronounce words using their L1 phonological system.

A similar phenomenon can be seen in the phonology of loanwords. When a language borrows a word from another language, it makes the word fit into its own phonological system. For example, as we saw in Chapter 3, when English borrowed the word *pterodactyl* from Greek, it reduced the onset cluster [pt], which is well-formed in Greek but not in English. However, no such change was made in the word *helicopter* (also from Greek) since it already complied with the phonological pattern of English.

Markedness

One question that has received a lot of attention in SLA research is whether some sounds are harder to acquire in a second language than others. Perhaps some sounds are simpler than others, or perhaps some sound systems are easier for speakers of a certain language to acquire. Would it be easier for a Japanese speaker to acquire English or Vietnamese? As might be expected, these are not simple issues. We cannot talk about the ease or difficulty of entire languages, but we may have something to say about individual sounds.

When linguists try to deal with the notions of ease or simplicity, they make use of the notion of **markedness**. Structures that are simple *and/or* especially common in human language are said to be unmarked, while structures that are complex or less common are said to be marked. So, we might say that a sound that is found in relatively few of the world's languages (e.g., [θ]) is marked, whereas a sound that occurs in many of the world's languages (e.g., [t]) is unmarked.

Markedness is commonly approached from the perspective of language typology, which is concerned with the comparative study of languages. As noted in Chapter 9, researchers have discovered certain implicational universals of the form "if a language has x, it will also have y". For example, if a language has nasal vowels (e.g., [ã]), then it will also have oral vowels (e.g., [a]). Significant to the understanding of implicational universals is the fact that the implication is unidirectional. Thus a language that has oral vowels does not necessarily have nasal vowels. This allows us to identify [a] as less marked than [ã], in accordance with the following generalization.

6)

X is more marked than *y* if the presence of *x* implies the presence of *y*, *but not vice versa*.

It is interesting to ask whether IL grammars obey such implicational universals and whether this can tell us something about the question of ease and difficulty of learning.

The **Markedness Differential Hypothesis** investigates second language acquisition in terms of typological universals by comparing the relative markedness of structures in the L1 and the L2. Remember the earlier example of Syllable Final Obstruent Devoicing in German, which explains why a word like *hund* 'dog' is pronounced with a [t] at the end. German speakers learning English typically transfer Syllable Final Obstruent Devoicing into their IL (producing [hæt] for [hæd] 'had') and must learn to make the contrast between [t] and [d] at the ends of words. We might be tempted to think that the principle underlying this phenomenon is something like "it's hard to learn to make contrasts that your L1 doesn't make". But when we look at another set of data we see that this is not the case.

French makes a contrast between [ʃ] and [ʒ] in places where English does not, as Table 13.7 indicates.

Table 13.7 The [ʃ] / [ʒ] contrast in English and French

	English [ʃ] / [ʒ]	*French [ʃ] / [ʒ]*
Initial	sure [ʃ] / * [ʒ]	chant ([ʃ]) / gens ([ʒ]) 'song' 'people'
Medial	assure ([ʃ]) / azure ([ʒ])	boucher ([ʃ]) / bouger ([ʒ]) 'to fill up' 'to budge'
Final	leash ([ʃ]) / liege ([ʒ])	hache ([ʃ]) / age ([ʒ]) 'h' 'age'

If it were invariably difficult for second language learners to make contrasts that are not found in their L1, we would expect English speakers to have difficulty learning to produce [ʒ] at the beginning of words. But they don't. English speakers seem able to learn to pronounce French words like *jaune* 'yellow' and *jeudi* 'Thursday' without trouble.

The notion of markedness can be used to explain why German speakers have difficulty making a new contrast in English, while English speakers don't have difficulty making a new contrast in French. The typological situation is as follows:

- There are languages that have a voicing contrast initially, medially, and finally (e.g., English).
- There are languages that have a voicing contrast initially, and medially, but not finally (e.g., German).
- There are languages that have a voicing contrast initially, but not medially or finally (e.g., Sardinian).

These generalizations allow us to formulate the following implicational universal.

7)

The presence of a voicing contrast in final position implies the presence of a voicing contrast in medial position, which in turn implies the presence of a voicing contrast in initial position.

We can represent this universal graphically as follows:

8)

initial < medial < final
C B A

The presence of A implies the presence of B (but not vice versa), and the presence of B implies the presence of C (but not vice versa). Therefore A is the most marked and C is the least marked. This markedness differential explains the degrees of difficulty exhibited by the German and English L2 learners. The German speakers learning English are attempting to acquire a contrast in a universally more marked position (final), whereas the English speakers learning French are attempting to acquire a contrast in a universally unmarked position (initial).

In addition to the segmental inventory, second language learners also have to acquire the prosodic phonology of the target language. For example, they have to acquire the principles of syllabification and stress assignment. We will now look at each in turn.

L2 syllabification

We saw in Chapter 3 that syllables have the hierarchical structure in Figure 13.4.

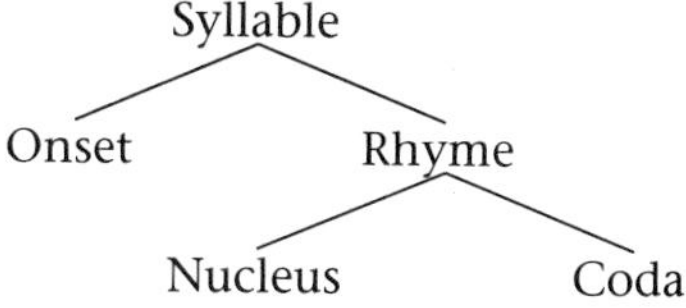

Figure 13.4 The internal structure of the syllable

The languages of the world vary in terms of whether syllabic nodes can branch. Some languages (e.g., Japanese) do not allow branching onsets or codas. Ignoring some complexities, let us assume that all syllables in such languages must be CV or CVC. More complex syllables such as CCVCC are not allowed. A common phenomenon in second language learning involves modifying an L2 word so that it fits the L1 syllable structure. Consider the following words spoken by someone whose L1 is Arabic:

9)

English target	*Nonnative speaker's version*
plant	pilanti
Fred	Fired
translate	tiransilet

Arabic does not allow branching onsets or codas, so an English word like *plant* cannot be mapped onto a single Arabic syllable. A characteristic of Arabic is that illicit consonant clusters are broken up by an epenthetic [i].

With this in mind, let us look at the steps that an Arabic speaker would go through in syllabifying 'plant'.

Step 1 Initial syllabification: Assign vowels to a nucleus (N) and the nucleus to a rhyme (R).

Step 2 Assign allowable onset (O) consonants (in Arabic, one).

Step 3 Assign allowable coda (C) consonants (in Arabic, one).

Step 4 Insert an epenthetic [i] to the right of an unsyllabified consonant.

Step 5 Assign vowels to a nucleus and the nucleus to a rhyme.

Step 6 Assign allowable onset consonants (in Arabic, one).

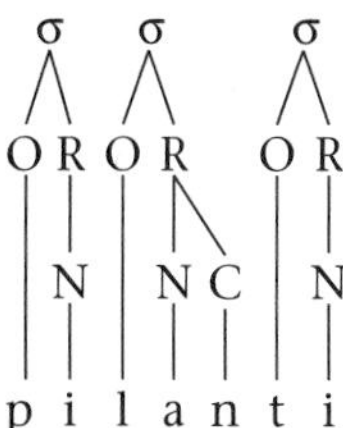

As this example shows, we can explain why Arabic speakers pronounce English words in the way that they do by investigating the principles of syllabification in the L1. Especially at the beginning levels of proficiency, the structure of the IL is influenced by the structure of the L1.

Stress assignment

L2 learners also have to acquire the stress patterns of the language they are trying to learn. Consider an example from Polish. Polish is a language in which word-level stress is assigned to the next-to-last syllable (regardless of syllable weight). Such principles transfer and result in one of the characteristics of a Polish accent in English: the tendency to place stress on the penultimate syllable regardless of syllable weight. Remember from Chapter 3 that in English heavy syllables tend to attract stress (e.g., *aróma, agénda*). The following examples illustrate a nonnative stress pattern in which the second to last syllable is always stressed.

10)

English target	*Nonnative form*
astónish	astónish
maintáin	máintain
cábinet	cabínet

2.2 L2 SYNTAX

L2 learners also have to acquire the syntax of their new language. In this section, we will look at two facets of syntactic structure: null subjects and verb movement.

Null subjects

As we saw in Chapter 5, **Universal Grammar** includes universal principles (that account for what all natural languages have in common), as well as parameters (that account for cross-linguistic variation). Parameters are like linguistic switches (often binary) that can be set to a particular value as a result of the linguistic input. One of the first parameters to be discussed in the generative literature was the Null Subject (or pronoun-drop) Parameter. Essentially, this parameter is designed to account for the contrast between languages like French and English, which require overt grammatical subjects (e.g., *He speaks French/*Speaks French*), and languages like Spanish and Italian, which allow subjects to be omitted (e.g., Spanish *Él habla español/Habla español* '[S/he] speaks Spanish').

11)

The Null Subject Parameter:
The subject of a finite clause {may/may not} be null.

Languages that allow null subjects tend to have other grammatical traits associated with them. For one, they tend to allow declarative sentences with the word order Verb + Subject as well as Subject + Verb, as in the following examples from Spanish.

12)

a. Juan llegó.
John arrived.
b. Llegó Juan
arrived John.

Secondly, they tend to allow sentences like the following, in which a complementizer (here *que* 'that') is immediately followed by the trace of a moved *Wh* word.

13)

Quién dijo usted que e̲ llegó?
who said you that arrived?
'Who did you say arrived?'

As the following example shows, such sentences are unacceptable in Standard English.

14)

*Who did you say [$_{CP}$ that [$_{S}$ e̲ arrived]]?
(deep structure = *you did say that who arrived*)

In other words, languages like English ([–null subject]) do not allow *that*-trace sequences, whereas languages like Spanish ([+null subject]) do.

Studies on L2 learners of English show that Spanish speakers are more likely to judge subjectless English sentences to be grammatical than are French speakers. This is consistent with the assumption that L1 parameter settings are transferred into the IL grammar, at least in the early stages. Learning a second language can be seen as involving the resetting of parameters that have different values in the L1 and the L2.

When Spanish subjects are given a task that requires them to change a declarative sentence into a question, they are more likely to produce a sentence that contains a *that*-trace sequence than are French subjects. For example, if Spanish subjects are given a sentence like *Joshua believed that his father would be late* and have to form a question asking about the underlined element, they are more likely than French subjects to produce a sentence like *Who did Joshua believe that t would be late?* This points toward the possibility that the admissibility of null subjects and the acceptability of *that*-trace sequences are somehow both related to the **Null Subject Parameter** (i.e., speakers of null subject languages are more likely to permit *that*-trace sequences).

There are complications, however. Remember that the study just described had the Spanish and French speakers form new sentences. Another study had both French and Spanish subjects judge the grammaticality of English sentences with a *that*-trace violation. Both groups were quite able to reject those sentences as ungrammatical. For some reason, there is a stronger L1 influence when learners have to form new sentences themselves.

Verb movement

One difference between French and English involves the setting of the **Verb Movement Parameter**.

15)

The Verb Movement Parameter:
V {raises/does not raise} to Infl.

We saw in Chapter 5 that the transformation of verb movement takes a verb from within the VP and moves it up in Infl. Simplifying slightly, let us say that English does not allow verb movement but French does. Thus, in French the verb raises to Infl past a preverbal adverb, but in English it does not. This difference can be seen in the following sentences, in which movement of the verb over the adverb separating it from the Infl position gives a bad result in English but a good result in French.

16)

a. *Marie watches often television.
b. Marie regarde souvent la télévision.

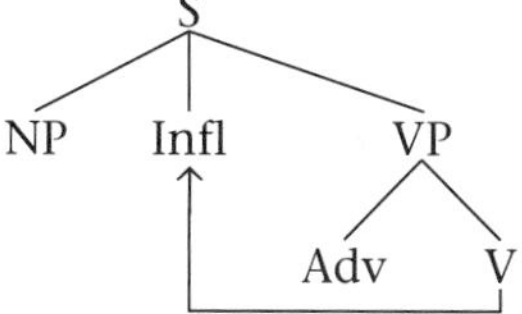

Figure 13.5 Verb movement

Studies have shown that French speakers learning English initially assume that English allows verb raising. In order to learn English they have to reset the value of their verb raising parameter.

Markedness and the Subset Principle

Another interesting facet of a parameter-setting approach to SLA has to do with whether adult L2 learners can reset their parameters, and whether the notion of directionality of difficulty associated with the Markedness Differential Hypothesis (see above, Section 2.1) can be captured in a parameter-setting model. The Null Subject Parameter can be used to address these questions. To understand how, we must first consider how a parameter-setting model instantiates the notion of markedness.

If we consider the two settings of the Null Subject Parameter (+/–), we can see that the different values generate different grammars, as shown in the following sentences from English and Spanish.

17)

[–null subject]:	I speak Spanish.
[+null subject]:	Yo hablo español.
	Hablo español.

As you can see, the [+null subject] setting generates more grammatical utterances than the [–null subject] setting does. Therefore, the [–] setting is said to be a subset of the [+] setting. This is represented graphically in Figure 13.6.

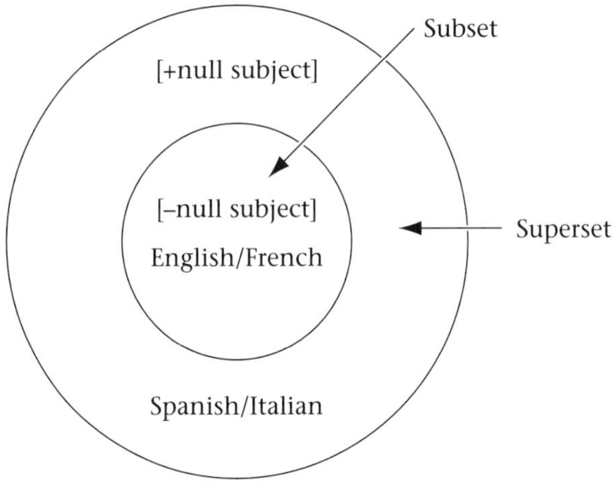

Figure 13.6 Subset/superset relation for the Null Subject Parameter

Parameter setting in such cases is guided by the **Subset Principle**.

18)

The Subset Principle:
The initial or default setting of a parameter will correspond to the most restrictive option (i.e., the option that permits the fewest patterns).

The Subset Principle stipulates that for first language learners, the initial or default setting will be the subset value (i.e., [–null subject]) in the case of the Null Subject Parameter.

Second language learners may have to reset their parameters. When attempting to reset from subset to superset or from superset to subset, there are different types of evidence available to the learner. Imagine a learner of English (who has the [–] setting) trying to learn Spanish. The learner's initial assumption will be the L1 parameter setting, which leads to the expectation that all sentences will have overt subjects. When faced with Spanish input, the learner will be exposed to grammatical utterances in the L2 that do not have overt subjects (e.g., *Hablo español* '[I] speak Spanish'), which indicates that the L1 setting is incorrect and needs to be reset. Data like these, which involve grammatical utterances to which one is actually exposed, are referred to as **positive evidence**.

Now imagine a learner whose L1 is Spanish ([+]) who is trying to learn English ([–]). The learner's initial assumption will be that English should be [+null subject], like the L1. The learner's IL grammar will allow sentences with overt subjects and sentences without. There will be no positive evidence in the English input directed at this learner to show that the L1 parameter setting is wrong. The learner will hear sentences with overt subjects, which are sanctioned by the current IL grammar, but there will be no direct indication that sentences with null subjects are not allowed. There is no pressure to reset the parameter. In this case, the learner will have to rely on **negative evidence** (i.e., observations about what is missing or ungrammatical in the data) to reset the parameter. In particular, the learner would either have to be explicitly told what is ungrammatical (direct negative evidence), or infer that it is ungrammatical based on the fact that no one else ever says it (indirect negative evidence).

Given that direct positive evidence is available in one case (English → Spanish), and negative evidence is required in the other (Spanish → English), we might predict that it is harder for Spanish speakers to learn the English value of the Null Subject Parameter than vice versa. In fact, the prediction is borne out. Studies have shown that it is easier for English speakers to reset to the Spanish value of the Null Subject Parameter, than it is for Spanish subjects to reset to the English setting.

Let us now consider how an approach based on typological universals would treat the same phenomenon. The possibility of null subjects implies the possibility of overt subjects, but not vice versa.

19)

overt subjects < null subjects

Therefore, null subjects would be thought of as more marked, and consequently, more difficult to acquire. The Markedness Differential Hypothesis predicts that structures that are more marked typologically will cause difficulty in SLA because they are more marked. The Subset Principle, on the other hand, predicts that structures that are more marked will not cause difficulty because there will be clear evidence that the L1 setting is wrong. Although only the Subset Principle seems to make the correct prediction in the case of the null subjects, further research is necessary in order to see which approach is better able to handle a wider range of data.

2.3 L2 MORPHOLOGY

The study of second language morphology has a slightly different flavor than the study of either L2 phonology or syntax. L2 phonology has been studied for a long time, though the analyses have changed to reflect changes in linguistic theory. L2 syntax is a much younger field, and much of it has been influenced by current linguistic theory. By contrast, L2 morphology has been studied more or less in a theoretical vacuum. In the 1970s, a number of studies collected data on the accuracy of second language learners on a variety of morphemes. This research drew on previous studies of first language acquisition that had attempted to determine the order of acquisition of morphemes in L1 development. The following developmental sequence was found.

Table 13.8 Developmental order for first language acquisition

1. *-ing*	the present participle affix (e.g., she is work*ing*)
2. Plural *-s*	(e.g., bottle*s*)
3. Irregular past	(e.g., she *taught* French)
4. Possessive *-s*	(e.g., a child'*s* toy)
5. Copula *be*	(e.g., I *am* happy)
6. Articles	(e.g., *a, the*)
7. Regular past	(e.g., she walk*ed* quickly)
8. Third person *-s*	(e.g., she walk*s* quickly)
9. Auxiliary *be*	(e.g., She *is* working)

Research on second language acquisition focused on whether the developmental sequence in L2 learning was the same as for L1 learning. The following order was found.

Table 13.9 Developmental order for second language acquisition

1. *-ing*
2. Copula *be*
3. Articles
4. Auxiliary *be*
5. Plural *-s*
6. Irregular past
7. Regular past
8. Third person *-s*
9. Possessive *-s*

There are many similarities but there are also some differences. For example, note that auxiliary and copula *be* are acquired at a relatively earlier point in L2 than in L1, and that the possessive morpheme *-'s* is acquired later in L2 than in L1. To attempt to explain these patterns, we need to look a little more closely at the structures that implement inflectional morphology.

In the syntax section we saw that in English main verbs do not raise to Infl. Now we note that the verb *be* does raise to Infl if no modal is present (see Section 4.3 in Chapter 5).

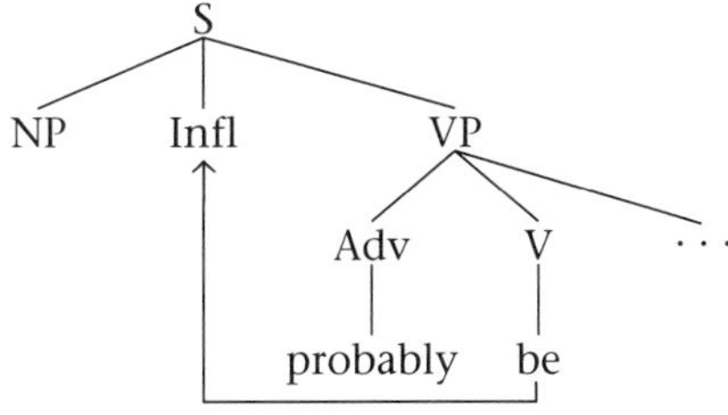

Figure 13.7 Raising of *be* to Infl

20)

a. No modal is present: the auxiliary verb moves from inside the VP to Infl.
He is [$_{VP}$ probably t eating].

b. A modal is present: the auxiliary verb does not raise.
He should [$_{VP}$ probably be eating].

c. Regular verbs do not raise.
He [$_{VP}$ probably likes eating] versus *He likes [$_{VP}$ probably t eating].

Children acquire *be* as a main verb before they acquire *be* as an auxiliary verb. So, children produce sentences that have only a copula verb (e.g., *He is hungry*) before they produce sentences that include an auxiliary plus a main verb (e.g., *He was working*) as shown in the trees in Figure 13.8.

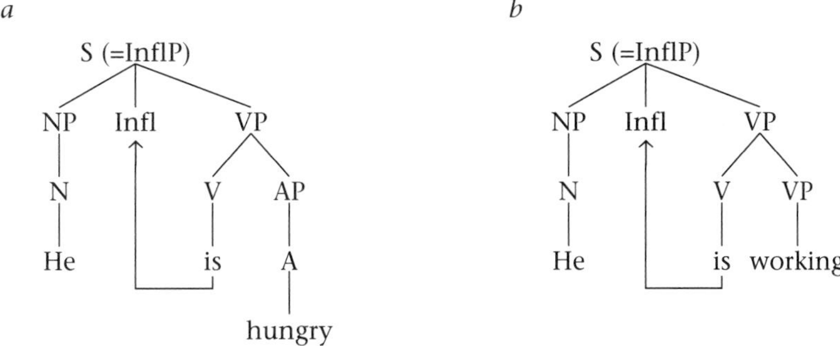

Figure 13.8 Copula versus auxiliary *be*

The structure in b has an extra level of complexity in that it has a complex verb phrase (one VP within another). Adults, on the other hand, appear to be able to use both the simple copula and auxiliary verbs quite early on. Whether this difference is because of the adult's greater ability to handle complexity in general cognitive terms or because children's linguistic systems are maturing remains a controversial and unresolved issue.

In addition, note that children acquire the three *-s* morphemes in the order plural, possessive, and third person in their first language. Phonetically, these morphemes have the same realization, so we can't say that the order reflects phonological complexity. The order might be explained by noting that plural is a word-level phenomenon (e.g., *dogs*), possessive is a phrase-level phenomenon (e.g., [*the king of England*]*'s horse*, not *[*the king*]*'s of England horse*), and third person marking involves a relation between the verb and a phrase (the subject) elsewhere in the sentence (e.g., [*That man*] *usually thinks too much*). Like the pattern noted for the development of copula and auxiliary *be*, children seem to be acquiring structures in order of complexity, as shown in Figure 13.9.

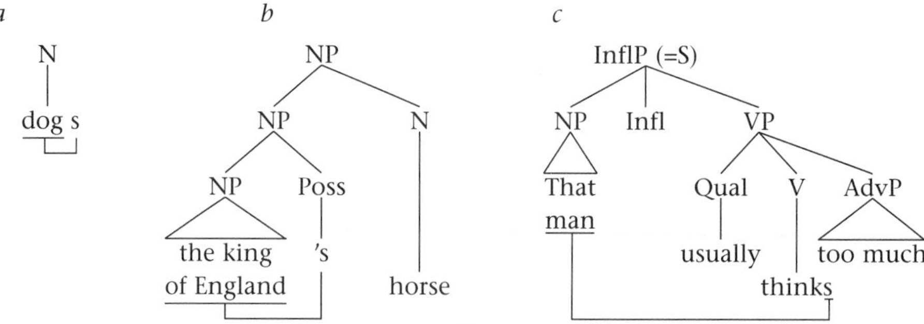

Figure 13.9 Three types of /s/ affix

In contrast, adults acquire the plural quite early, but then seem to get both the possessive and the third person marking quite late—perhaps for reasons involving processing. (When concentrating on getting the words right, we do not always have the processing capacity to produce well-formed higher-level structures.) Interestingly, the adults do not seem to find interphrasal morphology (like c above) more difficult than phrasal morphology (like b above). This may be because the adults have already acquired the grammar for their first language and that grammar most likely has both phrase-level and interphrasal morphological phenomena. In contrast, children have to set up a hierarchical structure of a grammar for the first time, and could conceivably be building the structure from the bottom up (words → phrases → sentences).

In summary, we note that the order of acquisition data are intriguing in both first and second language acquisition, even though we await a conclusive explanation of the facts.

3 FACTORS AFFECTING SLA

So far, we've looked at some of the characteristics of an IL grammar. Now let's turn to a variety of factors that can influence second language acquisition. It is clear that there is much more variation in the grammars of people learning second languages than in the grammars of people learning first languages. This brings us to the question of what factors might help to account for that variation.

3.1 AGE

One of the obvious ways that language learners vary is in their age. People start learning second languages at different points in their lives. Could the age of onset of L2 learning cause different levels of final proficiency?

This is a question usually considered under what is known as the **Critical Period Hypothesis** (see Chapter 12, Section 6.5). We know that biologically based critical periods exist in other species. For example, some birds can learn the song of their species if exposed to it only during a particular window of opportunity. If they hear the song too early or too late, then learning will not take place. (See Chapter 16 for further discussion.)

Is second language learning like this? Is there an optimal time (or critical period) to acquire a second language? The answer appears to be yes and no. Proficiency in a language is a remarkably complex thing (see the discussion of communicative competence in Section 1.4). Usually discussion of a possible critical period focuses on the area of phonological competence. While people who begin SLA as adults tend to retain nonnativelike phonology in the target language, it is much more difficult to predict knowledge or ability in any of the other areas of communicative competence (syntax, cohesion, sociolinguistics, etc.) based upon age of acquisition.

In fact, even L2 phonology is not so straightforward as it might first appear to be. We can predict with fair certainty that people who start learning their L2 before the age of seven will have nativelike L2 speech and that people who start learning after fourteen or fifteen will probably have nonnativelike speech. But the results for people who start learning between the ages of seven and fourteen are much more varied. Some end up with accents, and some do not.

There is no current evidence of anything biological that is preventing adults from acquiring proficiency in a second language. Factors that have been considered in the past (like brain **lateralization**—see Chapter 11) are now thought to be of little predictive value in determining L2 ability. The question of 'ultimate attainment' in L2 acquisition is still hotly debated, and the literature has cited cases of adult L2 learners who apparently perform virtually identically to native speakers in a variety of domains (including phonology).

Currently, the critical period debate in SLA research is usually couched in terms of the question "Do adults have access to Universal Grammar?" Rather than looking for changes in the brain that coincide with aging, researchers now look to see whether IL grammars are governed by the same constraints as primary languages (e.g., Swahili, Yoruba). If adults are engaged in the same kind of development process as children, then we would expect their IL grammars to be describable in terms of the same principles and parameters of UG that we use to describe primary languages. Conversely, if adults are acquiring their second languages using qualitatively different learning mechanisms than are used to acquire an L1 (e.g., if they use general problem-solving abilities), then we might expect them to adopt hypotheses that are not sanctioned by Universal Grammar. Something like this may in fact happen in the acquisition of gender in French. Children learning French as a first language seem to have very little trouble learning gender as they learn the words themselves (e.g., *le livre* 'the book' is masculine; *la table* 'the table' is feminine) and so on. On the other hand, adults whose first language does not have gender often have great difficulty learning French gender. They seem to set up complex (but incorrect) rules for predicting the gender of a given noun. For example, they may assume that words naming colors (or some other semantic category) are of one gender, or that words that end with a certain sound sequence are of another. Rules like this sometimes allow nonnative speakers to guess the gender correctly, but they still perform significantly differently from native speakers. This is an example of how adults' greater capacity to formulate general rules can sometimes lead them down the wrong path.

3.2 Individual differences

Learners vary in ways other than age. Broadly speaking, the research asks the question, "if learners have a particular quality *x*, does this make them better at second language acquisition?" For example, we might look at the effect of inhibition, left-handedness, or some other individual trait on L2 ability. As appealing as this avenue is, it is one that must be taken carefully. In particular, there are three points on which we must be explicit:

1. how we define and measure *x*
2. what it means to be *better*
3. what aspect of communicative competence we are referring to

Consider a trait like empathy. It has been argued that people who are empathetic are better language learners. This is an intuitively appealing notion. People who are empathetic can imagine what it feels like to be in someone else's shoes, and they can look at things from another perspective. And second language learning certainly involves looking at things from a different perspective. But in SLA research, we need to find a more precise way to evaluate this hypothesis.

There are tests that claim to measure a person's empathy, but is this notion really a well-defined construct? Is one simply empathetic or not, or are there degrees of empathy? If there are degrees, do we see a correlation between degree of empathy and degree of success? And what does it mean for empathetic learners to be better language learners than people who aren't empathetic? Do they make fewer errors? Less serious errors? Should we expect people with greater empathy to be better at everything in the L2? Or maybe just at phonology and sociolinguistic competence? On what basis could we make a prediction? These are not simple issues. We raise them not to argue that research on individual variation is misguided, but to show some of the complex areas that need to be addressed before we can hope to establish a causal connection between a particular personality trait and success at second language learning.

We can distinguish between two kinds of factors in terms of which individuals can vary: affective factors and cognitive factors. First we will look at the role of affect.

Affective factors

Affective factors have to do with the emotional side of learning a second language. Clearly there is a great deal at stake emotionally when learning a second language, and it is possible that emotions affect how successful a second language learner is. Affective factors that have been studied include empathy, anxiety, inhibition, and risk-taking. In this section we will look at another factor: motivation.

Learners can vary with respect to the amount or type of motivation they have to learn a second language. If someone is highly motivated to learn, will that person do better at learning? In order to answer this question, we need to say a bit more about what it means to be motivated.

Traditionally, two types of motivation have been proposed: **instrumental** and **integrative**. Instrumental motivation involves wanting to learn the L2 for a specific goal or reason. For example, someone might need to pass a language requirement in order to get a graduate degree or a job with a government agency. Integrative motivation, on the other hand, involves wanting to learn the L2 in order to learn more about a particular culture or fit into it better. For instance, someone might want to learn Japanese in order to learn more about a fascinating culture.

Studies have shown that the degree of integrative motivation correlates with the degree of success in language learning. That is to say, subjects who score highly on tests of integrative motivation do better on certain language tests than comparable subjects who score poorly on the same tests. Subjects with instrumental rather than integrative motivation, however, can also do well if their level of motivation is high. One study found that subjects who were offered a cash reward if they obtained a certain score on a language test performed much the same as subjects with high integrative motivation. All this seems to suggest that degree of motivation is a better predictor of future learning success than is type of motivation.

Cognitive factors

While affective factors have something to do with the emotional side of learning, cognitive factors involve the mechanics of how an individual learns something. Different people learn using different cognitive styles and different learning strategies. We will first address cognitive style.

As individuals, we tend to tackle mental tasks using a particular **cognitive style**. In contrast with an affective factor like motivation, which may vary from domain to domain (e.g., someone might be more motivated to learn French cooking than to learn the French language), cognitive style is a stable trait across domains.

The study of cognitive style often focuses on a contrast between field dependence and field independence. Learners who are field independent are not distracted by irrelevant background information when trying to learn something. These are people who can see the trees without being distracted by the forest. On the other hand, learners who are field dependent tend to see the forest but may miss the characteristics of individual trees. Of course, this is not to say that, overall, one trait is good and the other is bad. Field dependent learners probably are able to synthesize the overall picture better than field independent learners, but field independent learners are probably better able to pick out relevant facts.

In terms of second language acquisition, it seems that field independent learners do better on language tests that focus on analytic tasks such as providing the correct grammatical form in a given sentence:

21)

Yesterday, we ___ the kids to the zoo. (take)

In contrast, field dependent learners tend to do better on tasks that involve synthesizing their knowledge. For example, they may demonstrate broader communicative competence in that they are more concerned with getting the message across than with the grammatical accuracy of the form of their message.

Ultimately, the proficient L2 learner needs to be concerned with both **accuracy** and **fluency**. Broadly speaking, accuracy has to do with whether the learner has the correct representation of a particular linguistic structure (i.e., it involves *knowledge*). Fluency, on the other hand, has to do with the rapid retrieval or processing of those representations (i.e., it involves *skills*). Someone who is not fluent may well have accurate representations, but take considerable time and energy to retrieve them. Different learners, though, are probably going to have a natural affinity to emphasize either accuracy or fluency, depending perhaps on their individual cognitive style.

While cognitive styles appear to have relatively stable traits in individuals, there are elements of learning that we have some control over. Each of us has certain **learning strategies** that we can employ to try to fill gaps in our linguistic knowledge. These strategies can be contrasted with **communication strategies**, which are designed to keep communication happening in spite of gaps in knowledge—as when someone uses paraphrase to describe an object for which he or she has no vocabulary item (e.g., *Could you pass me the thing you use for hitting nails?*).

A learning strategy is used to discover something new about the L2. Many different learning strategies have been proposed. For example, using the strategy of directed attention, learners may decide in advance to focus on particular aspects of a task and to ignore others. So, when reading a text or listening to a lecture, they might decide to focus only on the main points. Another strategy involves repetition: To retain a lexical item or to improve the pronunciation of a sequence of sounds, the learner may repeat a word or phrase over and over. A third strategy makes use of clarification requests (to the teacher, a peer, or the others in a conversation) about something that is not understood (e.g., How come *stood* doesn't rhyme with *food*? What's a *liege*?). Learners have a variety of strategies at their disposal and have to discover which ones work best for them.

3.3 The good language learner

What makes a good language learner? One researcher has presented the following list of characteristics. For the most part, this list is concerned with the learning strategies that people invoke in an attempt to acquire an L2.

Table 13.10 Characteristics of the good language learner

1. Has an [effective] personal learning style or positive learning strategies.
2. Has an active approach to the learning task.
3. Has a tolerant and outgoing approach to the target language and empathy with its speakers.
4. Has technical know-how about how to tackle a language.
5. Has strategies of experimentation and planning with the object of developing the new language into an ordered system and revising this system progressively.
6. Is consistently searching for meaning.
7. Is willing to practice.
8. Is willing to use the language in real communication.
9. Has self-monitoring ability and critical sensitivity to language use.
10. Is able to develop the target language more and more as a separate reference system and is able to learn to think in it.

By focusing on such characteristics, the learning strategy approach seeks to account for differences in L2 proficiency by referring to the way in which individuals try to acquire new knowledge. Some people have gone so far as to suggest that this type of research will make it possible to teach not-so-good language learners the learning strategies necessary to be good language learners.

This brings us to the interesting question of second language learning in classrooms and the effect that instruction has on L2 learning. Is it really possible to teach someone a second language? Or can teachers simply create an environment in which second language learning can take place? We turn now to the research that has looked specifically at L2 classrooms.

4 THE L2 CLASSROOM

It has been flippantly said that people have been successfully acquiring second languages for thousands of years, but when teachers get involved, the success rate plummets. This comment is probably more a reflection of people's unfortunate experience in certain types of language classrooms (that may have been dull or even physically threatening, depending on the century) than it is a statement about general pedagogic utility. The fact remains, however, that language classrooms can be sheltered environments where students have the opportunity to learn and practice without being subject to the penalties for failure that may be imposed outside the classroom.

We should acknowledge at this point that there is really no such thing as the typical second language classroom. All classrooms are different because they have different people in them. Nevertheless, there are three relevant characteristics of a second language classroom that we wish to explore:

1. modified input
2. modified interaction
3. focus on form

4.1 MODIFIED INPUT

In Chapter 12, it was noted that adults do not talk to children in the same way that they talk to other adults. Just as the input directed to children has certain simplifying characteristics, so speech directed at nonnative speakers tends to be simplified compared to the speech directed at native speakers. In all communicative situations—whether dealing with a child or an adult, a nonnative speaker or a native speaker—we seem to make a rapid assessment of the level of proficiency or background knowledge of the listener, and adjust the input accordingly.

The input aimed at nonnative speakers is referred to as **foreigner talk**. The subset of this speech that takes place in classrooms is known as **teacher talk**. Teacher talk tends not to be as evenly matched to the proficiency of the listener as foreigner talk is, for the simple reason that teachers are usually addressing a class rather than an individual. As a result, some learners may find the modified speech too hard or too easy.

The pedagogic goal of teacher talk is crystal clear: Make sure the students know what is being talked about by providing **comprehensible input**. Perhaps surprisingly, this idea has generated an extraordinary amount of conflict in the field of SLA research. Although it seems to be useful to provide learners with comprehensible input, teachers must guard against simplifying too much, which might give the appearance of patronizing the learners or talking to them as if they were stupid rather than on the way to becoming bilingual.

4.2 Modified interaction

Second language classrooms also differ from the outside world in terms of the kind of interactions that go on there. The difference appears to be mainly one of degree, however, not quality. Inside a classroom, the teacher may engage in the following kinds of strategies:

- more comprehension checks, e.g., *Do you understand? OK?*
- more prompting, e.g., *Who knows where Council Bluffs is?*
- more expansions, e.g., Student: *Me red sweater.*
  Teacher: *Yes, you're wearing a red sweater, aren't you?*

This modified interaction appears to be one of the characteristics that differentiates classrooms from other communicative settings. While all these practices occur in nonclassroom discourse as well, they appear to occur more frequently in second language classrooms. Assuming that the teacher realizes that the purpose of the classroom is to prepare the student to understand input and interaction outside of the classroom as well, modified interaction is beneficial.

4.3 Focus on form

The final characteristic of the second language classroom to be discussed here involves **focus on form**. The term *focus on form* encompasses two practices that occur in most L2 classrooms: instruction about the language and explicit correction.

Most second language classes present the students with some sort of information about the language—noting, for example, that "The English sound [θ] is produced by placing the tongue between the teeth" or that "The *on* in French *bon* is pronounced as a nasal vowel." Instruction of this type is designed to improve the form (or **accuracy**) of the student's L2. In all likelihood, other activities that happen in the class will focus on giving the student a chance to improve fluency or particular sociolinguistic skills. Error correction is also designed to improve the form of the student's L2.

Regardless of the methodology used in most classes today, there is some focus on form, including some error correction. The interesting research question is whether either of these practices can be shown to have a positive effect on the learner. Do students who are corrected do better than students who don't? The question may not be as straightforward as it appears. Remember that it has frequently been argued in first language acquisition research that attempts at error correction are relatively infrequent and don't really affect children's grammars. Could it be different for adult second language learners? The learning environment is different in that adult learners (unlike children) are usually exposed to a fair amount of error correction. But does that make a difference? Not surprisingly, this question is difficult to answer. Some studies have argued that second language learners who receive correction develop at about the same pace as those who do not. Other studies have shown certain increases in accuracy as the result of correction.

These results may not be as contradictory as they seem, though. The areas where correction seems to be most useful involve the lexicon. When someone tries to learn the relevant properties of a lexical item, they benefit from feedback, but feedback concerning certain structural phenomena may not be as effective. For example, the study of French speakers learning about the lack of verb movement in English (see Section 2.2) found that while there were short-term improvements in the subjects who were explicitly taught the relevant facts, there were no significant long-term effects. When the subjects were tested a year later, they were found to have reverted to their pre-instructional performance.

This result doesn't necessarily mean either that students should not be corrected or that there should be no focus on form in the second language classroom. If a balance is struck between classroom activities that focus on form and those that focus on meaningful communication, then there is certainly no evidence that feedback causes any trouble. Indeed, to the contrary, there is evidence that students in classes that focus primarily on communication but also include some instruction on form are significantly more accurate than students who are exposed only to instruction that focuses on communication.

In sum, adult students usually expect error correction, and teachers are accustomed to providing it. Assuming that the class is not devoted entirely to instruction that focuses on form (with no opportunity for meaningful practice), error correction doesn't seem to cause any harm. And in a class with activities that focus on both form and fluency, the students tend to emerge with greater accuracy.

4.4 Bilingual education

We will conclude this chapter with a discussion of two types of bilingual education programs involving children: minority language maintenance programs and language **immersion** programs. Both are designed to produce bilingual children, but there are important differences. French immersion programs in Canada involve children from a majority language (English) being immersed in a minority language (French). As English-speaking children, they are in no danger of losing their first language since it is so dominant in the culture. Their situation is clearly different from that of children who speak a minority language (e.g., Spanish or Chinese) and who are submersed in the majority language (English). Not only are these children in some danger of losing their first language, but also the sink-or-swim approach can have strongly negative consequences on their future in school. For these reasons, it should be emphasized that even if we argue for the benefits of immersing English-speaking children in French classrooms, it does not follow that we should submerse speakers of other languages in English classrooms.

Let us look in more detail at some of the issues surrounding bilingual education. We begin with minority language maintenance programs.

Minority-language maintenance programs

Minority-language maintenance programs, which are also known as heritage language programs or L1 maintenance programs, have been introduced around the world to try to address the fact that minority-language children often have difficulty in majority-language schools. Even with separate classes of instruction, these children have more than their share of problems later in school (including a higher than expected drop-out rate). A reason for this becomes evident when one thinks of what such children face. Up until the age of five, they are exposed to a language at home (say, Greek). Then at age five, they are put into an English-speaking school in a class of primarily native English speakers. Typically, they do not understand everything that the teacher is saying and do not have the opportunity to develop the basic cognitive skills necessary for functioning in school. These children may thus suffer a setback from which they will never recover.

This poor beginning can lead to minority-language students' being placed in classes not designed for students intending to pursue postsecondary education, which in turn can lead to an exit from the educational system. To try to change this recurring pattern, a number of bilingual education programs have been set up in places like Canada, England, Finland, and the United States. In all of these programs the children of minority-language background receive their initial instruction in the minority language. Over the years of their elementary education, instruction in the majority language is gradually introduced so that by grades three to six, the children receive about half of their instruction in the majority language.

The question raised in evaluating these programs (and indeed the question that led policymakers to adopt the competing sink-or-swim approach to minority-language education) is, "What is the effect on the children's English?" Obviously, knowledge of English in places like the United States and Canada is essential. But is submersion in English the only way to acquire proficiency in English? It would seem that the answer is no, since children can become bilingual with relative ease. In virtually all of the bilingual education programs studied, the subjects ended up performing as well as their monolingual L1 and L2 peers by the end of grade six. So, for example, a child who received all instruction in Cree for the first couple of years of schooling and was getting 50 percent English and 50 percent Cree instruction by the end of grade six would be performing in Cree like a monolingual Cree speaker and in English just like a monolingual English speaker.

Thus, receiving instruction in the L1 does not have negative consequences on the L2. On the contrary, it seems to have significant positive effects on success in school, on linguistic proficiency, and even on the family situation of the students. The students can understand the teacher (which helps them at school), and they can understand their parents and grandparents (which helps them at home).

French immersion programs

Another very popular kind of bilingual education program in Canada involves immersing a majority-language student in a minority-language class. While any second language can be involved, we will refer to these as French immersion programs, since this is the most common type of program.

Immersion differs from traditional foreign language instruction and from submersion programs. It is different from a traditional foreign language course in that French is the medium of communication, not the subject of the course. It is teaching *in* French, not teaching *of* French. In a traditional foreign language course, French is just another subject (about 40 minutes a day). In French immersion, all of the instruction is in French, even when the content is geography or music.

Immersion is different from submersion in that no one in the class is a native speaker of the medium of instruction, so all the students are starting from approximately the same place. Contrast this with the experience of a native Chinese speaker who is thrown into an English-only class with a large number of native speakers of English.

The positive features of French immersion programs as they have been implemented in Canada can be stated as follows. Children who emerge from French immersion suffer no negative effects on their English, do well in school, outperform their monolingual counterparts in a number of ways, and know a lot of French.

Given the success of immersion programs in Canada, one might ask why similar programs are not popular in the United States. The simple answer is that bilingualism is not, by and large, considered worth the cost of immersion education. There are a few prestigious private schools in this country in which French immersion is practiced with success. But no single foreign language is perceived as important enough in any part of the United States for a public school system to be willing to invest the necessary funds in what amounts to setting up an entirely separate school curriculum in that language for what will always be a fairly small population of children whose English-speaking parents want them to be bilingual in that language.

SUMMING UP

This chapter has dealt with a number of issues in the field of second language acquisition. We investigated the notion of an **interlanguage** grammar and the influence of both the source and target languages on this grammar in terms of **transfer** and **developmental errors**. Proficiency in a second language requires both knowledge and ability, something captured in a model of **communicative competence**. Someone must acquire knowledge in all linguistic domains (phonetics, phonology, morphology, syntax, and semantics) as well as the ability to use that knowledge in a variety of social contexts.

What is easy or difficult to acquire in a second language has been investigated from a variety of perspectives. We focused on **Universal Grammar** (the **Subset Principle**) and typological universals (the **Markedness Differential Hypothesis**). It is not just universals that influence second language learning, however; the specific characteristics of an individual can also affect the process. Affective factors and cognitive factors both influence second language learning. So too do factors such as modified input, modified interaction, focus on form, and bilingual education.

The field of second language acquisition is remarkably diverse, in part because of what is involved in L2 learning. Someone who is attempting to learn an additional language must develop new mental representations, as well as a facility to access those representations in a variety of circumstances. The field of SLA research must therefore draw on psychology (theories of learning, theories of performance), linguistics (theories of linguistic structure), and pedagogy (theories of instruction). Although a comprehensive theory of how second languages are learned has not yet emerged, bit by bit, piece by piece, the puzzle is coming together.

Key terms

accuracy
bilingualism
cognitive style
communication strategies
communicative competence
comprehensible input
Critical Period Hypothesis
developmental errors
fluency
focus on form
foreigner talk
fossilized
grammatical competence
illocutionary competence
illocutionary force
immersion
instrumental motivation
integrative motivation
interlanguage
lateralization
learning strategies
markedness
Markedness Differential Hypothesis
negative evidence
Null Subject Parameter
Ontogeny Model
performance
positive evidence
second language acquisition
sociolinguistic competence
Subset Principle
target
teacher talk
text
textual competence
transfer
transfer errors
Universal Grammar
Verb Movement Parameter

Sources

The Ontogeny Model was proposed by R. Major in "Foreign Accent: Recent Research and Theory" in the *International Review of Applied Linguistics* 15:185–202 (1987). The model of communicative competence is an adaptation of L. Bachman's *Fundamental Considerations in Language Testing* (Oxford: Oxford University Press, 1990). The Markedness Differential Hypothesis was developed by F. Eckman in "Markedness and the Contrastive Analysis Hypothesis," *Language Learning* 27:315–30 (1977). The data from Arabic syllabification come from E. Broselow, "Prosodic Phonology and the Acquisition of a Second Language" in S. Flynn and W. O'Neil, eds., *Linguistic Theory in Second Language Acquisition* (Dordrecht: Kluwer, 1988). The stress data were reported in J. Archibald, *Language Learnability and L2 Phonology* (Dordrecht: Kluwer, 1993). The null subject analysis is drawn from L. White, *Universal Grammar and Second Language Acquisition* (Amsterdam: John Benjamins, 1989). The verb movement study can be found in L. White, "Adverb Placement in Second Language Acquisition: Some Effects of Positive and Negative Evidence in the Classroom" in *Second Language Research* 7:133–61 (1991). The L2 morphology data can be found in H. Zobl and J. Liceras, "Functional Categories and Acquisition Order" in *Language Learning* 44 (1): 159–80 (1994). The French gender information is discussed in S. Carroll, "Second-Language Acquisition and the Computational Paradigm" in *Language Learning* 39 (4): 535–94 (1989). The instrumental/integrative distinction comes from R. Gardner, J. B. Day, and P. D. MacIntyre, "Integrative Motivation, Induced Anxiety and Language Learning in a Controlled Environment" in *Studies in Second Language Acquisition* 14 (2): 197–214 (1992). The good language learner profile of Table 13.10 can be found in H. H. Stern, "What Can We Learn from the Good Language Learner?" in *The Canadian Modern Language Review* 34:304–18 (1975), but see also J. Rubin, "What the 'Good Language Learner' Can Teach Us" in *TESOL Quarterly* 9 (1): 41–51 (1975), and R. Ellis, *Understanding Second Language Acquisition* (Oxford: Oxford University Press, 1986). The L2 classroom discussion owes much to R. Allwright and K. Bailey, *Focus on the Language Classroom: An Introduction to Classroom Research for Language Teachers* (Cambridge: Cambridge University Press, 1991). The evidence from focus on form was presented by P. Lightbown and N. Spada, "Focus-on-Form and Corrective Feedback in Communicative Language Teaching: Effects on Second Language Learning" in *Studies in Second Language Acquisition* 12 (4): 429–48 (1990). Bilingual education and French immersion programs are discussed in J. Cummins and M. Swain, *Bilingualism in Education* (London: Longman, 1986).

Recommended reading

Archibald, J., and G. Libben. 1995. *Research Perspectives on Second Language Acquisition.* Toronto: Copp Clark.

Cummins, J., and M. Swain. 1986. *Bilingualism in Education.* London: Longman.

Larsen-Freeman, D., and M. Long. 1991. *An Introduction to Second Language Acquisition Research.* London: Longman.

Selinker, L. 1992. *Rediscovering Interlanguage.* London: Longman.

Sharwood Smith, M. 1994. *Second Language Learning: Theoretical Foundations.* London: Longman.

White, L. 1989. *Universal Grammar and Second Language Acquisition.* Philadelphia: John Benjamins.

Appendix:
L2 pedagogy

It has probably become clear that this chapter (and the field of second language acquisition research) is not directly concerned with second language *teaching.* Anyone interested in a catalogue of approaches to language teaching could consult *Approaches and Methods in Language Teaching* by J. C. Richards and T. S. Rodgers (New York: Cambridge University Press, 1986).

Historically, there have been a number of specific methods proposed as the best way to teach a language. There have been methods that emphasize physical activity (**Total Physical Response**), and methods that emphasize relaxed learning (**Suggestopedia**). Some methods encourage translation (**Grammar-Translation**), while others discourage it (**Direct Method**). There are approaches that encourage repetitive drilling (**audiolingualism**) and others that discourage it **Communicative Language Teaching**).

Recent trends in second language pedagogy have tended to downplay the idea that a single method of instruction will work for all people. As second language acquisition research identified the large number of ways in which second language learners can vary, it became evident that not everybody learns in the same way. Therefore, not everybody can be taught in the same way.

Currently, teachers tend to adopt an eclectic approach to second language instruction. What this means is that a variety of methods and approaches are used. A class may include some time for drilling and some time for physical activity (just to name two possibilities). The metaphor of multiple bridges may help to explain the rationale of this eclectic approach. If teachers want to get as many students as possible to a particular destination (call it proficiency) then they have a better chance if there are multiple bridges (i.e., techniques) than if there is only one bridge (i.e., a single methodology).

The activities that make up a class will be determined by the needs and preferences of the learners, as well as by the experience and preferences of the teacher. Together they attempt to negotiate a program of instruction that is best-suited for all concerned.

QUESTIONS

1. Some dialects of Arabic break up clusters by inserting an epenthetic vowel to the *left* of an unsyllabified consonant (unlike the dialect discussed in this chapter). How would a speaker of this dialect pronounce the words *plant, transport,* and *translate*? Draw the necessary syllable structures.

2. The following is a sample of nonnative writing. The assignment given was to write about whether you prefer to live in the city or the country. Look through the sample and 'correct' the errors. Compare your corrected copy with that of someone else in the class and see if you agree on the corrections.

   Are you among the number of people who have to choose their place to live? Whenever they have to move from another country, they even change the profession, they want to have a house outside the big city, or they can't find a place in Downtown.

   Its possible to move as well as you are supported by some essential condition of life I've mention in the following lines.

   Most of people are living in the Big city to have many of the opportunities that offer the Downtown lifestyle, jobs, studies, activities or whatever but nowadays for instance in TO [Toronto] its really difficult to find a place to live because the percentage of vacancy is slightly under 0% so many people are constrained to move on the suburb, because they want to avoid the noise, the smog of the city and even they try to find their own place to live with garden and everything, actually to invest money to owe their house which is better than to rent an apartment in downtown, therefore they have to consider the transportation problem to reach the city even to have a car or use the public transportation.

to have your own house outside the city required a great initial capital that you have to draft from any bank or you dispose in your account but afterwhat the house become your possession with the years and couple of more will increase the house value, although it is expensive furthermore it should be a great benefit for the owner even though he decided to rent the unoccupied room into the house.

Moreless the frienship beetween the person in the subrub is closer they are ore contact with each other and maybe can meet themselves doing yardwork or other kind of activities belong to the suburb lifestyle.

But in another (illegible) it should be difficult for the people who haven't ever lived in the suburb to move from th big city because they have to adapt their habits but they can fin amonst a great number of things that they use to have in the city. Otherwise during the last 15 years the business activites has developing around the city quickly in the North America also the supermarket company, manufacture and so on offered the job opportunity to the people outside the big aglomeration in that way it was created some apartments vacaint in the city.

For me I don't even care where I have to live but I will observe which part could be the less expensive as well as transportation to reach my job but I will be sure that I'd like to live outside the downtown.

3. Given what you know about implicational universals, do you think it would be easier for an English speaker to acquire French nasal vowels (e.g., *gant* [gã] 'glove') or for French speakers to acquire English oral vowels?

4. What explanation would you give for the fact that a native speaker of French produces an English sentence such as *I drink frequently coffee.* How could you explain the fact that the same speaker produces the sentence *He is frequently late,* which is grammatical? Do any other English verbs behave like this?

5. Which of the following sentences would you classify as positive evidence and which as negative evidence for the learner:
   a) Nonnative Speaker (NNS): He study a lot.
      Native Speaker (NS): He *studies* a lot.
   b) NS: What kind of books do you like to read?
      NNS: Mysteries.
   c) NNS: I was born in Saltillo.
      NS: Pardon me?
   d) NNS: I goed to Montreal on the weekend.
      NS: Remember that *go* has an irregular past.

6. Discuss why second language learners, regardless of their first language, might produce forms such as *goed, sheeps,* and *he felts* given that they never hear these forms in input from native speakers of English. Give some other forms analogous to the above that might be generated.

7. What factors can you think of that might influence fossilization? Do you think that some people are more likely to fossilize than others? Do you think it can be reversed? How?

8. Acquiring a second language involves both knowing something about the language, and being able to do something with the language. Do you think that knowledge and skills are related? Can you see any trade-off between accuracy and fluency?

9. Why do you think that nonnative speakers of English would be more at risk of leaving the education system than native speakers?

10. Respond to the following statement:
    It's the school system's job to make sure that nonnative speakers of English learn English. They need English in order to be able to succeed in this country. We want them to succeed. If we encourage them to speak their own language, then ghettos will form and they'll never learn English. And if we want them to learn English, then obviously they need to be exposed to more English. What good is it knowing how to speak another language in North America? What they need is English, English, and more English.

fourteen

Language in Social Contexts

Ronald H. Southerland

> *. . . it is clear that the causes of linguistic facts must be social in nature. . . .*
>
> – Antoine Meillet

This chapter treats a variety of social contexts in which one can examine both the use of language and the impact of extra-linguistic factors on language. The topics range from regional variation in language through social variation in language to studies of language use in interaction. The uses of language examined reflect the real world. Utterances are given in their natural form and are not edited or censored with respect to content or choice of vocabulary. A reading of this chapter should create an awareness that the reality of language in social contexts is not one of proper speech versus all other speech but of a set of complementary speech varieties that are used by members of the **speech community**. In promoting this awareness, the chapter also discusses analytical techniques and theoretical assumptions that underlie the topics examined.

1 FUNDAMENTAL CONCEPTS

The subdiscipline of linguistics that treats the social aspects of language is called **sociolinguistics**. In this chapter, this label will be used to refer to all research about language in social contexts. Such research ranges from the very limited and localized context of a single conversation to studies of language use by whole populations. Given these quite diverse areas of research interest, it might be assumed that many sociolinguists do not share the same fundamental concepts or goals. This is to some extent true.

Despite the fact that there are a number of ways of approaching the study of language in social context, there are nevertheless certain terms and concepts that are common to most of them. The locus of all sociolinguistic investigation is the speech community. A speech community can be as small as a town, village, or even a club or as large as a nation or a group of nations. The important characteristics of a speech community are that its members share a particular language (or variety of a language) as well as the norms (or rules) for the appropriate use of their language in social context, and that these speakers be distinguished from other comparable groups by similar sociolinguistic criteria.

The term **speech variety** is the label given to that language (or form of language) used by any group of speakers. It is an ambiguous term, which can refer to the basic lexicon, phonology, syntax, and morphology shared by members of the group or to the speech used by members of the group in particular situations. Speech varieties are of four types: the **standard language**, social speech varieties (also called social dialects or **sociolects**), regional speech varieties (or **regional dialects**), and functional speech varieties (or **registers**).

In modern, developed societies there is one variety, the standard, that ranks above the others. This superposed variety is employed by the government and communications media, used and taught in educational institutions, and is the main or only written language. It is more fixed and resistant to change than any other variety in the community and is something of a yardstick against which other varieties are measured. It is to the written standard that prescriptivists, those who seek to reg-

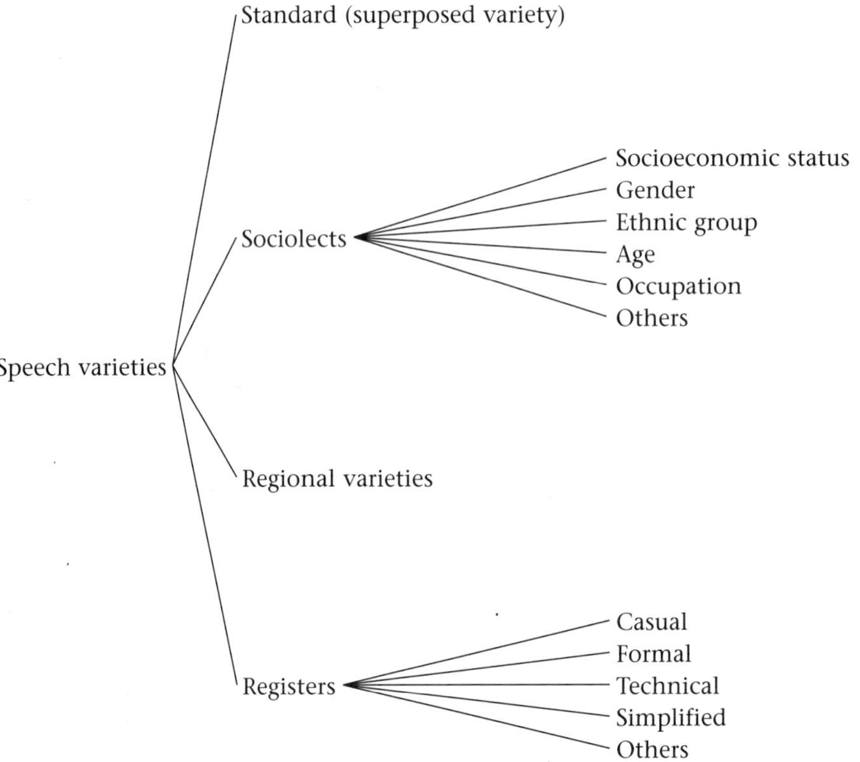

Figure 14.1 Types of speech varieties in the speech community

ulate how others use language, usually appeal when they condemn some usage as incorrect, improper, or even barbarous.

Sociolects are subdivisible into several smaller categories, largely as a function of the type of social group that shares the particular speech variety. Most often, one thinks of sociolects in terms of the socioeconomic status of the speakers. Other sociolects, however, may be associated with ethnic, gender, occupational, or age groups.

While sociolects are often seen as arranged along a vertical dimension corresponding to social status, regional dialects are usually thought of as distributed across a horizontal dimension. Their domains can be easily represented on a map. Regional dialects differ from each other systematically in terms of lexical or phonological criteria; they are not usually defined in terms of morphological or syntactic properties.

Functional speech varieties, more commonly called registers, are bits of talk that are appropriate to particular speech situations. This concept, along with other basic concepts and terms associated with interactional sociolinguistics, is somewhat different from the concept used by sociolinguists concerned with regional and social variation. Interactional sociolinguists are primarily interested in language use in speech situations, and their research thus centers on the dynamics of ongoing speech between people. The notions relevant to this type of study are treated in Section 5.

2 SOCIAL DIFFERENTIATION OF LANGUAGE

Social differentiation of language, in its broadest sense, refers to correlations between variation in language use and a speaker's membership in various social groups.

2.1 SOCIAL STRATIFICATION

As noted above, it is possible to correlate differences in how people speak with their membership in various social groups. Perhaps the most frequently invoked social correlate of language differentiation is socioeconomic status (SES). SES is associated with the income level, type of occupation, type of housing, educational level, and similar characteristics of speakers. Sociolinguistic investigations that focus on SES usually involve large random surveys of urban populations. These surveys are designed to elicit several types of data from speakers. They typically require respondents to read aloud passages, word lists, and sets of minimal pairs. They also attempt to elicit speech that more closely resembles natural (unaffected) language by asking respondents to tell a story about some interesting experience. The data obtained from these surveys are then subjected to statistically based quantitative analysis.

Approaches to the study of linguistic differentiation in the speech community that proceed from the assumption that SES is an important (or the most important) correlate of differences in language usage generally arrive at (or proceed from) a view of vertical variation that is referred to as the **social stratification** of language. It is probably fair to say that most sociolinguistic studies over the past two decades or so have been concerned with this vertical variation of language and that most have viewed it as a function of the speaker's membership in a particular socioeconomic class.

Stratification of language, while widespread in the world, is probably not universal. It is, on the other hand, reasonable to claim that social differentiation of one sort or another is universal. Underlying this claim is the belief that there are always differences in speech communities and that these differences correlate with the existence of social groups within the community. These social groups may be functions of the socioeconomic status, gender, age, ethnicity, or other characteristics of their members.

Until recently, most conventional sociolinguistic investigations have relied on random sampling in a speech community. Generally this research has also reflected the researcher's preconceptions about the most important social correlates of linguistic behavior in the community and, as well, has assumed that the individuals sampled were representative of such social categories as those listed in the previous paragraph. There is some concern, however, that, while linguistic variation clearly does correlate with social variation, the results of particular studies may be based on invalid (or incomplete) assumptions made by the investigator who has failed to consider a full range of possible correlates.

In other words, if one undertakes a study of social differentiation, assuming that the primary social correlate of observed differences in speech will be the socioeconomic status of speakers (however that may be defined), one may overlook other factors which could offer an equal or better explanation of the differentiation. Indeed, some recent studies (and attempts to reevaluate older studies in terms of newer methodologies) have suggested that assumptions about the primacy of SES as an explanation for linguistic variation have obscured the role of gender in that regard. Some research supports the conclusion that gender may, in fact, be a more powerful underlying cause for the social differentiation of language than socioeconomic status.

2.2 Other ways of studying social differentiation

Two alternative approaches that are challenging the traditional methodology are **social network analysis** and **Principal Components Analysis (PCA)**.

Social network analysis

A sociolinguist using the social network approach does not rely on large random samplings of a population but, rather, examines first-hand from the perspective of participant-observer the language use of a pre-existing social group. Just as more traditional sociolinguists may assume that social stratification exists and that this has significance for the interpretation of data, researchers using the social network approach also make certain assumptions. These researchers attach importance to the nature of the relationships (and resulting interactions) of a speaker and interpret linguistic variation in terms of the kinds and densities of relationships the individual enjoys in various groups.

The density of a network is related to the potential for communication among members of the network and can be either closeknit or looseknit. A person's social network will consist of everyone in every group in which the person plays some role. Closeknit networks, which typically characterize speakers of the highest and lowest

SES groups, exert a great deal of peer pressure on speakers. They are thus associated with language maintenance since speakers in such a network reinforce each other's speech habits, in that they interact with the same relatively limited set of people in a number of different kinds of relationships. Closeknit networks among the high SES groups reinforce either a standard speech variety or one with high status. Closeknit networks among low SES groups are loci for **nonstandard** speech varieties.

In social networks (as in Figure 14.2), each group is separate but at the same time exhibits overlap with other groups, and all groups converge on the center. Thus the nature and frequency of interactions in the family group will differ from those among fellow workers, members of the same sports team, neighbors, and the like. In a sense, such studies can lend weight to the notion that we 'talk like those we talk to', more especially where those interactants are in a closeknit network.

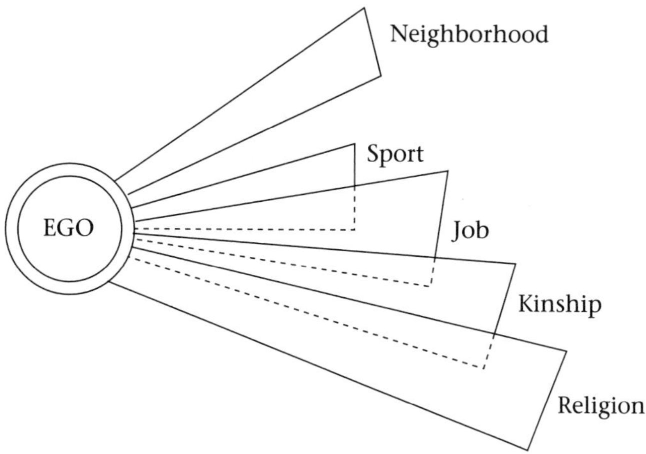

Figure 14.2 Social networks

Principal Components Analysis

The newest technique to challenge the traditional approach is Principal Components Analysis. This approach has been used in studies of the Sydney, Australia, and St. John's, Newfoundland, speech communities. PCA is highly quantitative. It uses statistical techniques that allow the investigator to examine a large number of linguistic variants, to compare speakers with similar linguistic characteristics (displayed on graphs in clusters) and, only as a last step, to determine what social similarities are shared by these linguistically categorized groups of speakers. A particular 'Principal Component' is a set of variables (such as the phonological ones in Table 14.1) which can be shown statistically to give the best account of the data. Groups of people who share particular linguistic features are categorized in terms of those sets of linguistic features rather than with respect to preconceived sociological features. Given the lack of *a priori* assumptions about the relevance of particular social categories, the results of PCA studies are seen by the investigators as more reliable pictures of social differentiation than was possible using traditional methodologies. In the section below on nonstandard phonological features we consider some of the results of the PCA study of St. John's, Newfoundland.

2.3 SOCIAL DIFFERENTIATION OF ENGLISH

The United States is distinctive in that, instead of a national language standard, there are a small number of regional varieties that are regarded as correct in their areas. We term this variety or varieties *Standard English.* These varieties differ principally in their phonology, and hardly at all in their written form. It is relatively easy to tell an educated Bostonian from an educated Charlestonian by listening to even their most careful speech; it is virtually impossible to distinguish the two on the basis of written works. Varieties other than the standard are termed *nonstandard.* This term is to be preferred to the designation *substandard,* which suggests some inherent inferiority of these varieties. In fact, the selection of standard and nonstandard varieties of English and other languages has to do with historical facts about who spoke which variety when; it has nothing to do with anything intrinsic to the varieties. Were English history a bit different, Cockney English might be standard English in Great Britain, and prescriptivists would have great fun criticizing those speakers who actually pronounce written *h*'s.

Nonstandard grammatical features

Certain features of nonstandard varieties of English are often singled out by prescriptivists as demonstrating the inherent illogic or lack of systematicity of nonstandard varieties. An oft-cited grammatical feature of this sort is the so-called double negative, seen in the first sentence in *1).*

1)

a. She don't know nothing.
b. She doesn't know anything.
c. She knows something.

A prescriptivist asserts that the two negations in the first sentence (*-n't* and *no-*) cancel each other out. Thus the speaker in *1a)* has supposedly uttered an affirmative sentence with the meaning of *1c).* Anyone who hears the sentence in *1a),* however, knows that its meaning is the same for the nonstandard speaker as the meaning of *1b)* is for the speaker of the standard. The nonstandard and standard negative sentences differ from the affirmative sentence in the same two ways: both verbs are marked as negative and both indefinite pronouns are marked differently from the pronoun in the affirmative sentence. When the verb is negated in Standard English, an indefinite pronoun in the verb phrase is also negated, by changing *some-* to *any-.* In the nonstandard variety, negating the verb causes the pronoun to be negated by changing *some-* to *no-.* Both varieties mark negation twice and thus are equally logical.

There is another nonstandard feature in *1a)*—the verb *do*—which co-occurs with the subject pronoun *she.* This sort of usage and the similar one seen in nonstandard *She know* are also condemned by prescriptivists. These two sentences violate the Standard English subject-verb agreement rule, which requires present-tense English verbs with third person subjects to have a special ending (*-s*). An examination of the morphology of Standard English verbs and a look at the historical development of these forms, however, show that over time all but the third person singular ending *-s* has been lost in the present tense. A nonprescriptivist view of those nonstandard varieties that lack a special ending in this form would hold that they have simply carried this particular linguistic change to its logical conclusion by eliminating the last remaining inflectional ending in the present tense.

Double negation, subject-verb agreement, and a number of other grammatical features are, of course, fairly superficial aspects of language. The following letter (which appeared in numerous newspapers) attests to their enduring importance for some people.

> Dear Ann Landers:
> I have been dating a young man for several years. Dan is everything a girl could want. Well, almost. He is kind, nice looking, considerate, fun to be with, and he makes good money. The only drawback is Dan's grammer. For example, he says "I seen," "youse," and "have went." I bite my tongue when he makes these awful mistakes, especially in front of my friends. I don't want to be ashamed of him, Ann, and I don't want to embarrass him either, but I'm afraid one day I might.
>
> Is there a chance that we can have a good marriage in spite of this? I am 26 and a college graduate. Dan is 27 and attended trade school. I do love him, but I fear I'll be a nagging wife—or worse yet, a silent wife who is ashamed of her husband's grammer. Please hurry your answer. He is waiting for mine.
> —York, Pennsylvania
>
> Dear York:
> Dan sounds too good to discard. Ask him if he wants to be corrected—when the two of you are alone, of course. Incidentally, you misspelled the word grammar throughout your letter. It is AR, dear. Perhaps you and Dan are not so far apart as you think.

Nonstandard phonological features

The phonological entities of interest to sociolinguists are called sociolinguistic variables. These variables are speech sounds (either single segments or syllables) that do not occur uniformly across a speech community or, occasionally, even in the speech of an individual. For instance, a particular variable may be realized one way in one speech variety and a different way in another speech variety. Similarly, a variable might be rendered one way by speakers when they are speaking carefully and another way in a more casual speaking style.

Perhaps the most widespread variable in English is (ing). We use parentheses to set off sociolinguistic variables, thus distinguishing them formally from phonemes and phones. Since (ing) is a variable, it is not always realized the same way in speech. Its two realizations are [ɪn] and [ɪŋ]. The same word might be pronounced with one or the other realization by the same speaker or by different speakers: *swimming* might thus be realized as [swɪmɪn] or as [swɪmɪŋ].

These realizations do not occur randomly in speech. There are well-established correlations between the two realizations of (ing) and such extra-linguistic factors as the socioeconomic status and gender of the speaker, the relative formality (or informality) of the speech situation, its physical location, and the nature of the particular lexical item. The variable tends to be realized as [ɪŋ] by speakers of higher socioeconomic status, by females, and in formal situations. Words such as *analyzing* (in general, formal vocabulary) are pronounced more frequently with [ɪŋ] than with [ɪn], while words such as *barfing* are more often heard with the [ɪn] than with [ɪŋ].

Words such as *everything* may be heard with either realization (depending often on the regional origin of the speaker), but we do not expect to hear any native speaker of English pronounce *sing* [sɪn], nor *sin* [sɪŋ]. Among children in school, more [ɪŋ]'s were heard in the classroom and more [ɪn]'s were heard on the playground.

The St. John's study mentioned above isolated some five consonantal and eight vocalic variables in the speech of its 120-person sample. Various statistically based groupings of these variables constituted particular Principal Components. Any one variable might appear in more than one Principal Component (PC) (along with other variables) but each PC was a set of variables linked to (and defining) some group of speakers. Principal Component 1 [PC1] was expressed in terms of the nonstandard realizations of each of the six variables given in Table 14.1.

Table 14.1 Phonological variables in Newfoundland English PC1

Variable	*Word*	*Phonetic realization*
(e)	bay	a) standard diphthongal [ej] b) nonstandard monophthongal [eː]
(o)	boat	a) standard diphthongal [ow] b) nonstandard monophthongal [oː]
(θ)	three	a) standard interdental fricative [θ] b) nonstandard alveolar stop [t]
(l) (postvocalic)	mole	a) standard dark [ɫ] b) Irish-like clear [l] c) vocalic [ɤ] (mid-back unrounded)
(or)	bore	a) standard [ɔr] b) nonstandard [ar]-like pronunciation
(ð)	them	a) standard interdental fricative [ð] b) nonstandard alveolar stop [d] or flap [ɾ]

Speakers evidencing high values (i.e., high percentages of occurrence) of the *nonstandard* realizations of the variables in Table 14.1 turned out almost exclusively to be older males. There were no correlations with socioeconomic status or religion.

Principal Component 2 [PC2], on the other hand, consisted of another grouping of variables.

Table 14.2 Phonological variables in Newfoundland English PC2

Variable	*Word*	*Phonetic realization*
(ing)	fishing	a) standard [ɪŋ] b) nonstandard or casual [ɪn]
(ð)	them	a) standard interdental fricative [ð] b) nonstandard alveolar stop [d] or flap [ɾ]
(θ)	three	a) standard interdental fricative [θ] b) nonstandard alveolar stop [t]

Speakers with high values of the *standard* realizations of the variables in Table 14.2 clustered together and showed a greater proportion of women than men and also a higher proportion of the uppermost SES groups than did other clusters of speakers. This is consistent with other findings that tend to show standard features occurring more in the speech of women and persons of higher socioeconomic status and less in the speech of men and persons of lesser socioeconomic status.

The Newfoundland examples also exhibit evidence of the sort needed to understand socially motivated linguistic change. Newfoundland English owes many of its characteristics to Irish English. But Newfoundland exists in the wider English-speaking North American community and for more than forty years has been a province of Canada. These phonological variables show something of the conflict between older linguistic norms and newer ones. Here the older men in the first group are adhering to older norms, while the women and higher status persons of the second group are reflecting incoming (general Canadian) norms.

2.4 Language and gender

Using the words *language* and *gender* in the same context can lead to confusion. Linguists use the word *gender* as the label for noun classes of certain kinds (see Chapter 4, Section 6.2). The word does not ultimately refer to sex. In popular usage, however, and in other social sciences *gender* refers to sexually based social distinctions. In the following section, *gender* used by itself will have this sociological sense and the term *grammatical gender* will be used when referring to purely linguistic categories.

There is a considerable literature on the general topic of language and gender, which may be taken as including all of the following:

- differences in language use associated with the gender (or sexual orientation) of the speaker or addressee (person spoken to)
- differences in language use associated with the gender (or sexual orientation) of the referent (person spoken about)
- efforts to alter the language with respect to ways gender is or is not encoded

Two different, but not necessarily contradictory, views have been advanced as to the relationship between language and gender. One view, which has characterized much sociolinguistic research in this area, holds that gender differences in language are simply a reflection of the way society works. Another view is that, far from merely reflecting the nature of society, language serves as a primary means of constructing and maintaining that society. The continued use, for instance, in English of male forms (such as *chairman*) in a generic sense (as we will see below) excludes women and is seen as perpetuating a social order in which women are invisible. Thus attitudes as to how people should talk and, indeed, how they are to regard their own status within society are formed by language and continue to be reinforced unless language changes (or is altered).

There is certainly truth in both of these views. Clearly language does mirror society with respect to what is seen as important and even normal. On the other hand, if groups (whether gender, ethnic, or other) are marginalized by the ways they are categorized or labelled by language, then this issue must be addressed and certain aspects of the language may need to be changed in order to include rather than exclude particular groups. In the following sections we will explore some specific types of gender differentiation in language and will examine some efforts to remove sexist language from English. The correlation between sexual orientation of speaker and language use is treated in Section 2.7.

Gender-exclusive differentiation

Gender-exclusive differentiation refers to the radically different speech varieties used by men and women in particular societies. In these societies, a woman or a man may, except in special circumstances, not be allowed to speak the variety of the other gender. It is in this sense that the varieties are gender-exclusive. A society in which this is the norm is typically one in which the roles assigned the genders are rigid, and in which there is little social change.

This phenomenon has been observed in some Amerindian societies but is no longer as widespread as it may have been in the remote past. A study of Koasati (a Muskogean language spoken in Louisiana) showed that members of this speech community possessed different verb forms based on the gender of the speaker. Some of these differences are illustrated in Table 14.3. The men's speech can be most efficiently described as being derived from the women's speech by rules. Where the women's form had falling pitch-stress (marked ˆ) on its final syllable and ended in a short vowel followed by [l], the men's forms showed high pitch-stress (marked ´) and [s] instead of the [l]. If the women's form ended in a short or long vowel followed by one or two consonants, the men's form added [s] ([t] + [s] → [ʧ]). If the women's form ended in [ʧ], the men's form was the same. (W in Table 14.3 stands for female speaker and M for male speaker)

Table 14.3 Gender-exclusive verb forms in Koasati

W	*M*	
lakawwîl	lakawwís	'I am lifting it'
lakáwʧ	lakáwʧ	'you are lifting it'
lakáw	lakáws	'he is lifting it'
lakáwwilit	lakáwwiliʧ	'I lifted it'

In traditional Koasati society, women and men normally used the forms appropriate to their gender, but they were not forbidden the use of forms associated with the other gender. In quoting a member of the other gender as in relating a story, a Koasati used the form appropriate to the person being quoted.

Gender-exclusive differentiation has assumed an even more radical form in some societies. In the most extreme form, which was decidedly rare, the gender of the speaker and that of the addressee were both encoded in an utterance. In Biloxi (an extinct language of the Siouan family), all of the following forms (each meaning 'carry it!') were found.

Table 14.4 Gender-exclusive differentiation in Biloxi

	One addressee	*More than one addressee*
M to M	kikankó	kítakankó
M or W to W	kitkí	kítatkí
W to M	kitaté	kítatuté

Gender-variable differentiation

Gender-variable differentiation is much more common in the languages of the world than is gender-exclusivity. This phenomenon is reflected in the relative frequency with which men and women use the same lexical items or other linguistic features. If, as is often asserted, female English speakers use words such as *lovely* and *nice* more often than do male speakers, we can claim that in this respect English speakers exhibit gender-variable differentiation.

Women have been shown to possess a greater variety of specific color terms than men in North American society. This is probably because of the tasks traditionally performed by women. There is no evidence to show that women have more acute color perception than do men. Indeed, one study showed that younger men had larger vocabularies of color terms than did older men but still less extensive ones than women. Thus there is evidence that gender-variability in this area is undergoing change.

Men are reputed to possess larger lexicons in areas associated with traditional male activities (such as particular occupations and sports). These examples may appear stereotypical, but they do reflect the sometimes subtle, sometimes blatant, differences between the activities and thus the language of members of the two genders.

Other differences between men's and women's language in North American society are seen in women's more frequent use of **politeness formulas**. There are a number of ways in which requests (or commands) can be mitigated in English. Instead of simply saying to someone *'Open the window!'* we might say *'Please open the window!' 'Would you please open the window?' 'Could you open the window?' 'Would you mind opening the window?' 'Do you find it stuffy in here?'* and so on. These are all less direct ways of requesting than is the straightforward imperative and, it is claimed, would more likely be employed by women. Similarly, some studies suggest that women use more **verbal hedges** than do men. These are words such as *perhaps* or *maybe* which are less assertive in conversations than utterances without hedges. Since we are discussing gender-variable usage here, we must emphasize that all of the above ways of phrasing a request are available to all speakers but may not be equally selected by male and female speakers.

Talking about men and women

The most obvious way in which gender differences with respect to a referent are manifested in English is grammatical gender. The use of English pronouns is instructive in this regard. We do not employ *he*, for instance, to refer only to males. In Standard English, it has been prescribed as a generic third person singular pronoun when the gender of the referent is unknown or irrelevant. Thus, we might hear sentences such as *'Did everyone turn in his assignment today?'* even if the entire group of referents is composed of women. However, in naturally occurring speech we more often hear utterances such as the following: *'No one can with impunity take the law into* their *own hands'* (asserted by former Mayor Koch of New York City) and *'Why don't we go to our first caller and see what* their *concerns are?'* (from a television talk-show host). In these sentences, we have instances of singular (gender-indefinite) *they*, which is widespread in nonstandard (or, perhaps better, nonprescriptivist) English and which denotes an indefinite number of individuals of unspecified (or possibly mixed) gender. For speakers who use singular *they*, the pronouns *she* and *he* are reserved for reference to individuals whose gender is known.

English nouns, though not overtly marked for grammatical gender like those in Latin, Russian, or many other languages, may distinguish between women and men. Generally in English, nouns referring to occupations are at once both masculine and generic, thus the terms *statesman* and *craftsman* are used both for men and women, although they contain the masculine suffix *-man*. There occasionally are female forms for the names of occupations (*sculptress, actress, usherette*) but these have evolved to connote more than just the gender of the practitioner of the occupation. Many observers feel that these and similar forms trivialize women so labeled. A woman who acts in films pointedly identified herself as an *actor* in an interview, not as an actress. She said that *actor* connoted for her someone who was serious about the craft, while *actress* did not.

The term *man* has been under considerable scrutiny in the recent past with respect to its reference. The pervasiveness of male-referential forms used generically (as in *chairman, mailman*, and *Museum of Man*) has disturbed many observers, who have felt that such language not only reflects sexist values but also perpetuates and reinforces them. This concern has resulted in moves to eliminate generic masculine forms from the language. In many instances, the suffix *-man* has been changed to gender-neutral *-person*. Other morphological processes have resulted in the creation of new forms (a *mailman* becomes a *letter carrier*, a *fireman* becomes a *fire fighter*, and a *chairman* becomes a *chair*). The *Museum of Man* became the *Museum of Civilization*. Changes have also come about in the use of pronouns. In many cases, regulations, laws, and the like have been rewritten to eliminate discriminatory masculine forms, replacing them with forms such as *he/she* or the gender-neutral singular *they*.

Replacement of sexist nouns with gender-neutral ones and a few adjustments in the use of third-person pronouns contribute, of course, to the creation of a less biased language. Advocates of the view (discussed earlier) that language does not merely mirror society but rather molds it would point to further and more wide-ranging examples of sexism that should be reformed. In this view, as long as these inequalities exist, they reinforce the status quo and leave women as a marginalized group. (For further examples of the unequal treatment of men and women—in the context of a university slang—see Section 2.6.)

2.5 Euphemism

Euphemism is the avoidance of words that may be seen as offensive, obscene, or somehow disturbing to listeners or readers. Items that are euphemized are said to be tabooed. The word **taboo** was borrowed from the Tongan language and, in its most general sense, refers to a prohibition on the use of, mention of, or association with particular objects, actions, or persons. As originally used in Polynesia, *taboo* had religious connotations, but in sociolinguistics it now denotes any prohibition on the use of particular lexical items. Taboo and euphemism are thus two faces of the same coin.

In the English-language speech community, the most obvious taboos are not religious but have to do with bodily functions, body parts, and death. In addition there is a noticeable tendency for governments to resort to euphemism to mask otherwise unpleasant concepts or to conceal aspects of their policy. Table 14.5 contains a variety of types of euphemisms that have been employed in the past or are currently in use.

Table 14.5 Some common euphemisms in English

Euphemism	*Definition*
privates	'male or female genitals'
make love	'engage in sexual intercourse'
perspire	'sweat'
pass away	'die'
collateral losses	'civilian casualties'

The existence of taboo and euphemism represent the exercise of power by dominant groups over their subordinates. Controlling what one can say is an aspect of controlling one's overall behavior. Taboos in English on language related to sex are, after all, not uniform across the speech community; men have historically been allowed much greater freedom to use such terms in public than have women. Taboos serve to support the status quo, the existing power structure. They may help to maintain the dominance of one gender over another, a political or religious elite over the general population or the like. Since no words are inherently 'dirty' or 'offensive', it is unclear what salutary effect taboos and euphemisms have. In Sections 2.6 and 2.7 there are examples of some terms which, although not seen as offensive by the speakers who use them, may cause offense (and thus may be tabooed) in the wider speech community.

2.6 Slang

Slang is a label that is frequently used to denote certain informal or faddish usages of nearly anyone in the speech community. The term was first attested in English in the mid-eighteenth century, used in reference to "special vocabulary used by any set of persons of a low or disreputable character; language of a low and vulgar type" (according to the *Oxford English Dictionary*). Nowadays, it is often applied to aspects of the language of adolescents or others who are perceived as speaking nonstandard varieties of the language.

Slang exists alongside jargon and argot (see Section 2.7) as members of a class of speech varieties of limited usage in the speech community. Each of these last two mentioned varieties, whether characteristic of an occupational or social group, is confined to a comparatively small number of speakers and is obscure to outsiders. Slang, while it may be fleeting and subject to rapid change, is more widespread and more familiar to large numbers of speakers. Particular 'slangs', however, are very much associated with membership in groups and, when used in the presence of another member of the same group, serve as an affirmation of solidarity.

Studies have shown that slang usage is abundant, creative, and socially important in high schools, colleges, and universities. High school students often divide themselves into groups, each distinguished from the other by clothing and hair styles, the kinds of music they listen to and their slang. It is sometimes reasonable to speak of a tripartite division of high school students into a (1) 'leading crowd' (called Jocks, Preppies, Collegiates, or Soc's [sowʃəz]); (2) a 'rebellious crowd' (termed Burnouts, Hoods, or Greasers); and (3) those who belong to no particular group (Lames). A study of a Calgary high school, carried out in the early 1980s, showed students being aware of some seven groups: (1) Jocks, (2) Freaks (or Heads), (3) Punks (or Rockers), (4) Snobs, (5) Preppies, (6) Brown-Noses (or Homework Gang), and (7) Nerds (or Hosers). There were links and similarities between some of the groups (Jocks and Preppies), and other 'groups' (Brown-Noses and Nerds) were said to consist of students not belonging to any of the first five categories. The slang of Freaks and Punks had, among other characteristics, numerous terms for drugs. The Jocks and Preppies had many of the exaggerated characteristics of California 'Valley Girl' speech (for example, extreme shifts in pitch or frequent use of *like*) in their slang.

A study of slang at a major American university (UCLA) produced a dictionary that included details of syntax and word formation as well as some indications of the origins of many of the slang expressions.

Table 14.6 Origins of UCLA slang

Slang expression	*Meaning*	*Origin*
homeboy	'very close male friend'	Black English
mazeh	'gorgeous guy'	Hebrew
happa	'half-Asian person'	Japanese
have missile lock	'concentrate on'	popular film

The students were also found to use particular word formation processes in producing slang.

Table 14.7 Processes of word formation in UCLA slang

Slang	*Meaning*	*Source*	*Process*
sucky	'awful'	suck	derivation [V → Adj]
mazehette	'gorgeous girl'	mazeh	derivation [N → N]
gork	'nerd'	**g**eek + d**ork**	blending
cas [kæʒ]	'all right'	**cas**ual	clipping
T.F.A.	'great!'	**T**otally **F**ucking **A**wesome	acronymy
fake-bake	'tanning salon'	fake + bake	compounding

In addition to these morphological techniques of word formation there was substantial use of the semantic technique of metaphor, in which an existing lexical item is replaced by another which suggests an image similar to that associated with the item replaced. Often the new coinage can be seen as more dramatic than the original. A typical instance of this process is seen in the phrase *blow chunks* 'vomit'. This replaces the older phrase *throw up* with a new phrase that has greater impact.

Although speakers of this slang can be expected to exhibit phonological variability with respect to (ing) (discussed in Section 2.1) in their usual speech, they consistently realize (ing) as [ɪn] in the slang word *bitchin'* 'good, excellent' so that there is no **bitching* alternating with it.

Interestingly, the slang items gathered in this study had a relatively limited semantic range. That is, the overwhelming majority of forms referred to comparatively few concepts. Many concerned the appearance of males (most were flattering, such as *hoss* 'stud; muscular male'; only a few were not: *eddie* 'ugly guy'). A large proportion of the terms referring to women were denigrating (as, *wilma* 'ugly girl', or *turbobitch* 'crabby female'). Some descriptive labels were gender-neutral (e.g., *studmuffin* both 'strong, muscular person' and 'cute person; achiever' and *gagger* 'disgusting person or thing'). Other frequently attested semantic domains in the UCLA slang included every aspect of university life, sexual relations, and bodily functions.

2.7 Jargon and argot

The terms **jargon** and **argot** are often used almost interchangeably to refer to 'obscure or secret language' or 'language of a particular occupational group'. Since the term *argot* arose in the seventeenth century as the label for a speech variety used by French beggars and street merchants and later was applied to the secret language of criminals, we will use it to denote 'secret language'. It is a label for speech varieties associated with social groups whose members wish to or must conceal themselves or some aspects of their communication from nonmembers. We will use jargon as the label for 'vocabulary peculiar to some field; occupational sociolect'.

'Gay lingo'

Language used by members of the male homosexual community is, in historical perspective at least, an example of an argot. Either it was used covertly, or its use in public was not meant to be understood by nongays. The lexicon of this argot covers a variety of concepts but is particularly rich in terms denoting sexual practices, categories of homosexuals, physical appearance, and matters of taste, among others.

Table 14.8 Some words from 'gay lingo' that have attained wider usage in the speech community

butch	'(of a woman) very "masculine"; (of a man) macho'
camp	'a playful appreciation of the ridiculous or kitsch'
come out	'disclosing one's homosexuality'
(in the) closet	'relating to the concealing of one's homosexuality (or other trait) from public knowledge'

Only *butch* preserves most of the original notion in nongay casual speech. The other three terms, though clearly arising in the gay subculture, have gained wider usage. Thus one can now refer not only to a 'closet homosexual' but, in an age that increasingly frowns on the use of tobacco, to a 'closet smoker'. While a homosexual can 'come out' so can anyone else who wishes to acknowledge some aspect of his or her identity that has previously been masked. The notion of camp has become so well-known that a philosopher wrote an essay on it, and it frequently appears in discussions of art and entertainment. These words are excellent examples of the fact that argots, jargons, and, especially, slang are productive sources of lexical items that later become part of the linguistic resources of the wider speech community.

'Hacker jargon'

Practitioners of many professions are often accused by others of having obscure jargons that deny communicative access to nonmembers of the group. Although jargons may offer effective and efficient ways of communication within the group, they are confusing to outsiders. One contemporary jargon that is notably unclear to the noninitiate but nevertheless important and increasingly influential in the language is hacker jargon. Hackers are perhaps best defined as 'particularly enthusiastic and resourceful computer users and programmers'. Their jargon is characterized by a substantial vocabulary associated with computers but also evidences unusual rules both in its syntax and word formation. The word *hardware* 'the computer or its attachments', for instance, provided via reanalysis of *-ware* the **neologism** *software* 'instructions, applications that are distinct from the computer and require use of the computer in order to function'. Over time the use of *-ware* has been further extended so that hackers have coined terms such as those in Table 14.9.

Table 14.9 Some instances of *-ware* in hacker jargon

freeware	'software provided without fee by its developer'
shareware	'software for which the developer requires a voluntary payment of a small fee by the user'
guiltware	'shareware that contains a message detailing how much effort the developer has put into it and implying that the user should immediately pay the fee'
crippleware	'shareware that has some important function removed, so as to entice the user to remit the fee in order to receive a full functional version'
crudware	'large quantities of low-quality freeware available from users' groups'
postcardware	'freeware for which the developer's only requested payment is a postcard from the user's hometown'
happiware	'freeware that contains a message stating the developer hopes it will make the user happy'
vaporware	'products (software or hardware) announced far in advance of their appearance, which may never take place'
wetware	'the human brain; human beings such as programmers'

Hackers, of course, very often use computers for communication. In so doing they have adapted some features of face-to-face interaction to this electronic medium. Thus an e-mail (electronic mail) message may be filled with typed utterances such as *<groan>* or *<chortle>*. These usages may then be transferred into the hackers' verbal interaction so that they actually say 'groan' in the course of speaking. There are also numerous 'emoticons' (use of standard keyboard characters to convey the emotions or attitudes of the communicator, such as **;-)** 'a smile and a wink' or **:-(** 'a frown or anger'). LISP, a programming language, uses a *p* suffix to denote functions resembling questions. A LISP programmer may then appropriate this (normally written) usage in his or her speech and utter *'Foodp?'* which means perhaps 'Do you want to eat?' All of the examples in this paragraph are instances of usage from one register (see Section 5.1) being adapted for use in another. Hackers offer in microcosm an example of a very resourceful use of the devices available to speakers of the language and an indication of ways in which language changes.

2.8 Politics and language

In countries with substantial populations speaking different languages, there may be a need for more than one standard language. Such countries often have designated official languages, which are recognized by the government for national or regional use. In Canada, French and English are official languages; in Finland, Finnish and Swedish are official languages; in Belgium, French and Flemish (Dutch) are similarly recognized. Countries with numerically significant localized minorities sometimes assign quasi-official status to the languages of these peoples. In such situations, the local language may be used on street signs, in the local media and, occasionally, even in local schools and administrative bodies. Examples of this type of limited local linguistic autonomy abound—in, for instance, the Inuit language in Canada, the Sámi (Lapp) language in Norway, and the Romansch language in Switzerland.

On a global scale, English has increasingly become the chief international language of communication. In many countries, this is perceived to present a threat to indigenous languages. English is by far the most common second language in the world. The more English is used for communication between persons who speak it as a second language, the less their own languages are used, and the less useful they may become for modern communication. It is to avoid the loss of their indigenous languages that many governments take action either by limiting the use of foreign languages (such as English) or by requiring the use of some indigenous language. Thus, we have the examples of both France and Quebec restricting the use of English and encouraging the use of French in business and technology. A more extreme example is Ireland, where the use of the Irish language is promoted, although it is spoken by only about five percent of the country's population.

Multilingualism

There is a great deal of variation in nations of the world with regard to language situations. At one extreme are countries such as Iceland and Portugal in which almost everybody speaks the same language. (Although this situation is limited to a very few relatively small countries, most Americans seem to think of this as the normal situation.) Next are countries such as the United States and Spain in which there is one dominant language spoken by a good-sized majority of the nation, but in which there are notable linguistic minorities. Then there are countries such as Canada and Belgium in which the great bulk of citizens are speakers of one of two major languages. At the other extreme are countries such as India, which had twenty-four major languages and hundreds of minor ones. (The designations *major* and *minor* are determined by number of speakers and legal position in the nation.)

Just as there are many language situations among the nations of the world, so there are many language policies adopted by these nations. One such policy, much favored, is to recognize only a single language for most official and educational purposes. This is the policy in Poland, Malaysia, and Senegal, among many others. It is important to note that the connotations of this policy may be very different depending upon the existing linguistic situation. Thus, in Poland, the national language, Polish, is spoken natively by the vast majority of the population. In Malaysia, the national language, Bhasa Malay, is spoken natively by the largest single ethnic group in the country, but there are significant minorities whose languages, Chinese and Tamil, have little official status. This creates the potential for tension between speakers of Chinese and Tamil on one side and Bhasa Malay on the other. In Senegal, a large percentage of the population speaks Wolof natively, but the national language is French, spoken natively by almost none of the population. This situation reflects the relative prestige of the two languages and the legacy of French colonial rule of Senegal.

In the United States, the preponderant portion of the population speaks English natively, and this is the *de facto* national language. However, the Supreme Court decision in *Lau* vs. *Nichols* (1974) and policies emitting from both the legislative and executive branches of the government have established safeguards for speakers of minority languages. Thus, voting materials must be made available in significant minority languages, and school boards must plan for the education of non-English-speaking children in ways that take into account their differing native languages.

Canada and Belgium, among others, follow a policy of absolute legal equality between two languages. While this sometimes is better followed in theory than in practice, it does provide a method by which two ethnic groups may live in a single political entity without either imposing its language on the other. In Canada and Belgium, this policy has provided a framework for continued political unity, which would have been seriously endangered if a single language policy had been pursued. Until recently, the Republic of South Africa followed an unusual version of this policy in that the two official languages, Afrikaans and English, were each spoken natively by a small minority of the country's population. Recent political changes in that country have seen the number of national languages increase to eleven, with the addition of nine indigenous languages. Switzerland is the only nation to attempt the policy of legal equality with more than two languages, German, French, and Italian all having equal status in Switzerland. Romansch, a Romance language, also has a legal status, albeit more restricted.

Nations such as India and the Philippines, in which a large variety of languages are spoken by significant groups, have opted for a national language-regional languages policy. In this arrangement, a single language, often the largest single language (e.g., Tagalog, in the Philippines) is chosen as the national language. All citizens of the country are expected to be able to function in that language. At the same time, other languages are recognized as official in specific geographical areas of the country. India follows this policy but has two national languages, Hindi and English;

twelve other languages have official status in particular states, while Sanskrit and Sindhi have official status but no designated territory.

3 REGIONAL DIFFERENTIATION OF LANGUAGE

Dialectology is the study of linguistic variation in terms of the geographical distribution of speakers. Dialectology arose in Europe about a century ago as a result of the interest of some historical linguists in observing the spread of sound changes across particular regions, especially rural areas. Later dialectological studies came to include lexical variation.

3.1 METHODS

Dialectologists gather data from speakers in a variety of ways. Originally, aspects of speech were recorded by hand on worksheets in interviews and then subjected to analysis. Today dialectologists use sophisticated interviews and record speakers' utterances on tape, thus lending greater accuracy to their work. Many dialectologists use computers for quantitative analysis or visualization of their data.

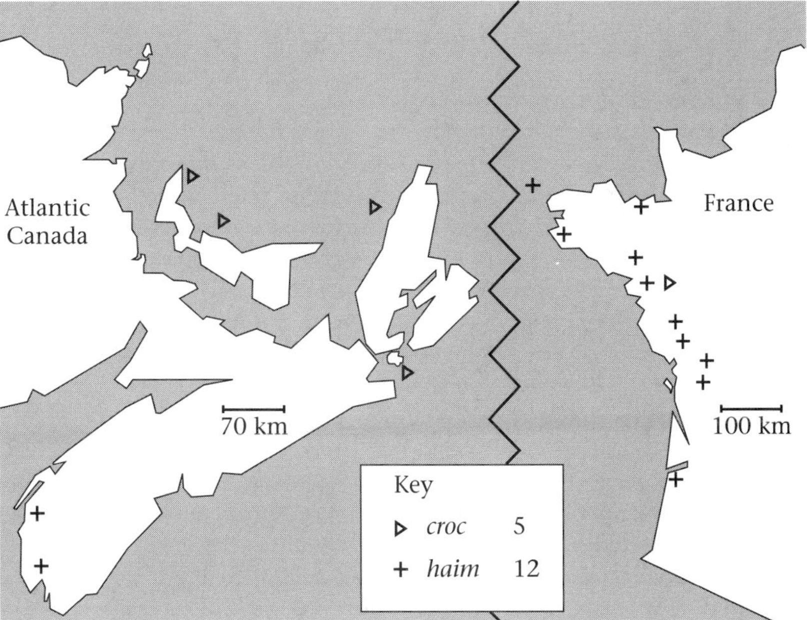

Figure 14.3 Words for 'fishhook' [Standard French *hameçon*] in French dialects of Atlantic Canada and western France (Péronnet and Arsenault, 1990)

The work of dialectologists may be published in the form of articles, but may take the form of a dialect atlas. A dialect atlas contains numerous maps that exhibit regional variation in a language. These maps may plot features that characterize a particular group of speakers or they may, for instance, be used to show features that separate one group of speakers from another. The computer-generated map in Figure 14.3 is designed to show similarities in shared vocabulary between French-speaking fishing villages in Atlantic Canada and France, thus demonstrating the probable geographical origins of the settlers of the Maritime villages.

Sometimes it is possible to discern clear boundaries between speakers of one dialect and speakers of another. These boundaries are represented on maps by means of lines called **isoglosses**. The latter may be drawn with respect to one feature (generally phonological or lexical) but the more significant boundaries occur in the form of **bundles of isoglosses**. These lines are meant to indicate that with respect to the feature or features in question, people on one side share one variant while those on the other share a different one.

The following are examples of lexical items elicited in dialect surveys. The questions are adapted from some used in actual surveys in different parts of North America. Respondents might be asked to circle the form they ordinarily used in each instance or to respond verbally to the question.

Table 14.10 Sample questions from some North American English dialect surveys

Definitions for the terms sought	*Possible responses*
Walking diagonally across a lot or an intersection	kitty-corner(ed), catty-corner(ed), going catty-wampus, caper-corner(ed), catty wompsum, antigoglin, bias-ways
Children's nicknames for one who tattles	tongue tattler, tattle-tale, tattle-box, tittle-tattle, squealer, rat, fink
Tired, exhausted	fagged out, perished, beat up, (plumb) tuckered (out), used up, done up, done in, petered out, give out, whipped, pooped, all in, bushed, wore (slam) out
Group of trees in open country	grove, motte, bluff, chênière, chenier, clump
Calls to horses (when getting them from pasture)	ku-jack!, co-jack!, kope!, curp!, curph!, quop!, quopy!, quoby!, quowa!, whistling

Early dialectologists typically surveyed large areas. They also believed that isolated rural speech was likely to be purer and of more interest than urban speech. They therefore emphasized rural and small-town speakers over urban ones. Thus, the *Linguistic Atlas of the Eastern United States,* with more than 2,500 informants, had only twenty-five from New York City. More recently, a number of sociolinguists have been interested in intensive studies of urban areas. William Labov interviewed well over 100 speakers from a single area of New York City. Similarly, there has been a change of emphasis from the written questionnaires of the early dialect studies to attempts to record speech in the most natural possible form.

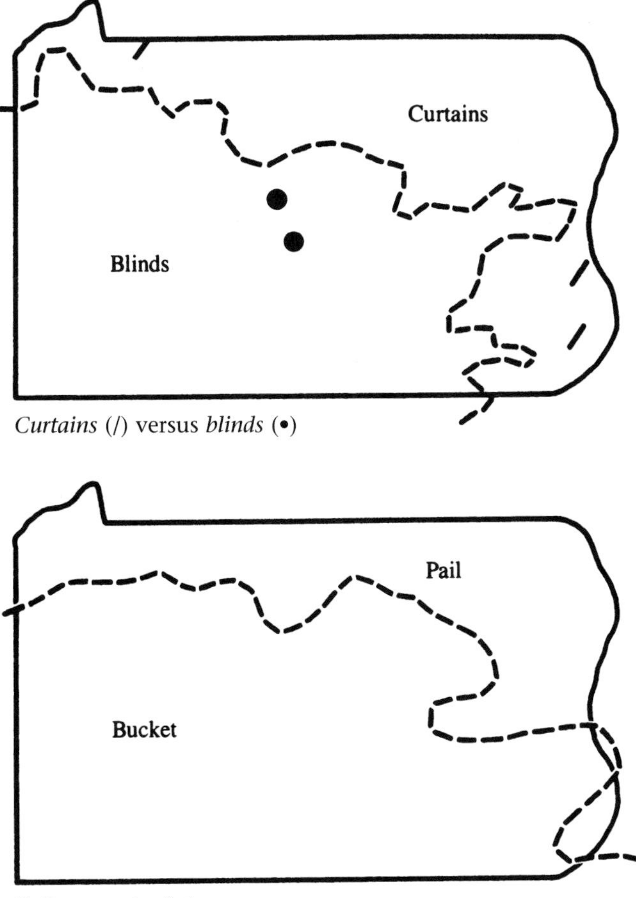

Curtains (/) versus *blinds* (•)

Pail versus *bucket*

Figure 14.4 Dialect areas in Pennsylvania

3.2 English in North America

Dialect differences in Europe often have hundreds of years of history. By the time of Alfred the Great (ninth century AD), there were already several distinct varieties of Old English, and some of these distinctions can be followed through to distinctions in Modern English varieties in Great Britain. Dialect differences in North America originated much more recently. Although there was some tendency for speakers of a single English dialect to settle together in North America, the net effect of immigration was a geographical mixing of English dialects and thus a leveling of dialect differences. The major geographical dialects of North American English, therefore, have histories of only a few hundred years of separation at most.

Within the United States alone, there are several major regional dialects. These are illustrated in Figure 14.5. The main dialect areas in the eastern United States are the Northern, Midland, and Southern regions. They are distinguished from each other primarily in terms of particular phonological and lexical features. The distinc-

Figure 14.5 Regional dialects of American English. Eastern dialects are numbered. Other (more tentative) dialect boundaries are indicated by dotted lines. Arrows indicate direction of major migrations.

tions among these regions tend to become less obvious as one moves to the west. This reflects the historical pattern of migration from east to west in North America in which dialectal differences have become blended.

American English

Generally speaking, the study of American dialectology has proceeded like the settlement of the United States itself, from east to west. The most extensively published studies and the most certain generalizations concern the Eastern Seaboard and adjoining states. Here we find three major dialect areas: Northern, encompassing the area north of a line running westward from central New Jersey through northern

Pennsylvania; Southern, including those areas south and east of a line starting at the Atlantic at the southern border of New Jersey and heading westward almost to West Virginia, and then heading south through North Carolina and South Carolina; and Midland, including the area between the Northern and Southern areas. The Northern dialect area contains Eastern New England (Maine, New Hampshire, Rhode Island, and eastern Massachusetts and Connecticut) as a major sub-area. The Midland dialect is divided into Northern Midland (Pennsylvania, southern New Jersey, northern Maryland, and northern West Virginia) and Southern Midland (southern West Virginia, western Virginia, western North Carolina, and northwestern South Carolina). Studies have been made of the westward extensions of these dialects, but the situation is more complicated and less well studied than along the Eastern Seaboard.

Northern English

The Northern dialect is set off by the use of such vocabulary terms as *pail* rather than *bucket, angleworm* for *earthworm,* and *pit* rather than *seed* in a cherry. Phonologically it has a phonemic distinction between the vowels in *morning* and *mourning,* /s/ instead of /z/ in *greasy*, and /u/ instead of /ʊ/ in *root.* Eastern New England is set off from the rest of the Northern dialect by the loss of postvocalic /r/ (i.e., in such words as *barn, four,* and *daughter*) and the use of /a/ for /æ/ in words such as *aunt, bath,* and *half.*

Midland English

The Midland dialect is distinguished by vocabulary items such as *skillet* for frying pan, *blinds* for window shades, and *poke* for a paper sack. Phonologically it retains postvocalic /r/ and has /θ/ finally in *with.* Northern Midland is distinguished by vocabulary items such as *run* for a small stream and /a/ in *frog, hog,* and *fog,* which do not rhyme with *dog.* Southern Midland has *redworm* for *earthworm, pack* for *carry,* and /a/ for /aj/ in words such as *write* and *ride.*

Southern English

Southern English is marked by the loss of postvocalic /r/, /z/ in *Mrs.,* and the use of *tote* for *carry* and *snap beans* for *string beans.* It shares with Southern Midland the use of *you-all* for the second person plural pronoun, /juw/ in words such as *news* and *due, shucks* rather than *husks* for the coverings of corn, and *might could* for *might be able to.*

4 MIXED LANGUAGES

No natural language is in any sense 'pure' or free from all influence from other languages and cultures. Some languages in the world are, however, mixtures composed of elements from many sources. This very quality of being 'mixed' rather than the product of one clear historical evolution lends a unique character to these languages.

4.1 PIDGINS

The term **pidgin** is used by linguists as the label for speech varieties that develop when speakers of two or more different languages come into contact with each other and do not know each other's language. A pidgin is not the native language of any group. Where pidgins still exist, their use may be confined to the marketplace or similar domain. There are numerous theories as to why and how pidgins have come about. Some pidgins have been called 'trade languages' or 'trade jargons' and have clearly arisen as the result of contact situations between people who were seeking to do business with each other. Sailors have been ascribed a particular role in the genesis of certain pidgins. Some scholars have claimed that jargons called 'nautical English' or 'maritime French' served as the basis for later pidgins in various parts of the world. Clearly, sailors did at least play an important role in spreading major colonial languages (English, French, Spanish, Portuguese, and Dutch) throughout the world but it is unclear that their jargons formed the basis for resulting pidgins.

There is some evidence to support the claim that pidgins may have arisen as a result of the apparently quite normal tendency for speakers in contact situations to 'simplify' their speech both syntactically and lexically. Linguists use the term *foreigner talk* for such simplified registers (see Chapter 13, Section 4.1). This term is used to describe the way an adult native speaker of English attempts to communicate with a non-English speaker, relying on simple concepts and avoiding more complicated syntactic devices such as embedded clauses or passives. Foreigner talk is similar to *baby talk*, which is the label for the simplified register adults use to talk with babies (see Section 5.1).

However they may have arisen, pidgins typically present a syntactic structure that is comparatively simple and exhibit certain characteristic relationships to their source languages. They normally reflect the influence of the higher status (or dominant) language in their lexicon and that of the lower status language in their phonology (and occasionally syntax). For example, the following sentence from the Hawaii Pidgin English spoken by Philippine laborers in Hawaii prior to 1930 consists of English words but has the verb in initial position (where it occurs in Philippine languages):

2)

wok had dis pipl
work hard these people
'These people work hard.'

Pidgins are an important subset of a larger group of languages termed *lingue franche* (plural of lingua franca). A **lingua franca** may be a pidgin or it may be the native language of a people (as is modern English). These are 'third' languages that are used for communication among speakers of different languages. The name derives from a medieval trade language (called Lingua Franca) used in the Mediterranean region and based largely on Romance languages (Italian, French, and Spanish) but also containing elements of Greek, Arabic, and Turkish. In the modern world, it is fair to say that English is the most important lingua franca, since it is used as a means of communication for purposes of business among large numbers of people who do not otherwise share a common language.

4.2 Creoles

A **creole** is a language that, having originated as a pidgin, has become established as a first language in some speech community. In most instances, creoles that have become established as first languages in particular countries continue to exist alongside the standard (higher status) language that was originally pidginized. The standard language usually serves as the language of education and administration. The creole, not having the stabilizing base of a written tradition and likely subject to the influence of the standard, tends to change more rapidly over time.

Typically, different varieties of the creole emerge, some resembling the standard more than the others. The standard may serve as a source for new lexical items in the creole. In such situations, the creole may develop varieties that to greater or lesser extents resemble the standard. Those varieties that show the greatest lexical influence from the standard and are otherwise most similar to the standard are labelled **acrolects**. Those that evidence the least influence from the standard are called **basilects**. Varieties between these two extremes are called **mesolects**.

Along with most pidgins, most creoles have existed in a relatively narrow belt between the Tropics of Cancer and Capricorn (see Figure 14.6). There are a number of them in the West Indies, the East Indies, and West Africa. Two important and opposing views on the origin and development of these creoles are the notions of **relexification** and the **language bioprogram hypothesis**. Both of these theories are based on the fact that creoles the world over show remarkable similarities in their grammars, such as SVO word order.

In brief, the relexification hypothesis holds that creoles either (1) all go back to a single historical source (such as the sixteenth-century West African slaver's jargon Pidgin Portuguese or the original Lingua Franca) and have essentially retained the grammar (syntax) of that pidgin but have undergone changes in their vocabulary (relexification) in different subsequent linguistic and cultural contexts, or (2) may have more than one historical source but still are largely re-formed over time through the replacement of lexical items while the comparatively simple grammars remain relatively unchanged.

The language bioprogram hypothesis holds that similarities among creoles are not the result of historical transmission from an original 'proto-pidgin' grammar but reflect linguistic universals both in terms of first language acquisition and with respect to processes and structures that are putatively innate in the human brain. A pattern of similar innovations in the development of the first generation of creoles has been observed which, it is claimed, can only be explained in terms of a theory of linguistic universals. These innovations include, for example, the use of various preverbal particles to indicate notions such as completeness, ongoing action, and the like. In the following sentence from Hawaiian Creole English, for example, the particle *stei* (from English 'stay') is used to indicate an action currently taking place:

3)

ai no kea hu stei hant insai dea
I no care who stay hunt inside there
'I don't care who's hunting in there.'

Figure 14.6 Some English- and French-based pidgins and creoles of the world

Pidgins are seen as structurally deficient in many respects and inadequate as input to children acquiring their first language. Children are thus said to be thrown back on their innate language bioprogram to provide a basic structure for the creole. This produces a language that can serve as the basis for further generations of learners and can, for instance, undergo the sorts of lexical changes mentioned above in which it may come to resemble the original higher status language more.

Cape York Creole

Among the English-based creoles of the world is Cape York Creole (CYC), spoken in the northern tip of Australia opposite Papua-New Guinea. The data from this creole in Tables 14.11 to 14.13 will help to illustrate the fact that creoles are not simply deformed or bastardized languages but, in fact, have interesting characteristics of their own that are not shared with the standard.

Table 14.11 Singular pronouns in Cape York Creole

1st person	ai, mi
2nd person	yu
3rd person	i, im

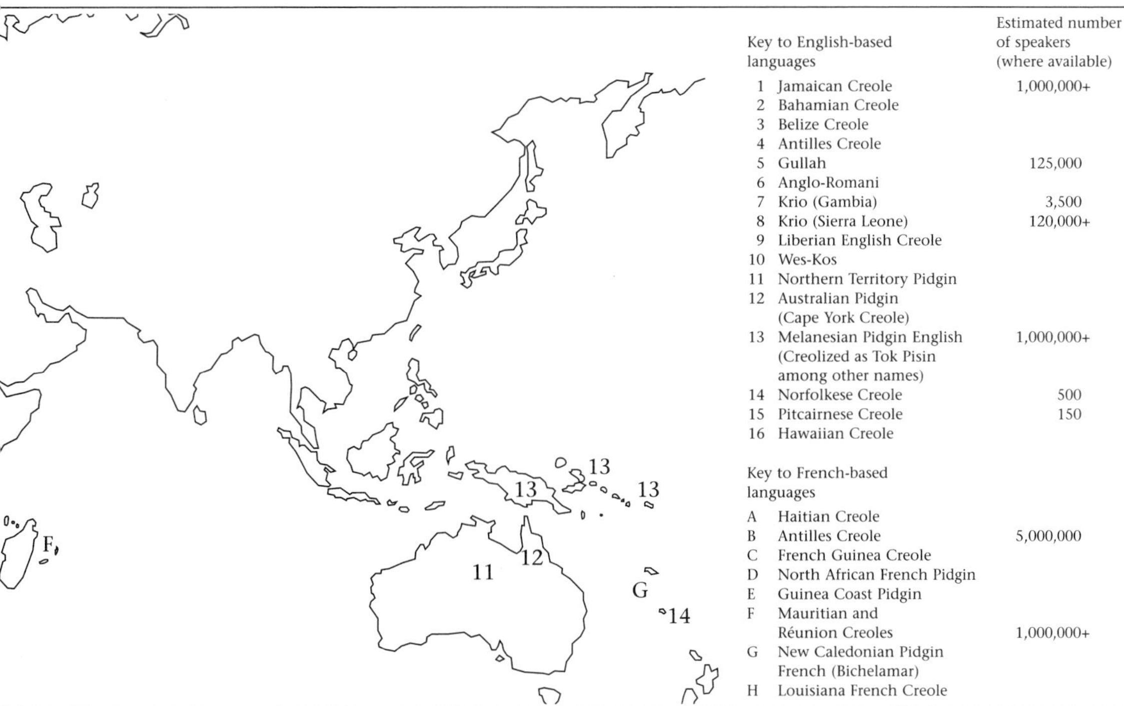

Differences from Standard English include the fact that in the third person there is no three-way gender distinction and that all of these pronouns can serve as a subject. Only *mi*, *yu*, and *im*, however, can serve as objects just like Standard English pronouns *me* and *him*. The main difference between the CYC pronominal system and that of Standard English lies in the nonsingular forms. CYC exhibits two nonsingular categories: dual and plural. The forms for second and third person are shown in Table 14.12.

Table 14.12 Dual and plural pronouns in Cape York Creole (second and third person)

Dual, 2nd person	yutu(pela)
Dual, 3rd person	tupela
Plural, 2nd person	yu(pela)
Plural, 3rd person	ol, dempela

The form *-pela* derives from English *fellow*. It occurs in several realizations, *-fela* being the acrolectal form. In the first person, a further distinction is made between *inclusive* and *exclusive* pronouns. Inclusive pronouns *include* the speaker and the addressee ('you and I'), while exclusive pronouns *exclude* the addressee but include the speaker and someone else. These pronominal categories are realized in CYC in the forms in Table 14.13, all of which are first person, nonsingular.

Table 14.13 Dual and plural pronouns in Cape York Creole (1st person)

Dual, inclusive	yumi, yumtu	(speaker plus one addressee)
Dual, exclusive	mitu	(speaker plus one other, not the addressee)
Plural, inclusive	mipela, wi	(speaker plus addressees)
Plural, exclusive	mitupela, wi	(speaker plus others, not addressee)

The following example illustrates the semantic differences among some of these categories. Assume that they are uttered in a situation in which three persons (A, B, and C) are present.

4)

a. If A says to B *yumi go nau,* A is saying that the two of them will go but not C.
b. If A says to B *mitu go nau,* A is saying that A and C will go but not B.
c. If A says to B and C *mipela go nau,* A is saying that all three of them will go.

It should be apparent from these few examples that creoles, far from being less than a standard, are capable of distinctions not found in the standard. The existence of a dual category of number alongside those of plural and singular, for example, affords CYC speakers a precision not available to speakers of Standard English. The dual is often seen in languages spoken in small-scale, mainly agricultural societies in which it is useful to be able to designate items as occurring in pairs. The distinction between inclusive and exclusive pronouns is widespread in languages of the world, being present in many Amerindian languages, for example. Note how, in the foregoing translations, English can only somewhat clumsily paraphrase the ideas expressed by these CYC pronouns. These distinctions are, however, important to CYC speakers—and probably to speakers of neighboring indigenous languages—and thus are incorporated into the pronominal system. Like other English-based creoles, CYC shares a number of features with Standard English but has its own linguistic system and its own history.

5 SPEECH SITUATIONS

. . . the social situation is the most powerful determinant of verbal behavior . . .

– William Labov

Speech situations are those social situations in which there is appropriate use of language. They are the main locus for research by interactional sociolinguists. **Interactional sociolinguistics** may be said either to include or to exhibit considerable overlap with the subdisciplines of ethnography of communication, discourse analysis, and pragmatics. The methods of description and analysis of language used in speech situations differ markedly from the techniques we have previously examined in this chapter, yet we have already referred to several concepts that can only be adequately discussed using this approach.

A speech situation consists of a number of components. In analyzing a speech situation, the sociolinguist (or an ethnographer of communication) seeks to specify how each of these components is realized. Once this has been done, an understanding of the how, what, and why of the interaction is achieved. In Table 14.14, the components of the speech situation have been mnemonically arranged to form the acronym SPEAKING.

Table 14.14 Components of the speech situation arranged mnemonically

S	the setting and scene of a speech situation, distinguishing between the physical locale and the type of activity
P	the participants, often characterized by terms such as addressor, addressee, speaker, performer, audience, questioner, answerer, caller, interviewer, interviewee, and so on
E	the ends, including both functions and outcomes; functions may be broadly classified as those in which the content of talk is important (transactional function) and those that serve to reinforce or establish social or interpersonal relations (interactional function); the outcomes have to do with what effect the speech has on the addressee or other aspects of the situation
A	the act sequence, including the content and form of speech
K	the key, tone, mood, or manner, distinguishing among serious, facetious, formal, sarcastic, and so on
I	the instrumentalities, including the 'channel' (verbal, nonverbal, face-to-face, written, electronic mail, and so on) and 'code' (the language and/or variety used)
N	the norms of interaction and interpretation (the basic rules that seem to underlie the interaction)
G	the genre, any one of a class of named speech acts (greeting, leave-taking, lecture, joke, and so on)

These notions become more concrete in the context of a specific example. Consider the following situations, which might occur in a university.

Setting, Scene A classroom could be the setting and might accommodate a number of scenes, among them a lecture, seminar, club meeting, or conversation.

Participants The different scenes provide for a number of possible relationships between interactants: teacher-student, leader-member, speaker-addressee, among others.

Ends Among the numerous possible functions might be the instructional (in a lecture), the consultative (in a tutorial), and the interactional (in a friendly conversation). The outcomes could include whatever has been learned in the lecture or tutorial, the plans for a party in the club meeting, or the sharing of gossip in a conversation.

Act sequence The content and form might vary from the structured lecture material, to the question and answer or problem solving of the seminar, to the agenda of the meeting, to the small talk of the conversation.

Key The mood would range from the comparative formality of the lecture to the relative informality (even jocularity) of the conversation.

Instrumentalities All the situations would be face-to-face, mostly verbal (aside from appropriate nonverbal aspects such as the raising of a hand for recognition and the performance of written tasks). The variety of English would likely be Standard English in the lecture but might contain significantly more nonstandard features in the conversation. Recalling the sociolinguistic variable (ing) from Section 2.3, we might expect to hear it realized as [ɪŋ] in the lecture but as [ɪn] more often in the conversation.

Norms The norms would vary considerably from situation to situation. The rights (or status) of participants would differ markedly. In the lecture, seminar, and, perhaps to a lesser extent, the club meeting, the teacher (or leader) would control the situation. He or she might do most of the talking and generally determine the course of the interaction. Other participants would normally be required to secure the permission of the leader in order to speak. In the conversation, there would be greater equality between participants.

Genre A lecture can be termed a genre in itself. It is recognizable by its form, limited number of topics, speaker-audience format, and relative formality. A seminar would include questions and answers, among other acts. A conversation consists of a number of possible speech acts (or genres). Among these might be an initial greeting (*'Hi!'*), a concluding leave-taking (*'Bye!'*), and intervening narratives (including perhaps a joke). Thus, it can be seen that genre is a component that can be understood on more than one level. A lecture can be a genre but so can a greeting or a joke, which is included in the lecture.

As we can see from these examples, speaking in social contexts involves more than simply being able to form grammatical sentences. Sociolinguists claim that speakers possess communicative competence, or underlying knowledge of the linguistic system combined with knowledge of the rules (or norms) for the appropriate use of language in speech situations. In interactional sociolinguistics, the concern is not so much with the grammaticality of utterances but rather with their appropriateness. The next section treats this matching of language with situation in its discussion of the concept of functional speech variety, or register.

5.1 Register

The form that talk takes in any given context is called a **register**. Different registers may be characterized in phonological, syntactic, or lexical terms. A register is also a function of all the other components of a speech situation discussed in the previous section. A formal setting may condition a formal register, characterized by particular lexical items, greater adherence to the rules of Standard English, absence of stigmatized sociolinguistic variables, and so on. An informal setting may be reflected in a casual register that exhibits less formal vocabulary, more nonstandard features, greater instances of stigmatized variables, and so on. Registers can also be categorized in terms of their relative explicitness.

Two good friends discussing a matter well known to both do not need to make every detail of their conversation explicit. Each may correctly assume that the other knows basically what the conversation is about. Such an assumption can result in the appropriate use of pronouns and elliptical sentences, both of which are less explicit (more implicit) than nouns or full sentences. The speakers' shared background knowledge will fill in the blanks. Similarly, shared knowledge in an ongoing situation, such as experienced by spectators at a hockey game, means that one fan can refer to the goalie (as in *'He sure blew that one!'*) and be understood by another. A university lecture (or a textbook), on the other hand, requires both a formal and an explicit register and perhaps a technical one as well, since new and unfamiliar concepts are being introduced and explained.

The following examples of some registers of spoken and written language are mainly differentiated from each other in terms of relative formality and explicitness.

5)

"This is close to a charge. Call it yourself. No, he did move over on him!"

This was uttered by a color commentator describing an instant replay in a basketball game. It was understandable in context and appropriately implicit. Only one noun was used in the quotation, and it is a technical term in basketball. The referents of the pronouns (other than the audience-directed "yourself") were entirely context-bound. It was reasonable to assume that anyone who could see the telecast could interpret their meanings.

6)

"That's what I ought to look like is like that."

This sentence is again entirely context-bound (and maximally implicit) in its meaning. It was appropriate, however, when uttered. Its speaker and addressee both understood what *that* referred to. Its syntax is also consistent with its informality.

7)

"In those pants you really look like a zhlub."

Again, the interpretation of the precise reference is limited to the context in which the sentence was uttered. Also, the use of an ethnic slang term *zhlub* (meaning 'gauche or coarse person' in Yiddish) signals an informal register.

8)

"Wilt thou have this man to be thy wedded husband . . ."

Lexical, morphological, and syntactic archaisms signal this formal (and ritualized) register.

9)

"Pellagra is characterized by cutaneous, mucous membrane, CNS, and gastrointestinal symptoms."

This quotation from a medical handbook illustrates features of a formal register (in the written channel) by its fully formed sentence, high degree of explicitness, use of the passive, and the presence of medical jargon. It is an example of a technical register.

10)

"Bruins harpooned"

This appeared as a caption to a graphic on a television newscast. Its elliptical form is obviously derived from the style of newspaper headlines. It is appropriate to the written channel of communication and illustrates the importance of shared knowledge in the interpreting of elliptical utterances. A hockey fan would know that the caption refers to the defeat of the Boston Bruins by the Hartford Whalers.

11)

"Time to go bye-bye."

The minimal syntax and choice of lexical items characterize this utterance as one which might be directed by a parent to a child. It is an example of a simplified register called *baby talk* (termed *motherese* in Chapter 12). Baby talk is widespread, perhaps even universal, in speech communities in the world. In English it is specifically characterized by its limited lexicon, simple syntax, and relatively high pitch. In these respects it is most similar to the registers we use to speak to a pet or a lover and is thus both nonthreatening and nurturing. With respect to its simplified grammar and lexicon, baby talk resembles the foreigner talk register mentioned above in the discussion of the genesis of pidgins (see Section 4.1).

The preceding quotations are a small sample of the variety of registers available to English speakers. All competent speakers of the language are able to produce at least a few registers, thereby making their speech appropriate for particular speech situations.

5.2 Forms of Address

One aspect of speech that has been productively analyzed by interactional sociolinguists is that of **address term** usage. This phenomenon has been observed in a variety of languages and cultures. It seems clear that all languages have address forms and specific rules that determine their appropriate use. Every time one calls someone, or refers to him or her by name, one indicates something of one's social relationship to or personal feeling about that individual. One might be on first-name terms with a friend but not with an uncle or a mother. A grandparent might be addressed by a pet name coined in one's childhood, but an employer might be called Ms. Smyth and might address an employee by using the latter's first name. There is nothing unusual about these examples. Not everyone functions with precisely this assortment of address forms, but they are probably quite representative of general usage in our society.

Compared to most of the world's languages, English has a relatively simple system of address terms, such as those shown in Table 14.15.

Table 14.15 Types of address terms in English

Term	*Example*
First name (FN)	Jane!
Title + last name (TLN)	Mr. Simpson!
Title alone (T)	Nurse!
Last name (LN)	Smith!
Kinterms (KT*)	Granny!

*alone or with FN or LN, as appropriate

Address terms can be used reciprocally or nonreciprocally. In the first case, speakers address each other with the same type of term (FN or TLN). This is a sign of a symmetrical social relationship in which both parties have the same status (friends, colleagues, and so on). In the case of nonreciprocal usage, there is an asymmetrical relationship, one in which the difference in status between participants is marked. Thus, one person might use FN, and the other TLN. This is typical of a doctor-patient or teacher-student relationship.

In English, and other languages as well, it is also possible to avoid address terms altogether when participants are unsure which term to use. This practice is called **no-naming**. In the case of English speakers, it results in participants using *you* while scrupulously avoiding terms such as FN or TLN. A familiar example of this occurs in the university setting when students no-name an instructor if unsure whether to call him or her by a more specific address term.

Other European languages have one complication that has been largely missing from our language since the seventeenth century: the choice of two pronouns in the second person. On one level in the grammars of these languages, choosing between these two pronouns (*tu* and *vous* in French) is a function of the number of people being addressed—singular versus plural. These pronouns, however, also encode the sociolinguistic dimensions mentioned above. Thus, the form *tu* is like our FN in connoting friendship or intimacy when used mutually and in connoting lower status of the addressee when used nonreciprocally. The form *vous* used with a singular addressee is similar to our TLN in these respects. The details of these usages vary from language to language, but these broad outlines are indicative of the general tendencies.

Outside of Europe and other areas where European languages dominate, these overall patterns still hold, but often in complex systems with vast numbers of address forms. In many instances, we also have to take into account not only the second person pronouns, but first and third person pronouns as well. In many languages (especially those in highly traditional, stratified societies), there are a number of first person singular pronouns. In Thai, for example, there are seventeen different forms that translate English *I*. Their appropriate use is based on the status of the speaker, that of the addressee, and the relationship between the two. In the same language, there are a further seventeen second person forms and eleven third person forms. In addition, there are numerous categories of nouns that can be used in direct address. The rules for deciding which form is appropriate are complex and require that participants have some knowledge about each other's status. Given these complications and the possibility that selecting an inappropriate form might be rude or insulting, there is also a provision for no-naming.

Table 14.16 Some Thai address forms

Speaker	*Addressee*	*Term*
friend/kin/spouse	friend/kin/spouse	/nii/
adult/superior	child/inferior	/nuu/
Buddhist monk	superior monk	/pradeedprakhun/
inferior/nonmonk	superior/monk	/than/

These forms, all equivalent to English *you*, are but a small sample of the set of address terms available in the Bangkok speech community.

5.3 Discourse and text

Language used in naturally occurring situations takes many forms. Any bit of talk produced by a speaker, which is distinct from other bits of talk from the same speaker and from other speakers in a speech situation, is an **utterance**. An utterance may be realized as a single sentence (*'I have to leave now'*), an elliptical sentence (*'Time to go'*), a sequence of sentences (as in a long response to a question), or a single word (*'Yes'*). Any utterance will also be analyzable in terms of the components of SPEAKING (discussed earlier in Section 5) and thus will have, in addition to a particular form, an appropriate speaker and hearer, function, and so forth. The set of utterances produced by a speaker can be referred to as that speaker's **discourse**. The written (or transcribed) version of any utterance or body of discourse is called a **text**. The field that deals with the organization of texts, ways in which parts of texts are connected, and the devices used for achieving textual structure is **discourse analysis**.

Discourse analysis is very much a multidisciplinary field. Its practitioners are drawn from linguistics, anthropology, sociology, philosophy, psychology, computer science, and other disciplines. Linguists working in this area tend to focus on the nature of the language used in texts, particularly on those devices that provide a structural framework to texts and those that provide the cohesion necessary for a text to be perceived as an organized whole.

Discourse markers

In either spoken or written discourse the 'utterer' produces not only strings of nouns, verbs, adjectives, adverbs, and the like, but, as well, makes use of forms called **discourse markers** to provide structure. One scholar who is concerned with this phenomenon of naturally occurring language use has defined discourse markers as 'sequentially dependent elements which bracket units of talk'. By this she means that these markers occur over the length of a bit of discourse, separating one 'unit of talk' from a previous one. The bits of talk are themselves defined by the markers. In English alone there are a number of such discourse markers. Not all of them have received a great deal of study and there remains much work to be done in order to reach a full understanding of what all of the markers are and how they function. Similar phenomena in other languages remain to be treated.

Two typical discourse markers in English are *well* and *y'know*. In *12)* we see an example of the use of *well* as a discourse marker.

12)

Speaker A: Did you enjoy your trip to the mountains?
Speaker B: Well, it rained the whole time, so we had to stay indoors and never got to do anything.

In this instance *well* serves to introduce a response that is possibly contrary to what might have been expected. It also avoids the most direct possible answer to the *yes-no* question posed by speaker A: *No!* English speakers tend to soften negative responses to such questions by using a hedge such as *well*, as seen in *13)*.

13)

Speaker C: Could you type this letter for me before you leave?
Speaker D: Well, I was really planning to get an early start on my weekend so I thought I'd leave a few minutes early.

A discourse marker such as *y'know* can be used to appeal to knowledge shared by speaker and addressee, to involve the addressee more in the interaction, to test whether the addressee does in fact share the knowledge or a combination of these.

14)

Say, I saw Betty last week. Y'know, the girl who used to live across the street?

15)

I was driving to Drumheller on Sunday and saw this incredible coulee on the way. Y'know, that's a sort of canyon where there's been a lot of erosion?

In *14)* the speaker apparently assumes that the addressee knows or recalls the girl in question. In *15)* the speaker assumes that the addressee does not share (or may not share) the information (what a coulee is) and thus uses *y'know* to bracket off the unit of talk that provides the clarification.

The long list of discourse markers in English includes such forms as *oh, I mean, anyway*, coordinating conjunctions (*and, but, or*), temporal adverbs (*then, now*), and others. Although speakers are not usually aware of them, they are essential and their use provides organization to discourse (especially spoken discourse).

Textual cohesion

While discourse markers bracket off units of talk and do provide some element of cohesion, there are other linguistic resources that are more typically thought of as the primary **cohesive devices** in English. Table 14.17 provides a list of some of these devices.

Table 14.17 Textual cohesion in English

(1) Reference (anaphoric):
I know Grant. He drives a red car.

(2) Reference (cataphoric):
It's awfully dry, this toast.

(3) Lexical cohesion (substitution):
Speaker E: Do you know San Francisco at all?
Speaker F: I've never been to the place.

(4) Ellipsis:
Speaker G: Do you speak French?
Speaker H: No.

In examples (1), (3), and (4) in Table 14.17 there are two sentences, either uttered by one speaker or by two speakers in sequence. Cohesive devices are not limited, however, to operating between sentences. Most of these can function within one sentence, as we see in example (2). In examples (1), (2), and (4) the underlined elements are the ones that exhibit cohesion; one underlined constituent presupposes the other. The more usual type of pronominal reference in English is **anaphoric**, in which the noun or noun phrase occurs earlier in the text than the pronoun with which it is coreferential. In the less frequent **cataphoric** reference, a pronoun is coreferential with a noun or noun phrase that occurs later in the text. In both of these one must know (or be able to find) the coreferential noun or noun phrase in order to be able to decode the pronoun. This link between the pronoun and the constituent with which it is coreferential is the cohesive tie between parts of the same text. Similarly, in example (3) *San Francisco* and *the place* refer to the same thing and understanding the second phrase requires one to have access to the first. One phrase has been substituted for the other and the two utterances are thus linked.

In example (4) the minimal utterance in response to a *yes-no* question can only be interpreted by the speakers' knowledge that this one word replaces (or stands for) a fuller reponse (*'No, I don't speak French'*) which, however, would probably be heard as inappropriate here. Another possible response would be *'No, I don't.'* This is also elliptical, since decoding it requires knowledge of the preceding utterance.

These are a few instances of cohesive devices in English. Other languages possess similar ones for the creation of texts. It is possible to observe these, as was the case with discourse markers, in written and spoken discourse. They are some of the most important and obvious linguistic means for connecting language and situation.

SUMMING UP

The field of **sociolinguistics** treats the social aspects of language use. This chapter focuses on three principal types of **speech variety**: **sociolects**, **regional dialects**, and **registers**, along with a number of related phenomena. All languages have such varieties, but in all communities, one variety, the **standard**, has more prestige than the others. Sociolects of a language correlate with such social factors as the socioeconomic status, gender, age, and occupation of their speakers. Approaches to the study of the social differentiation of language proceed from different perspectives, emphasizing the **social stratification** of speech varieties or focusing on the **social networks** of speakers. There are many instances of **euphemism** in language, which result in the replacement of **taboo** items. The most casual varieties of language (often associated with younger speakers) are the **slang** varieties. Some segments of any population develop secret languages or **argots**, while **jargons** are associated with specialized professions. **Dialectology** deals with regional variation in language. The interaction of different linguistic groups may give rise to **pidgins**, mixed languages without native speakers. **Creoles** arise when pidgins are learned as native languages. The components of **SPEAKING** provide a model for understanding language use in **speech situations**. They also serve as a framework for the discussion of **registers**, **address terms**, and specific aspects of **discourse analysis**, such as **discourse markers** and **textual cohesion**.

KEY TERMS

acrolects
act sequence
address terms
anaphoric (reference)
argot
basilects
bundles of isoglosses
cataphoric (reference)
cohesive devices
creole
dialectology
discourse
discourse analysis
discourse markers
ends
euphemism
gender-exclusive differentiation
gender-variable differentiation
genre
instrumentalities
interactional sociolinguistics
isoglosses
jargon
key
language bioprogram hypothesis
lingua franca
mesolects
neologism
no-naming
nonstandard (dialect)
norms
participants
pidgin
politeness formulas
Principal Components Analysis
regional dialect
registers
relexification
scene
setting
slang
social network analysis
social stratification
sociolects
sociolinguistics
speech community
speech situations
speech variety
standard language
taboo
text
utterance
verbal hedges

Sources

Underlying the discussion of the social network approach are Lesley Milroy, *Language and Social Networks* (Oxford: Blackwell, 1980), Lesley Milroy, *Observing and Analysing Natural Language* (Oxford: Blackwell, 1987), and Jeremy Boissevain, *Friends of Friends: Networks, Manipulators and Coalitions* (Oxford: Blackwell, 1974). Figure 14.2 comes from the latter. Background for the discussion of Principal Components Analysis and the later treatment of phonological variables in Newfoundland English came from a paper, "Problems in the Analysis of Sociolinguistic Variability: From Social to Linguistic Groupings," presented by Sandra Clarke at the 19th Annual NWAVE conference, held at the University of Pennsylvania, October 1990. The source for the section on nonstandard grammatical features, and, indeed, an underlying inspiration for sections dealing with the social stratification of English is William Labov's article "The Logic of Nonstandard English" in *Report of the Twentieth Annual Round Table Meeting on Linguistics and Language Studies*, edited by James E. Alatis (Washington: Georgetown University Press, 1970), pp. 1–43.

General sources on language and gender are: David Graddol and Joan Swann, *Gender Voices* (Oxford: Blackwell, 1989), Dennis Baron, *Grammar and Gender* (New Haven: Yale University Press, 1986), and Robin Lakoff, *Talking Power: The Politics of Language* (New York: Basic Books, 1990). Some of the terminology used in the language and gender section derived from Anne Bodine's article "Sex Differentiation in Language" in *Language and Sex: Difference and Dominance*, edited by Barrie Thorne and Nancy Henley (Rowley, MA: Newbury House, 1975), pp. 130–51. The Amerindian examples in this section were taken from Mary Haas's article "Men's and Women's Speech in Koasati" in *Language* 20:142–49 (1944).

Some concepts in the discussion of slang were derived from Penelope Eckert, *Jocks and Burnouts: Social Categories and Identities in the High School* (New York: Teachers College Press, 1989). The study of language use in a Calgary high school mentioned in the text is Janet P. Bowes, "Teenage Labelling: 'Are You a Jock or a Freak?'" in *Calgary Working Papers in Linguistics*, No. 9:7–16 (1983). Slang examples in Tables 14.6 and 14.7 are from Pamela Munro, ed., *U.C.L.A. Slang: A Dictionary of Slang Words and Expressions Used at U.C.L.A.* in *Occasional Paper in Linguistics* #8 (1989).

The examples of 'gay lingo' in Table 14.8 and some of the accompanying discussion are derived from Wayne Dynes, *Homolexis: A Historical and Cultural Lexicon of Homosexuality, Gai Saber Monograph No. 4* (1985). The discussion of 'hacker jargon' and the examples in Table 14.9 are adapted from the "Jargon File," version 2.2.1 (15 Dec 1990), an on-line publication.

General background for the discussion of contemporary methodologies in dialectology was adapted from Alan R. Thomas, ed., *Methods in Dialectology* (Clevedon: Multilingual Matters, 1988). The map in Figure 14.3 is taken from Louise Péronnet and Paul-André Arsenault, "Linguistic Atlas of French Maritime Terminology: Computerized Maps," *Journal of English Linguistics* 22 (1): 25–29 (1990). Material in Table 14.10 is adapted from Alva L. Davis, Raven I. McDavid, Jr., and Virginia G. McDavid, eds., *A Compilation of the Work Sheets of the Linguistic Atlas of the United States and Canada and Associated Projects,* 2nd ed. (Chicago: University of Chicago Press, 1969).

General discussion of the nature and origins of pidgins and creoles is adapted from Peter Mühlhäusler, *Pidgin and Creole Linguistics* (Oxford: Blackwell, 1986) and Derek Bickerton's article "The Language Bioprogram Hypothesis" in *The Behavioral and Brain Sciences* 7:173–221 (1984). Material on Cape York Creole is derived from the article "Cape York Creole" by Terry Crowley and Bruce Rigsby in *Languages and Their Status*, edited by Timothy Shopen (Cambridge, MA: Winthrop Publishers, 1979), pp. 153–207. The map showing the distribution of some English- and French-based creoles and pidgins is from Ian F. Hancock's article "A Survey of the Pidgins and Creoles of the World" in *Pidginization and Creolization of Languages*, edited by Dell Hymes (Cambridge, MA: Cambridge University Press, 1971), pp. 509–23 and from Ian F. Hancock's article "Repertory of Pidgin and Creole Languages" in *Pidgin and Creole Linguistics*, edited by Albert Valdman (Bloomington, IN: Indiana University Press, 1977).

The components of SPEAKING and the inspiration for the section in which they appear derive from Dell Hymes's article "Models of the Interaction of Language and Social Life" in *Directions in Sociolinguistics: The Ethnography of Communication*, edited by J. Gumperz and D. Hymes (New York: Holt, Rinehart and Winston, 1972), pp. 35–71. The section on register is inspired partially by M. A. K. Halliday, *Language as Social Semiotic* (London: Edward Arnold, 1978). Another source on register is Hywel Coleman, ed., *Working with Language: A Multidisciplinary Consideration of Language Use in Work Contexts* (Berlin: Mouton de Gruyter, 1989). An underlying source for the section on address terms is the article by Roger Brown and Albert Gilman, "The Pronouns of Power and Solidarity" in *Style in Language*, edited by Thomas A. Sebeok (Cambridge, MA: MIT Press, 1960), pp. 253–76. The discussion and examples of Thai address terms are taken from Angkab Palakornkul's work *A Sociolinguistic Study of Pronominal Strategy in Spoken Bangkok Thai* (Ph.D. diss., University of Texas, 1972).

Underlying the sections on text and discourse is Michael Stubbs, *Discourse Analysis: The Sociolinguistic Analysis of Natural Language* (Oxford: Blackwell, 1983). Discussion of discourse markers is based on Deborah Schiffrin, *Discourse Markers* (London: Cambridge University Press, 1987). Treatment of cohesive devices is derived from M. A. K. Halliday and Ruqaiya Hasan, *Cohesion in English* (London: Longman, 1976).

Recommended reading

Allan, Keith, and Kate Burridge. 1991. *Euphemism and Dysphemism*. New York: Oxford University Press.

Chambers, J. K., and Peter Trudgill. 1980. *Dialectology*. London: Cambridge University Press.

Coates, Jennifer. 1986. *Women, Men and Language*. London: Longman.

Fasold, Ralph. 1984. *The Sociolinguistics of Society*. Oxford: Blackwell.

———. 1990. *The Sociolinguistics of Language*. Oxford: Blackwell.

King, Ruth. 1991. *Talking Gender: A Guide to Nonsexist Communication*. Toronto: Copp Clark Pitman.

Saville-Troike, Muriel. 1989. *The Ethnography of Communication: An Introduction*. 2nd ed. Oxford: Blackwell.

QUESTIONS

1. Based on your knowledge of your speech community, design a simple questionnaire (along the lines of the sample in Table 14.10) testing for particular lexical items. If you live in a rural community, you might explore items similar to those in the table. If you live in a city, look, for example, at names for types of buildings or houses, streets, sidewalks, the spaces between streets and sidewalks, and so on.

2. Choose a particular field of endeavor (for example, farming, computers, or weaving) and, either by using secondary sources or by interviewing people, discover and describe the unique features of its jargon.

3. Find two English speakers who grew up in areas different from you. Determine what lexical items they use for the following notions:
   a) first meal of the day (morning)
   b) mid-day meal (weekdays)
   c) evening meal (weekdays)
   d) large, formal meal (weekend)
   e) mid-morning or mid-day first meal (weekends)
   f) meal midway through an evening work shift
   g) late afternoon quick meal

   Contrast their terms with yours. Does anyone have more than one term for any one of these notions? Under what conditions do they use these different terms? Did they volunteer any other meal names besides those elicited? In what ways do your findings provide evidence for social, regional, or situational differentiation of language?

4. English exhibits considerable variation (from region to region, from speaker to speaker in the same region, and even in the speech of individuals) with respect to the pronunciation of the vowel associated with the letters *oo* in the following sets of words. Most speakers of North American English use /uw/ or /ʊ/ in these words, but the vowel /ʌ/ also occurs in some. Examine these three groups and determine which vowel you use. If possible, contrast your pronunciation with that of a speaker of another variety of English. In which group(s) does the pronunciation appear to be most stable (uniform)? In which is the least uniformity seen? Are there any correlations between variations in pronunciation of *oo* in these words and the regional origin of speakers?
   a) pool, fool, mood, loop, boon, doom, loose
   b) good, foot, book
   c) hoof, roof, soot, room, coop, hoop

5. Carefully examine how your local newspaper, radio or television uses language with respect to matters of gender. Point out any instances of gender-biased or gender-neutral language. Pay particular attention to the coverage of sports and note to what extent the nature and amount of language used is biased or not.

6. Monitor the speech in your community, and determine whether there are any sociolinguistic variables such as the (ing), (ð), and (θ) discussed in the chapter.

If so, how are they reflected in speech? (*Hint*: You might examine the realizations of the phonemes /t/ and /d/ in words such as *sitting* and *reading*.)

7. Groups of people even as small as one's family can share linguistic features that set them off from other groups and provide a measure of solidarity. Consider your own family's sociolect and point out any lexical or other features that you believe to be unique. Contrast these with similar items from the family sociolects of two other students.

8. List and classify (both semantically and morphologically) as many slang words from your community as you can. Do all groups of adolescents in a particular community or school share the same slang? How do their ways of speaking differ? How are they alike?

9. In early Modern English, there were two functioning second person pronouns: *thou* and *ye*. *Thou* was used by social superiors to inferiors (including parents to children) and *ye* was used by the inferior in addressing the superior. *Thou* has been lost from general use in our language. Only *ye* (in the form *you*) has survived. In view of the discussion of address terms in this chapter, what has caused this change?

10. Choose a contemporary English-language play or film. Transcribe and examine some dialogue, if no published version is available for you to consult. List and discuss the discourse markers used in the dialogue. Point out how they may be used to achieve temporal sequencing of events, involvement of the addressee or audience, or interjecting the speaker's own point of view. Try to compare this fictional dialogue with real-life conversations. Show how the play or film resembles or fails to resemble naturally occurring talk.

11. Consult with a speaker of another language regarding cohesive devices in his or her language. Using reference items listed above under Sources try to determine some types of such devices used in that language. Look specifically for the two types of reference mentioned, ellipsis and substitution. Are all of these exhibited in the other language? Do they appear to work in much the same way as in English? What other devices does your consultant suggest you consider?

For the Student Linguist

WHEN LANGUAGE GOES BAD

Nothing shows more clearly how many rules and norms we have about language use than when something goes awry. The following example, from Tom Stoppard's *Rosencrantz and Guildenstern Are Dead,* would probably be an interactional sociolinguist's worst nightmare.

In case you haven't read the play or seen the movie, Rosencrantz and Guildenstern (whom you may recall as two minor characters from *Hamlet*) are killing time and decide to play a game. The rules of the game are actually straightforward. Unfortunately for the poor interactional sociolinguist, the guys aren't too consistent with their application of the rules. Thus, some of the statements they make about the game (e.g., "cheating") aren't scored as part of the game while others are (e.g., "I hadn't started yet.").

The speech norms seem even more dubious when you look at Rosencrantz and Guildenstern's decisions about what does (and does not) count as a synonym, as a *non sequitur,* or as rhetoric. However, it's surprising to me that many of the components of this speech situation are relatively easily identifiable in spite of this being such an absurd discourse. After you've identified the components, you might want to experiment with making just one or two of them absurd (choosing different ones than Stoppard did) while keeping the others logical, and see if there's any sort of system or pattern to effective humor. Then again, too much analysis always kills a joke. Maybe you should just rent the video, make some popcorn, and put off your homework for tonight.

ROS: We could play at questions.
GUIL: What good would that do?
ROS: Practice!
GUIL: Statement! One-love
ROS: Cheating!
GUIL: How?
ROS: I hadn't started yet.
GUIL: Statement. Two-love.
ROS: Are you counting that?
GUIL: What?
ROS: Are you counting that?
GUIL: Foul! No repetitions. Three-love. First game to . . .
ROS: I'm not going to play if you're going to be like that.
GUIL: Whose serve?
ROS: Hah?
GUIL: Foul! No grunts. Love-one.
ROS: Whose go?
GUIL: Why?
ROS: Why not?
GUIL: What for?
ROS: Foul! No synonyms! One-all.
GUIL: What in God's name is going on?
ROS: Foul! No rhetoric. Two-one.
GUIL: What does it all add up to?
ROS: Can't you guess?
GUIL: Were you addressing me?
ROS: Is there anyone else?
GUIL: Who?
ROS: How would I know?
GUIL: Why do you ask?

ROS: Are you serious?
GUIL: Was that rhetoric?
ROS: No.
GUIL: Statement! Two-all. Game point.
ROS: What's the matter with you today?
GUIL: When?
ROS: What?
GUIL: Are you deaf?
ROS: Am I dead?
GUIL: Yes or no?
ROS: Is there a choice?
GUIL: Is there a God?
ROS: Foul! No *non sequiturs,* three-two, one game all.
GUIL: (*seriously*) What's your name?
ROS: What's yours?
GUIL: I asked you first.
ROS: Statement. One-love.
GUIL: What's your name when you're at home?
ROS: What's yours?
GUIL: When I'm at home?
ROS: What home?
GUIL: Haven't you got one?
ROS: Why do you ask?
GUIL: What are you driving at?
ROS: (*with emphasis*) What's your name?
GUIL: Repetition. Two-love. Match point to me.
ROS: (*seizing him violently*) WHO DO YOU THINK YOU ARE?
GUIL: Rhetoric! Game and match!

fifteen

WRITING AND LANGUAGE

Michael Dobrovolsky
William O'Grady

Outside of a dog, a book is man's best friend; inside of a dog, it's too dark to read.

– GROUCHO MARX

Speaking and writing are different in both origin and practice. Our ability to use language is as old as humankind, and reflects biological and cognitive modification that has occurred in the evolutionary history of our species. **Writing**, the representation of language by graphic signs or symbols, is a comparatively recent cultural development, having occurred within the past five thousand years and only in certain parts of the world. The contrast between speech and writing comes into sharper focus when we consider that spoken language is acquired without specific formal instruction, whereas writing must be taught and learned through deliberate effort. There are entire groups of people in the world today, as well as individuals in every literate society, who are unable to write. While spoken language comes naturally to human beings, writing does not.

1 TYPES OF WRITING

As different as they are, speech and writing share one major characteristic: Just as spoken language shows an arbitrary link between sound and meaning, the various symbols and techniques used in written language show an arbitrary link between symbol and sound. All writing can be grouped into two basic types, called logographic and phonographic, depending on the technique of linguistic representation they use.

1.1 Logographic writing

The term **logographic** (from Greek *logos* 'word') refers to a type of writing in which symbols represent morphemes or even entire words.

Logograms

Logographic writing is the oldest type of genuine writing. Ancient Mesopotamian cuneiform inscriptions, Egyptian hieroglyphics, and primordial Chinese characters were all highly logographic in their early stages. In fact, all writing systems maintain some logographic symbols. Conventional abbreviations such as &, %, $, and the like are logographic, as are the symbols for numerals. To a certain extent, logographic writing can be read independently of its language of origin. For example, the Arabic numbers 1, 2, 7, 10, and so on can be read in any language.

1.2 Phonographic writing

No writing system is purely logographic, however. Nor can it be, since using a separate symbol to write each word in a language is simply too cumbersome. Throughout human history, writing systems have always evolved signs that represent some aspect of pronunciation. In **phonographic writing** (from Greek *phonos* 'sound'), the symbols represent syllables or segments.

Syllabic writing

As the name suggests, **syllabic writing** employs symbols to represent syllables (a set of syllabic symbols is called a **syllabary**). Languages with relatively simple syllabic structures such as CV or CVC (Japanese and Cree, for example) are well suited to this type of writing, since they contain a relatively limited number of syllable types. In Japanese, the word *kakimashita* '(s/he) wrote' can be written with the five syllabic signs か ka, き ki, ま ma, し shi, and た ta: かきました. Pure syllabaries perhaps do not exist; they are typically augmented with symbols that represent segments (see Figures 15.19 and 15.25).

Alphabetic writing

Alphabetic writing represents consonant and vowel segments. Unlike the International Phonetic Alphabet, which is devised expressly to represent details of pronunciation, ordinary alphabets generally ignore nonphonemic phenomena. Thus, the spelling of the English words *pan* and *nap* represents the phonemes /p/, /n/, and /æ/, but ignores consonant aspiration, vowel nasalization, stress, and other subphonemic variation. As we will see in Section 4 of this chapter, some spelling systems also capture certain morphophonemic alternations.

Writing systems emerged and spread around the earth over a long period of time. Though we can trace the spread of some systems over a wide area, writing may have emerged independently in several different places. The next sections trace the development of some writing systems from their pictorial origins.

2 THE HISTORY OF WRITING

It is surprising that we cannot say with certainty how a comparatively recent cultural phenomenon like writing originated. We do know that writing developed in historically recorded stages, the earliest of which involves direct representation of objects and which is sometimes called *prewriting*.

2.1 PREWRITING

Figures and scenes depicted on cave walls and rock faces in the Americas, Africa, and Europe twelve thousand years ago or perhaps even earlier may have been forerunners of writing. Some of these petroglyphs (scenes painted on stone) may represent a type of proto-literate stage that did not evolve into a full-fledged writing system.

These drawings depict a wide range of human and animal activity, and may even have been intended for purposes of linguistic communication. Some of them were doubtless a form of religious magic to guarantee a successful hunt or other benefits. Perhaps some were purely esthetic expression. Some illustrations, such as those depicting the phases of the moon, may have been part of some form of record keeping. Figure 15.1a shows a pair of elk from a rock wall drawing in Sweden dating from the Old Stone Age (Paleolithic) period, perhaps as far back as 20,000 BC. Figure 15.1b shows an incised eagle bone from Le Placard, France, that dates back some 13,000 to 15,000 years. The incisions, which vary subtly, have been analyzed as a record of lunar phases. Pictorial records thus link the origins of writing with the history of representative art.

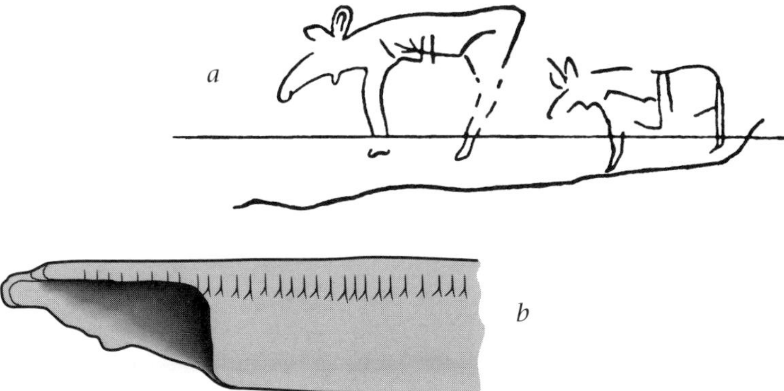

Figure 15.1 *a.* Paleolithic drawing, Sweden; *b.* Le Placard eagle bone

An even more direct connection links the origin of writing with record keeping. It has been suggested that the idea of writing had its origin in small clay tokens and counters that were used in record keeping and business transactions in the ancient Middle East. These small, fire-baked pieces of clay were apparently used for thousands of years before writing emerged. Counters representing cattle and other goods were stored on shelves or in baskets. Eventually, people began to make an impression of the tokens on soft clay tablets rather than storing and shipping the tokens themselves. This may have led to the idea that other objects and events in the world could be represented symbolically in graphic form.

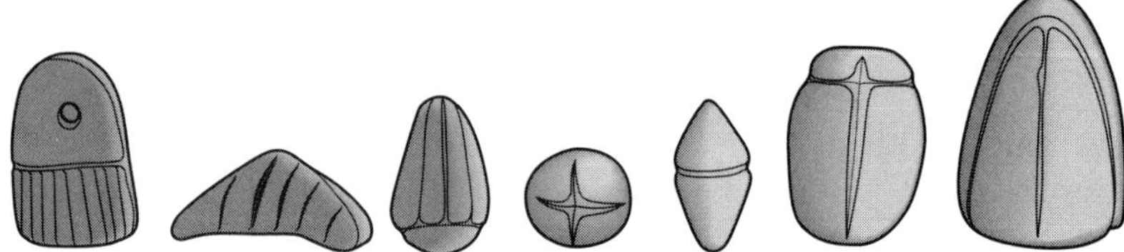

Figure 15.2 Ancient Mesopotamian tokens

2.2 PICTOGRAMS

Whatever their purpose, there is no doubt that pictures were among the precursors of the written word. Early writing systems all evolved from pictorial represention called **pictograms** or picture writing. Each pictogram was an image of the object or objects (and, in some cases, concepts) it represented, and, as far as we know, offered no clues to pronunciation. This kind of communication has been found among people throughout the ancient and modern world. Figure 15.3 is an example of Amerindian picture writing taken from a record kept by a Dakota named Lonedog; these pictures served as a kind of memory aid and not as a detailed record of events.

Like any other product of culture, pictography requires a knowledge of the conventions used by the author. Lonedog's record, for example, lists thirty Dakota

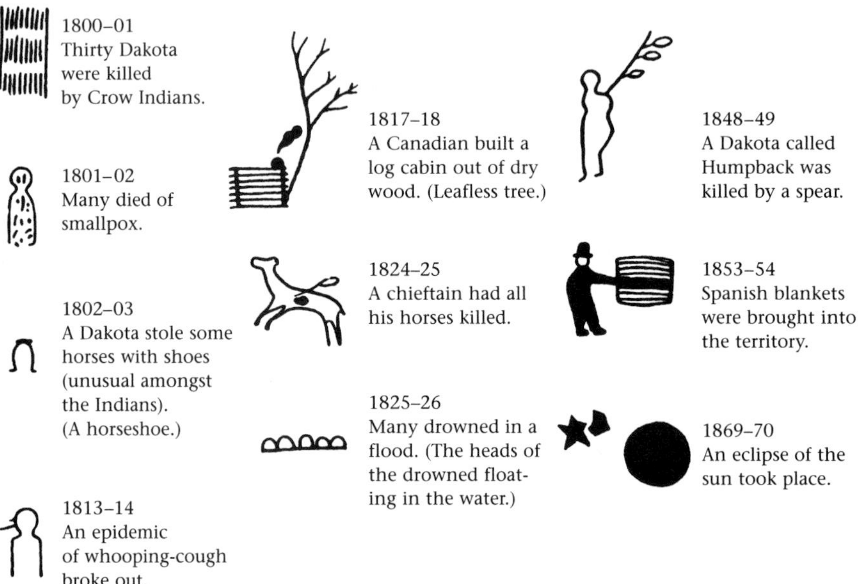

Figure 15.3 Amerindian pictography: A Dakota record of significant events

killed, but there are only twenty-four short vertical lines. To interpret the record correctly, it is necessary to know that the frame itself consists of six joined lines.

Pictograms are still used today, and they reflect the memory-aid nature of this form of prewriting. Signs indicating roadside services or information in parks are all pictographic in nature. The Olympic Association has developed a standardized set of pictograms to indicate sporting events.

Figure 15.4 Contemporary pictograms: Olympic signs for sporting events

A contemporary and very sophisticated development of pictographic writing, **Blissymbolics** (originally called semantography), was developed by Charles K. Bliss. It makes use of a number of recombineable symbols that represent basic units of meaning, as the following example illustrates.

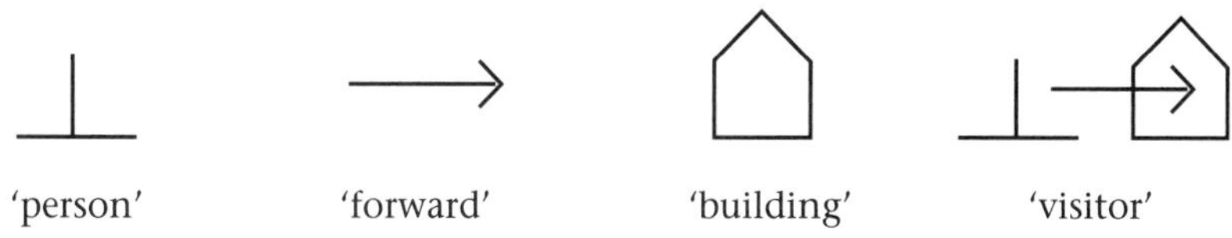

Figure 15.5 Blissymbolics

Though Blissymbolics was intended as a means of international, cross-linguistic communication by its inventor, its primary use today is as a means of augmentative communication for nonspeaking individuals. The Blissymbolics Communication Institute of Toronto sets the standard for the training and application of Blissymbols for this specialized purpose.

As we consider developments that emerge from pictographic representation, it is important to remember that pictograms are not writing in any sense of the word. They do not represent any linguistic elements such as segments, syllables, morphemes, or words; they are not associated with sequencing rules that parallel syntactic rules. Finally, pictograms typically lend themselves to more than one interpretation, and so provide only limited clues about their intended meaning.

3 THE EVOLUTION OF WRITING

The earliest known pictographic writing came from Sumeria, from where it spread to surrounding areas about five thousand years ago. The inherently ambiguous pictograms came to be used to represent abstract notions by extending their use to include concepts felt to be associated with them. A pictogram of fire could also mean 'inflammation', a hand 'hand', 'fist,' and a certain 'unit of measurement', and a foot 'to go', 'to move', or 'to go away'. It is possible that by the time such symbols appear, we are encountering writing in its logographic form.

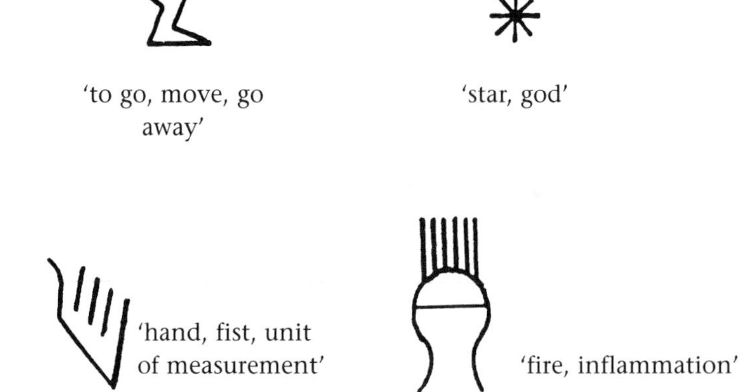

Figure 15.6 Sumerian logograms

Sumerian writing also combined signs to express abstract meanings. For example, a head with fire coming out of the crown indicated 'anger':

Although its evolution was gradual, we can state with some certainty that Sumerian writing was logographic because, from a fairly early stage on, it was written in a consistent linear order that would appear to reflect the order of words in speech. We cannot say with certainty at what date pictures began to be read as words, but once this practice had taken hold, the stage was set for the evolution to phonographic writing.

3.1 Rebuses and the emergence of writing

This major development in the history of writing took place around 3000 BC with the first use of Sumerian symbols to represent sound rather than just meaning. Known as the **rebus principle**, this innovation allowed a sign to be used for any word that was pronounced like the word whose meaning it originally represented. In the following inscription of an economic transaction, for example, the symbol in the upper left-hand corner, originally used to represent the word *gi* 'reed', here represents a homophonous word with the meaning 'reimburse'.

Figure 15.7 Sumerian rebus inscription (c. 3000 BC)

Thanks to the rebus principle, concepts that could not be directly depicted by a pictogram/logogram could be represented in writing. Thus, the sign for the word *ti* 'arrow', , was also used for the word *ti* 'life'.

3.2 Towards syllabic writing

Once the breakthrough towards phonographic writing had been made, it did not take long (in historical terms) before syllabic writing began to emerge. Within about five hundred to six hundred years, signs that clearly represent not just homophonous words, but parts of words—specifically, syllables—had become well established in Sumerian writing. Typically, the Sumerians overlapped their syllabic signs in order to use them more efficiently. Thus, a word like *kir* would be represented by the syllabic signs for *ki* and *ir* in sequence. Without this overlapping technique, a special sign for *r* would have had to be employed. Figure 15.8 illustrates this with Sumerian cuneiform signs, which are discussed in more detail in the following section.

Sumerian writing never developed into a pure syllabary. Logographic elements were interspersed with syllabic ones, and in addition, many syllabic signs were used to represent syllables with other pronunciations as well.

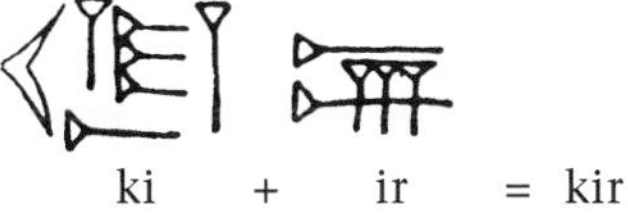

Figure 15.8 Overlapped Sumerian syllabic signs

Cuneiform

Over the centuries, Sumerian writing was simplified and eventually produced with the use of a wedge-shaped stylus that was pressed into soft clay tablets. This form of writing, initiated in the fourth millennium BC, has come to be known as **cuneiform** (from Latin *cuneus* 'wedge'). In time, a change in writing practices led the cuneiform signs to be rotated ninety degrees to the left. This resulted in their bearing even less resemblance to their pictographic origins than before. Figure 15.9 illustrates this development in two forms.

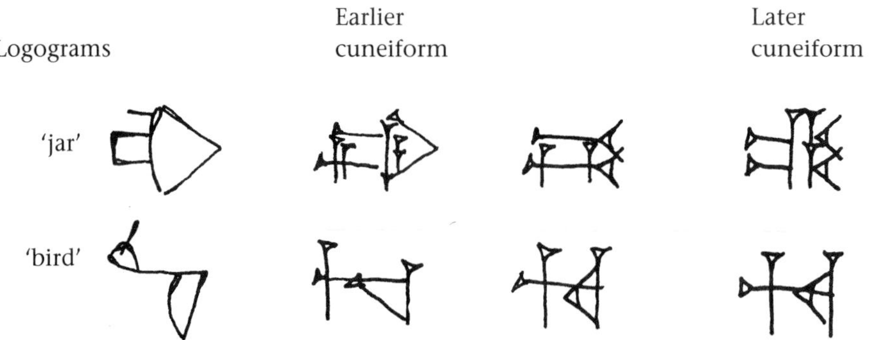

Figure 15.9 Changes in cuneiform writing

The cuneiform system was borrowed by the Elamites and Akkadians in the third millenium BC, a little later by the Persians, and in the second millennium BC by the Hittites far to the north in the ancient region of Anatolia (Modern Asian Turkey).

Cuneiform writing persisted until about the first few centuries of the Christian era in some areas, and then disappeared from use, not to be rediscovered until the nineteenth century. It was first deciphered from Old Persian texts, a breakthrough that led to the deciphering of Akkadian, Sumerian, and Hittite, among other languages that employed it. This script was used for thousands of years but then was generally replaced by systems of writing employed by the Semitic peoples of the Eastern Mediterranean.

3.3 ANOTHER MIDDLE EASTERN WRITING SYSTEM: HIEROGLYPHICS

At about the time Sumerian pictography was flourishing, a similar system of pictorial communication was in use in Egypt. The Egyptian signs have become known as **hieroglyphics** (meaning 'sacred inscriptions' in Greek). The earliest texts display about five hundred such symbols. Like Sumerian pictograms, the hieroglyphic signs at first represented objects, but later they became logographic in that they began to be associated with words.

Egyptian hieroglyphics developed into a mixed system of both word writing and phonographic writing. For example, the sign for a lute was a picture of a lute: 𓄤 ; this represented the word itself: *nfr*. (Only the consonants of words represented by hieroglyphics are known with certainty. The Egyptians did not represent the vowels—these can only be partially reconstructed from transcriptions in Greek and other languages that were made much later.) Eventually, the sign came to be disassociated from the word it represented and was used to transcribe other words that consisted of or included these sounds, such as the word for 'good', whose consonants were also *nfr*.

These symbols eventually came to be used to represent the consonant phonemes of words by application of what is called the **acrophonic principle** (from Greek *acros* 'extreme'): sounds are represented by pictures of objects whose pronunciation begins with the sound to be represented. In this way, the first consonant of a word-sign came to be what the sign stood for. For example, the hieroglyph for 'horned viper':

is read logographically as f(V)t; this sign is also used to represent the phoneme /f/ in spellings such as *fen* 'pleasant':

As we see in Section 3.4, this principle was crucial in the development of true alphabets. In Egyptian writing, however, it was only part of a system that mixed logographic and phonographic elements. Figure 15.10 shows some hieroglyphics. (Throughout this chapter, a macron over a vowel indicates a long vowel.)

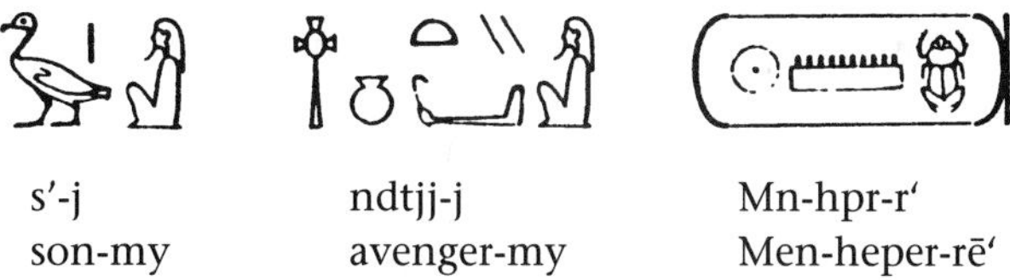

Figure 15.10 Egyptian hieroglyphics (c. 2000 BC)

Hieroglyphics continued in decreasing use down to Christian times. By the second century AD, Egyptian began to be written with Greek letters, and by the third century AD, hieroglyphics had been replaced by the Greek alphabet.

3.4 The emergence of alphabets

In the Middle East, alphabetic writing was slowly emerging from mixed writing systems over a long period. Building on this tradition, the Semitic peoples of ancient Phoenicia (modern Lebanon) had devised a writing system of twenty-two consonantal signs as early as 1000 BC. This system was written horizontally, right to left, without variation in the placement of the letters, as had been common in earlier scripts. It was ultimately to lead to the development of many alphabetic writing systems, including both the Greek and Latin alphabets.

The pictorial (and eventually logographic) origins of the Phoenician alphabet are evident in some of its symbols. The development of **logograms** for a stylized ox's head, throwing stick, and wavy flow of water are shown in Figure 15.11, along with the corresponding letter names.

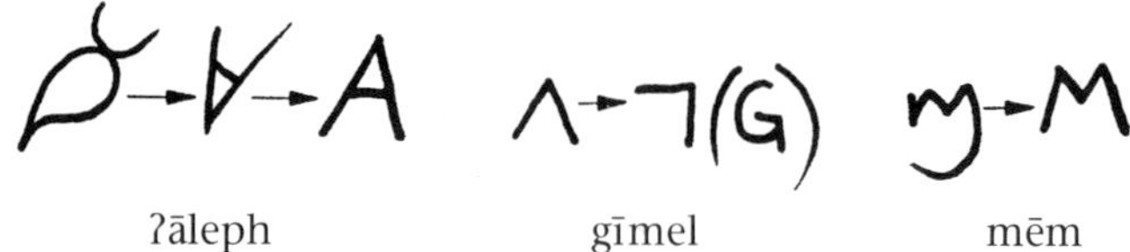

Figure 15.11 Pictorial and logographic origins of some signs evident in the Phoenician alphabet

These symbols eventually came to be used to represent the consonant phonemes of words by application of the acrophonic principle (see Section 3.3). In this way, *ʔāleph* was used to represent the glottal stop; *gīmel*, a /g/; and *mēm*, an /m/. Some of the symbols of the Phoenician alphabet had developed from Egyptian hieroglyphics, and, as in hieroglyphic writing, vowels were not represented (see Figure 15.10).

The Phoenicians were a trading people, and their alphabetic writing spread to adjacent countries and beyond. Eventually, the Greeks acquired and adapted the Phoenician alphabet.

The Greek alphabet

The Greeks developed the Phoenician writing system into a full alphabet: each symbol represented one phoneme and all phonemes were recorded by a symbol. A number of the Phoenician symbols represented consonant sounds that were not found in Greek. Some of these symbols were adapted to represent Greek vowels, and other unneeded consonant symbols were eventually dropped. Figure 15.12 illustrates the evolution of the Classical Greek and ultimately the Latin alphabet from the original Phoenician consonantal symbols.

Phoenician *ʔāleph*, as we have seen, represented a glottal stop. Since Greek had no glottal stop phoneme, the *ʔāleph* was employed to represent the vowel /a/ in Greek. Phoenician (*h*) was used to represent the Greek vowel /e/. Other signs were added to the system by the Greeks, such as ф /f/, X /x/, ψ /ps/, and Ω /ɔ:/.

The Semitic names for the letters (*aleph*, *beth*, *gimel*, *daleth*, and so on) were maintained by the Greeks (as *alpha*, *beta*, *gamma*, *delta*, and so on), but the possible pictorial origins had been lost and the names carried no other meaning. The writing system itself gained its name from the first two letters of the series: alphabet.

The Roman alphabet

When Greek colonists occupied southern Italy in the eighth and seventh centuries BC, they took their alphabet with them. It was in turn taken up and modified by the Etruscan inhabitants of central Italy, a non-Latin-speaking people who were a political and cultural power before the rise of Rome. It is believed that the Romans acquired their alphabet through the Etruscans. As the Romans grew in power and influence during the following centuries, first as masters of Italy and later of Europe, the Roman alphabet spread throughout the Empire.

Symbols			Greek			Latin	
Phoenician	Hebrew Name	Phonetic value	Early	Classical	Name	Early	Monumental (Classical)
𐤀	'Aleph	ʔ	A	A	Alpha	A	A
𐤁	Beth	b	B	B	Beta		B
𐤂	Gimel	g	Γ	Γ	Gamma		C
𐤃	Daleth	d	Δ	Δ	Delta	D	D
𐤄	He	h	E	E	Epsilon	E	E
𐤅	Waw	w	F		Digamma	F	F
							G
𐤆	Zayin	z	I	Z	Zeta		
𐤇	Ḥeth	ħ	H	H	Ēta	H	H
𐤈	Teth	ŧ	⊗	Θ	Theta		
𐤉	Yod	j	I	I	Iota	I	I (J)
𐤊	Kaph	k	K	K	Kappa	K	K
𐤋	Lamed	l	Λ	Λ	Lambda		L
𐤌	Mem	m	M	M	Mu	M	M
𐤍	Nun	n	N	N	Nu	N	N
𐤎	Samekh	s					
𐤏	'Ayin	ʕ	O	O	Ŏmicron	O	O
𐤐	Pe	p	Π	Π	Pi		P
𐤑	Tsade	ṣ	M		San		
𐤒	Qoph	q	Ϙ		Qoppa		Q
𐤓	Reš	r	P	P	Rho		R
𐤔	Šin	ʃ-s	Σ	Σ	Sigma	S	S
𐤕	Taw	t	X		Tau		T
				Y	Upsilon	V	V
				X	Chi		X
							Y
				Ω	Omega		Z

Figure 15.12 Evolution of the Greek and Latin alphabets (adapted from DeFrancis, p. 180)

Under the Romans, the Greek/Etruscan alphabet was again modified, this time with some symbols influenced by the Etruscans. The G in Greek writing developed into both *C* for the phoneme /k/ and *G* for /g/. The oldest inscriptions also retained *K* for /k/ in some words, but it was generally replaced by *C*. Similarly, *Q* was retained before /u/. Roman script also employed Greek *U* (= *V*), *X*, *Y*, and *Z* and moved *Z* to the end of the alphabet. The symbols Φ, Θ, ψ, and Ω were among those discarded, and *H* was converted back to a consonant symbol.

Some subsequent changes were made in the alphabet as it was adapted by various peoples of the Roman Empire. In English, for example, *W* was created from two juxtaposed *V's*. Spanish employs a tilde (˜) over *n* (ñ) to signify a palatal nasal, as in *año* /aɲo/ 'year', and French uses a cedilla under the *c* (ç) to indicate the dental fricative /s/, as in the spelling of *français* /frãsɛ/ 'French'.

3.5 Other developments, east and west

A great number of alphabetic systems evolved and flourished in addition to the Greek and Latin traditions. In this section, we briefly present some of these that are of historical significance or interest.

Runic writing

Germanic tribes occupying the north of Italy developed an early offshoot of the Greek/Etruscan tradition of writing into a script known as **Runic writing**. This system emerged shortly after the beginning of the Christian era, and its developments were eventually found as far north as Scandinavia. Runic writing persisted until the sixteenth century in some areas before giving way to the Latin alphabet.

Figure 15.13 illustrates some symbols from one of the oldest known Runic inscriptions, which dates from about the third century AD. The angular style of the letters arose because the alphabet was carved in wood or stone, the former especially not readily lending itself to curved lines. The script is read from right to left.

Figure 15.13 Runic script

Cyrillic script

Another offshoot of the Greek script was created for the Slavic peoples in the ninth century AD. The Greek missionary brothers Constantine (Cyril) and Methodius introduced a writing system for the translation of the Bible that is now known as **Glagolitic script**. A later development, which combined adaptations of Glagolitic letters with Greek and Hebrew characters, has come to be known as the **Cyrillic alphabet**. The current Russian, Byelorussian, Ukrainian, Serbian, Macedonian, and Bulgarian alphabets, as well as those used to represent many non-Slavic languages spoken in the former Soviet Union, have evolved from this early Cyrillic script. Some examples of its development and adaption are given in Figure 15.14, followed by a short passage in contemporary Russian Cyrillic, which is transliterated for its letter values.

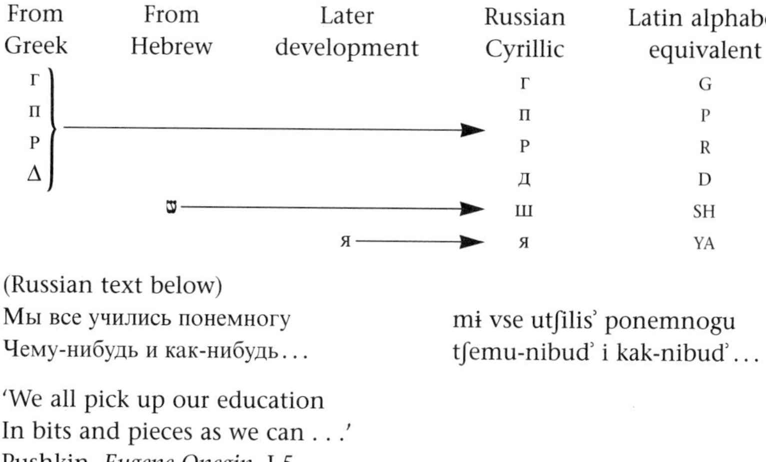

Figure 15.14 Contemporary Russian Cyrillic transliterated

Two Semitic alphabets

Both Arabic and Hebrew are written with alphabets that descend from or are closely related to **Phoenician script**. Both are essentially consonant-writing systems (vowels are indicated with diacritic dots), and both are written from right to left.

The contemporary Arabic alphabet is the most widespread of all the descendants of Middle Eastern writing except the Latin alphabet. Its earliest inscription dates back to the fourth century AD. In the latter half of the seventh century, this script was used to write the sacred text of Islam, the Koran, and accompanied the rapid spread of Islam over the next centuries. It contains twenty-eight consonants (vowels are indicated by diacritics above and below the consonants), and is written from right to left. An interesting feature of this alphabet is the fact that twenty-two of its twenty-eight symbols have different forms, depending on their position in (or outside of) a word. Figure 15.15 shows this variation for the forms of the letters *b* and *k* in initial, medial, and final position, as well as their forms when written in isolation.

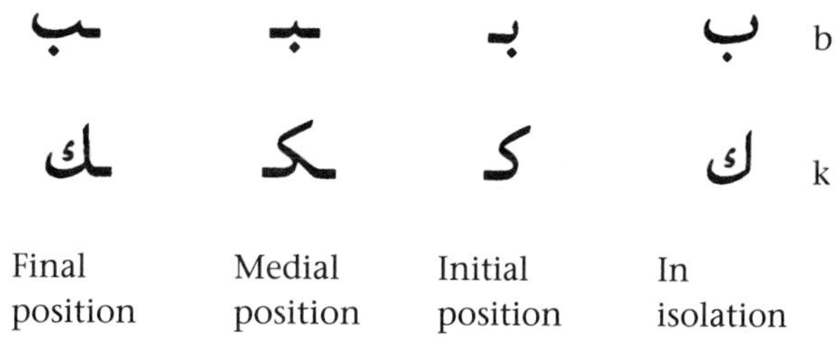

Figure 15.15 Variation in two Arabic letters according to position

The resemblances among the symbols shown in Figure 15.16 demonstrate the clear link between Phoenician script and the Hebrew and Arabic scripts.

Hebrew Letter name	Phonetic value	Phoenician	Modern Hebrew	Modern Arabic
'Alēph	ʔ	𐤀	א	ا
Bêth	b	𐤁	בּ ב	ب
Gimel	g	𐤂	גּ ג	ج
Dāleth	d	𐤃	דּ ד	د
Hē	h	𐤄	ה	ه
Wāw	w	𐤅	ו	و
Zayin	z	𐤆	ז	ز
Ḥēth	ħ	𐤇	ח	ح
Ṭēth	ŧ	𐤈	ט	ط
Yōdh	j	𐤉	י	ي
Kaph	k	𐤊	כּ כ ך	ك
Lāmadh	l	𐤋	ל	ل
Mêm	m	𐤌	מ ם	م
Nūn	n	𐤍	נ ן	ن
Sāmekh	s	𐤎	ס	س
'Ayin	ʕ	𐤏	ע	ع
Pê	p	𐤐	פּ פ ף	ف
Ṣādê	ṣ	𐤑	צ ץ	ص
Qōph	q	𐤒	ק	ق
Rêš	r	𐤓	ר	ر
Šîn	ʃ	𐤔	שׁ	ش
Tāw	t	𐤕	תּ ת	ت

Figure 15.16 The Phoenician, Hebrew, and Arabic alphabets

Other descendants of Middle Eastern systems

Early Middle Eastern scripts gave rise to Aramaic, Old Hebrew, and South Arabic syllabaries, which, in turn, led to a host of further writing systems eventually stretching across the Near East and North Africa from India to Morocco. Figure 15.17 illustrates this widespread diffusion on a time scale.

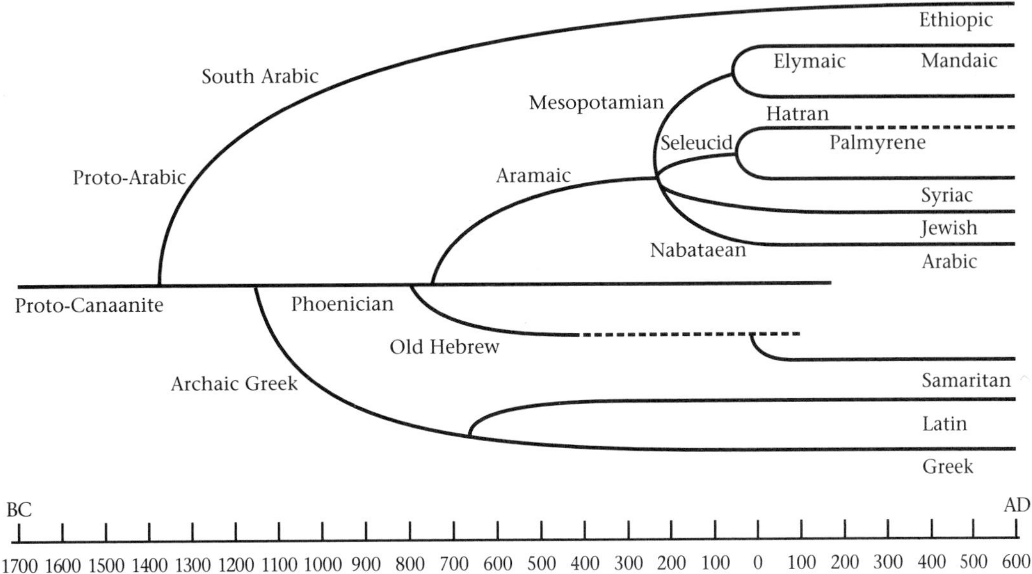

Figure 15.17 Development of writing systems (dotted lines indicate that the line of development is hypothetical)

4 SOME NON-EUROPEAN WRITING SYSTEMS

This section focuses on the nature and development of writing systems that originated outside the Middle East. While some of these systems emerged in response to external influences, others seem to have been entirely independent innovations.

4.1 CHINESE WRITING

The Chinese system of writing developed out of pictograms that eventually came to represent morphemes (most of which are also words). The oldest inscriptions are the oracle texts, written on animal bones and tortoise shells and dating back to about twelve hundred BC. These include many recognizable images, such as ⊙ 'sun' and ☽ 'moon'. A change toward more symbolic signs began at an early date as more abstract notions were represented, such as ◡ 'above' and ◠ 'below'. Symbols were also combined to extend meanings metaphorically. For example, the symbol for 'to tend' 牧 is composed of 牛 'cow' and 攴 'hand and whip'. 'To follow' 从 is two men in sequence, and so on. In time, the symbols became more abstract. Figure 15.18 shows the historical development of the symbol for 'dog'.

Calligraphy is an ancient and respected art in China, and Chinese writing exists in a number of styles. The modern script is usually written from left to right along a

Figure 15.18 Historical development of the Chinese symbol for 'dog'

horizontal axis, although newspapers and older texts begin in the right-hand margin and are read downwards.

The units of contemporary Chinese writing are called **characters**. Many monosyllabic words are presented in true logographic fashion by a character consisting of a single symbol. For example, the Mandarin words [ʃǒw] 'hand' and [mǎ] 'horse' are written 手 and 馬, respectively. However, the overwhelming majority of characters (one estimate is 99 percent) consist of two parts.

The main component of a multi-element character, called the **phonetic determinative**, provides information about the pronunciation of the corresponding morpheme. Although about four thousand different phonetic determinatives are used in Chinese writing, they represent pronunciation very imperfectly. Tone, which is contrastive in Chinese (see Chapter 2), is not represented at all, and many phonetic determinatives indicate only part of the morpheme's pronunciation. The determinative 敖, for instance, is used for a wide variety of words ending in *ao* without regard for whether the initial consonant is *j*, *n*, *r*, or some other element. Furthermore, due to sound changes over the last centuries, about one-third of all phonetic determinatives provide little or no useful information about current pronunciation. Finally, because Chinese has many homophones, even the most informative phonetic determinatives can be used for many different words.

Chinese characters also include a semantic component, called the **radical** or key, which provides clues about the morpheme's meaning. There are about two hundred different radicals in contemporary Chinese writing. Table 15.1 provides examples of some of the characters that can be formed by combining phonetic determinatives with radicals.

Table 15.1 Some Chinese characters

		Phonetic determinatives			
		A	B	C	D
	Semantic radical	敖 (*áo*)	參 (*cān*)	堯 (*yáo*)	甫 (*fǔ*)
1	亻 'person'	傲 (*ào:* 'proud')	傪 (*cān:* 'good')	僥 (*jiǎo:* 'lucky')	俌 (*fù:* 'help')
2	扌 'hand'	擙 (*ào:* 'shake')	摻 (*shǎn:* 'seize')	撓 (*nǎo:* 'scratch')	捕 (*bǔ:* 'catch')
3	木 'wood'	⿰木敖 (*āo:* 'barge')	槮 (*shēn:* 'beam')	橈 (*náo:* 'oar')	⿰木甫 (*fú:* 'trellis')
4	氵 'water'	滶 (*ào:* 'stream')	滲 (*shèn:* 'leak')	澆 (*jiāo:* 'sprinkle')	浦 (*pǔ:* 'creek')

Notice that only the phonetic determinative in column A indicates the pronunciation (ignoring tone) of the four characters in which it appears. The other determinatives supply helpful, but incomplete, phonetic information. For instance, the determinative *yao* (column C) has a pronunciation that rhymes with that of the four morphemes it helps to represent.

The usefulness of the information supplied by the radicals also varies. The characters in row 1 represent morphemes whose meaning is at best indirectly associated with that of the radical ('person'), but the radicals in rows 2, 3, and 4 are much more informative. For example, the characters in row 2 all denote actions involving the hand while those in row 3 refer to things made of wood and those in row 4 all have something to do with liquids.

Although neither phonetic determinatives alone nor semantic radicals alone suffice to identify the morphemes that they are used to represent, they are more than adequate when used in conjunction with each other. Despite its complexities—one authority has described the system as 'outsized, haphazard, inefficient, and only partially reliable'—Chinese writing provides its users with an effective way to represent the words and morphemes of the language. Moreover, the lack of efficiency is offset by the fact that the same literary script can be understood by speakers of different Chinese languages. Although a speaker of Mandarin and a speaker of Cantonese may pronounce the word for 'fire' differently—/xwǒ/ and /fɔ̀/, respectively—both can read it from the same character (火) since Chinese writing does not directly represent a word's phonemic segments.

In recent times, the government of the People's Republic of China has introduced simplified characters (some newly invented) in an attempt to promote literacy. At the same time, a system of writing Mandarin with a modified Latin alphabet, called **pinyin**, has also been introduced. Pinyin is used as a subsidiary system for writing such things as street signs, addresses, and brand names as well as for teaching children how to pronounce characters. It is also used for word processing and other computer-related activities, including electronic mail.

4.2 Japanese writing

The writing system of modern Japanese is arguably the most complicated in the entire world. Its use requires knowledge of three distinct scripts, including a pair of syllabaries—**katakana** and **hiragana**—which were created by modifying Chinese characters.

Although Japanese can be written exclusively with either syllabary, normal writing involves use of Chinese characters (called **kanji** in Japanese) in addition to hiragana and katakana. Kanji symbols are typically used to represent all or part of a word's root, whereas affixes are represented by hiragana symbols. The phrase *in the man's car*, for example, can be written as in Figure 15.20, with the roots 'man' and 'car' represented by kanji, and the possessive morpheme *no* and the locative morpheme *de* written in hiragana.

The katakana syllabary, whose symbols are less rounded than their hiragana counterparts, is used to write onomatopoeic words as well as words borrowed into Japanese from other languages. In addition, it is employed in advertising and in telegrams.

Katakana chart

COLUMN / LINE	A	I	U	E	O
SINGLE VOWEL	ア A	イ I	ウ U	エ E	オ O
K	カ KA	キ KI	ク KU	ケ KE	コ KO
S	サ SA	シ SHI	ス SU	セ SE	ソ SO
T	タ TA	チ CHI	ツ TSU	テ TE	ト TO
N	ナ NA	ニ NI	ヌ NU	ネ NE	ノ NO
H	ハ HA	ヒ HI	フ HU	ヘ HE	ホ HO
M	マ MA	ミ MI	ム MU	メ ME	モ MO
Y	ヤ YA		ユ YU		ヨ YO
R	ラ RA	リ RI	ル RU	レ RE	ロ RO
W	ワ WA				ヲ O
N (in a coda)	ン N				

Hiragana chart

COLUMN / LINE	A	I	U	E	O
SINGLE VOWEL	あ A	い I	う U	え E	お O
K	か KA	き KI	く KU	け KE	こ KO
S	さ SA	し SHI	す SU	せ SE	そ SO
T	た TA	ち CHI	つ TSU	て TE	と TO
N	な NA	に NI	ぬ NU	ね NE	の NO
H	は HA	ひ HI	ふ HU	へ HE	ほ HO
M	ま MA	み MI	む MU	め ME	も MO
Y	や YA		ゆ YU		よ YO
R	ら RA	り RI	る RU	れ RE	ろ RO
W	わ WA				を O
N (in a coda)	ん N				

Figure 15.19 Hiragana and katakana syllabaries and their phonetic values (The conventions for representing voicing, vowel length, and gemination are not indicated here.)

hito no	kuruma de
人 の	車 で
man Gen	car Loc
kanji hiragana	kanji hiragana

Figure 15.20 A phrase written in a mixture of kanji and hiragana

Finally, it should be noted that the Latin alphabet, which the Japanese call *romaji*, is also making inroads. It is not unusual to see all four scripts used together, especially in advertising.

New Tomato

ほんのり 甘味 さらっと あと 味
(honnori amami saratto ato aji)
'Subtle sweetness and light after taste.'

トマト の 新しい ジュース です
(tomato no atarashi juusu desu)
'It's a new tomato juice.'

—— --Hiragana
〰〰 --Katakana
═══ --Kanji

Figure 15.21 Kanji, hiragana, katakana, and romaji in a Japanese advertisement

Learning to read Japanese is a formidable task, in part because of the way the various scripts are intermingled and in part because of complexities in the use of kanji symbols, which can have more than one pronunciation depending on whether they are used to represent a word of Chinese or Japanese origin. (For example, Japanese has two morphemes with the meaning 'mountain'—/san/, which is of Chinese origin, and the native Japanese /yama/; both are written with the kanji character 山.)

4.3 Korean writing

Korean was once written with Chinese characters, which had been introduced in the first centuries AD. However, Korean suffixes could not be easily represented by Chinese writing. Various devices were tried to alleviate this problem but inadequacies persisted. Finally, King Sejong (1419–1452) commissioned an alphabetic script, called **hangul**, consisting of eleven vowels and seventeen consonants that, after some modifications over the centuries, became the standard Korean writing system. An especially interesting feature of hangul is that symbols are grouped together into syllable-sized clusters rather than being arranged in a completely linear fashion.

Hangul symbols

ㅂ	ㅜ	ㄹ	ㄱ	ㅗ	ㅣ
/p/	/u/	/l/	/k/	/o/	/i/

Grouped symbols

불	고기
'fire' /pul/	'meat' /koki/

Written form

불고기

'barbecued meat' *pulkoki*

Figure 15.22 Korean hangul

Like Japanese, Korean also makes use of Chinese characters (called **hanja**), although in a more restricted way. Slightly more than half the vocabulary of contemporary Korean is of Chinese origin and many words of this type are written with the help of Chinese characters in newspapers and in scientific articles. However, this practice has been reduced somewhat in recent years in South Korea and it has been eliminated entirely in North Korea.

4.4 AMERICAN SCRIPTS

A number of major civilizations developed on the American continents. In Mesoamerica alone more than eighteen writing systems have been discovered, including those of the Mayans of the Yucatan and the Aztecs of Mexico. In both systems, we can see the evolution of pictograms that leaned toward phonetic word signs, just as did the Egyptian hieroglyphics illustrated in Section 3.3.

Mayan symbols are called **glyphs**. Although some were read as word signs (logograms), they had other uses as well. The rebus principle was employed, although sometimes only partially, as in the use of the symbol for a smoking bun-

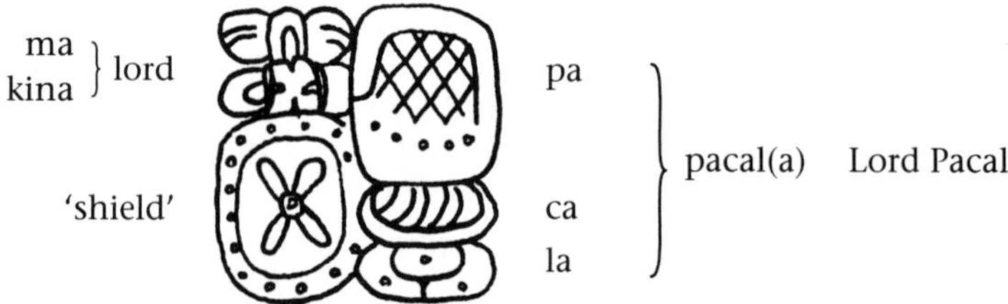

Figure 15.23 Six Mayan glyphs spelling 'Lord Pacal'

dle of pine, /taaʒ/, to represent the locative preposition /ta/. Moreover, Mayan signs could be used for their phonetic value in a form of syllabic writing. Glyphs that mix syllabic writing with logographic representation are also found.

Cherokee

Some American writing systems do not date back to a distant ancestor. After the colonization of North America by Europeans, a number of scripts were developed to provide native peoples with a form of written communication. In one well-known case, the Cherokee leader Sikwayi (Sequoia) devised a syllabic script of more than eighty symbols, some based on the shapes of English letters and others newly invented.

Symbol	Value	Symbol	Value	Symbol	Value	Symbol	Value	Symbol	Value
Ꭰ	*a*	Ꭱ	*e*	Ꭲ	*i*	Ꭳ	*o*	Ꭴ	*u*
Ꭶ	*ga*	Ꭸ	*ge*	Ꭹ	*gi*	Ꭺ	*go*	Ꭻ	*gu*
Ꭽ	*ha*	Ꭾ	*he*	Ꭿ	*hi*	Ꮀ	*ho*	Ꮁ	*hu*
Ꮃ	*la*	Ꮄ	*le*	Ꮅ	*li*	Ꮆ	*lo*	Ꮇ	*lu*
Ꮉ	*ma*	Ꮊ	*me*	Ꮋ	*mi*	Ꮌ	*mo*	Ꮍ	*mu*

Figure 15.24 Some Cherokee syllabic symbols

Cree

Professional linguists have often played a role in the development of American scripts, as have missionaries. The syllabic script of the Cree Indians was the creation of a missionary, J. Evans, in the nineteenth century. It was employed for religious literature, and by 1861, the entire Bible appeared in the Cree syllabary. Today, in somewhat modified form, this script is used by Cree speakers across Canada.

Cree morphemes are made up of syllables that combine one of ten initial consonants with one of seven vowels; in some cases, there is also a postvocalic consonant. The Cree writing system provides a separate symbol for each V and CV syllable. As in syllabaries in general, the symbols representing the CV syllables bear no resemblance to those representing syllables consisting of a single vowel; there is no connection, for instance, between the symbols for the syllable /ki/ ᑭ and the syllable /i/ ᐃ. However, the Cree system is not wholly syllabic since consonants that occur at the end of a syllable must be represented by a separate symbol.

A striking feature of the Cree syllabary is its phonetic symbolism. The vowel in a syllable is indicated by the direction in which the symbol faces. Symbols that face 'south' (downward on the printed page) contain /eː/; those facing 'north' (upward) contain /i/ or /iː/; those pointing 'east' (rightward) have /o/ or /oː/, and those looking to the 'west' (leftward) contain /a/ or /aː/. Vowel length is indicated by a superposed dot, as in = ᓰ /siː/.

Plains Cree, a variety of Cree spoken in Western Canada, is written with the following symbols (other dialects use slightly different ones).

ᐃ	*i*, *ī*	ᐁ	*ē*	ᐅ	*o*, *ō*	ᐊ	*a*
ᐱ	*pi*, *pī*	ᐯ	*pē*	ᐳ	*po*, *pō*	ᐸ	*pa*
ᑎ	*ti*, *tī*	ᑌ	*tē*	ᑐ	*to*, *tō*	ᑕ	*ta*
ᒋ	*ci*, *cī*	ᒉ	*cē*	ᒍ	*co*, *cō*	ᒐ	*ca*
ᑭ	*ki*, *kī*	ᑫ	*kē*	ᑯ	*ko*, *kō*	ᑲ	*ka*
ᒥ	*mi*, *mī*	ᒣ	*mē*	ᒧ	*mo*, *mō*	ᒪ	*ma*
ᓂ	*ni*, *nī*	ᓀ	*nē*	ᓄ	*no*, *nō*	ᓇ	*na*
ᓯ	*si*, *sī*	ᓭ	*sē*	ᓱ	*so*, *sō*	ᓴ	*sa*
ᔨ	*yi*, *yī*	ᔦ	*yē*	ᔪ	*yo*, *yō*	ᔭ	*ya*

Finals

ᑊ *p* ᐟ *t* ᐨ *c* ᐠ *k* ᒼ *m* ᐢ *s* ᐣ *n* • *y* ᐤ *w* ᐦ *h* ᕽ *hk* ᓬ *l* ᕒ *r*

Figure 15.25 Western Cree syllabary

The following examples illustrate the use of the Cree syllabary.

ᓃ ᐱ		ᓂ ᐱ		ᓰ ᐱ	
nīpi	'leaf'	nipi	'water'	sīpi	'river'

Figure 15.26 Three words in Western Cree syllabary

Some other American scripts

The Cree syllabary, appropriately modified, is used by the Inuit of Baffin Island to represent their language, which is unrelated to Cree. A word-writing system developed by Alaskan Inuit toward the end of the nineteenth century eventually evolved into a partially syllabic system, although it did not become fully syllabic. A number of different systems are in use in different regions of Alaska, and in some, tendencies toward alphabetization are discernible.

4.5 Some African scripts

In the past several centuries, societies in Central Africa have also produced syllabic scripts, which have either developed through stages from pictograms to refined syllabaries or have been invented by one or several individuals. Although the idea of writing appears to have been imported into these societies, the development of the various systems was indigenous.

The first Subsaharan African writing seems to have been that of the Vai peoples in the region of Sierra Leone and Liberia. In the nineteenth century, a native of the area developed a syllabary from a system of picture communication. The new system, which grew to consist of 226 syllabic symbols plus a few logographic symbols, appears to have spawned a number of imitations throughout the area.

The writing of the Bamum people in the Cameroons was invented at the end of the nineteenth century by a native leader. The current seventy syllabic symbols show tendencies toward alphabetization.

The only sure example of alphabetic writing developed in modern times among African peoples is the Somali alphabet. The originator, acquainted with Arabic and Italian, devised an alphabet composed of nineteen consonants and ten vowels. The symbols appear to have been freely invented, but their names are based on those used for the letters of the Arabic alphabet, and are listed and recited in the same order.

4.6 Some Indian scripts

A pictorial script appears to have had an independent origin in Northern India, where inscribed seals, pottery, and copper tablets dating back to the third millennium BC have been unearthed. The system seems to have consisted of about 250 symbols such as , , and , but died away long before another writing system, seemingly derived from Semitic (see Figure 15.27), was employed in the middle of the first millennium BC to record the ancient Sanskrit language.

The date of the first appearance of Indian Sanskrit symbols cannot be ascertained, but they resemble Aramaic and appeared as a full system of writing in the edicts of Ašoka (who ruled from 272 to 231 BC). They were set down in two types of writing: Kharosthi and Brahmi. The former continued in use until about the fifth century AD in Northern India. The Brahmi script gave rise to all later varieties of Indian writing.

One of these varieties, a cursive type called the Gupta script, was later employed to write Tocharian, Saka, and Turkish manuscripts discovered in eastern Turkestan. In India, it evolved into the Devanagari script, which became the most widespread type of writing in the subcontinent and which was used to record the voluminous literature of the Sanskrit language. Inscriptions in Devanagari are found throughout Southeast Asia, Indonesia, and as far afield as the southern Philippines.

Varieties of Indian writing were carried abroad by Buddhist missionaries and influenced writing systems in Tibet and Central and Southeast Asia. The Dravidian peoples of Southern India also developed a number of scripts under the influence of the Northern varieties. Another ancient Indian script, called Pali, gave rise to a number of Southeast Asian writing systems, including those used for Thai and Cambodian. Figure 15.27 illustrates Devanagari and some of the many other scripts found in India and Southeast Asia.

The examples cited in this chapter only touch on the variety of writing systems past and present that scholars have investigated. The index of one standard work lists 470 scripts. Many of these are historically related, but the number nonetheless testifies to human ingenuity and creativity in devising writing systems.

a

व्यवहारान्नृपः पश्येद्विद्वद्भिर्ब्राह्मणैः सह ।
धर्मशास्त्रानुसारेण क्रोधलोभविवर्जितः ॥१॥

b

ਕਿਉਂਕਿ ਪਰਮੇਸੁਰ ਨੇ ਜਗਤ ਨੂੰ ਅਜਿਹਾ ਪਿਆਰ
ਕੀਤਾ ਜੋ ਉਸਨੇ ਆਪਣਾ ਇਕਲੌਤਾ ਪੁਤ੍ਰ ਦਿੱਤਾ ਤਾਂ
ਹਰੇਕ ਜੋ ਉਸ ਉੱਤੇ ਨਿਹਚਾ ਕਰਦਾ ਹੈ ਉਹਦਾ ਨਾਸ
ਨਾ ਹੋਵੇ ਸਗੋਂ ਸਦੀਪਕ ਜੀਉਣ ਪਾਵੇ ।

c

തന്റെ ഏകജാതനായ പുത്രനിൽ വിശ്വ-
സിക്കുന്ന ഏവനും നശിച്ചു പോകാതെ നിത്യ
ജീവൻ പ്രാപിക്കേണ്ടതിന്നു ദൈവം അവനെ
നല്കുവാൻ തക്കവണ്ണം ലോകത്തെ സ്നേഹിച്ചു.

d ตาอ่อนเป็นคนจน บ้านอยู่ใกล้ๆป่า

Figure 15.27 *a*. Devanagari; *b*. Gurmuki; *c*. Modern Malayalam; *d*. Modern Thai

5 ENGLISH ORTHOGRAPHY

The set of conventions for representing language in written form is called an **orthography**. English employs an alphabetic orthography in which symbols are used to represent individual consonants and vowels rather than syllables or words. In this section, we will consider the nature and history of English orthography. We will then use Section 6 to examine the relationship between writing and reading.

5.1 IRREGULARITIES

A frequently expressed complaint about English orthography is that it does not establish a one-to-one relationship between symbols and phonological segments. Table 15.2 lists some well-known examples of this.

The following excerpt from a poem by Richard Krogh vividly illustrates the extent to which English orthography departs from the principle of one sound, one letter (one segment, one symbol).

Beware of heard, a dreadful word
That looks like beard and sounds like bird.
And dead; it's said like bed, not bead;
For goodness sake, don't call it deed!
Watch out for meat and great and threat
(They rhyme with suite and straight and debt).
A moth is not a moth in Mother,
Nor both in bother, broth in brother.

Table 15.2 Some problems with English orthography

Problem	*Examples*
Some letters do not represent any segments in a particular word.	through, sign, give, palm
A group of letters can be used to represent a single segment.	think /θ/, ship /ʃ/, philosophy /f/
A single letter can represent a group of segments.	saxophone /ks/, exile /gz/
The same letter can represent different segments in different words.	*o* in rot /ɑ/, bone /ow/, son /ʌ/, one /wʌ/
The same segment can be represented by different letters in different words.	/uw/ in rude, loop, soup, new, sue, to, two

Historical factors

The relationship between symbol and segment in English orthography has not always been so indirect. In fact, the spelling system used throughout England during the Old English period provided a regular set of direct symbol-segment correspondences. The foundation for today's system, it lacked the symbols *j*, *v*, and *w*, but made use of four symbols that are not part of our current alphabet.

Table 15.3 Old English symbols not found in Modern English spelling

Symbol	*Name*	*Segment(s) it represented*
æ	ash	[æ]
ð	eth	[θ] and [ð]
þ	thorn	[θ] and [ð]
ƿ	wynn	[w]

The relationship between symbol and segment in English orthography was significantly disturbed in the Middle English period, as the phonological pattern of the language began to change. To see an example of this, we need only consider the Great Vowel Shift and related changes, which dramatically altered the pronunciation of long vowels—converting /iː/ into /aj/, /eː/ into /ij/, /aː/ into /ej/, and so on (see Chapter 8). Because Old English orthography used the same symbol for long and short vowels, complications arose when the former vowels changed. Thus, the letter *i*, which had formerly been used only to represent the phonetically similar /iː/ and /i/, ended up representing the very dissimilar /aj/ (the descendant of /iː/) and /ɪ/ (the descendant of /i/). The end result can be seen in the spelling of *hide* and *hid*, *write* and *written*, *ride* and *ridden*, *wide* and *width*, and many other words.

Additional complications arose following the invasion of England by French-speaking Normans in the eleventh century. The use of English in official documents declined and regional orthographies developed in the absence of a national standard. To make matters worse, scribes who were trained primarily to write French and Latin introduced a number of conventions from those languages into English spelling. Among those that have survived are the use of *ch* rather than *c* for /tʃ/ (*cheese, chin,* etc.), *th* rather than *þ* (thorn) and *ð* (eth) for /θ/ and /ð/ (*thin, this*), and *c* rather than *s* for /s/ (*grace, ice, mice*).

Toward the end of the fifteenth century, yet another trend developed—the practice of spelling words in a manner that would reflect their etymological origin. Enduring examples of this influence are found in the spelling of the words *debt, doubt, receipt,* and *salmon* (formerly spelled *dette, doute, receite,* and *samon*), all of which were given a 'silent' consonant to make them look more like the Latin words from which they descended.

By the 1500s, English orthography had become increasingly irregular and idiosyncratic, with many different spellings in use for the same word. The word *pity*, for example, could be spelled *pity, pyty, pitie, pytie, pittie,* and *pyttye*. As printing presses came into greater use and books became more widely available, the need to reform and regularize English orthography became apparent. In the late 1500s and early 1600s, a number of individuals (most notably Richard Mulcaster and Edmond Coote) formulated and published spelling rules, which were gradually adopted by printers and other literate speakers of English. While these rules retained many of the practices discussed above, they at least had the effect of stabilizing English spelling. By the 1700s, English orthography was more or less fixed.

The vast majority of the spelling conventions introduced during this period are still in use today. One of the most famous, proposed by Mulcaster in 1582, involves the use of 'silent' *e* at the end of words to indicate a preceding long (tense) vowel, as in *name, same,* and *mate*. Even here, though, there are complications and exceptions. In an earlier period, word-final *e* had represented [ə]. Following the loss of this sound in this position in the fourteenth century, final *e* was used quite haphazardly and was often added to words that would otherwise end in a single consonant. The *e* in the modern spelling of *have, done,* and *gone*, which contain lax vowels, reflects this practice and has survived even though it does not comply with Mulcaster's rule.

5.2 Obstacles to reform

Over the years, there have been numerous proposals for the reform of English orthography, including those put forward by Benjamin Franklin, George Bernard Shaw, and Noah Webster. However, far-reaching reforms are unlikely for a variety of reasons. For one thing, they would require a long and difficult period of transition. As the following letter to *The Economist* by M. J. Shields illustrates, reform would not be painless even if it took place over a period of many years.

> For example, in Year 1 that useless letter 'c' would be dropped to be replased either by 'k' or 's', and likewise 'x' would no longer be part of the alphabet. The only kase in which 'c' would be retained would be the 'ch' formation, which will be dealt with later. Year 2 might reform 'w' spelling, so that 'which' and 'one' would take the same konsonant, wile Year 3 might well abolish 'y' replasing it with 'i' and Iear 4 might fiks the 'g-j' anomali wonse and for all.
>
> Jenerally, then, the improvement would kontinue iear bai iear with Iear 5 doing awai with useless double konsonants, and Iears 6 - 12 or so modifaiing vowlz and the rimeining voist and unvoist konsonants. Bai Iear 15 or sou, it wud fainali be posibl tu

meik ius ov thi ridandant leterz 'c', 'y' and 'x' - bai now jast a memori in the maindz of ould doderers - tu replais 'ch', 'sh' and 'th' rispektivli.

Fainali, xen, after sam 20 iers ov orxogrephkl riform, we wud hev a lojikl, kohirnt speling in ius xrewawt xe Ingliy spiking werld...

People who knew only the reformed spelling system proposed in this letter would have difficulty reading books written in traditional orthography. Those who wished to read any of the millions of books or articles currently in print would therefore have to learn either the traditional spelling system or have the documents that interested them converted into the new orthography.

A second factor militating against serious orthographic reform has to do with the dialectal variation found within English. Because English is spoken in more parts of the world than any other language, it has many different dialects. Any attempt to establish an orthography based on a principle of one segment, one symbol would result in serious regional differences in spelling. For instance, speakers of Boston English would write *far* as *fa* since they do not pronounce syllable-final /r/. Speakers of some dialects of Irish English would write both *tin* and *thin* as *tin* and both *day* and *they* as *day* since they have no /t/-/θ/ or /d/-/ð/ distinction. Moreover, while many Americans would have identical spellings for *cot* and *caught* (since these words are homophonous in their speech), speakers of English in many other parts of the world would spell the words differently to reflect the fact that they pronounce them differently.

Other considerations

Even if considerations relating to practicality and dialectal variation did not rule out major reforms to our orthography, there might still be reasons for retaining at least some of the current spelling conventions.

One advantage of the contemporary system is that it often indicates derivational relationships among words. For instance, if the words *music* and *musician* or *sign* and *signature* were spelled phonetically, it would be difficult to perceive the relationship between them since the root is pronounced differently in each case.

1)

music	[mjuzɪk]	musician	[mjuzɪʃ-ən]
sign	[sajn]	signature	[sɪgn-ɪtʃər]

There are many other such cases where English orthography ignores differences in pronunciation so that a morpheme can have the same or nearly the same spelling in different words.

Examples such as these show that English orthography does not simply represent phonemic contrasts. Often, it provides a single representation for the variants of a morpheme, even if this means ignoring morphologically conditioned alternations among phonemes. (For this reason, some linguists have concluded that English orthography is a type of *morphophonemic* spelling system; see Chapter 6, Section 1 for a discussion of morphophonemic alternations.) Once this fact is taken into account, it is possible to see the usefulness of orthographic conventions that allow *c* to stand for either /k/ (*electric*) or /s/ (*electricity*) and *t* to represent /t/ (*react*) or /ʃ/ (*reaction*).

Table 15.4 Some cases in which English orthography provides a single spelling for roots with different pronunciations

electric - electricity	[k] and [s] represented as *c*
insert - insertion	[t] and [ʃ] as *t*
right - righteous	[t] and [tʃ] as *t*
bomb - bombard	Ø and [b] as *b*
damn - damnation	Ø and [n] as *n*
impress - impression	[s] and [ʃ] as *ss*
allege - allegation	[ɛ] and [ə] as *e*; [dʒ] and [g] as *g*
resign - resignation	[aj] and [ɪ] as *i*; Ø and [g] as *g*
chaste - chastity	[ej] and [æ] as *a*
produce - productive	[uw] and [ʌ] as *u*
please - pleasant	[ij] and [ɛ] as *ea*

Morphological considerations are reflected in English orthography in other ways as well. Consider in this regard the spelling of the following words.

2)

mess	lapse
crass	dense
kiss	house
gloss	mouse

Although these words all end in the phoneme /s/, this segment cannot be represented as a simple *s*. Instead, the *s* is either doubled to *ss* (when preceded by a lax vowel, as in the first column) or followed by an *e* (all other cases, as exemplified in the second column). This reflects a general rule of English orthography, which reserves word-final *s* for inflectional suffixes (particularly, the plural and the third person singular). Thus, *s* is permitted in the word *laps* (the plural of *lap*) but not in *lapse*.

Another example of morphological influence is found in the rule that prohibits a final *ll* in polysyllabic words—*plentiful, excel, repel,* and so on. As the following examples show, this rule is systematically suspended in two morphological patterns: compounds (the first column) and derivations consisting of a prefix and its base (the second column).

3)

baseball	unwell
spoonbill	resell
landfill	recall

Yet another morphologically constrained rule of English orthography converts postconsonantal *y* to *i* in front of a suffix.

4)

carry	carri-ed
merry	merri-ly

marry	marri-age
candy	candi-es
beauty	beauti-ful

The existence of conventions and practices such as these demonstrate that English orthography is much more than a system for phonemic transcription. Its intricacies can be understood only through the careful study of the history and structure of the linguistic system that it is used to represent.

6 WRITING AND READING

The three types of writing described earlier in this chapter each represent different types of linguistic units—morphemes and words in the case of logographic systems, syllables in the case of syllabaries, and consonants and vowels in the case of alphabets. Because of these differences, each orthography places different demands on readers. We know that different parts of the brain are used for reading logographic writing systems and phonographic orthographies such as syllabaries and alphabets. Because phonological structure is largely irrelevant to logographic writing, people suffering from Broca's aphasia (see Chapter 11) typically do not lose the ability to write and read logograms. However, the use of syllabaries and alphabets can be severely disrupted by this type of brain damage. There are reports of Japanese patients suffering from Broca's aphasia who are unable to use hiragana or katakana (the Japanese syllabaries), but retain mastery of kanji (the logographic writing system).

Further information about the relationship between language and writing systems comes from the study of the congenitally deaf. Because such people have never heard speech, they have little or no understanding of the phonological units that alphabets represent. Significantly, congenitally deaf individuals have a great deal of difficulty learning to read English. Even after many years of instruction, their reading remains poor and few attain college-level skills in this area.

The type of linguistic unit represented by an orthography also has an effect on how children with normal hearing learn to read. Each system has its own advantages and disadvantages. Children learning Chinese characters, for instance, have little difficulty understanding what each symbol represents, but it takes them many years to learn enough symbols to be able to write and read all the items in their vocabulary. (Knowledge of several thousand separate symbols is required just to read a newspaper.) Even educated people typically know only a few thousand characters and must use dictionaries for new or unfamiliar ones.

This problem does not arise in syllabic and alphabetic orthographies. Because languages have far fewer syllables and phonemes than morphemes or words, the entire inventory of symbols can be learned in a year or two and then used productively to write and read new words. This is the major advantage of sound-based orthographies over word-based writing systems.

There is reason to think that children find syllabaries easier to master than alphabets. Children learning syllabaries (such as Japanese *hiragana*) are reported to have fewer reading problems than children learning alphabetic orthographies. Although at least some difficulties encountered by children learning to read English may be due to the complexity of English spelling conventions, Italian and German children learning to use their relatively regular alphabetic orthographies can also have reading problems.

The advantage of syllabaries over alphabets for young readers apparently stems from the fact that children have less difficulty identifying syllables than phonemes. One study revealed that 46 percent of four year olds and 90 percent of six year olds can segment words into syllables. In contrast, virtually no four year olds and only about two-thirds of all six year olds can segment words into phoneme-size units. Since learning to read involves an understanding of the type of unit represented by written symbols, it is not surprising that syllabaries are generally easier for young children to learn.

Of course, it must be remembered that syllabaries may have disadvantages of other sorts. While syllabic writing is feasible for languages such as Japanese that have a relatively small number of syllable types, it would be quite impractical in English where there are dozens of different syllable structures. Ultimately, an orthography must be judged in terms of its success in representing language for the purpose of reading and writing. There is no doubt that an alphabetic orthography is superior to a syllabary for representing the phonological structure of English.

Summing up

The development of writing has been one of humanity's greatest intellectual achievements. From **pictograms**, and **logograms**, the graphic representation of language has developed through **syllabic writing** to the **alphabet**. This was achieved through the creation of a relationship between graphic symbols and sounds.

Many of the large number of writing systems found throughout the modern world owe their origin directly or indirectly to the Semitic writing systems of the eastern Mediterranean. As the idea of writing spread, new forms of the symbols were independently invented and sound-symbol correspondences were altered in accordance with language structures. Some writing systems derived from the Graeco-Phoenician tradition are today scarcely recognizable as such, since so little remains of the original symbols. In cases where the entire system was invented, perhaps only the idea of writing is traceable to the early traditions.

In all cases, the historical line of development is clear. There seems to be no evidence of a culture that has developed an alphabet and then followed this with the development of, for example, a logographic script. But this cultural line of development does not imply that earlier forms of writing are inferior to alphabetic writing. In the case of languages such as Japanese or Cree, the syllabic writing system is as well suited to the phonological structure of the language as an alphabetic script would be.

Key terms

acrophonic principle
alphabetic writing
Blissymbolics
characters
cuneiform
Cyrillic alphabet
Glagolitic script
glyphs
hangul
hanja
hieroglyphics
hiragana
kanji
katakana
logograms
logographic writing
orthography
Phoenician script
phonetic determinative
phonographic writing
pictograms
pinyin
radical
rebus principle
Runic writing
syllabary
syllabic writing
writing

Sources

Comprehensive surveys of the development of writing and of the world's writing systems are found in Jensen, Gelb, and DeFrancis (all cited below). The point that pure syllabaries may not exist was called to the authors' attention by Prof. W. Poser of the University of Northern British Columbia (personal communication). The idea that writing may have originated in record keeping with clay tokens is taken from Schmandt-Besserat (cited below). The following figures are adapted: from Jensen, 15.1a, 15.3, 15.10, 15.13, 15.26, 15.29; from Alexander Marshack, *The Roots of Civilization* (New York: McGraw-Hill, 1972), 15.1b; from Schmandt-Besserat, 15.2; from René Labat, *Manuel d'Epigraphie Akkadienne*, 5th ed. (Paris: P. Geuthner, 1976), 15.6; from DeFrancis (see further references to origins of these figures therein), 15.7, 15.8, 15.12, 15.25 (adapted from *Visible Speech: The Diverse Oneness of Writing Systems* and reprinted by permission of the University of Hawaii Press); from Wayne M. Senner, "Theories and Myths on the Origins of Writing: A Historical Overview," in Senner (cited below and reprinted by permission of the University of Nebraska Press), 15.9; from Sampson (cited below), 15.11; from Frank Moore Cross, "The Invention and Development of the Alphabet," in Senner, p. 89 (cited below and reprinted by permission of the University of Nebraska Press), 15.17. The sport pictograms in Figure 15.4 are courtesy of the Olympic Trust of Canada, ™Official Mark © Canadian Olympic Association, 1972. Figure 15.5 is courtesy of the Blissymbolics Communication Institute, exclusive licensee, 1982, and is derived from the symbols described in the work *Semantography*, original copyright C. K. Bliss 1949.

Reference to Arabic writing is from James A. Bellamy, "The Arabic Alphabet," in Senner (cited below). John DeFrancis (University of Hawaii), Robert Fisher (University of Toronto), and Brian King (University of British Columbia) all provided insightful and helpful comments (especially regarding Chinese writing), so many, in fact, that we were not able to make use of all of them here. Their views are not necessarily those reflected in the chapter. The discussion of Chinese writing is derived from DeFrancis (cited below), as is Table 15.1; Figure 15.8 was adapted from Jerry Norman, *Chinese* (Cambridge: Cambridge University Press, 1988); Chinese characters were kindly provided by Lin Zhiqiu. The presentation of Japanese writing also owes to DeFrancis, as well as to M. Shibatani, *The Languages of Japan* (Cambridge: Cambridge University Press, 1990). The hiragana and katakana charts (Figure 15.19) are adapted from Len Walsh's *Read Japanese Today* (Tokyo, Japan: Charles E. Tuttle, 1971) and reprinted by permission of the publisher; Japanese examples were provided by Kazue Kanno. For a discussion of Cherokee writing, see "Native American Writing Systems" by W. Walker, in *Language in the USA*, edited by C. Ferguson et al. (New York: Cambridge University Press, 1981). Presentation of the Cree syllabary is adapted from D. Pentland, *Nēhiyawasi-nahikēwin: A Standard Orthography for the Cree Language* (Saskatoon: Saskatchewan Indian Cultural College, 1977). David H. Kelley of the University of Calgary provided corrective and helpful advice on Mayan and other Mesoamerican writing. The examples of Northern Indian pictorial script are from John Marshall, *Mohenjo-Daro and the Indus Civilization* (London: A. Probsthain, 1931).

The discussion of the history of English spelling is based on *A History of English Spelling* by D. G. Scragg (New York: Barnes & Noble, 1974). The examples of spelling rules sensitive to morphological structure come from the book by D. W. Cummings cited below. Data on children's ability to segment words into syllables and phonemes come from I. Y. Liberman, reported in Gibson and Levin (cited below). Peter Avery of York University, Toronto, caught several important errors. John Sören Pettersson of Uppsala University commented extensively and helpfully on the entire chapter.

Recommended reading

Cummings, D. W. 1988. *American English Spelling.* Baltimore: Johns Hopkins University Press.

Daniels, Peter T., and William Bright, eds. 1995. *The World's Writing Systems.* Oxford: Oxford University Press.

DeFrancis, John. 1989. *Visible Speech: The Diverse Oneness of Writing Systems.* Honolulu: University of Hawaii Press.

Gelb, I. J. 1963. *A Study of Writing.* Chicago: University of Chicago Press.

Gibson, E., and H. Levin. 1975. *The Psychology of Reading.* Cambridge, MA: MIT Press.

Gleitman, L., and P. Rozin. 1977. "The Structure and Acquisition of Reading I: Relations Between Orthographies and the Structures of Language." In *Toward a Psychology of Reading.* Edited by A. Reber and D. Scarborough, 1–53. Hillsdale, NJ: Erlbaum.

Jensen, H. 1970. *Sign, Symbol and Script.* G. Unwin, trans. London: George Allen and Unwin.

Sampson, G. 1985. *Writing Systems: A Linguistic Introduction.* Stanford, CA: Stanford University Press.

Schmandt-Besserat, Denise. 1989. "Two Precursors of Writing: Plain and Complex Tokens." In *The Origins of Writing*. Edited by W. M. Senner, 27–42. Lincoln, NE: University of Nebraska Press.

Senner, W. M., ed. 1989. *The Origins of Writing*. Lincoln, NE: University of Nebraska Press.

Wallace, Rex. 1989. "The Origins and Development of the Latin Alphabet." In *The Origins of Writing*. Edited by W. M. Senner, 121–36. Lincoln, NE: University of Nebraska Press.

Questions

1. Suppose you are the user of a pictographic writing system that can already represent concrete objects in a satisfactory way. Using the pictographic symbols of your system, propose and explain ideographic extensions of these symbols to represent the following meanings.

a) hunt	f) cook
b) cold	g) tired
c) fast	h) wet
d) white	i) angry
e) strength	j) weakness

2. Construct a syllabary for English that can be used to spell the following words. What problems do you encounter?

a) foe	law	shoe
b) slaw	slow	slowly
c) lee	day	daily
d) sue	pull	shop
e) ship	loop	food
f) lock	shock	unlock
g) locked	shocked	pulled
h) shops	locker	shod
i) float	splint	schlock

3. *i)* How does English orthography capture the morphophonemic alternations in the following words? Begin your analysis with a phonemic transcription of the forms.

a) hymn	hymnal	
b) part	partial	
c) recite	recitation	
d) reduce	reduction	
e) design	designation	
f) critical	criticize	criticism
g) analogue	analogous	analogy

ii) After discussing the forms in question *i)*, consider the following forms. Does the spelling system treat all cases of allomorphic variation the same way?

a) invade	invasion
b) concede	concession
c) assume	assumption
d) profound	profundity

4. Briefly outline the advantages and disadvantages of the three major types of writing that have evolved throughout history.

sixteen

ANIMAL COMMUNICATION

Michael Dobrovolsky

As I listened from a beach-chair in the shade
To all the noises that my garden made,
It seemed to me only proper that words
Should be withheld from vegetables and birds.

– W. H. AUDEN

Communication—the passing on or exchange of information—distinguishes what is living from what is nonliving in nature. Communication is found even in the apparently passive world of plants; trees, for example, have been found to pass on information about advancing predators by means of chemical signals. Animals communicate among themselves and with humans so effectively that they are frequently held to use 'language'. But communication and language are not simply words that mean the same thing. Human language is a specific *way* of representing the world and passing on information. From the linguist's point of view, not just any communication qualifies as language as it is defined in this book.

A question that therefore interests many linguists is whether animals make use of any system of communication that genuinely resembles or approximates human language. Just as the use of communication sets what is living apart from what is nonliving, the use of language is often said to set humans apart from all other animals. If animals communicate with a system that is structured like human language, then language as we know it is not the unique property of our species, and we will have to look for other ways of defining humanness. This chapter investigates the ways in which animal communication is like human language and the ways in which it is different.

1 NONVOCAL COMMUNICATION

One of the most striking things about animal communication is the variety of means with which it is carried out. Animals communicate not only with sounds but with scent, light, ultrasound, visual signs, gestures, color, and even electricity. From the slime mold to the giant blue whale, all living things appear to have some means of communication. Some nonvocal modes of communication are described here.

Scent Chemically based scent communication is used by species as different as molds, insects, and mammals. Chemicals used by animals specifically for communicative purposes are called **pheremones**. A female moth signals its reproductive readiness through the release of a pheremone into the air. Only a few of these molecules need to be sensed by a male moth for it to start flying zig-zag upwind towards its potential mate. Dogs and other canines leave a urine-based pheremone as an identification mark to stake out their territory, and many nonhuman primates have specialized scent glands for the same purpose.

Light Probably the most well-known light user in North America is the firefly or lightning bug. This small flying beetle uses light flashes in varying patterns to signal its identity, sex, and location. Different species of these insects have different and distinguishing light patterns.

Electricity Certain species of eels in the Amazon River basin communicate their presence and territoriality by means of electrical impulses at various frequencies. Each species signals at a specific frequency range, and the transmitting frequencies, like those of radio and television stations, do not overlap.

Color The color (or color pattern) of many animals plays an important role in their identification by members of their own species and other animals. The octopus changes color frequently, and this coloring is used for a range of messages that include territorial defense and mating readiness.

Posture This is a common communicative device among animals. Dogs, for example, lower the front part of their bodies and extend their front legs when they are playful. They lower their whole bodies to the ground when they are submissive. Postural communication is found in both human and nonhuman primates as well.

Gesture A gesture may be defined as active posturing. Humans wave their arms in recognition or farewell, dogs wave their tails in excitement, and cats flick their tails when irritated. Many birds perform elaborate gestures of raising and lowering the head or racing back and forth across the water in their mating rituals. Some fish, such as the male stickleback, perform a series of distinct movements in the water as part of their mating ritual.

Facial expressions These are specific types of communicative gestures. When a male baboon yawns, bares its fangs, and retracts its eyebrows, it is indicating a willingness to fight. A wide and recognizable variety of facial expressions is found among chimpanzees; a number of these are shown in Figure 16.1. Experiments have shown that humans can classify the meanings of these expressions quite accurately. For example, when humans draw back the corners of their mouths into a smile, they are generally indicating cooperation. A nonhuman primate's smile also indicates nonaggressiveness.

Figure 16.1 Some chimpanzee facial expressions: *a.* anger; *b.* fear-anger; *c.* affection; *d.* frustration-sadness; *e.* playfulness

2 COMMUNICATION STRUCTURE: THE STUDY OF SIGNS

Underlying the bewildering variety of communicative methods found in nature are certain common elements. An understanding of these is necessary for comparing the differences and similarities among systems of communication.

2.1 SIGNS

Communication relies on using something to stand for something else. Words are an obvious example of this: You do not have to have a car, a sandwich, or your cousin present in order to talk about them—the words *car, sandwich,* and *cousin* stand for them instead. This same phenomenon is found in animal communication as well. Instead of fighting over territory, for example, many animals produce sounds or make gestures that threaten and intimidate intruders—the message replaces the attack. Birds utter warning calls that represent the presence of a threat. A threatening animal or human need not be seen by other birds before they take flight—perception of the warning call replaces visual perception of the threat.

Each of these things that stand for other things is technically known as a **sign**. The sign is a unit of communication structure that consists of two parts: a **signifier**, be it a word, a scent, a gesture, or an electrical frequency, and something **signified** that exists in the real world, and which is mentally represented by the sign's conceptual content. The real world can be thought of as either external, mental, or emotional, and so what is signified by a sign can be as diverse as a tree, an abstract idea, a perception, or a feeling. Because their content is conceptual, all signs are associated with some **meaning**, such as 'danger', or 'item of furniture with legs and a flat top'. Individual instances of signs are called **tokens**. For example, in the sentence *The baby threw the rattle* there are five word tokens, but only four signs; *the* occurs twice as a token, but it is the same sign in both instances. Figure 16.2 illustrates these distinctions.

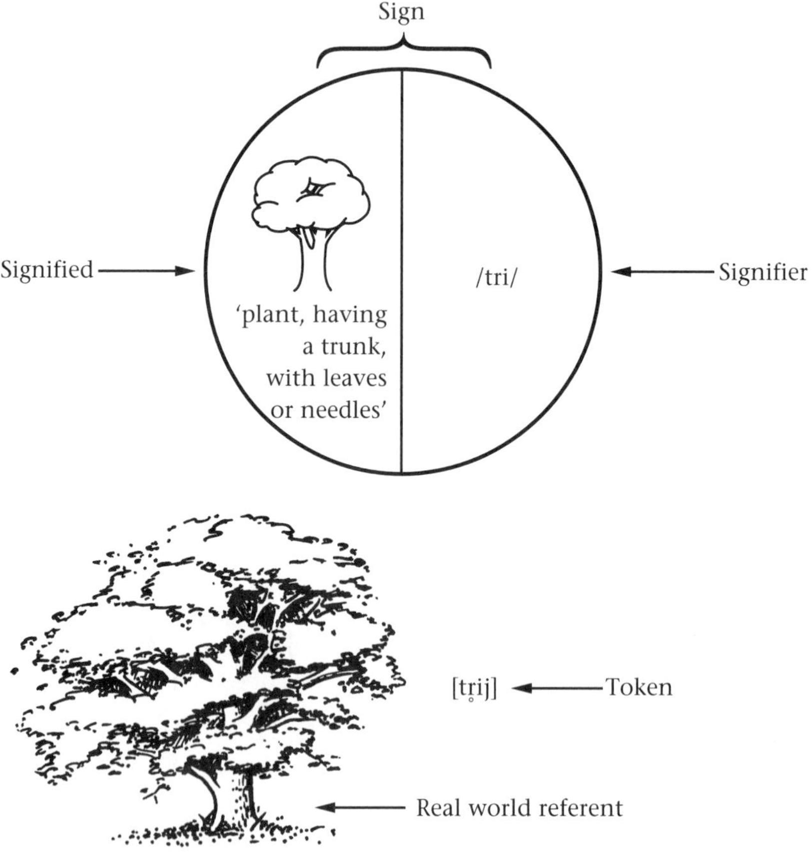

Figure 16.2 A sign

The study of signs is known as **semiotics**. Semiotics is a field of study that links many diverse disciplines, among them linguistics, anthropology, philosophy, zoology, genetics, literary study, and computer science. An understanding of signs is essential for understanding how messages are transmitted. To understand signs better before proceeding on to analyzing animal communication, the next section examines their structure in more detail.

The signifier

A signifier is that part of a sign that stimulates at least one sense organ of the receiver of a message. The phonological component of the word *tree*, represented as /tri/ and pronounced [tr̥ij] is a typical linguistic signifier. A signifier can also be a picture, a photograph, a sign language gesture, or one of the many other words for *tree* in different languages.

The signified

The signified component of the sign refers to both the real world object it represents and its conceptual content.

The first of these is the real world content of the sign, its *extension* or *referent* (Chapter 7, Section 1.1) within a system of signs such as English, avian communication, or sign language. In our example, the referent is a real tree represented by a drawing in Figure 16.2. (Of course, the signifier /tri/ could also have a picture of a tree as its referent.) It is easiest to think of referents as concepts or persons or things but they may be ideas or feelings as well.

The signified component of a sign also evokes an *intension* (Chapter 7, Section 1.3) to users of the system in question. A word for 'tree' evokes concepts that probably include 'plant', 'having a trunk', and 'bearing leaves or needles' in the minds of speakers of any language who are familiar with trees. Some animals appear to conceptualize in terms of classes or categories as well. Certain monkeys, for example, distinguish among various types of predators on the basis of size, shape, and motion (see Section 5.3).

2.2 TYPES OF SIGNS

Signs can be divided into three basic types, depending on (1) whether the signifier naturally resembles its referent, (2) whether the signifier is directly linked with the referent in a physical or mechanical sense, or (3) whether signifier and referent are arbitrarily associated.

Iconic signs

Iconic signs, or *icons*, always bear some resemblance to their referent. A photograph is an iconic sign; so too is a stylized silhouette of a female or a male on a restroom door. A baboon's open-mouth threat is iconic, resembling as it does the act of biting. Onomatopoeic words like *buzz*, *splat*, and *squish* in English and their counterparts in other human languages are also iconic in that they somewhat resemble what they signify.

Figure 16.3 Some iconic tokens: *a.* open-mouth threat by a Japanese macaque (*Macaca fuscata*); *b.* park recreation signs; *c.* onomatopoeic words in English

Icons are widespread in the communication systems of all animals; many postures and gestures that are critical to animal communication are iconic, as are the postures and gestures used by humans. Human linguistic communication, however, does not make extensive use of iconic signs.

Indexical signs

An **indexical sign**, or *index*, fulfils its function by pointing out its referent, typically by being a partial or representative sample of it. Indexes are not arbitrary, since their presence has in some sense been caused by their referent. For this reason it is sometimes said that there is a causal link between an indexical sign and its referent. The track of an animal, for example, points to the existence of the animal by representing a part of it. The presence of smoke is an index of fire.

Most important for our discussion here is a specific kind of indexical sign called a **symptomatic sign**, or *symptom*. Symptomatic signs spontaneously convey the internal state or emotions of the sender and thus represent the sender in an indexical manner. For example, the fact that our body temperature rises when we are ill is a spontaneous reflection of our internal state. When someone steps on our foot and we cry out, the cry is a spontaneous reflection of our internal state and thus constitutes a symptomatic sign.

Since symptomatic signs are spontaneous, we do not consider them to be deliberately selected by the sender for purposes of communication. We do not choose to cry out in pain in the same way as we might, for example, decide to call our dwelling place a *house*, *home*, *dwelling*, or *residence* in the appropriate circumstances. As forms of communication, symptomatic signs are therefore used primarily by the receiver of a message to assess the internal state of the sender. Since senders do not deliberately choose to transmit the sign, the message is assumed to be essentially beyond their control.

Symbolic signs

Symbolic signs bear an arbitrary relationship to their referents and in this way are distinct from both icons and indexes. Human language is highly symbolic in that the vast majority of its signs bear no inherent resemblance or causal connection to their referents, as the following words show.

hana	=	?
mazə	=	?
talo	=	?
kum	=	?
berat	=	?

Figure 16.4 Arbitrary sound-meaning correspondence in language

No phonological property of the words in Figure 16.4 gives you any hint as to their possible meaning. (*Hana* means 'flower' or 'nose' in Japanese, *mazə* is 'forest' in Kabardian, *talo* is 'house' in Finnish, *kum* means 'sand' in Turkish, and *berat* means 'heavy' in Indonesian.)

We encounter many other symbolic signs in everyday life. The octagonal shape of a stop sign is symbolic; it bears no inherent connection with the message it helps to communicate. The colors used in traffic signals are symbolic as well; red has no more inherent connection with the act of stopping than yellow.

Mixed signs

Signs are not always exclusively of one type or another. Symptomatic signs, for example, may have iconic properties, as when a dog opens its mouth in a threat to bite. Symbolic signs such as traffic lights are symptomatic in that they reflect the internal state of the mechanism that causes them to change color. Still, we classify a sign according to its major property: If it resembles its referent, it is iconic; if it is linked to its referent in some causal way or represents it partially in some non-arbitrary way, it is indexical (and symptomatic if it spontaneously expresses some internal state); and if its relationship to its referent is arbitrary, it is a symbol.

Signals

All signs can act as **signals** when they trigger a specific action on the part of the receiver, as do traffic lights, words in human language such as the race starter's "Go!", or the warning calls of birds. Typically, a signal releases more energy in the receiver than it takes for the transmitter to send it. For example, the simple release of a mating pheremone into the wind by a female moth (a symptomatic sign and also a signal) can cause the male to fly as much as six kilometres in search of her. Signals are very common in animal communication, but only a limited subset of human linguistic activity consists of signalling.

2.3 Sign structure

No matter what their type, signs show different kinds of structure. A basic distinction is made between **graded** and **discrete** sign structure.

Graded signs

Graded signs convey their meaning by changes in degree. A good example of a gradation in communication is voice volume. The more you want to be heard, the louder you speak along an increasing scale of loudness. There are no steps or jumps from one level to the next that can be associated with a specific change in meaning.

Gradation is common in many forms of communication. The hands of most clocks move (or appear to move) in a graded manner, as does the needle of an automobile speedometer. Many animal signs, such as the barking of dogs, are graded as well. A goose has essentially one type of honk, which may become louder and faster as it takes off in flight, but does not become another kind of honking. The gradually increasing fear in the facial expression of the monkey depicted in Figure 16.5 is also a graded sign.

Figure 16.5 Some graded signs: the facial expressions *a*, *b*, and *c* of the macaque monkey represent just three points on a continuum expressing fear; *a*. is a neutral face; *b*. expresses slight fear; and *c*. expresses extreme fear. Each expression grades into the next. The hands of the clock in *d* express minutes in a graded manner.

Discrete signs

Discrete signs are distinguished from each other by categorical (stepwise) differences. There is no gradual transition from one sign to the next. The words of human language are good examples of discrete signs. There is no intermediate stage between the words *stop* and *go* in English except that which can be expressed by other discrete words or combinations of words, such as *start to go*. The digital displays of

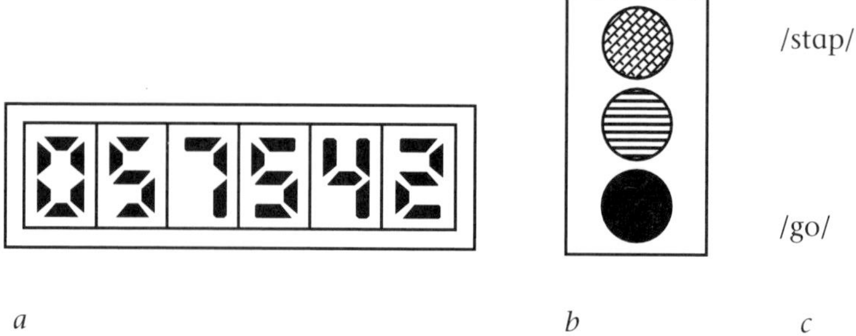

Figure 16.6 Some discrete signs: *a*. digital time display; *b*. traffic lights; *c*. words of a human language

watches are discrete as well, since they progress from one minute (or even second) to the next with no gradation. Traffic lights, too, are discrete signs; there is no gradual shifting from green to yellow to red.

Sign types and structure

All three types of signs—*iconic*, *indexical/symptomatic*, and *symbolic*—can be graded or discrete. A photograph is iconic and discrete, but a threatening canine's gradual baring of its fangs is iconic and graded. Morse code is symbolic and discrete, but a slowly dimming light that signals the beginning of a theatrical performance is symbolic and graded. Symptomatic signs, too, may be discrete (the traffic light again) or graded (the crying of a child or the act of blushing).

It is possible for a discrete sign to be internally graded, and even to slip over into another type by degrees. Human crying, for example, is interpreted by experimental subjects as becoming gradually more like screaming as the audible intake of breath between sobs becomes shorter and shorter. Figure 16.7 illustrates this phenomenon.

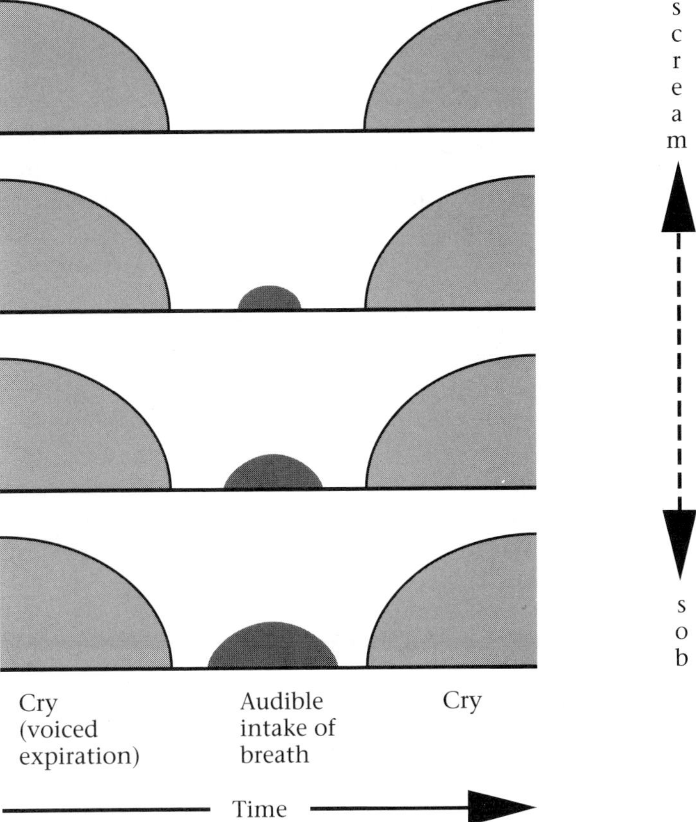

Figure 16.7 The graded continuum from sobbing to screaming (the height of the stippled and blackened areas represents the audibility of the vocalization and the width its time): both sob and scream are discrete signs, even though each grades into the other.

At the extreme ends of the continuum, there is no difficulty interpreting the sound as one or the other, although it is difficult to say precisely when a 'sob' becomes a 'scream'. Thus we can say that 'sobbing' and 'screaming' are discrete symptomatic signs, but each of them is internally graded, and their gradations overlap. The same is true of many vocalizations in animal communication.

2.4 A VIEW OF ANIMAL COMMUNICATION

They're like Swiss watches . . . they just react. Their genes and hormones and experience tell them what to do. They don't think about it.

Zookeeper Ben Beck (on golden lion tamarin monkeys)

Most animal communication, it is claimed, shows little arbitrariness. It is said to be largely iconic and symptomatic and hence not deliberate or conscious in intent, nor symbolic in its sign repertory. For example, if a monkey gives a certain cry in the presence of danger, it is assumed that the monkey is spontaneously signalling its fear by vocalizing, but is not deliberately warning other group members of the danger. The vocalization is interpreted and used by other members of a troop for their own benefit.

It follows from this view of animal communication that the acquisition of communicative systems by animals was in the past assumed to be largely devoid of learning and experience. Rather, it was claimed that the systems are rather strictly limited by genetic inheritance, and in this sense radically unlike human language, the acquisition of which requires exposure to a mature system. This limitation certainly appears to be true in some cases. When raised in isolation, animals as diverse as the fox, the elephant seal, the cat, and certain monkeys develop the full range of vocalizations typical of their species. However, as we will see in Section 4 of this chapter, the situation can be more complex than this.

It is further claimed that animal communication is neither conscious nor deliberate. It is not widely believed, for example, that a monkey assesses a situation and then deliberately chooses to warn group members of danger by selecting a sign from a repertoire of meaningful sound symbols at its disposal. For this reason, the term **stimulus-bound** is also used to describe animal communication, since it is often claimed that animal communication only occurs when it is triggered by exposure to a certain stimulus or for certain specific ends. Animals do not communicate about anything but the here and now. As the philosopher Bertrand Russell once noted, "No matter how eloquently a dog may bark, it cannot tell you that its parents were poor but honest."

With respect to structure, animal communication is said to show few traces of discrete structuring beyond the obvious fact that one group of symptomatic, graded signals may sound very different from another. Whining in dogs, for example, is clearly different from barking, but both are assumed to be symptomatic, and the two may grade into each other. Combining and recombining of discrete units of structure such as phonemes, morphemes, and words is not characteristic of the way animals communicate. Dogs do not combine whines and barks to produce novel messages.

This does not mean that animal communication consists of random emotional outbursts. Nor does it mean that animal communication does not show structure. Animal communication is both complex and organized. Evolutionary pressure has guaranteed that animal communication is optimally in tune with the survival requirements of each species. The electrical communication of Amazonian eels is an excellent means of communication in muddy waters. The danger whistle of a small, tree-dwelling primate like the galago is ideal for nocturnal communication in a dense forest. Small jungle frogs in South America communicate by sticking out their long and colorful legs, ideal for sending messages in the dim and noisy jungle. But jungle frogs do not try new combinations of leg movements in order to come up with an original message, any more than the electric eel recombines frequencies in order to signal something it has never conveyed before. Animal communication appears to be limited in the messages it can convey.

But is animal communication so very unlike human language in all respects? Recent work on animal communication has often focused on its relationship to human linguistic communication. The next sections examine the communication systems of several kinds of animals and compare them with human language.

3 THE BEES

I have no doubt that some will attempt to 'explain' the performances of the bees as the results of reflexes and instincts . . . for my part, I find it difficult to assume that such perfection and flexibility in behavior can be reached without some kind of mental processes going on in the small heads of the bees.

August Krogh, *Scientific American*

3.1 The system

Forager bees display a remarkable system of communicating the location of a food source to other bees in their hive. When a food source has been discovered, the forager flies back to the hive and communicates information about it by performing special movements (which humans call *dancing*) before other members of the hive. The dancing conveys information about the location of the food source, its quality, and its distance from the hive.

Distance

Distance is conveyed by one of three different dances performed on the wall or floor of the hive (some species have only two different dances, and so may be said to have a different 'dialect'). In doing the *round dance*, the bee circles repeatedly. This indicates a food source within five meters or so of the hive. The *sickle dance* indicates a food source from five to twenty meters from the hive. It is performed by the bee dancing a curved figure eight shape. The *tail-wagging dance* indicates distances further than twenty meters. In this dance, the bee wags its abdomen as it moves forward, circles to the right back to its starting point, repeats the wagging forward motion, and circles left. The cycle then begins again.

Direction

The round dance does not communicate direction, presumably since the food source is so close to the hive. The direction of more distant food sources is indicated in the other two types of dance.

As the bee performs the sickle and tail-wagging dances, it is simultaneously indicating the direction of the food source. Bees orient themselves in flight relative to the angle of the sun. When danced on the floor of the hive, the angle of the open side of the sickle dance's figure eight or the angle of the wagging path during the tail-wagging dance indicates the direction of flight. When the dancing is performed on the vertical wall of the hive, it is apparently 'understood' that the top of the hive wall represents the current position of the sun in the sky. During the sickle dance, the angle of the open side of the figure eight relative to the hive's vertical alignment indicates the direction of flight toward the food source relative to the sun. When the bee performs the tail-wagging dance, the angle of its wagging path relative to the hive's vertical angle indicates the path of flight toward the food source relative to the sun. Figure 16.8 illustrates the dances and their manner of indicating the direction of the food source.

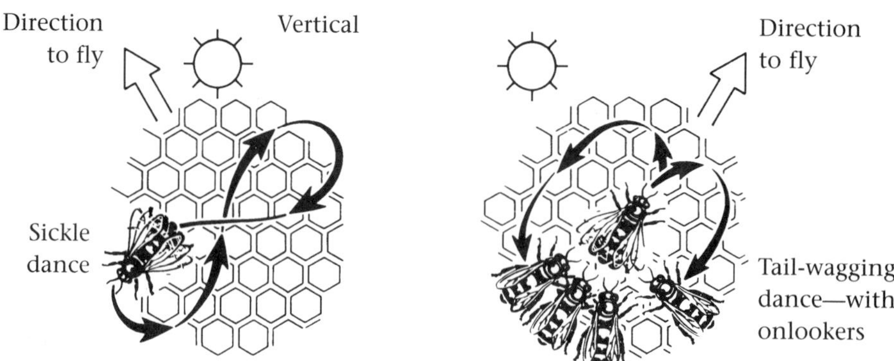

Figure 16.8 Bee dancing

Quality

Quality of the food source is indicated by the intensity of the dancing and the number of repetitions of the circling movements. As the food source is depleted, the dance is performed with less vivacity.

Other factors

These messages are not communicated with perfect accuracy, nor are they the only ones involved in bee communication. Bees also leave a hive-specific pheremone trace at the site of the food source, thereby directing their fellow foragers to the precise location. The bees also carry back traces of the food source odors, which further aid other bees in the search. A complex of communicative modes operating on different channels—a **constellation**—is thus employed in bee communication. The use of different modalities to communicate the same information is called **redundancy**. Redundancy helps guarantee that communication will succeed in the event one or the other modalities fails or is imperfectly transmitted. All communication systems make use of redundancy, and human language is no exception. For example, the presence of allophonic features such as voicelessness and aspiration on syllable initial voiceless stops, or both length and quality differences on vowels provides redundancy that assists in decoding the signals.

3.2 Bees and humans

How does bee communication compare with human language? The three patterns that the bees dance are not obviously connected with the messages they communicate and so are *symbolic* in nature (though it is possible to argue that relative distance is iconically represented in that a greater distance covered by the bee in each cycle of the dance corresponds to a greater distance of the nectar source from the hive). The communication of direction is *indexical* when carried out on the hive floor (in the sense that it points in the direction of flight), and in this sense may be comparable to a human gesture. Bees are, however, capable of transforming this information into a *symbolic* representation, since they transfer the horizontal flight path to a vertical representation on the hive wall. The expression of food source quality is, in all probability, symptomatic: The more stimulated a bee is by the quality of the food source, the faster it dances.

The total communicative constellation involves other, redundant sources of communication as well, such as pheremones and food source samples. The performance even involves audience participation. During its dancing, the returning bee is expected to provide samples from the food source. If it fails to do so, it may be stung to death.

Bee communication, then, like human language, shows symbolic, indexical, and symptomatic traits, and interaction between sender and receiver of the messages. But there is a major difference between the two systems of communication. The topic of bee language is severely constrained. Bees communicate only about food sources. Furthermore, their potential for communication is very limited. Only certain locations of food sources can be conveyed. Bees cannot communicate the notion of up or down. They can be easily tricked into communicating the wrong direction of the food source if a strong light source is placed in an incorrect position in relation to the food source. They can also be tricked into giving the wrong information about distance to the food source if they are forced to walk or stop several times during their trip. This indicates that they gauge distance by time. The bees show no means of assessing varying information and communicating this fact. Their system of communication appears to be close-ended and limited to a specific number of facts about a specific type of information.

It also appears that bee language is largely innate—that is, there is very little need for a new forager bee to be exposed to the system in the presence of other bees. Foragers on their first flight perform the appropriate dances, although they refine their performance to some extent with time and exposure to other dancing. Their flight orientation to the sun is imperfect at first, but it develops within a few hours.

The innateness of bee dancing has been tested by cross-breeding Austrian bees, which do not perform the sickle dance to express intermediate distance of the food source from the hive, with Italian honeybees, which do. The results of such experiments further support a genetic interpretation of bee communication. In the cross-breeding experiment, the bees that bore a physical resemblance to their Italian parent performed the sickle dance to indicate intermediate distance 98 percent of the time. The bees that bore a physical resemblance to their Austrian parent performed the round dance to indicate intermediate distance 96 percent of the time; they did not perform the sickle dance at all. The dance pattern used in a specific situation appears to be inherited from a certain parent along with other more obvious genetic traits.

In 1948, when the Danish physiologist August Krogh made the statement quoted at the beginning of this section, he struck at the widely accepted notion that animal behavior was either the result of some kind of conditioning, or, in some ill-defined way, instinctive. Much has been learned since then about the enormous quantity of information imparted by genetic transfer. It is now possible to state with a fair degree of certainty that the complex and sophisticated behavior of bees and other equally remarkable insects is in all probability largely genetically predetermined and, unlike human language, it relies very little on exposure to the mature system in order to be acquired.

4 THE BIRDS

How intelligent is a creature that can amuse himself for 15 minutes by uttering, over and over, the following sounds: uhr, uhr, uhr, Uhr, URH, URH, Wah, Wah, wah, wah, wah?

Jake Page (on his Amazon parrot)

4.1 Bird vocalization

Birds, as Jake Page later found out, can do a lot more than utter sounds over and over. Even the parrot, which has been labelled for years as nothing but a stimulus-bound mimic, has been shown to have some capacity for meaningful labelling (although it took one test parrot four years to acquire a vocabulary of eighteen nouns). The parroting of trained birds is generally accepted to be nothing more than nonintentional response to external stimuli arrived at through repetitive conditioning. But recently, it has been claimed that certain kinds of parroting have cognitive underpinning of a type shared with primates and perhaps even humans. Research on natural communication among birds has already shed light on parallels in human linguistic communication.

Bird vocalization can be divided into two types, **call** and **song**. Calls are typically short bursts of sound or simple patterns of notes. Songs are lengthy, elaborate patterns of mostly pitched sounds.

Calls

Calls serve very specific functions in the bird community. They typically warn of predators, coordinate flocking and flight activity, express aggression, and accompany nesting or feeding behavior. The cawing of crows is a typical call. It appears to convey a generalized mobilization to possible danger. When a crow hears cawing, it flies up to a tree if it is on the ground, or flies higher in a tree—or to another tree—if it is already in one. (If there are crows in your neighborhood, you can test this yourself, as cawing is easy to imitate.)

In some birds, individual calls are associated with specific activities; a danger call is quite different from a call given when birds are grouped in flight. A flight call is generally short, crisp, and easy for other group members to locate. The honking of geese in flight is a typical example of this sort of call. Because it is loud and easy to locate, it is well suited to enable the bird flock to stay together. The call given by small birds when larger avian predators threaten them is very different. It is typically thin and high-pitched. This kind of sound is difficult to locate, and so can be given as a warning without revealing the position of the caller. Such functional utility is typical of bird calls, and in fact, calls that serve the same communicative purpose are often remarkably similar among different species of birds.

Song

Birdsong is different from calling. Although calls are produced year round, singing is largely limited to spring, summer, and autumn. Furthermore, it is generally only male birds that sing.

The main purposes of song are, as far as we know, to announce and delimit the territory of the male and to attract a mate. Birds establish territory for breeding purposes and defend it vigorously. Across the country, it is a common sight in the spring to see a red-winged blackbird (*Agelaius phoeniceus*) and its mate team up to drive away a male of their species that has strayed into their territory. The use of song enables male birds to establish and maintain this territory without constant patrolling and fighting. Moreover, once a bird has established its territory, its song serves to attract and maintain contact with a mate. It follows that birdsong is unique from species to species, and even varies to some degree from bird to bird within the same species, since its purposes require species and individual recognition.

In some species, songs are nothing more than a successive repetition of calls. In others, songs consist of complex patterns of pitches—sometimes called syllables—that form longer repeated units or themes. The sometimes elaborate complexity of song structure reflects individual variation among the singers, and, as pointed out previously, serves a specific purpose. Figure 16.9 shows a **spectrogram** (an acoustic recording that shows pitch and intensity of sound along a time axis) of the song of the European robin (*Erithacus rubecula*). Note how the different subsections of the song are distinct and recognizable. There is also some evidence that sections of a song are combined in different orders by certain birds, but there is no evidence that recombination is associated with different meanings.

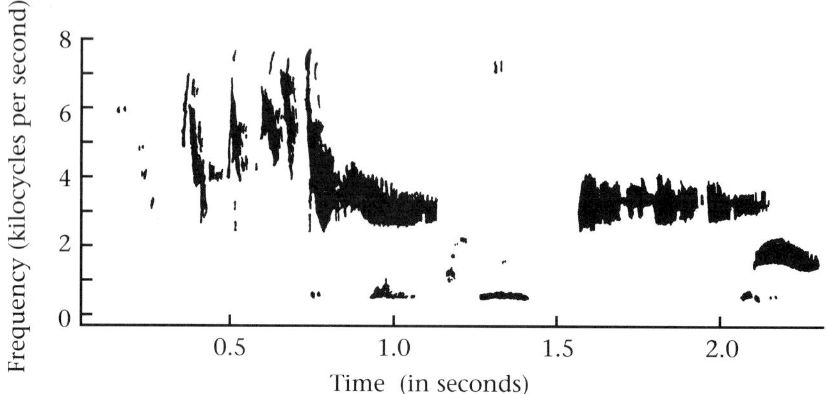

Figure 16.9 Spectrogram of a robin song; pitch is shown vertically, intensity by greater darkness

Avian dialects

There is evidence for both song and call dialects among bird species. Researchers even speak of avian *isoglosses* (lines drawn on a map to indicate shared characteristics among dialects; see Chapter 14, Section 3.1) that are based on variations in the melody of song 'syllables' or themes (see Figure 16.10). The reason for the existence of dialects is still unclear; it may be no more than a reflection of individual avian variation in song and call learning. If it is, we are led to an intriguing issue in the relationship of bird vocalization to human language—the question of how bird vocalizations are acquired.

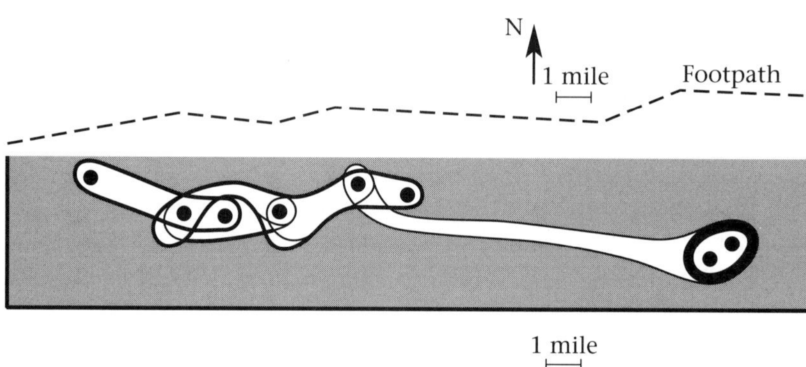

Figure 16.10 Avian isoglosses: call patterns of male Hill Mynas (black dots show myna groups; the shaded area shows forested hills and the unshaded, open plain; the heavier the black lines, the more song characteristics are shared by the group within its boundaries)

4.2 Birds and humans

The acquisition of call and song by birds shows interesting parallels with recent hypotheses about the acquisition of language by human children (see Chapter 12).

Though a great deal of bird vocalization—particularly calling—appears to be innate, there is much that appears to be acquired. Studies of avian dialects have shown that birds reared in the same nest acquire different song dialects when they live in different dialect areas. It also appears to be the case that singing ability is lateralized in the left brains of birds, as is linguistic ability in humans. Still more significant for linguistic study is the fact that some birds must acquire the species-specific characteristics of their song within a certain timespan or critical period. A number of bird species do not develop fully characteristic songs if they are deprived from hearing them during the early stages of their lives. The chaffinch (*Fringilla coelebs*) is one such bird. If chaffinches are reared in isolation, they sing, but replicate only in a general way the typical song of the species. If young chaffinches are reared away from fully developed singers, but with other young chaffinches, the entire experimental community develops an identical song. Finally, chaffinches that have been exposed to only some part of the fully developed song (those that are captured in the autumn of the first year of life) will, the following spring, develop a song that is partially typical but not completely well formed.

These experiments indicate that there are some songbirds that have both an innate and a learned component in their song. The innate component predisposes them to perform a general song that is extremely simplified. This has been called a **template** or a blueprint. Only exposure to the fully formed song of the species will enable them to produce the correct song. (Exposure to other song causes some species to imitate in this direction; other species simply do not acquire anything they are exposed to unless it is their own species-characteristic song.) Finally, it is clear that certain birds do not acquire their characteristic song in a brief span of time, but that several seasons of exposure are required. The evidence from songbird studies, while not transferable directly to humans, gives strong support to the idea that a combination of innate and learned components is one way that the acquisition of complex behavior takes place in nature.

5 NONHUMAN PRIMATES

Some animals share qualities of both man and the four-footed beasts, for example, the ape, the monkey, and the baboon.

Aristotle, *On Animals*

Fascination with nonhuman primates goes far back in human history. Their social behavior has long been seen as an amusing (and sometimes instructive) parody of human behavior. Since the recent establishment of the fact that we are closely related genetically to these animals—some 99 percent of our genetic matter is shared with chimpanzees and gorillas—the resemblance of their behavioral, social, and communicative traits to ours has been seen as more than an amusing counterpart to human activity. Recently, the question of our shared cognitive, and especially linguistic ability, has become more important; a better understanding of nonhuman primates may shed light on the evolution of human social and cognitive abilities.

Primates form a large class of mammals, which range from the tiny Tarsier to the imposing Mountain Gorilla. Among the nonhuman primates, some are nocturnal, some diurnal in their activity cycle. Some are solitary, some form part of complex social groups. Many are tree-dwelling, and many are ground-dwelling. Some are quadrupeds, and some show periods of bipedal locomotion. Figure 16.11 shows one widely accepted classification of the primates.

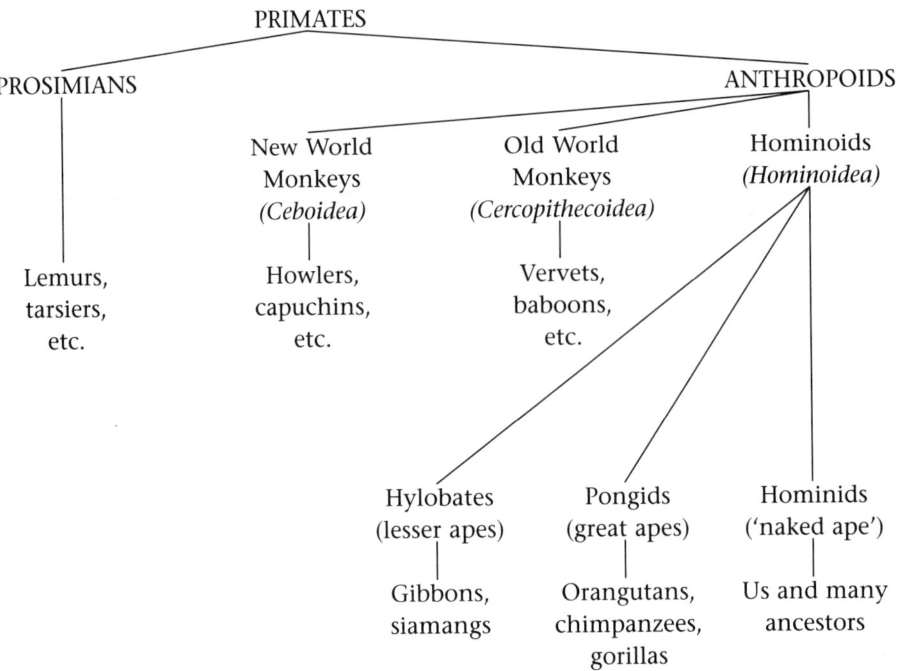

Figure 16.11 The primates

The prosimians are an evolutionarily early group found on the island of Malagasy, in Subsaharan Africa, and in Southeast Asia. New World Monkeys range from Mexico through South America. Among them are the only primates with prehensile (grasping) tails. Old World Monkeys include the many tree- and ground-dwelling species of Africa and the Far East. The larger nonhuman primates—baboons, chimpanzees, and gorillas—are not native to North and South America. Baboons, large, mainly ground-dwelling primates, are found from central to northern Africa. They show a high degree of social organization, intelligence, and aggressiveness. The hominoids include the agile gibbons, solitary orangutans (both found only in Southeast Asia), the large but peaceful gorillas, the chimpanzees, and humans.

The validity of studies of communication among captive primates has been criticized because the animals' social existence is highly limited and compromised in zoos. Studies of nonhuman primate communication have largely left the zoo and laboratory and moved into the animals' natural habitat. While careful observation of nonhuman primate communication is still the basis of this work, the use of playback experiments, in which tape recordings of natural calls are played back over hidden loudspeakers, has led to a greater understanding of the communicative systems of these animals.

In the next section, we first turn our attention to nonhuman primate communication in the wild. It is there that we can gain an initial understanding of how forms of nonhuman primate communication resemble or differ from our own in terms of function and structure.

5.1 Some functions of nonhuman primate communication

Although the social life of even the most gregarious nonhuman primate is relatively simple when compared to that of humans, primates, like humans, communicate for many different reasons.

Typical nonhuman primate communication serves to mark and announce territory, to warn other group members of danger, to seek or maintain contact with a mate or other members of the species, and to interact with members of the troop or species in various ways we can call 'socializing'. Socializing vocalizations are particularly important in mother-child bonding and in primate groups with a complex and hierarchical social structure. In these groups, it is important to know which members have a higher or lower rank so that group members can behave accordingly in their presence. Vocalization is a key factor in maintaining this behavior.

As we briefly survey some aspects of the structure of nonhuman primate communicative systems, we will also refer to the ways in which structure and function are linked.

5.2 Prosimian communication

Prosimian communication shows a small repertoire of sounds that are patterned into discrete groups. The lemur (*Lemur catta*) of Malagasy is a typical prosimian with respect to its vocal communication system. It has been described as making essentially two types of vocalization, noises and calls, each of which shows some grading. The vocalizations appear to be symptomatic. They are classified in Table 16.1; quasi-phonetic descriptions like *spat* should be interpreted as onomatopoeic.

Table 16.1 Lemur vocalization

Noises		*Calls*	
Sound	*Context*	*Sound*	*Context*
Single click	In response to strange objects	Light spat (yip)	When driving off threatening inferiors
Clicks, grunts	During locomotion, or for friendly greeting	Spat	When crowded or handled roughly
Purr	While grooming	Bark	When startled

Each graded set of sounds is used in a circumscribed range of situations. The calls, in particular, are limited to threat or fear encounters. They seem to form a graded series, ranging from the *light spat* to the *bark* in intensity. A small repertoire of distinct vocalizations is the norm among prosimians. The slow loris (*Nycticebus coucang*), an Asian prosimian, is reported to have no more than five calls.

5.3 Monkeys

The study of communication among the many varieties of New World and Old World monkeys is too vast for this chapter. An oversimplified picture reflects what most researchers agree is primarily a symptomatic system, but one that shows a larger number of signs, with more gradation among them, than does the communication of prosimians.

One study of the Bonnet Macaque (*Macaca radiata*), a South Asian monkey, presents a system of twenty-five different basic patterns that are used in various social interactions, including contact, agonistic encounters, foraging, greeting, sexual contact, and alarm giving. These vocalizations are determined by correlating observation with spectrographic analysis; descriptive labels are also given to the vocalizations, such as *whoo, rattle, growl, whistle,* and *bark.* These basic patterns are described as grading into each other. It is also claimed that they occur in combinations. There is no evidence, however, that these recombinations mean anything novel when they occur.

The communication systems of many monkeys appear to be genetically determined. This has been established by raising newborns in isolation. However, this statement cannot be made for all monkeys. For some monkeys, input from the adult system appears to be required. The study of one small monkey has suggested that not all monkey vocalizations are symptomatic, and that experience and learning can play a role in the acquisition of the communicative system.

The East African vervet monkey (*Cercopithecus aethiops*) is said to have three distinctive and arbitrary calls that announce the presence of either eagles, snakes, or large terrestial mammals posing a threat. These calls are associated with different responses by the monkeys. When they hear the eagle call, the monkeys look up or run into the bushes. The snake call causes them to look down at the ground near them. The mammal alarm sees them run up into the trees, or climb higher in a tree if they are already in one.

These findings, which appear to have been well established by playback experiments since they were first reported in 1967, suggest that not all nonhuman primates rely strictly on symptomatic signals to communicate or to trigger behavior in others. It is claimed rather that the vervets assess the potential danger situation and then choose a specific call with a clearly defined referent to announce the danger. Furthermore, each call is a vocalization signifier that is arbitrarily linked with its referent. Other monkeys respond appropriately to the calls without necessarily observing the danger themselves. All this taken together suggests a cognitive ability for classification of objects in the world and an ability to link this classification system to arbitrary sounds for purposes of intentional communication (see Figure 16.12).

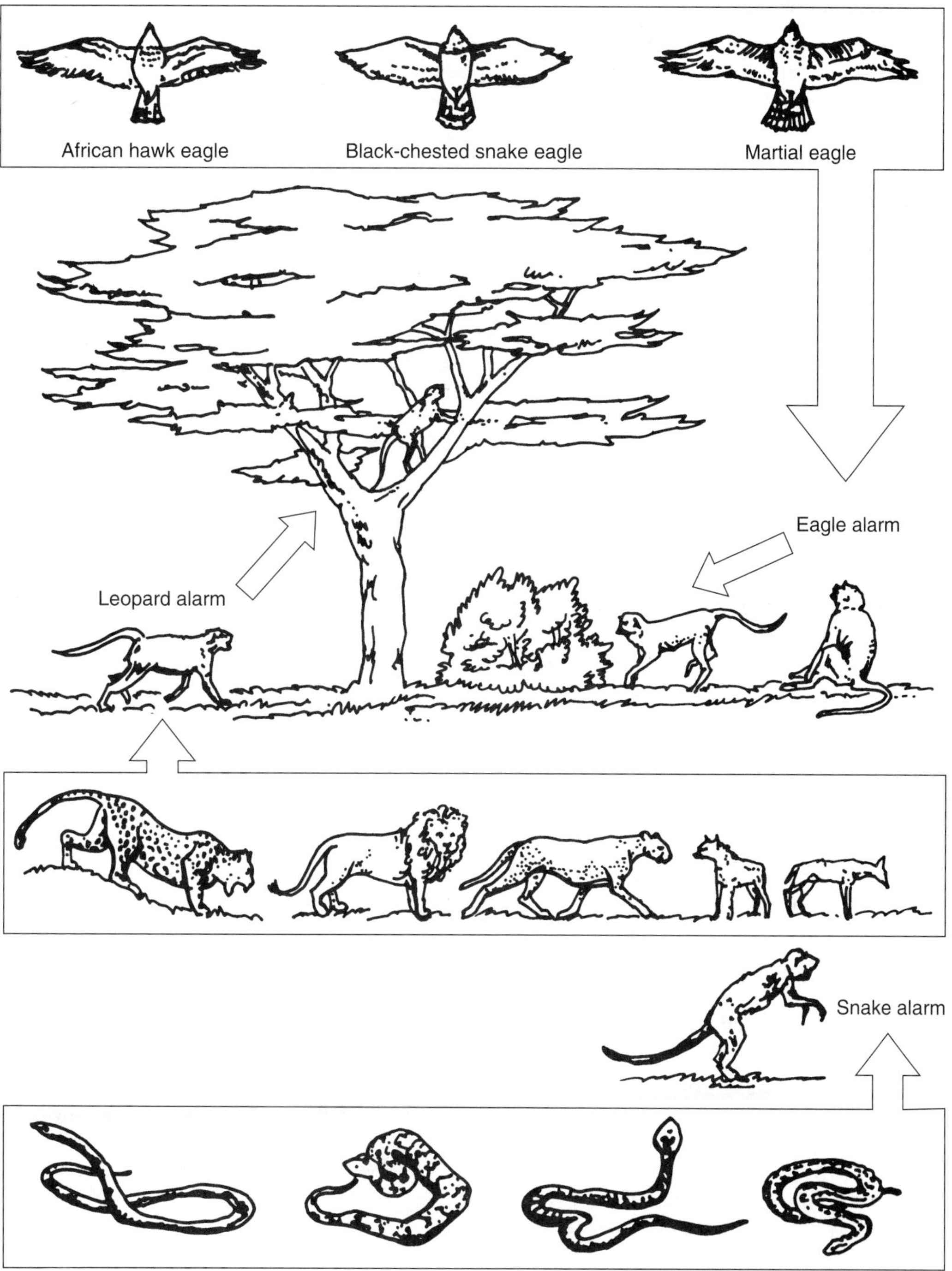

Figure 16.12 Responses of vervet monkeys to specific predators

The vervet may not be an isolated case. Goeldi's Monkey (*Callimico goeldii*), found in South America, is cited as having five different alarm calls, three of which are used when terrestrial predators approach, and two of which have been heard in the presence of large birds. Such observations support the claim that monkeys have the cognitive capacity to associate perceptual categories with vocalizations.

The acquisition of these signals among vervets is interesting. Infant vervets appear to distinguish innately among broad classes of mammals, snakes, and birds, but they also give the 'eagle call' when other birds appear and the 'leopard call' when other terrestrial mammals appear. Adults distinguish between leopards and less dangerous mammals, and eagles and less dangerous birds (as well as between snakes and sticks), and it is claimed that this ability must be perfected through experience. This once again suggests that a mixture of innate components and learning is typical of the way some communication systems are naturally acquired.

5.4 Gibbons, orangutans, and chimpanzees

Since the higher primates are close genetic relatives of humans, it is natural to expect their vocal communication to resemble that of humans. Perhaps surprisingly, communication among the higher primates does not show much indication of discrete vocal signs that could be interpreted as resembling human words. Rather, the communication systems of these animals are made up of groups of graded vocal signs.

Gibbons and orangutans

Gibbons display an interesting form of vocal interaction known as duetting. **Duetting**, the interchange of calls in a patterned manner between two members of a species, is found among certain birds, bats, and even antelopes. Duetting is, however, atypical of primate communication—among the hominoids, only gibbons perform it. Recent playback experiments show that duetting among gibbons serves to maintain spacing among territories much as does birdsong (see Section 4.1). Playback of duetting within a gibbon's territory will cause it to approach the apparent source of the vocalizations, possibly with the intent of driving the intruders out. Playback of singing and duetting from outside a group's territory only infrequently evokes a response. Recognition of individuals does not appear to play a role in these vocalizations.

Unlike gibbons, which live in family groups, orangutans largely keep to themselves (except for mother-child pairs). Among the solitary forest males, loud calls serve a territorial and spacing function. These calls also identify the individuals who produce them. High-ranking males approach calls, presumably to confront the intruder, while low-ranking males stay away from areas where they hear the calls of high-ranking males. These calls are, in other words, indexes, which stand in for the individual animals themselves, and orangutans must identify and assess each of these calls before acting on them.

Chimpanzees

Chimpanzees vocalize with a number of graded calls. As many as sixteen types have been reported. Some of these appear to show rather specific referents. Chimps typically hoot to signal location (a sound that carries well in dense forest). Hooting is also used in greeting or when chimps are excited about something. Another typical vocalization is known as rough grunting and is given in the presence of a favorite food source. A recent experiment has led to the claim that transmission of signs from one generation to the next plays a role in the acquisition of certain signs among chimpanzees. (For more on tradition, see Section 7.1.)

'Language' in the wild?

Especially among highly socialized species, nonhuman primate vocalizations all show a great deal of variation. There is every indication that their vocalizations form part of a constellation of redundant communicative acts including gesture, posture, gaze (eye 'pointing'), and the expression of affect, all of which must be interpreted by other troop members. The obvious complexity of communication systems among these animals suggests that the level of mental activity devoted to communicative behavior is quite high.

Despite the high degree of intelligence and social organization these animals demonstrate, there is very little evidence for arbitrary relationships between sound and meaning among apes. Even more significantly, there is no evidence of recombining various sections of a message to form new messages. Nothing that parallels the phonemic or morphological recombination of human language has been discovered in the natural communication systems of nonhuman primates.

It is possible that the lack of parallels with human linguistic communication in species closely related to our own may be because of the nature of their social organization. The small groups or family units typical of chimpanzees and gorillas living in a food-rich environment may not have required the development of any other mode of communication. What has evolved is suited to their needs. This does not mean, however, that our near-relatives do not possess any of the cognitive abilities necessary for using a system of communication akin to human language. There is some evidence, for example, of left hemisphere development of the type associated with human linguistic ability. A number of recent experiments with nonhuman primates have attempted to determine the extent—if any—of their linguistic abilities.

6 TESTING NONHUMAN PRIMATES FOR LINGUISTIC ABILITY

Much attention has been paid in recent years to nonhuman primates who communicate with humans through the use of sign language.

Controlled testing of the possible shared linguistic abilities of nonhuman primates and humans goes back to 1948 when two psychologists attempted to train Viki, a young chimpanzee, to say meaningful words in English. With great effort, Viki learned to approximate the pronunciations of a few words like *cup* and *papa* over a period of fourteen months. Unfortunately, the experiment was doomed to failure from the start, since the vocal fold structure and supralaryngeal anatomy of the chimpanzee is unsuited for producing human sounds.

Chimpanzee vocal folds are fatty and less muscular than those of humans, and the neurological pathways between the brain and vocal folds are less developed than in humans. The chimpanzee's epiglottis extends well up into the throat cavity, which lessens the range of sounds it can produce. Finally, the whole larynx-tongue linkage rests higher in the chimpanzee throat, which results in limitations on its human-like sound production as well. In short, the chimpanzee is unsuited for producing human speech, and concentrating effort on teaching it to articulate words was distracting from the more provocative question: To what extent is the chimp mentally capable of linguistic behavior?

6.1 Some experiments

An experiment conducted from 1965 to 1972 by Allen and Beatrice Gardner with a young female chimpanzee named Washoe created a new perspective on nonhuman primate linguistic abilities. The Gardners attempted to raise Washoe much as a human child would be raised, and to teach her American Sign Language (ASL), on the assumption that it was a genuinely linguistic form of communication (of which there is no doubt). Given the known manual dexterity of chimpanzees, it was felt that sign language might provide a window on chimpanzee linguistic abilities.

Washoe

The Gardners' reports claim that Washoe communicates intentionally with arbitrary signs in a creative manner, and thus shows the rudiments of human linguistic ability. Washoe learned to produce approximately 130 signs over a period of three years. (She recognized many more.) Most significantly, it is claimed that Washoe spontaneously combined these signs to form novel utterances. She is reported to have signed WATER BIRD (in this chapter, signs are indicated by capital letters) on seeing ducks. Washoe also is said to have spontaneously produced BABY IN MY CUP when her toy doll was placed in her drinking cup and she was asked WHAT THAT?

Washoe was the first, but not the only chimpanzee to be taught sign language. The results have suggested to some linguists that chimpanzees show greater ability to associate arbitrary tokens with referents than was believed earlier, and that they demonstrate rudimentary syntactic behavior. Other chimps, gorillas, and an orangutan that have been taught ASL since the pioneering Washoe experiment are reported to have performed even better.

Nim

Still other experiments in teaching chimpanzees sign language have produced contradictory results. The achievements of a chimpanzee named Nim have been interpreted by his teachers as consisting of frequent repetitions of a small number of all-purpose signs (NIM, ME, YOU, EAT, DRINK, MORE, and GIVE) that were largely appropriate to any context. These signs are said to have made up almost 50 percent of Nim's production. Furthermore, there are no reports of his engaging in creative combining of signs.

6.2 Nonsigning experiments

Much of the criticism levelled at Washoe's performance centered on the relative informality of her training and claims that ASL is a loose communicative system that does not require a strict adherence to syntactic rules. Two very different experiments with chimpanzees attempted to forestall such criticism.

Lana

A chimpanzee called Lana was trained to fulfill her needs for food, fresh air, grooming, and entertainment (in the form of slide shows) by requesting these from a computer-controlled apparatus. Communication with the computer was carried out by means of a simple rule-governed language of nine arbitrary symbols. The symbols were on buttons that lit up and activated the computer when pressed. Any deviation from the syntactic rule system invented for the experiment failed to get the desired responses from the computer. Human experimenters communicated directly with the chimpanzee through use of the same symbols. Lana learned to label and request food and other amenities through the computer. The experiment with Lana was criticized because she was said to have learned simple reflex associations among symbol, sequence, and reward. There was no evidence that she had acquired the rules underlying the sequences, and so could not be said to have displayed linguistic abilities.

Sarah

Another now classic experiment involved training a young female chimp named Sarah to manipulate arbitrary plastic symbols in a predetermined manner in order to obtain rewards. Sarah had to learn to use word order correctly, since only the following order would obtain a banana.

Figure 16.13 Arbitrary symbols used in experiments with the chimpanzee Sarah

She also seemed to show sensitivity to more abstract words like *if/then* in sentences like those shown in Figure 16.14. But was Sarah learning aspects of human language or was she, too, trained? Humans who are taught similar skills perform them as well as Sarah but find it difficult to translate them into human language. They approach the exercise of moving plastic symbols around to obtain a reward as a puzzle that is not necessarily associated with language. It has been suggested that Sarah was performing the same kind of puzzle-solving and not demonstrating human-like linguistic capacities.

These studies have led to a resurgence of interest in human-animal communication. Language-using dogs, cats, pigs, and even turtles have been reported for thousands of years. The basis of much of the current criticism of all of these experiments rests on the performance of a horse in Germany at the turn of this century.

Figure 16.14 A 'sentence' understood by Sarah

6.3 The Clever Hans controversy

When I play with my cat, who is to say that my cat is not playing with me?

Michel de Montaigne, *Essays*

In 1904, a Berlin school teacher named Wilhelm von Osten claimed to possess a horse that showed evidence of a human-like capacity to think. His horse, **Clever Hans** (*der kluge Hans*), could supposedly calculate and convey messages by tapping out numbers or numbered letters of the alphabet with a front hoof or by nodding its head.

Experimentation by a skeptical scientist, Oskar Pfungst, eventually showed that Clever Hans was not so much a creative thinker as a careful observer: The horse perceived cues that indicated that he had performed correctly. For example, van Osten involuntarily moved his head very slightly when a correct answer had been reached. This movement (less than five millimetres) was outside the normal perceptual range of human observers, but the horse had learned to associate it with the correct answer. When observers did not know the answer to a question, or when Clever Hans was blindfolded, he failed to perform his miracles.

Clever Hans's performance resulted from **dressage**, a type of interaction between trainer and animal that depends on the animal's interpreting subtle cues given by the trainer. The Clever Hans phenomenon is an excellent example of dressage, which need not involve conscious communication on the part of humans. The highly developed perceptual ability displayed by Clever Hans is common to many animals. Many scientists believe that chimpanzees and gorillas that use sign language and perform other language-like tasks are demonstrating nothing more than the Clever Hans phenomenon.

The position is explained as follows. Human trainers want very much for their animal charges to succeed. This desire is translated into involuntary actions, which can be seized on by the animal because of its keen perceptual abilities; it is these cues that determine the animal's performance. A typical example of this is pointed out in

Washoe's signing of BABY IN MY CUP which has been recorded on film (*First Signs of Washoe*). A careful examination of this interchange shows that the human repeatedly holds out the object to be signed and then points rapidly at the cup. Probably none of this cueing was intentional on the human's part.

Some so-called linguistic activity may be the result of factors other than the Clever Hans effect. Some reports of creative signing, such as Washoe's WATER BIRD, are dismissed as reflex signing that shows no intention of forming combinations on the part of the chimp. Reports of the gorilla Koko's displays of wit (she occasionally produces the opposite sign of the one requested, such as UP for DOWN) are also considered to be exaggerated or simply wishful thinking by researchers.

Some reports of linguistic behavior are attributed to nonsystematic or inaccurate observing. (For example, if Washoe answered WHAT THAT with any noun sign, the answer was considered correct.) Other reports are attributed to overoptimistic interpretation of signs. (Koko is reported to intentionally produce 'rhyming' signs—those that are very similar to the ones asked for or expected.) In short, those who do not view chimpanzee signing and symbol manipulation as linguistically relevant claim that this behavior is more simply explained as arising from straightforward response-reward association and/or from dressage, and not a reflection of linguistic competence. As one researcher noted, training two pigeons to bat a ping-pong ball across a net does not mean that the birds know the rules of ping-pong.

6.4 The Great Ape Debate

We believe that . . . there is no basis to conclude that signing apes acquired linguistic skills.

Mark S. Seidenberg and Laura Petitto

When these projects [Washoe, Lana, Sarah, and Nim] are taken together, it can be seen that chimpanzees are within the range of language behavior of humans and therefore have the capacity for language.

Roger Fouts

Researchers involved with the chimpanzees and gorillas who are being taught to sign attest to the emotional bonds they form with them, and also emphasize that in using human language, such bonds are a prerequisite to normal communication. They strongly insist that apes communicate spontaneously and creatively with humans. Roger Fouts, who has spent many years in close contact with Washoe and other chimpanzees, puts the case this way.

> I reject the notion that there is some ultimate cut-and-dried criterion that distinguishes language from all other social and cognitive behaviors, or that distinguishes human communication and thought from that of all other species.

It is important to emphasize that most researchers sympathetic to the idea that apes show human linguistic abilities employ a broader definition of language than many of their critics. For these researchers, language use includes socialization and the use of communicative constellations.

For many linguists critical of these projects, a definition of language that rests on its social or functional aspects is unacceptable. In much current linguistic thinking, language is viewed as independent of the purposes it serves. This view, sometimes called the *linguistic autonomy hypothesis*, equates language with grammar—the "mental system that allows human beings to form and interpret the words and sentences of their language," to quote from Chapter 1 of this text. It follows from this definition that linguistic ability in nonhuman primates can only be claimed to exist if the animals produce, at the very least, spontaneous and intentional symbolic signs that are manipulated in a rule-governed manner.

Symbol use

All researchers who support the claim that nonhuman primates can employ intentional symbolic communication deny that cueing is a major factor in the apes' abilities, although most admit that it might be present on occasion. In order to refute charges of the Clever Hans effect, researchers employ a strict form of experimentation.

Primate sign language researchers try to avoid cueing by the use of a **double-blind test**. In this test, the ape is shown objects or pictures of objects that are invisible to a second human researcher. The ape's signing is then recorded by this researcher and the record is interpreted by a third researcher who has not seen the signing. In this way, unintentional cueing is said to be avoided.

Critics of this research claim that even double-blind tests can be affected by human-animal interaction. First, the apes must be taught to perform the task. During this process they may be conditioned to provide certain responses. Secondly, it is difficult to avoid any human-animal interaction during these tests, and this could lead to subliminal cueing. As we have also seen, many claims for symbolic behavior on any ape's part have been dismissed as stimulus-response conditioning—the mere mimicking of behavior in order to obtain a reward. We still have no way of knowing whether Washoe's use of a sign sequence like TIME-EAT indicates that she has a concept of time.

Ongoing work with two chimpanzees named Sherman and Austin has led to their exchanging signed information about classes of objects such as 'tool' and 'food'. These experiments are claimed to have circumvented any reliance on the Clever Hans effect and shown that signing apes can communicate about whole referential classes of items rather than be bound to simple stimulus-response association with individual items such as 'banana' and 'ice cream'.

Careful control of experiments has convinced some linguists that limited symbol use has been exhibited by some apes, perhaps even up to the level of a two-year-old human child. But some linguists who allow that a level of symbolic signing has been achieved have also denied this is a critical feature for defining language. Rather, rule-governed, creative symbol combinations and syntactic behavior are said to be the critical features.

Creative signing?

A feature of language that sets it apart from most animal communication is its creativity—the fact that humans can use language to create novel messages. Sign researchers claim that such creativity is present in the many instances of novel combinations signed by the animals.

An early and famous instance of alleged creative signing was Washoe's WATER BIRD (referred to in Section 6.3), which she signed on seeing a duck in the water for the first time. Such alleged compound signing behavior has been noted in various signing apes. Some of the gorilla Koko's novel combinations are provided in Table 16.2.

Table 16.2 Some sign combinations produced by Koko

Compound	*Referent*
MILK CANDY	rich tapioca pudding
FRUIT LOLLIPOP	frozen banana
PICK FACE	tweezers
BLANKET WHITE COLD	rabbit-fur cape
NOSE FAKE	mask
POTATO APPLE FRUIT	pineapple

Critics say either that such combinations are accidental or that the ape produces the two signs independently of each other and thus does not display true compounding. There is no doubt that Washoe signed both WATER in the presence of water, and BIRD in the presence of the bird, but there is no consistent indication from her other output that she has a rule of compound formation.

It has been claimed that in more recent and carefully controlled experiments with a pygmy chimpanzee (*Pan pansicus*) named Kanzi, statistically significant differences in the spontaneous ordering of symbols has been observed. The conclusion that has been drawn from this is that Kanzi has exhibited a form of grammatical rule. For example, Kanzi frequently used combinations of signs that link two actions, such as CHASE HIDE, TICKLE SLAP, and GRAB SLAP. In fifty-four out of eighty-four cases, the first sign corresponded to the invitation to play and the second to the type of play requested.

Is there syntax?

Claims for syntactic behavior among signing apes have also been made. Even though it has been claimed that the general (though loose) syntax of ASL is copied by the apes, reports on the signing chimp Nim (Section 6.1) showed that the animal had no consistent word order patterning. In fact, Nim's syntactic output was structurally incoherent. His longest sentence is reported as GIVE ORANGE ME GIVE EAT ORANGE ME EAT ORANGE GIVE ME EAT ORANGE GIVE ME YOU.

Koko is said to have developed her own word order in noun phrases—the adjective consistently follows the noun it modifies. It is difficult to prove claims for syntactic behavior in animal signing, because (all) signing forms constellations with facial expression and gestures and so may be said to reduce the need for rigorous syntax. Koko, for example, can sign a meaning like 'I love Coca-Cola' by hugging herself (the sign for *love*) while signing *Coca-Cola* at the same time with her hands.

In spite of what is now widely considered to be the disappointment of the earlier studies (possibly because they expected too much), some controlled experimentation continues. Recently, the pygmy chimpanzee Kanzi is reported to have produced significant (though not wholly consistent) differences in the placement of animate agents in sign combinations. When another chimpanzee named Matata was grabbed, Kanzi produced GRAB MATATA, but when Matata performed an action such as biting, Kanzi produced MATATA BITE.

Lingering doubts

As we have seen, supporters of language use among apes have not yet proved to the satisfaction of all their critics that genuine symbolic behavior is occurring, much less anything resembling rule-governed creativity in compounding or syntactic patterning.

Researchers who see the results of ape studies as positive evidence for linguistic ability in these animals claim that their opponents keep raising the stakes every time a chimp or a gorilla accomplishes something that could be interpreted as linguistic behavior. Possible evidence of symbol use or creative signing to indicate linguistic ability is dismissed by these opponents as unsurprising or irrelevant. Supporters of ape studies note that such critics are motivated by a long tradition of viewing animals as 'organic machines' that are locked into specific behavioral and communicative repertoires by their genetic inheritance, and that can therefore only respond automatically to a given situation with a narrow range of signs. Their own view, they claim, is at once more ancient and more modern in granting animals a certain as yet unknown degree of intentionality and cognitive ability in their behavior.

In general, recent experiments have established more convincingly than earlier ape studies that symbol use and referential behavior form part of the cognitive makeup of some nonhuman primates. Taken together with naturalistic studies, they help circumvent the claim that all evidence of symbol use among nonhuman primates is caused by the Clever Hans phenomenon.

Nonetheless, questions about creative sign combination and syntactic use still remain. Kanzi's alleged rules have been equated with those of a two-year-old child. But the major difference between a chimpanzee and a child at that point in their lives is that the elementary grammar of a two year old is the first hint of a full system that is rapidly developing and that will be in place in a matter of a few more years. While Kanzi's communicative behavior constitutes interesting evidence for a chimpanzee's awareness of the world, it does not unequivocally imply a system of grammar. It has been noted, for example, that Kanzi's 'rules' are often bound up with a natural order of action or relationships (as when the sign GRAB precedes the sign SLAP).

The apparent lack of rule-governed behavior among signing apes (especially in the realm of syntax) remains to critics of these experiments the linguistic hurdle that the animals have not overcome. It is certain that apes do not show syntactic behavior to any degree that humans do (for example, embedding is completely lacking) and many linguists claim that without such behavior, the apes cannot be said to be using language. Syntax, in the strict linguistic sense, provides a system of rules capable of producing a sentence of potentially infinite length (even though in practice this is never required). There is no evidence that primates have shown this ability.

6.5 Implications

Critics of the ape studies have at this time carried the day. Many funding sources for ape-human research have dried up, and most of the subjects have lost their privileged relationships with humans and been returned to zoos. But the severe reaction to the apparent failure of ape-human linguistic communication research has had positive effects on the field as well. Recent trends—the number of experiments on animal cognition in the wild, and the more carefully controlled experiments with apes like Kanzi—are leading us slowly closer to new ideas on this age-old issue.

The real significance of these experiments in ape-human linguistic communication goes far beyond popular enthusiasm about what an ape might say to us if it could talk. It has often been pointed out that an animal's view of the world must be totally unlike our own. It is perhaps not surprising that apes appear to communicate largely about their fundamental emotions and such basic needs as food and play.

In time, this research may help illuminate what is truly unique about human linguistic ability. As we have seen, many linguists claim that there is no connection between the communicative behavior of nonhuman primates and the complex structures of human language. The opposing view claims that the capacity for true grammatical activity can be found in nonhuman primates. This implies that what we call language reflects a cognitive difference in *degree* and not in *kind* between humans and these animals. The optimistic view is that such research may ultimately shed light on the evolutionary origins of our species and its language use by demonstrating the degree of shared cognitive abilities between ourselves and our nearest genetic relatives.

7 COMPARING COMMUNICATION SYSTEMS: DESIGN FEATURES

Throughout this chapter, we have emphasized the distinction between communication and language. In this final section, we will compare human linguistic communication with what we have learned about systems of animal communication.

7.1 THE FEATURES

Differences and similarities between human language and natural animal communication systems can be highlighted by comparing essential characteristics of the systems. These characteristics are called **design features**, and are set up (perhaps unfairly) with reference to human language. Since this book emphasizes the essentially mental nature of linguistic ability, the design features that follow do not include the traditional reference to vocal-auditory transmission. What is emphasized is the nature of the semantic and organizational structuring of each system. These design features represent an adaptation of those of Charles Hockett and W. H. Thorpe, as noted at the end of this chapter.

1. ***Interchangeability*** All members of the species can both send and receive messages.

   This is obviously true of human language. It is not the case with bee dancing (performed only by foragers) or birdsong (performed only by males). Nonhuman primate vocalizations appear to be interchangeable.

2. ***Feedback*** Users of the system are aware of what they are transmitting.

   Humans monitor their linguistic output and correct it. It is debatable whether bees do so when they dance, or whether birds monitor their calls. It is not known if birds monitor their song; it is likely that they do.

3. ***Specialization*** The communication system serves no other function but to communicate.

   Human language represents reality—both external (real world) and internal (states, beliefs)—symbolically in the mind. Manifested as speech, language serves uniquely as a communicative system. Bee dancing and birdsong also appear to be specialized communicative activity. Alarm calls of any species may be symptomatic but at the same time are specialized for different types of predators. Symptomatic tokens, on the other hand, are unspecialized. Crying is a symptomatic sign that may be interpreted by someone else and thus function communicatively, but its primary purpose is physiological (the clearing of foreign matter from the eye, the release of emotional tension). If animal communication is primarily symptomatic—a claim that is hotly disputed by specialists in animal communication—then it would not qualify as a specialized communicative system.

4. ***Semanticity*** The system conveys meaning through a set of fixed relationships among signifiers, referents, and meanings.

   Human language conveys meaning through arbitrary symbols. Bee dancing conveys meaning, but within a very limited range, as do bird calls and song. The range of meaning is broader and more subtle in nonhuman primate vocalizations. Although we cannot claim to know the minds of such near relations as chimpanzees and gorillas, it appears that the range of meanings suggested by their behavior in the wild does not approach the vastness of human semanticity (see feature 8).

5. ***Arbitrariness*** There is no natural or inherent connection between a token and its referent.

   This is true of human language, with the possible exception of a few onomatopoeic terms. Bee dancing shows arbitrariness in that there may be no connection between the form of the dance and the distance from the hive. Expressions of food source quality and direction are not arbitrary, however. Many bird calls are highly suited for their purpose, such as danger calls which are difficult to locate, and in this sense are not arbitrary. Most nonhuman primate vocalization appears to be equally adaptive. Arbitrariness has, however, been claimed for vervet monkey alarm calls.

6. ***Discreteness*** The communication system consists of isolatable, repeatable units.

   Human language shows distinctive features, phonemes, syllables, morphemes, words, and still larger combinations. There are two (three, in some dialects) discrete types of bee dances, but these dances are not combined in various ways to produce novel messages. There is some evidence for subunits in birdsong. They are also present in primate call systems.

7. ***Displacement*** Users of the system are able to refer to events remote in space and time.

   Bee dancing shows displacement. No evidence for displacement is found in bird calls or songs. Baboons occasionally produce threat and fight vocalizations long after an aggressive encounter, but there is no evidence that this is reflecting displacement; it probably reflects a slow winding down of the animal's affective state. Among apes, it is not yet clear whether some degree of displacement is a feature of either their communication in the wild or the systems they have learned from humans. Nonhuman primates do not appear to communicate about imaginary pasts or futures, which humans are able to do with language.

8. ***Productivity*** New messages on any topic can be produced at any time.

   This is obviously true of human language. Bees show limited productivity. Bird calls show none. Birdsong shows evidence of recombination (the songs of laughing gulls are well documented in this respect), but it is doubtful whether these recombinations transmit novel messages. This is also true of recombination in the calls of certain monkeys, such as macaques.

9. ***Duality of patterning*** Meaningless units (phonemes) are combined to form arbitrary signs. These signs in turn can be recombined to form new, meaningful larger units.

   In human language, phonemes can be combined in various ways to create different symbolic tokens: *spot*, *tops*, *opts*, and *pots*. These tokens in turn can be combined in meaningful ways: *Spot the tops of the pots*. There is no evidence of this type of patterning in any known animal communication system.

10. ***Tradition*** At least certain aspects of the system must be transmitted from an experienced user to a learner.

    This is obviously a factor in the acquisition of human language. It is possibly present in a very limited way in bee communication, and it is definitely present in the acquisition of birdsong for some species. As noted in Section 5.3, there is some recent evidence for a degree of tradition among chimpanzees.

11. ***Prevarication*** The system enables the users to talk nonsense or to lie.

    Undoubtedly, this property is found in human language. There are specialized mimics among birds, fishes, and even insects. A few examples of animal deception have been noted among the arctic fox and among vervets, but it is not clear whether this is normal species-specific behavior or the acts of a few isolated individuals. The question of intentionality is crucial here. Current work with birds suggests that some species learn as many songs as possible and use this repertoire to maintain territorial advantage by 'impersonating' other species. This may well be purely genetically determined behavior, but, in any event, it is highly complex.

12. ***Learnability*** A user of the system can learn other variants.

    Humans can learn a number of different languages. Bees are limited to their own genetically specified dialect. Bird calls are apparently limited in this same way. As noted previously, some birds learn the songs of other species, but this may well be simply mimicry. Nonhuman primates seem restricted to their own systems.

13. ***Reflexiveness*** The ability to use the communication system to discuss the system itself.

No evidence exists that any other species writes grammars or linguistics textbooks.

Tables 16.3 and 16.4 summarize this survey of design features.

Table 16.3 Summary of design features for bees and birds

Design feature	*Bees*	*Birds*
1. Interchangeability	no; foragers only	no; only males sing
2. Feedback	?	?
3. Specialization	yes	yes
4. Semanticity	yes, very limited	yes, limited
5. Arbitrariness	yes, for expressing distance	yes, though highly adaptive
6. Discreteness	in a limited way	yes, in song
7. Displacement	yes	no
8. Productivity	yes, very limited	possibly
9. Duality of patterning	no	no
10. Tradition	possibly, but highly limited	yes, limited
11. Prevarication	no	possibly
12. Learnability	no	possibly
13. Reflexiveness	no	no

Table 16.4 Summary of design features for nonhuman primates and humans

Design feature	*Nonhuman primates*	*Humans*
1. Interchangeability	yes	yes
2. Feedback	probably	yes
3. Specialization	in part	yes
4. Semanticity	yes	yes
5. Arbitrariness	limited confirmation; selectively adaptive	yes
6. Discreteness	in call systems	yes
7. Displacement	no	yes
8. Productivity	possibly	yes
9. Duality of patterning	no	yes
10. Tradition	possibly	yes
11. Prevarication	possibly	yes!
12. Learnability	no	yes
13. Reflexiveness	no current evidence	yes

Summing up

This brief overview of animal communication systems emphasizes that human language is one communication system among the many that life forms on this planet employ.

Communication can be described with reference to the **sign**, which is composed of two components, a **signifier** and that which is **signified**. Tokens may be **iconic**, **symbolic**, or **indexical** (the latter including the **symptomatic** token), and structured as **graded** or **discrete** types. Most animal communication has traditionally been viewed as symptomatic, though studies of communication among birds and bees suggests symbolic signs are used. A significant innate component may interact with some exposure to the communication system, especially among birds. Nonhuman primate communication consists of graded series of vocalizations and appears to show little arbitrariness, though some has been reported for the alarm calls of several monkeys.

Experiments with nonhuman primates have created controversy over whether chimpanzees and gorillas have shown symbolic behavior and a capacity for linguistic behavior. Many researchers have dismissed the work as an example of **dressage** or the **Clever Hans** phenomenon.

Human language and systems of animal communication share certain **design features**. Humans, however, lack many communicative skills that animals possess. We are hopelessly inadequate at following scent trails, a feat that prosimians accomplish with ease; we cannot change color for communicative purposes with the facility of an octopus; and we are not as gifted as horses and many other mammals at assessing and interpreting subtle body gestures. Humans do possess an ability to symbolize which far exceeds that of chimpanzees and gorillas (our nearest genetic relatives), even allowing for the most generous interpretation possible of recent experiments. Human language is also more flexible and productive in manipulating these symbols than any known animal communication system. Language is as suited for and as much a part of human life patterns as the communication systems of our fellow creatures are for their modes of existence.

Key terms

arbitrariness
call
Clever Hans
constellation
design features
discrete (sign)
displacement
double-blind test
dressage
duality of patterning
duetting
feedback
graded (sign)
iconic sign
indexical sign
interchangeability
learnability
meaning
pheremones
prevarication

productivity
redundancy
reflexiveness
semanticity
semiotics
sign
signals
signified
signifier
song
specialization
spectrogram
stimulus-bound (communication)
symbolic sign
symptomatic sign
template
tokens
tradition

Picture credits

Chimpanzee facial expressions in Figure 16.1 and question 3, and monkey facial expressions in Figure 16.5, are adapted from S. Chevalier-Skolnikoff's "Facial Expression and Emotion in Nonhuman Primates" in *Darwin and Facial Expression*, edited by P. Ekman (New York: Academic Press, 1973), pp. 11–90. The baboon open-mouth threat in Figure 16.3 is adapted from a photograph in K. R. L. Hall and I. DeVore's "Baboon Social Behavior," in *Primate Behavior*, edited by I. DeVore (Toronto: Holt, Rinehart and Winston, 1965), pp. 53–110; park information signs in Figure 16.3 are courtesy of Alberta Provincial Parks. Figure 16.7 is adapted from D. Todt's "Serial Calling as a Mediator of Interaction Processes: Crying" in *Primate Vocal Communication*, edited by D. Todt, D. P. Goedeking, and D. Symmes (Berlin: Springer-Verlag, 1988), pp. 88–107 and reprinted by permission of the publisher. Bee dancing (Figure 16.8) is adapted from K. von Frisch's *The Dance Language and Orientation of Bees*, p. 57 (cited in sources). Copyright © 1967, 1993 by the President and Fellows of Harvard College. Reprinted by permission of Harvard University Press. The spectrogram of the robin song (Figure 16.9) is from *Bird-Song* by W. H. Thorpe (cited in sources) copyrighted and reprinted with the permission of Cambridge University Press. Avian isoglosses in Figure 16.10 are from Paul Mundinger's "Microgeographic and Macrogeographic Variation in Acquired Vocalizations of Birds," in *Acoustic Communication in Birds*, Vol. 2, edited by D. E. Kroodsma, E. H. Miller, and H. Ouellet (New York: Academic Press, 1982), pp. 147–208 and reprinted by permission. Figure 16.12 illustrating the response of vervet monkeys to predators is taken from *Animal Language* by Michael Bright (cited in sources). Tokens used in the Sarah experiments (Figures 16.13 and 16.14) are taken from D. Premack and A. J. Premack as cited on p. 179 in E. Linden's *Apes, Men, and Language* (Baltimore, MD: Pelican Books, 1974).

Sources

The theory of semiotics outlined in this chapter is drawn from several recent works on semiotics, including T. Sebeok's *Contributions to the Doctrine of Signs*, Studies in Semiotics 5 (Bloomington, IN: Indiana University Press, 1976), *I Think I Am a Verb*

(New York: Plenum Press, 1986), and U. Eco's *Semiotics and the Philosophy of Language* (Bloomington, IN: Indiana University Press, 1984). Bee communication is drawn from K. von Frisch's "Dialects in the Language of the Bees" in *Scientific American* 202 (2): 78–87 (1962) and his work *The Dance Language and Orientation of Bees,* translated by C. E. Chadwick (Cambridge, MA: Harvard University Press, 1967). Bird vocalization is based largely on W. H. Thorpe's *Bird-Song* (Cambridge, MA: Cambridge University Press, 1961). Jake Page's parrot is reported in *Science* (1982). Lemur vocalizations in Table 16.1 are drawn from A. Jolly's *Lemur Behavior* (Chicago: University of Chicago Press, 1966). Vervet communication is drawn from R. M. Seyfarth and D. L. Cheney's "How Monkeys See the World," edited by Snowden et al. (cited below). Creative signing by Koko is reported in F. Patterson and E. Linden's work *The Education of Koko* (New York: Holt, Rinehart and Winston, 1981). The reference to cultural transmission of signs among chimpanzees is drawn from Michael Tomasello's "Cultural Transmission in the Tool Use and Communicatory Signaling of Chimpanzees?" in Parker and Gibson (cited below), pp. 274–311; some of the material on invented rules by the pygmy chimpanzee Kanzi is drawn from Patricia Marks Greenfield and E. Sue Savage-Rumbaugh's "Grammatical Combination in *Pan paniscus,*" also in Parker and Gibson, pp. 540–76; this volume contains a number of other articles relevant to the question of nonhuman primate cognitive and linguistic abilities. Some question material is drawn from various articles in *How Animals Communicate,* edited by Thomas A. Sebeok (Bloomington, IN: Indiana University Press, 1977).

Recommended reading

Bright, Michael. 1984. *Animal Language*. London: British Broadcasting Corporation.

Cheney, Dorothy L., and Robert M. Seyfarth. 1991. *How Monkeys See the World.* Chicago: University of Chicago Press.

de Luce, Judith, and Hugh T. Wilder, eds. 1983. *Language in Primates: Perspectives and Implications*. New York: Springer-Verlag.

Hockett, Charles. 1960. "The Origin of Speech." *Scientific American* 203 (3): 88–96.

Lieberman, Philip. 1984. *The Biology and Evolution of Language*. Cambridge, MA: Harvard University Press.

Parker, Sue Taylor, and Kathleen Rita Gibson. 1990. *"Language" and Intelligence in Monkeys and Apes: Comparative Developmental Perspectives*. Cambridge, Eng.: Cambridge University Press.

Sebeok, Thomas A., and Jean Umiker-Sebeok. 1980. *Speaking of Apes*. New York: Plenum Press.

Sebeok, Thomas A., and Robert Rosenthal, eds. 1981. *The Clever Hans Phenomenon: Communication with Horses, Whales, Apes, and People*. Annals of the New York Academy of Sciences 364. New York: The New York Academy of Sciences.

Snowden, C. T., C. H. Brown, and M. R. Petersen, eds. 1982. *Primate Communication*. London: Cambridge University Press.

Thorpe, W. H. 1974. *Animal Nature and Human Nature*. Garden City, NY: Doubleday.

Questions

1. The following signs are all symptomatic.
   a) Dogs wag their tails when happy, cats flick their tails when irritated.
   b) An octopus, when showing aggressive behavior, becomes bright red.
   c) The Canada goose shows aggressive intentions by opening its mouth, coiling its neck, and directing its head toward an opponent. When it is unlikely to attack, its mouth is closed, its head is horizontally extended, and its head is directed away from an opponent.
   d) Tree leaves change color in the fall.
   e) The presence of stratocumulus clouds accompanies good weather.

   i) Explain why we can say that each case involves a symptomatic sign.
   ii) Signs in some cases may be iconic or symbolic in addition to being symptomatic. Identify which cases contain mixed signs, and which sign is the primary sign.

2. Find two examples each of *iconic, symbolic,* and *indexical* signs you encounter in the course of a day. Is it possible to classify unambiguously each sign as to type? If not, state why in each case.

3. What do the following chimpanzee facial expressions convey? Using a mirror, try to imitate the facial expressions; does this make it easier for you to label them? What characteristics of the signs lead you to your conclusion in each case?

4. Observe an animal in a zoo or at home for at least one-half hour. Try to discover at least three unambiguous signs the animal employs to communicate. Describe each one in terms of both *signifier* and *signified.* (A good way to do this is to note carefully the context in which the sign is given, to whom it is addressed, and what the receiver's response is to the communication.)

5. Add two columns to the list of design features presented in Tables 16.3 and 16.4. For one column, take the perspective of a researcher who believes that apes show

Answers to question 3: *a)* submission; *b)* excitement, perhaps affection; *c)* desiring, perhaps mixed with frustration true linguistic ability in their signing, and fill in the column from this point of view. Fill in the other column from the perspective of a researcher who does not believe such ability has been shown. Be sure to comment on each design feature.

6. Now that you have been exposed to both sides of the ape language issue, summarize your own conclusions about it. Do you believe that human language is different in degree or in kind from the communicative behavior of the great apes? Why?

seventeen

COMPUTATIONAL LINGUISTICS

Judith Klavans

How comes it that human beings, whose contacts with the world are brief and personal and limited, are nevertheless able to know so much as they do know?

– BERTRAND RUSSELL

Imagine that you have a robot, but the robot does not talk or understand language. It is your job to program the robot to speak English (or any other language), and to program it to understand what you say to it. One of the central questions in **computational linguistics** is this: What would a computer program have to contain to enable the computer or the robot to analyze, understand, and create sentences and paragraphs correctly? These sentences could be either spoken or written. This is something that we humans achieve effortlessly. However, consider the amount and type of information that a computer would have to know about language in order to understand a simple sentence like this:

1)

The essay reads well and provides strong arguments.

First, the computer would have to understand the meaning and use of each of the words. For example, the computer would need to know that when the determiner *the* is used, this indicates a specific essay. The determiner *a* or *an* would indicate that it is the class of items or entities known as *essays* which read easily; this is the kind of usage found in a sentence like *An apple a day keeps the doctor away.* Since the subject of the sentence, *essay,* is a singular noun, then the computer would have to know that the verb must be singular, in order to avoid sentences like **The essay read well.* But this is only true in the present tense, since in the past, the verb *read* would serve both for singular or plural, as in *Yesterday's essay read well.* This is because *read* is an irregular verb, with homophonous verb forms (as discussed in Chapter 4 on morphology, and Chapter 7 on semantics).

In addition to this grammatical knowledge about *the* and about agreement between subject and verb, there is a great deal of other information people have about sentence *1)*. For example, we know that essays are written and thus are likely to be read, and that essays are likely to contain arguments. This is called **real-world knowledge** as distinct from **grammatical knowledge**. For example, although telephone messages are written, and are likely to be read, they are unlikely to contain arguments. Furthermore, when analyzed carefully, the verb *read* has several uses. One is the transitive use, in which the subject is the Agent (the entity that performs the action), as in *The professor read forty essays*. The other is the intransitive use in which the subject of the sentence, in this case *essay*, is the Theme (the entity undergoing the action).

In sentence *1)*, the Agent is not explicit; we do not know who is doing the reading. These two ways of using the verb *read* are related, but their interpretation is quite different. Finally, the word *strong*, like many adjectives, has many different meanings in context. The most common use of *strong* is to mean *powerful* as in *strong muscles*; another common use is found in *strong odor*. The interpretation of the word *strong* depends on the noun argument, relating to the fact that arguments have a gradation of effectiveness, measured from weak or unconvincing to strong or persuasive.

What sort of knowledge about pronunciation would a computer need to know to utter this sentence? The rules of pronunciation, like the rules of grammar, are different for each language. They are likely to vary within the same language depending on many factors. For example, the vowel in *the* when preceding a consonant is pronounced as a schwa /ə/ (see Chapter 2), whereas when preceding a vowel, it is pronounced as /i/. English speakers know that the letter *e* in *the* is to be pronounced differently depending on the initial phoneme in the word that follows. But this is not true for every word ending in the sound /i/. For example, the words *we* and *flea* do not change pronounciation so drastically according to the word that follows, although there is always some adjustment in spoken language. Another fact of pronunciation concerns the verb *read*: is this present or past tense? Of course, there is more to pronunciation than just converting letters to sounds, as is shown in Chapters 2 and 3, and in later sections of this chapter.

These examples are sufficient to illustrate the quantity and variety of information that humans know about language. We take this knowledge for granted. Until we try to write computer programs to understand or generate even the most simple sentences, there is no need to pick apart the knowledge about language that we possess. However, computers are only as capable as the humans who program them, so it is the task of the linguist to spell out this knowledge for the computer. This is a major undertaking, involving all aspects of knowledge of language.

Computational linguistics is a relatively new discipline that lies at the intersection of the fields of linguistics and computer science. It is but one of many new hybrid disciplines involving computers that require computational expertise as well as a background in another field. The term *computational linguistics* covers many subfields. It sometimes refers to the use of computers as a tool to understand or implement linguistic theories. This means that linguists and computer scientists can gain a better understanding of the scientific and research questions by using computers.

On the other hand, the term is sometimes used to refer to working systems or applications in which linguistic knowledge is needed. In this case, the questions and issues are usually ones of software engineering as well as of theory.

This chapter is organized around subfields of linguistics that are discussed in other chapters in this book: phonetics and phonology, morphology, syntax, and semantics. There is also a section on computational lexicology. The first part of the chapter shows how each linguistic subfield is used as the basis for a computational linguistic subfield. The second part of the chapter shows some ways in which these various subsystems are combined to create computer systems that use language.

1 COMPUTATIONAL PHONETICS AND PHONOLOGY

1.1 THE TALKING MACHINE: SPEECH SYNTHESIS

At the 1939 World's Fair in New York, a device called a vocoder was displayed. The machine, developed by scientists at Bell Laboratories, reconstructed the human voice by producing a sound source which was then modified by a set of filters. The values for the filters were derived from the analysis of human speech. The vocoder system consisted of a source of random noise for unvoiced sound, an oscillator to give voicing, a way to control resonance, and some switches to control the energy level. This was to simulate the vowel sounds and fricatives (see Chapter 2). Then there were controls for the stop consonants /p,b/, /t,d/, and /k,g/. An amplifier then converted the modified source signal into sound that resembled the human speech it was originally modeled after.

The vocoder was nicknamed the Talking Machine. It was a crude device, but it demonstrated that good speech synthesis could indeed be achieved, given the right values for the major frequencies, and the right methods of concatenating and modifying adjacent values. Early systems used different technology from that used today, but the principles remain the same. The goal is to replicate the wave forms that correctly reflect those of human speech in order to produce speech which, at the very least, will be intelligible and aesthetically pleasing and, in the ultimate, could not be distinguished from the speech of a human being.

Chapter 2 gave a summary of articulatory phonetics, that is, how sounds are made when humans speak. Chapter 3 covered some aspects of sound systems. Speech recognition and speech synthesis rely on a detailed knowledge of acoustic phonetics as well as articulatory phonetics, although there are correlations between the acoustic and articulatory properties of sounds. Acoustic phonetics is the study of the structure of the wave forms that constitute speech. As was explained in Chapter 2, the lungs push a stream of air through the trachea. The air stream is modified first at the glottis and then by the tongue and lips.

Each sound can be broken down into its fundamental wave forms, as shown in Figure 17.1. The figure shows a spectrographic analysis or **spectrogram** of the words *heed, hid, head, had, hod, hawed, hood,* and *who'd* as spoken by a British speaker.

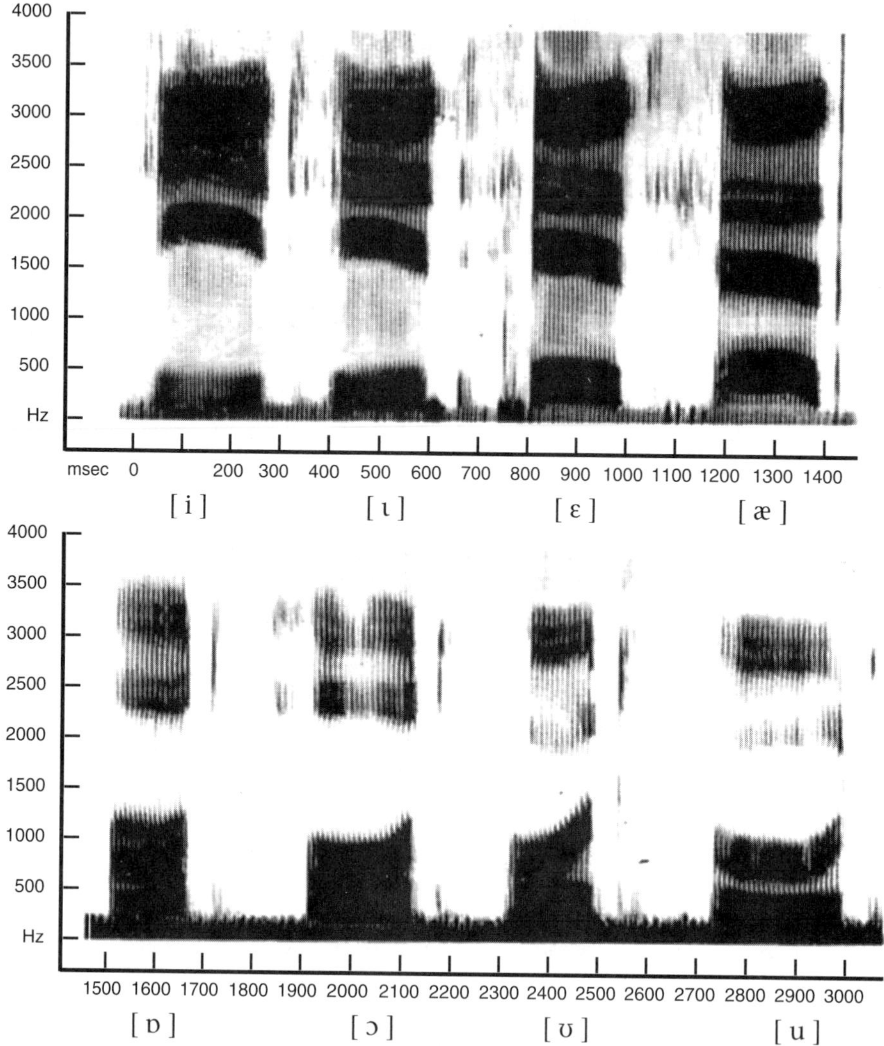

Figure 17.1

The diagrams give a visual representation of the duration of the utterance on the horizontal axis, and the different frequencies in the wave form on the vertical axis. The main frequencies, or **formants**, show up because they have more intensity than other frequencies. Note the different locations of the formants along the frequency dimension for the different vowels. The sound /h/ is only slightly visible as fuzzy lines across the spectrum because /h/ is a voiceless fricative with little or no glottal constriction (see Chapter 2, Section 5). The acoustic effect is weak "white noise" resembling fuzz or static. The /d/ is a stop, so there is just a low-frequency "voice bar" resulting from the vibrations in the glottis, but there are no vowel formants for the period of closure since the air flow is blocked. This shows up as blank space on the spectrogram. For speech synthesis, the first three formants are the most critical for identifying different vowels. The others add some refinement to the sound, but they do not determine intelligibility or naturalness with the same significance as the first three formants.

Since different vowels are composed of different frequencies, in theory the task of the speech synthesizer is simply to replicate those vowel sounds, put in a few consonants, and string them together just as letters are strung together to make words and sentences. Unfortunately, the matter is not so simple, since sounds are not fixed. Rather, they vary according to the segments that surround them. Effects occur on adjacent segments and across groupings, sometimes as far as six phonemes away. For example, Figure 17.2 shows the same phonetic vowel [æ], but notice the rises and slumps in the formants. The figure shows how adjacent consonants can modify vowels. Similarly, vowels modify consonants. Nasal sounds modify larger chunks of surrounding speech. On top of these local changes, there are changes to entire phrases based on suprasegmental features such as stress and intonation (see Chapter 2, Section 9).

Many steps are involved in achieving speech synthesis, and there are many different choices in ordering these steps. The text to be spoken has to be analyzed syntactically, semantically, and orthographically. Pronunciations for exceptional words such as *have* /hæv/ or *four* /fɔr/ must be found. These words do not follow the predictable letter-sound correspondences of English: *have* does not rhyme with *nave* or *rave*, and *four* does not rhyme with *sour* or *glamour*. Contrastive sounds need to be assigned based on the letters and other information about the word. After the correct phoneme is chosen, a system must look at the environment to see which allophone of the phoneme to choose. For example, to return to Figure 17.2, if the system were trying to pronounce *bab* /bæb/, the vowel /æ/ corresponding to the labial onset and labial offset would be chosen, since labials tend to lower adjacent formants.

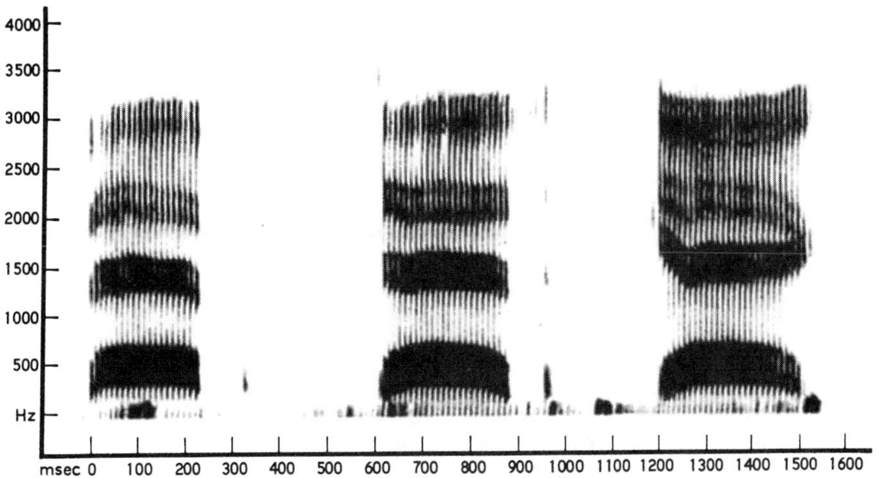

Figure 17.2 Spectograms of the words *bab, dad, gag*

A syntactic analysis of a sentence permits a system to identify words that might go together for phrasing. This is particularly important for noun compounds in English. As many as six nouns can be strung together, and the pronunciation of the compound can change the listener's interpretation of the meaning. For example, the phrase *Mississippi mud pie* could have two interpretations, depending on its structure. The most likely interpretation is shown in Figure 17.3, where the mud pie is Mississippi style.

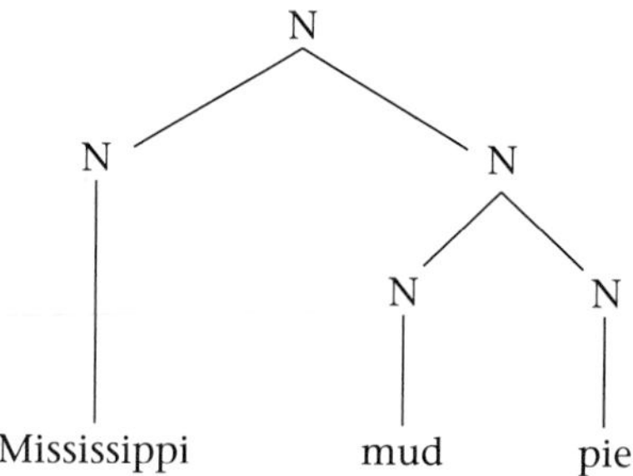

Figure 17.3

Alternatively, the pie could be made of mud from Mississippi, in which case the syntax of the phrase is different, as shown in Figure 17.4, and so is the pronuncia-

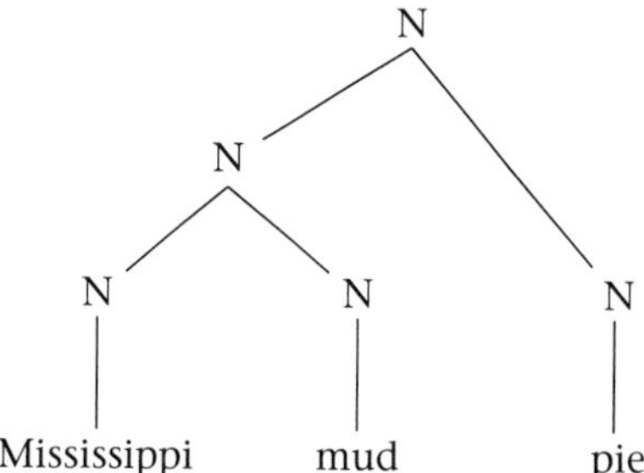

Figure 17.4

tion. Syntactic analysis can also determine the part of speech for noun/verb pairs that are spelled the same but pronounced differently, such as the verb *record* /rəkɔ́rd/ and the noun *record* /rɛ́kərd/.

Also, parentheticals will be identified, as in these sentences:

2)

Here are the apples, as you can see.

3)

He said, although I don't believe it, that he was a good driver.

Parentheticals are typically pronounced at a lower pitch and loudness. When pronounced with main phrase intonation, they are difficult to understand. Finally, a semantic analysis of a sentence, and of a text, gives an idea of focus and stress. These features must be translated into duration (length), pitch, and loudness in order for synthetic speech to sound completely natural.

Given advances in computer technology, along with advances in electronics and acoustics, intelligible speech synthesis has already been achieved. However, everyone who has seen popular science fiction films knows that even now, synthetic speech still sounds synthetic. In addition to the syntactic and semantic issues raised above, a number of difficult problems remain, such as incorporating intonational variety into the rules to eliminate the droning quality of synthesized speech, and improving individual sounds.

1.2 Speech Recognition or Speech Analysis

As we have seen, speech consists of very complex wave forms changing rapidly across time and in subtle ways, which can affect the perception of a message. The task of speech recognition is to take these wave forms as input and decode them. This is exactly what we humans do when listening to speech. The wave form that reaches the ear is a continuous stream of sound; we segment the sound into words, phrases, and meaningful units so we can determine the meaning of the utterance. The task of a speech recognition system is to teach a computer to understand speech, whether the system models human mechanisms or not.

Even though human beings have no trouble decoding speech wave forms, computers do. The problems are immense. First of all, as is shown in Chapter 2, Section 9, speech sounds are modified by adjacent sounds in natural speech. The faster and more informal the speech, the more sounds are merged and dropped. Guessing what sounds have been dropped based on faulty and limited input is an extremely difficult task. Knowledge of context, of syntactic structure, and of probabilities of occurrence is helpful, but the problem is still not solved.

Since decoding of continuous speech presents such problems, some systems impose the requirement that words be pronounced slowly, and separated by a slight pause. The pause gives a clear cue that the word has ended, so a system has much less guesswork to do. Also, if the speech is said more slowly, fewer sounds will be dropped. In addition to the constraint of pronouncing words in isolation, limiting a system's vocabulary means that the recognition machine will have less guesswork to do. Finally, yet another way to reduce the guesswork is to require that an individual user "train" the system to be tailored to his or her voice alone. Anyone who is skilled at recognizing voices can attest to the fact that no two people sound alike. The purpose of "training" a computer is to familiarize it with the unique and distinguishing features of the user's voice.

Another very difficult problem for speech recognition is what is called the **cocktail party effect**, such as that of being in a crowded room. Even though there is much noise from other people, from music, or from the street, humans manage to filter out the background noise and pick out a particular sound or conversation to listen to. Everyone has had the experience of not hearing a sound, such as a leaking faucet, until someone points out the sound, and the annoying sound then becomes the only one to be heard. Whatever mechanisms were used to suppress the noise of the faucet were deactivated when brought to the listener's attention. Computer recognition systems cannot distinguish the speech signal from the noise, so they perform poorly in noisy environments. Thus, another condition—a reasonably quiet environment—must be imposed on systems in order for them to function adequately.

Each of these constraints can be imposed to result in more reliable systems, but the overall research problem still remains: Why is it that humans are so adept at decoding speech yet computers cannot be easily taught to do so?

2 COMPUTATIONAL MORPHOLOGY

Morphology is the study of the internal structure of words, covering such topics as affixation, compounding, and infixation (see Chapter 4). Most research in computational morphology arose as a by-product of developing natural language processing systems. Looking up words in a computational dictionary for these systems turned out to be more complicated than met the eye, precisely because of morphological processes that can conceal the base word. For example, if a dictionary has the word *book*, the word *books* would not be found by a simple search. Unless a system is explicitly told that *book* is related to *books* by a productive and regular rule of inflectional morphology, it would not be able to infer that those words are related. Thus, a program needs to include the rule of pluralization in English as well as other rules in order to recognize or generate the morphological permutations of words.

2.1 MORPHOLOGICAL PROCESSES

Most morphologically conditioned changes in written English involve spelling, with some changes in stems. Examples are *stop/stopped, sing/sang,* and *tolerate/tolerant.* In general, morphological variations in English are not as opaque as in other languages. Some languages, such as German, have very productive compounding, whereas others have infixation and reduplication, or complex stem changes. Words altered by morphological processes cannot be easily recognized by a natural language processor unless they are properly related to their bases for lexical lookup.

Implementing morphological processes: method one

Broadly speaking, there are two approaches to computational morphology. Historically, the first was called a **stemming** or **stripping algorithm**. An algorithm is a set of rules for solving a problem; the term was first used in mathematics to describe the rules for solving mathematical problems. Since algorithmic procedures usually involve a sequence of repeated steps, the term is naturally suited to computer programs in general, and to programs for computational linguistics in particular. In the stemming or stripping algorithm, affixes are recursively stripped off the beginnings and ends of words, and base forms are proposed. If the base form is found in the base-form dictionary, then the word is analyzable. Successful analyses provide information about the internal structure of the words as well as whatever other information is produced by the rule for a given affix, such as part of speech change, inherent semantic changes (e.g., *-ess* is +feminine), or other information (e.g., abstract, Latinate, singular, plural). Most of these systems are sensitive to constraints on affix ordering such as described in the chapter on morphology. Inflectional affixes occur outside of derivational affixes, and there may be some derivational affixes that occur outside of other derivational affixes.

Two different types of dictionaries are possible with the stemming method: word-based and stem-based. A word-based system has a dictionary with words only. For word generation, all input to morphological rules must be well-formed words, and all output will be well-formed words. For word analysis, all proposed stems will be words. The word-based system has proven to be very useful for projects that use large machine-readable dictionaries, since dictionaries list words, not stems. A machine-readable dictionary is a dictionary that appears in computer form, such as that available in spelling checkers or thesauruses. Machine-readable dictionaries have definitions, pronunciations, etymologies, and other information, not just the spelling or synonyms. (See Section 4 for more on machine-readable dictionaries.)

Table 17.1 presents an example of the type of analyses given by a word-based stemming system. To analyze *conceptualize* as an infinitive verb (V form(inf)), first

Table 17.1 Input word: conceptualize

Analysis	*Part of speech*	*Features*
concept	N	num(sing)
-ual	A	
-ize	V	form(inf)

conceptual must be analyzed as an adjective (A). This would be done by a rule stating that the suffix *-ize* can attach to certain adjectives to create verbs. *Conceptual* can be analyzed as an adjective if *concept* can first be analyzed as a singular noun (N num(sing)). This would be done by a rule for *-ual* stating that the suffix *-ual* can attach to certain nouns to create adjectives. *Concept* is stored in the dictionary as a singular noun, so this lexical lookup serves as the final step of the analysis. The analyses shown here actually result from recursive calls to the morphological rules. Each rule has conditions that restrict its operation. In this example, the *-ual* rule states that the base must be a singular noun. The condition for the *-ize* rule is that the base must be an adjective (but compare *terrorize* and *hospitalize*, where in each case the base, namely *terror* and *hospital*, is a noun). Since each condition is met, an analysis is possible. The word *conceptualize* is deemed a well-formed infinitive verb.

How would the system analyze a more complex form? Consider the analyses in Table 17.2 of the word *conceptualizations*, which is based on the previous example.

Table 17.2 Input word: conceptualizations

Analysis	*Part of speech*	*Features*
concept	N	num(sing)
-ual	A	
-ize	V	form(inf)
-ation	N	num(sing)
-s	N	num(plur)

In this example, the suffix *-ation* attaches to infinitival verbs. Notice that when *-ation* attaches to *conceptualize*, there is a spelling change. If no spelling rules were written, then the word **conceptualizeation* would be allowed by the system. Finally, the plural marker *-s* is attached at the outside of the noun. For the plural suffix *-s*, there is no change in the part of speech, but only in the number feature of the word from singular to plural. Observe that these examples illustrate a word-based system. Both the dictionary entry, in this case *concept*, and the complex words *conceptualize* and *conceptualizations* are well-formed words of English.

How would this system differ if it were stem-based? For this example, the morpheme *-cept* might be listed in a stem dictionary, due to its presence in other words in English, such as *reception, conception, inception,* and *perception.* Since *-ceive* and *-cept* are related in a regular way, this relationship might also be given in the stem dictionary, or the words could be related by rule. Consider again *conceptualizations*, analyzed down to a stem in Table 17.3. In this example, the prefix *con-* attaches to *-cept.*

Table 17.3 Input word: conceptualizations

Analysis	*Part of speech*	*Features*
con-		
-cept	N	num(sing)
-ual	A	
-ize	V	form(inf)
-ation	N	num(sing)
-s	N	num(plur)

The point was made earlier that a word-based morphology system can use a regular dictionary as its lexicon, but no such convenience exists for a stem-based system. In order for stem-based morphology to get wide coverage, a large dictionary of stems is required. (More on this topic is found in the section on computational lexicology later in this chapter.)

Implementing morphological processes: method two

The other common approach to computational morphology, the two-level approach, is fundamentally different from the stemming approach. This results in basic differences in computational properties. Both systems contain a lexicon or dictionary, although two-level morphology *requires* a stem-based lexicon. Both systems have rules, but the rules are very different. In two-level morphology, the rules define correspondences between surface and lexical representations; they specify if a correspondence is restricted to, required by, or prohibited by a particular environment. *Lexical* roughly corresponds to *underlying*, whereas *surface* usually means *orthographic* but sometimes *phonemic*. In Figure 17.5, the lexical representation of *try* followed by the *+s* is compared with a surface representation *tries*.

Lexical and surface representations are compared using a special kind of rule system called finite-state transducer. Simply put, the rules would decide whether the lexical *y* could correspond to the surface *i* based on information the rules have already seen. The rules that compare lexical and surface form move from left to

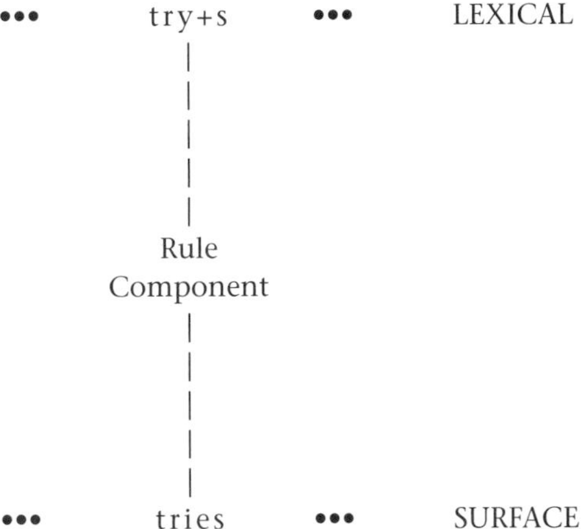

Figure 17.5

right, so when a successful correspondence is made, the rule moves along. One of the claimed strengths of this method is that, since the procedure moves from left to right, it accurately reflects the way that people process words. Since people hear and read English from left to right (i.e., the beginning of the word is encountered before the end), a system that incorporates this directionality might be an actual model of processing. Furthermore, since the two-level system processes from left to right for morphological analysis, it can easily be reversed and function from right to left for morphological generation. The primary drawback of the two-level system is that it requires a specialized stem dictionary, complete with restrictions on the stems so that not all affixes attach without restrictions. For example, a dictionary would need to include *-cept* or *-mit* (for *transmit, submit, permit,* and so on).

2.2 Some problems in computational morphology

Compounding is a particularly thorny problem since it tends to be so productive that compounds are often not listed in a dictionary. The word *bookworm,* for example, does not appear in *Webster's Seventh New Collegiate Dictionary.* A good morphological analyzer should be able to analyze *bookworm* as shown in Table 17.4. However, what about a word like *accordion?*

Table 17.4 Input word: bookworm

Analysis	*Part of speech*	*Features*
book	N	num(sing)
worm	N	num(sing)

The analysis in Table 17.5 shows *accordion* to be composed of the noun *accord* plus the noun *ion.* This is obviously incorrect because *accordion* is not a compound analogous to *bookworm.* Since *accordion* does not ever have this analysis, it might be marked as an exception to morphological decomposition.

Table 17.5 Input word: accordion

Analysis	*Part of speech*	*Features*
accord	N	num(sing)
ion	N	num(sing)

A related problem arises due to overenthusiastic rule application. Table 17.6 presents an analysis of *really*. Here *really* is analyzed as [*re*- [*ally*- $_{\text{verb}}$]$_{\text{verb}}$], meaning "to ally oneself with someone again." This analysis is correct, although highly improbable. Cases like that of *re*- in *really* bring up a difficult issue. Should a word like *really* be specially marked in the dictionary as a nonanalyzable word, an exception to the rules that would apply to regular formations like *reapply, redo,* and *reduplicate*? Or should the rules be allowed to apply freely? What about a word like *resent,* which could either be [*re*-[*sent*$_{\text{verb}}$]$_{\text{verb}}$] as in *He didn't get my letter, so I resent it,* or [*resent*$_{\text{verb}}$] as in *Did he resent that nasty comment*? The spelling of this word is truly ambiguous, so a decision about its analyzability requires knowledge of syntactic and semantic features in the sentence and context. Usually the decision is driven by practical concerns. A system that is designed to implement a theory, but that does not need to perform well on a task that applies the theory, would probably allow the rules to apply freely. A system that needs to perform accurately on large texts would probably mark *really* and *resent* as nonanalyzable words, even though strictly speaking they are not.

Table 17.6 Input word: really

Analysis	*Part of speech*	*Features*
re-		
ally	V	form(inf)

3 COMPUTATIONAL SYNTAX

Research in computational syntax arose from two sources. One was the practical motivation resulting from attempts to build working systems to analyze and generate language. Some of these systems, such as machine translation and database query systems, are discussed in Section 6. The other source was a desire on the part of theoretical linguists to use the computer as a tool to demonstrate that a particular theory is internally consistent. In this case, less value was given to efficiency or broad coverage since this was not the goal. The emphasis was instead on theory testing and on formal issues in natural language analysis. Ideally, builders of practical systems should take more advantage of theoretical insights, and linguistic theoreticians should pay more attention to practical problems. This has been the case in recent research on parsing, although this is a fairly new friendship.

3.1 Natural language analysis

Parsers and grammars

Chapter 5 showed how sentences can be analyzed by rules into substructures such as noun phrases, verb phrases, prepositional phrases, and so on, as shown in Figure 17.6. Given a system of rules, an analyzer will be able to break up and organize a sen-

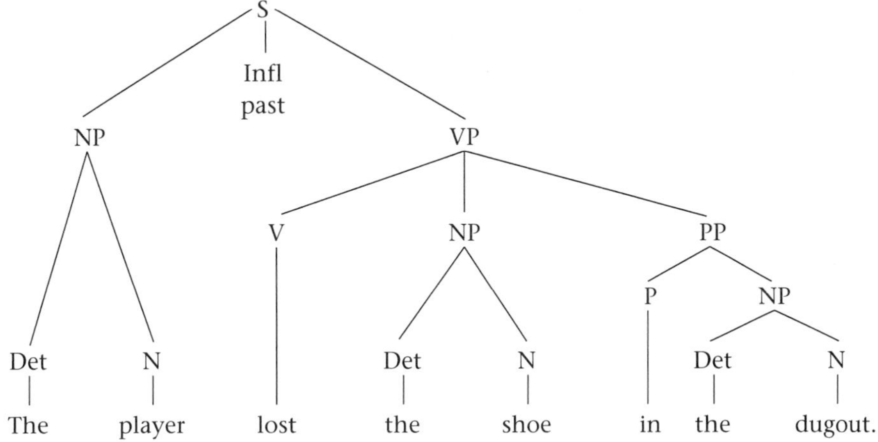

Figure 17.6 A syntactic analysis done by a parser

tence into its substructures. A grammar can be viewed as the set of rules that define a language. These rules can be of different shapes or formats, which give them different properties. A **parser** is the machine or engine that is responsible for applying the rules. A parser can have different strategies for applying rules. Chapter 5 showed how the rules for sentence structure differ between languages. These differences are reflected in the grammars for these languages, although the parser that drives the grammars can remain constant. (Recall the discussion of the role of parsers in language processing in Chapter 11.)

Determinism vs. nondeterminism

Any time a syntactic parser can produce more than one analysis of the input sentence, the problem of backtracking is raised. For example, if the beginning of the sentence in Figure 17.7 is read word by word, there is more than one possible end-

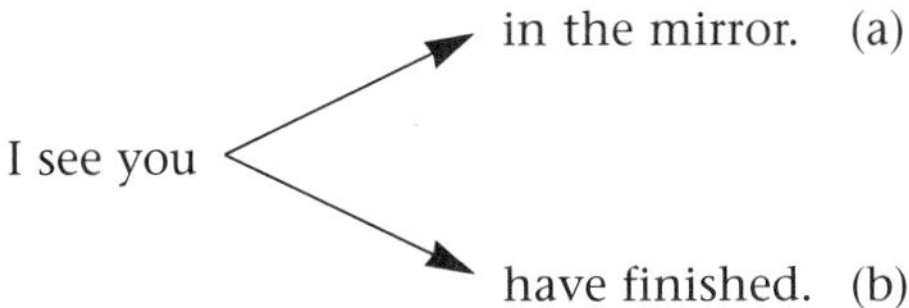

Figure 17.7

ing. In choice (a), the word *you* is the object of the main verb *see.* For (b) the word *that* has been left out, as is permitted in English, so the word *you* is the subject of the clause *you have finished.* If the parser follows path (a), and if that path turns out to be the wrong one, how can the situation be rectified to get the right analysis? Or can choices be controlled so that a parser never has to undergo the time-consuming task of going back and starting over? (See also the discussion of garden path sentences in Chapter 10.)

The term **nondeterministic** may refer to going back or backtracking if the first analysis turns out to be impossible. It may also mean following multiple paths in parallel, meaning that both analyses are built at the same time but on separate channels. By contrast, the term **deterministic** means that the parser has to stick to the path it has chosen. There have been many proposals about controlling the backtracking of parsers. The problem is a serious one since the number of alternatives increases as the coverage of a system increases. The result is that as an analyzer improves, it also becomes more and more cumbersome because each time it is presented with more and more options.

Top-down vs. bottom-up parsing

Consider the following phrase structure rules for English (introduced in Chapter 5):

4)

a. S → NP Infl VP
b. NP → (Det) (AP) N (PP)
c. VP → V (NP) (PP)
d. PP → P NP

There are two ways to build an analysis of a sentence, using just these rules. This section illustrates the principles of what is called **top-down** and **bottom-up parsing**. Working systems may not be built to function exactly like this, but the principles are the same.

In addition to the rules in *4),* we also need to give some lexical items, or **terminal nodes**, for each category or **nonterminal nodes**.

5)

N → Larry
Infl → past
V → sat
P → on
Det → the
N → grass

Generally speaking, a nonterminal is not a word in the language. Rather, it is a category or a phrase, such as N or NP. A terminal can be thought of as a word (although sometimes a terminal is a part of a word or several words). In top-down parsing, the analyzer always starts with the topmost node, in this case S, and finds a way to expand it. The only rule in the set *4)* for S is shown in Figure 17.8. Both NP and VP are nonterminal nodes. The next rule to apply is the NP expansion rule and then the

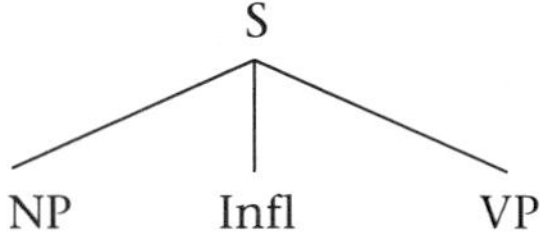

Figure 17.8 Top-down parsing: first step starts with S

VP expansion rule. The results are shown in Figure 17.9. Although N is a nonterminal, it has no expansions, so the next rule to apply would be the VP rule. If the subject of the sentence had been *the batter*, then the NP would have been expanded to Det and N. This process continues until no more expansions could apply, and until all the lexical items or words in *5)* occur in the correct position to match the input

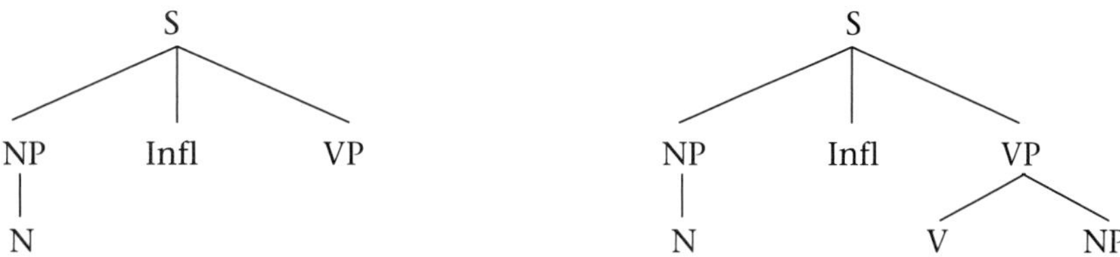

Figure 17.9

sentence *Larry sat on the grass*. Top-down parsers suggest a hypothesis that a proposed structure is correct until proven otherwise.

In contrast, bottom-up parsers take the terminals (words) of a sentence one by one, replace the terminals with proposed nonterminal or category labels, and then reduce the strings of categories to permissible structures. For the same example, the analysis would be built as follows: First the word *Larry* would be assigned the cate-

Figure 17.10

gory N; then *sat* would be assigned to V, and so on. The partial analysis up to this point is shown in Figure 17.10. None of the rules in *4)* permit the combination of N

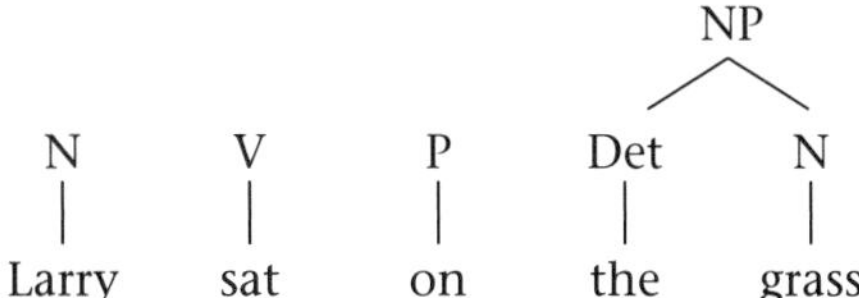

Figure 17.11

and V; none permit V and P nor P and Det to combine. But the NP rule does combine Det and N to build up a structure, as shown in Figure 17.11. This continues until the structure of a sentence is built. It has been proposed that the building of the structure from the terminal nodes up to the topmost S node from left to right reflects the way human beings process sentences more accurately than the top-down approach, but this is a controversial issue.

Generative capacity

The term *generative* in this context refers to formal properties of grammars as mathematical systems. It does not refer to language generation, which is discussed below. Recall that a grammar consists of a set of rules that describe a language. Assume also some finite set of symbols, *V*, the vocabulary of a language. For English, examples of *V* would be:

6)

V_L = [*player, shoe, child, lost, a . . .*]

In the vocabulary *V* are other symbols and categories, such as *N* and *Det*. Formally, a language *L* over *V* is a finite set of strings of symbols taken from *V*. Informally, a language consists of strings from the vocabulary. Of course, a sentence is more than just a string of words, as shown in Chapter 5. Furthermore, the set of strings is greater than the set of well-formed sentences, as sentences *7)* to *9)* show. Even though the vocabulary *V* may be a finite list, the language *L* may be finite or infinite. This is because of recursion, a very powerful property of natural languages. (Chapter 5 contains a discussion of recursive rules.) The application of a finite number of recursive rules results in languages that can contain an infinite number of well-formed strings.

The following sentences consist of vocabulary from the set in *6)*. While *7)* is a well-formed sentence in English, *8)* and *9)* are not.

7)

A child lost a shoe.

8)

*child shoe a.

9)

*Lost a shoe a child.

Although *9)* is not in the language *L* for English, it could be found in the language *L* for Spanish, given the same vocabulary.

10)

Perdió un zapato un niño.
lost a shoe a child

The grammar of English would give a correct description of *7)*, but not *8)* or *9)*. On the other hand, the grammar of Spanish would allow both *7)* and *9)*, but not *8)*. The goal of an implemented grammar is exactly the same. An **implementation** is simply a practical system. The grammar rules are programmed into a computer, and the computer program then decides if the string is permitted in the language. If the string is permitted, it then has the task of giving the sentence the correct description.

Natural languages (as opposed to computer languages) are highly complex, so discovering the correct grammar for a given language is an extremely difficult task. The complexity and subtlety of natural languages continue to present a challenge to linguists. There are many competing theories of what the "correct" grammar of natural languages will be like. Even the grammar for English, a very well-studied natural language, is not at all well-understood. One issue that all theories agree upon, however, is that a grammar should have certain properties. Grammars should give a correct description of the following:

A. The strings of a language *L*
B. The structures corresponding to the strings in *L*

Property A is called **weak generative capacity**. Property B is called **strong generative capacity**. (Generative here does not mean "create" but rather "describe.")

To explain, Figure 17.6 shows an analysis in which the first two words *the* and *player* are joined into a noun phrase (NP). Infl is dominated by S. The verb phrase (VP) is described by the grammar as consisting of a verb (V), followed by a noun phrase (NP), followed by a preposition phrase (PP). These three constituents are immediately dominated by the VP node. What if a different grammar were to claim a different structure for this sentence? Consider the structure in Figure 17.12. This

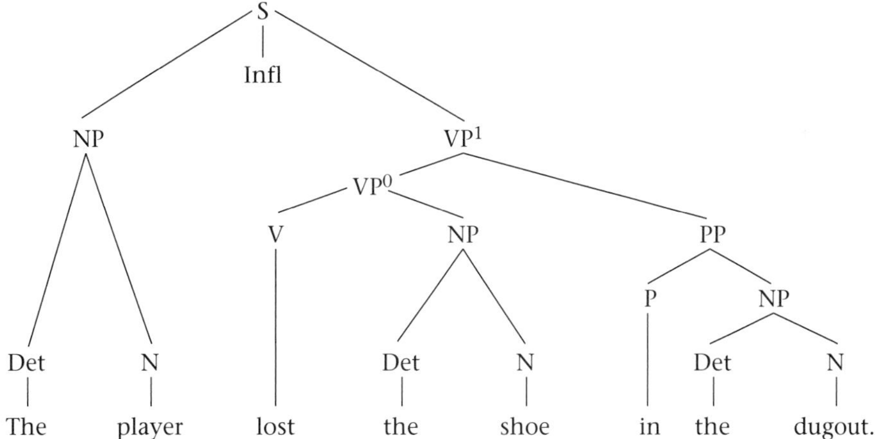

Figure 17.12

analysis makes different claims about the structure of the sentence, but the actual string of words stays the same. The tree in Figure 17.12 has two levels of verb phrase. One is VP^1, which dominates everything in the predicate of the sentence (everything in the sentence except the subject and Infl). The other is VP^0, which dominates only the main verb and the direct object. The grammar generating the structure in Figure 17.12 differs in strong generative capacity from the grammar for Figure 17.6.

However, both grammars may have the same weak generative capacity since they both have the ability to describe the string *The player lost a shoe in the dugout.*

The role of syntax and semantics

The preceding section dealt with syntactic analyzers, but it is important to note that the division between what should be handled by the syntactic component of a system and what is properly in the semantic component is a matter of great debate. For example, some systems might claim that selections of prepositions by verbs, often considered a syntactic property, is actually dependent on the semantic category of the verb. For example, not all verbs can take the instrumental, as in the reading of *11)* in which *the bone* was used to reward the dog.

11)

He rewarded the dog with a bone.

If a different verb is substituted for *rewarded,* would the sentence be semantically or syntactically ill-formed?

12)

?He told his story with a bone.

Some systems assume that a syntactic analysis precedes a semantic one, and that the semantics should be applied to the output of syntactic analyses. This is the position of the earliest transformational models, which was incorporated into many computational systems. Some systems perform syntactic and semantic analyses hand-in-hand. Other systems ignore the syntactic, viewing it as a second-step derivative from semantic analyses.

3.2 Natural language generation

What is generation?

To utter a sentence, a speaker first must decide on goals, plan the information to be included, and then express that information in a sentence of his or her language. The language generation problem is often viewed as the reverse of the language analysis problem, but this is not accurate. In the same way, the generation of speech, discussed in Section 6, is in no way simply the reverse of speech recognition. Certain problems are the same, but many are not.

Language generation has been the underling of computational linguistics. The reason for this may be that it is a more difficult area to work in than language analysis. For language analysis, the linguist is given a set of data (i.e., strings of the language) with which to work. For language generation, the linguist has ideas and plans that need to be turned into language. A language generator must be able to make decisions about the content of the text, about issues of discourse structure, and about cohesion of the sentences and paragraphs. In contrast, a language analyzer might be invoked to make proposals about discourse and content, but the raw material upon which guesses are based is already there. For the language generator, only concepts and ideas are available to work with. Choices of words (lexical items) and syntactic structures are part of decisions to be made in building a text.

As with syntactic analyzers, there are two approaches to generation: top-down and bottom-up. In the top-down approach, first a very high-level structure of the output text is determined, along with very abstract expressions of meaning and goal. Then lower levels are filled in progressively. Subsections are determined, and examples of the verbs with their subjects and objects, if any, are proposed. This is refined, until the prefinal stage when lexical items are chosen from the dictionary. After all sentences have been decided upon, and after all lexical items have been inserted, there is a component to "smooth" and provide low-level coherence to the text. This component makes sure that pronouns are used correctly, for example, and that connecting phrases such as *in the preceding paragraph* or *on the other hand* are used correctly. In contrast, the bottom-up approach builds sentences from complex lexical items. First, words to achieve the goals are hypothesized. Then sentences are composed, and finally high-level paragraph and text coherence principles are applied.

The generation lexicon

The lexicon is just one link in many difficult steps involved in generating natural and cohesive text for an underlying set of goals and plans. Imagine that you have determined an underlying message, plan, or goal. In order to figure out how to translate the underlying message into some actual words in a language, your generation system will have to figure out such matters as what verbs to pick and how to pick the subjects and objects, if any, for those verbs.

Suppose you want to express how fast time is going by in your life. You might use the verb *elapse. Elapse* is said to be a one-place predicate or a one-place verb. It is intransitive, so it takes just one argument, the subject. (The term *argument* here refers to grammatical dependents of a verb.) If you want to talk about baseball, you need to describe the action. You might use the verb *hit. Hit* is transitive; it takes two arguments. *Hit* is also often used with an instrumental, a phrase that tells what the subject hit *with,* as in *with a bat.* In this case, *hit* can take three arguments. Finally, a verb like *give* takes an agent, theme, and goal, and those three arguments can be expressed as a subject, object, and indirect object, indicated by *to* as in *13).* Alternatively, *give* can undergo what is called Dative Movement, as in *14),* in which case the indirect object *dog* appears next to the verb and is not preceded by the preposition *to.*

13)

He gave a stick to the dog.

14)

He gave the dog a stick.

Often verbs with very close meanings take different numbers of arguments and in different order. For example, *give* can also mean *donate,* but *donate* does not permit the same alternations as *give.*

15)

He donated a stick to the dog.

16)

*He donated the dog a stick.

A system must be capable of deciding what the meaning to be conveyed is, and then it must be capable of picking very similar words to express that meaning. The lexicon or dictionary must supply items to instantiate the link between meaning and words.

The design and content of the generation lexicon is one of the most difficult areas in language generation. The lexicon needs to contain many different types of information, such as syntactic facts about verbs, facts about usage and focus, and facts about types of modifiers. Building lexicons for generation is one of the goals of computational lexicology, as discussed in the following section.

4 COMPUTATIONAL LEXICOLOGY

Since phrases, sentences, and paragraphs are composed of words, computer systems need to contain detailed information about words. The section on morphology dealt with the structure and analyses of word forms, but there is more to know about words than this.

Computational linguists are realizing that an analyzer or generator is only as good as its dictionary or lexicon. The lexicon is the repository of whatever information a particular system needs. The individual words in the lexicon are called lexical items. Chapter 5, Section 2, shows how lexical insertion occurs in syntactic structure. For example, in order for a bare structure such as Figure 17.13 to be "filled out"

Figure 17.13

with real words, a program would need to have a match between a word marked Det in the lexicon and the slot in the tree requiring a Det. The same goes for any part of speech, such as noun, verb, or adjective. Given the items in *5)*, a valid match for Figure 17.13 would be Figure 17.14. Figure 17.15 would not be a valid match. Notice that the preposition *on* occurs under the determiner node, and the verb *sat* occurs

Figure 17.14 ***Figure 17.15***

under the noun node. At the very least, the condition of matching part of speech has to be met.

A computer program would need to know more than just part of speech to analyze or generate a sentence correctly. Subcategorization, that is, the number of arguments a verb can take, must be considered (see Chapter 5). Knowledge of thematic roles, such as agent, patient, and goal, is also needed (see Chapter 7, Section 2). A syntactic analyzer would also need to know what kinds of complements a verb can take (see Chapter 5).

17)

I decided to go.

18)

*I decided him to go.

19)

*I persuaded to go.

20)

I persuaded him to go.

The verb *decide* can take the infinitive *to go* as in *17)*, but it cannot take an NP object and then the infinitive, as in *18)*. The verb *persuade* is the opposite. It cannot take the infinitive *to go* as in *19)*, but it must have an NP object before the infinitive, as in *20)*.

The lexicon needs to know about the kinds of structures in which words can appear, about the semantics of surrounding words, and about the style of the text. For example, sentence *21)* is strange in meaning, but the structure is fine.

21)

I broke the concept.

The verb *break* is transitive and so can take an object, but the problem here is the type of noun. Only concrete objects are breakable, unless the meaning is metaphorical as in *The disease broke his will to live.* (See Chapter 7 for more discussion of semantics.)

What does a computational lexicon look like? So far the list of information includes:

22)

Lexical Entry
1. Part of Speech
2. Sense Number
3. Subcategorization
4. Semantic Properties

Keeping in mind that a computational lexicon has to contain as much information as possible in order to correctly analyze and generate phrases, sentences, and text, the following are also needed:

22) (continued)

5. Pronunciation
6. Context and Style
7. Etymology
8. Usage (e.g., taboos)
9. Spelling (including abbreviations)

The task of collecting all the important information for every existing word in the English language is awesome. In addition, given that the kind of information needed cannot be found in conventional dictionaries, how are computational lexicons built? There are several approaches. One is to hand-build a lexicon specifying only those features that a given system needs and using only the lexical items that are most likely to occur. For example, assume that an analyzer is reading the *Wall Street Journal,* and assume that the sentence to be analyzed is *His interest is high this month.* If the analyzer is to assign a meaning to this sentence, it has to know at least the information below.

Word: interest-1
1. Part of Speech: Noun
2. Inherent Semantic Features: [+concrete], . . .
3. Context: Financial

In just this usage, there is no reason to know about the abstract meaning of *interest* as "attention" or "concern." The lexical entry for this other sense would include the information below.

Word: interest-2
1. Part of Speech: Noun
2. Inherent Semantic Features: [+abstract], . . .
3. Context: Emotional

Most words have many different senses, and sometimes the different senses have very different grammatical behavior. Every time a new word is added to the lexicon, if a new feature is also added, then the dictionary builder has to go back through the lexicon and modify every word to match the new expanded word. When *interest-2* was added to the dictionary, new features had to be added, namely that *interest-1* does not have a context "Emotional" and that *interest-2* does not have a context "Financial." One of the major problems in building computational dictionaries is extensibility. The problem is how to add new information, and modify old information, without starting over each time.

Another option in building large lexicons is to use two resources: the power of the computer and the data of machine-readable dictionaries. A machine-readable dictionary (**MRD**) is a conventional dictionary, but it is in machine-readable form (i.e., on the computer) rather than on the bookshelf. (An example is the *Longman Dictionary of Contemporary English,* which has been widely used for computational purposes.) MRDs are useful in building large lexicons because the computer can be used to examine and analyze automatically information that has already been organized by lexicographers, the writers of dictionaries. Unfortunately, the type of information that is needed by a computational dictionary is not always easy to find in a conventional dictionary. However, with some clever approaches to exploiting the hidden information in conventional MRDs, it appears that many important facts can be pulled out and put into a computational lexicon. This work is at a fairly early stage, so it is uncertain how far it can be pushed, but it is an important line of research in computational linguistics.

For example, the knowledge that a word has a sense that is [+human] is needed in a computational lexicon for both syntactic and semantic reasons. *Webster's Seventh New Collegiate Dictionary*, which has about seventy thousand headwords, has just over a thousand nouns that are defined in terms of the word *person*. Some examples are given below:

accessory
  a *person* not actually or constructively present but contributing as an assistant or instigator to the commission of an offense—called also accessory before the fact
acquaintance
  a *person* whom one knows but who is not a particularly close friend
intellectual
  a very intelligent or intellectual *person*
scatterbrain
  a giddy heedless *person*: FLIBBERTIGIBBET
unbeliever
  one that does not believe: an incredulous *person*: DOUBTER, SKEPTIC

Notice that each word can have other senses. *Accessory*, for example, can mean an object or device that is not essential but that enhances the main object. A program has been written to extract these words. The headwords are then marked [+human], and synonyms such as *flibbertigibbet, doubter,* and *skeptic* can also be marked as [+human] in one sense.

Although this approach is appealing, caution is in order. In the first place, lexicographers are people, and dictionaries are huge undertakings written by many different contributors. Therefore, there is less internal consistency than would be ideal. Finally, and most seriously, there is the problem that most words have more than one sense. Keeping track of which senses have which features is not an easy task. Furthermore, the decision on what is a sense is also not clear-cut. The problem of extensibility enters into play again. Even with all these restrictions, however, using machine-readable dictionaries as a resource for constructing large lexicons looks very promising.

Another approach to building large lexicons for natural language analysis and generation is **corpus analysis**. The larger the corpus, or text, the more useful it is, since the chances of covering the language as it actually is used increase. In addition to size, a good corpus should include a wide variety of types of writing, such as newspapers, textbooks, popular writing, fiction, and technical material. As an example of the way large corpora (the plural of corpus) are useful, consider the verb of movement *flounce*. The definitions given for the verb in *Webster's Seventh New Collegiate Dictionary* are:

flounce 1
  to move with exaggerated, jerky motions
  to go with sudden determination
  to trim with flounces

These definitions tell nothing about likely subjects. Looking at corpus data will yield this information. From a large corpus, about twenty occurrences of the verb *flounce* were extracted. Thirteen had subjects that were female, as in sentences *23)* and *24)*.

23)

Carol flounced out to the kitchen for an apron.

24)

She flounced off with a following of hens behind her.

Four had subjects that were clothing:

25)

The white cashmere dressing-gown flounced around her.

One had *horses* as the subject, and the other subjects were pronouns. The point is that, given a good parser, it would be possible to extract automatically all the subjects of a given verb, and then to look for properties of those subjects. For *flounce*, that information would appear in the lexicon as:

Word: flounce-1

1. Part of Speech: Verb
2. Subcategorization: Intransitive
3. Semantic Properties: Female human subject

Word: flounce-2

1. Part of Speech: Verb
2. Subcategorization: Intransitive
3. Semantic Properties: Clothing subject

Using computers to extract linguistically useful information from dictionaries and texts for the purpose of constructing large lexicons is a new field within computational linguistics. The use of statistical methods to analyze language has seen great advances in recent years, giving promise in providing a solution to the difficult but fundamental problem of building computational lexicons out of already existing resources. At this point, clever programs give large and comprehensive lists of words with a potential characteristic, but human judgments are still necessary. If the computer is viewed as a tool to be used in collecting lists of words, then the endeavor is successful. If the goal is to view the computer as the only tool, and to eliminate the human judge, then computational lexicon builders still have a long way to go.

5 COMPUTATIONAL SEMANTICS

So far in this chapter, we have focused on structure: the structure of sentences and words. However, in order to understand what a word, sentence, or text means, a computer program has to know the semantics of words, sentences, and text. This section treats briefly some of the semantic representations and processes that have been proposed in computational linguistics.

Semantic issues were touched on in the preceding section. The lexical item contains a field for semantic information, including such information as what kind of semantic features a verb requires for its subject or which thematic roles a verb requires or permits. The semantic fields for the two senses of *flounce* are:

Word: flounce-1
Semantic Restrictions: Female human subject
Word: flounce-2
Semantic Restrictions: Clothing subject

Although the semantics of words is an important component of any language system, there is yet a broader issue: the semantics of sentences and paragraphs.

Two approaches to semantics and language analysis have been proposed: syntactically based systems and semantically based systems. Considering for the moment the analysis of sentences, in the first approach the sentence is assigned a syntactic analysis, much in the way outlined in Chapter 5 and earlier in this chapter. A semantic representation is built after the syntactic analysis is performed (see Figure 17.16). The problems arise in getting from one representation to the other. This is sometimes called the mapping problem. However, in the semantically based system, first a semantic representation is built. Sometimes there is no syntactic analysis at all (see Figure 17.17). Consider a response to the question *Who got the coffee today?*

Syntactically Based Systems

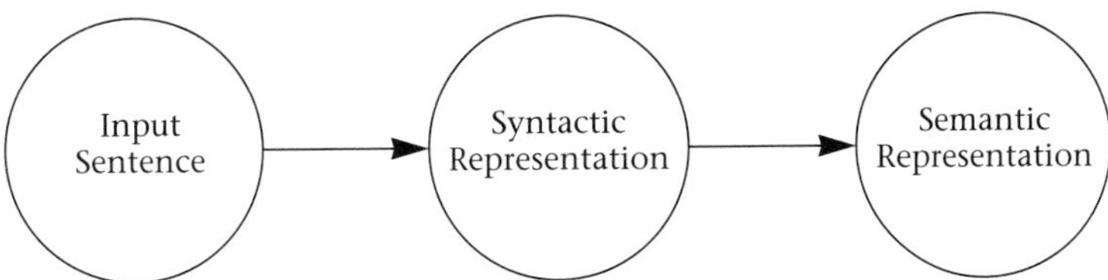

Figure 17.16

26)

The new student went.

Semantically Based Systems

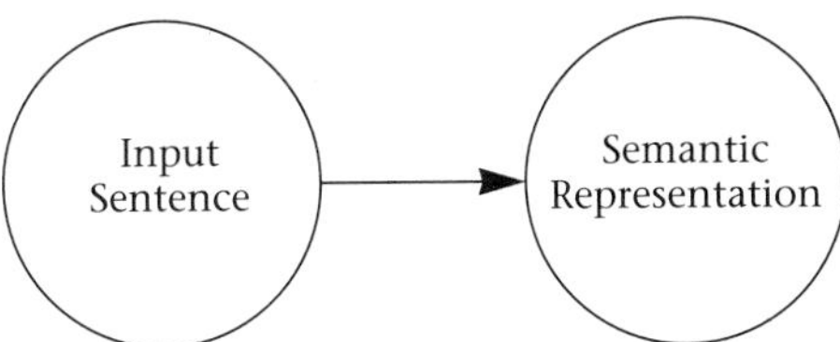

Figure 17.17

A syntactic analysis of the sentence would show that *the new student* is the first NP directly dominated by S (see Figure 17.18). From there, the parser might guess that

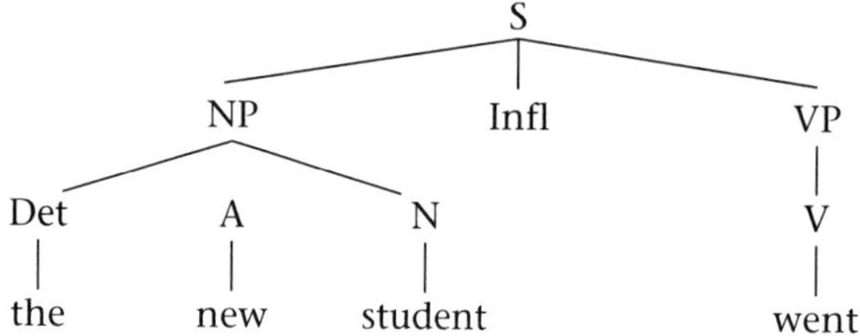

Figure 17.18

the subject is *the new student*. This is often true in English, although it is not always the case. Still, nothing is said about the fact that the subject is the actor (i.e., the one who performs the action) with a verb like go. Compare this to the intransitive version of the verb *open*.

27)

The door opened.

In this case, the subject *door* is not performing an action. Something or someone opened the door. A syntactically based system obtains this knowledge about a sentence after a structure is built.

In contrast, a semantically based system builds a semantic representation first. For sentence 26, it might look something like the one in Figure 17.19.

Go — Actor
NP
went the new student

Figure 17.19

The word order is not represented, but the underlying semantic information is expressed. The semantic representation of related sentences might be the same.

28)

It was the new student who went.

The mapping into the various syntactic forms of what is basically the same sentence occurs after the semantic representation is decided upon. Semantically based systems have been used for text and discourse analysis, such as for understanding stories.

Both approaches still need to accomplish the same goal, namely that of assigning word meaning, sentence meaning, and text meaning. The problem of semantic representation will not be covered here. However, it must be mentioned that determining matters like reference, as in *29*, and scope, as in *30* to *32*, are part of what needs to be achieved.

29)

Chris wants to marry an Australian.

30)

Pregnant women and children get out first.

31)

Ripe apples and peaches make a good fruit salad.

32)

Every person speaks two languages.

For *29)*, is this a specific Australian, or would any Australian at all do? For *30)*, what is the scope of *pregnant*? Is it *pregnant women and pregnant children*? This is unlikely. But in *31)*, the likely interpretation is *ripe apples and ripe peaches*. Finally, in *32)*, does every person speak the same two languages? Or different languages?

5.1 PRAGMATICS

The word *meaning* itself has many meanings. In addition to word meaning, logic, paragraph meaning, and so on, it has also been loosely applied to the field of **pragmatics**. Pragmatics is the study of how language is used in communication. Consider the following telephone conversation.

33)

Caller: Is George at home?
Answer: Yes.

This dialogue is amusing because the answerer has broken some basic conversational principles. The caller is not really asking the literal question *Is George at home?* although the semantic analysis of the sentence would indicate that this is a request for information about whether or not George is at home. The syntactic form of the question requires the answers *yes* or *no*, but nothing else. The dialogue in *34)* does not have the amusing quality of *33)*.

34)

Caller: Are you tired?
Answer: Yes.

Conversational principles (see Chapter 7) require that an answer be as informative as possible. This is not the case in *33)*, which violates the maxim of quantity. Another example of conversational principles is illustrated in *35)* and *36)*.

35)

Sue got on the horse and rode into the sunset.

36)

Sue rode into the sunset and got on the horse.

Why is *36)* strange? The coordinating conjunction *and* should just be a simple joining of two like parts. The nouns from *31)*, for example, could be reversed with no strange result (the scope problem remains unsolved, however):

37)

Ripe peaches and apples make a good fruit salad.

The reason for the problem in *36)* is that the word *and* is often given a temporal interpretation. This may not be part of the meaning of *and* but rather a matter of how it is used.

Whether pragmatics is a subfield of semantics is controversial, but there is no disagreement on the fact that knowledge of pragmatic principles is necessary to understanding and generating language.

6 PRACTICAL APPLICATIONS OF COMPUTATIONAL LINGUISTICS

The previous sections of this chapter have shown how the use of computers has forced linguists to formulate rigorous statements of theory and facts, because all of the implicit knowledge that humans have about language has to be made explicit. Theories become testable in a concrete way. Implementations of practical systems tend to force researchers (and students) to understand a particular language process in very detailed terms. Since related skills are needed both for linguistic analysis and for programming, the field of computational linguistics has flourished. This section discusses some specific types of computer systems that involve using linguistically sophisticated programs.

An **application** can be defined as the use to which a program or set of programs is put, for example, a payroll application, an airline reservation application, or a word processing application. Most early applications in computational linguistics fell into three categories: indexing and concordances, machine translation, and information retrieval. Other applications included speech synthesis and recognition and database applications.

6.1 Indexing and concordances

Indexing means finding, identifying, and usually counting all occurrences of a certain word in large texts. This application of computers to language study does exactly what computers are best at doing: locating a word, recording the location by line or sentence number, and counting how many times it appears. The examples of the use of the word *flounce* in the lexicology section were extracted from text using an indexing program. The program searched text on the computer to find any occurrence of the string *flounce, flouncing, flounced,* or *flounces*. When the string was found, the computer program took out the sentence and saved it in a separate file. A tally was kept of each time a targeted word was found.

A **concordance** tells which words occur near other words. Concordance and indexing programs are used widely in literary analysis. Some authors seem to favor using certain words in the context of other words. Concordance programs can find these relationships. A concordance program could tell, for example, how many times the word *she* occurred next to *flounce*.

Perhaps the most widely used word count was performed by Henry Kucera and Nelson Francis in 1962 on a corpus of one million words. The corpus is referred to as the Brown corpus since the work was completed at Brown University. Kucera and Francis took fifteen different texts and wrote a program to count the number of times each word appeared. The ten most frequent words of English are:

the	69,971
of	36,411
and	28,852
to	26,149
a	23,237
in	21,341
that	10,595
is	10,099
was	9,816
he	9,543

The numbers after the words indicate how many times they appeared in the one million words. Word frequency lists derived from these data have been useful to psycholinguists who need to pay attention to frequency when designing experiments.

These early applications are still very useful, but they are not linguistic in nature. They used the power of the computer to count and categorize words, so the results were of use to the linguist, but they did not rely on any linguistic knowledge. For example, to find *flounce*, the related words *flounced, flounces, flouncing* also had to be looked for. Early systems were not endowed with morphological knowledge, so they could look only for the exact string given. The program could not figure out that *flounce* and *flouncing* were related forms. Furthermore, all occurrences of the strings *flounce, flounces,* and so on were pulled out, without regard to part of speech. Since the goal was to look at subjects of verbs, it was necessary to distinguish between the verb *flounce* and the noun *flounce* as in *The women always flounce out* and *The chair had a lacy flounce around the bottom.* Notice the implications of this: Two of the top ten most frequent words are forms of the verb *be*, but since the system counts only strings, the forms *is* and *was* are counted separately. The inability of early systems to relate words had other problems. For example:

Minute	53
Min	5
Min.	1
Min,	1

are probably all variations of the word *minute,* although this would have to be verified by checking the original text. The count of *minute* is 53, but it really should be 60. (Note, however, that there is a possible complication: Some of the occurrences of *minute* may be examples of the noun *minute* meaning 'memorandum' rather than 60 seconds, or the unrelated differently-pronounced adjective *minute* [majnút] meaning 'very small', or it could be an abbreviation of *minister, ministry, minimum* or *minim* (a fluid measure roughly equivalent to a drop). We cannot be sure.

Most current concordance and indexing programs have solved some of the easier problems such as abbreviations. Much larger bodies of text are being used to overcome some of the problems of sparse and limited data, and more sophisticated statistical techniques are being employed. But most of the harder problems still remain. First of all, morphological knowledge is needed in order to relate various forms of the same word to just one base word. Second, syntactic knowledge is needed in order to establish the part of speech of the word in the sentences and in order to determine the arguments of the verbs, such as subject and object. Finally, semantic knowledge is needed to know the thematic roles of the arguments and to know which meaning of a word is intended.

6.2 Information access and retrieval

The Internet and the World Wide Web have created a growing body of text and images that can now be searched by anyone with access to a computer and modem. Furthermore, there are dozens of freely available search systems or engines for roaming through titles, articles, captions, and other sections of texts. However, anyone who has ever tried to search for articles on a particular topic has had the frustrating experience of having to wade through masses of irrelevant material to find what was wanted. For example, when the word *morphology* was searched in the *Library Index of Book Titles*, the following titles were among those returned:

Principles of Polymer Morphology
Image Analysis and Mathematical Morphology
Drainage Basin Morphology
French Morphology

If a linguistically sophisticated program had been used to retrieve these titles, it is likely that they would have been divided according to the semantic subject field. Thus a chemist would not get titles on French, just as a linguist would not get titles on chemistry.

What linguistic expertise could text retrieval systems use? Again, as with indexing and concordance, the three critical subareas are computational morphology, syntax, and semantics. For example, someone wanting to know about the theory of light might want to find all references to the word *light* in an encyclopedia. Searching for the string *light* anywhere in the text might give *lightning, enlightenment,* and *lighthearted,* but also *delight* and *candlelight.* On the other hand, if the user searches only for *light* surrounded by blanks, then words like *lighting* or *lights* would be missed. The user might want to find synonyms or related words, such as *colorless* or *clear* for the adjective, or *illuminate* for the verb. Without a parser and semantics, there is no clue about the nature of the word *light* when it is found in the text. The problem appears simple, but in fact it is quite complex.

6.3 Machine translation

The purpose of a machine translation system is the same as that of any translation system: taking text written or spoken in one language and writing or speaking it in another (see Figure 17.20). Translation poses challenging problems both for the human translator and for the machine attempting to do what the human does.

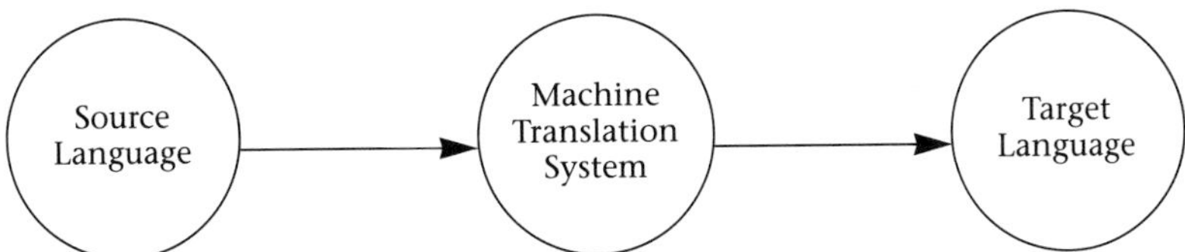

Figure 17.20

Projects in machine translation in the 1940s and 1950s spawned much of the early research in computational linguistics. Consider the written case first, and think of a single institution like the United Nations. Every day millions of words need to be translated from one language to another. Add to that other political and scientific institutions, plus businesses and publishers. This results in an overwhelming need for help in translation, since the process, when done correctly, is time-consuming and mentally demanding. Since computers are suited to tasks requiring memory, it would seem that, with careful programming, the problem of translating by computer could be solved.

This was the thinking of computer scientists and linguists, but the problems turned out to be far more difficult than was imagined. Much government money was poured into the machine translation task from the late 1940s to the early 1960s, but results were slow to emerge due to the complexity of unforeseen problems. The subtlety of language, the nuances and lack of precision, caused problems because computers are suited to mathematical computation where subtleties do not prevail. Funding agencies became disillusioned, and although most researchers were still hopeful, they were humbled by the difficulties encountered in early years.

Researchers are now more realistic about their goals. Rather than attempting to build full-fledged machine translation systems that automatically convert a text from one language to another, some projects are aiming toward machine-assisted translation. In these projects, the computer is viewed as a tool to aid the translator. The computer makes suggestions, but the human translator makes final decisions. Another simplification is to aim the translation at a specific subject area; this way, word ambiguities are reduced to a minimum. For example, in the financial domain, the word *vehicle* is probably an investment device, but in the automobile domain, *vehicle* is most likely a device for driving. Yet other projects are developing ways to take texts and pass them through a preprocessor. A preprocessor is a system that looks at sentences and figures out which ones might present problems. The computer can identify the problem, and then ask the original writer to clarify. Take the following example:

38)

Many elephants smell.

Since this sentence could be confusing (because the verb *smell* is ambiguous—is the intended interpretation that many elephants stink or that many elephants are capable of perceiving odors?), it might be sent back to the writer to be clarified.

Machine translation applications encompass many aspects of computational linguistics. For this reason, the venture is one of the more challenging to researchers. In addition, the notion of a machine that is capable or nearly capable of mimicking a very complex and subtle human activity constitutes an intriguing enterprise. The source language needs to be analyzed syntactically and semantically. Lexical items need to be matched. This is a particularly difficult task. Not only do words in one language often not exist in another, but sometimes several words are used for one. One example involves the German words *essen* and *fressen*. Both words mean *eat* in English, but the verb *essen* is used for humans, whereas *fressen* is used for animals. If the system made the mistake of using *fressen* for people, it would be an insult. Syntax can also be a problem. An example from Spanish concerns a missing word, as shown in *39)* and *40)*. Sentence *41)* gives the word-by-word translation of the Spanish in *40)*.

39)

The elephants slept but didn't snore.

40)

Los elefantes durmiéron pero no roncaron.

41)

*The elephants slept but not snored.

The word-by-word translation in *41)* is not English. What's wrong? In English, in a negative sentence without an auxiliary verb, the properly inflected form of the verb *do* needs to be inserted. Since *39)* is in the past tense, and since the subject is plural, the correct form is *did*. There is no word for *did* in the Spanish version of the same sentence. Just as the human translator has to know this fact, so does the machine translation system. If the input language were Spanish and the input sentence were *40)*, then the English generation system would need to know to insert the verb *do*, properly inflected, and not to inflect the main verb. The difficulties increase with languages that are fundamentally different in nature, such as English and Japanese, or Spanish and Finnish, or French and Chinese.

If the machine translation system is required to take spoken language as input and give spoken language as output, then the system becomes even more complex, as shown in Figure 17.21.

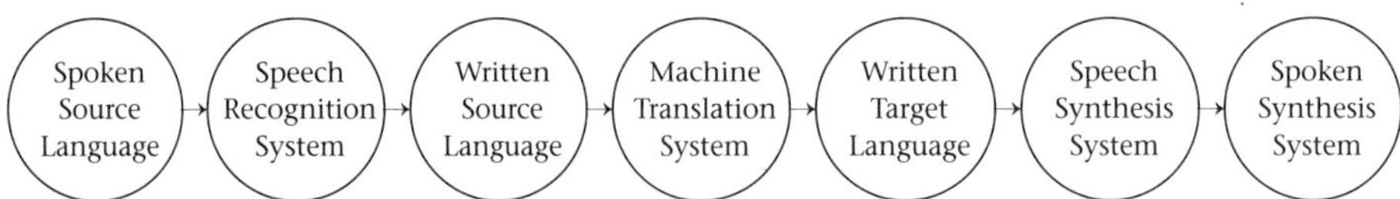

Figure 17.21

6.4 SPEECH RECOGNITION

A speech recognition system takes spoken language as input and understands it (see Figure 17.22). The result could be the written text of what was said, or it could be orders to another machine. For example, a smart typewriter equipped with a recognition device will take orders to delete a line. The typewriter follows orders, but the

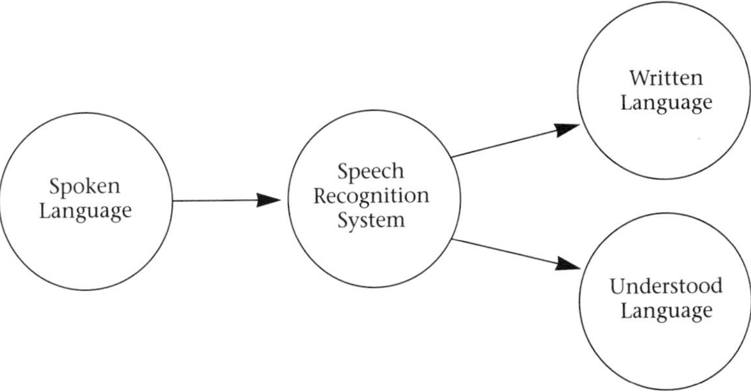

Figure 17.22

words *delete line* will not be written. Speech recognition is a process that humans perform effortlessly, but teaching computers to recognize speech has turned out to be more difficult than was originally thought. Some of the linguistic problems involved were outlined in the sections on computational phonetics and phonology.

What are some applications that would benefit from a speech recognition system? One that has been explored is in the area of medical record keeping. Writing down details of examinations is time-consuming; often doctors leave out critical information due to these time pressures. With a speech recognition system, the doctor would simply talk while doing an examination. The speech would automatically and instantly be translated into text, which could be printed out immediately. In this way, the doctor could examine the report with the patient there to make sure everything has been covered. Medical terminology is fairly controlled, so the computer would have an advantage in guessing words. The examination room is relatively quiet, reducing the problem of background noise. Finally, a speech recognition system would allow the doctor to use both hands while speaking. Medical records could immediately go into a central library, which could be referred to by researchers studying symptoms and diagnoses. Last but not least, no one would ever have to struggle to read the doctor's illegible handwriting!

Such a system would have to be absolutely perfect. However, it is easier to correct an error in a report than to write one. Other applications that have been explored include quality control devices for inspecting assembly lines. For example, a worker would be able to say words like *pass* or *fail,* and the machine would then know whether to accept the part or refuse it. A very important application of speech recognition is in developing aids for the physically disabled. These include devices such as voice-operated appliances, machines, and tools. Applications such as these have great promise.

6.5 SPEECH SYNTHESIS

A speech synthesis system has the opposite goal from a speech recognition system (see Figure 17.23). Applications for speech synthesis systems abound. One of the most important uses is "reading" to the visually impaired. Previously this required a

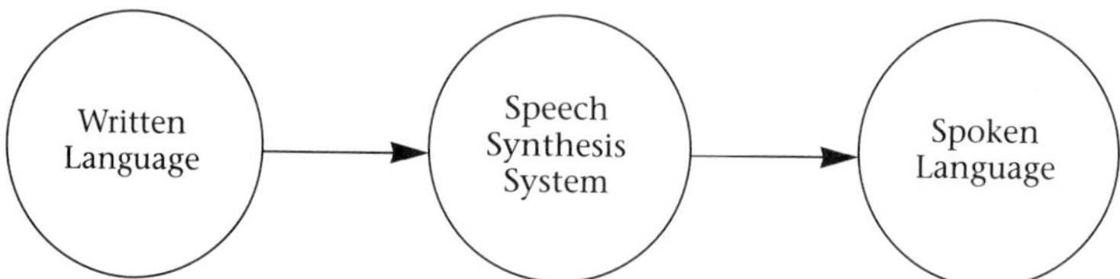

Figure 17.23

human either to do the actual reading or to pre-record books and other material. This is not only expensive but also limiting, since what the person wants or needs to read may not be available on tape. Another important application is as a talking aid for the vocally handicapped. Communication boards and talking typewriters show the value of converting text to spoken language.

Another fairly common application is in an area called *database query*. A database is a large source of information, such as bank records, billing records, airline schedules, and theater and movie schedules. Imagine wanting to find out about ticket availability for the theater, movies, or other cultural events. This information is constantly changing as people buy tickets and as agencies release tickets. When you call, the text-to-speech machine can read the information aloud directly out of the database. No one has had to record it, which is time-consuming and expensive. Furthermore, the information is completely up-to-date. Other applications include use in machine translation systems, for robots, for expert systems, and for novel medical applications.

Summing up

This chapter has covered the relatively new field of **computational linguistics**, which is the application of computers to the study of linguistic problems. There are two goals in computational linguistics. One is to use the computer as a tool to build programs that model a particular linguistic theory or approach. For this goal, the computer becomes a testing ground for the theory. The other goal is to build working systems that use linguistic information. The chapter covers the fields of computational phonetics and phonology, morphology, syntax, lexicology, and semantics and pragmatics. A section on **applications** presents some of the devices that have incorporated linguistic tools, such as machine translation systems and reading machines for the visually impaired.

Key terms

application
bottom-up parsing
cocktail party effect
computational linguistics
concordance
corpus analysis
deterministic parsing
formants
grammatical knowledge
implementation
indexing
MRD (machine-readable dictionary)

nondeterministic parsing
nonterminal nodes
parser
pragmatics
real-world knowledge
spectrogram
stemming (or stripping) algorithm
strong generative capacity
terminal nodes
top-down parsing
weak generative capacity

Recommended Reading

Allen, James. 1995. *Natural Language Understanding*. 2nd ed. Menlo Park, CA: Benjamin/Cummings.

Grishman, Ralph. 1986. *Computational Linguistics: An Introduction*. Cambridge University Studies in Natural Language Processing. Cambridge: Cambridge University Press.

Journal of the Association for Computational Linguistics. 1987. Volume 13, Numbers 3–4.

King, Margaret, ed. 1983. *Parsing Natural Language*. London: Academic Press/Harcourt Brace Jovanovich.

Klatt, Dennis. 1987. "Review of Text-to-Speech Conversion for English." *Journal of the Acoustical Society of America*. Volume 82, Number 3.

Leech, Geoffrey, and Steven Fligelstone. 1992. "Computers and corpus analysis." In *Computers and Written Texts* edited by C. Butler. Oxford: Blackwell.

Levinsohn, Stephan E., and Mark Y. Liberman. 1981. "Speech Recognition by Computer." *Scientific American*. April.

Pullman, Steve. 1997. *Computational Linguistics*. Cambridge: Cambridge University Press.

Savitch, Walter J., Emmon Bach, William Marsh, and Gila Safran-Naveh, eds. 1987. *The Formal Complexity of Natural Language*. New York: D. Reidel/Kluwer.

Questions

1. What kinds of problems might a computer have with these sentences?
   a) Sue bought red apples and plums.
   b) It was a large animal house.
   c) Susan baked in the kitchen.
   d) Susan baked in the sun.
   e) Susan baked.

2. What are the main uses of a text-to-speech system? What information does the computer need to know in order to pronounce these sentences in informal style?
   a) What are you doing tonight?
   b) The woman was delighted.
   c) That article misled me.
   d) That's a new car, isn't it?
   e) It was a tough test, although I did well.
   f) Can't you sing better?

3. What rules are necessary for a computer program to analyze these words? (*Hint:* First figure out the prefixes and suffixes. Refer to the chapter on morphology if necessary.)
   a) kindness
   b) kindly
   c) kindnesses
   d) nationalism
   e) countability
   f) nontransformational
   g) reusable

4. What different structures might a syntactic analyzer propose for the following ambiguous sentences?
   a) She saw the man with a telescope.
   b) Watch dogs bark.
   c) Broadcast programs like 60 Minutes.

5. Think of a word that has many different meanings, such as *bank* or *interest.* Then give information about that word using the categories in Section 4. Give at least two senses for each part of speech. The following example has one sense for the noun part of speech, and two senses for the verb part of speech.

   WORD: bank
   a) Part of Speech: Noun
   b) Sense Number: 1
   c) Semantic Properties: Of a river
   d) Pronunciation: /bæŋk/
   e) Context and Style: Normal
   f) Example: The bank of the river was grassy.

   WORD: bank
   a) Part of Speech: Verb
   b) Sense Number: 1
   c) Subcategorization: Transitive, requires the preposition *on*
   d) Semantic Properties: Object of preposition is either a person or thing
   e) Pronunciation: /bæŋk/
   f) Context and Style: Informal
   g) Example: I can't bank on him to do it.

   WORD: bank
   a) Part of Speech: Verb
   b) Sense Number: 2
   c) Subcategorization: Transitive
   d) Semantic Properties: Object is money
   e) Pronunciation: /bæŋk/
   f) Context and Style: Normal
   g) Example: She banks her money at the local branch.

6. Give three applications of computational linguistics. How can these systems improve the quality of life for people with physical disabilities?

7. The use of the internet and the World Wide Web has changed the way people access information. In the context of requesting information from an electronic source:
   a) List three cases where linguistic information would help you to find your way around the net. For example, if you are looking for information on *attorney*, it would help in your search to know that the British equivalents are *barrister* and *solicitor*.
   b) List three cases where linguistic ambiguity will hurt you in search for information electronically. For example, in looking for articles on the word *bank*, you will find articles on rivers and financial institutions. What are some words and phrases that would give you problems? Explain for each example what the problem is, and how you could solve it.

FOR THE STUDENT LINGUIST

ONE SECOND

Mike is driving the kids to the game. It's a simple sentence; you probably have no problem understanding it and can do so within the few seconds it takes to utter this sentence. But by now you've learned something about phonetics, phonology, morphology, and syntax, and so you can recognize that there's a lot of structure hidden inside this seemingly simple sentence. In computational linguistics we deal with the ways in which individual components of grammar interact. One place where this happens is during parsing.

I think parsing is one of the most fascinating parts of language. To illustrate how complex parsing must be, I've listed some of the steps your brain might be following as you hear this sentence. Imagine how much work you'd have to do for a more complicated sentence.

M

As soon as you hear the first sound, you're already coming up with possible words:

my	Mabel	microphone	magazine	meat
music	Midol	migraine	mine	mud
might	make	mat	miss	mice
Mike	mascara	moped	mitochondria	model

Mi

Each new sound eliminates some possibilities and makes others more likely.

my	microphone	mitochondria
might	Midol	mine
Mike	migraine	mice

Mike

Already there's a conflict: this string of sounds could be *my* plus another word (starting with [k]), or *Mike, microphone,* etc.

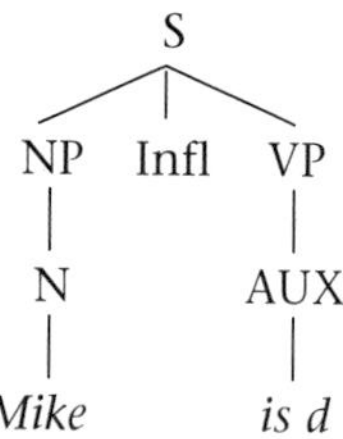

By now these sounds are probably identified as *Mike is . . .* , since a possibility like *My kismet . . .* is ruled out by the [d] and *my* followed by some unknown word has a low probability. So syntax can kick in, and start making tree structures. You might wonder when your brain knows it's going to get a sentence. It might assume it right away, and postulate an *S* node as soon as the first word starts. Or maybe it waits until it hears something verb-like. What do you think? Let's assume that as soon as it hears a noun or a determiner, it knows it's going to get an NP, and as soon as it gets an AUX or a verb it knows it's going to get a VP.

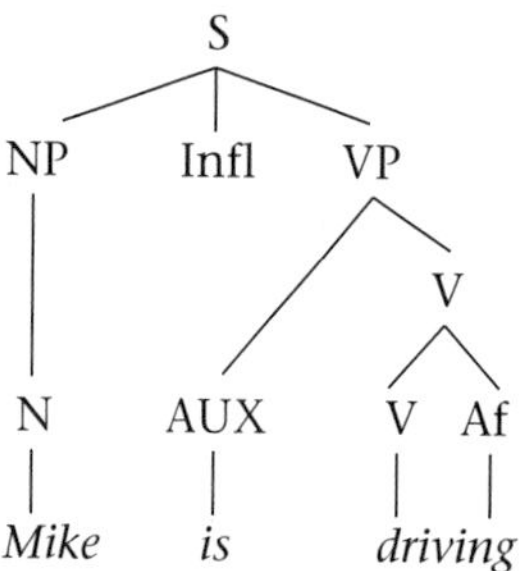

The morphology component of the parser didn't have to do much with the first two words, but once it reaches *driving* it has to identify the verb stem and the affix. Meanwhile, phonology and morphology together have to rule out something like *Mike is dry . . . ving. . . .* Notice how misleading it could be to pick the first legitimate-sounding sequence as the real sequence; it's *Mike*, not *My k . . .* , it's *Mike is driving,* not *Mike is dry.* So your brain has to delay decisions a bit, until it has confirmation that it has made the right choice.

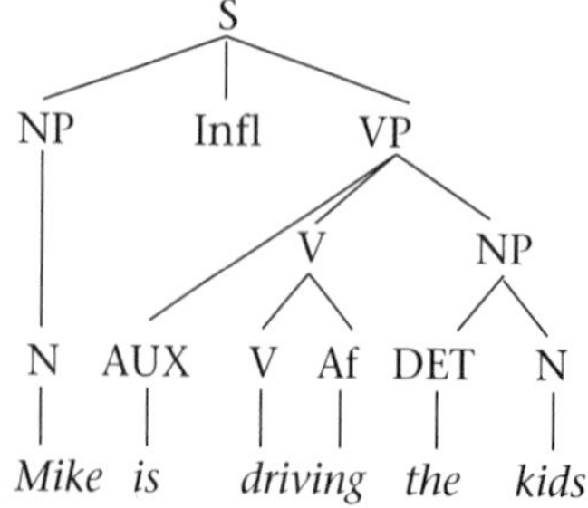

Now the morphology component has a dilemma. *Kids* could be plural or possessive (remember, you're hearing this, so you can't see any punctuation), so the morphology and syntax components can't tell whether the NP is complete (if it's just *the kids*) or to expect more material in the NP, waiting for whatever object follows *the kid's* or *the kids'*.

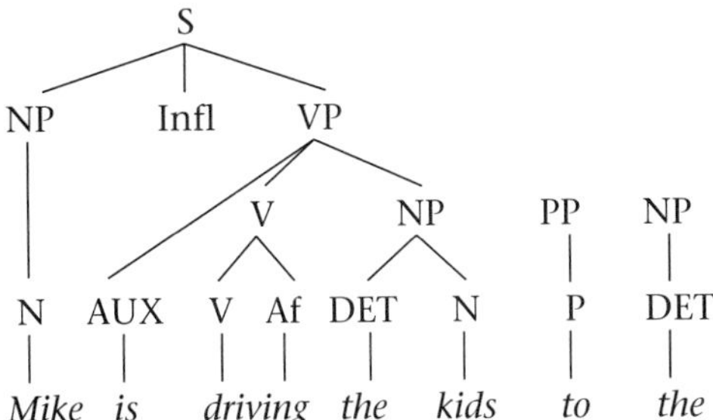

Once you hear *the*, you can rule out something like *the kid's two cars . . .* or *the kids' two cars . . .* and "close" the NP (decide that it's complete). Or can you? What if the PP following *kids* modifies it (and therefore the PP for *to the game* is a sister of the N for *kids* instead of a sister of the NP *the kids*)? Again, the different components have to interface to determine the structure as quickly as possible without locking into an incorrect decision prematurely.

Why am I emphasizing the need to figure out when you've reached the end of some phrase? Because it might require more memory to hold a group of words as an open, active unit than to declare it a complete constituent. Sort of like having a limited amount of desk space; it's easier to file away things you know you're done with than to keep them spread all over your desk surface and in your way.

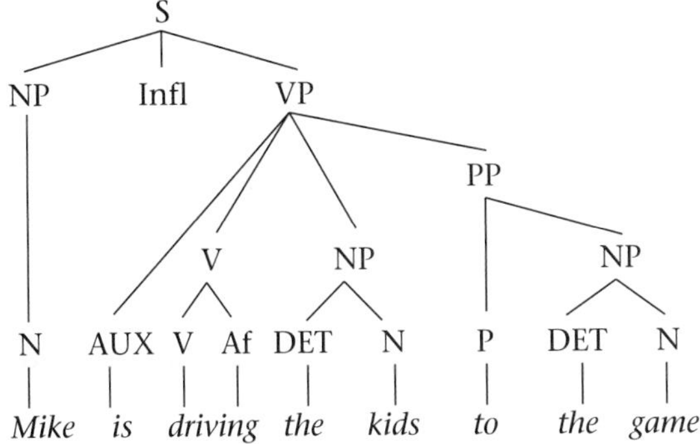

And finally you're done. Pretty amazing that you can do all that parsing in a few seconds, isn't it? Now you can try to explain why sentences like the following are so hard to understand. Good luck.

The dog walked past the kennel barked.

Since Sheila kept on eating the brownies burned.

The reporter that the dog that Mary owns bit last week slept late.

GLOSSARY

Ablaut A vowel alternation that marks a grammatical contrast (e.g., *mouse/mice*).

Absolute universals Patterns or traits that occur in all languages.

Absolutive In some languages, the case associated with both the direct object of a transitive verb and the subject of an intransitive verb.

Abstract Hypothetical, not phonetically realized. *See* **underlying**.

Abstract representation A phonological description that is to a greater or lesser degree distinct from its phonetic realization.

Accidental gaps Nonoccurring but possible forms of a language (e.g., in English, *blork*).

Accuracy Second language production in which the structures are nativelike.

Acoustic phonetics An approach to phonetics that is concerned with measuring and analyzing the physical properties of sound waves produced when we speak.

Acquired agraphia *See* **Acquired dysgraphia**.

Acquired alexia *See* **Acquired dyslexia**.

Acquired dysgraphia The impairment of writing ability in patients who previously possessed normal writing ability (also called **acquired agraphia**).

Acquired dyslexia The impairment of reading ability in patients who previously possessed normal reading ability (also called **acquired alexia**).

Acrolect A creole variety that is relatively similar to the standard language from which it arose. (*See also* **Basilect** and **Mesolect**.)

Acronym A word that is formed by taking the initial letters of (some or all) of the words in a phrase or title and pronouncing them as a word (e.g., *NATO* for *North Atlantic Treaty Organization*).

Acrophonic principle The representation of sounds by pictures of objects whose pronunciation begins with the sound to be represented (e.g., the sound [b] might be represented by a picture of a bird).

Act sequence A component of the speech situation, which includes the content and form of speech.

Active sentence A sentence in which the NP with the agent role is the subject (e.g., *Helen painted the room*).

Address terms The various forms that are used to address people, indicating something of one's relationship to the individual addressed (e.g., in English, *Ms Callaghan, Professor Van Haar, Jake*).

Adjective (A) A lexical category that designates a property that is applicable to the entities named by nouns, can often take comparative and superlative endings in English, and functions as the head of an adjective phrase (e.g., *red, obese, hearty*).

Adstratum influence The mutual influence of two equally dominant languages on each other (e.g., the influence of English and French on each other in Montreal).

Adverb (Adv) A lexical category that typically names properties that can be applied to the actions designated by verbs (e.g., *quickly, fearfully*).

Affix (Af) A bound morpheme that modifies the meaning and/or syntactic (sub)category of the stem in some way (e.g., *un-* and *-able* in *unreadable*).

Affixation The process that attaches an affix to a base.

Affricates Noncontinuant consonants that show a slow release of the closure (e.g., [ʧ, ʤ]).

Affrication A process in which stops become affricates.

Agent The thematic role of the doer of an action (e.g., *Marilyn* in *Marilyn fed the dolphin*).

Agglutinating languages Languages in which words typically contain several morphemes, of which usually only one is a lexical category. The others are clearly identifiable affixes, each of which typically encodes a single grammatical contrast.

Agrammatism An aphasic disturbance characterized by the omission of function words and inflectional affixes and by syntactic comprehension deficits.

Agreement The result of one category being inflected to mark properties of another (e.g., the verb marked for the person and/or the number of the subject).

Allomorphs Variants of a morpheme (e.g., [-s], [-z], and [-əz] are allomorphs of the English plural morpheme).

Allophones Variants of a phoneme, usually in complementary distribution and phonetically similar (e.g., voiced and voiceless *l* in English).

Alpha rules Phonological rules stated in a conventional formula in which variables (α, β, etc.) are introduced for the value of distinctive features.

Alphabetic writing A type of writing in which symbols represent consonant and vowel segments.

Alveolar ridge The small ridge just behind the upper front teeth.

Alveopalatal (area) The area just behind the alveolar ridge where the roof of the mouth rises sharply (also called **palatoalveolar**).

Ambisyllabicity The simultaneous presence of a segment in two adjoining syllables.

Amelioration The process in which the meaning of a word becomes more favorable (e.g., *pretty* used to mean 'tricky, sly, cunning').

Amerind The group into which all the Native American languages (except for Na-Dené and Eskimo-Aleut stocks) have been placed, according to one controversial classification system.

Amerindian languages Languages spoken by the aboriginal peoples of North, South, and Central America.

Analogy A source of language change that involves the generalization of a regularity on the basis of the inference that if elements are alike in some respects, they should be alike in others as well (e.g., *bring* becoming *brung* by analogy with *ring/rung*).

Analytic languages *See* **Isolating languages**.

Anaphoric reference The use of a pronoun that refers to an NP earlier in the discourse (e.g., *her* in *Hilary ate her dinner*).

Angular gyrus An area of the brain that plays an important role in reading.

Animate In some languages, a class consisting of nouns, most of which have living referents.

Antecedent The element that determines the interpretation of a pronoun (e.g., *Jeremy* in *Jeremy looked at himself in the mirror*).

Anterior A place feature that characterizes sounds articulated in front of the alveopalatal region.

Antonyms Words or phrases that are opposites with respect to some component of their meaning (e.g., *big* and *small*).

Aphasia A language deficit caused by damage to the brain.

Application The use to which a computer program is put.

Apocope The deletion of a word-final vowel (e.g., *name* used to be pronounced with a word-final schwa).

Arbitrariness A property of communication whereby there is no natural or inherent connection between a sign and its referent.

Archaism A lexical item that was previously widely used but has survived only in a particular dialect (e.g., the absolute form of the possessive pronouns *hisn, hern, yourn* in Appalachian English).

Areal classification An approach to language classification that identifies characteristics shared by languages that are in the same geographical area.

Argot A secret language associated with social groups whose members wish to conceal some aspect of their communication from nonmembers.

Articulatory phonetics An approach to phonetics that studies the physiological mechanisms of speech production.

Articulatory simplification A process that facilitates acquisition (e.g., by deleting a consonant in a complex cluster or inserting a vowel to break up a cluster).

Arytenoids Two small cartilages in the larynx that are attached to the vocal folds, enabling the vocal folds to be drawn together or apart.

Aspiration The lag in the onset of vocalic voicing, accompanied by the release of air, that is heard after the release of certain stops in English (e.g., the first sound of *top* is aspirated).

Assimilation The influence of one segment on another, resulting in a sound becoming more like a nearby sound in terms of one or more of its phonetic characteristics (e.g., in English, vowels become nasal if followed by a nasal consonant).

Association line A line linking a symbol that represents a sound segment with a symbol that represents a tone or feature.

Audiolingualism A method of second language teaching based on the notion that second language learning should be regarded as a mechanistic process of habit formation.

Autopsy studies Studies based on a post-mortem examination.

Autosegmental (notation) The type of notation in phonology that links segments with tones or individual features by **association lines**.

Autosegmental principles Rules that account for phonological processes, including rules that associate **features** to **segments** and segments to features and rules that prohibit the crossing of **association lines**.

Autosegments Phonological features (such as **manner features** and **place features**) that operate more or less autonomously.

Auxiliary verb (Aux) A verb that serves as the specifier of the main verb (e.g., *was* in *was talking*).

Babbling Speech-like sounds produced as babies acquire and exercise articulatory skills.

Back A feature of sounds articulated behind the palatal region in the oral cavity.

Back (of the tongue) The part of the tongue that is hindmost but still lies in the mouth.

Back vowel A vowel that is made with the tongue positioned in the back of the mouth (e.g., the vowel sounds in *hoot* and *board*).

Backformation A word formation process that creates a new word by removing a real or supposed affix from another word in the language (e.g., *edit* came from *editor* through the removal of *-or*).

Base The form to which an affix is added (e.g., *book* is the base for the affix *-s* in *books*, *modernize* is the base for the affix *-ed* in *modernized*).

Basilect A creole variety that shows the least influence from the standard language from which it arose. (*See also* **Acrolect** and **Mesolect**.)

Bilingualism The state of possessing knowledge of two languages; the discipline devoted to the study of the simultaneous acquisition of two languages by children.

Blade (of the tongue) The area of the tongue just behind the tip.

Blend A word that is created from parts of two already existing items (e.g., *brunch* from *breakfast* and *lunch*).

Blissymbolics A contemporary development of pictographic writing that uses a number of recombineable symbols representing basic units of meaning; primarily used for nonspeaking individuals.

Body (of the tongue) The main mass of the tongue.

Borrowing A source of language change that involves adopting aspects of one language into another.

Bottom-up parsing A method of speech analysis that starts with individual words and builds structures upwards in successively larger units.

Bottom-up processing A type of mental processing in which more complex representations (e.g., words) are accessed through simpler constituent representations (e.g., phonemes).

Bound morpheme A morpheme that must be attached to another element (e.g., the past tense marker *-ed*).

Boustrophedon The practice of reversing the direction of writing at the end of each line, which was typical of many old writing systems.

Broca's aphasia A nonfluent aphasia in which speech is very halting, there are numerous phonemic errors, and there is a lack of intonation.

Broca's area The area in the lower rear portion of the left frontal lobe of the brain that plays an important role in language production.

Bundles of isoglosses Convergence of several lines drawn on a dialect map to represent boundaries between dialects.

Call In avian communication, short bursts of sound or simple patterns of notes, typically used as warnings or other group-related signals.

Caregiver speech *See* **Motherese**.

Case A morphological category that encodes information about an element's grammatical role (subject, direct object, and so on) (e.g., the contrast between *he* and *him*).

Case Filter, The The requirement that every NP in a grammatical sentence be in a position to which case can be assigned.

Cataphoric reference The use of a pronoun that refers to an NP later in the discourse (e.g., *she* in *When she heard the news, Ann smiled*).

Category change A change in the part of speech of a word as a result of **affixation** (e.g. adding *-ize* to *modern,* an adjective, makes it into a verb, *modernize*).

C-command A syntactic notion that is involved in pronoun interpretation and is formulated as: NP_a c-commands NP_b if the first category above NP_a contains NP_b.

Central sulcus The fold that extends from the top of the cerebral cortex to the lateral fissure (also called the fissure of Rolando).

Cerebral blood flow study A technique for observing activity in the brain that uses a radio-isotope detector to produce images of how much blood is going to particular parts of the brain.

Cerebral cortex The grey wrinkled mass that sits like a cap over the rest of the brain and is the seat of cognitive functioning.

Cerebral hemispheres The left and right halves of the brain, separated by the longitudinal fissure.

Cerebrovascular accident *See* **Stroke**.

Characters The units of contemporary Chinese orthography, many of which consist of two parts, a phonetic **determinative** and a **radical**.

Class, (sound) A group of sounds that shares certain phonetic properties (e.g., all voiced sounds).

Class 1 A group of affixes that (in English) often trigger changes in the consonant or vowel segments of the base and may affect the assignment of stress.

Class 2 A group of affixes that tend to be phonologically neutral in English, having no effect on the segmental makeup of the base or on stress assignment.

Class node A label that represents each phonological feature grouping in the feature hierarchy (also called simply a **node**).

Clever Hans A horse that seemed to have a human-like capacity to think.

Clipping A word formation process that shortens a polysyllabic word by deleting one or more syllables (e.g., *prof* from *professor*).

Clitic A word that is unable to stand alone as an independent form for phonological reasons.

Cliticization The process by which a **clitic** is attached to a word.

Closed syllable A syllable with a coda (e.g., both syllables in *camping*).

Coarticulation An articulation in which phonemes overlap to a certain extent.

Cocktail party effect The ability to filter out background noise and pick out a particular sound.

Coda (C) The elements that follow the nucleus in the same syllable (e.g., [rf] in *surfboard*).

Cognates Words of different languages that have descended from a common source, as shown by systematic phonetic correspondences (e.g., English *father* and German *Vater*).

Cognitive development The emergence of the various mental abilities (such as language) that make up the human intellect.

Cognitive style The way in which we are predisposed to process information in our environment.

Cohesive device A device that establishes a connection among two or more elements in the discourse (e.g., anaphoric reference, cataphoric reference, lexical cohesion, ellipsis, and so on).

Cohort model A model of spoken word recognition according to which word recognition proceeds by isolating a target word from a set of words that share initial segments.

Coinage *See* **Word manufacture**.

Communication strategies Strategies used by L2 learners when they are lacking the necessary linguistic knowledge to say what they want to say (e.g., paraphrasing).

Communicative competence A speaker's underlying knowledge of the linguistic system and the norms for the appropriate sociocultural use of language in particular speech situations.

Communicative language teaching method (CLT) Second language teaching method that emphasizes functional language in the attempt to attain the goal of communicative competence.

Comparative reconstruction The reconstruction of properties of a parent language through comparison of its descendant languages.

Complement A syntactic constituent that provides information about entities and locations implied by the meaning of the head.

Complement clause A sentence-like construction that is embedded within a larger structure (e.g., *that his car had been totalled* in *Jerry told Mary that his car had been totalled*).

Complementary distribution The distribution of allophones in their respective phonetic environments such that one never appears in the same phonetic context as the other (e.g., the distribution of long and short vowels in English).

Complementizer (C) A functional category that takes an S complement, forming a CP (complementizer phrase) (e.g., *whether* in *I wonder whether Lorna has left*).

Complex word A word that contains two or more morphemes (e.g., *theorize, unemployment*).

Componential analysis The representation of a word's intension in terms of smaller semantic components called features.

Compound level A descriptive term indicating where stress is placed in compounds.

Compound stress **Primary stress** assigned to the first word in an English compound (e.g., bláckbòard).

Compounding The combination of lexical categories (N, V, A, or P) to form a larger word (e.g., *fire* + *engine*).

Comprehensible input The linguistic input to which the L2 learner is exposed that is slightly beyond his or her competence in the target language (i+1).

Computational linguistics The area of common interest between linguistics and computer science.

Computerized Axial Tomography A technique for observing the living brain that uses a narrow beam of X-rays to create brain images that take the form of a series of brain slices (also called **CT scanning**).

Concordance An index of words showing every occurrence of each word in its context.

Conditioned allomorphs The different forms of a **morpheme** whose distribution depends on the phonological and morphological environment in which they occur (e.g., the English plural has several allomorphs whose distribution depends on phonological and morphological factors).

Conjugation The set of inflected forms associated with a verb (also called a verbal paradigm).

Conjunction (Con) A functional category that joins two or more categories of the same type, forming a coordinate structure (e.g., *and* in *a man and his dog*).

Connotation The set of associations that a word's use can evoke (e.g., in Canada *winter* evokes ice, snow, bare trees, etc.). (*See also* **Denotation**.)

Conservative language A language that shows comparatively few changes over time.

Consonant deletion A phonetic process that deletes a consonant (e.g., the deletion of [θ] in *sixths*).

Consonant weakening A lessening in the time or degree of a consonant's closure.

Consonantal A major class feature that characterizes sounds produced with a major obstruction in the vocal tract.

Consonantal strength Increasing the time or degree of a consonant's closure.

Consonants Sounds that are produced with a narrow or complete closure in the vocal tract.

Constellation A complex of communicative modes operating on different channels.

Constituent One or more words that make up a syntactic unit (e.g., *the apple* in *the apple fell onto the floor*). (*See also* **Coordination test, Substitution test**, and **Movement test.**)

Constricted Glottis ([CG]) A laryngeal feature that characterizes sounds made with the glottis closed (in English, only [ʔ]).

Continuant A manner feature that characterizes sounds made with free or nearly free airflow through the oral cavity: vowels, fricatives, glides, and liquids.

Continuants Sounds that are produced with a continuous airflow through the mouth.

Contour tone A tone that changes pitch on a single syllable.

Contradiction A relationship between sentences wherein the truth of one sentence requires the falsity of another sentence (e.g., *Raymond is married* contradicts *Raymond is a bachelor*).

Contralateral The control of the right side of the body by the left side of the brain and vice versa.

Contrast Segments are said to contrast when their presence alone may distinguish forms with different meanings from each other (e.g., [s] and [z] in the words *sip* and *zip*).

Conversational implicature Information that is understood through inference but is not actually said.

Conversion A word formation process that assigns an already existing word to a new syntactic category (also called **zero derivation**) (e.g., *nurse* (V) from *nurse* (N)).

Cooperative Principle, The The general overarching guideline thought to underlie conversational interactions: Make your contribution appropriate to the conversation.

Coordinate structure A phrase that is formed by joining two (or more) categories of the same type with a conjunction such as *and* or *or* (e.g., *those men and that woman*).

Coordinate Structure Constraint, The A constraint on transformations that does not allow an element to be removed from a coordinate structure.

Coordination The process of grouping together two or more categories of the same type with the help of a conjunction (e.g., *Mary and the white horse*).

Coordination Rule A syntactic rule that allows similar categories (e.g., N, V, A) at the same structural level (e.g., X, XP) to be joined by a **conjunction**.

Coordination test A test used to determine if a group of words is a constituent by joining it to another group of words with a conjunction such as *and* or *or*.

Coronal A place feature that characterizes sounds made with the tongue tip or blade raised (e.g., [t d s θ]).

Corpus analysis A technique for building lexicons by means of automated analysis of a body of texts.

Corpus callosum The bundle of nerve fibres that serves as the main connection between the cerebral hemispheres, allowing the two hemispheres to communicate with one another.

Creativity The characteristic of human language that allows novelty and innovation in response to new thoughts, experiences, and situations.

Creole A language that originated as a pidgin and has become established as a first language in a speech community.

Cricoid cartilage The ring-shaped cartilage in the larynx on which the thyroid cartilage rests.

Critical period A particular time frame during which children have to be exposed to language if the acquisition process is to be successful.

Cross-sectional (research) Research that investigates and compares subjects selected from different developmental stages.

CT scanning *See* **Computerized Axial Tomography**.

Cuneiform Writing invented in the fourth millenium BC and produced by pressing a wedge-shaped stylus into soft clay tablets.

Cycle Each application of a rule on a particular level of representation.

Cyrillic alphabet An alphabet that combined adaptations of Glagolitic letters with Greek and Hebrew characters, evolving into the alphabets that are currently used to represent some of the languages spoken in the former Soviet Union and in the Balkans.

D-structure *See* **Deep structure**.

Deaffrication A type of segmental simplification that turns affricates into fricatives by eliminating the stop portion of the affricate (e.g., [ʤ] becoming [ʒ]).

Declension *See* **Nominal paradigm**.

Deep dyslexia A type of acquired dyslexia in which the patient produces a word that is semantically related to the word he or she is asked to read (e.g., producing *father* when asked to read *mother*).

Deep structure The structure generated by the phrase structure rules in accordance with the subcategorization properties of the heads.

Degemination The weakening of a geminate consonant to a nongeminate consonant (e.g., [tt] becoming [t]).

Degree word (Deg) A functional category that serves as the specifier of a preposition or an adjective (e.g., *quite* in *quite tired, very* in *very near the house*).

Deictics Forms whose use and interpretation depend on the location of the speaker and/or addressee within a particular setting (e.g., *this/that, here/there*).

Delayed release A manner feature that refers to the release of the stop in affricate consonants.

Deletion A process that removes a segment from certain phonetic contexts (e.g., the pronunciation of *fifths* as [fɪfs]).

Denasalization A common substitution process in child language acquisition that involves the replacement of a nasal stop by a nonnasal counterpart (e.g., *come* is pronounced [kʌb]).

Denotation Entities that a word or expression refers to (also called its **referents** or **extension**).

Dentals Sounds made with the tongue placed against or near the teeth.

Dependent variable In an experiment, the behavior or event that is measured.

Derivation (a) In morphology, a word formation process by which a new word is built from a stem, usually through the addition of an affix, that changes the word class and/or basic meaning of the word. (b) The set of steps or rule applications that results in the formation of a sentence in syntax and of a phonetic representation from an underlying form in phonology.

Derived (phonology) Resulting from the application of phonological rules to underlying representations.

Descriptive (grammar) A grammar that seeks to describe human linguistic ability and knowledge, not to prescribe one system in preference to another. (*See also* **Prescriptive (grammar)**.)

Design features Essential characteristics of communication systems that have been established with reference to human language.

Determiner (Det) A functional category that serves as the specifier of a noun (e.g., *a, the, these*).

Deterministic parsing A means of processing sentences in which no more than one analysis at a time is pursued.

Developmental (errors) Errors that occur in language acquisition and provide evidence of the learner's attempts to create a grammatical system based on his or her hypotheses about the target language (e.g., *why didn't he came to work?*).

Developmental sequences The stages of linguistic development that are relatively invariant across language learners.

Devoicing Voicing assimilation in which a sound becomes voiceless because of a nearby voiceless sound (e.g., the *l* in *place* is devoiced because of the voiceless stop preceding it).

Diacritic A mark added to a phonetic symbol to alter its value in some way (e.g., a circle under a symbol to indicate voicelessness).

Dialect A regional or social variety of a language characterized by its own phonological, syntactic, and lexical properties.

Dialectology A branch of linguistics concerned with the analysis and description of regional varieties of a language.

Diaphragm The large sheet of muscle that separates the chest cavity from the abdomen and helps to maintain the air pressure necessary for speech production.

Diary study A type of naturalistic investigation in which a researcher (often a parent) keeps daily notes on a child's linguistic progress.

Dichotic listening An experimental technique in which the subject listens to different sounds in each ear.

Diphthong A vowel that shows a noticeable change in quality within a single syllable (e.g., the vowel sounds in *house* and *ride*).

Diphthongization A process in which a monophthong becomes a diphthong (e.g., [iː] became [aj] during the Great English Vowel Shift).

Direct method (DM) A method of second language teaching that is based on the belief that an adult L2 learner can learn language in the same manner as a child and therefore involves no grammar instruction but rather concentrates on communicating.

Direct negative evidence Language instruction involving correction or focus on form.

Direct object The NP complement of a verb (e.g., *a fish* in *Judy caught a fish*).

Discourse A set of utterances that constitute a speech event.

Discourse analysis The field that deals with the organization of texts, including ways in which parts of texts are connected and the devices used for achieving textual structure.

Discourse markers Markers that occur over the length of a bit of discourse, separating one 'unit of talk' from a previous one (e.g., *well, y'know*).

Discrete sign A sign that is distinguished from other signs by stepwise differences (e.g., voiced and voiceless sounds, the numbers of a digital clock).

Displacement A property by which the users of the communication system are able to refer to events that are remote in space and time.

Dissimilation A process whereby one segment becomes less like another segment in its environment (e.g., *anma* 'soul' in Latin became *alma* in Spanish).

Distinctive feature A feature that serves to distinguish contrastive forms (e.g., the feature [voice] is distinctive in English because it underlies the contrast between /p/ and /b/, /t/ and /d/, etc.).

Distribution The set of elements with which an item can co-occur.

***Do* insertion** The syntactic rule that places *do* into an empty Infl position, making **inversion** possible in English questions.

Dorsal features Features that represent placement of the body of the tongue.

Dorsum (of the tongue) The body and back of the tongue.

Double-blind test A test in which a subject's responses are interpreted independently by someone other than the administrator of the test.

Downdrift The maintenance of a distinction among the pitch registers of an utterance even as the overall pitch of the utterance falls.

Dressage Interaction between trainer and animal in which the animal responds to subtle cues given by the trainer.

Duality of patterning A property of communication systems in which meaningless units are combined to form arbitrary signs that, in turn, are recombined to form new larger signs.

Duetting The interchange of calls in a patterned manner between two members of a species.

Dysprosody The lack of sentence intonation, a common characteristic of the speech of Broca's aphasics.

Enclitic A clitic that attaches to the end of a word.

Endocentric compounds Compound words in which one member identifies the general class to which the meaning of the entire word belongs (e.g., *dogfood* is a type of food in English). (*See also* **Exocentric compound**.)

Ends A component of the speech situation, which shows the function and the outcome of the speech.

Entailment A relation between sentences in which the truth of one sentence necessarily implies the truth of another (e.g., *Gary is Bernice's husband* entails the sentence *Bernice is married*).

Environment The phonetic context in which a sound occurs.

Epenthesis A process that inserts a segment into a particular environment (e.g., the insertion of a schwa in the pronunciation of *athlete* as [æθəlijt]).

Ergative The case associated with the subject of a transitive verb (but not that of an intransitive verb).

Euphemism A word or phrase that is less direct than the taboo word it replaces and is considered to be more socially acceptable (e.g., *passed away* for *died*).

Event-related potentials (ERP) A measurement of electrical activity in the brain that is correlated with the presentation of particular stimulus events.

Exclusive A type of first person plural pronoun whose referents do not include the addressee. (*See also* **Inclusive**.)

Exocentric compound A compound whose meaning does not follow from the meaning of its parts (e.g., *redneck*, since its referent is not a type of neck).

Experimental approach An approach to investigating child language in which researchers make use of specially designed tasks to elicit linguistic activity relevant to a particular phenomenon.

Experimental paradigm A method of investigation that involves a particular way of presenting stimuli and a particular way of measuring responses.

Extension The set of entities to which a word or expression refers (also called its denotation or referents).

Feature hierarchy A hierarchical representation of how features are related to each other.

Feature (phonetic) The smallest unit of analysis of phonological structure, combinations of which make up segments (e.g., [nasal], [continuant]).

Features (semantic) The semantic components that make up a word's intension.

Feedback A property of communication in which users of the system monitor what they are transmitting.

Feeding (rule order) A rule ordering where the first rule makes the application of the following rule possible.

Field dependence A learning style in which the learner operates holistically, perceiving the "field" as a whole rather than in terms of its component parts.

Field independence A learning style in which the learner operates analytically, perceiving the "field" in terms of its component parts rather than as a whole.

Field technique A method of study that does not involve manipulation and control of factors in a laboratory, but rather involves observing phenomena as they occur.

Fissure A relatively deep sulcus of the cerebral cortex.

Fixed stress Stress whose position in a word is predictable.

Flap A sound commonly identified with *r* and produced when the tongue tip strikes the alveolar ridge as it passes across it (e.g., in North American English, the medial consonant in *bitter* and *bidder*).

Flapping A phonetic process in which an alveolar stop is pronounced as a voice flap between vowels, the first of which is generally stressed (e.g., [bʌ́tr̩] → [bʌ́Dr̩]).

Fluency Second language speech that is produced automatically and without noticeable hesitation.

Fluent aphasia The aphasia that occurs due to damage to parts of the left cortex behind the central sulcus, resulting in fluent speech but great difficulty selecting, organizing, and monitoring language production (also called **sensory aphasia**).

Focus on form In second language teaching, the practice of giving explicit instruction about the second language and overtly correcting errors.

Folk etymology Reanalysis of a word that is based on an incorrect historical analysis (e.g., *hamburger* being reanalyzed into two morphemes, *ham* and *burger*).

Foreigner talk The type of speech that is typically addressed to second language learners, characterized by such properties as simple word order and more common vocabulary items (also called **teacher talk**).

Formants The main frequencies of a speech wave.

Fossilized Characteristic of an interlanguage grammar that has reached a plateau, that has ceased to improve.

Free form An element that can occur in isolation and/or whose position with respect to neighboring elements is not entirely fixed.

Free morpheme A morpheme that can be a word by itself (e.g., *fear*).

Free rule application Unordered application of rules in a **derivation**.

Free stress Stress whose position in a word is not predictable and must be learned on a case-by-case basis.

Free variation The free alternation of allophones and/or phonemes in a given environment (e.g., *sto*[pˀ], *sto*[p]; /ɛ/*conomics*, /i/*conomics*).

Frequency effect The common experimental finding that words that occur more commonly in a language are processed more quickly and more accurately.

Frication The weakening of a stop to a fricative (e.g., [d] becoming [ð]).

Fricatives Consonants produced with a continuous airflow through the mouth, accompanied by a continuous audible noise (e.g., [f], [ʃ]).

Front vowel A vowel that is made with the tongue positioned in the front of the oral cavity (e.g., the vowel sounds in s<u>ea</u>l and b<u>a</u>t).

Frontal lobe The lobe of the brain that lies in front of the central sulcus and in which Broca's area is located.

Fronting A common substitution process in child language acquisition that involves the moving forward of a sound's place of articulation (e.g., *cheese* pronounced as [tsijz]).

Full reduplication A morphological process that duplicates the entire word (e.g., in Turkish, ʧabuk 'quickly'/ʧabuk ʧabuk 'very quickly').

Function words Words such as determiners and conjunctions that specify grammatical relations rather than carry semantic content.

Functional analysis An approach to syntactic analysis that attempts to understand syntactic phenomena in terms of their communicative function.

Functional category A word-level syntactic category whose members specify grammatical relations rather than carry semantic content (e.g., auxiliary verbs, conjunctions, determiners, and degree words) (also called **nonlexical category**).

Fusion A morphological change where a word becomes an affix (e.g., English affixes such as *-hood, -dom,* and *-ly* used to be words).

Fusional languages Languages in which words typically consist of several morphemes and the morphemes that are affixes often mark several grammatical categories simultaneously (e.g., Russian).

Fuzzy concepts Concepts that do not have clear-cut boundaries that distinguish them from other concepts (e.g., the concept 'poor').

Garden path sentence A sentence that is difficult to process and interpret because its structure biases sentence parsing toward an incorrect analysis.

Gender A grammatical category dividing nouns into classes often based on shared semantic and/or phonological properties (also called **Noun class**).

Gender-exclusive differentiation A type of social differentiation in which the use of some linguistic forms depends on the gender of the speakers.

Gender-variable differentiation The relative frequency with which men and women use certain features of language.

Genetic classification The categorization of languages according to the ancestor languages from which they developed.

Genetically related languages Languages that have descended from a common parent (e.g., German and Italian have both descended from Indo-European).

Genre A component of the speech situation, which refers to any one of a class of named speech acts (e.g., greeting, leave-taking, lecture, joke, and so on).

Given information Knowledge that the speaker assumes is available to the addressee at the time of the utterance, either because it is shared by both or because it has already been introduced into the discourse (also called **old information**).

Glagolitic script A script that was introduced in Slavic-speaking areas in the ninth century AD for the translation of the Bible.

Glide strengthening The strengthening of a glide to an affricate (e.g., [j] becoming [ʤ]).

Glides Sounds that are produced with an articulation like that of a vowel, but move quickly to another articulation (e.g., [j], [w]).

Gliding A common substitution process in child language acquisition which involves the replacement of a liquid by a glide (e.g., *play* is pronounced [pwej]).

Global aphasia The most severe form of nonfluent aphasia, in which the patient is completely mute.

Glottals Sounds produced by using the vocal folds as the primary articulators (e.g., [h], [ʔ]).

Glottis The space between the vocal folds.

Glyphs The symbols used in Mayan writing.

Goal A **thematic role** that describes the end point for a movement (e.g., *'Mary'* in the sentence *'Terry gave the skis to Mary'*).

Graded concept A concept whose members display varying degrees of the characteristics that are considered typical of the concept.

Graded sign A sign that conveys its meaning by changes in degree (e.g., voice volume, a blush).

Grammar The mental system of rules and categories that allows humans to form and interpret the words and sentences of their language.

Grammar translation method (GTM) A method of second language teaching that emphasizes reading, writing, translation, and the conscious learning of grammatical rules, its primary goal being to develop a literary mastery of the target language.

Grammatical (sentence) A sentence that speakers judge to be a possible sentence in their language.

Grammatical competence Competence in the structural aspects at or below the sentence level.

Grammatical hierarchy A hierarchy of grammatical relations such as subjects and objects in terms of markedness.

Grammaticalization The change of a lexical form into a grammatical form (e.g., an affix or member of a functional category).

Grammatical knowledge Knowledge of the meaning and use of words in sentences. (Compare **real world knowledge**.)

Grammaticized concepts Concepts that are expressed as affixes or nonlexical categories (e.g., the concept of 'obligation' as expressed by the auxiliary verb *must*).

Great English Vowel Shift A series of nonphonetically conditioned modifications to long vowels that occurred from the Middle English period to the eighteenth century.

Grimm's Law A set of consonant shifts that took place between Proto-Indo-European and Proto-Germanic.

Gyrus An area where the cerebral cortex is folded out.

Hangul The alphabetic script used to represent Korean, the symbols of which are grouped to represent the syllables of individual morphemes.

Hanja The Korean word for the Chinese characters used in Korean writing.

Head (of a phrase) The lexical category around which a phrasal category is built (e.g., V is head of VP, N is head of NP, A of AP, P of PP).

Head (of a word) The morpheme that determines the category of the entire word (e.g., *bird* in *blackbird*).

Hieroglyphics An Egyptian pictorial writing system, which later developed into a mixed writing system.

High A dorsal feature that characterizes sounds produced with the tongue body raised.

High vowel A vowel that is made with the tongue raised (e.g., the vowel sounds in *b<u>ea</u>t* and *l<u>o</u>se*).

Hiragana The Japanese syllabary that is used in conjunction with katakana and kanji to write Japanese.

Historical linguistics The linguistic discipline that is concerned with the description and the explanation of language change over time.

Holophrases Utterances produced by children in which one word expresses the type of meaning that would be associated with an entire sentence in adult speech (e.g., *up* used to mean 'Pick me up').

Homophony The situation in which a single form has two or more entirely distinct meanings (e.g., *club* 'a social organization', *club* 'a blunt weapon').

Hypercorrection Overgeneralization of particular rules in a language in an attempt to speak (or write) correctly.

Iconic sign A sign that bears some resemblance to its referent (e.g., a picture of a woman on a washroom door).

Illocutionary competence The ability to understand a speaker's intent and to produce a variety of forms to convey intent.

Illocutionary force The communicative intention of an utterance.

Immersion A method of teaching a second language to children in which students are given most of their content courses and school activities in the target language.

Implementation A practical application of a formal system.

Implicational universals A universal of language which specifies that the presence of one trait implies the presence of another (but not vice versa).

Inanimate A noun class category in some languages generally assigned to non-living referents. (*See also* **Animate**.)

Inclusive A contrast in some languages which indicates that the addressee is to be included in the interpretation of the first person plural morpheme. (*See also* **Exclusive**.)

Incorporation The combination of a word (usually a noun) with a verb to form a compound verb.

Indexical sign A sign that fulfills its function by pointing out its referent, typically by being a partial sample of it (e.g., the track of an animal).

Indexing Finding, identifying, and counting all occurrences of a word in large texts.

Indirect negative evidence The assumption that nonoccurring structures in the linguistic environment are ungrammatical.

Indo-European family The language family that includes most of the languages in a broad curve from northern India through western Asia (Iran and Armenia) to Europe.

Infix An affix that occurs within a base.

Inflection The modification of a word's form to indicate the grammatical subclass to which it belongs (e.g., the *-s* in *books* marks the plural subclass).

Inflectional language *See* **Fusional languages**.

Insertion rule An operation that adds an element to a tree structure.

Instrumental motivation The desire to achieve proficiency in a new language for utilitarian reasons, such as job promotion.

Instrumentalities A component of the speech situation, which includes 'channel' (verbal, written, electronic mail, etc.) and 'code' (the language and/or variety used).

Integrative motivation The desire to achieve proficiency in a new language in order to participate in the social life of the community that speaks the language.

Intension An expression's inherent sense; the concepts that it evokes.

Interactional sociolinguistics Sociolinguistic research that is mainly concerned with the language used by participants in speech situations.

Interchangeability A property of communication in which all users can both send and receive messages.

Intercostals The muscles between the ribs that help to maintain the air pressure necessary for speech production.

Interdentals Sounds made with the tongue placed between the teeth (e.g., [θ], [ð]).

Interfaces The ways in which components of a grammar (such as phonology and syntax) are related to each other.

Interlanguage The changing grammatical system that an L2 learner is using at a particular period in his or her acquisition of a second language as s/he moves towards proficiency in the target language.

Internal change A process that substitutes one nonmorphemic segment for another to mark a grammatical contrast (e.g., *sing, sang, sung*).

Internal reconstruction The reconstruction of a proto-language that relies on the analysis of morphophonemic variation within a single language.

International Phonetic Alphabet (IPA) A system for transcribing the sounds of speech that attempts to represent each sound of human speech with a single symbol.

Intonation Pitch movement in spoken utterances that is not related to differences in word meaning.

Intransitive verb A verb that does not take a direct object (e.g., *sleep*).

Inversion A transformation that moves Aux from its position within the VP to a position in front of the subject, formulated as: Move Aux to C.

Island A constituent that does not permit extraction of a component part (e.g., a coordinated phrase like *Jerry and Pam*).

Isoglosses Lines drawn on a dialect map to represent boundaries between dialects.

Isolate A language that is not known to be related to any other living language (e.g., Basque, Kutenai).

Isolating languages Languages whose words typically consist of only one morpheme (also called **analytic languages**) (e.g., Mandarin).

Jargon Vocabulary peculiar to some field, also called occupational sociolect.

Jargonaphasia A symptom of severe cases of Wernicke's aphasia in which speech contains very few real words of the language.

Kanji The Japanese word for the Chinese characters used to write Japanese.

Katakana The Japanese syllabary that is used in conjunction with hiragana and kanji to write Japanese.

Key (a) A component of the speech situation that specifies the mode, such as serious, facetious, formal, sarcastic, and so on. (b) *See* **Radical**.

Labial A place feature that characterizes sounds articulated with one or both lips.

Labials Sounds made with closure or near closure of the lips (e.g., the initial sounds of *win* and *forget*).

Labiodentals Sounds involving the lower lip and upper teeth (e.g., the initial sounds of *freedom* and *vintage*).

Labiovelars Sounds made with the tongue raised near the velum and the lips rounded at the same time (e.g., the initial sound of *wound*).

Language bioprogram hypothesis The hypothesis that similarities among creoles reflect linguistic universals both in terms of first language acquisition and with respect to processes and structures that are innate.

Language contact Interaction between speakers of one language and speakers of another language or dialect.

Laryngeal features Phonological features that represent laryngeal states (e.g., [voice], [spread glottis], and [constricted glottis]).

Laryngeal node A node in the feature geometry in autosegmental phonology, which dominates laryngeal features such as voicing, spread glottis, and constricted glottis.

Larynx The box-like structure located in the throat through which air passes during speech production, commonly known as the voicebox.

Late closure A parsing principle that claims that, in sentence comprehension, humans prefer to attach new words to the clause currently being processed.

Lateral (sound) A sound made with the sides of the tongue lowered (e.g., varieties of [l]).

Lateral fissure The fissure that separates the temporal lobe from the frontal and parietal lobes.

Lateral fricative A lateral sound made with a narrow enough closure to be classified as a fricative.

Lateralization The unilateral control of cognitive functions by either the left or the right side of the brain (e.g., language is lateralized to the left hemisphere in most people).

Laterals Sounds made with the sides of the tongue lowered (e.g., varieties of *l*).

Lax vowel A vowel that is made with a placement of the tongue that results in relatively less vocal tract constriction (e.g., the vowel sounds in *hit* and *but*).

Learnability A property of communication in which a user of the system can learn other variants.

Learning strategies The ways in which language learners process language input to develop linguistic knowledge.

Length The subjective impression of time occupied by the duration of a phone.

Lesion Severe damage to the brain.

Levelt's model of speech production A **psycholinguistic model** of how constellations of activities such as conceptualizing, formulating, and articulating a message interact when speech is produced.

Lexical ambiguity A situation in which a single form has two or more meanings (e.g., a *trunk* is a 'piece of luggage' or an 'elephant nose').

Lexical category The word-level syntactic categories noun (N), verb (V), adjective (A), and preposition (P).

Lexical decision An experimental paradigm in which a person sees or hears a stimulus and must judge as quickly as possible whether or not that stimulus is a word of his or her language.

Lexical diffusion Linguistic change that first manifests itself in a few words and then gradually spreads through the vocabulary of the language.

Lexical gaps Gaps in the lexicon that result from technological innovation or contact with another culture.

Lexicalization The process whereby concepts are encoded in the words of a language (e.g., the concepts of 'motion' and 'manner' are both encoded by the word *roll*).

Lexicon A speaker's mental dictionary, which contains information about the syntactic properties, meaning, and phonological representation of a language's words.

Lingua franca A language that is used when speakers of two or more different languages come into contact and do not know each other's languages.

Linguistic competence Speakers' knowledge of their language, which allows them to produce and understand an unlimited number of utterances, including many that are novel.

Linguistic typology An approach to language classification that classifies languages according to their common structural characteristics without regard for genetic relationships.

Linguistic universals Structural characteristics that occur across the languages of the world.

Linguistics The discipline that studies the nature and use of language.

Lobes Substructures of the hemispheres of the brain that appear to have distinct responsibilities (e.g., **frontal lobe**, **temporal lobe**).

Location A thematic role that specifies the place where an action occurs (e.g., *'the SkyDome'* in the sentence *'The athletes practiced in the SkyDome'*).

Logogram A written symbol representing a morpheme or word.

Logographic writing A type of writing in which symbols represent morphemes or even entire words.

Longitudinal fissure The fissure that extends from the front of the brain to the back and separates the left and right cerebral hemispheres.

Loudness The subjective impression of a phone's volume relative to the sounds around it.

Low (sound) A sound made with the tongue lowered (e.g., [a], [ɑ], [æ]).

Low vowel A vowel that is made with the tongue lowered (e.g., the vowel sounds made in the word *c<u>a</u>t* and *t<u>o</u>p*).

Macrofamilies *See* **Phyla**.

Major class features Phonological features that represent the classes consonant, obstruent, nasal, liquid, glide, and vowel.

Majority rules strategy A secondary strategy used to reconstruct proto-forms which stipulates that the segment found in the majority of cognates should be assumed to be part of the proto-form. (*See also* **Phonetic plausibility strategy**.)

Manner features Phonological features that represent manner of articulation.

Manner node A node in the feature geometry in autosegmental phonology, which dominates features that relate to manner of articulation (e.g., continuant, lateral).

Manners of articulation The various configurations produced by positioning the lips, tongue, velum, and glottis in different ways (e.g., nasal, fricative, liquid).

Marked traits Complex or less common features or characteristics of languages.

Markedness Differential Hypothesis The hypothesis that L2 elements that are different and more marked than the L1 elements will cause difficulty in learning.

Markedness theory A theory that classifies traits or patterns of languages as marked (those that are considered to be more complex and/or universally rarer) and unmarked (those that are considered to be less complex and/or universally more common).

Matrix A representation of sounds, where all the relevant distinctive features and their values are placed in an array.

Matrix clause The larger S in which a complement clause occurs.

Maxim of Manner A principle that is thought to underlie the efficient use of language and is formulated as: Avoid ambiguity and obscurity; be brief and orderly.

Maxim of Quality A principle that is thought to underlie the efficient use of language and is formulated as: Try to make your contribution one that is true. (Do not say things that are false or for which you lack adequate evidence.)

Maxim of Quantity A principle that is thought to underlie the efficient use of language and is formulated as: Do not make your contribution more or less informative than required.

Maxim of Relation A principle that is thought to underlie the efficient use of language and is formulated as: Be relevant.

Maxims The specific principles that ensure that conversational interactions satisfy the Cooperative Principle.

Meaning The message or content that a sign or utterance conveys.

Mental lexicon See **Lexicon**.

Merger A change in a phonological system in which two or more phonemes collapse into one, thereby reducing the number of phonemes in that language.

Mesolect A creole variety that falls between an acrolect and a basilect in terms of the amount of influence from the standard language.

Metaphor The understanding of one concept in terms of another, sometimes responsible for language change (e.g., 'argument' understood in terms of 'war': *She annihilated him in the debate*).

Metathesis A process that reorders a sequence of segments (e.g., in child language, pronouncing *spaghetti* as [pəskɛɾij]).

Mid vowel A vowel that is made with the tongue neither raised nor lowered (e.g., the vowel sounds in s*e*t and C*o*ke).

Minimal attachment A proposed parsing principle that claims that, in sentence comprehension, humans tend to attach incoming material into phrase structure using the fewest nodes possible.

Minimal pair Two forms with distinct meanings that differ by only one segment found in the same position in each form (e.g., [ʃɪp] and [ʃip]).

Mixed type language A language that simultaneously has some characteristics of two or more morphological types such as isolating, polysynthetic, agglutinating, and fusional types.

Modifier An optional element that describes a property of a head (e.g., *blue* in *that blue car* or *that Gloria likes* in *the car that Gloria likes*).

Module A unit of processing that is relatively autonomous from other processing units.

Morph A meaningful sequence of sounds that cannot be divided into smaller meaningful component parts. Morphs that have the same meaning and are in **complementary distribution** are members of the same **morpheme** (e.g., the English plural morpheme includes a number of morphs, including /z/, /s/, /əz/, and /ən/).

Morpheme The smallest unit of language that carries information about meaning or function (e.g., *books* consists of the two morphemes *book* + *s*).

Morphology The system of categories and rules involved in word formation and interpretation.

Morphophonemic rules Rules that account for alternations among allomorphs.

Motherese The type of speech that is typically addressed to young children (also called **caregiver speech**).

Motion verbs Words that can describe motion through space (e.g., *come, go,* and *move* in English).

Motor aphasia *See* **Nonfluent aphasia**.

Movement test A test used to determine if a group of words is a constituent by moving it as a single unit to a different position within the sentence.

MRD Machine-readable dictionary.

Murmur The glottal state that produces voiced sounds with the vocal folds relaxed enough to allow enough air to escape to produce a simultaneous whispery effect (also called **whispery voice**).

Mutual intelligibility The criterion that is sometimes used to distinguish between language and dialect: Mutually intelligible varieties of a language can be understood by speakers of each variety and are therefore dialects of the same language.

Nasal A manner feature that characterizes any sound made with the velum lowered.

Nasal sounds Sounds produced by lowering the velum, allowing air to pass through the nasal passages.

Nasalization The nasalizing effect that a nasal consonant can have on an adjacent vowel.

Native speaker One who has acquired a language as a child in a natural setting.

Nativism The view that certain grammatical knowledge is inborn.

Natural class A class of sounds that shares a feature or features (e.g., voiced stops).

Naturalistic approach An approach to investigating child language in which researchers observe and record children's spontaneous verbal behavior.

Naturalness A criterion that guides language reconstruction by determining whether or not changes are natural.

Negative evidence Information as to the ungrammatical nature of utterances.

Neologism A lexical innovation (e.g., *fishocracy* in Newfoundland English).

Neurolinguistics The study of how language is represented and processed in the brain.

Neurons The basic information-processing units of the nervous system, also called nerve cells.

Neuroscience The scientific study of the brain.

New information Knowledge that is introduced into the discourse for the first time.

Node *See* **Class node**.

Nominal paradigm The set of related forms associated with a noun (also called a **declension**).

No-naming The practice of avoiding address terms when participants are unsure which term to use.

Nondeterministic parsing A means of processing sentences in which more than one analysis at a time can be pursued.

Nonfluent aphasia Aphasia that results from damage to parts of the brain in front of the central sulcus and is characterized by slow, effortful speech production (also called **motor aphasia**).

Nonlexical category *See* **Functional category**.

Nonstandard (dialect) A variety of language that differs from the standard dialect in systematic ways.

Nonterminal (intonation) contour Rising or level intonation at the end of an utterance, often signalling that the utterance is incomplete.

Nonterminal nodes Parts of a structure which are not lexical items, for example VP, NP, Det, N. Compare with **terminal nodes**.

Norms Basic rules that seem to underlie speech interaction.

Noun (N) A lexical category that typically names entities, can usually be inflected for number and possession (in English), and functions as the head of a noun phrase (e.g., *key, Bob, perception*).

Noun class *See* **Gender**.

NP Movement A transformation that moves a noun phrase into the subject position.

Nucleus (N) A vocalic element that forms the core of a syllable (e.g., the vowel [æ] is the nucleus of the first syllable of *Patrick*).

Null Subject Parameter A cross-linguistic variation that allows some languages to drop subject pronouns, while other languages require an overt grammatical subject.

Number The morphological category that expresses contrasts involving countable quantities (e.g., in English, the two-way distinction between singular and plural).

Object permanence A developmental milestone characterized by the child's ability to recognize that objects have an existence independent of one's interaction with them.

Oblique NP A noun phrase that combines with a preposition.

Obstruent Any non-sonorant consonant: fricatives, affricates, oral stops.

Obviative A verb form used in some languages to indicate that the referent of the subject is not the entity previously chosen as the focus of the conversation. (*See also* **Proximate**.)

Occipital lobe The area of the brain to the rear of the angular gyrus in which the visual cortex is located.

Old information *See* **Given information**.

One-word stage A stage of first-language acquisition where children characteristically produce one-word utterances.

Onomatopoeic words Words that sound like the thing that they name (e.g., *plop, hiss*).

Onset The portion of a syllable that precedes the nucleus (e.g., /spl/ in *spleen*).

Ontogeny Model Predicts that during the course of SLA, transfer errors start out high in number and subsequently decrease, while developmental errors start out low in number, then increase, and finally decrease.

Oral sounds Sounds produced with the velum raised and the airflow through the nasal passage cut off.

Orthography A set of conventions for representing language in written form.

Overextension A developmental phenomenon in which the meaning of a child's word overlaps with that of the equivalent adult word, but also extends beyond it (e.g., *dog* is used to refer to other animals as well as dogs).

Overgeneralization A developmental phenomenon that results from the overly broad application of a rule (e.g., *falled* instead of *fell*).

Overregularization *See* **Overgeneralization**.

Palatalization The effect that front vowels and the palatal guide [j] typically have on velar, alveolar, and dental stops, making their place of articulation more palatal (e.g., the first sound of *keep* is palatalized).

Palatals Sounds produced with the tongue on or near the palate (e.g., [j]).

Palate The highest part of the roof of the mouth.

Palatoalveolar *See* **Alveopalatal (area)**.

Paragraphia Writing errors made by Broca's aphasics that have characteristics corresponding to their speech.

Parameter The set of alternatives for a particular phenomenon made available by Universal Grammar to individual languages.

Paraphrases Two sentences that have the same basic meaning (e.g., *A Canadian wrote that book* is a paraphrase of *That book was written by a Canadian*).

Parietal lobe The lobe of the brain that lies behind the central sulcus and above the temporal lobe.

Parser A program or mental process for doing grammatical analysis.

Parsing The procedure through which speech or text is analyzed by assigning categories to words and structure to strings of words.

Partial assimilation A phonological process by which neighboring segments become more like each other, e.g., by sharing the same **place of articulation** or the same **manner of articulation**.

Partial reduplication A morphological process in which part of a stem is repeated to form a new word (e.g., in Tagalog, *takbuh* 'run' and *tatakbuh* 'will run').

Partial suppletion A morphological process that marks a grammatical contrast by replacing part of a morpheme (e.g., *think/thought*).

Participants A component of the speech situation, characterized by terms such as addressor, addressee, speaker, performer, audience, and so on.

Passive sentence A sentence whose theme is encoded as grammatical subject (e.g., *The report was prepared by the committee members*).

Pejoration A semantic change where the meaning of a word becomes more negative or unfavorable (e.g., the meaning of *wench* used to be 'girl').

Performance Actual language use in particular situations.

Person A morphological category that typically distinguishes among the first person (the speaker), the second person (the addressee), and the third person (anyone else) (e.g., in English, the difference between *I*, *you*, and *she/he/it*).

Pharyngeals Sounds made through the modification of airflow in the pharynx by retracting the tongue or constricting the pharynx.

Pharynx The area of the throat between the uvula and the larynx.

Pheremones Chemicals used by animals specifically for communicative purposes.

Phoenician script An early writing system, which had twenty-two consonantal signs, devised by the Semitic peoples of ancient Phoenicia as early as 1000 B.C.

Phone Any sound used in human language (also called a **speech sound**).

Phoneme A contrastive segmental unit with predictable phonetic variants.

Phonemic paraphasias Speech errors that result from phonemic substitutions and omissions (e.g., *spoon* may be pronounced as *poon*).

Phonemic transcription A type of transcription of sounds where phonetic details are ignored and only phonemic contrast is recorded.

Phonetic determinative The part of a Chinese character that provides information about the pronunciation of the corresponding morpheme.

Phonetic plausibility strategy The primary strategy used to reconstruct protoforms that requires any sound changes posited to be phonetically plausible. (*See also* **Majority rules strategy**.)

Phonetic sound change A sound change that results in a new allophone of an already existing phoneme.

Phonetic transcription A type of transcription of sounds where not only phonemic differences but also phonetic details are recorded.

Phonetically conditioned sound change Sound change that begins as subtle alterations in the sound pattern of a language in particular phonetic environments.

Phonetics The study of the inventory and structure of the sounds of language.

Phonographic writing A type of writing in which symbols represent syllables or segments.

Phonological change A sound change that results in the addition, elimination, or rearrangement of phonemes (e.g., splits, mergers).

Phonological dyslexia A type of acquired dyslexia in which the patient seems to have lost the ability to use spelling-to-sound rules and can only read words that they have seen before.

Phonological rules Rules that relate the underlying forms of words to their phonetic forms.

Phonology The component of a grammar made up of the elements and principles that determine how sounds pattern in a language.

Phonotactics The set of constraints on how sequences of segments pattern.

Phrase One or more words that are built around a 'skeleton' consisting of two levels, a phrase level and a word level, and act as a syntactic unit (e.g., *the apple, Bob, hurried to class*).

Phrase level A descriptive term indicating where stress is placed in phrases.

Phrase structure rule A rule that specifies how a syntactic constituent is formed out of other smaller syntactic constituents (e.g., S → NP VP).

Phyla The groups into which purportedly related language stocks are placed (also called superstocks).

Pictograms Pictorial representations of objects or events.

Pidgin A lingua franca with a highly simplified grammatical structure that has emerged as a mixture of two or more languages and has no native speakers.

Pinyin The system of writing Mandarin with a modified Latin alphabet, used for such things as street signs and brand names.

Pitch The auditory property of a sound that enables us to place it on a scale that ranges from low to high.

Place features Phonological features that represent place of articulation.

Place node A node in the feature geometry in autosegmental phonology, which dominates major place features.

Places of articulation The point at which the airstream is modified in the vocal tract to produce a phone (also called *point of articulation*).

Plural An inflectional category associated with nouns with more than one referent.

Politeness formulas Modifications of a simple expression so that it can convey politeness (e.g., Open the window! → Please open the window.).

Polysemy The situation in which a word has two or more related meanings (e.g., *bright* 'intelligent', *bright* 'shining').

Polysynthetic languages Languages in which single words can consist of long strings of lexical categories and affixes, often expressing the meaning of an entire sentence in English (e.g., Inuktitut).

Positive evidence Grammatical utterances in the learner's linguistic environment.

Positron Emission Tomography (PET) A brain imaging technique that uses radioactive isotopes to measure changes in brain metabolism associated with particular cognitive and behavioral tasks.

Postposition A P that occurs after its complement. (*See* **Preposition**.)

Pragmatics Speakers' and addressees' background attitudes and beliefs, their understanding of the context of an utterance, and their knowledge of how language can be used for a variety of purposes.

Prefix An affix that is attached to the front of its base (e.g., *re-* in *replay*).

Preposition (P) A minor lexical category whose members typically designate relations in space or time (e.g., *in, before*); they come before the NP complement with which they combine to form a PP.

Prescriptive (grammar) A grammar that aims to state the linguistic facts in terms of how they should be. (*See also* **Descriptive**.)

Presupposition The assumption or belief implied by the use of a particular word or structure.

Prevarication A property of communication in which the system enables the users to talk nonsense or to lie.

Primary stress The most prominent stress of a word.

Prime In a priming experiment, this is the stimulus that is expected to affect a subject's **response accuracy** and **latency** to the following stimulus.

Priming A situation in which the presentation of a stimulus makes it easier to process the following stimulus.

Priming effect In a priming experiment, this is the extent to which a priming stimulus facilitates the processing of the next stimulus.

Principal components analysis (PCA) An approach to studying social differentiation, where the statistical investigation of a large number of linguistic variants precedes determining what social similarities are shared among them.

Principle A The syntactic principle that constrains the interpretation of reflexive pronouns and is formulated as: A **reflexive pronoun** must have an antecedent (within the same clause) that c-commands it.

Principle B The syntactic principle that constrains the interpretation of pronominals and is formulated as: A **pronominal** must not have an antecedent (within the same clause) that c-commands it.

Principle of Compositionality, The A principle underlying sentence interpretation that is formulated as: The meaning of a sentence is determined by the meaning of its component parts and the manner in which they are arranged in syntactic structure.

Processes Articulatory adjustments that occur during the production of speech (e.g., deletion, epenthesis, assimilation).

Proclitic A clitic that attaches to the beginning of a word.

Productivity In morphology, the relative freedom with which affixes can combine with bases of the appropriate category.

Progressive assimilation Assimilation in which a sound influences a following segment (e.g., liquid-glide devoicing).

Pronominal A pronoun whose interpretation may, but does not have to be, determined by an antecedent in the same sentence (e.g., *he, her*).

Pronoun (Pro) A minor lexical category whose members can replace a noun phrase and that look to another element for their interpretation (e.g., *he, herself, it*).

Prosodic properties *See* **Suprasegmental properties**.

Proto-form The form that is reconstructed as the source of cognate words in related languages.

Proto-Indo-European (PIE) The proto-language from which evolved most of the languages of Europe, Persia (Iran), and the northern part of India.

Proto-language The reconstructed language that is presumed to be the common source for two or more related languages (e.g., Proto-Indo-European).

Prototypes The best exemplars of a concept (e.g., robins or magpies are prototypes of the concept 'bird').

Proximate A verb form used in some languages to indicate that the subject of the verb has been chosen as the focus of the conversation and any further use of which (without an overt subject) indicates a reference to that focused entity. (*See also* **Obviative**.)

Psycholinguistic model A schematic representation based on experimental results of how language is processed mentally.

Psycholinguistics The study of the mental processes and representations involved in language comprehension and production.

Radical The part of a Chinese character that provides clues about the morpheme's meaning (also called a **key**).

Reading The interpretation for a particular utterance.

Real-world knowledge Knowledge of what is likely in real life.

Reanalysis A source of language change that involves an attempt to attribute an internal structure to a word that formerly was not broken down into component morphemes (e.g., *ham* + *burger*).

Rebus principle In writing, the use of a sign for any word that is pronounced like the word whose meaning the sign represented initially.

Reduced A phonological characteristic of schwa [ə], indicating a weakly articulated, unstressed variant of stressed vowels.

Reduced vowel *See* **Schwa**.

Redundancy The use of different modalities to convey the same information.

Reduplication A morphological process that repeats all or part of the base to which it is attached. (*See also* **Partial reduplication** and **Full reduplication**.)

Referents The set of entities to which a word or expression refers (also called its **denotation** or **extension**).

Reflexive pronoun A pronoun that must have a c-commanding antecedent usually in the same clause (e.g., *himself, herself*).

Reflexiveness A property of communication where the communication system is used to discuss the system itself.

Regional dialect A speech variety spoken in a particular geographical area (e.g., Appalachian English).

Register A speech variety appropriate to a particular speech situation (e.g., formal versus casual).

Register tone A tone that has a stable pitch over a single syllable.

Regressive assimilation Assimilation in which a sound influences a preceding segment (e.g., nasalization in English).

Regressive saccades Eye movements in which the eyes dart backward to a section of text that has been previously read.

Related languages Languages that developed historically from the same ancestor language.

Relational analysis A syntactic analysis in which phenomena are described in terms of grammatical relations such as subject and direct object rather than morphological patterns or the order of words.

Relative clause A sentence-like construction that is embedded within an NP and provides information about the set of entities denoted by the head noun (e.g., The meteor *that she saw*).

Relexification The hypothesis that creoles are formed through the replacement of vocabulary, with little change in grammar.

Representations Models of one aspect of language (e.g., phonological representation, syntactic representation).

Response accuracy The correctness of a subject's responses to particular stimuli in an experiment.

Response latency The amount of time taken by a subject in an experiment to respond to a stimulus.

Retroflex Sounds produced by curling the tongue tip back into the mouth (e.g., American English [r]).

Rhotacism A type of weakening that typically involves the change of [z] to [r].

Rhyme (R) The nucleus and the coda of a syllable (e.g., [uwts] in the word *boots*).

Right ear advantage A phenomenon where speech is louder and clearer when it is heard in the right ear than in the left ear for right-handed people.

Root (of the tongue) The part of the tongue that is contained in the upper part of the throat.

Root (of a word) In a complex word, the morpheme that remains after all affixes are removed (e.g., *mind* in unmindfulness).

Root node The highest node of the feature hierarchy.

Round A place feature that characterizes sounds made by protruding the lips (e.g, [ɔ], [w]).

Rounded (sounds) Sounds made with the lips protruding (e.g., [ow], [ɔ]).

Runic writing A writing system that was developed shortly after the beginning of the

Christian era by Germanic tribes and lasted until the sixteenth century.

S Rule, The The phrase structure rule that states the composition of a sentence: S → NP Infl VP.

S-structure *See* **Surface structure**.

Saccades The quick and uneven movements of the eyes during reading.

Scene *See* **Setting**.

Schwa The mid unrounded lax vowel that is characterized by briefer duration than any of the other vowels (also called a **reduced vowel**) (e.g., the underlined vowels in *Canada, suppose*).

Second language acquisition (SLA) The acquisition of a language that is not one's native language.

Secondary stress The second most prominent stress in a word.

Segmental change A sound change that affects a segment.

Segments Individual speech sounds.

Semantic broadening The process in which the meaning of a word becomes more general or more inclusive than its historically earlier form (e.g., the word 'aunt' used to mean only father's sister).

Semantic decomposition *See* **Componential analysis**.

Semantic features The components of meaning that make up a word's intension (e.g., *man* has the feature [+human]; *dog* has the feature [-human]).

Semantic narrowing The process in which the meaning of a word becomes less general or less inclusive than its historically earlier meaning (e.g., the word *meat* used to mean any type of food).

Semantic shift The process in which a word loses its former meaning, taking on a new, often related, meaning (e.g., *immoral* used to mean 'not customary').

Semanticity A property of communication, in which the system conveys meaning through a set of fixed relationships among signs, referents, and meanings.

Semantics The study of meaning in human language.

Semiotics The study of signs.

Sensory aphasia *See* **Fluent aphasia**.

Sentence (S) A syntactic unit consisting of a noun phrase and a verb phrase.

Sentence ambiguity The possibility that a sentence can be interpreted in more than one way.

Sequential change Sound change that involves sequences of segments (e.g., assimilation).

Setting Contextual information having to do with the physical environment in which a sentence is uttered.

Shift A change in a phonological system in which a series of phonemes is systematically modified so that their organization with respect to each other is altered (e.g., the Great English Vowel Shift).

Sibilants *See* **Stridents**.

Sign A unit of communication structure that consists of two parts: a signifier (such as a sequence of sounds [trij]) and something signified (such as a tree in the real world).

Signal A sign that triggers a specific action on the part of the receiver (e.g., traffic lights).

Signified The real world object that a sign represents, as well as the sign's conceptual content.

Signifier That part of a sign that stimulates at least one sense organ of the receiver of a message.

Simple vowels Vowels that do not show a noticeable change in quality during their production (also called **monophthongs**) (e.g., the vowel sounds of *cab* and *get*).

Simple word A word that consists of a single morpheme (e.g., *horse*).

Singular An inflectional category associated with nouns with a single referent.

Slang An informal nonstandard speech variety characterized by newly coined and rapidly changing vocabulary.

Social network analysis An approach to sociolinguistic research in which the researcher is a participant-observer of a social group and interprets linguistic variation in terms of the kinds and densities of relationships experienced by speakers.

Social stratification The differentiation of language varieties along the vertical continuum of socioeconomic status.

Sociolect A speech variety spoken by a group of people who share a particular social characteristic such as socioeconomic class, ethnicity, or age.

Sociolinguistic competence The ability to understand and produce a variety of social dialects in appropriate circumstances.

Sociolinguistics The study of the social aspects of language.

Song In bird communication, lengthy elaborate patterns of mostly pitched sounds.

Sonorant A major class feature that characterizes all and only the 'singables': vowels, glides, liquids, and nasals.

Sound change A systematic change of sounds that took place over a long period.

Sound class *See* **Class, (sound)**.

Sound shift The systematic modification of a series of phonemes (e.g., Grimm's Law).

Source A **thematic role** that describes the starting point for a movement (e.g., *Maine* in the sentence *The senator sent the lobster from Maine to Nebraska*).

Spatial metaphor Use of a word that is primarily associated with spatial orientation to talk about physical and psychological states.

Specialization A property of communication in which the system serves no other function but to communicate.

Specifier A word that helps to make more precise the meaning of the head of the phrase and that occurs immediately beneath XP (e.g., *the* in *the book*).

Spectrogram An acoustic recording that graphically shows the frequency, intensity, and time of sounds.

Speech community A group whose members share both a particular language or variety of language and the norms for its appropriate use in social context.

Speech situation The social situation in which language is used.

Speech sound *See* **Phone**.

Speech variety The language or form of language used by any group of speakers.

Spelling pronunciation One factor in sound change, where a new pronunciation reflects the spelling of the word (e.g., *often*).

Splits Phonological changes where two allophones become separate phonemes due to the loss of the conditioning environment.

Split brain experiments Studies that investigate the effects of surgically severing the corpus callosum.

Spoonerisms A type of speech error, named after Reverend William A. Spooner, in which words or sounds are rearranged with often humorous results.

Spread Glottis ([SG]) A laryngeal feature that refers to the position of the vocal folds and that distinguishes unaspirated from aspirated sounds.

Spreading Association of a feature to neighboring segments in autosegmental phonology.

Standard language The prestige variety of a language that is employed by the government and media, used and taught in educational institutions, and is the main or only written variety.

Stem The base to which an inflectional affix is added (e.g., *modification* is the stem for *-s* in the word *modifications*).

Stemming (or stripping) algorithm A computer program for doing automated morphological analysis.

Stimulus-bound communication Communication that only occurs when it is triggered by exposure to a certain stimulus or for certain specific ends (e.g., the warning call of a bird).

Stocks In language classification, groups of related language families.

Stopping In child language acquisition, the replacement of a fricative by a corresponding stop (e.g., *zebra* is pronounced [dijbrə]).

Stops Sounds made with a complete and momentary closure of airflow through the vocal tract (e.g., [p], [t], [k]).

Stress *See* **Stressed vowels**.

Stressed vowels Vowels that are perceived as relatively more prominent due to the combined effects of pitch, loudness, and length.

Strident A manner feature of fricatives and affricates characterized by greater acoustic noise (in English, [s z ʃ ʒ ʧ ʤ]).

Stridents The noisier coronal fricatives and affricates (in English, [s z ʃ ʒ ʧ ʤ]) (also called **sibilants**).

Stroke A hemorrhage in the brain or the blockage or rupture of an artery, causing brain damage (also called a **cerebrovascular accident**).

Strong generative capacity Capacity to describe correctly the structures of the strings of a language.

Structurally ambiguous A property of phrases or sentences whose component words can be combined in more than one way (e.g., *fast cars and motorcyles*).

Subcategorization The classification of words in terms of their complement options (e.g., the verb *devour* is subcategorized for a complement NP).

Subject The NP occurring immediately under S (e.g., *Irene* in *Irene is a tailor).*

Subject Constraint, The A constraint on transformations that prevents elements from being moved out of a subject phrase.

Subset Principle, The The initial or default setting of a parameter will correspond to the option that permits fewer patterns.

Substitution (of sounds) Replacement of one segment with another similar sounding segment.

Substitution test A test used to determine if a group of words is a syntactic constituent by replacing them with a single word.

Substratum influence The influence of a politically or culturally nondominant language on a dominant language in the area (e.g., the borrowing of words into English from Amerindian languages).

Suffix An affix that is attached to the end of its base (e.g., *-ly* in *quickly*).

Suggestopedia A method of second language instruction in which students assume fictitious identities, instruction takes place in a relaxed living room setting, and L2 input is provided by the instructor reading a text to the background of classical music.

Sulcus An area where the cerebral cortex is folded in.

Superstratum influence The influence of a politically or culturally dominant language on a less dominant language in the area (e.g., the effects of Norman-French on English during the Middle English period).

Suppletion A morphological process that marks a grammatical contrast by replacing a morpheme with an entirely different morpheme (e.g., *be/was*).

Suprasegmental properties Those properties of sounds that form part of their makeup no matter what their place or manner of articulation: pitch, loudness, and length (also called **prosodic properties**).

Surface dyslexia A type of acquired dyslexia in which the patient seems unable to recognize words as wholes, but must process all words through a set of spelling-to-sound rules (e.g., *yacht* would be pronounced /jæʧt/).

Surface structure The structure that results from the application of whatever transformations are appropriate for the sentence in question.

Syllabary A set of syllabic signs used for writing a language.

Syllabic A major phonological class feature assigned to segments that function as the nuclei of syllables (vowels and liquids).

Syllabic liquids Liquids that function as syllabic nuclei (e.g., the *l* in *bottle*).

Syllabic nasals Nasals that function as syllabic nuclei (e.g., the *n* in *button*).

Syllabic writing A type of writing in which each symbol represents a syllable.

Syllable A unit of linguistic structure that consists of a syllabic element and any segments that are associated with it. (*See also* **Onset**, **Nucleus**, **Coda**.)

Symbolic sign A sign that bears an arbitrary relationship to its referent (e.g., nononomatopoeic words, a stop sign).

Symptomatic sign A sign that spontaneously and involuntarily conveys an internal state or an emotion, as in crying.

Syncope The deletion of a word-internal vowel (e.g., the deletion of the schwa in *police*).

Synonyms Words or expressions that have the same meanings in some or all contexts (e.g., *buy* and *purchase*).

Syntactic category The category into which an element is placed depending on the type of meaning that it expresses, the type of affixes it takes, and the type of structure in which it occurs (includes both lexical and functional categories).

Syntactic parser The theoretical construct that accounts for the human ability to assign grammatical categories and hierarchical structure to elements in a stream of language input.

Syntax The system of rules and categories that underlies sentence formation in human language.

Systematic gaps Nonoccurring forms that would violate the phonotactic constraints of a language (e.g., in English **mtlow*).

Systematic phonetic correspondences Sound correspondences between two or more related languages that are consistent throughout the vocabularies of those languages.

Synthetic language A language that makes extensive use of polymorphemic words (e.g., words containing a root and one or more affixes) (also called an **Inflectional language**) (e.g., Spanish).

Taboo Expressions that are seen as offensive and are therefore often euphemized.

Target In a priming experiment, this is the stimulus to which a subject must respond and for which response accuracy and latency are measured.

Target language The language that an L2 learner is learning.

Teacher talk *See* **Foreigner talk**.

Telegraphic speech Speech lacking functional categories and bound morphemes.

Telegraphic stage The stage in child language acquisition in which children's utterances are generally longer than two words but lack bound morphemes and most functional categories.

Template The innate blueprint of birdsong that predisposes birds to perform a general song that is extremely simplified.

Temporal lobe The lobe of the brain that lies beneath the lateral fissure and in which Wernicke's area is located.

Tense (feature) A dorsal feature that expresses the distinction between **tense** and **lax vowels**.

Tense (verb) In syntax and morphology, an inflectional category indicating the time of an event or action relative to the moment of speaking.

Tense vowel A vowel that is made with a relatively tense tongue and greater vocal tract constriction than a **lax vowel** (e.g., the vowel sounds in *heat* and *boat*).

Terminal (intonation) contour Falling intonation at the end of an utterance, signalling that the utterance is complete.

Terminal nodes The lexical items or prefixes, suffixes, stems, or words of a language.

Text The written version of any utterance or body of discourse.

Textual competence Competence in the organization of language beyond the sentence.

Textual reference References recovered from the text itself (e.g., anaphoric, cataphoric, lexical cohesion, and ellipsis).

Thematic role The part played by a particular entity in an event (e.g., agent, theme, source, goal, location).

Theme The thematic role of the entity directly affected by the action of the verb (e.g., *the ball* in *Tom caught the ball*).

Thyroid cartilage The cartilage that forms the main portion of the larynx, spreading outward like the head of a plow.

Tier A level of phonological description in which only certain phonological elements are represented (e.g., a syllabic tier, a tonal tier).

Tip (of the tongue) The narrow area at the front of the tongue.

Token An individual instance of a sign.

Tone Pitch differences that signal differences in meaning.

Tone language A language in which differences in word meaning are signalled by differences in pitch.

Top-down parsing A method of sentence analysis in which the entire sentence is considered first, before its component parts.

Top-down processing A type of mental processing using a set of expectations to guide phonetic processing and word recognition.

Topic What a sentence or group of sentences is about.

Total assimilation The assimilation of all the features of neighboring segments.

Total physical response (TPR) A method of L2 teaching in which the student is initially not required to speak, but rather carries out simple commands in the second language (e.g., *close the door*).

Trace The empty element, marked by the symbol *e*, that is left in syntactic structure after an element has been moved.

Trachea The tube below the larynx through which air travels when it leaves the lungs, commonly known as the windpipe.

Tradition A property of communication whereby at least certain aspects of the system must be transmitted from an experienced user to a learner.

Transfer The process by which the first language (L1) influences the interlanguage grammar of the learner of a second language.

Transfer error An error made by a second language learner that can be traced to the first language.

Transformation A type of syntactic rule that can move an element from one position to another.

Transformational syntax A widely accepted approach to syntactic analysis in which syntactic phenomena are described in terms of phrase structure rules (which generate deep structures) and transformations (which generate surface structures).

Transitive verb A verb that takes a direct object (e.g., *hit*).

Tree structure A diagram that represents the internal organization of a word, phrase, or sentence.

Trill An *r*-like sound that is made by passing air over the raised tongue tip, allowing it to vibrate.

Truth conditions The circumstances under which a sentence is true.

Two-word stage A stage of first language acquisition, where children normally utter two succeeding words.

Typological plausibility A criterion that guides language reconstruction by referring to universals or existing properties of language.

Umlaut The effect that a vowel (or sometimes a glide) in one syllable can have on the vowel of another (usually preceding) syllable.

Underextension A developmental phenomenon in which a child uses a lexical item to denote only a subset of the items that it denotes in adult speech (e.g., *car* used to refer to only moving cars).

Underlying The unpredictable features of a phonemic segment are basic or underlying.

Underlying form In phonology, a form from which phonetic forms are derived by rule.

Underlying representation *See* **Underlying form**.

Universal Grammar The system of categories, mechanisms, and constraints shared by all human languages and considered to be innate.

Universal tendencies Patterns or traits that occur in all or most languages.

Unmarked traits Those characteristics of language that are considered to be less complex and/or universally more common in languages.

Utterance Any bit of talk produced by a speaker that is distinct from other bits of talk in a speech situation.

Uvula The small fleshy flap of tissue that hangs down from the velum.

Uvulars Sounds made with the tongue near or touching the uvula.

Velars Sounds made with the tongue touching or near the velum (e.g., [ŋ], [k]).

Velum The soft area towards the rear of the roof of the mouth.

Verb (V) A lexical category that typically designates actions, sensations, and states, can usually be inflected for tense, and functions as the head of a verb phrase (e.g., *see, feel, remain*).

Verb Movement Parameter A cross-linguistic variation involving whether the verb does or does not raise to Infl.

Verb raising A syntactic rule that moves the verb to the Infl position in **S-structure** in languages such as French.

Verbal hedges Words or phrases that make statements less assertive (e.g., *maybe, sort of*).

Verbal paradigm The set of inflected forms associated with a verb (also called a **conjugation**).

Verner's Law A generalization made by Karl Verner, which states that a word-internal voiceless fricative resulting from Grimm's Law underwent voicing if the original Proto-Indo-European accent did not immediately precede it.

Vocal cords *See* **Vocal folds**.

Vocal folds A set of muscles inside the larynx that may be positioned in various ways to produce different glottal states (also called **vocal cords**).

Vocal tract The oral cavity, nasal cavity, and pharynx.

Voice A laryngeal feature that distinguishes between **voiced** and **voiceless** sounds.

Voiced The glottal state in which the vocal folds are brought close together, but not tightly closed, causing air passing through them to vibrate (e.g., [æ], [z], [m] are voiced).

Voiceless The glottal state in which the vocal folds are pulled apart, allowing air to pass directly through the glottis (e.g., [t], [s], [f] are voiceless).

Voicing A historical process of **consonant weakening** in which voiceless stops or fricatives become voiced.

Voicing assimilation Assimilation in which one segment becomes more like a nearby segment in terms of voicing (e.g., liquid-glide devoicing).

Vowel reduction A process that converts a full vowel, typically unstressed, to the short, lax schwa.

Vowels Resonant, syllabic sounds produced with less obstruction in the vocal tract than that required for glides.

Weakening (phonetic) A type of assimilation in which a lessening in the time or degree of a consonant's closure occurs (also called lenition).

Weakening (semantic) The process in which the meaning of a word has less force (e.g., *soon* used to mean 'immediately' but now means 'in the near future').

Weak generative capacity Capacity to describe properly all the strings of a language.

Wernicke's aphasia The aphasia that results in fluent but nonsensical speech, sometimes characterized by **jargonaphasia**.

Wernicke's area The area of the brain involved in the interpretation and the selection of lexical items.

***Wh* movement** A transformation that moves a *wh* phrase to the beginning of the sentence, formulated as: Move a *wh* phrase to the specifier position under CP.

***Wh* question** A sentence that begins with a *wh*-word such as *what, where, when* (e.g., *Who did you see?*).

Whisper The glottal state in which the vocal folds are adjusted so that the front portions are pulled close together, while the back portions are apart.

Whispery voice *See* **Murmur**.

Word A minimal free form.

Word level The level of representation above the syllable level.

Word manufacture The creation of a word from scratch, sometimes with the help of a computer (also called **coinage**) (e.g., *Kodak*).

Word-based morphology Morphology that can form a new word from a base that is itself a word (e.g., *re-do* and *treat-ment* in English).

Words The smallest free forms found in language.

Writing The representation of language by graphic signs or symbols.

X´ rule A phrase structure rule that deals with intermediate categories, which states that an intermediate category X´ consists of a head, X, and any optional complements.

XP rule A phrase structure rule that deals with maximal categories, which states that a maximal category XP consists of an optional specifier and an X´.

Zero derivation *See* **Conversion**.

Acknowledgments (continued from page iv)

Page 422: Figure 11.5. Pet scans. Source: By Marcus E. Raichle, M.D. from "Mind and Brain" by Gerald D. Fishbach in *Scientific American* (September 1992). Reprinted by permission of Marcus E. Raichle, M.D., Washington University School of Medicine, St. Louis, Missouri.

Pages 424–425: C. S. Moss. Excerpt from *Recovery with Aphasia* by C. S. Moss. Copyright © 1972 by C. S. Moss. Reprinted by permission of the University of Illinois.

Page 515: Ann Landers. "Dan's Grammer." Copyright © Creators Syndicate. Permission granted by Ann Landers and Creators Syndicate.

Pages 534–535: Map: Some English- and French-based pidgins and creoles of the world. Source: *Pidginization and Creolization of Languages* edited by Dell Hymes, pp. 509–23. Copyright © 1971 by Dell Hymes. Reprinted with the permission of Cambridge University Press; "Repertory of Pidgin and Creole Languages" by Hancock in *Pidgin and Creole Linguistics* edited by Albert Valdman, pp. 532–33. Reprinted by permission of Indiana University Press.

Pages 549–551: Tom Stoppard. Excerpt from *Rosencrantz and Guildenstern Are Dead* by Tom Stoppard. Copyright © 1967 by Tom Stoppard. Used by permission of Grove/Atlantic, Inc.

Pages 555, 559, 563, and 574: Figures 15.1, 15.7, 15.8, 15.12, and 15.25. Paleolithic drawing, Sweden, and Le Placard eagle bone; Sumerian rebus inscription; Overlapped Sumerian syllabic signs; Evolution of the Greek and Latin alphabets; Western Cree syllabary. Source: *Visible Speech: The Diverse Oneness of Writing Systems* by John DeFrancis. Copyright © 1989 by John DeFrancis. Reprinted by permission of the University of Hawaii Press.

Page 556: Figure 15.2. Ancient Mesopotamian tokens. Source: From "Two Precursors of Writing Plain and Complex Tokens" by Denise Schmandt-Besserat, in *The Origins of Writing* edited by Wayne M. Senner. Copyright © 1989 by Wayne M. Senner. Published by the University of Nebraska Press. This figure is owned by the Musée du Louvre, Paris, France. Reprinted by permission.

Page 557: Figure 15.4. Contemporary pictograms. Source: Courtesy of the Olympic Trust of Canada. ™ Official Mark, © Canadian Olympic Association, 1972.

Page 557: Figure 15.5. Blissymbolics. Source: Courtesy of Blissymbolics Communications Institute, exclusive licensee (1982) and is derived from the symbols described in *Semantography,* original copyright C. K. Bliss 1949.

Page 558: Figure 15.6. Sumerian logograms. Source*: Manuel D'Epigraphic Akkadienne,* Fifth Edition, by Rene Labat. Copyright © 1976 by Rene Labat. Reprinted by permission.

Page 560: Figure 15.9. Changes in cuneiform writing. Source: *The Origins of Writing* edited by Wayne M. Senner. Copyright © 1989 The University of Nebraska Press. Reprinted by permission.

Page 567: Figure 15.17. Development of writing systems. Source: *The Origins of Writing* edited by Wayne M. Senner, p. 89. Copyright © 1989 The University of Nebraska Press. This figure was created by Joseph Haveh, The Hebrew University, Mount Scopus 91905, Israel. Reprinted by permission.

Page 568: Figure 15.18. Historical development of the Chinese symbol for 'dog.' Source: *Chinese* by Jerry Norman, p. 564. Copyright © 1988 by Jerry Norman. Reprinted with the permission of Cambridge University Press.

Page 570: Figure 15.19. Hiragana and katakana syllabaries and their phonetic values. Source: *Read Japanese Today* by Len Walsh. Copyright © 1971 by Charles E. Tuttle Publishing Company, Inc. of Tokyo, Japan. Reprinted by permission.

Pages 589, 594, and 624: Figures 16.1, 16.5, and figures in question 3. Some chimpanzee facial expressions; Some graded signs. Source: Adapted from "Facial Expression and Emotion in Nonhuman Primates," (pp. 11–90) in *Darwin and Facial Expression* edited by P. Ekman. Copyright © 1973 by P. Ekman. Reprinted by permission of the author and Academic Press, New York.

Page 595: Figure 16.7. The graded continuum from sobbing to screaming. Source: Adapted from "Serial Calling as a Mediator of Interaction Processes: Crying" (pp. 88–107) in *Primal Vocal Communication* edited by D. Todt, D. P. Goedeking, and D. Symmes. Copyright © 1988 by D. Todt, D. P. Goedeking, and D. Symmes. Reprinted by permission of Springer-Verlag, New York.

Page 598: Figure 16.8. Bee dancing. Source: Adapted from *The Dance Language and Orientation of Bees* by K. Von Frisch (p. 57). Copyright © 1967, 1993 by The President and Fellows of Harvard College. Reprinted by permission of the publisher.

Page 602: Figure 16.9. Spectrogram of a robin song. Source: *Bird Song* by H. H. Thorpe. Copyright © 1961 by W. H. Thorpe. Reprinted with the permission of Cambridge University Press.

Page 602: Figure 16.10. Avian isoglosses: call patterns of male Hill Mynas. Source: From "Microgeographic and Macrogeographic Variation in Acquired Vocalizations of Birds" by Paul Mundiger in *Acoustic Communication in Birds,* vol. 2, edited by D. E. Kroodsma, E. H. Miller, and H. Ouellet. Copyright © 1982 by D. E. Kroodsma, E. H. Miller, and H. Ouellet. Reprinted by permission of the authors and Academic Press, New York.

Page 605: Table 16.1. Lemur vocalization. From *Lemur Behavior* by A. Jolly. Copyright © 1966 by A. Jolly. Reprinted by permission of The University of Chicago Press.

Pages 611 and 612: Figures 16.13 and 16.14. Arbitrary symbols used in experiments with the chimpanzee Sarah; A 'sentence' understood by Sarah. Source: Adapted from *Apes, Men, and Language* by E. Linden (p. 179). Copyright © 1974 by E. Linden. (Baltimore, MD: Pelican Books.) Reprinted by permission.

Page 615: Table 16.2. Some sign combinations produced by Koko. Source: From *The Education of Koko* by Francine Patterson and E. Linden. Copyright © 1981 by Francine Patterson and E. Linden, The Gorilla Foundation, Woodside, CA 94062. Reprinted by permission of the authors.

LANGUAGE INDEX

INDEX